MASTERPLOTS II

POETRY SERIES
REVISED EDITION

MASTERPLOTS II

POETRY SERIES
REVISED EDITION

4

Hero and Leander–The Listeners

Editor, Revised Edition
PHILIP K. JASON

Project Editor, Revised Edition
TRACY IRONS-GEORGES

Editors, Supplement
JOHN WILSON   **PHILIP K. JASON**

Editor, First Edition
FRANK N. MAGILL

SALEM PRESS

Pasadena, California   Hackensack, New Jersey

Editor in Chief: Dawn P. Dawson

Project Editor: Tracy Irons-Georges   *Research Supervisor:* Jeffry Jensen
Production Editor: Cynthia Beres   *Research Assistant:* Jeff Stephens
Copy Editor: Lauren Mitchell   *Acquisitions Editor:* Mark Rehn

Some of the essays in this work originally appeared in *Masterplots II, Poetry Series*, edited by Frank N. Magill (Pasadena, Calif.: Salem Press, Inc., 1992), and in *Masterplots II, Poetry Series Supplement*, edited by John Wilson and Philip K. Jason (Pasadena, Calif.: Salem Press, Inc., 1998).

∞ The paper used in these volumes conforms to the American National Standard for Permanence of Paper for Printed Library Materials, Z39.48-1992 (R1997).

Library of Congress Cataloging-in-Publication Data
Masterplots II. Poetry series.— Rev. ed. / editor, Philip K. Jason ; project editor, Tracy Irons-Georges
  p. ; cm.
  Rev. ed.: Masterplots two / Frank Northen Magill, 1992-1998.
  Includes bibliographical references and indexes.
  ISBN 1-58765-037-1 (set : alk. paper) — ISBN 1-58765-041-X (vol. 4 : alk. paper) —
  1. Poetry — Themes, motives. I. Title: Masterplots two. II. Title: Masterplots 2. III. Jason, Philip K., 1941-   . IV. Irons-Georges, Tracy.

PN1110.5 .M37 2002
809.1—dc21

                                                                2001055059

Second Printing

TABLE OF CONTENTS

TABLE OF CONTENTS

TABLE OF CONTENTS

MASTERPLOTS II

POETRY SERIES
REVISED EDITION

HERO AND LEANDER

Author: Christopher Marlowe (1564-1593)
Type of poem: Epic
First published: 1598

The Poem

Hero and Leander is a short, amorous epic written in rhymed couplets of iambic pentameter. It is divided into cantos called "sestiads," after a verse form which gains its name from the isle of Sestos, where the action takes place. Apparently, Christopher Marlowe wrote the entire first two sestiads of 484 and 334 lines. Some believe these two chapters were meant in themselves to be a complete poem; others believe that Marlowe did not live to finish his work. In any case, George Chapman, the famous translator of Homer, took up the work and completed it by adding four more sestiads. Although appreciated, the Chapman augmentation is not cherished, venerated, or studied with the same interest as the Marlowe chapters, which are considered the best poetic work in that genre during the Elizabethan period.

Hero and Leander could be called an "amorous epic" to distinguish it from the longer Homeric epics which are on heroic subjects. It lacks the sober dignity and solemn tragedy of classical Greek tragedy and epic. Some critics have suggested calling it an epyllion, which carries the sense of a shorter and less serious narrative work. The classical models for these works, so popular in the sixteenth century, were the long, sensuous, and humorous poems of Ovid, particularly the *Amores* (c. 20 B.C.E.), the *Heroides* (before 8 C.E.), and the *Metamorphoses* (c. 8 C.E.). Ovid was popular in the Middle Ages, providing the literary material for a cult of love which expressed itself in verse romances and the poetry of the troubadours, though the explicit sections of his works were treated as allegory.

The English Renaissance—gay, vigorous, delighting in the senses and a newly discovered sense of personal freedom—disrobed classical love literature of its embarrassed indirection, and sensual, worldly, playful poetry abounded. Marlowe's *Hero and Leander* was one of the most popular and influential works following this tendency. It describes the brief and illicit courtship of Hero, a young priestess of the temple of Venus on Sestos, and Leander, a handsome young man of the city of Abydos. The two are separated by the rough seas of the Hellespont, and Leander braves the waters in order to spend evenings with Hero.

The complete legend involves the tragic death of the lovers. Neptune, the god of the sea, becomes enamored of Leander as he swims across the Hellespont. Leander rejects Neptune's love, and the god drowns Hero in anger. This tragic tale was told by the Greek fifth century poet Musaeus, and it is the Greek or a Latin translation of this poem which is the textual basis for Marlowe's work. Marlowe, however, barely foreshadows the lovers' unhappy fate in his two sestiads; this grave duty has been left by history to Chapman. It is possible to read Marlowe alone, therefore, and see nothing but a bright, humorous, sexy poem about two young lovers enjoying their first carnal knowledge, as well as Leander dealing embarrassedly with the homosexual love interest of Neptune, who, showering Leander with jewels and lasciviously fondling him as he swims, seems the picture of an aroused, wealthy, older bon vivant.

The poem begins with a straightforward exposition and then veers instantly into a florid description, full of classical allusions, of Hero's beauty. Marlowe fills the text with such allusions, an ostentatious display of knowledge of antiquity that is part of the genre. Hero's beauty is so great that the god Apollo once offered her his throne. Her sleeves are decorated with a representation of naked Venus chasing her beloved Adonis; the figured border of Hero's dress is stained with the blood of desperate lovers who killed themselves because she rejected them. In a spirit of humorous exaggeration, Marlowe describes her breath as so sweet-smelling that bystanders praise it and honeybees swarm about her mouth. Marlowe calls her "Venus' nun," which means literally that she is a virgin serving the cult of Venus in the temple at Sestos. Yet, "Venus' nun" is also an Elizabethan expression for a prostitute.

The description of Leander is equally exaggerated and even more replete with classical allusions. The allusions recall stories from Homer, Vergil, Ovid, and Greek tragedy. Leander's tresses are like the Golden Fleece—the Argonauts would have traveled to Colchis for them. Cynthia, the moon, is pale in grief that she cannot have Leander. His body is as straight as the magic wand of Circe, the enchantress from the *Odyssey* (c. 800 B.C.E.). Jove would have accepted drink from Leander's hand and replaced the lovely servant Ganymede with him. Hippolytus, who preferred hunting to love and died rather than accept improper amorous advances, would nevertheless have fallen in love with Leander.

The narration is taken up again with a description of the annual festival at Sestos of Adonis, the boy loved by Venus. Since the festival is in honor of the goddess of love, guests journey there to find new lovers. Hero stands out as the most beautiful woman there. She is compared with the stars and all sorts of heavenly bodies. People rush to see her; many fall in love with her and die of her indifference (to "die" is, in Elizabethan parlance, colloquial for sexual climax).

There is a moment of tragic foresight when Hero and Leander first see each other, but instead of continuing with a description of the meeting of the lovers, Marlowe provides an elaborate digression by describing the fabulous temple of Venus. It is adorned with representations of mythology; these frescoes and bas reliefs, a convention in heroic literature, are usually an evocation of battle and heroic deeds. Yet in this light, amorous epic, they are a list of amorous indiscretions by the gods—appropriate adornment for a temple to Venus. The courting scene begins tenderly with commonplaces about love at first sight. Then, however, follows a long speech by Leander against virginity. One sophism after another, it is designed to seduce Hero at all costs.

Hero's answer expresses her maidenly ambivalence, for although she is attracted to the young man, she nevertheless makes a show of defending her virtue. She supplicates Venus to save her from this threat to her chastity, but Cupid, the god of love, hovers above her and beats back her prayers from heaven. He then flies to the "palace of the Destinies," where the Fates, three old women, weave each person's fortune and future. Cupid asks the Fates to arrange a happy outcome for Hero and Leander, but they will not, because of an injury received from the god at an earlier time. The story of this ancient insult to the Fates, another lengthy digression, ends the sestiad.

The second sestiad is devoted to the actual seduction of Hero. She flees to her tower on Sestos. Leander follows. They kiss and embrace, but no more than that, because Leander does not yet know the facts of life. As instinct instructs him further, however, he again presses Hero to have intercourse with him. The narrator describes in delicious detail their amorous contention and Hero's attempt to maintain her virginity. This level of description proceeds throughout the entire poem as an alternative to the mythological allusions and classical tone. Leander leaves without having completed "the rites of love." Soon, however, he swims again to Sestos, this time attracting Neptune as his naked body cleaves the waters. Leander's rejection of the sea god is the basis for his downfall, which will occur in the Chapman section of the epic.

The rest of the sestiad is the actual final seduction of Hero and an evening of lovemaking. In the morning, the sun rises to find Hero standing by the bed, watching Leander. Marlowe achieves a grand climax by paralleling her early rise with the rise of the sun, which chases away embarrassed night. The 1598 edition contains at this point a cryptic Latin expression, *Desunt nonnulla*, which means "something is lacking." That probably indicates the publisher's understanding that Marlowe broke off in his composition before it was completed.

Forms and Devices

Hero and Leander has been considered by many to be the finest of the English Renaissance's "mythological poems." One of the chief devices of a mythological poem is classical allusion, references to texts and legends of Greek and Roman antiquity. The allusions in *Hero and Leander*, however, are uneven in tone and often have an unmeasured quality. For example, in praising Leander's beauty, Marlowe writes, "Even as delicious meat is to the taste,/ So was his neck in touching, and surpass'd/ The white of Pelops' shoulder." Pelops's shoulder is indeed white, because it is made of ivory, a god having in fact eaten the fleshly shoulder when it was served up by Tantalus, Pelops's father, in a stew. Yet there is also the poet's description of the carvings on the walls of Venus's temple: "There might you see the gods in sundry shapes,/ Committing heady riots, incest, rapes." The poet then tells of Zeus's seduction, as a golden shower, of Danae; his marriage to his sister, Hera; his love play with the boy Ganymede; and his appearance as a bull to rape Europa. Marlowe then describes Mars and Venus, who were trapped in an iron net by Vulcan after they committed adultery together; and the destruction of Troy because of the rape of Helen.

Nineteenth century critics such as A. C. Bradley saw in the sensuality of Marlowe's imagery and the flamboyance of his classical allusions a certain Renaissance enthusiasm and "frank acceptance of sensuous beauty and joy." M. C. Bradbrook introduced in the mid-1930's, however, a new reading of Marlowe's poem which sees these allusions as ironic, parodic, and generally humorous. The reference to Pelops, for example, is not infelicitous or inapt but sharp-edged and complex; it means that Marlowe is not taking Leander's gratuitous beauty utterly seriously. He creates an ironic distance and does not uncritically portray Leander's amoral sensuality. The poet's list of rapes, incests, and acts of sexual violence by the gods could be seen as sarcasm or at least not the acceptance without regard to taste and decorum usually attributed to Elizabethan "enthusiasm."

In general, the devices of Marlowe's poem parallel those of true heroic narrative, but because the subject is love, not war, there is a deliberate contrast as well. When aggression is replaced by passion, romantic wooing replaces mighty heroic deeds.

Themes and Meanings

During the Renaissance, respect for classical antiquity, for Greek and Roman culture, expressed the idea that mortal man with his abilities and limitations should be at the center of human perspective, that is, should be the measure of human values. This view contrasted with medieval thought, in which the Christian god and theological absolutes were the measure of all things. *Hero and Leander* is an expression of the Renaissance "humanistic" perspective, for the work takes human physical love as its subject and gives the reader a psychological portrait of the development of passion and romance in callow youth. The classical references and constant evocation of antique mythology underscore the humanistic point by posing a nonmetaphysical, nontheological cosmology instead of the allegorical Catholic Christian worldview.

Recent criticism has improved scholars' understanding of the humanity of this approach by pointing out the complexity and ambivalence of Marlowe's acceptance of classical models. He does not receive the violent and irascible sexual life of the Greek gods as a model of authenticity or self-liberation; he regards it with a critical eye. Expressing Renaissance enthusiasm, he rejoices in the richness of the story materials, the colorful tales of the loves of the gods. Yet there is also irony and parody, subtle shifts of perspective and changes of voice, which indicate that his moral perspective is complex.

Hero, for example, is beautiful but disingenuous. Her defense of her virginity is half-hearted. She spurns Leander but drops her sixteenth century fan so that he will follow. Leander's behavior reflects no moral position but rather pure concupiscence. Hence Marlowe's harsh aphorism: "Love is not full of pity (as men say)/ But deaf and cruel where he means to prey." Moreover, Leander may be beautiful and winsome, but he is also embarassingly naïve. He does not know even the basic facts about human intercourse. He fails to recognize Neptune's homosexual love for what it is and ignorantly says, "You are deceiv'd, I am no woman, I."

Robin Kornman

THE HEROES OF CHILDHOOD

Author: Thomas McGrath (1916-1990)
Type of poem: Elegy
First published: 1947, in *To Walk a Crooked Mile*

The Poem

An "elegy" at one time indicated a poem of mourning for an admired member of the nobility or for a deceased loved one. Though this meaning sometimes still holds, the term is now applied to virtually any verse meditation on loss. "The Heroes of Childhood" is a modern folk elegy which romantically laments, not a particular human death, but the death of childhood and the illusions of youth. Written in five five-line stanzas, the poem's end rhyme and regular metrics contribute to its innocent, songlike quality. That quality reinforces the poem's very subject—with mounting irony.

The "childhood heroes" of the poem's first stanza are immediately described in terms of the American West: "their pearl-handled six-guns never missed fire," and "In a town full of badmen they never lost face." The point of view is first-person plural, which serves to generalize or universalize the subject. Faith in human goodness and infallibility is a typical experience of childhood, and the objects of admiration are like frontier heroes with their perfect aim and absolute goodness.

Stanza 2 continues the fictitious Wild West analogy but introduces two names from nonfictitious history: "Big Bill Haywood" and "Two Gun Marx." Marx is Karl Marx, the father of socialism and Communism, and Haywood was William Dudley Haywood, the American labor leader. These are the outlaw heroes who "stood against the bankers" to give to the poor. (From about the time of his college years, Thomas McGrath himself was a Marxist, and he was even blacklisted during the McCarthy era.) At this point in the poem, the speaker seems to be describing the heroes, not of childhood and myth, but of young adulthood and history, the perspective of youth coming to an awareness of real-world events and politics.

Even this faith in historical heroes, however, is eventually disturbed: "But we in our time are not so sure." When "we"—as opposed to childhood's god-heroes—are called to account, "our hearts" are "strung up" by hard thought about the realities of attempting political revolution. The childhood analogy of Wild West heroes is continued here, but the speaker now acknowledges the difficulties of living up to childhood ideals. The efforts this speaker has made to eliminate social injustice (through the labor movement and socialist reform) are condemned by the very society those efforts were meant to assist.

The natural next step in disillusionment is to examine anew one's childhood heroes and to consider whether, indeed, they too awaken at night, feverish with doubts. The tone of this fourth stanza is distinctly elegiac: "Perhaps we were mistaken, it has been so long. . . ." Each sentence here ends with a question, and the stanza is itself about raising ultimate questions. The speaker ends with an admonition that "The heart must build its own direction—/ Which only in the future has a permanent shape." The fall from faith has left only a romantic hope for future revolution, one constructed out of the "heart" rather than faith in human gods. Childhood and this poem itself thus come to their grim, though stubbornly idealistic, conclusion.

Forms and Devices

McGrath's poems are characterized by incredible formal variety. Though much of his later work is free verse, he sets an adroit pen to seemingly any formal exercise, including "The Heroes of Childhood." The poem is written in fairly regular iambic tetrameter, with an end-rhyme scheme of *aabba*. Though these formal choices contribute to the folk-songlike quality of the piece, the meter is never so regular and the end rhyme never so direct as to reduce the poem to pure playfulness or silliness. The first stanza, in fact, demonstrates his skill at slant rhyme: "austere," "fire" and "there," as well as "dice" and "face." The second stanza includes "pure," "car," and "poor," as well as "Marx" and "works." These off rhymes blunt the potential singsong effect of true end rhyme. In a poem about both childhood innocence and hard adult realities, McGrath's rhyme scheme seems here to be just right.

Typical also of McGrath's work is an impersonal point of view. Though some of his poems are indeed intimate, he more often employs distancing devices to address universal political issues. In the case of "The Heroes of Childhood," McGrath accomplishes this distance through a first person plural angle of vision. One could easily substitute "I" for each "we" in this poem; the particularly American childhood, the conversion to Marxism, the subsequent doubts and even blacklisting—these are biographical elements of McGrath's own life. His choice of the plural pronoun, however, generalizes the poem, and underscores the universality of social concerns he felt took precedence over personal biography.

Point of view and sound patterns are important devices in "The Heroes of Childhood." More than anything, however, the poem relies on a central, extended figure: the American West as an emblem of American innocence. The Hollywood-style Wild West described in this piece, with its "Dead Eye Dans" and pure-hearted outlaws, is like the philosophic childhood of the speaker, and perhaps America generally. The key feature of such a philosophy, as of Hollywood popular film, is illusion. According to this vision, morality is unambiguous, the good guys always win and the good guys are always on our side. By the end of the poem, however, the figurative West has become "this dead world's Indian Nation." The immature vision of the speaker thus gives over to a single, real, and terrible image: the mass grave of America's native people.

Themes and Meanings

At the center of McGrath's poem is the idea of direction and its loss, or illusion and disillusion. This is a well-worn theme. In the work of writers from every part of the globe, there appears in imaginative writing some notion of the Fall, a loss of original innocence and faith, and the subsequent troubles of mortality and incapacity.

The first illusion for McGrath is the American Dream—Hollywood-style heroes with their white hats and horses—but this is soon replaced by a young man's Communist ideals. In the Marxist view, direction is all-important because it is predetermined. The world is on an inevitable course toward a workers' utopia, free of class struggle. Yet in stanza 4, the speaker's faith in absolute direction, absolute ideals of any kind, is eroding: "Did they too wake at night . . ./ And wonder when direction would be clear if ever?" At the far end of both the American and the Marxist dream is loss of moral certainty and purpose.

Interestingly, "The Heroes of Childhood" ends with a reaffirmed faith in a new type of direction through what McGrath calls "the heart." This is not the heart of any particular person, group, or view, but is *the* heart, and so is perhaps intended as some essential self, a romantic source or spring. It might be the imagination as well, casting forward its shapes and building its own spontaneous paths, independent of worldly change and ideologies. "The heart must build its own direction—/ Which only in the future has a permanent shape."

Such indefinite, rather wistful sentiments are not necessarily typical of McGrath. Throughout much of his work, he seems to insist on tangible, earthly remedies for tangible human problems. He is critical of Platonic idealism and notions of afterlife salvation. He wants change right here and now, in the world we know. Nevertheless, in such poems as "The Heroes of Childhood," efforts to change the world are found to be untenable, fraught with ambiguities. He thus comes to rely on the less practical redemption of "the heart."

Certainly no other American poet has demonstrated such an unlikely interlocking of elements as we find in McGrath. Few poets write from both artistic expertise as well as overt political convictions—and Communist ones, at that—but despite those life-long convictions, in this poem McGrath seems to affirm, instead, creative imagination as the source of change and goodness. The imagination is an imperfect assurance, however, and some readers may find the poem's conclusion unconvincing, or at least difficult: The heart "left hanging" must somehow now start building.

Cynthia Nichols

HIGH WINDOWS

Author: Philip Larkin (1922-1985)
Type of poem: Lyric
First published: 1974, in *High Windows*

The Poem

"High Windows" consists of five quatrains; it has a variable metrical pattern and an irregular but discernible rhyme scheme (basically *abab*). Like many of Philip Larkin's poems, "High Windows" is written in the first person with no attempt to separate himself from the speaker. "I write poems," Larkin has said, "to preserve things I have seen/thought/felt (if I may so indicate a composite and complex experience) both for myself and others."

In "High Windows," an older man describes his thoughts and feelings on seeing a young couple during the late 1960's at the height of the sexual revolution. With cynical envy, and in blunt language, the speaker assumes that they have sex and that "she's/ Taking pills or wearing a diaphragm."

It is a situation that to him (and his generation's way of thinking) seems like the "paradise/ Everyone old has dreamed of all their lives"—without consequences and free of shame. All social restraints of "Bonds and gestures" have been thrown aside like "an outdated combine harvester" in favor of this new freedom, and now everyone can go down the "long slide/ To happiness."

At this point, the speaker wonders whether anyone looked at him when he was young, "forty years back," and thought the same things: *"That'll be the life;/ No God any more, or sweating in the dark/ About hell and that."* The church and its priests, too, *"will all go down the long slide/ Like free bloody birds."* Here it is unclear whether the slide leads to happiness, hell, or (in the absence of God) simply into nothingness.

The speaker concludes enigmatically by refusing to state his conclusion in words. "Rather than words comes the thought of high windows." Larkin is conveying (in words) the idea that some mental processes are beyond words. In this case, there is only the image, like a revelation, of the "sun-comprehending glass,/ And beyond it, the deep blue air, that shows/ Nothing, and is nowhere, and is endless."

Forms and Devices

It is one of the privileges of the contemporary poet working in traditional forms to play with those forms for ironic effect. Larkin once said that "Deprivation is for me what daffodils were to Wordsworth"; his tone is typically that of a cynic for whom life has not made good on its promises. Larkin's technique in "High Windows," as elsewhere, is based on the frustration of form, just as his theme is often frustration itself.

At first glance, "High Windows" appears to be written in traditional quatrains, but the first stanza immediately frustrates such an assumption. Whatever one may have assumed about the decorum of lyric poetry is contradicted by the opening lines, as much by the tone set by the vulgar and technical diction as by the lack of perfect rhyme.

Like Wilfred Owen, Larkin is a master of slant or off rhyme, setting up sonorous expectations that turn out to be as off-key as life itself is. The "she's/paradise" slant rhyme makes sense in that it displays the speaker's envy; the "kids/diaphragm" pairing does not rhyme at all. Its dissonance is as much a thing of sense as of sound, implying the irony of kids using birth control to keep from having kids. After this unconventional opening, the poem becomes increasingly traditional, in diction and meter as well as rhyme, as the speaker begins to make sense of a situation that at first merely baffles him. His conclusion, though, is startling.

The three verbs of the opening stanza set the agenda for the stages of the poem: the speaker can "see" the couple, can "guess" what they are doing, and can "know" that they are in paradise. His initial observation reveals more about his own desires and fears than theirs. Through an imaginative shift in perspective, he is able to look at himself more objectively. This double perspective inexplicably leads to the vision of high windows.

Tonally, the speaker moves from a cynical stance of envy (stated in vulgarly degrading diction) to a more reasonable viewpoint (mildly blasphemous in comparing priests with "bloody birds"), until he comes to rest in the meditative reconciliation with the world and himself in the high-toned final stanza.

This tonal modulation is matched by the poem's thematic development. It moves from a literal interpretation of the couple's freedom (the freedom from restraint to couple as they please), to an act of imaginative speculation (if there is no God, then the priests have no power), to a symbolic interpretation of freedom that acknowledges that beyond the physical and social realm lies another sort of freedom—beyond desire, envy, and everything transient and human.

Themes and Meanings

"High Windows" is a poem about the nature of freedom. The technology of birth control has granted sexual license to the young couple by freeing them from the inevitable sequence of love-marriage-children, but old "Bonds and gestures" die hard. A generation reared on the restraints of religion envies the young's relative "paradise." Deeper than envy, however, is the fear of freedom. Without restraints, society dissolves into anarchy, and the universe becomes meaningless. Such fears are what William Blake called "the mind-forg'd manacles" of self-enslavement. In the course of the poem, the speaker casts off envy and fear to accept the absolute freedom promised by the endless emptiness of "the deep blue air."

The poem (dated February 12, 1967) takes as its point of departure the free love of the sexual revolution. Old and new views of sex are contrasted in a pair of images: the combine versus the slide. The old view of sex has been "pushed to one side/ Like an outdated combine harvester." It suggests something mechanical, useful, and economically profitable, and it carries the symbolic baggage of a moralistic grim reaper: Ye shall reap what wild oats ye sow. The new view re-forms the old metal into a smooth playground slide, down which the young are going "To happiness, endlessly." The mechanical social duties of sex have been replaced by the free play of the pleasure principle.

With the obsolescence of social bonds, the power of the church, the chief agent of restraint, is lessened. The priests, too, will go down the long slide, like "*free bloody birds*," but not to happiness. In the existential philosopher Jean-Paul Sartre's phrase, they will be "condemned to be free." They will disappear into the empty heavens.

In situation and point of view, Larkin's poem resembles "Sailing to Byzantium" by William Butler Yeats. An old man observing "the sensual music" of "The young/ In one another's arms" decides that "That is no country for old men." Leaving the sensual world to the young, the speaker finds his solace in "monuments of unaging intellect" and is left contemplating "God's holy fire/ As in the gold mosaic of a wall" in the ideal city of Byzantium. Yet Larkin's tone is wryer, drier, and more down to earth. Larkin's speaker finds neither monuments of culture nor God in his "high windows." For all their majesty, they are not the stained glass of an old church, but clear "sun-comprehending glass."

The absence of God in Larkin's sky, as well as the absence of culture, has led some critics to see Larkin as a pessimist. Far from conveying any sense of hopelessness, however, the transparency of the glass, the purity of the blue sky, and the clarity of the vacant heavens are supremely peaceful. Above and beyond any thoughts of youth or age, unsullied by human desire or deprivation, social or even divine expectations, are the sun and sky—nature, pure and brutally simple, without judgment or explanation.

The image is a vitalistic, life-affirming view of nature. The "sun-comprehending glass" may be uncomprehending, leaving the big metaphysical questions unanswered, but it does understand the sun's life-giving warmth. The pagan sun god of sensual joy has replaced the Christian God of restraint and punishment. The last word of the poem is "endless," but the poem's motion does not end there. Instead, it circles back to the young couple "going down the long slide/ To happiness, endlessly." The linkage affirms the connection between their literal freedom and the absolute freedom of the speaker's vision beyond the "high windows."

The revelation suddenly reconciles the speaker not only with the couple (he now seems free of envy for their slide to happiness) but also with the priests (who may be pitied for their illusory slide into a vacant heaven). For him there may be "Nothing" in the way of transcendental or metaphysical solace above and beyond man and nature, but with the disappearance of God there is also the disappearance of shame and therefore a rediscovery of "paradise." Instead of "sweating in the dark/ About hell and that," the speaker stands in the light of a new kind of peace and freedom, where he must find, or make, his own meaning of a seemingly meaningless universe.

Richard Collins

THE HILLS

Author: Guillaume Apollinaire (Guillaume Albert Wladimir Alexandre de Kostrow-itzky; 1880-1918)
Type of poem: Lyric
First published: 1918, as "Les Collines" in *Calligrammes*; English translation collected in *Calligrammes*, 1980

The Poem

"The Hills" is a poem in blank verse divided into forty-four stanzas of five lines each. The title is a metaphor that will continue throughout the poem, thus giving coherence to a long sequence of apparently disparate images. The hills suggest altitude and, implicitly, the possibility of a better vision: One can have a better perspective and see farther from the top of a promontory. This elevated position becomes the equivalent of foresight and superior knowledge.

Like traditional lyric poetry, "The Hills" is written mainly in the first person, but, in the original French version, poet Guillaume Apollinaire sometimes uses the second-person singular (*tu*) when addressing his old self in order to make a clear distinction between his old nature and his new one, between past and future. He also uses the second-person plural (*vous*) when he addresses the whole of humankind in a prophetic voice.

The poem begins with an image that could be related to Apollinaire's experience in World War I: two planes involved in combat over Paris. However, one of the planes symbolizes the poet's childhood and youth, and it is brought down by the other one, which symbolizes the future. This metaphoric victory of the future over the past announces a new era of unlimited knowledge and magic, where poets can perceive, as if from the top of a hill, things that had not been seen before and where they can announce "Billions of prodigies" to come.

Each of the following stanzas contains a prophecy, a memory, or a dreamlike image that implicitly continues the oscillation between future and past. The origin of these images is not observation but rather something that may evoke psychoanalysis: the productive "Depths of consciousness" to be explored in a near future. It is from these "abysses" that the poet-prophets emerge like hills and bring a different type of knowledge of the world that is as precise and valid as scientific knowledge. In a reversed time perspective specific to many poems by Apollinaire, this new predicted era is actually "coming back," as if the future has already happened. The world is cyclic: "Here nothing ends nothing begins" and the "Helpful spirits" of the ancestors mingle among the new generations.

The poet talks about his own role as a prophet and his ability to remember and foresee at the same time. The instrument of his magic tricks is language, that "talisman . . ./ Dead and yet subtler than life." Language has a history and therefore has its roots in the past, but it also belongs to the fugitive present of the utterance and to the future by the poetic legacy of innovation. As a prophet, the poet can levitate and raise himself above "all natural things." Like a shaman, he can explore realms that nobody else has ever imagined. He can view his past, and poetry becomes a way by which the poet can freely contemplate himself, split into a subject and an object, author and matter of the poem: "it is I/ Who am the flute I play."

All these trancelike images end when the poet is reunited with himself as he hears his "footsteps coming back." He sits at his desk to write about his experiences of travel in time, and each stanza represents disparate images meant to break any connection with tradition, literary convention, or prosaic semantics: The orange tastes like a fireworks display, a maître d'hôtel pours unreal champagne for his dead customers, and a chauffeur discovers new universes around every corner. The poem ends with a complex image of a multilayered world, like a rose whose hidden essence needs to be discovered.

Forms and Devices

Although it has no punctuation, "The Hills" may seem more traditional than other poems published by Apollinaire in *Calligrammes* because of its regular stanzas. (*Calligrammes* is famous for its poems that are shaped like objects such as cigars, trees, guitars, and the Eiffel Tower.) In spite of its regular pattern, however, "The Hills" experiments with new poetic language and imagery. Each stanza contains a global and instantaneous image of the world. The poem is made of several such independent frames that succeed each other in an order that seems arbitrary; it is actually the result of a different temporal perspective that is specific to a poetic vision that covers present, past, and future in one glance. The poet uses the future tense to mark his prophetic tone ("A time will come for suffering" or "Man will become a god"), and he alternates it with both the past tense, which indicates a return in time, and the present tense, which he uses to describe himself experiencing the future he predicts.

Many critics have contrasted the Apollinaire of *Calligrammes* to the Apollinaire of *Alcools* (1913; *Alcohols*, 1964) and other early works in prose and verse, stating that the war experience marked a turning point in the writer's style and themes. However, the unique graphic arrangement of some poems in *Calligrammes* should not prevent readers from seeing the continuation of certain images and themes throughout his work. Thus many of the metaphors in "The Hills" can be better understood when placed in the context of other poems or writings in prose. For instance, the whole sequence describing Italy in stanzas 21-23 is a literary allusion to Apollinaire's short story "Giovani Moroni," in which Rome during carnival represents a powerful childhood memory. The "dead talisman" in this poem is a metaphor for language, as is the "dead purple" in the earlier collection entitled *Le Bestiaire* (1911; *Bestiary*, 1978). Even the image of the dual or split persona appears in the poem "Cortège" (*Alcools*), in which the poet is described as waiting to meet himself and calling his own name as if calling a friend's name.

What is definitely new in this poem, however, is the sequence of dismantled visual fragments evocative of cubist or Dadaist painting. The images are decomposed, and their separate elements are juxtaposed: The still life in stanza 37, for example, gathers different and unrelated objects (a hat, fruit, gloves) on a table. The dreamlike sequences (stanzas 37 and 38) anticipate the incongruous associations in surrealist art. Apollinaire, after all, is said to have invented the word "surrealism" and also wrote the first surrealist play, *Les Mamalles de Tirésias* (1917; *The Breasts of Tiresias*, 1961). These elements allow the reader to establish a connection between Apollinaire's poetry, his art criticism, his aesthetic vision, and even his relationship with contemporary artists such as Pablo Picasso and Marcel Duchamp.

Themes and Meanings

"The Hills" is considered to be one of Apollinaire's poetic testaments (a quote from it is engraved on the poet's tombstone) in which he develops his vision of the future of art and literature. In this poem, he predicts a new kind of aesthetic ideal, superior to the traditional one that "arose from symmetry." This idea of new aesthetic creation is expressed in an allusion to a Greek myth. In stanza 8, when he foresees that "Seafoam would once more be mother," the poet refers to Venus, the goddess of beauty born from the sea foam, and he announces the advent of a new type of beauty.

Apollinaire refers to another Greek myth when defining his vision of the poet's new mission. For him, the poet is also similar to a magician or a prophet gifted with almost supernatural powers. In this definition, the reader can identify the mythical figure of Orpheus who, in Greek mythology, was a poet, musician, and prophet with magical powers. His art could charm the most ferocious beasts and bring peace and harmony. He traveled to the underworld to bring his wife, Eurydice, back from the dead. This myth is one of Apollinaire's favorites, and, in "The Hills," the imagery of travel in time and space, beyond life and death, can be interpreted as a modern replica to Orpheus's journey.

In Apollinaire's interpretation, the myth of Orpheus also incarnates the idea of the poet as a martyr and of poetry as a sacred and sacrificial gesture (Orpheus, who appears in many of Apollinaire's poems and stories, is killed and torn to pieces by bacchantes who do not understand his art). "A time will come for suffering," the poet predicts in stanza 25, and this theme of poetry as suffering and martyrdom is continued throughout the poem in images inspired also by Christian parables and medieval legends. In "The Hills," the poet's words become vegetal: They are "sweet fruits" and "grain" (in stanzas 27 and 28) that can be shared and eaten. The suffering (converted into vegetal food) is always mentioned in relation to the goodness of heart (in stanzas 24, 25, and 35, for example), so it appears like a deeply humanitarian sacrifice. The image of the poet-martyr sacrificing himself for humankind and offering himself to be eaten as fruit or grain is derived from the Eucharist (in which Christ symbolically offers his body to be eaten).

The presence of numerous archetypes, timeless stories, and myths in Apollinaire's poetry may seem surprising when one considers that he was trying to promote what he called "a new lyricism" and a "new spirit." However, his temporal perspective explains this intermingling of ancient figures (references to myths and legends) and modern descriptive elements (such as airplanes, car drivers, and elevators): In "The Hills," Apollinaire expresses his belief that the poet must include in his view both tradition and innovation. The past and the ancestors must somehow be permanently present in an artist's life. Thus, the new aesthetic ideal that he predicts is not the destruction of older models but rather the continuation of a heritage.

Anca Mitroi Sprenger

THE HIND AND THE PANTHER

Author: John Dryden (1631-1700)
Type of poem: Narrative
First published: 1687

The Poem

    The Hind and the Panther is a long poem in three parts totaling 2,592 lines. In this poem, John Dryden employs his favorite verse form, the heroic couplet. Taken as a whole, *The Hind and the Panther* is an allegorical and argumentative treatment of the religious conflicts that took place in England during the reign of King James II. More specifically, the poem is a defense of the Catholic faith and of Dryden's conversion to Catholicism in 1685. The hind of the poem's title is an allegorical deer representing the Catholic church, while the panther represents the Anglican church.

    In part 1 of *The Hind and the Panther*, Dryden introduces the various religious factions of his time as allegorical beasts. Thus, the bear represents religious independents, the hare represents Quakers, the ape represents atheists, the boar represents Baptists, the fox represents Unitarians, and the wolf represents Presbyterians. The fox and the wolf are described with special satiric intensity. Also in part 1, Dryden includes a moving and beautifully expressed confession of his own religious faith. Part 1 concludes with a meeting between the Catholic hind and the Anglican panther, which sets the stage for part 2.

    Part 2 is essentially a vigorous debate between the hind and the panther in which the main differences between Catholicism and Anglicanism are argued in verse of great power and discursive clarity. The issues discussed include church authority, biblical interpretation, the value of Catholic oral tradition, the Catholic doctrine of infallibility, and the 1673 Test Act, which prevented Catholics from being appointed to important state positions. Consistent with the general purpose of the poem, the Catholic positions are expressed with overwhelmingly persuasive force.

    Part 3 continues the debate between the hind and the panther but deals less with doctrine than with the political future of Catholics in England. The panther tells an animal fable dealing with swallows and martins in which the swallows, representing Catholics in general, and the martins, representing the Catholic clergy, are fooled by mild weather into delaying migration until they are destroyed by the coming of winter. This fable within a fable not only expresses Anglican antipathy toward the Catholics but also serves as Dryden's warning to his fellow Catholics that they should not depend too much on King James's pro-Catholic policies. By way of answer to the panther, the hind tells her own fable of the pigeons and the buzzard in which she warns of the dangers to the Anglican church if the Anglicans ally themselves too closely with the sectarian supporters of the anti-Catholic Test Act. Following this fable, the poem ends with a beautiful passage that suggests the divine nature and the glorious future of the Catholic church.

Forms and Devices

Dryden's most obvious literary technique in *The Hind and the Panther* is the allegorical animal fable. Not only is the poem as a whole an animal fable, but part 3 also presents two distinct animal fables within the larger fable. As Dryden makes clear at the beginning of part 3, he is very much aware of the tradition of the animal fable, which goes back to ancient times. By using the fable, he is able to deal with very controversial and potentially explosive religious and political matters with humor, detachment, clarity, and simplicity. His use of the animal fable gives *The Hind and the Panther* a lightness and playfulness that the reader might not expect from the poem's serious subject matter.

Dryden balances the lightness of his fable with another literary technique that is important in both *The Hind and the Panther* and his poetry in general. Dryden was a great master of the verse essay. There are few poets in all of world literature who can equal his ability to reason and debate within the restrictions and formal demands of verse structure. Thus, especially in part 2, the debate between the hind and the panther regarding complex religious issues is handled with a precision, force, logic, and polish that are uniquely Drydenian. Much of the success of *The Hind and the Panther* stems from Dryden's remarkable combination of fabulistic charm and discursive strength.

Dryden's poetry as a whole is famous for its satire, and satire is, predictably, an important element in *The Hind and the Panther*. In part 1, Dryden sharply satirizes religious sectarianism in general and Unitarianism and Presbyterianism in particular. Moreover, the history of Anglicanism, the contradictions of the Church of England, and the political effects of radical Protestantism are handled with flashing ridicule.

Dryden's imagery is also important in *The Hind and the Panther*, especially imagery associated with light. Light is most often used to describe the purity and truth of Catholicism. Thus, the Catholic church is "a blaze of glory that forbids the sight," while the Anglican church is seen as a moon that reflects the higher light of Catholicism: "The rays she borrow'd from a better star." Dryden also uses a wide variety of imagery to clarify arguments or to sharpen satiric points. Thus, he communicates the doctrinal instability of Anglicanism with a simple but effective image: "Her wild belief on ev'ry wave is toss'd." In discussing the intellectual darkness of radical sectarianism, Dryden reduces the followers of such sects to blind insects. They are "such souls as shards produce, such beetle things/ As only buzz to heav'n with ev'ning wings." His wonderfully diminishing imagery also describes the origins of Calvinism on the shores of Lake Geneva near the Alps: "What tho' your native kennel still be small,/ Bounded betwixt a puddle and a wall."

Finally, Dryden's complete mastery of the neoclassical heroic couplet is crucial to *The Hind and the Panther*. His handling of narrative, argument, and satire in the poem depends on the compression and energy of his couplets. As an example, note how Dryden uses rhythm, parallel structure, and alliteration within the heroic couplet to define the weakness of the Anglican church surrounded by sectarian enemies: "Rul'd while she rules, and losing ev'ry hour/ Her wretched remnants of precarious pow'r."

Themes and Meanings

In his formative years, Dryden saw the chaos and destruction brought by a religiously inspired civil war in England. Most of Dryden's major poems, including *Absalom and Achitophel* (1681-1682), *Mac Flecknoe* (1682), and *Religio Laici* (1682), deal with his search for an authority and a coherent tradition that could stand against anarchy and the destructive power of radical individualism. *The Hind and the Panther* is Dryden's longest and most ambitious treatment of this theme. His fear of and scorn for the radical individualism that leads to extreme sectarianism is evident throughout the poem. In part 1, the sectarian animals (the wolf, the fox, the hare, and the boar) are all satiric portraits revealing the dangers of "private reason." For Dryden, all religious sects are tainted by pride, arrogance, confusion, violence, and a generally rebellious spirit. This sectarian rebelliousness has dangerous political and religious implications. Also for Dryden, sectarian belief in the efficacy of reason presents a fundamental and profound problem. In Dryden's view, the very essence of religion is that it deals with things beyond reason. Reason is valuable in those areas where it is appropriate, but it is helpless and misleading in the higher sphere of divinity: "Let Reason then at her own quarry fly,/ But how can finite grasp Infinity?"

In part 2 of *The Hind and the Panther*, Dryden sees the Anglican church as the least tainted of non-Catholic faiths. It is "least deform'd, because reform'd the least." Still, with great argumentative and poetic skill, Dryden expresses what he sees as the essential faults of the Anglican hind: It has no real apostolic authority, it is the dubious result of English political history, it is inconsistent and wavering in its basic doctrine, and it relies on a belief in individual biblical interpretation that can only produce chaos. In part 3, Dryden goes on to emphasize what he sees as the Anglican church's destructive willingness to enter into unscrupulous political alliances.

Since, for Dryden, no church based on "private reason" and sectarianism can provide a true authority and a valid tradition, it is in the Catholic church that he finds what he calls the "one central principle of unity." For Dryden, the Catholic church is "Entire, one solid shining diamond." It has the majesty of the bride of Christ. It is an authoritative and unwavering source of doctrine. It has a unity, a sanctity, a universality, and a claim to apostolic succession that form a telling contrast to the intellectual and spiritual chaos which, for Dryden, marked the English religious sects of the late seventeenth century. Certainly, from one point of view, Dryden's poem is a brilliantly versified defense of Catholicism. It is, however, something more: the dramatization of a powerful mind's search for certainty in a world of political and religious confusion.

Phillip B. Anderson

HIS SHIELD

Author: Marianne Moore (1887-1972)
Type of poem: Lyric
First published: 1951, in *Collected Poems*

The Poem

"His Shield" is a thirty-three-line poem in five stanzas, with an end-line rhyming scheme. Moore chose the title "His Shield" (originally "The Magic Shield") in an attempt to explain the life of Presbyter John, a legendary Christian of medieval times from Asia or Africa who was said to wear a salamander's skin for protection, thus shielding him from heat, fire, and other natural phenomena. Making the name "John" doubly interesting is the fact that her own father was named John, as was her grandfather, who was himself a "Presbyter": He was a Presbyterian minister in St. Louis, Missouri, where Moore was born in 1887.

Moore's poetry has been compared to the poetry of John Donne and, like Donne's poetry, is often called "metaphysical" because she uses images from nature and expands them by using metaphors. The central metaphor of nature's protective devices is used throughout "His Shield." In the first stanza Moore immediately mentions a number of animals, including the hedgehog, porcupine, and rhinoceros, that wear some sort of protection on their bodies. Her point is that many animals are prepared for life as they might be prepared for war; life is so dangerous that animals must evolve shields to battle the elements, as well as other animals, every day: "everything is battle-dressed."

In the second stanza Moore recognizes that human beings have very little protection in life, and she turns to the legendary Presbyter John for a clue as to how to save herself from the dangerous elements that might bombard her skin. She decides to use salamander skin, which supposedly has asbestoslike qualities, to shield her from fire and the sun. If John could protect himself in Africa with salamander skin, she too can become "asbestos-eyed asbestos-eared" to "withstand fire" and avoid drowning.

Attending to the Presbyter John legend in greater detail in stanza 3, Moore states that in Africa, where Presbyter John might have lived in perhaps the twelfth century, the land was rich with gold and rubies, yet no one valued these items greatly. No one was envious or greedy. Presbyter John was able to gird himself even more effectively than with salamander skin: He donned a coat of humility that deflected all jealousy and harm.

Stanza 4 explains that a shield of humility, similar perhaps to that used by Presbyter John, could provide protection for the leader of the African country of Ethiopia in the 1940's (the time when the poem was written). This dimension of the poem is difficult to grasp from the text alone, but Moore provided some explanation in other writings and interviews. Haile Selassie (also called the "Lion of Judah") was the emperor of Ethiopia, which was being besieged by Italy during World War II. Perhaps, Moore suggests, Selassie and Ethiopia could remain free without actually being free. Surrounded by his enemies, Selassie is advised to stay humble, avoid greed, avoid pomp, and avoid provoking the enemy.

In the final stanza Moore gives direct advice to readers on how they might avoid battles in their own lives. "Become dinosaur-/ skulled" and "ironshod," she suggests. More important, along with this armor, readers are urged to "be/ dull. Don't be envied." In other words, they should not be pompous, should not appear proud and haughty. People should stop counting their money and counting their victories. They should put aside their "measuring-rod" for sizing up their enemies and their friends. Remaining humble and avoiding confrontations is the way to survival.

Forms and Devices

Marianne Moore often used works of art, photographs, or newspaper articles to trigger ideas for poems. In addition, common animals such as porcupines, elephants, swans, and snakes often inspired her. As Patricia C. Willis explains in her book *Marianne Moore: Vision into Verse* (1987), "His Shield" was inspired by an article in *The New York Times* entitled "Rare Animal Freak Is Echidna in Zoo." Moore read and clipped the article, and later she combined what she had read with a book she had been reading about Haile Selassie. This book also included the legend of Presbyter John. The newspaper article described the echidna as an animal with "spines as defense armor." Moore added to this the idea of Presbyter John living his life in humility and the World War II theme of protection for Ethiopia, where Haile Selassie was facing the enemy in a battle for freedom.

Thus Moore began with an animal and built a metaphor that is challenging for the reader to decipher. The echidna, an Australian animal, is somewhat like a porcupine except that it hatches its young from eggs and then raises them in a kangaroolike pouch. The echidna is a very obscure creature to use as the central metaphor in a poem. Moore explained the problem of challenging the reader, yet being understood, when she said to Donald Hall (*A Marianne Moore Reader*, 1961), "I think the most difficult thing for me is to be satisfactorily lucid, yet have enough implication in it to suit myself."

The problems in understanding "His Shield" are not resolved once one can picture the echidna. One must also be able to picture a religious man living centuries ago in Africa, perhaps Ethiopia, preaching the gospel and wearing the skin of the salamander (another unusual animal) to protect himself from the heat. There is also the problem of understanding the situation in 1944 Ethiopia, where Haile Selassie was in reality battling his Italian enemies, using weapons and armor to save his country. In a sense, Moore's poem seems to be written to the world at large in 1944. The poem is sufficiently ambiguous that the reader wonders exactly what Moore intends. Is "His Shield" an antiwar poem? Is Moore advocating that Selassie become humble to avoid death? Should he and Ethiopia put down their armor and rely only on being humble and "dull"?

Themes and Meanings

"His Shield" uses nature as a model, as a provoking influence, to guide humans to make the right decisions. Moore suggests that people can find metaphors—and answers—for human problems by studying nature carefully. However, she goes beyond the physical to the metaphorical and the psychological. Perhaps, she muses, people can use a state of mind—in this case, humility—to foil their enemies. They can be "dull," paradoxically relinquishing their freedom to keep it alive. They can become "dinosaur-skulled" to protect the brain and can use the brain to be humble.

Moore's themes, though they typically start with a simple, obscure image, grow until they encompass a way of life, a way of living, that can protect and enlighten. Moore gave a hint at the meaning of "His Shield" when she spoke of humility in a speech she gave at the Grolier Club in 1948:

> Humility, indeed, is armor, for it realizes that it is impossible to be original, in the sense of doing something that has never been thought of before. Originality is in any case a by-product of sincerity . . . of feeling that is honest and accordingly rejects anything that might cloud the impression.

"His Shield" could also be described as a sort of "metaphysical satire." If satire pokes fun at the pompous, if it shows that a common way of dealing with life is false or egotistical, then "His Shield" is satirizing those who rely on weapons, verbal darts, and other offensive tactics to dominate others. Whether in actual warfare or in coffeehouse conversation, Moore admonishes people to put away armor, greed, and envy and to replace these ineffective tools with a humble approach. After all, since there is nothing new in nature, humans have little that is new. Therefore, perhaps they should stop measuring one another for greatness in life or imagination. Instead, Moore would have people put away their "measuring-rod" in order to be safe and free.

Larry Rochelle

A HISTORY OF CIVILIZATION

Author: Albert Goldbarth (1948-   )
Type of poem: Lyric
First published: 1981; collected in *Original Light: New and Selected Poems, 1973-1983*, 1983

The Poem

Reading "A History of Civilization" is somewhat like opening a box within a box within a box. The poem consists of four six-line stanzas organized so that each stanza focuses on a particular place and each place suggests a particular past. Each of the first three stanzas ends on the open phrase "In back," thus sending the reader quickly into the next stanza. For all its brevity, "A History of Civilization" does not quite fit the definition of a lyric. The reader does not "overhear" a speaker, but is treated to a complex layering of scenes.

The poem opens in the present, in a "dating bar" where everything is a bit suggestive. All the details evoke the contemporary—silk blouses, sweet brie. In back of the dating bar is the "last one-family grocer's," with its strings of vegetables, coffee, kidney beans. The lush details of the store—the "millet barrel" and the cash register "as intricate as a Sicilian shrine"—seem to be of another era. The woman here is proud of her clean linen apron rather than a silk blouse.

In back of the grocery is a room with a fireplace where a ring of "somber-gabardined grandpas" play dominoes: "Even their/ coughs, their phlegms, are in an older language." This scene evokes America's immigrant past. The final stanza takes place "in back/ of the back room" where cats are eyeing other cats, spraying the sacks and baskets with their scent. Here, in the animal world, it's mating season too. "The dust motes drift, the continents." Time moves inexorably on, and very little has changed over the "history of civilization." All species must reproduce themselves in order to move into the future, and the poem concludes, "In the fern bar a hand tries a knee, as if unplanned."

Although the poem presents these rooms as opening into each other, as though they were linked in physical space, the subtle shifts in vocabulary hint that they may inhabit a continuum in time, as though there were only one room that has gone through the transformation from storage vault to "back room" to grocery to dating bar, following the needs of the new generations. Either "reading" is acceptable, since history is not only a series of successive events but also a fluid connection *between* events—a layering of time and place and interpretation.

The title of the poem makes large claims, but the details of the poem are so particular—and sometimes humorous—that the reader understands that the title is at least partly tongue-in-cheek. Take any place and peel back the layers, the poem seems to say, and you will find just such a "history." The progress of the human race depends on rooms such as these. "A History of Civilization" honors the daily lives of ordinary people even as it pokes some fun at the concepts of "history" and "civilization."

Forms and Devices

The most notable device in "A History of Civilization" is the use of subtle shifts in tone and language. Goldbarth not only lingers lovingly on the details of each specific place but also looks at each scene with a slightly altered eye. In the dating bar, sexual innuendo is extended to inanimate objects; the ferns are seen as "spore-studded/ elopement ladders." There is a sardonic eye that equates "slices of smiles" with "slices of sweet brie." Even the atmosphere of the bar ("dark and its many white wedges") is reduced to pockets of light where the single people can eye one another. In the grocery, however, Goldbarth illuminates the past, as though it were imperative to "fix" it in memory. His adjectives and similes make the objects almost palpable. The coffee barrel has a "cordovan sheen," and the millet scoops "stand at attention." "Sheen" extends to the woman polishing the cash register until "sheen" elides to "shrine."

The next stanza finds its core in the repeated imagery of insubstantiality. The old men doze and wake in "fitful starts" by a "guttering" fire. Their beards "flicker" in the light. In the shimmer of such vocabulary, the people appear and fade, half-seen, nearly legend. There is an almost formal tone as the poet pays homage to their simplicity. The vocabulary and tone of the final stanza returns to the informal, almost hip, language of the opening. (Both stanzas have to do with sexuality and procreation, the first of humans, the last of cats.) Cats "eye" cats, and everything "comes down to a few/ sure moves." There are "sure moves" in language, too, as Goldbarth deftly describes an era in a few chosen words.

"A History of Civilization" relies heavily on alliteration and assonance. "Two top buttons" emphasizes the letter *t*, and "white wedges" and "flicker like filaments" are other obvious examples of these techniques. Goldbarth also carefully orchestrates his phrases more subtly to take advantage of consonants, as in the parallel sounds of "coffee barrel" and "kidney beans" or the elegance of "unlit lengths." Vowels are given similar importance, starting with the short *a* of "back," which is echoed throughout. The short *u* of "rut" and "estrus" weds them in sound as well as sense. But the *tour de force* of assonance remains the "register as intricate as a Sicilian shrine." The shift from a hard to a soft *c* and the repeated *n* make the tongue "polish" the phrase just as the woman lingers over her dusting.

There is a ghost of meter behind this poem—"In the dating bar, the potted ferns lean down" has more than a hint of iambic pentameter, and this rhythm is repeated just often enough to remind the reader of its presence. Never singsong, the poem builds toward the metrical authority of its most important sentence: "The dust motes drift, the continents."

Themes and Meanings

Albert Goldbarth's poems are spun from an encyclopedic mind that engages odd snippets of information as well as the whole of scientific treatises. The "larger" issues have been Goldbarth's themes, but he treats them in unique, even spectacular ways. Funny, ironic, bitter, hilarious, irreverent, sexy, serious—this list of adjectives could apply to almost every one of his poems. "A History of Civilization" is a relatively early poem. It is less experimental, more traditional, than Goldbarth's later poems. Yet through its title and its complex structure, it predicts the poet who went on to write books with such titles as *Heaven and Earth: A Cosmology* (1991) and *Across the Layers: Poems Old and New* (1993) and to win the National Book Critics Circle Award. Goldbarth's style developed into one of excess—excessively long sentences packed with an excess of fact, speculation, memory, data of all kinds. Images and incidents fuse, break apart, then connect again. Everything is part of a larger chaos that, in the end, belongs to an even larger order.

Whether it is like the short journey of the dust mote or the more dramatic shifting of tectonic plates, the life of any individual is insignificant when measured against eternity. History, however, creates a context and reveals significance. "A History of Civilization" peels back layers of remembered time to uncover the basic values of America, to shine the spotlight briefly on the hard work of the immigrant family before the poem veers off (or back) to the one procreative force that shapes animals and humans alike. Lives are composed of an amalgam of history, coincidence, and imagination; one goes on layering the quotidian until the past becomes so distant it needs to be reinvented.

When Goldbarth introduces the old men playing dominoes, firelight flickering on their beards "like filaments still waiting for the bulb or the phone to be invented," he describes the scene with the benefit of hindsight, naming the technology that will pull them into the present even as it thrusts the scene into the past. But Goldbarth looks through both ends of the telescope at once. The rooms become a palimpsest, time superimposed on place, until they fuse into one story. Thus, in the way of all "stories," history is being made this evening in the dating bar.

In the poem's final line, "In the fern bar a hand tries a knee, as if unplanned," the "as if" is important. It knows something of human nature. The planning is part of the age-old ritual of courtship that keeps the world spinning. This final line is also the moment when the reader becomes aware of the speaker as a shaping presence. More than an omniscient author, he is someone with a wry commentary, a point of view. If a cosmology implies a philosophy, Goldbarth's might be simply this: In a universe so vast, people have one another.

Judith Kitchen

THE HOLLOW MEN

Author: T. S. Eliot (1888-1965)
Type of poem: Dramatic monologue
First published: 1925, in *Poems, 1909-1925*

The Poem

"The Hollow Men" is both a single hundred-line poem and a sequence of five po-ems (or parts). Although almost entirely lacking in simple narrative cohesiveness and linear development, and defying simple classification ("The Hollow Men" is at once dramatic monologue, soliloquy, choric ode, lyric, elegy, and meditation), T. S. Eliot's highly and at times allegorically abstract text nevertheless achieves a remarkable unity of effect in terms of voice, mood, and imagery. The simplicity and seeming transparency of the title—a conflation of William Shakespeare's *Julius Caesar* (c. 1599-1600) and poems by Rudyard Kipling and William Morris—serve as an ironic indicator of Eliot's rich and complex texture. The two epigraphs—one from Joseph Conrad's novel, *Heart of Darkness* (1899), and the other a child's line from the yearly observance of Guy Fawkes Day (November 5) in England—serve a similar purpose; they contextualize the poem literarily and historically while underscoring the poem's thematization of spiritual hollowness and failure of will.

The poem is chiefly narrated in the first-person plural; a "we" that serves to broaden the speaker's predicament beyond the individual to encompass a more nearly universal figure who is emblematic of his age and who may well be speaking for, as well as to, the reader. Against the dying Kurtz's last words, "The horror! The horror!" in *Heart of Darkness*, Eliot's narrator can only rouse himself to utter a "quiet and meaningless" "Alas!" of resignation and despair.

The very fact that this "we" does speak (although monotonously) holds out at least the possibility that this "we" is not yet completely resigned to human inconsequential-ity and to a spiritual void—that, whether from guilt or from need, "we" yearns for something more. The wasteland depicted here looks back to Eliot's 1922 poem *The Waste Land* but more especially to Dante's *Inferno* (c. 1320). "We" are modern-day versions of Dante's tormented souls suffering in "our" low-grade way the pain of loss, whispering rather than howling. The Dantean allusion helps to explain the otherwise inexplicable shift from plural "we" to singular "I" in part 2 and helps explain the in-tensification of wasteland and inferno imagery here and in part 3. Part 4 holds out the distinct, slight possibility of redemption for those otherwise condemned to groping blindly "in this valley of dying stars," of dying hope.

On the very verge of entering the saving (baptismal) waters of "the tumid river," of crossing over Eliot's version of the River Styx from the land of death in life to that of life in death, the choric narrator fails to make the necessary Kierkegaardian leap of faith. He remains where he is, poised between spiritual as well as sexual sterility and the promise of a redemption, which, he also perceives, holds the threat of judgment and damnation.

The fifth and concluding section is structurally the most complex and thematically the most disturbing. The unresolved mix of pronouncements, prayer, and nursery rhyme (with its substitution of "prickly pear" for "mulberry bush") offers no entry into purgatory, no glimpse of paradise. Instead, it leaves speaker and reader alike still poised between two states of being and therefore still very much in the grip of paralyzing despair.

Forms and Devices

In his review of James Joyce's prototypical high modernist novel, *Ulysses* (1922), written at the very time he began work on the poems that would later make up "The Hollow Men," Eliot explained that "in manipulating a continuous parallel between contemporaneity and antiquity, Mr. Joyce is pursuing a method which others must pursue after him. . . . It is simply a way of controlling, of ordering, of giving a shape and a significance to the immense panorama of futility and anarchy which is contemporary history." Eliot had himself already employed the mythic method to devastating effect in *The Waste Land*. That method, along with the richly allusive style to which it is closely tied, plays a less insistent but arguably more integral role in giving shape and direction to the considerably less diversified but still disconcerting flux of materials (or "stuffing") from which Eliot assembled "The Hollow Men."

Rudyard Kipling, William Morris, Joseph Conrad, William Shakespeare, Ernest Dowson, and Paul Valéry play their parts, but none so importantly, pervasively, and unobtrusively as Dante. His *Divine Comedy* (c. 1320) serves as both the foundation upon which Eliot's otherwise fragmented text rests and as the yardstick by which the choric speaker's spiritual plight may be measured. The point of the mythic method is not to show how far modern man has fallen from some nostalgically regarded golden age, but to show how similar, even static, the human condition actually is. Such a procedure transforms Eliot's paralyzed narrator into a figure capable of Dantean grandeur—and anguish.

In addition to perfecting the mythic method, Eliot began structuring his poetry in dramatic terms. The two procedures are in fact clearly connected, for Eliot's interest in drama focused on its origin in primitive rituals. The choric voice and "drum-beat" rhythms of "The Hollow Men" manifest a dramatic quality that Eliot adds to and plays against the Dantean parallel. The prevalence of short lines, of elliptical and fragmentary phrasings, and the repetition of a handful of key words and images (eyes, shadow, and kingdom, for example), as well as the inclusion of two framing quasi-rituals (the children begging on Guy Fawkes Day and the "here we go round the mulberry bush" children's rhyme), highlight the poem's dramatic quality, even if they do not direct attention to it overtly, and add not only to the work's incantatory effect but also make it at once mythic and modern, strangely primitive yet remarkably up-to-date.

Themes and Meanings

Although sufficient evidence exists to warrant reading "The Hollow Men" as autobiographical revelation, Eliot's commitment (particularly at this point in his career) to an "impersonalist" aesthetic and to finding "objective correlatives" that would transform private experience into subjective terms requires a less narrow approach. "The Hollow Men" reflects the lingering post-World War I malaise that affected not only Eliot but his age as well.

The poem succeeds admirably in registering a mood not merely of disillusionment but of personal weakness. The choric speaker, either speaking in unison with others about their common condition or speaking alone for them, perhaps because they do not yet perceive or understand their plight, wearily yet, in his own way, steadfastly resists the self-knowledge to which his whispering leads him. This resistance is, however, tempered by the fact that he mocks himself for his failure. He fears the judgment that will expose his failure of nerve to others and to himself at least as much as he fears the death that will just as surely expose the meaninglessness of his life as a spiritual coward or zombie.

Although he fears the "eyes" that will know and pass sentence on his evident inadequacy, he also longs for the "eyes" that see what he does not. These are the eyes (of Dante's Beatrice and Christ's mother Mary) evoked in the poem's most intensely lyrical moment: "The eyes [that] reappear/ As the perpetual star/ Multifoliate rose/ Of death's twilight kingdom/ The hope only/ Of empty men." The moment—"Alas!"— does not last; it is followed by the highly fragmented fifth and final section, which ends, as does *The Waste Land*, with a shoring of fragments against the ruin. Unlike *The Waste Land*, however, here poetic word and world end not with madness and not "with a bang but a whimper." The shadow of spiritual death—doubt and despair— falls; the mood of spiritual paralysis prevails.

Robert A. Morace

HOMAGE TO PAUL CÉZANNE

Author: Charles Wright (1935-   )
Type of poem: Meditation
First published: 1977; collected in *The Southern Cross*, 1981

The Poem

Charles Wright's "Homage to Paul Cézanne" consists of eight unnumbered sections of sixteen lines each that examine the nature of the relationship between the living and the dead. "Homage to Paul Cézanne" opens Charles Wright's fifth volume of poems, *The Southern Cross*, which inaugurates a departure in both technique and outlook from his earlier volumes. It stands on the threshold of the poet's mature style, and, as the poet himself acknowledged, "Homage to Paul Cézanne" holds a special place in his entire work.

The poem begins by describing the dead and what they are wearing at night, when their presence is both visible and ascertainable. Although some specific features are singled out, the speaker's voice (presumably the poet's) keeps reassuring the reader that the dead are "like us," in many respects, and act accordingly: "Like us,/ They keep on saying the same thing, trying to get it right." After putting together some familiar and some less familiar traits, in the second section their presence is further qualified by pointing out some rules or even laws underlying their behavior: "Each year the dead grow less dead, and nudge/ Close to the surface of all things."

The third section of the poem deals with the degree of integration with nature and the landscape, which the dead have succeeded in achieving in order to communicate both their story and their utmost desire—never to be forgotten: "*Remember me, speak my name*." The fourth section, or variation on the theme, brings the reader closer to a metaphysical understanding of their condition, which in terms of color—after all, the poem is in praise of a great French painter, Paul Cézanne (1839-1906)—is a certain kind of blue, endowed with psycho-intellectual abilities, such as understanding.

Once this identity is established, it can be further naturalized either by requiring the dead to do various domestic chores or by pointing to their involvement in the greater drama of the elements: "Over our heads they're huge in the night sky" and "Their sighs are gaps in the wind." Next, the reader becomes acquainted with the minute acts of communication that occur through the day between the dead and the living "we," their initiatives and their solicitude:

> The dead are waiting for us in our rooms,
> Little globules of light
> In one of the far corners, and close to the ceiling, hovering, think-
>   ing our thoughts.

In the seventh part the claim of omnipresence is greater still: "The dead fall around us like rain." Finally, the poem concludes by returning to the mundane, palpable reality of the humble and helpless condition of the living. If the dead are so involved in what "we" do and think, then, it seems, the living are less able to reciprocate: "Whose tongue is toothless enough to speak their piece?" Against this background of who can do what and, especially, of who can transcend what, the poet rather humorously reminds his readers of another presence with other concerns. Nonchalantly, screened by the clouds, bears "Amble across the heavens, serene as black coffee."

Forms and Devices

Having opted, in his fifth volume, for a less elliptical and encoded poetic mode, and in favor of a more discursive type of utterance, implicitly Wright moved, on the whole, in the direction of a more fully fledged sentence structure, more classical in form and, therefore, more transparent and explicit. This strategy imparted to the poem a greater rhetorical forcefulness, without losing the flexibility of a modern free form. Each section has a specific inner structure, which can be further examined in terms of a center or of a symmetry axis in order to observe the way meaning gets organized in smaller or larger syntactical units.

The best way to assess how meaning emerges in a Wright poem is to consider the individual line, which in this poem varies in length (number of syllables and of stresses) and, moreover, is not vertically grouped or linked by means of rhyme. This way of building a complex poem imparts a sense of an overall pattern whose intricate order is coupled with much local (horizontal) freedom. The poet achieves his line in the same manner the painter employs his palette knife or brushstroke.

Both the beginning and the ending of the poem—the first and the eighth sections—are more daringly "poetic" than the rest. There is room for language employed figuratively in the traditional sense. In the first section, moonshine is "fish-light"; leaves have gotten "little arks"; envelopes "wait" on desks; water "unsettles" (erases) dead people's names; "We [the living] rub" the dead people's answers "off our hands." In contrast, the imagery in the closing section is full of movement: Stars are "streaming"; the mountain "glides"; bears "amble across the heavens"; "Our gestures salve for the wind."

In the remaining—middle—sections the utterances are less tentative, plainer in their intent. Hence a rhetoric of insistent stress and repetition is served by shorter, terse sentences. An explanatory mode, as in the climactic fourth section, creeps in. Even when states of mind get more complex, as in the sixth section, and the sentences more elaborate and less manageable, what prevails is an argumentative stance in which a sense of temporal reality—however misleading and unreal the temporality of the dead is—has to be established in terms of spatial coordinates and activities: "The voices rising around us like mist// And dew, *it's all right, it's all right, it's all right.*"

Themes and Meanings

The theme of the poem is clearly specified and underlined throughout, namely "the dead." By this syntagma the poet means primarily his parents and other departed relatives or friends. Later in his career, Wright embarked upon a related topic when—in six numbered, separate poems bearing the generic title "The Appalachian Book of the Dead"—he tackled a mythology of death and dying. What is less clear, and of no little consequence to the understanding of "Homage to Paul Cézanne," is the relation between the topic and the poem's title.

Paul Cézanne was the towering figure of modernity at the turn of the twentieth century. Both cubism, exemplified by Pablo Picasso, and Fauvism, by Henri Matisse, sprang from him. His characters, landscapes, and still lifes yield an overpowering sense of reality. At the same time, one of his chief concerns was to establish a parallel between the harmony at work in nature and the one inherent in his art. Wright's insight was that the dead daily imbue reality with their presence as, for instance, the color blue, which was used in everything Cézanne painted. This is particularly visible in the later landscapes, including the series of sixty works dedicated to Mont Sainte-Victoire, which dominates the sights at Aix-en-Provence, a historical and cultural region in southern France.

The American critic and novelist William Gass, in his essay "On Being Blue: A Philosophical Inquiry" (1975), examined that color's symbolism. Blue is credited with expressing both emotional and intellectual states. In addition, blue embodies two of the primeval elements, air and water. Historically, blue was related to ancient cultures, such as those of Egypt and China, and to some of the major world religions, including Christianity. It was dealt with by such philosophers as Plato and Kant and by some major romantic poets, for both its lofty and pure connotations.

Cézanne's palette of blues included cobalt, ultramarine, and Prussian blue. In the fourth section of the poem, Wright, however, uses the term "cadmium blue," a combination which seems impossible, because cadmium oxides yield only ocher pigments. In his finely crafted first line, Wright says, "The dead are a cadmium blue." He therefore hints in a subtle way at the singularity of the metaphor and, by implication at the condition of the dead. They are blue for they are dematerialized, spiritual; yet they are also of the earth. Hence the cadmium component, for their so-called fingerprints can be seen everywhere.

To lend some additional weight to such a reading, Wright elaborated that

> such a color does not exist. Which is precisely the reason I made the color up and used it in the poem. The "dead," the subject of the poem, don't exist either, and yet they do. The same thing goes for the color, cadmium blue—it does not exist but I try to make it so by describing it in terms of something else which does not, but which we can apprehend, the "idea" of the dead. The whole poem deals in the attempt to make abstractions representational.

Stefan Stoenescu

HOMAGE TO SEXTUS PROPERTIUS

Author: Ezra Pound (1885-1972)
Type of poem: Poetic sequence
First published: 1919, in *Quia Pauper Amavi*

The Poem

   Homage to Sextus Propertius is essentially Ezra Pound's translation of books 2 and 3 of the *Elegies* by the Roman poet Sextus Propertius, who lived during the latter part of the first century C.E. Calling this poem a "translation," however, is misleading. Although many of Pound's lines are accurate translations of the Latin verses, other stretches of the English-language poem depart widely in sense from the Latin original. Nevertheless, the subject matter of *Homage to Sextus Propertius* is that of the original books of the elegies, though the ordering of the various sections is often Pound's own.

   Section I encompasses the standard elegiac introduction of classical poetry: Propertius establishes his credentials as a young poet, with a new way of saying things. He acknowledges that his fame might be some time in coming, but when it does come, he will have a better memorial than the finest, most elaborate tomb. Part of Propertius's novel poetic manner is his subject matter: Instead of glorifying the exploits of Imperial Rome, he intends to be part of the lyric tradition of classical poetry, which emphasizes love and intense personal emotion.

   In the first stanza, Propertius calls up the ghosts of past lyric poets, thereby establishing his poetic heritage. He then contrasts the lyric tradition, in the second stanza, with popular contemporary poets whose subject is war. In the third stanza, he heightens the contrast through irony, speaking with contempt of poets whose chief role seems to be publicists of the Roman state and its "celebrities." Propertius concludes this section with the traditional prediction that those who are mentioned in his poems will enjoy eternal fame along with the poet.

   In section II, Propertius extends his opening theme, explaining how he came to turn from the currently popular subjects of war and conquest to poems having to do with pining lovers, sorcery, and midnight trysts. The impetus behind his change of heart, Propertius claims, comes from two visions: one of Apollo ("Phoebus") and one from Calliope (the Greek muse of epic poetry). These two supernatural beings, both of whom were traditionally associated with poetic inspiration, remind Propertius that his gifts do not lie in the area of public poetry.

   In section III, Propertius turns, then, to what he does best—writing about love. In this section, he receives a late-night invitation from Cynthia, his lover, to visit her. Out of timidity, however, he refuses.

   At midnight, Cynthia demands that Propertius come to her—the implication is that their meeting will be for lovemaking. Propertius experiences a conflict, however; on the one hand, he is eager to visit his mistress (and he knows how angry she can be if he fails her). On the other hand, he worries about muggers. The unlit streets of ancient Rome were probably no safer at midnight than those of modern New York City, and Propertius imagines his robbery and death.

He tries to bolster his courage in the third stanza by recalling that lovers are sacred. Even if he does meet violence, he tells himself, such a death is worth dying for Cynthia's sake. Still, in the end, he decides he would rather not die on a public street.

In section IV, Propertius talks with his slave, Lygdamus, who is his go-between with Cynthia. During this conversation, he imagines how Cynthia has received his rejection of her earlier offer. Throughout this section, Propertius implies that Cynthia is little more than a prostitute and that she has been unfaithful to him with Lygdamus. Evidently, Lygdamus has described the desolation that has fallen over Cynthia's household as news of Propertius's rejection has reached her. Lygdamus tells him that his mistress remains in bed, copiously weeping, dressed simply, without her usual ornaments. Moreover, Cynthia accuses Propertius of unfaithfulness.

In stanzas 3 and 4, Lygdamus quotes Cynthia's description of Propertius's quite literal enchantment by another woman: The other woman has used potions and spells to snare her lover. This is followed by Cynthia's curse on her rival, and the prediction of her own death following Propertius's rejection. Propertius, however, responds sardonically to these histrionics. He believes neither in Cynthia's protestations nor in Lygdamus's fidelity.

Meanwhile, in section V, Propertius proves to have other problems besides those with his mistress. His patron, Maecenas, is pressuring him to write martial epics in the manner of Vergil. In classical Rome, poets commonly were supported by rich men eager to add to their own fame by being associated with well-known writers. Such patrons often lent their financial backing to several writers. Maecenas was perhaps the most important of such men because he included in his literary circle such great writers as Vergil and Horace. Propertius, however, struggles to maintain his poetic integrity. He stubbornly restates his initial intention to write lyric poetry instead of the public verse of Maecenas's other poets.

In the first part of section V, Propertius gives Maecenas a literal example of why it would be a bad idea for him to attempt Vergilian epics. Propertius makes a pretended attempt to write on "great" subjects—the extensions of the Roman Empire, the triumphs of Augustus Caesar, the battles of the Roman legions. The result is bombast, badly written, and ridiculously described.

In the second part of this section, however, Propertius turns to his true gift: love poetry. He explains to Maecenas that his muse is his lover, that everything she does provides him with material for volumes of poetry. Her lyre playing, the way her hair falls on her forehead, the clothes she wears, and especially, her lovemaking—all these are so fascinating to him that he has no time for writing poetry about war and history. In fact, Propertius tells Maecenas in the final part of this section, his lover disdains epic poetry, especially Homer. Her distaste for the greatest of ancient writers, Propertius ironically reveals, is that she disapproves of Helen of Troy's "conduct."

Section VI introduces a somber note to the course of the poem. Propertius imagines his death and funeral and Cynthia's response to his death. Much of the content in this section is conventional to classical poetry. In death, the high and the low, the conqueror and the conquered, are equal, sharing Charon's ferry over the river Acheron in the underworld. As far as Propertius himself is concerned, his death will be humble. His funeral cortege will comprise few followers, and those will be not very distinguished. Cynthia will lament her dead lover, to be sure, but perhaps only because "it is a custom." In any case, Cynthia's cries of grief will be in vain, since, obviously, the dead are past hearing.

Section VII is also conventional in theme: Love is contrasted to death. Propertius is keen to assert that lovemaking—the sensory joy of the physical—is the only antidote to mortality. The poet describes Cynthia's insistence on a lighted chamber so that the lovers can see each other, thus increasing their joy. Their nightlong embraces have great variety, and these are interspersed with intimate conversation and with each gazing into the other's eyes.

In contrast to section VI, in which Propertius reflects on his own death, in section VIII, he imagines Cynthia's death. The content here is gently ironic. The poet imagines the jealousy of the goddesses over Cynthia's arrival in the afterworld. He briefly retells the stories of other mortal women who suffered the goddesses' wrath: Io, who was turned into a cow by Hera because Zeus admired her; Andromeda, whose beauty incurred the wrath of Poseidon; Callisto, whose affair with Zeus spurred Hera to change the mortal girl into a bear. Nevertheless, Propertius claims, Cynthia's beauty is so great that, once she arrives on Olympus, the goddesses may permanently lose favor.

Propertius continues this theme in section IX, where he implores the gods to extend Cynthia's life. He argues that there are already enough beautiful women in the underworld and that, besides, he himself will die if Cynthia perishes. He then goes on to admonish Cynthia to keep up her devotions to the gods in thanks for her continued life, and he also insists that she show her "thanks" to the poet by spending ten nights with him.

In section X, Propertius describes his kidnapping by a group of small boys who have been commissioned by Cynthia to bring him to her. The poet has been up most of the night carousing, so he is fairly drunk when the boys accost him. They drag him to Cynthia's house at daybreak, and he enters. He finds Cynthia asleep, and he stands gazing at her, stunned by her beauty. As his senses return, so do his doubts of Cynthia's fidelity. He carefully inspects her bed for signs of a rival. At this point, Cynthia awakes and knows what her lover is thinking. She haughtily denies having other lovers; in fact, she implies, she's tired of love—so tired, in fact, that she is on her way to make her devotions at the temple of the vestal virgins and will have nothing more to do with Propertius.

The aftermath of Cynthia's rejection is described in section XI. Tormented by love, Propertius glumly reflects on the fact that there is no escaping desire. Even if he could mount Pegasus or wear Perseus's flying sandals, he could not escape his love for Cynthia. Meanwhile, Cynthia herself seems to have forgotten him. He hears tales of her other affairs, but he tries to dismiss these as the inevitable rumors surrounding beautiful women. In an attempt to forget his worries, he reconsiders old stories of the loves of gods and mortals, but even in retelling these he finds no escape. In the poem's conclusion, section XII, Propertius discovers that his worst imaginings are true: His best friend, Lynceus, another poet, is conducting an affair with Cynthia. Nevertheless, Propertius reaffirms both his love for Cynthia and his intention to continue to write love poetry against the contemporary fashion for epics.

Forms and Devices

Like nearly all Pound's poetry, *Homage to Sextus Propertius* uses free verse—poetic lines that have no set rhythm or consistent number of feet and that do not rhyme. This does not mean, however, that the poem lacks strong verse structure. Moreover, certain distinct rhythms recur, which often suggest certain classical patterns. For example, anapestic feet (two unstressed beats followed by a stress) occur frequently, as in the poem's first stanza: "Who hath taught you so subtle a measure." Such rhythms were used in classical poetry for a variety of purposes, especially for Latin comic drama.

Generally, however, the rhythms here are those of speech: Pound believed that Propertius's lines were meant to mimic the rise and fall of conversation, in the same rhythmic fashion as Pound's own verse. The result is often a rhythmic line, or sequence of lines, followed by an ironic, nonrhythmic conclusion. The generally anapestic rhythm of "And expound the distentions of Empire," for example, is interrupted by the lack of distinct rhythm in the line immediately following: "But for something to read in normal circumstances?" In the preceding example, Pound uses structural irony—the pompous beat of the first line contrasted with the idiomatic rhythm of the second—to reinforce the thematic irony, which contrasts the windy subject matter of Imperial Rome with Propertius's own more personal verse.

The other striking structural feature of the poem is its use of allusion. Such use would obviously be natural to any classical poet. Although Pound, through Propertius, makes reference to a number of contemporary historical events (mainly the conquests of the Roman emperors), generally the poem's allusions are to the loves of the gods, discussed above.

Finally, the poem includes many lyrical, imagist passages, especially in lines describing Propertius's love for Cynthia. Imagism was a poetic movement, largely "invented" by Pound himself, that sought to impart to the reader highly vivid sensory impressions of natural images. These impressions were to be appreciated for their own sake and not for any symbolic weight they might hold. The images were usually coupled, so that two distinct impressions might together create a third. In section III's first stanza, for example, "Bright tips reach up from twin towers,/ Anienan spring water falls into flat-spread pools" combines two distinct sensory images—the glowing tops of the Roman cityscape with the trickle of water into shallow pools. This juxtaposition of images is done for its own sake, to instill in the reader a feeling of the reality of the sensory world.

Themes and Meanings

The thematic basis of *Homage to Sextus Propertius* is reflected in the poem's most obvious feature: that it is a creative translation by one poet of another poet's work. The key, then, to what Pound was attempting with this poetic form lies in the word "homage" of the title. The poem is an attempt by Pound to recapture the living spirit of Sextus Propertius, to enable a modern English audience to understand how an ancient Latin audience would have read, and appreciated, this classical poet. Thus, "homage" means "a loving tribute" by the modern writer "in the manner of" the ancient one.

Moreover, Pound has chosen to translate Propertius's *Elegies* because the Latin poet's themes coincide closely with Pound's own cultural concerns. A clue to this coincidence lies in Pound's many modern, idiomatic renderings of Latin passages having to do with Roman Imperial politics. Pound's "celebrities from the Trans-Caucasus," for example, uses the twentieth century "celebrities" to focus on the parallels between ancient imperialism and the modern British variety.

Like Propertius, Pound believed that many popular contemporary writers were little more than public relations experts for the powerful. *Homage to Sextus Propertius* was written during the close of World War I, when the war's futility and horror had become widely known. In the aftermath, the prewar colonial empires began to collapse, making poetry that glorified imperial power seem highly ironic. So Pound discovered in the works of the first-century Roman poet a precursor to his own concerns.

Among these concerns was the conflict between public and private in literature. *Homage to Sextus Propertius* exalts the permanence of highly personal lyric poetry and emphasizes the transience of "public" verse. Pound's lively re-creation of Propertius's life and milieu is itself proof that individual experience is poetry's most enduring subject. Gifted people, the poem implies, will always be underestimated by the ruling elite; yet those writers who fully record their own emotions will enjoy fame long after the conquests of empire are forgotten.

As Propertius/Pound turns to examine the private life, the poem introduces themes having to do with love and with the subtleties of personality. As the reader learns of Propertius's joys, sorrows, and ironic doubts in love, he or she also begins to learn much about the poet's personality. In fact, as the poem develops, the psychology of the poet himself will turn out to be a main theme. Propertius is a complex, "modern" figure—at once passionate and timid, self-reflective and naïve, sincere and ironic. Through this Latin poem, Pound gives voice to a twentieth century sensibility.

John Steven Childs

HOME BURIAL

Author: Robert Frost (1874-1963)
Type of poem: Narrative
First published: 1914, in *North of Boston*

The Poem

"Home Burial," a dramatic narrative largely in the form of dialogue, has 116 lines in informal blank verse. The setting is a windowed stairway in a rural home in which an unnamed farmer and his wife, Amy, live. The immediate intent of the title is made clear when the reader learns that the husband has recently buried their first-born child, a boy, in his family graveyard behind the house. The title can also be taken to suggest that the parents so fundamentally disagree about how to mourn that their "home" life is in mortal jeopardy—in danger of being buried. Further, Amy, because of her intro-spective grieving, risks burying both her marriage and her sanity.

The husband enters the stairway from below and sees her before she sees him, because she is wrapped up in herself. He tardily observes that she has been looking out the stairway window at the graveyard, already containing four of "my people" and "the child's mound." She doubts that he ever noticed the graveyard from that window and cries out for him to stop talking. Avoiding his touch, she shrinks past him down the stairs. When he asks why a man cannot speak of his "lost" child, she counters first by saying "Not you!" and then by doubting that any man can. She abruptly announces that she must get some air. He tells her not to take her grief to "someone else this time," sits so as not to seem domineering, and, calling her "dear," says he wishes to ask her something. When she replies that he does not know how to ask, he requests her "help," grows bitter at her silence, and generalizes: Men must give up some manliness when married, and further, two who love should to be able to discuss anything. He wants to be allowed into her grief, which he thinks she is "overdo[ing] . . . a little," and hints that their love could produce a child to replace the dead one, whose "memory might be satisfied" by now.

Her rejoinder that he is "sneering" makes him upbraid and half-threaten her and ask why he cannot talk about "his own" dead child. This provokes her longest speech, briefly interrupted by his comment that he feels so "cursed" that he should laugh. The essence of her complaint is that he does not know how to speak, that she could not even recognize him when he dug the grave so energetically that he made "the gravel leap and leap," and that his voice then was too "rumbling" when he commented that foggy and rainy weather will rot good birch fences. Concluding that he cannot care, she in turn generalizes: Friends grieve for another's loss so little that they should not bother "at all," and when a person "is sick to death" he "is alone, and he dies more alone." Even when survivors attend a burial they are busy thinking of their own lives and actions. She calls the world evil and adds that she will not have grief this way if she "can change it."

He mistakenly feels that she has said her say, will stay now, and should close the door. She blurts out that he thinks "the talk is all" and that she must "go—/ Somewhere out of this house." He demands to know where and vows to "bring you back by force."

Forms and Devices

"Home Burial" achieves tension first of all through its use of unpretentious wording in blank verse, a poetic form with a tradition going back centuries, to tell a tragic domestic story in a homely locale. More obvious tension results from the fact that Amy and her husband have no meeting of either heads or hearts. He speaks fifty-eight lines, many of which are incomplete, while she speaks forty-five such lines. In contrast to the rhetoric of William Shakespeare's flowing blank-verse dialogue, Frost's is full of rushes, interruptions, and pauses. Amy tells her husband to stop talking thus: "Don't, Don't, Don't, Don't." Frost called this burst the best part of the poem. The husband puts too much faith in words, saying at one point, "There, you have said it all and you feel better." In Amy's reply—"oh, you think the talk is all"—that "oh," which Frost also said he liked, is more effective than a dozen words.

Much remains unarticulated. Frost never tells readers the husband's name, what the house looks like inside or out, how long ago the child died, or where Amy plans to go as she leaves. The poem is partly about the ineffectiveness of words. When the husband says that he must laugh because he is cursed, Amy does not even hear him but chooses to quote—and misunderstand—his earlier talk about wet days and birch fences.

Frost freights his sparse words with much meaning, often subtle, sometimes symbolic. When he talks of rotting birch wood, Amy says only that his comment has nothing to do with their child's body when it was "in the darkened parlour." The astute reader, however, will connect wood rot with human decomposition. When the husband compares the graveyard to a bedroom in size, he is being harmlessly literal. The reader, however, will think that Amy is recalling with displeasure the bedroom in which their child was conceived. When the husband pleads, "Let me into your grief," there is another sexual overtone of which he is not conscious. The stairway should be a place where the two might walk together, connecting levels of shared living; instead, it is merely a stage where body language reinforces the poem's words. Amy silently spies on her husband through the window instead of calling and waving to him. He climbs the stairs until his nearness makes her "cower . . . under him," at which he promises not to "come down the stairs." Frost intends a pun when the husband complains that his words to Amy "are nearly always an offence." Truly the two are fenced apart, by words and acts.

Amy's most effective verbal barrage, loaded with *l* alliteration, is her description of her husband's fiercely digging the grave with the leaping, leaping gravel "roll(ing) back down the mound beside the hole." Surely Frost wants the reader to connect this up-and-down motion with sexual activity but also, and more important, with the birth-life-adulthood-love-death cycle of humankind.

Themes and Meanings

Frost's primary concern in "Home Burial" is to present modes of grief and communication. The Frosts' first child, a son, died in 1900 at the age of four. Their grief, which permanently wrenched their long marriage, took conflicting forms, during which his wife, unlike the more talkative Frost, bottled up her grief and called the world evil exactly as Amy does. Frost, who gave innumerable public and private readings of his poetry, never included "Home Burial," explaining that it was too sad.

Amy and her husband are disastrously contrasting spouses. She is masochistic and rebellious. When she says, "I won't have grief so/ If I can change it. Oh, I won't, I won't!," she risks losing not only husband but reason itself. He moves coarsely from trying to question her to protesting and threatening. He never explains his sense of loss or his mode of grieving and never tells her that his commonplace talk and actions might represent a flinching from heartbreak. He never says that when he buried their baby he wished she had been standing beside him. Amy too misses a chance to replace discord with harmony, by not helping him frame the question he wants to ask; instead she stifles him by saying that neither he nor "any man" can speak acceptably to her. Never once do they speak of "our" child.

They communicate by body language more expressively than by words. At first she is at the top of the stairs, and he is at the bottom. After they have reversed positions of seeming dominance, he sits—but with his chin in "his fists," not his hands. When he generalizes about off-limit topics between couples, her only response is to "move . . . the latch" of the door. Her intention is to get out of the house. It, along with her husband in it, is smothering her. Frost offers two messages in "Home Burial," one for pessimists such as himself, another for optimists. Its action exposes barriers to communication even among people "wonted" to intimacy. On the other hand, the dreadful aftermath of such barriers should encourage readers of good will to speak from the heart, listen, and be sympathetic.

Robert L. Gale

HOME COURSE IN RELIGION

Author: Gary Soto (1952-   )
Type of poem: Narrative
First published: 1991, in *Home Course in Religion*

The Poem

"Home Course in Religion," a long narrative poem, does not adhere to a specific rhyme or rhythm scheme. Instead, this prose poem relies on a variety of structural devices to provide unity. As with many of his other poems, Gary Soto is more concerned with creating and conveying an image with short, tight lines and direct, succinct diction than he is with rhyme and rhythm. For example, Soto consistently juxtaposes two seemingly ordinary, terse words (such as "Top Ramen" and "cereal bowl") that together reinforce the reality of the persona's poverty, a poverty that influences his every action: "I was living on Top Ramen and cold cereal." The socioeconomic concept of poverty and its resulting oppressiveness is pervasive in the poem. Building on this sense of poverty, the poem, written in the first person, allows Soto to create a persona whose view of the world and whose experiences are very similar to his. Thus, the poet speaks directly to and intimately with the audience, conveying an experience that is immediate and authentic.

The poem universalizes the archetypal journey of an eighteen-year-old college student as he struggles to find the "quiddity," or essence, of his life. As the title "Home Course in Religion" implies, the student undertakes his introspective journey by turning to religion. He begins by reading "a really long book" that "*ought to be read by anyone/ Who has had a formal or home-study course in metaphysics.*" Unable to understand the convoluted images, he turns to other sources such as the Bible and *The Problem of Evil*. Although "much clearer," neither source alleviates his sense of separateness; rather, both books further obfuscate his search.

Throughout the poem, the young man's attempts to find answers through prescribed religion are thwarted. He then turns to other venues: politics, society, and education. For example, when he and his roommates discuss former U.S. president Richard Nixon's Watergate debacle and try to make sense of it, their ability to communicate with one another is impeded by a language barrier: "none of us understood what the other/ Was saying." In college, his teachers lecture about "pumice" and the "Papuan people," and, even though he takes notes, he is more intent on watching the teacher sweat—perhaps implying the nonrelevance of the subject matter. None of these institutions provides him with answers or helps him reconcile the ideal of the American dream with the reality of his world of "cracker crumbs" and the jar of peanut butter he regards as a "present" that he and his girlfriend used on their "last three crackers."

The poem concludes with the gradual, and sometimes painful, disintegration of the young man's belief in organized religion and institutions and with the deep personal sense of disorientation that results from his discovery. His three-day journey leads him to a rather dark, almost nihilistic, epiphany: "I realized I might be in the wrong line of belief." This statement conveys a sense of growth and maturation; he realizes prescriptive religion can neither abate his suffering nor ease his socioeconomic hunger. He is now a stronger person because he knows that he will have to survive on his own.

Forms and Devices

Soto defines himself as "an imagist, one who tries to provide a stark, quick image." His definition could well apply to the prominent images and metaphors he creates in "Home Course in Religion." Although he employs biblical allusions, ambiguities as a rhetorical device, and irony, Soto relies on central images and metaphors to convey the physical, psychological, and spiritual hunger of the young man.

Soto directly addresses the physical hunger the young man and his brother experience as they exist on Top Ramen, crackers, and cold cereal, which he eats in his Top Ramen bowl. Occasionally, the brothers are treated to "oranges that rolled our way" or peanut butter that the narrator's girlfriend gives them. Soto's continued, matter-of-fact references to these images resonates and heightens their emotional impact. By understating the multifaceted deficiency, the author explicitly conveys a deep sense of hunger that is reinforced when he says, *"People with big cars don't know how much it hurts."* This hunger precipitates the young man's spiritual quest as a means of abating, or at least understanding, his pain and suffering; therefore, he begins reading religious books.

After trying to understand the content of one of his religion books, the young man plays basketball to "get the air" back into his brain. At first, the image of "air" conveys a positive, vibrant, life-affirming quality. When juxtaposed with reading a religion book, however, the connotation becomes subtly negative. Once again, after reading ten pages in another book that seems clearer (*"Costly grace . . ./ . . . comes as a word of/ Forgiveness to the broken spirit/ And the contrite heart"*), the "good air" leaves him and he falls asleep. The metaphorical suggestion in both examples is implicit: Prescribed religion cannot alleviate his suffering if the messages it conveys are too esoteric or too difficult to understand.

Nonetheless, the young man continues to search for a sense of reassurance through religion by reading about a "French mystic." Instead of providing him with insight and hope, however, he learns that she talked "in weird/ Ways and no longer reached people with her thoughts." Later, he reads another numbing text and again falls asleep. Once again, his efforts to understand his plight are thwarted. Ironically, on the second day of his journey, he learns "more about life" from a karate instructor in physical education class than he does with the help of a book: *"Pain doesn't exist . . ./ . . . Pain is in the mind./ The mind is the spiritual nature/ That follows your body."* He learns that he must control his pain and that pain is part of the human condition.

Metaphorically, by juxtaposing the images of "good air" leaving the brain or falling asleep with religious texts, the author conveys a sense of the young man's alienation that is reinforced throughout the poem. Whether reading the Bible or *The Problem of Evil*, the young man experiences the same dullness in his senses. His vitality and energy are seen when he talks to and jokes with his roommates and when he makes love to his girlfriend. Again, when he plays basketball and returns home, "sweaty in every hole," he feels revived and alive. In contrast to the deterioration of his vitality or life force when he delves into religious dogma, all of these interpersonal activities reaffirm his existence, evidence that neither his physical nor his spiritual hunger have been alleviated.

Themes and Meanings

"Home Course in Religion" is a poem about hunger (literally and figuratively) and the human pain or suffering that is a prerequisite to growth. In the poem, Soto explores the motif of hunger and universalizes one man's search for spiritual meaning in a world that seems devoid of spirituality.

Soto addresses the issues of hunger and poverty in several of his poems. The poem "Salt," in *Where The Sparrows Work Hard* (1987), poignantly describes two young boys whose hunger destroys their energy, even their will to live. "The Wound," in *Tale of Sunlight* (1978), focuses on the pain and anguish one young child endures as a result of his abject poverty. Although not directly stated, the boy suffers from a disease endemic to the impoverished. While hunger in both "The Wound" and "Home Course in Religion" begins as actual physical deprivation, it becomes a catalyst to attain a deeper understanding, a metaphysical explanation for the persona's pain.

The young man's quest in "Home Course in Religion" is complicated by his increasing involvement with his girlfriend. As his physical attraction to her intensifies, so too do his feelings of guilt and its accompanying remorse. One evening after his girlfriend leaves, he prays in his room, then crosses himself with his "fingertips\ Pushed into [his] flesh." His sense of guilt leads him to punish himself masochistically for what he perceives to be sins of the flesh. As he searches for answers to his conflicting feelings in a religious book, he falls asleep.

On the third and final day of his journey, the young man once again tries to sort through another book, but the "good air" leaves his brain, and he falls asleep. When his girlfriend arrives, she wakes him, literally and metaphorically, from his slumber. During the course of the evening, they become physically intimate, an intimacy that leads him to a deeper understanding of himself: People feel lonely "because they don't know themselves." By becoming sexually involved with her, he begins to acknowledge his need for life-affirming vitality. His immediate reaction to the sexual contact is similar to their first physical experience: He begins to feel "ashamed." His need to expiate his guilt drives him again to the Bible and to his futile search for divine affirmation. However, the sense of shame escalates when he realizes that the same hand that touched her turns the pages of the Bible. Out of a sense of remorse, he washes his hand, an act of physical, emotional, and spiritual purification. After performing this act, he begins to contemplate the evening during a "cat-and-dog storm" and realizes that he "might be in the wrong line of belief." This simple understatement symbolically underscores his epiphany, and the "line" he refers to implies a simultaneous movement away from systematic, organized religious dogma and toward more subtle, subjective, and life-affirming personal insights.

Sharon K. Wilson

HOMECOMING

Author: Paul Celan (Paul Antschel, 1920-1970)
Type of poem: Lyric
First published: 1959, as "Heimkehr," in *Sprachgitter*; English translation collected in *Paul Celan: Poems*, 1980

The Poem

"Homecoming" is a free-verse poem of nineteen lines. Its title is somewhat ironic, suggesting a joyous return, a celebration of reunion. The actual "homecoming" that Paul Celan describes in the poem is a bleak return to a landscape of the dead.

The poem comes from a collection that marks the point at which Celan became re-nowned throughout Europe. The title of this collection, *Sprachgitter* (speechmesh), illustrates the increasing darkness and obscurity of his work. The title suggests the dif-ficulty of speaking through a mesh or grid, and perhaps implies that speech itself is a mesh or grid, filtering and distorting the feelings it attempts to represent, perhaps causing pain and injury to the one who attempts to speak. The word is Celan's in-vented compound, and such inventions abound in his later work.

In the case of many poems, it is important to distinguish the speaker of the poem from the poet. In Celan's case, however, no such division is necessary. Celan's life speaks through his poems. They tell of the loss of his parents in the Holocaust and of his attempts to factor this loss into his life and come up with a product other than zero. They also tell of his failure to do this, describing again and again the void left by the Holocaust and the silence of God in response to his anguish.

The poem refers to an unidentified "you," but the "I" is suppressed. The word "I" is used once, but it is not the usual use of the first-person singular—it refers to "an I," a consciousness. The English version has only about seventy-five words (the total de-pending on how compounds are counted), and although "Homecoming" is not as sparse and compact as his later poems, no word is wasted.

The opening three-line section provides the basic scene and coloration of the poem: snowfall, gray-white or "dove-coloured." The second segment lifts the vision upward, but there is no change in mood. Above the landscape stretches the white sky, "the sleigh track of the lost." There is no respite from this overall blankness in a downward glance either, for there, "hidden," are "what so hurts the eyes," presumably the graves of the dead, which are what the speaker most sees although they are hidden by the snow.

Each of these "hills" represents "an I slipped away into dumbness." In the snow and ice, "a feeling" blown across the cold and empty scene ceases its drifting and plants its gray-white flag: Perhaps the flag is the poem, a grave-marker for the unnamed dead.

Forms and Devices

"Homecoming" is spare and stark, having little use for ornament. The truth it de-scribes trivializes conventional attempts at ornamentation. Its nineteen lines contain a number of words that have a falling rhythm—words such as "hidden," "dumbness," and "feeling," each of which contains a stressed syllable followed by an unstressed one. These words, often placed at the ends of lines, contribute to the mood of snowfall and of sadness. (The words in the original German have the same effect.) The other patterns of stressed and unstressed syllables in the poem produce the effect of chords in a minor key, and contribute to the overall impression of grief. The musical quality of "Homecoming" is also found in many of Celan's other poems, some of which make specific reference to musical forms and themes.

Metaphor in this poem is very basic. Snow and winter traditionally suggest death, and here the snow is becoming "denser and denser"—obscuring more and more the possibility of any vision of light. The snow is described as "the sleigh track of the lost." One of the recurrent images in Celan's earlier poems is the picture of the ashes of the dead rising over the Holocaust ovens, and this suggestion is recalled by the image of the dead rising in this poem into the air in a sleigh. The gray of the remembered ashes pollutes the purity of the snow, so that although the snow should be white, it is seen as gray, "dove-coloured."

The gray and white colors of this poem, combined with the insistent snow and ice, produce a feeling of isolation and desolation, the lowest level of the psyche. It is a mental state not far removed from the coldness at the center of Dante's inferno, where the deepest damned are immobilized in a pit of ice. At the level of complete loss, all freezes to "dumbness." This paralysis comes not from sin but from total grief, deprivation of all that centers one in the world and makes it livable.

At the conclusion, the only sign of life is a "feeling"—an emotion divorced from the speaker who experiences it. The poem combines the concrete with the abstract to explain how this feeling attaches "its dove-its snow-/ coloured cloth as a flag." The feeling has thus been brought into the world of real things.

By the end of "Homecoming," the reader has been led through a series of winter images to a closure that is ambivalent. The last image is the "flag," which suggests labeling, identifying, or claiming. The speaker may be using the poem to reclaim his lost loved ones by memorializing them. On the other hand, this attempt may be vain. The flag is barely discernible from the snow, its color almost indistinguishable from the surroundings of the same neutral hue.

Themes and Meanings

All Celan's poems are about loss, even those rare ones that carry some glimmer of hope, a possible substitution, such as love, for past losses. The deaths of his parents in the concentration camp, as well as those of all other victims of the Holocaust, haunt the poems. His best-known works ("Death Fugue," for example) are direct treatments of the Holocaust. The colors of all of his poems are gray and somber; his works reflect the experience of one who has survived the ordeal and at the same time not survived it, because so much has been lost that not enough is left to sustain him. Celan committed suicide in 1970, despite having married and having become internationally famous as poet and translator.

The death-in-life theme is present from the onset of "Homecoming." The title suggests meetings and greetings, but neither is forthcoming. The dense snow, suggesting death, is thickening. The third line is mysterious, but it too suggests death in life: The snow falls "as if even now you were sleeping." The "you" is addressed nowhere else in the poem and, as usual in Celan's poems, is indeterminate; but the lines state that the addressee is "as if" sleeping. He (or she, or they) is not sleeping; the suggestion is that he is absent, dead.

The white and gray of the scene extend from the top to the bottom of the field of vision, and everything the speaker sees in the sky or on the earth connotes death. The sky is the "sleigh track of the lost"; the ashes of the incinerated Holocaust victims rose skyward. The snowy hills on the ground are the graves, and each one contains "an I slipped away into dumbness." The use of "I" gives two suggestions to the line: Each individual consciousness has been silenced, and the speaker is identifying with each one of the lost. "I" in this poem may mean both "ego" and "self." (The German "Ich" also has this dual meaning.)

The final four lines raise the issue of the possibility of the speaker's survival. He has come "home" to homelessness; everything is frozen and dead. The earth and sky are full of graves. Still, something moves in this bleak landscape—a feeling, which finds its substance in cloth, white or gray-white. A question might arise from this enigmatic conclusion: Is the flag thus formed visible enough to identify the landscape? So much of the speaker has been lost, drained away, identified with the dead, diffused into the earth and the sky. Can there be enough self left to sustain him?

The question of how poetry could be written at all after the Holocaust has been raised, and some critics have accused Celan of aestheticizing the death camps—making them into art and thus glossing over their horror—but critic and translator Michael Hamburger's comment on another Celan poem could also be applied to "Homecoming": "[T]he personal anguish was transposed into distancing imagery and a musical structure so incompatible with reportage that a kind of 'terrible beauty' is wrested from an ugly theme."

Janet McCann

HOMECOMING

Author: Friedrich Hölderlin (1770-1843)
Type of poem: Elegy
First published: 1802, as "Heimkunft. An die Verwandten"; English translation collected in *Poems and Fragments*, 1966

The Poem

"Homecoming" is the last of Friedrich Hölderlin's eight elegies. It consists of six stanzas of eighteen lines each, for a total of fifty-four elegiac distichs. The poem begins with unqualified expressions of joy in the sight and sounds of a world disclosing itself in its pristine relation. It then moves to a somberness still marked by joy but wrought with care: The poet must care, if others cannot, about apprehending the divine source of joyousness and finding names for the High Ones to supersede the outworn terms that have lost the glory of radiant holiness. The naming of God, in the deity's disclosure of himself, is a participation in creation as a constant reality. The poet, still joyous in his ability to address the higher powers (the great Father and the angels), confronts incipient despair at the apparent impossibility of new efficacious naming.

The first stanza picks up the ambiguity of the poem's dedication, "An die Verwandten," which might be dedicating the poem to relatives to whom the poet is returning or simply to like-minded persons whom the poet is addressing. It exhibits creation as gloriously fraught with inherently resolved contradictions: bright night under a cloud; a cloud in the act of composing the poetic lines that the poet is composing about the cloud; a *gähnende* valley (a valley that is gaping or yawning as it comes awake and that is swallowing—presumably swallowing the night covered by the cloud in infantile self-sustenance). The stanza begins, "There inside the Alps it is still bright night, and the cloud, composing/ Joyousness, covers it within the yawning valley." The darkness is bright within a yawning (deep) valley that is waking with a yawn and gapingly devouring the night, covered by a cloud that is creating, as a writer creates, joyousness. The joyous pangs of beginning then issue from a young-looking, roaring and rushing Chaos, shaking in joyousness and reveling in bacchanalian discord, as dawn, like a newly born universe, moves toward order and temporality.

Above this terrestrial upheaval there is, in the second stanza, a silvery silence in which roses bloom in the snow of the mountain peaks. Above the snow, and above the light itself, dwells the pure, blissfully silent radiance of God dispensing beams of joyousness and perpetually creating life and the accoutrements of happiness. The vision of God is followed in the third stanza by assertions that whatever poets meditate upon or put into poetry is of concern or value to angels and God. Poetry, then, is a joyous acknowledgment of divinity's constant gift, and it is directed not to recipients but to the agency of donation. The acknowledgment includes, paradoxically, an apostrophe to the poet's fellow country-dwellers, reminding them that what he is experiencing is theirs to experience, if only through his relation of his vision to the Spirit providing that vision.

The fourth and fifth stanzas elaborate upon the homeland, the clear view or fully subjective experience of which is Spirit's unfolding itself to the viewer. Specific parts of the German Fatherland are identified by name: Lindau, the Rhine, and the tree-filled valleys of the Neckar. Here the note of care enters into the poet's joy at his vision of God, which is a full and clear experience of universal reality's unfolding itself to him. The poet senses that the unfolding is in process but that the process will not be completed. To this sense of incompletion is added his care that his compatriots, who feel the joy of their homeland do not know that they feel it. Consequently they do not fulfill the provisions of their destiny. The best thing, the discovery—actually the re-covery—under the holy rainbow of peace, of their native truth, is reserved from—or reserved for and yet kept from—the young and the old.

The conclusion of the fifth stanza moves into the beginning of the sixth as an invo-cation of the angels. The elegy concludes with the recognition that deity must be named: The outworn names have become names of names, mere words, and the poet must—but knows that he cannot—name afresh the divinity that constantly creates afresh and must always be named afresh.

Forms and Devices

Hölderlin applies the literary devices of ambiguity and paradox to an inversion of the biblical experience of Saul of Tarsus on the road to Damascus. Saul, leaving his home, was blinded by the divine light and was changed by his audience with God into Paul, God's emissary to those whom he must persuade to eschew their earthly homes. The poet in "Homecoming" is enlightened by the darkness and is restored by his audience with God to appreciation of the joys of his homeland at the same time that he is tenta-tively saddened by the impossibility of relating this vision and its significance to those whom he must nonetheless encourage to fulfill themselves in their earthly homes.

Inversion is also extended to the effective use of indirection—that is, achieving a goal by distancing oneself from it. Hölderlin's poet is seeing his home not as he had seen it while he lived there but in an entirely fresh Chaos of joyousness occasioned by his hav-ing been away from it. This achievement through indirection is analogous to the experi-ences of other characters in literature: Odysseus gets home by being kept away from it, Parzival finds the Grail by departing from the castle in which it is housed, Dante gets to the Blissful Mountain by going through the Inferno, Franz Kafka's K gets closer to the Castle when he is moving away from it than he does by heading straight for it, and Pär Lagerkvist's Tobias sustains his pilgrimage to the Holy Land by choosing to sail on a pi-rate ship going in a direction opposite to that of a Pilgrim ship.

Even the development of reference and allusion entails an inverseness that informs readers by disorienting them. The first stanza, for example, includes both direct refer-ences and allusions to Greek and Roman myth. Subsequent stanzas depart from such mythic terms in favor of general references to God, Spirit, and angels, alluding to the passage from classical antiquity to the Judeo-Christian Middle Ages and then to the modern age. However, they invert the Christian movement from earth to heaven so as to posit heaven's potential disclosure of itself constantly to earth-dwellers who can apprehend heaven within the truth of home. The subjective return to the home is an almost complete removal of the anxieties and uncertainties and uneasiness of human life.

This passage, or progression, is narratively enforced by the cabalistic device of beginning each of the six stanzas with a key word: "Inside" (*Drinn*), "Quiet" (*Ruhig*), "Much" (*Vieles*), "Definitely" (*Freilich*), "There" (*Dort*), and "Angels" (*Engel*). This succession provides a sense that there is great restfulness within oneself and that there are certainly angels outside oneself. The body of the poem intones the potentiality of the angels' provision of this great peace.

Themes and Meanings

"Homecoming" is a profound meditation upon the nature, or essence, of home. The blessings of home are brightness, friendliness, the experience of belonging, a sense of rightness, and ultimately a communion with the divinity who confers the blessings.

Martin Heidegger has provided a cogent essay on the meanings inherent in "Homecoming"; it was published as "Heimkunft / An die Verwandten" in *Erläuterungen zu Hölderlins Dichtung* (1944; a translation of the essay as "Remembrance of the Poet," along with its foreword, "Prefatory Remark to a Repetition of the Address," appears in the collection *Existence and Being*, 1949): "The innermost essence of home is already the destiny of a Providence, or as we call it: History. Nevertheless, in the dispensation of Providence, the essence is not yet completely handed over." It is reserved, given to be discovered but kept back from all. Heidegger identifies the reserved as that which introduces care (*Sorge*) into joyousness. He observes that the poem ends with a recognition that the poet must dispel care by caring rightly, not as he may wish or choose to care. He emphasizes the fact that the last word of the poem is a "blunt not'" (*nicht*).

Following Heidegger's lead, one could add that *nicht* is an element of the *Sorge* theme as it develops from the expression of joyousness. *Nicht* is absent from the first two stanzas; it then appears once in each of the next three stanzas and five times, in all, in the last stanza. The increasing note of negativity serves as a check on the joyousness that the poet feels. Words denoting joy appear fourteen times in the poem, five times in the sixth stanza, and are missing only from the fourth stanza—which does, however, include the word "happy" in modification of Lindau, the locale of the homecoming.

Heidegger selected Hölderlin's poetry as the prime example of his notion that poetry alone is receptive of Being's reserved unfolding of itself. Poetry, he says, is not about homecoming: poetry is the actual homecoming. The homecoming is serenification, the return to the serenity of Being. The unfolding of this serenity is best and most nearly fully experienced in one's existential home, where long residence effectively inhibits one's ability to achieve the experience. Distancing oneself from home ultimately serves to sharpen the ability to experience serenity upon returning or drawing near to home once again. The sensibility of the poet, exclusively, is attuned to the joyousness of homecoming and its attendant quality of care.

Roy Arthur Swanson

HOMECOMING: ANSE LA RAYE

Author: Derek Walcott (1930-   )
Type of poem: Lyric
First published: 1969, in *The Gulf and Other Poems*

The Poem

"Homecoming: Anse La Raye" is a poem of moderate length, with sixty lines of free verse divided unevenly into four stanzas. The title of the poem indicates the work's subject: the speaker's return to the village of Anse la Raye on the Caribbean Island of St. Lucia. This island is the birthplace of Derek Walcott, who can be identified as the speaker in the poem.

The poem begins in the first-person plural, but by the second stanza the voice shifts to the second person as the speaker begins to address his poetic self. The speaker states that his poetic self experiences many difficulties when he attempts to fulfill his desire to return and be an intrinsic part of his birthplace. The speaker's tone is imbued with estrangement and meditative reflection as the problems of his return to Anse la Raye are examined.

The first stanza begins by linking the peoples of the Caribbean region with other cultures. The speaker indicates that in the island's school the works of antiquity were taught but that these works and their mythological associations, although significant in some ways, were products of other cultures and soon forgotten. For the moment, the speaker's poetic self concentrates only on the sea and a "well-known passage." The speaker views the setting without romantic illusions. The "well-known passage" mentioned in the first stanza becomes a "fish-gut-reeking beach." The ominous tone suggests something more threatening and less comforting is taking place, not what one would expect for a homecoming. As the speaker's poetic self looks over the scene, children appear. The children think that he is a tourist and hope to receive money from him. A feeling of disenchantment is apparent as the speaker tries to interpret and react to what he sees.

The third stanza begins with another reference to the children who "swarm like flies" around the speaker's poetic self. At first, he does not reject the children but pities them, because they are unaware of the larger world and that the "silvery freighter" might "pass them by." Their ignorance is met with an equal amount of ambivalence as the speaker muses on what it would be like to share their lives. For a brief moment, he imagines a return to a physical state where the sea and island life are enough. A tone of resignation, however, enters as the stanza concludes with the thought that the experience of homecoming can be bereft of feelings of warmth and security.

The final stanza brings the reader back to the children. The speaker's poetic self has given them nothing, and they curse him for his lack of generosity. The natural environment remains threatening. He is tired and walks back to the village past an esplanade where "dead/ fishermen move their draughts in shade," probably a reference to the game of checkers rather than the fishermen's hauls. One of the fishermen smiles and nods in recognition, but the speaker views this gesture with the same detached mood, sarcastically commenting that the fisherman who nods gestures "as if all fate/ swayed in his lifted hand."

Forms and Devices

Walcott employs a tone of detachment in "Homecoming: Anse La Raye." At the beginning of the poem, the speaker uses the pronoun "we," implying that the speaker is addressing others who happen to share similar experiences. By the end of the second stanza, the speaker begins using the pronoun "you," referring to his separate poetic self. Because the poem plays on the idea of detachment and even alienation, the use of "you" is more effective but not totally exclusive: The speaker maintains a connection between the "we" of the first stanza and the "you" of the remainder of the poem. As a partially detached observer who uses the second person to observe his own actions, the speaker creates another less-subjective level of interaction with the surrounding environment and its people. This objectivity allows him to remove or dismiss most of the illusions one might possess when considering the experience of homecoming, especially on a Caribbean island.

The speaker gives the island and its people a voice. In a way, the speaker becomes the island. He employs alliteration, as in the use of the "s" sound to mimic the hissing sound of the surrounding sea as well as the ever-present trade winds. The repetitive nature of this device creates a lulling effect for the reader that imitates the constant and somewhat prosaic rhythms of island life.

The imagery in the poem is also symptomatic of the speaker's unbridled and sometimes harsh view of his home. Early in the poem, he refers to "Afro-Greeks" and "Helen." As the poem progresses, the speaker maintains contact with the world of antiquity and the world at large through the use of metaphor, simile, and personification. The fronds of the coconut palms are "salt-rusted/ swords," while the shells of sea crabs become "brittle helmets." The "barbecue of branches" on the beach are like "the ribs/ of sacrificial oxen on scorched sand." The use of these rather violent images strikes an unpleasant chord, as the reader is forced to wonder why the speaker thinks of his home this way. Yet the connection of the Caribbean culture with the cultures of the outside world is positive. The Caribbean region is associated with the "Middle Passage"—not a separate entity but part of the larger European, African, and American whole. The island and other islands like it, however, are encircled by an "infinite, boring, paradisal sea," an ocean that "sucks its teeth," where "frigates tack like buzzards." The black cliffs are not majestic, but they do "scowl" at the speaker's poetic self. This imagery gives the reader a glimpse at the actual place with its gloom, decay, and connection to the historical past.

Themes and Meanings

"Homecoming: Anse La Raye" is about estrangement from one's own culture as well as from the larger world. The title of the book in which this poem originally appeared supports this idea of separation or division. At one point in the poem, the speaker's poetic self becomes poignantly aware of the fact that "there are homecomings without home." His quandary is not easily explained. The island is viewed with an unbiased eye but also with a restrained rage. He attempts to see its natural beauty, but his attempt is stifled by the decay around him. The ocean becomes boring; its movement creates "the doom-/ surge-haunted nights." The comfort that one might associate with the constant caress of the sea gives way to rumbling turmoil. Standing on the beach with the children, he contemplates their fate and suggests that they may never get a chance to ride the "silvery freighter," which appears on the horizon as a symbol of human potential and freedom.

When the speaker's poetic self leaves the beach, he sees the "dead/ fishermen." One of the men appears to greet him, but the speaker's poetic self remains aloof. In one last reference to the fishermen, the speaker states that one of the men has "a politician's ignorant, sweet smile." This smile is benign, at least on the surface. The speaker possesses a negative yet sympathetic attitude toward these men. He has already pronounced them "dead." They are racked by a pervasive and destructive apathy. Their lack of concern creates a dilemma that borders on cannibalism—they are described as "eating their islands." Yet the speaker's pronouncement is paradoxical; fishermen are part of his personal history, but their apathy only reinforces his bittersweet feelings of estrangement. The gulfs that exist between the speaker and his past, the speaker and his island home, the speaker and the environment, the speaker and his people, and the speaker and himself all add to this alienation.

Another theme that is preponderant in the poem is the theme of rage, especially the rage that manifests itself as a reaction to the political, social, and economic domination of the Caribbean region by the old colonial powers. In the first stanza, the speaker refers to the lessons once learned and now forgotten involving "borrowed ancestors." He refers to himself (and others such as him) as "Afro-Greek." The speaker seems to relish the idea of cultural pluralism yet also finds it slightly distasteful. He is a victim, a castaway, the product of a colonial past. The resignation that he sees around him— the children who respond to the lure of the tourist's money and the dead fishermen who do not seem to find their lives bankrupt—is disturbing. He moves among his people as if he is a stranger, always guarded, never indicating that he feels totally comfortable or at ease. When the "silvery freighter" appears but then becomes a "silvery ghost," hope vanishes as well. The islanders' dreams and ambitions are dependent on a world still dominated by outside forces. The larger world seems content to ignore this island even though a few of its people, including the speaker, would welcome the opportunity to embrace it with a renewed spirit. Ultimately, their dilemma is emblematic of a far greater issue: The world abounds with all types of recognizable gulfs, and these gulfs, whether personal, cultural, or political, are not easily bridged.

Robert Bateman

HOMESICKNESS

Author: Marina Tsvetayeva (1892-1941)
Type of poem: Lyric
First published: 1936, as "Toska po rodine . . ."; in *Izbrannoe*, 1961; English translation collected in *Selected Poems*, 1981

The Poem

"Homesickness" is a short lyric poem in ten stanzas, each composed of four irregular lines. The meter of the poem is fundamentally iambic, but, as is characteristic of Marina Tsvetayeva's lyrics, there are breaks formed by the ellipsis of verbs and nouns as well as by emotional exclamations. The rhythmical intonation creates a counterpoint to the formal metrical pattern.

"Homesickness" was written immediately before Tsvetayeva's return to the Soviet Union. Tsvetayeva had emigrated to Europe (first to Berlin, then Prague, and finally to Paris) in 1922. Although the title of the lyric suggests that the poet is longing to return to her homeland, it becomes clear that the poem actually expresses the poet's ambivalence about returning to a place that may no longer be home. The title, instead, concerns the poet's desire to find a place where she and her poetry will be understood and welcomed.

Although Tsvetayeva often projected herself in the image of mythic or literary figures, this poem is written in the first person with no distinction implied between the poet and the speaker. Tsvetayeva's work is often noted for its intimate tone and emotional candor. Considering that most of Tsvetayeva's work is autobiographical in nature, and often confessional, it is helpful for readers of her poetry to be aware of certain biographical details.

Tsvetayeva left the Soviet Union, like many of her contemporaries, disillusioned with the outcome of the October Revolution. The time she spent outside her country, particularly the last decade in Paris, was also difficult. She found little acceptance for her writing in either the Soviet Union or among the Russian writers in the Parisian émigré community, which made her living situation difficult for most of her life. Ultimately, Tsvetayeva chose to return to the Soviet Union, where she later committed suicide.

The first four stanzas of the poem describe the alienation she feels from society: She has no place to call her own. The next three stanzas elaborate on the isolation she feels from other human beings. She exclaims that she will be misunderstood in any language, implying that she'll be misunderstood in Russia as well as in Europe. People with someplace to call their native land and with a nationality to serve as an identity will not understand her since she lacks this sort of "native stain." Furthermore, she will be misunderstood because she seeks to escape everyday reality, while the nameless, faceless "they" of the poem are immersed in it.

In the seventh stanza, she explains that her soul is outside the measure of time, so she will never be understood by readers of the twentieth century. In the last two stanzas, she emphasizes her detachment from her homeland in particular. In the last two lines of the poem, however, she suggests that, if she had to call someplace home, she would choose Russia, which is symbolized by the rowanberry bush.

Forms and Devices

The meaning and language of Tsvetayeva's later lyric poetry is concentrated. It is designed to frustrate the reader looking for standard poetic forms and formulae. Since experimentation in sound and rhythm is vital in Tsvetayeva's poetry, much of the poem's charm is lost in translation. Tsvetayeva's experimentation with language, in combination with her unofficial status in the world of Soviet literature until the 1960's, explains why much of her work is not yet translated into English.

Tsvetayeva's elliptical style is striking. Because of the inflected nature of the Russian language, the omission of verbs and nouns (as well as flexibility in word order) is possible and common in everyday speech. Tsvetayeva exploits this aspect of the Russian language to experiment with new rhythms. Her language is bound closely with the expression of feeling. The feelings expressed in her poetry always seem intense because of its highly personal content.

Many of her lyrics are syntactic and thematic variations on one theme. Repetition of certain words and sounds is an important element of Tsvetayeva's poetry. The phrase that is repeated throughout this lyric is "it's all the same." This repetition functions in several ways. It emphasizes the indifference of the world toward the poet, but more significantly, indicates the poet's detachment from society. While every other person is part of a group, she remains an outsider. Other people have an identity defined by nation, yet the poet has no nationality. The repetition of "all" and "every" also emphasizes the lack of distinction between all people and places. Places and people seem to merge into one amorphous whole. The poet remains an outsider to this group.

The isolation of the poet is further emphasized by the use of plurals and the images of the crowd. While the rest of society is compared to a group of trees, she is the log that is left behind. Other people are "readers of newspapers," signifying not only their uniformity but also their attachment to the reality of present time. In contrast to this group, she is a poet who lives in all centuries.

Tsvetayeva's employment of plurals to describe people with whom she shares nothing in common and places to which she does not belong seems to present a dehumanized world. Houses are no longer homes. Instead, they are described as hospitals or barracks. People are not human. They have become "readers of newspapers" or part of a forest. Tsvetayeva's portrayal of herself is also dehumanized but in the sense that she is not part of the human world. She describes herself as a "captive lion." She adds that while her body may be trapped in this century, her soul is beyond time. The poet seems to be the only one with a soul and with an individual identity.

Notably, only one another image that does not directly refer to the poet is mentioned. The one thing that emerges out of the uniformity is the rowanberry, a bush indigenous to Russia and significant in the Russian literary tradition. Even though she does not truly feel a part of any society, Russia is the closest thing to a home that is possible for her in this world.

Themes and Meanings

"Homesickness" is a lyric about the poet's alienation from society, and about Tsvetayeva's alienation from society in particular. Tsvetayeva often takes a broad theme that has been traditional to lyric poetry and personalizes it. She was very familiar with the Western European literary tradition as well as the Russian tradition. The theme of the poet as an émigré from all nations is common in Romantic poetry, in which the poet is considered to be a visionary. The poet essentially is different from other human beings. In that respect, the poet is isolated from society.

Tsvetayeva herself reiterates this idea in the essay "Poet i vremia" (1932), or "The Poet and Time." She writes that "every poet is essentially an émigré, even in Russia." Tsvetayeva, however, personalizes this theme by expressing her own alienation as well. Not only is she isolated from others by her status as a poet, but she is essentially exiled from her homeland. She felt—although her poetry actually did have many admirers—that her poetry was not accepted or understood among the Russians living in emigration and, in later years, that there was no place for her poetry in the Soviet Union either. Tsvetayeva sought escape in her poetry, which, in effect, isolated her to an even greater extent.

Her conception of the poet in exile differs from that of other Romantic poets in an important respect. Even though she often seems proud of the way in which she stands out from the crowd, Tsvetayeva also admits that her role is a burden to herself and to others. The Symbolists, who were also writing while Tsvetayeva was active, saw poets as prophets in an almost religious sense. Tsvetayeva may have considered the poet's role to be like that of a prophet, but she emphasized the loneliness and misery rather than the glory of the poet.

Pamela Pavliscak

HOMILY

Author: Jim Harrison (1937-   )
Type of poem: Satire
First published: 1985, in *The Theory and Practice of Rivers: Poems*

The Poem

"Homily" is a free-verse poem written in thirty-five lines with no stanza breaks. The construction of the poem is free from most formal conventions of poetry, including patterned rhyme, rhythm, and meter. Its organization follows the development of the poem's content, which is aptly described by its title. The term "homily" refers to a sermon often delivered in church to a congregation. The subject of the sermon is often designed to instruct or enlighten the audience for moral or spiritual improvement. In "Homily," Harrison offers his readers a list of "do's and don'ts" that escalates through the vices of indulgence in wine, song, pornography, and lust, culminating in the dissolution of the subject as he is torn apart by his desires. Though the persona of this poem could be said to speak to its readers (its congregation), the speaker in "Homily" also appears to be speaking only to himself, as if the reader were listening to someone talking alone in an attempt to find a balanced and moderate middle road in life.

The poem begins with a statement of "simple rules to live within." The first image is related to writing with one pen in the morning and another at night. Soon the poem's imagery moves to the kinds of indulgences that traditional church homilies often spoke against: "avoid blue food and ten-ounce shots/ of whiskey . . .// . . . don't read/ dirty magazines in front of stewardesses." The catalog of images includes a number of activities that might prove hazardous to one's physical health; other images relate to one's positive mental health. A few of the images are based on stereotypical words of common sense, such as "don't point a gun at yourself" and "don't use gas for starter fluid." The reader is reminded that a balanced life is not as easy as simple choices between right and wrong. Harrison asks, "who can/ choose between the animal in the road/ and the ditch?" These lines suggest that at times the choices one faces may not offer easy alternatives or clear avenues to a decision. Further, the lines imply a situation where the only offered alternatives are to do harm to another (the animal in the road) or to do harm to oneself by avoiding harming the other.

As the poem continues, images become more peculiar and inventive. The catalog of images focuses on the subject of love: self-love, love of another, infatuation, and fantasy. The climax of the poem is the admonition not to "fall in love/ with two at once." In the final set of lines, the reader is asked to look down upon the person who is now part of a threesome, "though one might be elsewhere." The person looked down upon from above tears himself apart and whirls in a circle: "he whirls so hard everything he *is* flies off." Because of this indulgence, this lack of moderation, the subject crumbles, only to experience the same fate again: "He crumples as paper but rises daily from the dead."

Forms and Devices

One of the significant features that individualize Harrison's poetry in comparison to so many of his contemporaries is the lack of consideration he gives to formal constraint. His poems often encapsulate wild flights of the imagination and surreal images that lack any definite closure and that do not demonstrate the least hint that any of the language was constructed in advance. Even when he has written in form, Harrison has most often employed the ghazal, a short series of couplets that allows a "metaphorical leap" from couplet to couplet, thus offering the kind of freedom within the form that Harrison continually appears to seek. He has stated that his tendencies "run hotly to the impure, the inclusive, as the realm of poetry."

"Homily" demonstrates Harrison's exuberance and wit as well as his facilities with language. The main device Harrison relies on to create the poem is the blazon, the catalog of images related to a single idea. The blazon supports Harrison's desire for inclusiveness and helps to develop the tone of dark humor that the poem suggests. The poem is a satire of the homily, a form delivered over many years in church services that, in the cleanest and most socially acceptable language possible, warned churchgoers of their potential for sin. Harrison's images warn against excess, but the images are so stark, so free of self-consciousness, that the reader can respond to the honesty and authenticity of the lines.

Harrison employs a number of the more common literary devices, including an early pun on the word "snipe" and a late series of similes that concretize the ways in which one might "fall" in love. Harrison's similes offer heterogeneous comparisons and unusual connections between images whose disparate natures create a high level of energy. There is also a natural cadence to the lines despite the lack of a patterned rhythm or meter. The sound cadences resemble those of speech, as the poem attempts to replicate the building intensity of an orally delivered homily. The sentence patterns employed in the poem are similar, usually consisting of imperatives that, because of their identical structure, create a rhythmic cadence. Though the poem is constructed in lines, conventional patterns of sentence structure and punctuation are used. The opening lines build with images in the longest sentence of the poem, quickening the pace of the reading. After the opening ten lines, sentence lengths vary but are generally relatively short as the poet's admonitions become more unusual and complex. In addition, the use of comparable phrases embedded within sentences of the poem supports the flowing cadence of the homily.

Themes and Meanings

"Homily" is concerned with the continuing challenge to find balance in life in the face of numerous seductions. Instead of the traditional, socially accepted language and subject matter offered in the church tradition, Harrison uses graphic images of temptations and behaviors that create humor on the surface of the piece. Underlying these comedic aspects, however, Harrison suggests the complexity involved in attempting to live a moderate life.

The poem begins with the relatively easy "rules to live within." These rules become habits that allow for a structured life. In addition to practicing certain kinds of habitual behavior, the speaker of the poem offers a few of the more obvious rules related to dangerous behavior, variations on the clichés most young people are told as they are growing up. The poem creates humor by employing more distinctive images of those things to avoid, including "blue food and ten-ounce shots/ of whiskey." The theme of the poem moves from a foundation of the basic principles of practicing positive behavior as an outcome of good habits and avoiding negative behavior by practicing common sense.

As the poem continues to develop, Harrison complicates the theme by introducing choices that are less easily defined and less easy to make. The poem moves to those experiences that are healthy and positive at a certain level but become increasingly dangerous with excess. The poet insists that dangers are not always a result of the kind of choice that has been made; they are sometimes a result of the degree to which one engages in these behaviors. Food is a life-giving necessity at one level and an unhealthy danger if consumed in overabundance. The imagination is a wonderful invention, but fleeing from real experience to a solely imagined life leads to misery. After the right choices are made, one must be on guard against excess to live a balanced life.

The continuing tension between the free will of choices and the fatalism of what happens builds to an extended set of images related to the dangers of love. One of the images warns not to fall in love "with photos of ladies in magazines," which suggests the harm of investing emotion in appearances. A series of images cautions not to fall in love so intensely as to be swept off one's feet. Each of the images shows the damage that results from this excess born innocently from the heart. The final stage of development related to this theme issues from the admonition against falling in love "with two at once." This excess is described with language that shows the individual "spinning" and "whirling," resulting in disintegration. The loss of self resulting from this experience is enacted repeatedly as the person "rises daily from the dead" only to travel the same circle to his or her own deterioration. The poem ends its series of warnings with this image of annihilation. The reader can then leave the poem in fear, though resolved to avoid these temptations. The satire of the traditional homily is complete.

Robert Haight

HOPE

Author: William Matthews (1942-1997)
Type of poem: Lyric/meditation/narrative
First published: 1987, in *Foreseeable Futures*

The Poem

William Matthews's "Hope" consists of five three-line, free-verse stanzas that examine the swift passage of time, the weight of mortality, and the cycle of life. The relationships between father and daughter and humanity and nature are examined simultaneously and are linked by the poem's assertion that time both obliterates and facilitates these relationships. The poem begins by listing two ambitions of the poem's protagonist: "Beautiful floors and a lively/ daughter." By juxtaposing these two unlike desires the poem propounds that humans are at once preoccupied with frivolity and concerned with posterity, perhaps even some form of provisional immortality. Based on these assertions, Matthews suggests to the reader that despite the fact that all people must die, there is hope not only in desires but also in fulfillment of the most benevolent ambitions.

The two ambitions spelled out in the first stanza are elaborated upon in the second stanza. The desires of the protagonist are made more complex, and the story and circumstance of life become more complicated: "that the dear piñata of her head/ not loose its bounty." The imagery here is not only playful but also serious, as it points to the trepidation and helplessness parents and caregivers—humanity as a whole—feel as they watch the continuance of their life force venture out into the world. The second stanza also notes the careful, minute precautions many take so those they love remain unharmed: "the girl's/ father scored the soles of her new shoes/ with a pocketknife, that she not slide." Here, irony is introduced to the poem as the protagonist's two desires are placed in conflict: His smooth, beautiful floors combined with his precious daughter's new shoes threaten to empty her head of "its bounty." The irony set in motion here prepares the reader for the more universal irony that concludes the poem.

The third stanza further demonstrates how irony infuses itself into the most mundane activities. The reader is once again reminded of the conflicting desires and how one desire can damage or negate another, more precious desire, such as the daughter, whom the father wants to protect from turning "finally upside-/ down on the oak floors he'd sanded/ and buffed slick."

This leads into the fourth stanza, which possesses the poem's strongest turn: "long before she first// gurgled from her crib. Now he's dead/ and she's eighty." Part of the passage's strength comes from the surprising turn in the poem's narrative. While the poem's first three stanzas tell a story of a father's care for his daughter alongside his nearly harmless obsession with hardwood floors, the fourth stanza focuses on the dark truths of time's passage and the human condition. Although the reader may be shocked when reading this fourth stanza, one must keep in mind that the revelation given here is, finally, not surprising at all. To kill the father off, so to speak, and to present the girl as an elderly woman gives the poem pathos, lifting it out of the realm of mere levity.

The final stanza, however, shifts the focus once more. A poem concerned with time's dominion over living things suddenly becomes a meditation on nature itself, including humankind and its relationship with nature. Time is "a tough nut to crack// and then a sapling, then a tree, and/ then somebody else's floor long/ after we ourselves are planted." The poem's cyclical trajectory completes itself with this universal gesture. "Hope" finally offers a view of the human condition that is equally pessimistic and optimistic; in order for one to remain hopeful, Matthews's poem asserts, one must die, which, ironically enough, one must.

Forms and Devices

Matthews's ironic vision relies not only on the specificity of details but also on the anonymous nature of his characters. They are at once intimate and distanced. This detached quality affords the poem's characters a multiplicity of personality, for they are emblematic of humanity. Irony can also be found in the poem's tone, which again is supported by the details' specificity. To describe one's head not simply as a piñata but as a "dear piñata" forges a voice that is simultaneously wise, idiosyncratic, and endearing. This is the first of only two metaphors in the poem. The second comes in the last stanza, which describes time as a nut, a sapling, and a tree. The absence of analogy, upon which most poetry supports itself, suggests that "Hope" should be read as a symbolic tale, a fable without an obvious moral. Readers are subtly introduced to the nimble activity of Matthews's mind.

In addition to the tonal irony, the poem's enjambments and inverted syntax give the poem its leisurely energy, its illusion of calm spontaneity. The first three stanzas are composed of one sentence that ends in the first line of the fourth stanza. The loose tetrameter paces the flourish of this sentence. Perhaps subconsciously, the reader's attention is grabbed by the sentence's ambling down the page. On a conscious level, one's attention focuses on the details within this sentence; the imagery is clear, fresh, and quirky. One such example is in the first line of the fourth stanza: The juxtaposition of the daughter's crib with the father's death is a microcosm of the poem's larger project.

The poem's epigrammatic quality—a narrative concerned with the human cycle of birth, death, and rebirth, in only fifteen lines—is the poem's most notable technical achievement. Its economy prevents the poem from slipping into something that could be dismissed as sentimental or histrionic. Its façade of simplicity and nonchalance, supported by the details and meter, further support the wit and irony of not only the poem's structure and devices but also its meaning.

Themes and Meanings

While "Hope" focuses on the darker aspects of time's passage and the human condition, it ultimately is a poem that desires an optimistic vision of the cycle of life. The poem subscribes to a tentative belief in pantheism alongside a fearful awareness of mortality. This paradox—in order to sustain life in the larger sense, the individual must die—is at the very heart of the poem; all its devices and meanings stem from it.

The poem's tone mimes its meaning: It is a poem that does not brood on the temporal, but rather attempts to find something humorous and tender in it. "To see oneself as struggling," Matthews said in an interview, "and funny at the same time is the richer and more complicated view." The protagonist's obsession for beautiful floors is purposefully trite, quirky, and silly. It is emblematic of the frivolous component of personality; it is part of being human. Conversely, the desire to have a beautiful, healthy child signifies more serious concerns and desires, the same concerns and desires that conceivably bring the greatest fear and supply the deepest love in life.

For a poem that confronts mortality, there is no mourning, no lamentation explicitly stated. Death in "Hope" is a merely a fact, a transaction that perpetuates life in the grander sense. Implicitly—tonally—the poem's acknowledgment of mortality proposes another complexity: Should one read "Hope" as an ironic or sincere interpretation of the human experience? It would seem off the mark to call "Hope" a gloomy poem because Matthews finds joy and humor in unlikely places. The lightness of the tone further exemplifies this; the best of light poems, it should be noted, are rarely as light as they appear. Matthews offers no clear answer, but he does base his vision on a belief that humanity is part of a larger scheme whose motion is dictated by the forces of nature. Despite this ambiguity, Matthews's message in "Hope" is clear: Regardless of all ambitions, desires, fears, and hope, one finally must succumb to the will of nature and, in that submission, become one with the whole, surviving only in what one leaves behind.

Alexander Long

THE HORSE SHOW AT MIDNIGHT

Author: Henry Taylor (1942-   )
Type of poem: Dramatic monologue
First published: 1966, in *The Horse Show at Midnight: Poems*

The Poem

"The Horse Show at Midnight," by Henry Taylor, is part dream, part fantasy, and part wish fulfillment. This 104-line poem relates the same story from two different points of view; part 1 relates the story from the perspective of the horse rider, and part 2 is told from the horse's point of view. From the opening lines to the eerie conclusion there is an air of the otherworldly, of a time and place not fixed nor even fixable. This is fable and fairy tale narrated by the id.

Set in a horse-show ring at the mystical hour of midnight, a rider summons sleeping horses from the stables with thought-commands and instructs them to perform beyond their waking abilities. As judge he commands them; then, transformed, he is also the rider. The horseman mounts the horse and strains to become one with it. They take "the fences one by one/ Not touching the poles or the ground." Horse and rider achieve a kind of perfection that the poem suggests is not possible in the world of the everyday. It takes a bit of the "willing suspension of disbelief" to enter the poem's altered state of consciousness, but once inside it is disorientingly fascinating

When the ride ends, the horse disappears, leaving the rider "Left behind by one horse that [he] love[s]." Almost desperately the rider seeks the horse, but it is gone. The rider sinks to his knees "Kneeling in nothing but bones." Horse flesh, and worse, spirit, have departed. The perfection sought, the poem warns the reader, is impossible in the real world. People must accept what is achieved in dream or altered state because it is there alone that they might realize their greatest desires.

In the second section, "The Horse," the narrative is also delivered from a first-person point of view. This time the reader is privy to the horse's consciousness as it receives the command while sleeping in a stall in the stables outside the ring. Rising, it "march[es] to the sound of a heart." From the horse's perspective the melding of rider and mount is more complete: "This man is only partly a rider/ And the rider in him is within me." However, as in section 1, when the perfect ride is over, the horse retreats to the stable, accepting the fantastic events that have just taken place. The horse seems in psychic contact with the man, as if the two have actually become one. The poem dissolves on this note:

> He kneels out there in the moonlight
> . . . .
> His heart singing deeply within
> A shape that moves with new life.
> I believe in the singing, and sleep.

At first glance the final line seems merely conclusive. The horse, because it does not judge or examine what has happened, is not self-reflective; it accepts all that has happened and goes to sleep. However, the line is ambiguous. An alternate reading suggests that the horse believes in the singing and it also believes in sleep, or the power of sleep and the dreams it contains to transform those involved. This is precisely what the human rider sought and believes he failed to achieve. Perhaps, this reading suggests, humans do not want too much; rather, they simply fail to see the miraculous within simplicity. Whichever reading one embraces, the poem resolves on a powerful note of acceptance by the dream horse, a note quite different from the quiet despair of the human rider at the end of part 1, who resides in solitude with no affirmation from horse or human clearly apparent to him.

Forms and Devices

In "The Horse Show at Midnight" Taylor demonstrates his command of meter, his ability to manipulate and complement meter with language, and his ability to distort vision for added visceral and emotional impact. The most obvious device in the poem is the powerful yet ponderous anapestic trimeter lines. From the outset, the poem refuses to advance more quickly than a canter, it never gallops as the horses do around the ring. It is not the nature of anapests to move quickly. The meter is self-regulating; even as it describes in metrical precision the sound of hooves striking the dirt of the ring it also insists that the lines be read slowly, every metrical foot being absorbed by the reader. Anapests are often associated with dirges and other serious forms. They can easily turn on a poet and work against a mood or an effect. That does not happen here, the anapests are stolid and advance the story at its own dreamlike and deliberate pace. By the end, it is hard to imagine the poem being said in any other meter; subject, setting, and rhythm all work to support each other, and all are stronger because of the others.

With assistance from trochaic and iambic substitutions, and at times with catalexis, the poem moves in a stately advance, accumulating its detail from adverbs that are often coupled for greater impact: "They march/ Around the ring, proudly, like men./ I stand on my toes and speak softly—/ They all start to gallop at once/ Noiselessly, weightlessly." Like the meter, the adverbs contribute to the fairy tale, otherworldly air of the poem. It is unhurried and floating in time. A poet in a hurry to offer narrative or lyric does not slow down for the intricacies of adverbs or the slow but steady beat of anapests.

Adverbs here also provide something else that supports the dream quality of the poem. They tend to distort, very slightly, the reader's expectations, sometimes bringing together seemingly conflicting notions. Like the moonlight by which the poem is lit, which distorts even as it enlightens, the adverbs move from the expected to the unexpected. In the end, the reader may feel as if he or she has just woken from a dream, or a pair of dreams, and may not be completely surprised by the conflicting sad-glad emotions.

Themes and Meanings

"The Horse Show at Midnight" can be interpreted in a number of ways. On one hand it is about the ancient human longing to communicate and connect with that which is not human. It is also about some primitive, id-driven desire not only to contact, but also to become "the other," to break utterly and finally from the confines and limitations of the human body and consciousness and become something absolutely different.

The judge-rider of the poem recognizes this desire, and through dream or fantasy or some other altered state of consciousness attempts to meld body and spirit with the horse. When the horse departs and the rider is left in the ring alone, he despairs for having failed to become the horse, left "Kneeling in nothing but bones." The "bones" symbolize the desire for physial metamorphoses, but because there is no physical transformation from man into horse, he considers his efforts an utter failure.

At the conclusion of part 2, in which the reader experiences the same events through the horse's point of view, the reader accepts the melding of the spiritual man and spiritual horse. The horse in some primordial way understands that the man "moves with new life," even if the man does not. The poem suggests that despite humans' self-awareness and superior intellect, they are unable, like the "dumb" animals, to connect with the primitive or unseen and subtle parts of life. If it is not physical and obvious, people do not, sometimes, see it or feel it. In other words, the horse's consciousness can cut through all the complications and be accepting of what is. The man needs proof, needs the experience to be absolute and complete on all levels. When it is not, he is saddened by what he perceives as failure.

On one level, at least, "The Horse Show at Midnight," the title poem of Taylor's third book, announced a topic that he would return to many times in both his poetry and his prose. Taylor, a horseman of the first order, has drawn from his deep knowledge of the animal and the art of riding to bring a distinctness to contemporary American poetry. As poets' early poems often do, this one points in a sure direction and begins to map out themes, rhythms, and devices for an entire career.

H. A. Maxson

THE HORSES

Author: Ted Hughes (1930-1998)
Type of poem: Lyric
First published: 1957, in *The Hawk in the Rain*

The Poem

"The Horses" is a thirty-eight-line poem in free verse, written mostly in two-line stanzas. Like many of Ted Hughes's poems, it reflects his fascination with nature, especially animals—their appearance and behavior, their own peculiar places in the world. The poem begins with the narrator in a bleak state of mind. Taking a walk in the dark before dawn could be invigorating, but he perceives "Evil air, a frost-making stillness," and his breath leaves "tortuous statues in the iron light." In these first few lines, Hughes paints a stark, dreamlike picture in black and gray.

Horses, a familiar enough sight during the day, become strange when the narrator sees ten of them in the gathering dawn. They do not react when he passes by. They seem to be objects, not living beings, chiseled out of a frigid landscape: "Grey silent fragments/ Of a grey silent world." The narrator, who listens "in emptiness on the moorridge," appears emotionally depleted. His spiritual emptiness leaves him vulnerable to the morning breaking dramatically around him. He hears a bird (a curlew) cry out in the stillness. He sees the sun light up the landscape in orange and red. The single sound and the vibrant colors expose a new world—complete with water and distant planets in the sky—lurking immediately below the winter night's seemingly impenetrable surface.

In this poem, the sun does not rise; it erupts: "Silently, and splitting to its core tore and flung cloud,/ Shook the gulf open, showed blue,/ And the big planets hanging." As is often the case in Hughes's poems, a familiar occurrence in nature takes on a muscular force, a startling violence. The narrator, having watched the landscape erupt into color, turns again to the horses. Like the landscape, they are waking up. Their stony stillness gives way to small signs of life: "Their draped stone manes, their tilted hind-hooves/ Stirring under a thaw." The horses, however, remain stoically silent, at one with their surroundings.

The horses shape the observer's memory of the scene. He is overwhelmed by their appearance in a landscape transformed so swiftly from icy desolation to apocalyptic beauty. Described early in the poem as "huge" and "megalith-still," the horses are powerful creatures with the will to remain controlled and quiet even as the "frost showed its fires." While the narrator has described himself as empty and stumbling about as if he were "in the fever of a dream," the horses appear calm, sure of their place in the world, able to endure all things. The poem ends with the narrator hoping, in a sentence construction reminiscent of prayer, that he will always remember the horses. Significantly, he now identifies them as "my memory." They have become something both personal and abstract, and they seem to embody a spiritual resilience of which the narrator did not seem capable in the first lines of the poem.

Forms and Devices

"The Horses" is somber in style as well as content. Its many monosyllabic words help create its weighty, serious sound. It is necessary to pause repeatedly in a monosyllabic line such as "The frost showed its fires. But still they made no sound." The rhythm is further slowed in this instance by the long vowel sounds and the full stop in the middle of the line. Frequent alliteration adds to the poem's intensity. The repetition of initial sounds ("draining the darkness," "making no move," "hung heads patient as the horizons") creates a solemn, lingering echo.

The repetition of key words is also significant to the poem's overall effect. In stanza 6, for example, Hughes describes the horses with their "draped manes and tilted hind-hooves," and in stanza 15, he again mentions their "draped stone manes, their tilted hind-hooves." The repetition of words and images heightens the horses' unchanging quality. They have a permanence about them that is both unnerving and awe-inspiring.

Hughes also repeats the word "still" to great effect. It first appears as a noun in the second line, "a frost-making stillness," paradoxically suggesting a kind of active stasis. Then the horses are portrayed as "megalith-still." Though alive, the animals seem as fixed and static as enormous stones. After the sun rises, the description of the horses ("still they stood") suggests resilience as well as lack of movement. The next time they are described as still ("But still they made no sound"), the word evokes restraint, the power to resist the upheaval of the overwhelming sunrise. In its last use, "still" describes the poet's desire to remember the horses' quiet power ("May I still meet my memory").

Such a shift in usage is a subtle analogue to the shift in the poet's perceptions of the horses and the landscape. One can see a similar effect in Hughes's use of color imagery. In the poem's opening lines, everything is black and gray, dark and empty. Then the sunrise brings violent orange and red into the picture and exposes the blue gulf.

The colors are so powerful that the poet attempts to retreat to the dark woods where he had been earlier. Outside the woods, however, he sees the horses calmly tolerating the exposure that comes with daylight. In this new context, "the red levelling rays" and, in the last stanza, "the red clouds" are transformed into images as beautiful and memorable as the horses.

For a poem so loaded with visual images, "The Horses" places an intriguing emphasis on listening. This emphasis is underscored by the poem's own echoes and solemn rhythms. Yet the landscape described is profoundly silent, except for the curlew's cry in stanza 9. At the end, the speaker (in the "din of the crowded streets") wants to remember not only "hearing curlews" but also "Hearing the horizons endure."

The silent horizon, paradoxically, becomes an enduring sound in the poet's mind. Sight and sound, sound and silence, shape his memory of a scene. Hence his memory—to continue the process of silence naturally evolving into sound—becomes the poem that is read silently yet heard in one's own mind.

Themes and Meanings

While Hughes's longstanding interest in animals, birds, and fish does not always provide him with positive imagery—one thinks of his macabre "Crow" poems, for example—this early poem portrays horses in an admirable light. Horses, in fact, stand up better to Hughes's scrutiny than most other creatures. They seem to represent a strength of will and a natural grace that humans would do well to emulate.

Cold and darkness are initially supplanted by the feverish brilliance of red and orange light. Then the horses, lit by these fiery hues, give the revelation some substance. They are stoic figures capable of surviving brilliant light as well as gray silence, and the narrator seems to identify with them. He wants to remember their resilience, their ability to endure.

This poem is, in retrospect, rather poignant, because not much of Hughes's later work provides for redemption. Many of his poems, in fact, contain grotesque analogies highlighting human shortcomings and self-degradation. In "Crow's First Lesson" (1970), for example, God attempts to teach the bird to say "love." The experiment is an abject failure, as these two strange lines suggest: "Crow retched again, before God could stop him./ And woman's vulva dropped over man's neck and tightened." Unlike the majestic horses, the crow evokes all that is sordid and unresolved in man's relationship with God, as well as in men's and women's relations with each other.

Another perspective on Hughes's animal poems is presented by the poem "Roe Deer" (1979). Similar to "The Horses" in its first-person consideration of animals at dawn, the poem describes two deer making their way past the narrator. Impressed with "their two or three years of secret deerhood," he wants to enter their world but cannot do so. "Roe Deer" ends with the animals vanishing in the snow.

In the later poem, Hughes seems preoccupied with the fleeting quality of inspiration. Although the deer are depicted in a positive light, they vanish before the narrator can grasp their full meaning. "The Horses," by contrast, depicts an emblem of endurance. Like the fleeting image of the deer, however, the horses now exist only in memory. The poet must evoke the huge, silent animals in words in order to savor that memory fully.

It is hard—particularly in the light of Hughes's later work—to ignore the poem's equally memorable images of despair and emptiness. The narrator's vulnerability in the face of the sunrise and the horses is extreme. There is not much separating the sustaining image of the horses and the poem's other images of violence and despair.

It seems possible, given the attention he pays to the frigid darkness, that he will recollect the "evil air" as often as he recollects the horses. The poem's prayerful conclusion may also be interpreted as unfulfilled longing, since even the powerful memory of the horses may not stem the tide of noise and years.

Hilary Holladay

THE HORSES

Author: Edwin Muir (1887-1959)
Type of poem: Narrative
First published: 1956, in *One Foot in Eden*

The Poem

Edwin Muir's "The Horses," a free-verse narrative poem of fifty-three lines, opens to the reader a future that may have seemed all too possible at the time of its composition in the 1950's. In the opening lines, "Barely a twelvemonth after/ The seven days war that put the world to sleep," Muir ushers the reader out of the realm of the everyday. Brief wars have occurred in the past, but have such wars put the entire world to sleep? The notion seems outrageous. Yet that sense of outrage in itself helps to color the passages that follow and put them into perspective. The reader learns, line by line, that things in the world have gone seriously awry. Technology has reached an impasse. "On the second day," Muir's narrator says, in chronicling the war, "The radios failed; we turned the knobs; no answer." The nature of the calamity comes gradually clear. "On the third day a warship passed us, heading north,/ Dead bodies piled on the deck. On the sixth day/ A plane plunged over us into the sea. Thereafter/ Nothing." An enormous but quiet disaster has overcome the world. In a dreamlike state, the weapons of war appear to the survivors less as machines than as mysterious signs of new times. When the warship appears, no pursuing ships follow. No enemy planes land to disgorge conquerors. The survivors of the "seven days war" emerge into a world in which only defeat is visible. They see no victors. From these cues, readers of Muir's poem may guess he is imagining the aftermath of atomic war, the one kind of conflict that might "put the world to sleep."

Muir's vision is by no means lacking in hope. Readers know from the beginning that some have survived. The survivors even thrive in an odd way: They remember certain ways of the past and return to a preindustrial level of coping. They learn again to produce food from the earth with their own hands. The horses of the title unexpectedly intrude upon the lives of these postapocalypse people. They initially possess a fearsome aspect, being "strange" and making their appearance with a haunting and "distant tapping on the road,/ A deepening drumming; it stopped, went on again/ And at the corner changed to hollow thunder./ We saw the heads/ Like a wild wave charging and were afraid."

The survivors know their forefathers had abandoned these horses in favor of tractors, which makes the unasked-for reappearance all the more unsettling. The animals return to the farms as if the "long-lost archaic companionship" between horses and the workers of the land is to be restored. The reestablishment of this relationship marks the return of natural order to the world. The horses also signal the return of validating emotional life. "That free servitude can still pierce our hearts," Muir's narrator says. "Our life is changed; their coming our beginning."

Forms and Devices

While "The Horses" is a speculative poem in that Muir uses a poetic narrative form to speculate into the future from an existing situation in the world, the poem may also be read as a conceit or an extended metaphor. The future world that has been brought to stillness and silence by technology may be none other than the contemporary world in which humans have become so divorced from their "natural," or at least traditional, modes of living that they are no longer fully in touch with their own true nature. Rather than being a future danger, the rift between humankind and the world has already grown wide.

Muir uses the narrative to take a hopeful view of the situation. By having the horses return to the farmers of their own volition, he suggests that humans may look to the world itself for the closing of the rift. A natural order may reestablish itself, even at a time when people appear unwilling to make the effort on their own. The narrator of the poem makes clear the attitude of the survivors toward the horses: "We did not dare go near them." The horses, nevertheless, offer their "free servitude," which allows the survivors to then rediscover their own place in nature. Muir gives depth and resonance to his free-verse lines with a series of intertwined repetitions and contrasts. Using the same adjective in the first three occurrences of "horses" in the poem, Muir emphasizes the dilemma of the survivors through a subtle oxymoron: The very animals that should have been most familiar to the farmers have instead become "strange" to them. Muir refers to the state of the world and, by inference, to the state of the survivors by speaking of the war "that put the world to sleep" and of nations "lying asleep." That it is an unnatural sleep Muir suggests obliquely: The poet refers to "days" and "noon" in speaking of the aftermath of war. It is a daytime sleep in which the nations are plunged. If the war was indeed atomic in nature, this daytime sleep would have been brought on not only by the artificial sun of the atom bomb but also by the figurative "light of reason" of science.

In contrast, when evening comes to the survivors, they confront an odd spectacle. The once-useful tractors now "lie about our fields; at evening/ They look like dank sea-monsters crouched and waiting." The approach of true sleep casts a mythological shadow over the machines. Evening also brings the horses and gives them similar shading: "Now they were strange to us/ As fabulous steeds set on an ancient shield/ Or illustrations in a book of knights." The parallel Muir draws between different animals at the plough also underlines a contrast. "We make our oxen drag our rusty ploughs," the narrator initially says. The horses then return. "Since then," the narrator says, "they have pulled our ploughs and borne our loads." Muir distinguishes the unwilling and forced relationship between farmer and land in the first line from the willing and unforced relationship in the latter by speaking immediately afterward of the "free servitude" offered by the horses. The farmers need no longer "make" nature do their will. Muir also links the changes brought on by war and those brought on by the horses through parallel phrases: "it was so still/ We listened to our breathing and were afraid," the narrator says of the first days of the war. After the farmers hear the approaching horses, they "saw the heads/ Like a wild wave charging and were afraid." First, unusual silence brings fear. In striking contrast, the noise of life does the same.

Themes and Meanings

In its imagery and its contained events, "The Horses" focuses upon communication, both failed and successful. At least initially, silence represents the former. The war itself starts with stillness and silence without the violence and clangor normally associated with major conflicts. Its first result, moreover, is added silence: The radios fall quiet. The passage of the warship and the falling of the plane seem noiseless events in Muir's emotionally muted, or numbed, lines. By the time the horses arrive, the survivors have already made a "covenant with silence" and have reached the point of preferring that the radios do not speak again. Muir conveys the anxiety with which they regard the notion of working radios and, by extension, the return of the technological world in emphatic lines of repetition: "But now if they should speak,/ If on a sudden they should speak again,/ If on the stroke of noon a voice should speak,/ We would not listen." No sounds are mentioned in the poem before the arrival of the horses except for a few words, presumably spoken by one farmer to another. The words relate to the return to soil. People are returning to the soil as farmers, and their old machinery is doing likewise in a more literal way: "'They'll moulder away and be like other loam,'" one says of the old tractors. Sound returns forcefully with the horses, beginning with an insistent tapping, followed by drumming and then the "hollow thunder" of their hooves.

In discriminating between the failed and the successful, Muir suggests there may be two kinds of communication. One kind, which relates to intellectual and technical knowledge, is represented by the radios, now fallen silent. This kind of speaking, and this kind of knowledge, has let down the survivors. War has transformed it to silence. The second kind, relating to the communication between people and their world, is, ironically, also represented by silence, even though it is ushered in by the stamping of hooves. The farmers do not, and cannot, speak with the strange horses, after all. The ancient relationship between humankind and horses restores itself without words. A new silence replaces the old. In this silence, however, the people are no longer alone.

Mark Rich

THE HORSESHOE FINDER

Author: Osip Mandelstam (1891-1938)
Type of poem: Ode
First published: 1923, as "Nashedshii podkovu"; in *Stikhotvoreniya*, 1928; English
translation collected in *Modern Russian Poetry*, 1967

The Poem
"The Horseshoe Finder" is an ode patterned, to a degree, after Pindar, as attested by
its subtitle, "A Pindaric Fragment." Its ninety-seven lines compose nine stanzas of
various length. It is the longest poem written by Osip Mandelstam; it is also one of the
very few poems he wrote in unrhymed free verse.

The poem opens with a choruslike description of a pine forest. The observers look at
the forest primarily from a utilitarian point of view, wondering how many ships could be
built from these tall trees and how the trees would fare in storms. The seafarer, "in his
thirst for space" and eagerness to go to sea, is also trying to figure out how a ship can be
built, comparing the raggedness of the sea to the firmness of the earth.

In stanza 2, the point of view is again that of the "we" of the chorus. They empathize with the planks and boards of the ship built long ago, not by the peaceful carpenter of Bethlehem but by another one, the father of wanderings and friend of seafarers.
They envisage, now in retrospect, that the boards were once tall trees standing on a
mountain ridge. Having completed the introduction, the poet is ready to "tell his
story," but he is uncertain at which point to begin. The perspective shifts to a more
modern time, in which everything "cracks and rocks" and the ships are replaced by
two-wheeled carts breaking themselves to pieces at a racetrack.

In the next stanza, the poet hails the maker of a song, not the anonymous one but the
one who put his name to it, thus assuring its long life and gaining for himself a head-
band reserved for heroes of antiquity. The fifth stanza presents the poet's musing
about the transformation of the air into water, of water into crystal, and finally of crystal into earth, tracing the normal process throughout history. Suddenly, after he has
been concerned with the course of history and the passage of time, in the sixth stanza
the poet makes a statement that divides the poem in half: "The fragile chronology of
time comes to an end." Expressing his gratitude for all that has transpired in the past,
the poet, switching to the first person, complains that he is confused, that he has lost
count, and that an erstwhile glorious era now rings hollow. Even though the sound is
still ringing, the stallion lies in the dust, unable to run anymore.

In the last two stanzas, the poet seems to be resigned to his fate. He has nothing
more to say, even though his lips still keep the shape of the last word; yet not everything is hopeless. Someone finds a horseshoe of the stallion long gone, polishes it, and
puts it over his threshold. Thus, even though time and the era have cut the poet like a
coin, so that "there's not even enough of me left for me," the final prognosis is that
there will still be horseshoes and coins to be found by later generations.

Forms and Devices

"The Horseshoe Finder" is an ode to the nameless horseshoe finder—and to Mandelstam's poetry. It was written at a time when Mandelstam thought that his poetry had become a fossil itself.

Connections with Pindar are obvious. Among the Pindaric features is, for example, a tendency to leap from one subject to another without transition. The myths are presented only in their essentials, while the rest is left for the reader to supply. The subject of a horse is also very Pindaric, as is the elegiac mood. Mandelstam's own poetic power, though, makes the poem distinctly his own.

As in most of his poems, Mandelstam relies here on images and metaphors as his strongest poetic devices. The image of stately pine trees, "free to the very top from their shaggy burden," adds beauty to their usefulness as material for ships. The poet returns to this image to point out once again that they are living beings as they moan under the saltless downpour, clamoring for a pinch of salt—that is, flavor. When describing the transformation of the elements, the poet says that "the air is kneaded until thick as earth." Perhaps the most beautiful image is that of a dying horse; the sharp arch of the neck still preserves the memory of a race, but the legs are now gone.

The most important metaphor is that of a ship, which has been used often in literature, both classical and modern, to represent poetry, among other things. When coupled with another metaphor, the racing two-wheeled carriage, which stands for modernization, the antithesis is complete. Furthermore, the change from boundless seas to a limited racetrack signals a loss of great proportions. Two other metaphors, the horseshoe and the coins, also play important roles in the poem. The horseshoe stands for two things: the glory that has been lost, and the value that has been recovered. While all glory must eventually pass, the value resulting from it can be preserved forever, provided it has been passed on to new generations. The horseshoe represents the preservation of great achievements in general, and of Mandelstam's poetry in particular. The fact that the horseshoe has been found and restored to its original beauty speaks for the validity of the poet's expectations.

The coin metaphor is somewhat less important and more negative; the poet seems to reverse himself and begins to doubt the permanence of things. Just as the coins can lose their value or be cut and disfigured, so the poet feels that "the era, trying to gnaw them in two, left the marks of its teeth on them." Through this metaphor, Mandelstam voices his pessimism about the future, in contrast to the optimism expressed by the horseshoe.

Themes and Meanings

By placing his emphasis on history and art in "The Horseshoe Finder," Mandelstam defines the poem's two basic themes: the passing of an era, and the capacity of art to survive throughout the ages.

Mandelstam often warned against the demise of civilization, most notably in his prose work "Gumanizm i sovremennost" ("Humanism and the Present," 1923). In many of his poems ("A Wandering Light at a Fearful Height," "The Age," and others), he raises the same issue, bemoaning the fact that the values of "the Golden Age" on which Western civilization is based are in danger of being replaced by a new, barbaric age. "The Horseshoe Finder" is the best example expressing those thoughts and sentiments.

The first two stanzas reveal Mandelstam's basic concept of history. The pristine world of antiquity, with its uncomplicated ways and closeness to nature, is personified by stately pine trees and ships, as well as by daring seafarers who were at home on boundless seas. Ships were built not by the peaceful carpenter of Bethlehem—a clear reference to Christ—but by an unnamed carpenter who loved travel and was a friend of sailors. The latter figure has been variously identified by critics as Joseph, Poseidon, and Peter the Great. Whichever interpretation is correct, the shipbuilder is a man of action, daring, and adventure—a mover of history.

The poet shifts to a different view of history when he states that the reckoning of the years of our age is coming to an end, presumably referring to the drastic changes in modern times in general and to the revolution in his own country in particular. The era now rings hollow, supported by no one, revealing indecision and hypocrisy. The deterioration of values is further underlined by a change from seafaring ships to race carts.

This pessimistic view of history is alleviated by the possibility that true values will survive, after all, as depicted by the metaphor of a horseshoe, which gives Mandelstam a chance to express his view of art. By finding a horseshoe, a future finder will be able not only to gain a correct picture of the past but also to realize the indestructibility of true art.

Toward the end of the poem, Mandelstam modifies the metaphor from a horseshoe to coins, undoubtedly to give vent to his despair about his personal situation in the 1920's and about his doubts of the survival of his own poetry. This momentary faintness of heart notwithstanding, Mandelstam's faith in the ultimate survival of art has been justified (by this poem, among others) and confirmed by the esteem he now enjoys more than ever.

Vasa D. Mihailovich

THE HOUSE IN THE HEART

Author: Naomi Shihab Nye (1952-   )
Type of poem: Lyric
First published: 1982; collected in *Yellow Glove*, 1986

The Poem

"The House in the Heart" is a free-verse poem with lines and stanzas of irregular length. The poem is written in the first person, with no particular distinction being made between the author and the one speaking; thus it takes on a confessional or private tone. The opening statement presents the problem of the poem—how to get through the day (and life) when one feels spiritually and emotionally empty. One does not know the specific occasion for this feeling of emptiness. It seems to exist almost like a form of weather, a depression that moves in like the "dark rain" outside. The speaker makes chamomile tea and watches the "little flowers" as they float in hot water. The chamomile flowers are desiccated and dead, inanimate, something the water uses. She says, "the water/ paint[s] itself yellow," while the flowers merely "float and bob"—a projection of her own feelings.

The speaker seems detached from life as the cars outside go "somewhere," but she does not venture to guess where. She feels no connection with them. Looking for some way to escape her depression, she makes the odd statement, "This is my favorite story," then talks about a "man with a secret jungle growing/ in his brain" who "says chocolate/ can make him happy." At this point, it is not clear whether her "favorite story" refers back to the cars swishing past or ahead to the man with the jungle in his brain. One is curious as to why either should be a "favorite story," especially since there is no real feeling of enjoyment here; perhaps she is simply trying to cheer herself up as one would distract and cheer a child by telling a story. Whatever the "favorite story" is, the reader does not get to hear it because when she imagines how much chocolate it would take to overcome her gloomy feelings, she says it would have to be "a bar/ heavy as a brick." The heaviness of the image conveys the heaviness of her mood. In an afterthought that is oddly amusing, given the melancholy tone of the poem, she adds that this chocolate bar would also have to have almonds. Then, she says, she would begin to whisper about "the house in the heart."

This "house in the heart" is a literal image of the chambers of a human heart, the "moth-wing ceilings" suggesting the heart's flutter and beat and the "cat-lip doors" its opening and closing valves. At the same time, the heart is a symbol of emotion. When one imagines the "penny-size rooms" of the heart, it becomes an image of diminution of feeling, small in size and in value.

At this point, at the center of the poem, there is a short, four-line stanza in which she tries to confront and accept the situation. Up to this point, she has been imagining some solution in making tea or eating chocolate—actions to satisfy the body. Now she rejects the importance of the body and says, "it's a porch, that's all." Her frustration is summed up in the words, "but I don't know/ what to do about it."

The wording at the beginning of the next stanza parallels that in the beginning of the poem as she returns to the problem of how to deal with the emptiness she feels. Common objects, such as the tea strainer she uses daily, seem unfamiliar. Some unhappy event has taken away the comfort and meaning of ordinary daily life so that her body is nothing but an envelope carrying messages she cannot remember.

She looks out the window at the darkness and bad weather, reflecting that the streetlights "will stay on late" in the unusual darkness. The poem ends with an image of the "house in the heart" in which there is "no one home." Love, emotion, maybe someone who once lived there—all are gone. One still does not know exactly what happened to bring things to this state, but the heart is an empty house, and the speaker is painfully aware of that emptiness. The word "cries" in the next-to-the-last line and the repetition of the words "no one home" end the poem on a note of mourning.

Forms and Devices

The form of the poem is open and improvisational: Line and stanza breaks are used to emphasize and to control the pace of the poem. The third stanza is a pivotal one, and the rest of the poem is organized around the resignation in that stanza.

Naomi Shihab Nye uses a fragmentary statement punctuated with a dash in the first stanza to give a questioning, inconclusive feeling to the poem. In general, punctuation and line breaks give a somewhat rambling feeling to the language, as if thoughts come slowly and with difficulty. When the speaker says, "With almonds," the two words come as an afterthought, simulating the speaker's meandering thoughts. Punctuation in the fourth stanza, which also ends with a dash, similarly contributes to this feeling.

Dramatic metaphors and startling images are extremely important in this poem, particularly the extended metaphor of the house as a heart and the body as its porch. Images of the "moth-wing ceilings" and "cat-lip doors" of the heart are beautiful and fantastic, yet slightly morbid.

Other objects and actions in the poem work metaphorically as outward signs of inner feelings. The act of brewing tea, the rain at the window, and the cars going by outside are used to externalize the speaker's state of mind. As her house feels strange to her and isolated by rain, darkness, and cold weather, so, too, her feelings are cut off by some sort of emotional bad weather. The frozen palm fronds outside suggest a death or loss. The dried flowers of the chamomile, the imagined bar of chocolate, and the idea of herself as an envelope containing no message she can remember all externalize her feelings dramatically. This is particularly important in a poem where the writer gives little specific information about any events that led to the poem and where the poem focuses on some pivotal moment extracted from some larger picture. Nye is particularly adept at such vivid capsule dramas, full of concrete detail and action, economical in development. One can only infer a world outside the focus of the poem— for the moment, the poem is the world. The repetition of "no one home, no one home" at the end simulates the ghostlike echo in an empty house and dramatizes the emptiness expressed by the speaker.

Themes and Meanings

Nye's poem is about dealing with grief or depression and the process of sustaining life when it seems that there is neither joy nor the will. One knows that the speaker is someone who in the past has brewed tea and has gone about her life full of "messages." She lives in a house in a neighborhood somewhere and has believed the body to be "important." What has gone wrong? One does not know, nor does one know how permanent this state is.

Presumably, people recover from grief and depression, but in the depths, it is hard to see past the moment and to imagine that things will ever be any better. If there is any hope in the poem, it is in a subdued feeling of amazement in the speaker's voice. The opening lines are not a question but a statement—"it is possible," the speaker says. No matter how empty one feels, it is possible to go through the motions of living, moving "through your own kitchen," trying to make sense of life.

The poem may be dealing with a spiritual crisis, or it may be an existential statement about the loss of meaning in life. Images of absence and the image of the palm tree injured or killed by cold weather suggest that this is about a particular loss—the loss of love or the death of a loved one—in which case, "no one home" means that someone is actually missing from the speaker's life, someone who occupied that place she calls the house in the heart.

Finally, however, one cannot know what circumstance gave rise to the poem, nor does one need to know. Like a piece of music that conveys a mood or state of mind, the poem uses concrete images to depict a state of profound depression. Though the speaker maintains an effort to go through the motions of life—making tea and looking out the window—the poem ends without any real comfort.

Barbara Drake

HOUSE ON A CLIFF

Author: Louis MacNeice (1907-1963)
Type of poem: Lyric
First published: 1955; collected in *Visitations*, 1957

The Poem

"House on a Cliff" is a sixteen-line poem in flexible iambic pentameter rhymed *abcb* and divided into three stanzas of four lines each. The title sets the scene and, to a certain extent, the mood as it creates an image of a life lived in a precarious place exposed to the elements. The poem is written in the third person, and the narrator is seemingly omniscient, moving quickly and repeatedly from descriptions of the interior of a house and its inhabitant to descriptions of the night outside and back again.

"House on a Cliff" begins indoors, where the poet notes "the tang of a tiny oil lamp," a detail that gives the impression of a confined, stifling space. The scene then switches immediately to a view of the "waste of sea" outside. This formal procedure of alternating between descriptions of the interior of the house and the outside environment will be followed throughout the rest of the poem. The stanza continues with a mention of the wind before concluding indoors with images of emotional frigidity: "the locked heart and the lost key."

The alternation of outdoors and indoors continues in the second stanza, which begins with a depiction of the inhospitable elements outside. There is, however, an important difference in this stanza: A character, the inhabitant of the house, is introduced. From this point on, this man, rather than the physical setting, is the focus of the indoor sections of the poem. The description of him in this stanza—"The strong man pained to find his red blood cools"—implies that he is aging and growing less vigorous. He is also very much aware of the ticking clock. However, the clock does not really grow "louder, faster" as the poem says it does; rather, this description is an indication of the man's preoccupation with time. The stanza ends outdoors with "the silent moon," another symbol of time.

The final stanza begins, "Indoors ancestral curse-cum-blessing," a phrase that characterizes the situation of the man mentioned in the previous stanza. The poet, by his use of the Latin preposition *cum* (together with), suggests that the man is both cursed and blessed by all the things—biological and cultural—he has inherited from his ancestors. When the perspective switches back to the outdoors, the reader is presented with a picture of the "empty bowl of heaven, the empty deep." The moon was out in the previous stanza, so the heavens cannot be literally "empty" nor does empty seem a plausible description of the sea, with all of its creatures. The poet means that the sky and sea are empty because they are missing the god or gods once thought to dwell there. The last two lines of the poem bring the reader back to the inhabitant of the house, who has fallen asleep. The man, described as "purposeful," "talks at cross/ Purposes, to himself, in a broken sleep." When two people are talking at cross purposes, they have somehow misunderstood each other. The poem ends, therefore, with the image of a man troubled by his lack of self-understanding.

Forms and Devices

In "House on a Cliff," Louis MacNeice is able to convey a sophisticated worldview in a very few lines, chiefly because of his use of form. The most striking formal device in the poem is the way the poet switches back and forth between "indoors" and "outdoors," consistently using these two words as signposts for the reader. It is not unlike the quick cuts a film director might use. This technique, combined with the metaphors it allows the poet to pair, ensures that the reader will find parallels and relationships between the two environments. The poem's short length makes it ideal for this technique. If it was any shorter, the poet would not have sufficient space for the picture he wants to paint; if it was any longer, the constant alternation would grow tiresome.

The correspondence between indoors and outdoors is not always as simple as in the first two lines, where the "tiny oil lamp" is paired with "the winking signal." Indeed, if the relationships between the indoor and outdoor sections were always this close, the poem would seem too neat. MacNeice sidesteps this danger by making the pairings that follow less closely related. What is the reader to make, for example, of "the locked heart" and "the lost key" being compared to "the chill, the void, the siren"? The first is much more obviously a metaphor. The second, aside from an allusion contained in the word "siren," which could be either a warning sound or a creature from Greek myth who lures sailors to their deaths, could be a straightforward naturalistic description. The poet, by placing them side by side, compels the reader to search for resemblances. "The chill, the void, the siren" become, in this context, a counterpart to the stunted emotional life being lived in the house.

MacNeice, like his contemporary and friend W. H. Auden, was a master of traditional forms and an expert at using meter, rhyme, alliteration, and assonance in such a way that they reinforce meaning. The last line of the first stanza is a good example of this: The crowding together of strong stresses, combined with alliteration and assonance—"the locked heart and the lost key"—creates a feeling of tension that reinforces the sense of the words. Another example is the second line of the second stanza, where the use of one-syllable, strongly stressed words in "The strong man pained to find his red blood cools" causes the line to move very slowly, thus complementing this description of the man's ebbing vitality. The reader should not take this sort of analysis to extremes. Meter cannot be expected to match meaning perfectly in every case, and there are other effects in the poem that are more or less ornamental. Taken as a whole, however, "House on a Cliff" is a fine example of how a poet can use meter to convey a message more effectively.

Themes and Meanings

"House on a Cliff" is a poem about the human condition and, more specifically, the perceptions of that condition in the twentieth century. MacNeice came of age as a poet in the 1930's when the ideas of thinkers such as Charles Darwin, Sigmund Freud, and

Karl Marx were beginning to gain widespread acceptance. Darwin, with his book *On the Origin of Species by Means of Natural Selection*, published in 1859, had undermined faith in the biblical account of creation. Freud had posited the existence of the unconscious, a part of the mind ruled largely by drives for sex and power. Marx, in *Das Kapital* (1867, 1885, 1894; translated 1886, 1907, 1909) and *Manifest der Kommunistischen Partei* (1848; *The Communist Manifesto*, 1850) had described a purely materialistic world in which change was driven by struggle between different economic classes. MacNeice realized the importance of these thinkers for his own time. In an earlier poem, "Autumn Journal," he called Marx and Freud "The figureheads of our transition."

By the time "House on a Cliff" was written, the universe in which many had come to believe was both much older and much larger than previously thought. Suddenly, many people doubted that God had created the universe or, if He had, that He had much to do with its day-to-day operation. Doubts about the existence of God crop up in a number of other poems by MacNeice, such as "The Blasphemies" and "London Rain." The outdoor portions of "House on a Cliff," with their descriptions of vast, empty spaces, of the "waste of sea" and "the empty bowl of heaven," exemplify the bleakness MacNeice saw as inherent in this new view of the universe. The indoor portions symbolize a human civilization that, though it may afford a certain amount of shelter and comfort, is still a very fragile thing. It is important to note also that the man, while sheltered, is unhappy and alone. There are many problems society cannot cure and some it may well make worse.

The view of human nature had also changed considerably. Darwin's idea that human beings were, in some fashion, descended from lower animals was a considerable blow to the ego. In addition, Freud's theories of the unconscious made the ancient Greek admonition to "know thyself" seem far more difficult. The contents of the unconscious were either those drives that society required be kept in check or incidents in childhood that were simply too painful for the conscious mind to remember. These drives and memories were thought, however, to reveal themselves in dreams. The man in "House on a Cliff," as he "talks at cross/ Purposes, to himself, in a broken sleep," provides readers with a concrete picture of this newer, more conflicted picture of human nature. This is not to say that such a bleak view of human life must necessarily follow from the conclusions of Darwin, Marx, and Freud. Some poets have been inspired by what they see as humankind's new freedom from divine interference. Wallace Stevens's poem "Sunday Morning," for example, invests the idea of a godless world with considerable grandeur. MacNeice, however, was never able to share this optimism uncritically.

Bill Coyle

HOUSEBOAT DAYS

Author: John Ashbery (1927-   )
Type of poem: Lyric
First published: 1976; collected in *Houseboat Days*, 1977

The Poem

"Houseboat Days" is a free-verse lyric divided into two irregular stanzas, one of thirty-nine lines and one of twenty-nine. The title "Houseboat Days" comes from a 1929 *National Geographic* article by Florence H. Morden, "Houseboat Days in the Vale of Kashmir," a phrase that seems to mingle the exotic with the ordinary.

"Houseboat Days" begins with an unattributed quotation, shifting abruptly from someone speaking, apparently in the immediate present, to a sentence placing that immediacy in the past on "that day." "Day" echoes the title and signals time as a subject of the poem. With the verb "walk," the poem moves into a new present. The setting, where blue hills are visible from a vantage point "along the shore," gives readers an anchor as they bob along among sentences and phrases that appear not to make much sense. John Ashbery likes to link abstract and concrete terms in humorous and disorienting combinations.

In the first stanza, the pain, "like an explosion in the brain," gives way to banal clichés: "life is various./ Life is beautiful." Then Ashbery makes the mock portentous observation that one who reads that cliché wisdom "Knows what he wants, and what will befall." The second stanza comes back to pain, implied in the "Pinpricks of rain" falling again. The constantly oscillating mind is in danger of letting the rain wash away that moving houseboat window in the first stanza through which varied and beautiful life is visible. The meditation on pain tries to move toward hope, but it is only "The picture of hope a dying man" cannot have. Now the poem/houseboat floats toward evening and sleep, making it clearer that the poem's overall shape is that of a houseboat day, from memories of breakfast china to the "pressure of sleep." The day is summed up this way: "mornings of assent/ Indifferent noons leading to the ripple of the question/ Of late afternoon projected into evening."

The ending leaves the reader with a slightly more comforting conundrum than pain and its automatic cancellation and return. Instead, the poet reassures the reader that "a little simple arithmetic tells you that to be with you/ In this passage, this movement, is what the instance costs." This self-referring statement is blurred by uncertainty about who is to be with whom. However, that statement is followed by a peaceful specific metaphor, "A sail out of some afternoon, beyond amazement." This elegant and "astonished" mood of peace is "not tampered with" by the gathering rain (or pain). Just as earlier pain carried its own cancellation, this peaceful mood now "protects/ Its own darkness." The poem closes with the teacups with which it began, the point of departure for each houseboat day.

Forms and Devices

Ashbery's free verse pushes toward the limits of prose. Deliberately avoiding both blank verse and the carefully measured lines of free verse, Ashbery seems to break his lines haphazardly, as if he were more concerned with the rhythms of his sentences and paragraphs than with the effects of pauses at the ends of lines. Thus the line breaks and the syntax of a sentence are sometimes at cross purposes. However, Ashbery wants to challenge readers' expectations and explore the effects of conflicting and well as complementary relationships between poetic measure and sentence sense.

"Houseboat Days" is more about imagination than about consciousness in general. Abstract language makes up most of the first stanza, from "The mind" to "And then it . . . happens." The passage says that insincere "reasoning on behalf of one's/ Sincere convictions" leads to pain, whether the convictions themselves are true or false. Although pain immediately gives way to "triumph over pain," the triumph is paradoxical, "pain/ . . . created just so as to deny its own existence." The word "pain," which rhymes with "brain" in one of the poem's few end rhymes, is repeated four times. Readers are then reminded of it again by "train" in the penultimate line of the first stanza and by "rain" in the opening line of the second stanza. Thus pain is played with, mocked and made light of, but it remains the poem's strongest emotional reference.

Not only does the poem begin with an unattributed quotation clearly indicated as a quotation, but it also includes actual transcriptions of the words of Walter Pater, not set off by quotation marks but identified with "he said." The pedantic-sounding passage in the first stanza, beginning with "that insincerity of reasoning" and ending with "At times," is taken verbatim from Pater's *Plato and Platonism* (1910). Another passage later in the same stanza also comes word for word from the same source. Ashbery's appropriation of these passages gives him an opportunity to gently mock abstract diction while, at the same time, using it for his own purposes, significantly changing the contexts from the originals. It also allows him to absorb into his poem all kinds of language, from the colloquial "Poking ahead" to the foreign "trouvailles" (French for the noun "find," including godsends and windfalls).

This inclusiveness, as well as the long lines, suggests a generosity of spirit, a willingness to accept anything. Ashbery, however, leaves out a great deal, carefully avoiding any details readers can clearly identify as personal or confessional and refusing to give readers specific information about places, times, and characters. As with Ashbery's grammatical manipulation of tenses, this disorienting approach detaches the poem from conventional time and space.

Themes and Meanings

The fact that Ashbery chose the title of this poem as the title of the collection in which it first appeared suggests the importance of the poem to the body of Ashbery's work. Ashbery is well known for assigning whimsical titles to his poems, titles that have nothing obvious to do with the poem. However, this poem is, in a sense, about what its title says: days spent in a dwelling that moves with time. A synopsis of the poem might make it sound more weighty and melancholy than it is. In fact, the tone of the poem is often quite light as Ashbery takes such serious subjects as pain and the nature of time and space and parodies the language poets and others might use to talk about them.

Ashbery is concerned with the passage of time and the way memory and perception bounce back and forth in the mind to give people a sense of what they call reality. In "Houseboat Days," reality is the interchange between perception and the world and, within perception, between sensing, thinking, and feeling. Odd though the poem's opening is, it is an opening, for the quotation ends with the word "began," and, as the first stanza ends, Ashbery brings readers back to the vague "beginning, where/ We must stay, in motion," flashing light into the "house" of consciousness (imagination) within, with its memories and associations. Ashbery's transcription of mental associations at first makes "Houseboat Days" jumpy and incoherent. Out of the seemingly random associations, however, Ashbery develops an abstract coherence metaphorically similar to a houseboat day, moving and standing still, rocking on gentle waters.

Uncertainties of time and place put the reader "beyond amazement." In fact, "Houseboat Days" is full of evasions and deflections. Pronoun shifts, quotations that are not obviously quoted, and quotations in unidentified voices all put readers in a realm that challenges their normal expectations of time and space. One cannot tell exactly to whom events are happening or when they are happening. Even in relation to each other, time references shift suddenly back and forth. The vague pronoun references in the first stanza refer to unspecified situations and people to suggest vague generalizations about life and consciousness. These vagaries are given weight and specificity by lively back and forth movement into and out of specifics.

A key generalization in the first part of the poem is the sentence beginning, "The mind/ Is so hospitable, taking in everything." Cut free of the conventions of narrative or lyric verse, Ashbery's poetry has a certain exhilarating freedom and seems almost infinitely open to interpretation. In a sense, Ashbery has deconstructed his own work and left it to readers and critics to put the pieces back together, however they see fit.

Thomas Lisk

HOW THE WORLD WORKS
An Essay

Author: Albert Goldbarth (1948-   )
Type of poem: Verse essay
First published: 1989; collected in *Heaven and Earth: A Cosmology,* 1991

The Poem

Albert Goldbarth's "How the World Works: An Essay" is a blend of vivid narration, verse essay, and meditation about the interrelation of the various cycles and circles of life, from the very large to the very small. Its form—including variation between un-rhymed lines as long as eighteen or as short as ten syllables—incorporates the contrast or cycling within the poem between macrocosm, the very large, and microcosm, the very small. While also considering small incidents in the speaker's life, the poem, a small thing in the universe, considers the grand cycles of life and death, the cosmological development and interconnectedness of life on earth, meteorology, and societal and global ecologies.

Further, its seven stanzas, with their fourteen lines each (based on a multiple of seven), symbolize the foundation of calendar time, the week, and the biblical account of creation; likewise, the enjambment of the last line of the first six stanzas to the first line of the next stanza mimics the poem's subjects of time's forward momentum and the interconnectedness of things.

As with an essay, a term used in other titles of Goldbarth's poems and reflecting his several books of essays, the poem's title and first stanza constitute an introduction, complete with thesis sentence, of the kind to be found in an essay's first paragraph; the speaker, indeed, uses the term "topic," saying in his first words after the title, "That's my topic." Suggesting the topic's scope and grandeur, the speaker alludes to epic invocation by summing up his large and small illustrations in the first stanza as "singing the rings-in-rings song of the planet," repeating this reference to singing several more times throughout the poem.

Illustrations of the world's working are provided in the second and third stanzas, from the speaker's childhood relationship with his father to an incident of the father's being stopped for a speeding traffic ticket in Chicago while the eight-year-old son was a passenger; in the fourth stanza, from episodes in the speaker's later-life sexual affair with a dyslexic woman; and in the fifth stanza, with the speaker's consideration of his father's death, circuitously associated with the gaudy "Pimp Prince" described in stanza 1.

Like the fifth stanza's cyclical reference to the Pimp Prince, the sixth stanza recycles the third stanza's illustration of various symbiotic interrelationships radiating from a bull, which becomes the breakfast steak of a salesman, the occupation of the speaker's father, in Washington State in 1929. The seventh stanza details an incident from the speaker's late adolescence, cycling back to the traffic ticket episode, which seems a counterexample to the world's working, illustrating "our own small break-down days" when the speaker and the reader are "sure that nothing ever does, or/ ever had really, or ever would, work."

When the speaker was eight years old, his father had been able to oil ("unctious functioning") the wheels of societal working by bribing the traffic "copper," but when the adolescent joyriding son, years later, tries in the same Chicago area to recycle this behavior, formally inculcated by his father years earlier, he ends up temporarily in jail and, after returning many hours later to the lakeshore, suffers the crowning insult of finding his car not working.

Forms and Devices

Repeated contrast between the formal level of usage and abstract diction on one side, and colloquialism (even an occasional vulgarity) and specific, sometimes scientific technical diction and imagery on the other side, helps convey how grand patterns and particular individuals interconnect. Thus, details of weather seen on computer screens or on the tiles of the Islamic architectural masterpiece in Granada, Spain, the Alhambra, help "construe a grander pattern." Further, the speaker's humorous awareness of the ironies in the contrasts and connections in the world's working often emerges from these contrasting stylistic components, as in the eight-year-old's embarrassed misery that the "copper's" motorcycle flasher was, the child thought, "calling all of Heaven's attention" to the traffic stop.

Specific or general settings are associated with the specific or general diction in the poem, showing the interconnectedness in the world's working. The Alhambran—the beautiful curvilinear swirls of Islamic art—weather patterns on computer screens resemble the rain patterns on the tiles of the actual Alhambra, and a poacher in Nepal kills a deer for the small quantity of musk that the Pimp Prince "reeks of" in mid-Manhattan. The speaker engages in "explaining the planet," a general or abstract setting, to his paramour on a cocktail napkin, implying the specific setting of the cocktail lounge to which he has taken her in his earlier "days of believing repeated sex/ meant knowing a person."

Specificity in setting also helps create the poem's looping, cyclical pattern, as the first stanza's implied view of the earth and its oceans on the computer screens connects with the last stanza's exhausted, dejected speaker's staring view of the ocean, as he is seated on the hood of his non-operating car. In contrast to his exuberant epic singing of the first stanza, the speaker can only "sit stupidly humming—not singing just humming" in the last stanza, while the description of the sea, "the first gray rhythmic swashing/ in-and-out of the water," associates it with the cyclicity of the world's working.

The poem's pervasive wordplay or punning is as important as its imagery and figurative language. The word "arabesques" not only suggests the swirling patterns on computer screens and courtyard tile, related to the circular or spiral connecting patterns in the world's working, but also suggests the medieval Arabs' Islamic culture, originating the beautiful Alhambra, which is connected to the modern Western meteorologists at their computer screens. The word "weathering" in the reference to the "weathering eddies on tiles" in the Alhambra's courtyards and other areas suggests not only the weather that generates the rain but also the rain's erosion of the artifact over time. The speaker's reference to the planet's song as "rings-in-rings" suggests the connecting concentric circles of the world's working; the enormous time of the world's working, implied by tree ring growth; the chains of the Pimp Prince's jewelry, or the different rings not really differentiating the Pimp Prince from a rival; and the play on "links" in "chlorophyl links," the chain-like interconnectedness of the world's working.

The ignorant malaprop of the speaker's dyslexic girlfriend in asking whether humanity is derived from monkeys "or little/ enemas in the water" in stanza 4 punningly displays her error for the word "amoebas," later linked to the protozoa-bull feces-salesman's breakfast steak chain in stanza 6, as well as the scatological imagery of the mini-ecosystem surrounding the bull described in stanza 3. The speaker's initial "ripplings" of pity when hearing his paramour's malaprop, both in the word and figure of speech, convey not only an emotional stirring but also a backward reference to the watery locus of her "enemas." Finally, the speaker's statement about needing to remember the world's "networking" or working "against our own small breakdown days" in stanza 6 plays on the meanings of "breakdown" not only as generally going badly but also, as revealed in the next, final stanza, as the episode in which the breakdown of the speaker's car capped a day on which the world apparently did not work for him, suggested also in the malfunctioning grammar of the poem's final two lines.

Themes and Meanings

The speaker's opening imagery of the "weathering eddies" accumulating on the tiles of the Alhambra's "courtyards and intimate tryst-rooms and policy chambers" conveys the focus in the poem, as in many other of Goldbarth's poems, on the workings and networkings of the external or natural world, often including a scientific perspective and vocabulary; human artifacts, ranging from architecture and painting to music and poetry; the various spheres of love, whether in the family or romantic relationship; and society's functioning. The poem shows that the world's working is a combination of harmony and discord, of order and disorder. While the social order works for the speaker's father in bribing the "copper," inviting the boss to dinner and being sycophantic, and "shmoozing" the waitress for better service, it painfully fails for the son years later when attempting to recycle the same behavior. While the bull, the "ecoconnected" cattle egret, lice on the egret, and dungbugs exist in harmony, the Pimp Prince and butterfly fish have their colorful rivals, the speaker's youthful love affair fails (though he has later gained important knowledge about connectedness in the romantic relationship), and the speaker's father—who seems so "high" and demonstrative of "mastery" to the eight-year-old son—is simply one of the "counters/ in some global game, 'Advantage,' tycoons and brigadiers play." Art, exemplified by the Alhambra, is both in harmony with nature, reflecting the weather's arabesques, and in conflict with nature, exemplified by the "weathering eddies" attacking and eventually eroding its beautiful tiles.

Goldbarth's poem is a virtuoso performance, from large structural connections and patterns to subtle metrical effects, such as the consonance on the *s* sound to convey the swish of the wind or water (lines 5-6) or the shortest lines of the poem—lines 56, 70, and 98—being used to convey things having smallness. Just as impressive are the poem's several metaphors and similes, such as nature, represented by Lake Michigan, "unhoarding" the "clear blue afternoon" at "winter's thinner end," suggesting not only the miserly bitterness of Chicago winters but also connecting with the bribery of the "copper" in the same stanza, the riches of the Pimp Prince in the preceding stanza, and the implied motif of money's role in the poem's depiction of the world's working. While the poem will repay study of Goldbarth's skill in using any of the main components of poetry (even rhyme makes a brief appearance in one line), perhaps most notable is his adroit diction or word choice, which in its range and precision recall another modern American master, Wallace Stevens.

Norman Prinsky

THE HUG

Author: Tess Gallagher (1943-   )
Type of poem: Narrative
First published: 1984, in *Willingly*

The Poem

Tess Gallagher's "The Hug" moves through four stanzas relating an experience of the female speaker giving a hug to a stranger and coming to an illumination about the human ability to connect. Central to the poem is the speaker's relationship to the lover taking a walk with her when this experience occurs. Their closeness sparks the stranger's request to receive one of the hugs the woman gives to her lover. Curiously, the speaker appears lost at the end of the poem, the hug over, her lover not much of a presence anymore.

Serendipity characterizes the poem's movement. Events seem to just happen, and one thing follows another. The oddity of a woman "reading a poem on the street" is not remarked upon. The lovers, "arms around each other," stop and listen; the street life is free-flowing and "open." The only ominous note is the contrast to the houses surrounding them: "no one is entering or leaving."

This stasis is offset by the woman's sudden desire to hug her lover: "a hug comes over me." She feels emotion; she acts, being spontaneous and loving. So attractive are her actions that a male bystander approaches and asks, "Can I have one of those?" The speaker is baffled by this man and wonders where he came from. His sudden appearance is as serendipitous as the sidewalk poetry reading or the speaker's desire to give her lover a hug. She says she is "surprised" at this request but even more taken aback that her lover agrees to it, not feeling possessive of her. The speaker's ordinary notion about love has been shaken: "love/ that nabs you with 'for me/ only' and holds on."

She matches her lover's nonchalance by hugging the stranger. This hug is the heart of the poem, and the woman gives it everything she has, although doubts creep in: "How big a hug is this supposed to be?" The man wears an overcoat, and "he is so big" she cannot reach her arms all the way around him. Instead, she "snuggle[s] in." He returns the hug, the two of them acting "So truly, so tenderly" they transcend their bodies; the speaker even forgets her lover. Then she thinks of the houses on the street and possibly the people inside looking out at them.

Gallagher concludes the poem with several insights, some ironic: "a little permission is a dangerous thing." In giving the hug so fully, she neglects her lover. Even so, she defends the intensity of the hug. If one is going to give a hug, it should be "a masterpiece of connection." She is left with an "imprint" of the man's coat button on her cheek, but when she tries to return to the way things were before, she is disoriented and can not seem to find "some place/ to go back to."

Forms and Devices

Gallagher's poem is conversational and depends little on traditional poetic devices, though there are some. The image of the houses in the first stanza seems initially just incidental background. They are self-contained houses with "no one . . . entering or leaving." If there is no departure, there must not be a journey; thus the houses function as a contrast to the speaker who makes a journey of self-discovery. The houses reappear in stanza 3 as if to remind readers of their stolid presence.

Stanza 2 contains two similes. The desire to hug her lover "comes over" the woman "like a variable star shooting light/ off to make itself comfortable, then/ subsiding." A "variable star" would be like the Sun going through periodic solar storms because of the pressures of internal gases. Solar flares exude an enormous amount of energy and may even interrupt communication systems on earth. There is no way to predict them. Likewise, Gallagher's simile places emphasis on the spontaneous quality of the woman's feelings. One does not know why the hug occurs at that particular moment. It must have something to do with the poem being read on the street by another woman. No overt connection is made in the poem, however. The hug is inexplicable, "like a variable star."

The second simile speaks of the relationship between the two lovers as being defined differently by the lover's acquiescence to the stranger's request. The woman is surprised to discover that her lover does not regard her as his, that is, "exclusive as a nose to/ its face." Gallagher's word choice reinvigorates the cliché of something obvious being as "plain as the nose on one's face." Her lover's surprising lack of sexual possessiveness propels her into the intimacy of hugging the stranger. This surprise generates more surprise.

Although hugging the stranger was not her idea, the speaker gets totally involved in it, so much so that in the last stanza she exhorts: "when you hug someone you want it/ to be a masterpiece of connection." Speaking as an authority, the woman adopts metaphorical language: the hug is a "masterpiece," a work of high order connecting one human being to another in a direct, sensuous, but ultimately nonsexual way. Gallagher compares the intensity of this connection to "the way the button/ on his coat will leave the imprint of/ a planet in my cheek/ when I walk away." The stranger has left a mark on her, the roundness of his coat button suggesting "a planet." In hugging him, she has entered another world. Coming back to the ordinary world, she has problems reentering and can not seem to "find some place/ to go back to." There is no mention of the lover.

Themes and Meanings

Gallagher's main focus in this poem is on expanding the borders of love. Instead of shunning the stranger, who "looks homeless because of how/ he needs," both she and her lover let him into their world. The speaker of this poem grows beyond notions of a love "that nabs you with 'for me/ only' and holds on." Love so constructed might as well wear manacles.

There are dangers, however, in developing a different perception or experience of love. In hugging the stranger, the speaker enters the unknown. The experience, for both her and the stranger, has positive effects: They hug "So truly, so tenderly/ [they] stop having arms." They become as one and lose sense of the physical. This is the spiritual center of the poem, where the temporal becomes the eternal. On the negative side, the speaker suffers a loss of awareness: "I don't know if/ my lover has walked away or what, or/ if the woman is still reading the poem." Up to this point, the poem has been addressed to the lover. Mirroring her distance from him, the woman refers to him ("My lover") rather than addressing him. She gains the transcendence of the hug but loses contact with her beloved. This is why she states in her last stanza, "Clearly, a little permission is a dangerous thing." The lover permitted the stranger to hug the woman, and the woman permitted herself to follow through on the hug. The stranger "give[s] it back so well I know he's/ getting it." The woman accepts the danger; it is worth it to achieve "a masterpiece of connection." The speaker is a different person at the end of the poem, not so smug or so grounded in coupledom.

Willingly, the volume in which "The Hug" appears, explores different faces of love: father and daughter, mother and son, sister and sister, and a reader and the blind man to whom she reads. There are many possibilities for loving in this world. In its generosity of spirit and its openness to experience, "The Hug" is typical of Gallagher's verse. The voice in the poem is natural, and yet what begins in the ordinary goes through a process of transcendent expansion and then reflection. What might appear wanton behavior in a restrictive culture comes across in this poem as deeply moral despite the surrounding houses, unmoved and unmoving. The stranger, essentially "homeless," is embraced. Included rather than excluded from the lovers' sphere, he leaves the mark of his own world on the woman's cheek. In expanding the boundaries of her self, the poem's speaker becomes more compassionate and humane. This poem's impulses are central, therefore, to Gallagher's main concerns throughout her work.

Claire Keyes

THE HUMAN ABSTRACT

Author: William Blake (1757-1827)
Type of poem: Lyric
First published: 1794, in *Songs of Innocence and of Experience*

The Poem

"The Human Abstract" is a short poem of twenty-four lines divided into six quatrains. The title refers to the human capacity to create false structures of belief through excessive use of the rational part of the mind.

In the first quatrain, the speaker offers his opinions on moral and social issues in a way that justifies the existing order. He says that without poverty, there would be no way for people to exercise pity or compassion, and that if everyone were happy, there would be no opportunity to relieve the suffering of others.

The same speaker, who obviously includes himself among the compassionate and merciful, continues in the first two lines of the second quatrain. He gives his explanation of how order is preserved in a society. When there is "mutual fear" among people, the result is peace; fear keeps everyone from breaking the rules of society. Although self-love (what the speaker here calls "selfish loves") always predominates, it is in everyone's interest to accept the social order and the restrictions it imposes. If every individual were allowed to gratify every personal desire, everyone would feel threatened and insecure.

In line 7, another speaker takes over, and the poem is given over to his attack on the views of the first speaker. This is clearly William Blake's own voice. He states that when people accept the views of the first speaker, the result is a cruel society. A false philosophy spreads its tentacles everywhere and traps the innocent. In the name of religion and compassion, the seeds of Christian "humility" are planted. The word has a bitter edge to it, because humility to Blake meant only subservience to a pernicious and illusory view of God and human nature. The seed grows into a tree, an imposing edifice that overspreads everything and cuts out the light of the sun to produce a "dismal shade/ Of Mystery." Mystery was another pejorative term for Blake. Taking his cue from the Book of Revelation (17:5), in which the Whore of Babylon is said to be named Mystery, Blake often used the term to refer to false religion. Here the speaker adds that caterpillars and flies (the representatives of organized religion) feed on this Tree of Mystery.

In the fifth quatrain, the speaker explains what this tree of false religion and false morality produces: deceit, but it is a deceit that seems sweet and healthful to those who are under its spell and appears to provide them with all the sustenance they need. The speaker, however, points to what he sees as the truth of the matter: In the tree, where its branches are thickest, lives the raven, a symbol of death.

The final quatrain brings the speaker's point home with considerable force. The tree that contains such poison is not to be found in nature or in anything that exists outside the mind of man; it grows in the human brain itself.

Forms and Devices

Blake's poems often grow in meaning when the illustrations that accompany them are taken into account. The design for "The Human Abstract" shows a bearded old man sitting under a tree, tangled up in its fallen branches. The branches resemble ropes or chains and seem to sprout directly from his brain. They also seem to be arranged to resemble part of a human skeleton, which brings out the idea implied in the text of the poem that conventional religion sucks the life out of people. The old man is an early depiction by Blake of his mythological figure Urizen, who represents the rational faculty of man when it no longer works in harmony with man's other faculties. Setting himself up as the sole God, Urizen becomes a tyrant, but, as the design shows, the enslaver is himself trapped by his own creation. This illustrates the images of snares and baits in the poem. Even the lines of Urizen's beard seem to suggest the branches of the Tree of Mystery.

"The Human Abstract" is the first poem in which Blake used the symbol of the Tree of Mystery. He was to use it many times afterwards, notably in *The Book of Ahania* (1795), in which Urizen, having broken away from the other faculties, finds the Tree springing up from under his own heel. The symbol is derived from the tree of the knowledge of good and evil, of which Adam and Eve ate the fruit, as recorded in Genesis 2:9. Blake interpreted this tale as indicative of a fall into the strictures of conventional morality, under which human desires and actions were classified into good and evil. To Blake this was a piece of judgmental nonsense that perverted the innocence and purity of human desire and led to corruption and self-deceit. The Tree of Mystery, for example, also appears in another of the *Songs of Experience*, "The Poison Tree," in which the devastating effects of the self-restraint known as "Christian forbearance" (the original title of the poem) are laid bare.

The other symbols in this heavily didactic poem are related to the tree symbol and form a straightforward part of the poem's allegory. The seed of the tree is Cruelty, and the seed forms a root, Humility, which develops into branches. The identification of the caterpillar as a symbol of the priesthood is clear when the following passage in Blake's *The Marriage of Heaven and Hell* (1790-1793) is noted: "As the caterpillar chooses the fairest leaves to lay her eggs on, so the priest lays his curse on the fairest of joys." Continuing the allegory, the fruits of the Tree are Deceit, and the true nature of the tree is revealed by the presence in its branches of the raven, ready to prey on those who have fallen victim to the great illusion.

Themes and Meanings

When Blake published *Songs of Innocence* (1789) and *Songs of Experience* together, in 1794, he subtitled the collection, "Shewing the Two Contrary States of the Human Soul." The state of experience is shown as a cramped, fearful, and introspective attitude to life, completely opposed to the free-flowing, open, joyful impulses enjoyed by the speakers in the *Songs of Innocence*.

Many of the poems in the two books are deliberately paired. In a draft version of "The Human Abstract," Blake called it "A Human Image," which shows that it was intended as a contrast to "The Divine Image" in *Songs of Innocence*. Blake altered the title to convey, more directly, the true nature of the human image portrayed in the poem.

"The Divine Image" celebrates the virtues of mercy, pity, peace, and love as divine qualities dwelling within man. "The Human Abstract" satirizes each of these virtues, showing what happens to them when calculation replaces spontaneity and self-righteous morality usurps innocent joy and self-understanding. In "The Divine Image," mercy and pity are innocent expressions of the essence of humanity—the natural tenderness that flows from one human being to another and makes the human divine. The qualities do not depend for their existence on the presence of unhappiness or suffering. In "The Human Abstract," all this is changed. Mercy and pity somehow must be manipulated into existence and can be manifested only in an imperfect society created by human beings; they are not intrinsic to the soul.

The other two virtues become even more sinister. Peace results only from fear, quite unlike the sense conveyed in "The Divine Image," in which peace is "the human dress," its natural state of being. The same applies to love, which, in the innocent poem is "the human form divine," but in "The Human Abstract" is a state of mind that seeks its own advantage in everything and all love is self-love. The tragedy that Blake conveys with such force is that to those who are enmeshed in this web of limitation, self-deceit, and man-made cruelty it seems normal, inevitable, divinely ordained, and good, while the speaker who attacks these premises with such withering scorn is fully aware of the battery of interlocking rationalizations and phony arguments that are used to seduce the minds of the unwary.

Although Blake would later develop a complex mythological system to convey his ideas, this short poem contains the essence of his vision in stark simplicity: his opposition to any philosophy or creed that diminishes man's capacity to enjoy the unbounded bliss that is his birthright.

Bryan Aubrey

THE HUNTING OF THE HARE

Author: Margaret Cavendish, Duchess of Newcastle (1624?-1674)
Type of poem: Satire
First published: 1653, in *Poems and Fancies*

The Poem

Margaret Cavendish's poem begins in a field where a small hare, Wat, lies close to the ground between two ridges of plowed earth. The poet notes that Wat always faces the wind, which would otherwise blow under his fur and make him cold. Wat rests in the field all day. At sunset he begins wandering, which he continues to do until dawn. Huntsmen and dogs discover Wat, who begins to runs away. As the dogs bark, Wat becomes terrified and believes that every shadow is a dog. After running a distance, he lies under a clod of earth in a sandpit. Soon he hears the huntsmen's horns and the dogs' barking, and he begins to run once more, this time so quickly that he scarcely treads the ground. Wat runs into a thick wood and hides under a broken bough, frightened by every leaf that is shaken by the wind. Hoping to deceive the dogs, he runs into unenclosed fields. While the dogs search for his scent, Wat, being weary, slows down. Sitting on his hind legs, he rubs the dust and sweat from his face with his forefeet. He then licks his feet and cleans his ears so well that no one could tell he had been hunted.

Wat sees the hounds and is again terrified. His fear gives him the strength to move more quickly. Ironically, he has never felt stronger than during this time of crisis. The poet notes that spirits often seek to guard the heart from death but that death eventually wins. The hounds approach Wat quickly. Just as the hare resigns himself to his fate, the winds take pity on him and blow his scent away. The dogs scatter, each searching bits of grass or tracts of land. Soon the dogs' work, which the poet compares to witchcraft, brings them back on task. When one dog discovers Wat's scent, the horns sound and the other dogs follow. The poet now provides an extended analogy comparing the barking dogs to members of a choir. The large slow dogs are the basses; the swift hounds are the tenors. Beagles sing treble, and the horns keep time as the hunters shout for joy. The hunters, seeming valiant, spur their horses, swim rivers, leap ditches, and endanger themselves only to see the hare, who has died with weeping eyes. The hunters begin rejoicing "as if the devil they did prisoner take."

The poet now satirizes hunting, noting that the sport is not valiant. Although men think that hunting provides good exercise, the poet argues that men are cruel when they kill harmless creatures which are imagined to be dangerous game. Hunters, the poet continues, destroy God's creation for sport, and in so doing make their stomachs "graves" for the murdered animals. The poet states that, although men believe themselves to be gentle, they are actually the cruelest creatures. Proud men, Cavendish concludes, believe that they possess a godlike entitlement and that all creatures were made for them to tyrannize.

Forms and Devices

"The Hunting of the Hare" is written in rhymed lines of iambic pentameter, or heroic couplets, which would become the most important verse form of Restoration and eighteenth century poetry. Cavendish uses this form and several poetic devices and conventions to create a sustained effect, one that shows the cruelty and senselessness of hunting.

Early in the poem Cavendish anthropomorphizes (gives human characteristics to) the hare, first by naming him and then by assigning to him human emotions. When first startled from his hiding place, Wat hopes to outrun the dogs and is then "struck with terror and with fear" as the dogs pursue him. By making the hare appear human, Cavendish accentuates the drama of the hunt and enhances her appeal to the reader's emotions. She furthers her intention by manipulating the rhythm and sounds of her lines. Describing the dogs' pursuit, for example, she reverses the iambic rhythm and offers trochaic lines: "But they by nature have so quick a scent/ That by their nose they trace what way he went." These lines re-create the bouncing and running of the dogs, which is accentuated by the tapping *t* sound. In contrast to these fast-paced lines, the poet offers slow lines to describe the hare: "Then Wat was struck with terror and with fear,/ Thinks every shadow still the dogs they were." In this couplet the repeated *s* sound, the *oz* sound in "was," the *ur* in "terror" and "were," and a pause all cause the lines to drag, while the jumbled syntax of "still the dogs they were" gives the line an almost nightmarish quality of paralysis.

Later the poet accentuates the barbarity of the hunt by allowing nature to function on behalf of the hare. After running through field, wood, and plain, the exhausted Wat is momentarily saved by the winds that "did pity poor Wat's case." Here the poet is using a poetic trope later critics would call the pathetic fallacy: assigning human sympathies to the natural world. Feeling pity for Wat's fate, nature tries to prevent the unnaturalness of the dogs' pursuit. After Wat is killed, the poet depicts the senselessness of the hunt. The huntsmen endanger their lives only to recover the pathetic hare. By showing the ridiculousness of the hunters risking their lives for so inconsequential a prize, Cavendish introduces to her poem a mock-heroic quality. Cavendish, like John Dryden and Alexander Pope, uses the mock heroic, which treats trivial issues with exaggerated seriousness, to ridicule human folly. Finding the poor hare, the hunters appear silly and deluded: "Men hooping loud such acclamations make/ As if the devil they did prisoner take,/ When they do but a shiftless creature kill." Near the end of the poem, Cavendish uses metaphor to heighten her message. The hunters' stomachs become "graves" which hold the "murthered bodies" of the prey. This metaphor prepares the reader for the poem's unsettling conclusion, in which Cavendish exposes the unnaturalness of the hunters' pride.

Themes and Meanings

"The Hunting of the Hare" explores several issues that are important to understanding Cavendish's poetry. Early in the poem the narrator describes how the hare lies close to the ground and faces the wind in order to stay warm. Cavendish had a keen interest in natural history. Herself an amateur scientist, she used her poetry as a vehicle for scientific speculation. As the critic Steven Max Miller has noted, her poetry "abounds with a sense . . . of wonder and delight in nature," and it sometimes questions "whether animals might know more natural science than man is capable of learning" (*Dictionary of Literary Biography* 43). Not only does the hare shield himself from the wind, he also executes a thoughtful initial escape from the dogs. Until his death, Wat appears to have an acute perception of his surroundings.

The poem is also an antihunting statement, one of the earliest in the language. Cavendish depicts the hare's death as a result of unnecessary cruelty. The hunters have no reason to kill the innocent creature except "for sport, or recreation's sake," and Cavendish makes clear that in indulging their desires they commit the equivalent of a crime. Earlier poems, such as Sir John Denham's *Cooper's Hill* (1642), used the hunt as a metaphor for man's political intrigues. used the hunt as a metaphor for man's political intrigues. Alexander Pope's *Windsor Forest* (1713), published sixty years after Cavendish's poem, explores the ambivalence and responsibility that accompany the "pleasing Toils" of the hunt. With its exaggerated pathos, Cavendish's poem is unique for its time, standing as seventeenth century England's strongest poetic condemnation of blood sport.

Cavendish condemns more than hunting, however; she also attacks the pride that causes individuals to engage in such activities. Near the end of the poem, the narrator reveals that hunters believe that God provided them with a "godlike nature"; all creatures were made for human domination. Believing in their own superiority, the hunters become morally inferior to the animals they hunt. In satirizing the hunters' pride, Cavendish anticipates a central theme of Restoration and eighteenth century poetry. Disrupting an implied natural order, the hunters become the embodiment of pride as understood by poets such as Pope, who wrote, "In Pride . . . our error lies;/ All quit their sphere, and rush into the skies./ . . . And who but wishes to invert the laws/ Of ORDER, sins against th' Eternal Cause" (Pope's *Essay on Man*).

Christopher D. Johnson

THE HUNTING OF THE SNARK
An Agony in Eight Fits

Author: Lewis Carroll (Charles Lutwidge Dodgson, 1832-1898)
Type of poem: Ballad
First published: 1876

The Poem

The Reverend Charles Lutwidge Dodgson used the pseudonym Lewis Carroll when he published *The Hunting of the Snark: An Agony in Eight Fits.* Although this work is often called "nonsense verse" or "children's literature," it is complex and dark. On a superficial reading it may seem a childish, laughter-filled romp, but it draws the thoughtful adult back to read it again and again as the laughter dies.

Carroll subtitles his poem *An Agony in Eight Fits.* The word "agony" derives from the Greek verb meaning "to act," which is also the root of the word "protagonist" and "action." The poem is divided into eight parts, which are quite properly called "fits," for in Old English the word for divisions of a poem is "fitts." Moreover, Carroll is suggesting that an "agony" suitably accompanies "fits," perhaps convulsive fits of madness.

In "Fit of the First," the captain of a ship gathers a band of companions for the venture. The captain is called the Bellman, perhaps because the life aboard a navy ship is governed by the ship's bell, with each watch changing at eight bells, like the eight fits of this text. Perhaps, on the other hand, a bellman is like a bellwether, the sheep that wears a bell and leads a herd of animals. There are ten in the band of hunters: the Bellman (captain), Boots (a boot boy who shines shoes), a Bonnet-maker, a Barrister (lawyer), a Broker (stockbroker), a Billiard-marker (a man who keeps score in a billiards game), a Banker, a Beaver (a furry animal who, in this story, makes lace), a Baker, and a Butcher. All the comrades have names beginning with the letter *B*. As the alliterative accented syllables fall in the lines of the poem, the sound of that *B* "Bombastically Booms until it Boggles" the mind. This is a motley crew; no great kings or noble knights gather to hunt the Snark, merely ordinary folk, except for one anthropomorphic animal, the Beaver.

The Bellman leads his band on a voyage to hunt the Snark. Carroll used the term "portmanteau" to mean a single word that is a combination of several other words, like a *portmanteau*, the French word for "suitcase," packed with odd contents. "Snark" might be a portmanteau word containing "to snag," "snail," and "shark," for example. No one knows what a Snark is, although many readers suggest a symbolic meaning for the word.

When the Baker joins the crew in the first section, he brings with him forty-two boxes of luggage. Carroll was forty-two years old when he wrote these lines, and sometimes the Baker is thought to be a caricature of the author himself. The Baker is forgetful and cannot remember his own name, but he is obsessed with a single idea, "Snark."

In "Fit of the Second, The Bellman's Speech," the companions arrive at an island wasteland of chasms and crags, where the Bellman delivers a speech, describing the Snark and warning the crew that some Snarks are Boojums. Readers may speculate that "Boojum" is a portmanteau word combining "boo," "bogeyman," and "fee, fi, fo, fum."

In "Fit of the Third, The Baker's Tale," the Baker observes that his uncle told him once that if one catches a Snark that is a Boojum, one will vanish away into nothingness. "Fit of the Fourth, The Hunting" shows the members of the crew each making preparations for the hunt. In "Fit of the Fifth, The Beaver's Lesson," the Beaver and the Butcher plan separately to hunt the Snark in a desolate valley. As they enter the valley, it grows narrower and narrower until they are marching side by side. Suddenly they hear the terrifying cry of the Jubjub bird. Through this frightening experience the Beaver and the Butcher become fast friends and return hand in hand to the crew.

"Fit of the Sixth, The Barrister's Dream" is a mock commentary on the complications of the British legal system. The Barrister, a lawyer, dreams that he is in court observing the Snark play simultaneously the roles of advocate, judge, and jury in a case of a pig that is charged with desertion of its sty. The Snark finds the pig guilty and sentences it to be transported (presumably to a distant penal colony) and fined. Unfortunately, the pig cannot serve his sentence, for he has been dead for many years.

"Fit of the Seventh, The Banker's Fate," tells that the Banker has rushed ahead of the others in search of the Snark and has fallen into the clutches of a Bandersnatch. When the rest of the crew arrive, the Bandersnatch flees, but they find that the Banker was so frightened that his waistcoat has turned white, while his face has turned black. The Banker cannot speak properly and merely rattles a couple of bones.

"Fit of the Eighth, The Vanishing" begins by repeating the formula for hunting a Snark:

> They sought it with thimbles, they sought it with care;
> They pursued it with forks and hope;
> They threatened its life with a railway-share;
> They charmed it with smiles and soap.

The Baker, rushing ahead of the others, cries that he has found the Snark. Then they hear him say that it is a "boo—" and there follows a long sigh that sounds like "jum." He has vanished. The concluding line of the poem is, "For the Snark *was* a Boojum, you see."

Forms and Devices

Carroll was a lecturer in mathematics at Christ Church College, Oxford University, and also a pioneer in the early stages of photography. He was a shy man who never married but from time to time formed close friendships with several young girls. *The Hunting of the Snark* begins with a dedication to such a young friend, Gertrude Chataway, whom Carroll had befriended at the beach on a summer vacation. The dedicatory poem is an anagram in which the first letter of each line, read from top to bottom of the text, spell out Gertrude Chataway's name. Moreover, it is composed of four stanzas of four lines each, and the first syllables in each stanza also combine to make the name: "Girt," "Rude," "Chat," "Away." The dedication expresses the joy Carroll felt in the companionship of the beautiful child on a summer's day at the seashore.

The dedication plus the eight "fits," or parts, of *The Hunting of the Snark* are in ballad measure. This is the poetic form found in nursery rhymes, children's game songs, Protestant hymns designated as common measure, or poems such as *Rime of the Ancient Mariner* (1798) by Samuel Taylor Coleridge. Carroll's ballad measure in *The Hunting of the Snark* is constructed of four-line stanzas, rhymed *abab*.

Lines 1 and 3 of each stanza have four accented syllables. Lines 2 and 4 have three accented syllables and conclude with a full stop or musical rest. The accented syllables often alliterate or display similar sounds. The number of unaccented syllables per line is variable. This ballad measure is thought to be related to the metrical structure of Old English alliterative verse as used in the epic of Beowulf. It is time-based, like common measure hymns or popular ballads designed to be sung to music with a time signature.

Themes and Meanings

The Hunting of the Snark belongs to the family of narratives called romance quest: A band of comrades sets out on a journey into a perilous domain on a quest for something of value. Often the exact nature of the object of the quest is a mystery. In the perilous domain the comrades encounter obstacles that test their heroic virtue. In medieval literature the knights of King Arthur's Round Table engaged in a quest for the Holy Grail. In a mock heroic journey in Victorian England, Carroll's "The Hunting of the Snark" depicts a similar journey into the perilous unknown carried out by a motley crew, ranging from a banker to a bootblack. In order to find the Snark, they must lose themselves.

Carroll claimed that the poem originated when a single line of nonsense randomly came into his mind, "For the Snark *was* a Boojum, you see." Many readers have suggested a symbolic meaning for the Snark: wealth, power, glory, honor, love. Unfortunately, the price for attaining the desire is annihilation. The poem invokes the trope of the "possessor possessed." The hunter thinks he is going to capture the Snark, but the Snark always gets him instead. Perhaps the reader enters the text of Carroll's poem looking for a meaning, like the Bellman's crew hunting the Snark, but the meaning is elusive.

The world of the Snark is surreal and absurd. The poem's central concern is being and nothingness. French surrealist Louis Aragon translated Carroll's poem into French and believed that such nonsense writings were a subversive political protest against the rigid social and economic structures of Victorian England. The Banker and the Broker are wasting their lives along with the lives of every Baker, Butcher, and Bonnet-maker in a crazy search of worthless, destructive wealth.

Psychological critics see the lonely, shy, celibate Carroll with his penchant for making friendships with pretty, young girls as a fertile domain for exploration. Carroll desperately sought love, approval, and human contact, but the only source of these values in his emotional wasteland was the forbidden and shameful affection of very young girls. Overt expression of such love was strictly forbidden, so what he wanted most was repressed deep in his subconscious.

Todd K. Bender

HURT HAWKS

Author: Robinson Jeffers (1887-1962)
Type of poem: Verse essay
First published: 1928, in *Cawdor and Other Poems*

The Poem

Because of its stark, powerful imagery and arguably misanthropic, even nihilistic, overtones, "Hurt Hawks" is probably Robinson Jeffers's most renowned and frequently anthologized poem. It consists of two numbered parts, of seventeen and fifteen uneven lines, respectively. These two parts are essentially two separate, though closely related, poems. Read in dialectical fashion—as thesis and antithesis—they produce a meaning far greater than the sum.

In part 1 the poet presents, in an objective and distanced way, a red-tail hawk with a hopelessly shattered wing that trails the bird "like a banner in defeat." The hawk will never fly again, will never hunt nor taste the freedom and power that are its birthright. It awaits the "salvation" of death with what appears to be "intrepid readiness." Empathizing deeply with the wounded hawk, the poet notes that Nature, the "wild God of the world," is sometimes merciful to its creatures but "not often to the arrogant"—by whom he doubtlessly means human beings, the "communal people" who do not know or have forgotten that wild God in humanity's comfortable alienation from Nature. The hawk, "beautiful and wild," remembers God, as do "men that are dying," because they are leaving civilization's cloister and returning, alone, to the natural world that spawned them.

Part 2 begins with one of the most provocative statements in all of modern poetry: "I'd sooner, except the penalties, kill a man than a hawk." One could argue, as Jeffers later did, that there is "no misanthropy involved, but only a comparison" meant to underscore the poet's intense love for the hawk. Be that as it may, such harsh rhetoric is meant to shock the reader into becoming conscious of the habituated anthropocentrism that marks human beings' relation to the natural world. As Jeffers asserts in "Carmel Point," "We must uncenter our minds from ourselves;/ We must unhumanize our views a little, and become/ confident/ As the rock and ocean that we were made from." Declaring hawks more valuable than people is one way to "unhumanize" and subvert modernity's dominant paradigm, which tends to presume human superiority over all other living things.

The statement also dramatizes the poet's extreme reluctance to kill the hopelessly injured raptor. After feeding the bird for six weeks the poet can no longer evade the fact that the hawk's wing is "too shattered for mending." He gives it its freedom so that nature can take its course. The hawk wanders "over the foreland hill" but returns in the evening, "asking for death." The poet finally obliges with "the lead gift in the twilight." The poem's great irony inheres in the fact that the act of killing is, in this instance, the ultimate sign of reverence. In death the ferocious hawk's body becomes a relaxed mass of "owl-downy, soft feminine feathers," but its spirit—the spirit of life that animates the universe—soars upward in a "fierce rush" that frightens the night-herons "at its rising/ Before it was quite unsheathed from reality."

Forms and Devices

In the first part of "Hurt Hawks" Jeffers forges a series of pointed contrasts between strength and freedom and their opposites: infirmity and limitation. Formerly indomitable and free "to use the sky forever," the wounded hawk must passively await its fate on the ground. While delineating the unique tragedy of a noble, entirely self-sufficient creature brought low, Jeffers is equally avid to emphasize that the bird was meant to inhabit a world utterly alien to humans. Banished from that free and wild world, the hawk nonetheless "remembers" its freedom and its God. Even in its diminished state the hawk remains fierce; it retains its essentially "intemperate and savage" nature. Its "terrible eyes" manifest no self-pity.

Having established the tragic magnificence of the hawk without resorting to sentimentality or bathos, Jeffers concludes part 1 by positing a related contrast, between nature and humanity. The poet castigates his brethren for their alienation from nature, an estrangement that is tantamount to an inability to deal with death. Conversely, only "men that are dying" remember the "wild God of the world."

Part 2 of the poem introduces other kinds of oppositions and antimonies. In marked contrast to the hawk's undivided nature, the poet's heart is fractured by sorrow, hesitation, and ambivalence. His desperate reluctance to shoot the hawk is opposed by the absolute necessity of the act. In the final lines of the poem this contradiction is resolved on an imagistic level. The hawk falls down dead after it is shot, but its spirit soars back to the sky that is its natural home. Thus, the divergence of spirit and matter in death echoes the cleavage of the poet's desire and will but resolves his self-division with a triumphal image of departure and liberation.

Tellingly, the poem is titled "Hurt Hawks," suggesting that the poet is also a kind of hawk, hurt not physically but by grief for the great creature he has to destroy—which makes him a predator, like the bird. Indeed, the distanced, objective tone of part 1 gives over to the more subjective, personal, and agonized tone of part 2 as the poem shifts focus from hawk to man. The plainly bifurcated nature of the poem suggests that the natural world and the human sensibility that seeks to confront that world have become ineluctably alien from each other. Perhaps they will always remain so.

Themes and Meanings

For Jeffers the majestic hawk epitomizes nature and embodies nature's purest form of freedom. Although he does not report how it was injured, given the type of the injury it is not unreasonable to assume that it was caused by a gunshot. Thus, the hawk may be a victim of human "arrogance," its perfect freedom curtailed by the more limited human freedom to choose violence. Nature's balance, disrupted by the hawk's injury, can be recovered only by the administration of another bullet. It is as if humankind has the power only to damage nature or to finish off what it has damaged in order to alleviate misery.

Full of admiration for the hawk, the poet himself feels wounded by the hawk's plight and further wounded by the duty he must carry out. In the acting of killing the stricken bird, the poet counters his species' arrogance with an example of compassion that can perhaps be viewed as a gesture of atonement as well. It would be wrong, however, to read the mercy killing in moral terms. In other poems, most notably "Birds and Fishes," Jeffers takes pains to insist that moral precepts are human inventions that can only be applied to human affairs. Such ideas have no relevance to the processes of nature, which remain brutally alien to us: "Justice and mercy/ Are human dreams, they do not concern the birds nor/ the fish nor eternal God."

In many of his poems Jeffers condemns ecological degradation and defilement in the name of "progress." Certainly this feature is present, in a muted way, in "Hurt Hawks." The poem's central concern, though, is with the spiritual alienation that the human race has suffered in its quest to detach itself from and master the natural world. Humanity's lost connection to the wild results in epistemological blindness, an inability to intuitively understand the ground of Being. In so doing, humans cease to comprehend true freedom, life, and death in any profoundly meaningful way. Because the hawk is in nature with all its soul, it has no fear of nonbeing; it instinctively wishes to die rather than live bereft of the exquisite freedom that it once enjoyed. Making the anthropocentric mistake of mourning for a creature that has no need to mourn itself, the poet comes to the realization that the death he has had to confer on the hawk is no occasion for sadness or guilt. The hawk is as comfortable in death as it is in life, whereas human beings seem displaced in either realm. Ultimately then, people are the hurt hawks—predators that aspire to transcend nature but succeed only in compromising themselves by adopting a muddled and egocentric relation to the world. The hawk's magnificent indifference and beautiful death can at least inspire humans toward greater equanimity.

Robert Niemi

HUSWIFERY

Author: Edward Taylor (c. 1645-1729)
Type of poem: Meditation
First published: 1960, in *The Poems of Edward Taylor*

The Poem
"Huswifery," written in the late seventeenth century, is perhaps the best known work of Edward Taylor's poetic canon. It is meditational in form, one of several periodic exercises designed to place Taylor in a correct spiritual posture for communion with Christ, literally through the Lord's Supper and metaphysically through a spiritual union brought about by faith. Almost always religious, Taylor's poetry is influenced by the great English Metaphysical poets John Donne, George Herbert, and Richard Crashaw. Like them, he joined disparate fields of experience and often offered bizarre juxtapositions of images.

"Huswifery" takes its unusual rural imagery not only from the primitive location of Taylor's pastorate but also from his memories of his boyhood home in England, where he earned a living from the soil and perhaps sheared and spun wool as part of his daily labor. In his early youth, Taylor may also have been employed in the weavers' shops of the nearby town of Hinckley.

Stanza 1 implores God to use Taylor as His spinning wheel and to provide a holder for the flax of faith in the words of Holy Scripture. Taylor breaks down the weaving image further by associating functions of the parts of the spinning wheel with various human characteristics. His affections become the "flyers" (revolving arms which twist the wool into yarn); the soul is the spool which collects the thread; and conversation is seen as the reel which winds the spun wool.

Stanza 2 continues the clothes-making metaphor as Taylor becomes the loom whereon the refined thread is transformed into cloth. As in stanza 1, a part of the Trinity, the Holy Spirit, is necessary for this new function to occur. The Spirit will wind bobbins or spindles, and God Himself will create a web, an organized pattern in the material. The speaker will weave the pattern of faith into the fabric and will complete the materials needed to construct the garment of salvation. Ordinances (God's law) will then shrink and thicken the cloth (the fulling process) by means of moistening, heating, and pressing. Finally, the finished product will be dyed in radiant and heavenly colors and ornamentally patterned with a lustrous finish of Edenic beauty.

The third stanza portrays the transformation of the cloth into a garment that will cover humanity's rebellious nature: his "understanding, will, affections, judgment, conscience, memory." Wearing the garment will also illuminate and affect Taylor's words and actions so that they will glorify God and lead Taylor himself to the ultimate glory of heaven. There, clothed with the holiness provided by the Father, Son, and Holy Spirit, he will be ready for the final judgment and eventual translation into eternal glory.

Forms and Devices

"Huswifery" may be placed in a category of emblematic poetry—collections in which engravings or woodcuts of moral symbols or types were printed with a motto or a series of short verses. Although the poem is grammatically simplistic, it revolves around a complex metaphysical conceit, the art of clothes making. Taylor's three stanzas (a Trinitarian reference) break down the conceit, extending the meaning by an analytic comparison of its parts. Thus Taylor first portrays the spinning of the yarn, then the weaving of a fabric on a loom, and finally the construction and completion of a finished garment or robe. Other rhetorical devices used by Taylor are polyptoton, the repetition of a word functioning as different parts of speech (for example, "reel" in lines 5 and 6 as both a noun and a verb), and ploce, a core or base word modified by various affixes (for example, "glory" becomes "glorify" in line 16 and returns to its original form in line 18).

Rhyme in the six-line stanzas follows an *ababcc* pattern, with some near rhyme illustrated in the use of "memory" and "glorify" (lines 14 and 16) and "choice" and "paradise" (lines 11 and 12). Taylor also utilizes syntactical inversions ("my conversation make," line 5) and stylistically parallels Old English alliterative verse by maintaining a caesura or pause at the middle of each line.

Since Taylor has been known to use anagrams and acrostics in his verse, some mention should also be made of the first and last letters in each line. The letters *m, t, a,* and *e* occur consistently and may be rearranged to form the words "team" and "mate," suggesting the symbolic joining of God and man that is mirrored in the text.

Although there is an occasional roughness in Taylor's word choice and awkward rhyming, the colloquial diction often attains the cosmic meaning desired by the author. It symbolizes the joining of the sinner with the Savior, the eventual union of the elect with Christ, and the predestination of all saints, no matter how lowly, to transcendent glory.

Themes and Meanings

A close reading of "Huswifery" suggests a variety of meanings for the central conceit of clothes making. In fact, the extended metaphors reveal an obsession with typology, finding theological meanings in ordinary events. Thus the coat or dress taken from Job 29:14 in the Bible can be seen as a symbol of righteousness. Other biblical referents include Psalm 30, where clothes equal joy, and Psalm 31:25, where clothes equal strength and dignity. Isaiah 61:10, however, offers the most specific parallel: Here the chosen is clothed in "garments of salvation and arrayed in a robe of righteousness as a bridegroom adorns his head like a priest and as a bride adorns herself with jewels." This passage also invokes the New Testament reference to being clothed with Christ (Galatians 3:27).

The robe, like Joseph's coat of many colors in Genesis, is a symbol for being the chosen one of God and for having put on Christ's flesh and His robe of blood through faith and baptism. The biblical associations with robes thus recall Jesus' roles as prophet, priest, and king, all of which require a ceremonial garment. The associations also suggest a sacramental preparation for receiving the Lord's Supper. Like several of Taylor's preparatory meditations, "Huswifery" also implies the necessity to be clothed in Christ before approaching the eucharistic table.

A meditation, the form "Huswifery" takes, is a secret prayer composed of praise and petition. By using this form, Taylor acknowledges the complete sovereignty of God and the inefficacy of good works to attain salvation. He implores God to use him as a pastor and as a poet to spread the Gospel. The poet becomes a weaver of lovely cloth, Christ's truth made more attractive in verse. As an artist, Taylor decorates theological images, utilizing speech as a cloth for constructing thought and English as a literary yarn to create a linguistic web of beauty. This writing image is also reinforced in the double meaning of the word "quills" (line 8), which indicates the inspiration of written verse by the Holy Spirit.

The transformation of wool into yarn and then into cloth and a garment also suggests a type of spiritual marriage. Here, putting on the robe suggests an assumption on Christ's honor and accomplishments. At the marriage feast, Christ becomes one with Taylor, imputing redemption through the sacrament. This creates a mystic union, a close and personal relationship that Taylor desires to share with others. Taylor appeals to God to continue to robe him with the sanctification necessary to minister, the grace needed to attend the nuptial feast of Christ and His Church, and the forgiveness required to participate in communion. The analytic breakdown of the clothes-making process mirrors the achievement of a state of grace. It too is gradual and Christ-centered in its reliance on God to bring about conversion, motivate repentance, and offer divine grace.

Ultimately, the title not only reflects Taylor's desire to parallel what he saw as a woman's tasks of spinning, weaving, and sewing but also displays his goal of becoming the bride of Christ, integrated and perfected as both pastor and poet by the sacrifice of the Lamb. Taylor's puns on "dye" and "die" as well as "pinked" (cut, or punctured as in the wounds of Christ) emphasize that the robed priest's sacrifice satisfies God's requirement for justice, at the same time pleading for His grace and for humanity's salvation.

Michael J. Meyer

THE HYENAS

Author: Rudyard Kipling (1865-1936)
Type of poem: Satire
First published: 1919, in *The Years Between*

The Poem

Rudyard Kipling's "The Hyenas" consists of seven stanzas, written in quatrain form. Using the hyena as a metaphor for humanity, the author compares and contrasts that wild scavenger, with its traditional reputation for slyness and cowardice, with the human animal, who only too often, according to the poet, exhibits the same vicious qualities, the same beastly characteristics. Kipling goes even further, suggesting that the actions of the hyenas, as instinctively brutal as they first appear, are more understandable and thus in reality less devious because they are readily recognized as uncivilized wild animals, unlike the human animal with its claims to be civilized and its pretensions to superior morality.

The poem, told in a relatively straightforward narrative style, begins with a burial party which, having completed its task, has left an unidentified grave site. Kites, vultures with their own reputation as scavengers, have also abandoned the field with the coming of night, and now the hyenas have entered the scene to ravish and rend the recently buried body. Neither knowing nor caring anything about the dead victim, they have come to dig up the corpse. Their only goal is food in the form of dead flesh. Kipling uses the traditional image and reputation of the hyenas as opportunistic but cowardly scavengers, who feed only when there is little threat to themselves; the beasts consume the dead as food because "the dead are safer meat," noting that even goats, worms, and children could pose at least a potential, if distant, threat to their safety. It is here, in the fourth stanza, that the reader discovers explicitly what is already known implicitly, given Kipling's long identification with the life and fate of the common soldier, that the once-buried body is that of "a dead soldier of the King." Yet since he is dead the soldier can inspire no fear in the cowardly hyenas.

With "whoop and halloo" the hyenas unearth the corpse, exposing the body once more to earth's sight, but only briefly, and only to a few. God, perceiving everything, sees the face of the dead soldier, but, as the poem relates, so do those who have no souls. Here, the obvious reference is to the hyenas as wild animals. As beasts, the hyenas are free from shame, a quality endemic in humanity since the Fall and the expulsion from the Garden of Eden. Kipling argues that human beings can also be without shame and without souls, and are thus no better than wild animals, and in reality even worse. They are more despicable, for they "defile the dead man's name" and "that is reserved for his kind." "The Hyenas" is an angry poem, bitter in its satirical argument that humanity can often be a lesser breed outside the moral law of civilization, worse even than the lowly and disreputable hyena.

Forms and Devices

"The Hyenas" is a relatively short poem written without a significant number of poetic devices. It is composed in an *abab* quatrain form, and the first and third lines of each stanza are longer than the second and fourth lines. The latter two lines, strongly punctuated, give the reader a periodic feeling of closure, or the completion of a statement. Although the meter of the poem is irregular, the general consistency of form and punctuation gives "The Hyenas" an easily accessible narrative line. In the early stanzas in particular, there is an almost matter-of-fact ballad quality, a characteristic that T. S. Eliot called the major defining element of most of Kipling's poetry.

One of the few obvious literary devices that Kipling does make at least some limited use of in "The Hyenas" is alliteration. For example, in the first stanza, the phrase "burial-parties" in line 1 is linked with "baffled kites" in the following line. Later a similar use of alliteration is found in line 7—"They snout the bushes and stones aside"—which also is an interesting use of the noun word "snout" as a verb. There is more alliteration throughout the poem, but its use is never excessive nor obtrusive. There are some archaisms in Kipling's choice of words—"shewn" and "ere," for example—but "The Hyenas" could not in any way be described as an obviously "poetic" poem.

Of the seven stanzas that make up "The Hyenas," the fourth, or middle, stanza is central to the poem. The entire stanza is enclosed in a parenthesis, a device not used elsewhere in the poem, and Kipling makes use of it here to provide an opportunity for an authorial aside to the reader, or as an explanatory pause, and it is effective in breaking the poem's seemingly simple narrative line. In the stanza the buried body is identified, and Kipling elaborates upon the cowardly character of the hyenas. The previous stanza closes with the observation that the hyenas are scavengers because "they know that the dead are safer meat/ Than the weakest thing alive." To a cowardly beast like the hyena, any life, even the weakest life, has the capacity to engender fear, "For a goat may butt, and a worm may sting,/ And a child will sometimes stand." In contrast to the potency of life, even that of a worm or a child, is the impotence of the dead and the permanence of death. In the last two lines of the stanza, the identity of the grave's now powerless inhabitant is revealed as "a poor dead soldier of the king/ [who] Can never lift a hand."

The metaphor of the hyena as a representative of humanity is suggested in the following stanza, when the hyenas begin to unearth the corpse, for "They whoop and halloo" just like human beings might do when engaged in sport, hunting, or play. The dead soldier is again briefly visible to God as well as to the hyenas before they consume the body, but because they are wild animals, lacking a soul and thus human shame, they are at least acting in a fashion appropriate to their species; unlike human beings, the hyenas "do not defile the dead man's name—/ That is reserved for his kind."

Themes and Meanings

As in much of Kipling's verse, there is an obvious political or social motive in "The Hyenas." In the late nineteenth and early twentieth centuries he was one of the most famous poets of the English-speaking world, and the popularity of his verse rested in large part upon its accessibility, both in its style and in its substance. It has been noted that anyone, even at first reading—or hearing—could at least superficially enter into his poetic world, whatever additional depths and insights might be obtained in further study and contemplation. Although generally perceived to be an unreconstructed supporter of the British Empire, his major focus was less upon the Empire as such and more on the plight of the ordinary soldier, and not necessarily only the British soldier. The plight of the common person was a theme that ran through Kipling's oeuvre, including "The Hyenas," where "the poor dead soldier of the King" is the helpless victim of the hyenas' hunger.

The important question is who Kipling's hyenas are. Obviously, in the literal sense, they are the traditional scavengers from the deserts and wildernesses who have been digging up battlefield corpses since humankind's earliest conflicts. In this sense, the poem can be considered timeless, with dead soldiers eternally serving as carrion for wild animals. However, given that "The Hyenas" was first published in 1919, it can be argued that Kipling's cowardly scavengers were not just those of the four-footed variety. Human beings could also be hyenas. After four years of the bloodiest conflict humanity had experienced, World War I had finally come to an end in November, 1918. During those four years an estimated ten million soldiers died, including Kipling's own son. Ultimately all the soldiers—British, German, Russian, French, American, and others—"were the poor dead soldiers of the King." They were all the victims of the statesmen and diplomats whose machinations had caused the conflict, the generals who ordered the doomed millions into the quagmire of no-man's-land, and the public, far from the front lines back at home, who thoughtlessly allowed the slaughter to continue for years without a resolution. It was these latter hyenas who, through their actions and inactions in thought and deed, "defile(d) the dead man's name."

The Hyenas is not the best known of Kipling's World War I poems. "Gethsemane," with its soldier-as-Christ figure, is more widely anthologized, but in his satirical use of the hyena as the metaphor of humanity, Kipling revealed a nadir of bleakness and bitterness.

Eugene Larson

HYMN TO INTELLECTUAL BEAUTY

Author: Percy Bysshe Shelley (1792-1822)
Type of poem: Lyric
First published: 1817; revised and collected in *Rosalind and Helen: A Modern Eclogue, with Other Poems*, 1819

The Poem

"Hymn to Intellectual Beauty" is written in seven twelve-line stanzas with an *abbaaccbddee* rhyme scheme. The word "intellectual" means nonmaterial, and "intellectual beauty" refers to an "unseen Power" that shines on "human thought or form." As a mental phenomenon, intellectual beauty is an ideal that transcends "This various world," which it visits like an "awful shadow." The poem's religious attitude toward this power is reflected in the use of the word "hymn" in the title.

In the first stanza, the speaker of the poem uses a series of similes to describe intellectual beauty to the reader. Its main characteristics seem to be universality and evanescence: Intellectual beauty visits "This various world" and "Each human heart and countenance," but it is "inconstant" and fleeting, "Like memory of music fled." The number of contrasting similes in the stanza suggests that this power is essentially ineffable, "yet dearer for its mystery."

The second stanza mourns intellectual beauty's inconstancy. The poem asks why this "Spirit of BEAUTY" is not always present to illuminate "our state,/ This dim vast vale of tears, vacant and desolate," but decides that this question is unanswerable. In the third stanza, the poet considers the sages and poets who use the names of "Gods and ghosts and Heaven" in a "vain endeavour" to explain away "Doubt, chance, and mutability." He insists, however, that "life's unquiet dream" will be given "grace and truth" by intellectual beauty, not by the myths of religion.

Stanza four continues the praise of intellectual beauty which, according to the poet, has the power to make man "immortal, and omnipotent" if it remains in man's heart. Although intellectual beauty does not provide people with ideas, it does nourish "human thought . . ./ Like darkness [does] a dying flame." The stanza ends with a prayer to the spirit to stay with man, "lest the grave should be,/ Like life and fear, a dark reality." The poet turns to autobiography in the fifth stanza, describing himself as a boy searching for ghosts and hoping for "high talk with the departed dead." He "called on poisonous names," which in the context of the poem are words such as "God and ghosts and Heaven," and was not answered, but then the shadow of intellectual beauty fell over him and he "shrieked, and clasped [his] hands in extacy!" Stanza six goes on to describe how he dedicated himself to intellectual beauty in the hope that this "awful LOVELINESS" would liberate "This world from its dark slavery."

The seventh and final stanza shifts to a "solemn and serene" autumn afternoon. Having given the reader a sense of intellectual beauty and his own relationship to that mysterious power, the poet asks it to give an autumnlike "calm" to his "onward life."

The poem ends with a prayer reaffirming the poet's allegiance to intellectual beauty and his commitment "To fear himself, and love all human kind."

Forms and Devices

"Hymn to Intellectual Beauty" takes the form of a religious address to an object of worship, beginning with an invocation, in which intellectual beauty is described and praised, and ending with a prayer. Moreover, the language used throughout the poem is religious. With its "own hues," the invisible power "consecrate[s]" everything human, giving "grace and truth to life's unquiet dream"; it has the power to make man "immortal, and omnipotent" and may even be able to redeem "This world from its dark slavery." The poet presents himself as having been intellectual beauty's ardent follower from the time the spirit's shadow fell over him when he was a boy. In fact, the poet's conversion is nearly hysterical in intensity: He shrieks as he clasps his hands in an attitude of prayer. Even in the present, the older poet dedicates himself to the "awful LOVELINESS" with "beating heart and streaming eyes," and his final prayer is for intellectual beauty to grant him "calm."

Although the poem uses religious terminology, it does not advocate an established religion. The beliefs of Christianity, for example, are described scornfully as "Frail spells," and the poet describes the religious phrases he learned as a child as the "poisonous names with which our youth is fed." According to the poet, intellectual beauty teaches him "To fear himself, and love all human kind"; God is not included in this formula. Thus the religious language of "Hymn to Intellectual Beauty" serves to express both the poet's reverence for the spirit of ideal beauty and his repudiation of traditional beliefs.

While the religious sentiments of "Hymn to Intellectual Beauty" are clear, intellectual beauty itself remains a vague concept, and Percy Bysshe Shelley uses similes throughout the poem to suggest, but never to limit, intellectual beauty's qualities. Some of these similes describe the invisible power as being "Like moonbeams . . . behind some piny mountain shower," "Like clouds in starlight widely spread," "like mists o'er mountains driven," and "like the truth/ Of nature on my passive youth." Since intellectual beauty is invisible, it cannot be given an exact physical description, so Shelley uses imagery that is partially obscured, cloudy, or misty. At times he even turns to another abstraction, such as "the truth of nature." When it manifests itself to the poet, intellectual beauty is described as an "awful shadow." The image of the "shadow" must be taken in a figurative rather than literal sense—it gives the reader a sense of the spirit's mysteriousness and indicates that intellectual beauty can never fully manifest itself in the physical world. At most, the poet can apprehend its reflection or shadow.

Shelley's decision to write a hymn to a nonmaterial power is typical of the poet, who believed that the physical world was less important than "human thought or form." Moreover, it is significant that "Hymn to Intellectual Beauty" is a prayer to an invisible spirit rather than to the kind of anthropomorphic deity that Shelley deplored.

Themes and Meanings

The central problem of "Hymn to Intellectual Beauty" has to do with the meaning and significance of intellectual beauty, in terms of both humanity as a whole and the poet's life in particular. Although many readers of the poem have tried to define intellectual beauty, it cannot be identified with any one ideal. In fact, the poem links this spirit with several abstractions, including beauty, grace, thought, form, harmony, and calmness.

Perhaps the key to understanding intellectual beauty is to focus on what it is not, and it is clear that it is not part of the physical world. Many of Shelley's philosophical notions derive from Plato's, and in his poetry Shelley often uses (and transfigures) Plato's belief that there are two kinds of reality: the visible or physical realm, made of constantly changing matter, and the intelligible realm of forms, or such purely mental phenomena as truth and beauty. Intellectual beauty resides solely in the intelligible realm and can only be apprehended in the visible world as an obscure, shadowy presence. It is nevertheless important to humankind, because it contains the ideals toward which each person must strive in order to achieve perfection. That is why Shelley associates intellectual beauty with human thought and insists that it is a crucial element in the attainment of human immortality and omnipotence, and the abolition of "dark slavery." The fact that intellectual beauty is identified with man suggests that this power, despite its divine attributes, does not derive from God or the supernatural. It teaches humanity to love, esteem, and fear itself rather than a separate divinity—in essence, "Hymn to Intellectual Beauty" is an attempt to replace traditional worship with a religion that celebrates humankind and its potential to perceive and attain perfection. The role of intellectual beauty in this religion is to dispel the fears and sufferings associated with the physical world by revealing to its disciples the deeper truth of the realm of ideals.

Beyond intellectual beauty's significance to humanity as a whole, the poem describes the importance of the spirit in the poet's life. As a boy, the poet sought to communicate with beings existing beyond the physical world, ghosts and heavenly spirits, but was not answered. When the boy turned to philosophy, however, "musing deeply on the lot/ Of life," the shadow of intellectual beauty fell over him in a sudden visitation. This suggests that intellectual beauty is to be found through philosophy rather than simple religious faith in "God and ghosts and Heaven." The autobiographical section of the poem is important because it allows the poet to speak with the authority of a prophet who has had direct communion with the object of his worship. Inasmuch as he represents humanity, the poet's experience supports the idea that humankind as a whole could be inspired and transfigured by intellectual beauty, escaping through this spirit the "dark reality" of death.

William D. Brewer

HYMN TO PROSERPINE

Author: Algernon Charles Swinburne (1837-1909)
Type of poem: Dramatic monologue
First published: 1866, in *Poems and Ballads*

The Poem
"Hymn to Proserpine" is a dramatic monologue of 110 lines, not divided into stanzas. The mythological Proserpine, the daughter of Zeus and Demeter, became queen of the underworld; Algernon Charles Swinburne invokes her in the title and throughout the poem as the goddess of death.

The poem is supposed to be spoken by the Roman Emperor Julian the Apostate (331-363 C.E.), who opposed Christianity and supported the traditional Roman pantheon. The poem has as an epigraph the Latin phrase *Vicisti, Galilaee* (thou hast conquered, Galilean), supposed to be Julian's dying words. The Galilean is Jesus Christ, and Julian meant that Christianity had triumphed. Although the hymn is ascribed to Julian, it presents Swinburne's own views rather than a historical reconstruction of Julian's doctrines.

Most people fear death, but the Julian of the poem does not. He states that death is greater than "the seasons that laugh or weep" (line 3). Life has its joys and sorrows but is ended by death. Yet this view of the world, Julian claims, has come under challenge. A new religion denying that life is cruel appears to have triumphed; Julian means Christianity, which under his ancestor Constantine had become the state religion of the Roman Empire. Julian looks with dismay at the strife caused by religious conflict, and he calls for an end to it: "I say to you all, be at peace" (line 21).

As for himself, the new religion has no appeal. It cannot destroy the pleasures of life or offer anything as good as they are. Although life has pleasures, however, everything is changeable, and death brings a welcome relief. Death ends all, and Julian rejects reincarnation and resurrection: "For no man under the sky lives twice, outliving his day" (line 31).

The poem shifts around line 40 to a sharp assault on Christianity. Julian mocks the worship of Jesus, who was beaten and crucified. To the Romans, the gods were beings of superhuman strength. Worshiping a being whom humans could injure and kill made no sense to the devotees of ancient paganism.

Julian declares that Christianity will eventually be overthrown; nothing can withstand the power of fate, which changes everything. A long comparison between fate, "impelled of invisible tides (line 54), and the sea concludes with the prophecy that the new religion will perish: "Ye shall sleep as a slain man sleeps, and the world shall forget you for kings" (line 70). Julian turns to a comparison between Mary, the mother of Jesus, and Proserpine, very much to the advantage of the latter. He concludes with the declaration that Proserpine is greater than all other gods, because she brings death.

Forms and Devices

The reader of "Hymn to Proserpine" will immediately be struck by Swinburne's unusually strong rhythms. This is characteristic of his poetry: "Hymn to Proserpine," like most of his verse, was written to be declaimed dramatically, not read silently.

In the line "Thou has conquered, O pale Galilean; the world has grown gray, from thy breath" (line 35), the stresses on the first syllable of "conquered," the third syllable of "Galilean," "gray," and "breath" have the effect of a continued drumbeat. Again, in "For these give labour and slumber; but thou, Proserpina, death" (line 104), the accents on "thou" and "death" jump at the reader. By his use of this device, Swinburne turns the poem into rhetoric: Although no audience is indicated, one can imagine Julian delivering it as a speech. Twentieth century poets such as T. S. Eliot turned away from this declamatory style, instead seeking to reproduce the sound of natural conversation. In spite of its artificial character, Swinburne's tone achieves great force.

The poem uses another technique characteristic of Swinburne—alliteration. When one encounters the line, "O ghastly glories of saints, dead limbs of gibbeted gods!" (line 44), the repeated *g* sounds capture one's attention. Swinburne grabs the reader by the lapels to put forward his view of Christianity. This line also uses contrast effectively: "glories" are usually the opposite of "ghastly," and "gibbeted" is hardly the first adjective that comes to mind for "gods." The unexpected adjectives add to the alliteration in highlighting the line.

Swinburne uses alliteration several times. In speaking of the sea, he says: "Waste water washes, and tall ships founder, and deep death waits" (line 50). Several lines later, one finds "And bitter as blood is the spray" (line 60). These phrases accent the importance of the sea, a key theme. In some of his poems, Swinburne overuses alliteration (the device is basic to the frequent parodies of his verse). In "Hymn to Proserpine," he keeps it under control.

Reference to the sea brings out another basic technique of the poem—symbolism. Much of the work presents the sea as a symbol of change; Swinburne makes it clear that he does not mean the literal sea. He speaks of it as "impelled of invisible tides" (line 52). He draws out the symbol in detail: The spray is "bitter as blood" (line 60); its crests are "fangs that devour" (line 60); it is "shark-toothed and serpentine curled" (line 53).

Swinburne's depiction of the sea displays another characteristic touch. The symbol has metaphors and similes included within it. It is not the crests of the real sea that he calls "fangs"; it is the "crests" of his symbol that are characterized by a further literary figure. The "foam of the present that sweeps to the surf of the past" (line 48) and the "whitening wind of the future" (line 54) are other metaphors lodged within the symbol.

Themes and Meanings

The poem presents an unusual view of life. Proserpine, the goddess of death, is celebrated. She has destroyed previous gods and will, Julian alleges, destroy Christ as well. Destruction and cruelty receive praise and are welcomed. The repeated "but thou, Proserpina, [give] death" praises the goddess rather than laments her effects. The poet turns to her—"Goddess and maiden and queen, be near me now and befriend" (line 92)—because she brings death.

One might think that if Swinburne welcomed death, then he hated life, but this mistakes the precise nature of his pessimism. He does not say that because life is bad, one should welcome death as a release. Rather, it is the destructive power of death that is welcomed. Swinburne admires the "poisonous-finned, shark-toothed" sea creatures (line 53). Although "grief is a grievous thing" (line 33), and death brings this to an end, life in itself is not exclusively evil. It includes many sensual pleasures; these, even—or perhaps especially—when destructive, are the chief glories of life. Not even these pleasures can withstand death.

Given his praise for destruction, it is hardly surprising that Swinburne scorned Christianity. It teaches that the world is governed by love and that death is a prelude to resurrection. Nothing could be more alien to Swinburne than these tenets. He notes, "They are merciful, clothed with pity, the young compassionate gods./ But for me their new device is barren" (lines 16-17). To replace wrath with pity and compassion is no step forward.

To Swinburne, those sentiments express weakness. Christianity's "ghastly glories" consist of the fact that its saints are martyrs. Jesus was executed as a criminal. The spread of the new religion thus represents the triumph of weakness. In speaking of "compassionate gods" and "gibbeted gods," Swinburne uses the plural to denigrate Christianity further. Although it taught belief in one God, the poet holds this of no account and simply refers to the new gods.

The view of death presented in the poem provides an even more essential reason to reject the new religion. Life may not be entirely, or even preponderantly, bad, but eventually people tire of it. Death is a permanent sleep and releases men from care. Christianity defies this key to the world's nature by teaching that death is not final. Fortunately, in Swinburne's view, this doctrine will fall before life's "mutable wings" (line 30).

To understand the poem, one must take account of the period when Swinburne wrote. Many of the Victorians questioned Christianity. Historical criticism of the Bible and the publication of Charles Darwin's *On the Origin of Species* (1859), which challenged the account of creation in Genesis, led to furious battles about religion.

Another issue arose from this one: Without belief in Christianity, what was the basis of morality? Swinburne's poem gives a decisive response to this question. The rules of morality inhibit pleasure; Christianity, by teaching compassion and self-sacrifice, has made the world grow gray. Had the times been less given to religious doubt, Swinburne's praise of destruction might have been easily dismissed as an aberration. Given the actual situation, high-minded humanists such as John Morley anxiously distanced themselves from the poem's message and condemned Swinburne.

Bill Delaney

HYMNS TO THE NIGHT

Author: Novalis (Friedrich von Hardenberg, 1772-1801)
Type of poem: Lyric
First published: 1800, as *Hymnen an die Nacht*; English translation collected in *Hymns to the Night and Other Writings*, 1960

The Poem

Hymns to the Night is a group of six organically related poems or hymns of praise and religious devotion. The hymns record the poet's struggle to overcome his grief at the death of his young fiancée, Sophie von Kühn, in 1797, shortly after her fifteenth birthday and shortly before they were to be married. The death of Sophie, the inconsolable loss of an unspoiled and idealized love, becomes for Novalis the occasion of a spiritual awakening, the opening of a new religious vision. The spiritual world opened to Novalis is represented as the world of the night.

Though the first hymn opens with praise of light, the inexpressible, secretive night soon exceeds the lavish wonders of day. As the world darkens and the busy activity of daytime fades away, distant memories, the wishes of youth, childhood dreams, and brief joys reemerge. The soul stirs its heavy wings and comes to life, returning to spiritual matters of its deepest concern. The night opens our spiritual eyes, which look at last toward the depths of the soul. Night becomes the realm of the life of the spirit.

Late in this hymn, the poet addresses night's messenger as his beloved. This messenger is Sophie, who "called the night to life" for him and opened his eyes, and to whom he owes his spiritual birth. Her love and her death broke the hold of the practical daylight world. He calls upon her to consume him with spirit fire, so that he may join her in the pure spiritual world of night, where the union denied them in the daylight world can be everlasting.

The second hymn laments the interruption of night by the return of day and entreats the night not to abandon her intimates utterly to the affairs of daylight. Novalis, however, comes to see that the daylight world secretly depends on the hidden processes of the night, which make a grape fill with juice or bring a young girl to her flowering. Similarly, the hidden processes that created the oldest stories and even the concept of heaven have their origins in the night world. Night and darkness bring the keys to our most infinite mysteries.

In the third and most personal hymn, Novalis recalls standing at the foot of Sophie's grave with nowhere to turn, consumed in grief. At the depths of despair, "Night inspiration" comes to him. The mound becomes transparent (in the next hymn it is called a "crystal wave"). As he gazes into it, he sees his beloved. In her eyes he first glimpses eternity.

This timeless moment, also recorded in Novalis's journals, is the point of origin of the hymns, which explore and develop the new vision this experience opened to him. Sophie's grave thus becomes symbolic, the crossover point from the world of daily preoccupations to the mysterious and infinite world of the spirit.

In the fourth hymn, Novalis attempts to reconcile his new vision with the practical demands of life. He resolves to work untiringly in his daytime pursuits yet adds that his secret heart will stay true to the night and to "creative love, her daughter." In this hymn, the author finds a mission that gives meaning and direction to his life and art. His mother, the night, sends him, and his brothers and sisters in this religious awakening, to transform the world with creative love and infuse it with spiritual meaning. The fourth hymn ends: "I live by day/ Full of faith and courage/ And die by night/ In holy fire."

In the fifth hymn, Novalis constructs a brief history of religion. He begins with the emergence of Greek gods, whose reign is pictured as a classical feast. Such early mythologies failed to address adequately the issue of death. The immortal gods were not concerned with it. For mortals, once life in the daylight world ended, there was only a dull dream in a world of shades. Death of a loved one brought sadness without consolation. The problem remained unresolved until the birth of Christ. A poet from Greece, present at the Nativity, sings of Christ as the savior whose death will open the world of the eternal spirit to humanity. Death, which once plunged humanity into despair, will now draw humankind forward in longing for eternal life.

Like Sophie, Christ opens the realm of eternal night, and like Sophie, Mary becomes the blessed virgin, the merciful messenger of the night world. The classical feast parallels the daylight world before Sophie's death. The larger context of cultural history thus parallels and illuminates the poet's new religious vision, and his revelation attains a broader cultural significance as a guide to a new spiritual awakening.

The sixth and final hymn, entitled "Longing for Death," envisions death as a desirable passage to the realm of the night. Remote from the time when Christ was in the daylight world, humankind's spiritual thirst can be quenched only in the world of the night. The poet praises night because in it individuals may join their lost loved ones and, guided by Mary and Christ, be settled forever in the lap of God.

Forms and Devices

The hymns are extremely innovative, formally mixing prose poetry and several forms of metrical, rhymed verse in a single work. In manuscript, the hymns were even more innovative, for the entire first hymn and several other lengthy passages were originally written in free verse. In the *Athenäum* version, on which almost all translations are based, the long passages of free verse were reorganized as paragraphs of poetic prose, or prose poems.

In the *Athenäum* version, the first three hymns are prose poems, the fourth begins in prose and shifts to rhymed verse, the fifth alternates forms, and the sixth is entirely rhymed, metrical verse. Thus, as Novalis's vision becomes more developed and unified in the hymns, his poetry becomes more formalized.

Novalis first introduces rhymed verse in the fourth hymn. In the second section, the speaker addresses the light, insisting that he will remain true to the night without which day is nothing. Then, in one of the highest moments of inspiration of the hymns, the speaker's point of view becomes identified with eternal spirit. Still addressing the light, he says, "Truly I was, before you existed. . . ." The speaker has become identified with pure spirit, which, unlike the body, can be said to be older than light itself, because it is eternal. In a way, he speaks with the voice of the night. This important shift in point of view reflects a leap of faith and is closely related to the shift in poetic forms.

From this inspired perspective, this union of the higher self and night, Novalis sees clearly his mission in life as an apostle of night. Shortly hereafter, Novalis breaks into rhymed verse, in a poem of devotion and celebration of the mission he has discovered. Written with inspired confidence in his vision, this poem is a part of Novalis's private litany, written as an expression of a confirmed faith.

Much of the fifth hymn, the historical one, is printed as paragraphs of prose poetry. Death's arrival at the table of the classical feast becomes the subject of an allegorical ballad, reminiscent of medieval morality tales. It is composed in rhymed iambic pentameter, in eight-line stanzas that end in a rhymed couplet. The form is reminiscent of folk song. The same stanza form is used for the song of the poet who attends Christ's nativity later in the hymn.

When the history is completed, the fifth hymn, again from a position of commitment to the vision and mission, breaks into metrical verse very much like that which closes the fourth hymn in line-length, measure, and rhyme scheme. As at the end of the fourth hymn, the shift in verse form corresponds to the construction of a liturgy of devotion to the night, the beloved, Christ and Mary. The sixth hymn, similarly, is an extended song of devotion written entirely in rhymed, metrical verse.

Thus, as Novalis gains certainty of his vision and the mission of the hymns, he leaves the exploratory forms of free verse and prose poetry in which he has developed his vision and the history that confirms it. He turns to forms in which a liturgy to sustain devotion and commitment may be created. The formal trend also marks a transition toward his metrically regular, rhymed *Geistliche Lieder* (1801-1802; *Devotional Songs*, 1910), which Novalis completed after the hymns. Some of the *Devotional Songs* later became hymns in German hymnals.

The symbolic connotations of night and day, of light and dark in religion, and the usual ascent associated with spiritual enlightenment are inverted in the hymns. Novalis attains his vision looking down into the grave and descending into the night. Christ and Mary are enthroned in the darkness, and daylight and light are, for the most part, reserved for the banal affairs of daily living. At the end, the movement toward God is downward. Readers soon become naturalized in this imagery, however, and even come to accept the premise that darkness, since very much larger than the realm of daylight, is perhaps a better metaphor for the realm of the eternal spirit.

An important romantic symbol is also introduced in the fourth hymn as Novalis finds his mission. He and his spiritual brothers and sisters are to plant the world of light with flowers that will never fade. Yet, the flowers of the daylight world always fade, and fade quickly. Only through creative love, perhaps through creative arts, or imagination, can there be flowers that never fade. This is the germ of the idea for the famous "blue flower" of Novalis's novel *Heinrich von Ofterdingen*, (1802; *Henry of Ofterdingen*, 1842), an unfading flower that became a central symbol of the German romantic movement.

Themes and Meanings

The inversion of light and dark imagery raises important questions about the relation between Novalis's vision and the Christian tradition that he invokes, as does the predominantly artistic mission the hymns outline. The mission of creative love, of transforming the world and giving it meaning rather than discovering an already existing meaning, emphasizes the importance of the individual imagination in religion. Like other Romantics, Novalis identified the soul with imagination, and the religion he would propound must be internalized and transformed, as it is in the hymns. It must awaken the soul. Also like other romantics, Novalis believed that poets must create the religious texts of the new awakening.

The emphasis on darkness and night tempts one to place Novalis in a lineage of Christian mystics that would include Saint John of the Cross. The role of Sophie as the virgin messenger who opens the realm of the spirit to the poet suggests a comparison with Dante, who is led through the world of the afterlife by the grace of Beatrice, who died in her youth. Yet the romantic emphasis on creative individual imagination and the absence of the concept of sin from Novalis's vision distinguish him from these more Catholic religious poets.

The last stanza of the fifth hymn contains one of the most problematic passages in the hymns. Novalis writes of the pure realm of the night, of the paradise of spiritual life, which he says is "Just a Single Night of Ecstasy—/ An eternal poem—/ And our sun of all suns/ Is the countenance of God." Many commentators find this passage problematic or offensive, since it blends sensual and aesthetic pleasure with religious devotion in language that lovers might apply to an earthly paradise. Novalis's highest paradise seems, to many commentators, not too high, and more an expression of perverse fantasy than of truly religious devotion and insight.

These questions point out the uniqueness and originality of the *Hymns to the Night*. In them, Novalis creates a magnificent romantic religious vision with a courage and height of inspiration few romantic writers were able to equal. His hymns resonate with passionate grief, love, and religious longing, and ultimately attain an aspiring faith in a compelling personal vision of the spiritual message and the life of Christianity. Novalis died young, at the age of twenty-nine, and the hymns stand as perhaps the purest expression of his youthful creative power and as a monument for his beloved, Sophie von Kühn.

Von E. Underwood

HYPERION

Author: John Keats (1795-1821)
Type of poem: Epic
First published: 1820, in *Lamia, Isabella, The Eve of St. Agnes, and Other Poems*

The Poem

Hyperion is a fragment of an epic poem in blank verse, divided into two complete books and a third incomplete book: Book I contains 357 lines, book II has 391 lines, and book III leaves off in mid-sentence at line 136. John Keats turned from this poem to compose his great odes in the summer of 1819 before returning to the subject of *Hyperion.* Instead of completing this epic, however, he began an entirely different poem (also incomplete) called *The Fall of Hyperion* (1856).

The title of *Hyperion* indicates the name of its hero, the ancient Greek god of the sun. Hyperion was one of the Titans, the offspring of Coelus (the sky) and Tellus (the earth). Saturn was ruler of the Titans, overthrown by his three Olympian sons, Jupiter, Neptune, and Pluto. Keats's epic is based upon this episode of mythology, when the Olympians overthrew the Titans and Olympian Apollo took the place of Titanic Hyperion. The story of the poem begins at the point when all the Titans except Hyperion have been defeated.

Book I opens in a dark valley of great stillness, where Thea (wife of Hyperion) is searching for Saturn. She finds him alone, massive but deeply dejected and utterly stunned. Thea urges him to look up; then she ceases, realizing that theirs is a hopeless cause. The two of them do not move for four months. Then Saturn opens his eyes and asks Thea to help him understand what has happened; he is supposed to be king of the gods, but he is so impotent he must have lost his identity. He makes himself believe that he can still command a force to recover his throne. Thea feels hope and urges Saturn to follow her to where other fallen Titans have gathered.

The poem then shifts to observe the behavior of the only Titan not yet fallen. Hyperion is in his sky-palace, stalking its hallways nervously, feeling great dread. He asks if he is also about to fall, like all of his brethren. He cries out in defiance that he will attack the rebel Olympians. Hyperion threatens to drive the sun through the sky to start the day at an unnatural time, but not even a god can disturb "the sacred seasons." His father, Coelus, sympathizes, urging Hyperion to use his remaining powers to help the Titans, to act and not wait to be acted against: "Be therefore in the van of Circumstance." The first book ends with Hyperion plunging into the darkness below, "like to a diver in the pearly seas."

Book II describes the arrival of Saturn and Thea at the dark den where the Titans have congregated. It is a woeful scene, where giant forms lie listlessly about in angry astonishment. They are roused when Saturn appears. He cannot explain their defeat, but he asks them how to respond to the Olympians.

The first to give advice is Oceanus, who counsels resignation. The triumph of the

Olympians is a phase in the process of natural law, which governs history and creates progress, as the old must give way to the new in all things. The Titans should be wise and recognize the truth of natural process. Oceanus says that the Olympian gods are young and beautiful, a new generation of advancing truth; "first in beauty should be first in might." The only consolation available to the Titans, he says, is to "receive the truth, and let it be your balm."

While the other Titans remain quiet, little-regarded Clymene timidly ventures to express her feelings. She describes how she had tried to console herself by blowing into a seashell to make music. She threw away the shell when she heard a strange, enchanting "golden melody" that seemed to drift across the ocean. She tried to stop her ears, but she heard the cry of a sweet voice, calling "Apollo! young Apollo!" Clymene tells her tale without interpreting it, simply illustrating the fact of a new regime.

Her brother Titan, huge Enceladus, is indignant at both the timidity of Clymene and the resignation of Oceanus. Enceladus offers to lead an assault on their conquerors, and he reminds them that Hyperion remains unfallen. At that moment, Hyperion appears, brightening the dark den with his burning presence. The Titans see that Hyperion is himself dejected, so they are tempted to become despondent again despite the fighting words of Enceladus. Some shout out the name of Saturn, and Hyperion answers the same. On this note, the second book ends.

Book III shifts to the young Apollo, about to assume his divine mission. He is wandering alone, perplexed about the strange emotions he feels. He sees a goddess approach, and he believes that he knows her from his dreams. She announces that she has been watching over his growth for some time, that she has forsaken her own people to be with him. Suddenly, Apollo recognizes that she is Mnemosyne (memory, mother of the Muses), and he struggles to control his feelings of sadness even as he speaks. Apollo explodes with a barrage of questions, asking Mnemosyne to account for the universe itself. Abruptly he halts his questioning and exclaims, as he looks into the eyes of the goddess, "Knowledge enormous makes a God of me." Then he writhes in pain, his face grows pale, and even his hair begins to move. He shrieks in agony, and the poem stops without completing its last sentence.

Forms and Devices

Hyperion was designed to follow the epic form of John Milton's *Paradise Lost* (1667). The opening is an imitation of the scene that opens Milton's epic, describing the army of angels who have followed Satan in their rebellion against God and who have been cast down into Hell. The summoning of the Titans to a conference by Saturn is a repetition of the call by Satan. Keats's poem strikes a new direction, however, by leaving its titular hero unfallen, awaiting the challenge from young Apollo. Yet perhaps there is an imitation here also, with some similarities between Hyperion/ Apollo and Satan/Christ. Where the poem would have gone if finished cannot be known, and perhaps Keats abandoned it because he could not take it beyond Milton's epic in a way satisfactory to Keats himself. When he returned to the subject in *The Fall of Hyperion*, Keats chose a new form and adopted a new style altogether, as he made himself the heroic medium for the transfiguration of Apollo into a god.

There is more to *Hyperion*, however, than an imitation of the narrative introduction and heroic characters found in *Paradise Lost*. The blank verse is "Miltonic" in its construction, using similar metric design and sentence structure. The normal subject-verb order is inverted, and the subject comes at the end of a long sentence, following a series of parallel modifying phrases. This device is a typical way to imitate the classic English epic style; thus, the poem opens in Book I with "Deep in . . ./ Far sunken from . . ./ Far from . . ./ Sat gray-hair'd Saturn." This sentence is still not finished with the identification of its subject, for it continues with more balanced clauses for another two-and-a-half lines. The catalog of identifying features used here, and elsewhere, is representative of epic style as well.

There are distinctive figures of speech, usually similes, which mark *Hyperion* as a poem of epic ambition. The most common kind of epic simile is the extended comparison, as when Thea is compared (or contrasted) with an Amazon in book I and when the forest where Saturn lies is compared with a meeting of a senate, also in book I.

Long set speeches, particularly in the first two books, contribute to the epic form of the poem. These occur in book III as well, but they are interrupted by exclamations and hurried expressions of surprise and recognition. The style of book III seems deliberately varied, then, to reflect the changes which are occurring in the character of Apollo as well as in the order of divine government. The poem further imitates classic epic form by setting its action throughout the cosmos, transcending human affairs, and exploring all possible realms of being. When Keats wants to suggest how far the Titans have fallen, in fact, he compares them with human beings, as in book II, when he says, "As with us mortal men," Saturn moves with a heavy heart.

The poet's apostrophe to the Muse to ask for inspiration is another typical device of the epic, and it is employed, with some individuality, in *Hyperion* to open book III: "O leave them, Muse! . . ./ Leave them, O Muse!" The poet who calls out to the muse actually is commanding rather than pleading or requesting. This aggressive and demanding attitude by the speaker as epic and prophetic poet is maintained through most of the poem, as Keats uses the privileged voice of a bard to pass judgments on his characters and to surround them with an understanding which surpasses their own—even if they are gods and he is merely human. This attitude will be more completely realized as a shaping form of the poem when it is presented as dream and vision in the later *The Fall of Hyperion*.

Themes and Meanings

The three main themes of *Hyperion* are: process, power, and poetry. The epic narrative examines how change in status and perception is a characteristic of all process. The conflict between generations of gods is a dramatization of the resistance of the past to claims of the present; while the poem focuses on the utterances of the Titans as signs of recovering energy, its thrust is toward the futility of efforts by the Titans to prevent their defeat. History is a succession of discrete generations, governed by a universal law of change. Whether Oceanus's interpretation of this process as progressive is correct the poem does not confirm, because it does not conclude.

Certainly, however, the poem confirms the pain of dislocation and disorientation which occurs in the process of transferring power, as the Titans are impressively miserable in their monumental, static condition. They barely relieve their misery by talking about it, yet that is the only means available to them for mitigation of their humiliation. There is irony at work in the poem's use of changing point of view, because the huge Titans ineffectively bluster about revenge while the young, troubled Apollo wanders aimlessly toward his divine destiny. In all instances, furthermore, the heroic gods are guided by heroic goddesses, to suggest that the physical power of males is administered by the greater power of females (manifested in their pity, their sensitivity, and their respect for the past).

The feelings of Thea, Clymene, and Mnemosyne are focused by their responses to the new powers of beauty manifested in the Olympian gods; that beauty is especially promised by the young Apollo, who will inspire a new era of civilized loveliness. Since Apollo is particularly the god of poetry, his birth into divinity is a fitting climax to a poem which ends without concluding. A new kind of poetry is born with the birth of a new god.

The meaning of *Hyperion* is caught by the crossing of these three themes. History and nature command change as a universal law of process, affecting the gods themselves. Natural process passes through discontinuous stages of self-awareness (the generations of gods and creatures), but it is also continuous, because it is a passage of power. The assumption of power by a new generation, a new body, and a new consciousness is the responsibility of all successive life, including the poets who, like Keats, suffer for their talent as they follow their inspiration by Apollo and reject the past of Hyperion.

Richard D. McGhee

I AM

Author: John Clare (1793-1864)
Type of poem: Lyric
First published: 1848; collected in *Poems of John Clare's Madness*, 1949

The Poem

"I Am" is a short poem of three six-line stanzas. Each stanza is regular iambic pentameter, rhyming *ababab*. The verse form is slightly unusual, not surprisingly for John Clare who experimented freely with different meters and forms. The poem begins with the simplest assertion of identity—"I am." The reader knows only the bare fact of the speaker's existence—no particulars are given. One does not learn who this speaker is and what his specific conditions are, though one is told in the first stanza that the speaker is friendless and forsaken. This speaker, paradoxically asserting his identity but providing no identification, repeats "I am" three times more in the opening stanza; however, he does so with qualifications that increasingly diminish his strange self-assertiveness. He tells the reader that no one cares who he is, that he has no one with whom to share his sorrows, and that he merely "lives," tossed about as aimlessly as "vapours." The aimlessness suggested by "vapour" in this final line of stanza 1 is powerfully reinforced by the enjambment, or running over, of the grammatical focus of its verb "tost" into the first line of stanza 2.

In the second stanza, the speaker is thrown helplessly "into the nothingness of scorn and noise." This paradox of a "nothingness" that is noisy and scornful is immediately followed by the pure oxymoron of "waking dreams." In this uncanny and contradictory world, the speaker likens himself to a shipwrecked sailor awash in a nightmare "sea" without a "sense of life or joys." The speaker, drifting insensibly in this "nothingness," now propounds his most fearsome paradox: Those whom he loves dearly are the most estranged from him. Although this stanza draws upon the conventional metaphor of shipwreck, with its suggestions of isolation and loneliness, there is evidence in this stanza that the speaker is not alone in his strange suffering. In fact, it appears that he suffers, in part, because he is not alone. Hostile ("scorn") or indifferent ("strange") witnesses may be present, but the speaker is separated from them as if lost at sea.

The concluding stanza confirms this, for the speaker now expresses a desire to escape to a world without men or women, without either joy or sorrow—a refuge of passive peace and detachment. This paradise is the past, the early years of childhood when the speaker imagines he was in unity with God and nature: "untroubling and untroubled." In "I Am," one encounters a nameless and faceless sufferer entertaining the impossible wish to return to the innocence of childhood. Exactly what and why he suffers is not known, but the terror and hopelessness of his sufferings are plain.

Forms and Devices

John Clare was the son of poor English farmers. At various times, Clare was a farm-hand, a militiaman, a kiln stoker, and a mendicant. His formal schooling was slight, and until late in life, his access to books was limited. One book Clare knew early and well was the Bible, and its influence is especially evident in "I Am." The Psalms are perhaps the best analogue for Clare's testament of sorrow, for like the Psalms, "I Am" is at once personal and impersonal, impassioned yet restrained. Like the Hebrew psalmist, who expressed his *de profundis* within a highly formal system of poetic parallelism, Clare closes his lyrical passion and despair in almost perfectly regular iambic pentameter. The speaker of the Psalms is often unidentified, as is the speaker in "I Am," and both tell much about the speakers' sorrows but little about the speakers themselves. The characteristic plea of the psalmist to be delivered from his "gathered enemies" is also echoed by the speaker of "I Am": He is surrounded by "scorn" and "noise" and, finally, in the closing lines, looks toward God for his deliverance.

The opening phrase of the first stanza, "I am—yet what I am," may allude to the divine tautology of Exodus, "I am that I am" (Exodus 3:14). If this is so, however, the allusion is ironic, for the speaker of this poem asserts his identity despairingly, emphasizing his impotence and helplessness. The speaker's description of being "tost into the nothing of scorn and noise" recalls biblical language describing the damned thrown into hell: "cast into the lake of fire" (Revelation 20:10). Finally, the idyllic image of the sleeping child "abiding" with God echoes the confidence of the psalmist who hopes to "abide before God for ever" (Psalms 61:7). Certainly, in a more general sense, the simplicity and grandeur that have so often been noted in this poem owe a debt to the lofty cadences of the King James Bible.

From another perspective, "I Am" is a poem intimately connected with the sensibilities of its own era, for it expresses with great intensity the Romantic conflict between innocence and experience, a theme central to the poetry of Clare's contemporaries. Clare is often compared to William Blake, since both were mystics who suffered eventual madness, but there is a more significant link between them. Clare shares Blake's Romantic exhaltation of childhood. In "I Am," childhood is figured as paradise before the Fall, a region in which there is no man (Adam) and no woman (Eve), only the isolated consciousness alone with God. The poem's speaker seeks to recover the infantile condition of moral neutrality and irresponsibility free of the knowledge of sexual distinctions and the emotional extremes of either joy or sorrow. Recognizing Clare's Romantic division of innocence and experience, one can appreciate the terrible irony of his reiterated "I am," for the poem is really a passionate longing after "I was." For William Wordsworth, Clare's other Romantic analogue, adult experience involves a falling away from the glories of childhood, a diminishment with compensations of greater knowledge; but for Clare, adult experience is a virtual hell from which the only escape is a fantasy of return to childhood, even to a prenatal unconsciousness.

Themes and Meanings

It has been said of Clare's lyrics, of which "I Am" is perhaps the greatest, that they possess "a penetrating simplicity which neither requires nor permits of analysis." In a sense, this is true. "I Am" is a cry from the depths, an utterance of terrible sorrow passing into an imagined calm that is as deep and absolute. Part of its power is its perfect directness; it is not a confession so much as a prayer, and its language is unmarred by sentimentality or ornament. It is perhaps too profound for literary criticism and strains the limits of secular literature. What does cast light on the poem—as is not the case with many poems—is the author's biography.

Clare was a man who crossed many boundaries. Son of a semiliterate father and a wholly illiterate mother, he began life in terrible poverty. His schooling was meager and brief, and his first poems were written on chance scraps of paper while he worked as a farmer or laborer. When a collection of these poems was published in 1820, he came to the attention of a sympathetic nobleman who helped raise an annuity for his support. For a time, Clare was a celebrity, a kind of "natural wonder," appealing in his uncouthness to the current taste among intellectuals for primitive genius. The farmer's son toured London and met the literati, but the "peasant poet" soon found himself on the outs again trying to sell his books door-to-door.

At this time, an unhappy love affair of Clare's youth began to haunt him. He began to have delusions, added to a serious drinking problem, so his family placed him in an asylum. Clare remained in various asylums for the last twenty-seven years of his life, writing poetry in the brief lucid intervals of his madness. The "living sea of waking dream" in "I Am" is a vivid image of a madhouse common room where patients act out delusions and fantasies that the sane experience only in dreams. Thus, the reader can now recognize that the oxymoron of "waking dream" is really no more than a matter-of-fact description of a terrible reality. The obsessive return to assertions of identity in "I Am" is the desperate affirmation of a self threatened by distintegration into madness, into "the nothingness of scorn and noise" from which the poet briefly emerges through the clarity and nobility of his poem.

Clare was not the only poet of humble origins in this time who found fame only to die miserably. Robert Burns, Robert Bloomfield, and William Thom suffered much the same fate. This group is sometimes known as the "unlettered poets," and the name is indicative of the kind of condescension and half-comprehension they often encountered. Clare's repeated "I am" may share something—but far more mournful—of Burns's angry "a man's a man for a' that," which Burns wrote in defiance of all the monied privilege and pretension he grew to hate. Having escaped the confines of their class, these poets had a need to assert their identities, because this assertion was all the identity they had: "I am—yet what I am, none cares or knows."

Whitney Hoth

1828

I AM A PARCEL OF VAIN STRIVINGS TIED

Author: Henry David Thoreau (1817-1862)
Type of poem: Meditation
First published: 1841, as "Sic Vita"; as "I am a parcel of vain strivings tied" in *A Week on the Concord and Merrimack Rivers*, 1849

The Poem

"I am a parcel of vain strivings tied" by Henry David Thoreau is a shaped-verse poem of forty-two lines consisting of seven six-line stanzas that meditate upon the brevity of life, the delicate and complex forces that bind experience together, and the sources of artistic inspiration or rebirth. The poem begins with a startling, almost paradoxical image that compares the poet to a package that cannot hold its dynamic, struggling contents. The second and third stanzas further develop this theme with the image of a bouquet of flowers held together by a mere "wisp of straw" and of a single flower scooped up in haste. The third stanza also introduces a new conflict, the power of time, which threatens the flowers cut from their native soil.

Stanzas 3 and 4 reflect on the insights gathered in the images—parcel, bouquet, and flower—about the power of time and the source of a second blooming, yet "unseen," of the artist. This theme is complicated in stanza 5 by the poet's assertion that "woe" has filled the "tender buds" of life and by the idea in stanza 6 of a purpose provided by a "kind hand" that has brought the flowers, as it were, to a second life in a new place. In the poem's conclusion, the poet asserts that when thus preserved this "stock" will "soon redeem its hours" and flourish again in new soil.

Forms and Devices

This poem foregrounds the poet through the use of first person and is developed around an extended metaphor. The poet's life is considered using an analogy with nature. This vision begins with the startling first line, "I am a parcel of vain strivings tied," which creates a contradictory image—that of a package that might have been neatly tied, but which actually is full of disunity. It is composed of "strivings" that are the more contradictory because the poem knows that they are "vain." The force of unity is a mere "chance bond." As a result, the nature of humanity is captured in an image of struggles and "dangling" parts. This plain image describes the poet's person, which is, at the final line of the first stanza, a vulnerable thing made "For milder weather."

In the second stanza, the image of a parcel is modified. The reader learns that the parcel is a bundle of flowers. Through combination of line lengths and rhyme scheme, this poem then takes the shape of a carefully structured bouquet. Each line length contributes to this visual effect. The informing metaphor gives each stanza its shape on the printed page. Each stanza repeats this form while also using a consistent rhyme scheme. By the end of the second stanza the poem has unified both form and content.

The remaining stanzas discuss the flowers and their relationship to the poet's concerns for time, the vitality of life, and the difficulties of life. Stanza 3 focuses on a single flower, "A nosegay which Time clutched" from out of "weeds and broken stems." This stanza is directed at misspent life by focusing on a single flower chosen from less desirable plants.

Stanzas 4 and 5 introduce the conflict in the poem's central metaphor and increase the drama of the metaphor. Stanza 4, for example, focuses on the rootlessness of the blooms that "stand/ In a bare cup." The fifth stanza allows that some "tender buds" of vitality remain only in "mimicry of life." These buds are "rife" with "woe." The central image of the poem, then, is problematic, and the bulk of the poem focuses on the paradox of life "in a bare cup." The final stanzas develop each of these problems from stanzas 3, 4, and 5.

After the poet has established the metaphor and explored it, the final two stanzas are used to discuss the philosophical meaning of the metaphor. Stanza 6 begins with a shift in direction. "But now I see," the poet writes. The poem's tone shifts to focus on survival and what life might be possible when flowers are set in "a strange place" by a "kind hand." In the final stanza, the meaning of the poem becomes more problematic and unclear because as the poet asserts that hope exists—the "stock" of flowers will "soon redeem its hours"—the poem ends with a reassertion of his own hopelessness. "I droop here" are the final words, which bring back to view the earlier, pessimistic of a life "in a bare cup." Whatever transcendence had come through the agency of the "kind hand" has been limited by the image of the final line.

Themes and Meanings

This poem should be read in the meditative tradition of John Donne and George Herbert, which uses startling or paradoxical first lines, plain images, and ordinary events to make philosophical statements guided by a clear vision of humanity, nature, and time which yield the poet's vision of his proper place in the universe. Thoreau's reputation as a poet has been slow in developing because many critics and readers think his prose is far more poetic than this poetry. Thoreau's poem "I am a parcel of vain strivings tied" clearly was not dashed off hurriedly but is the product of a poet who worked to achieve a synthesis of form and content.

As a shaped poem, this work illustrates the craftsmanship of Thoreau's poetic output. By establishing a concrete image, developing the metaphor, and then considering its meaning, the poem's impact is made profound. The transcendent qualities of life are fragile but are "alive" when one sees that one is not "plucked for nought" but instead is guided by the purposes of a "kind hand." Just what those forces of life are is not established by the poem. Thoreau's other work is needed to flesh out just what those forces might be.

The structure of this poem is impressive, if playful. The combination of stanza shape and rhyme scheme demonstrates Thoreau's care and mastery as a poet even if the poem occasionally seems unclear or static. It is a poem intended to grow more clear and dynamic upon reflection. From the first two stanzas, which establish the metaphor, the poem moves into a more abstract consideration of time and the nature of life. It is in the final four stanzas that the poet forces the reader to confront his complex, sometimes paradoxical, concepts of what real life is and where its essences are to be found.

Thoreau's poetry, especially "I am a parcel of vain strivings tied," is guided by a subtle quality that yields greater depths as one understands the transcendentalism that he espoused. In "I am a parcel of vain strivings tied," the poet and the poem each require an organic connection to nature to remain vital. This becomes clear in the last two stanzas, which begin,

> But now I see I was not plucked for nought,
> And after in life's vase
> Of glass set while I might survive
> But by a kind hand brought
> Alive
> To a strange place.

The symbolism of the flowers here contains a deep "dis-analogy" that Thoreau exploits and, finally, redeploys to assert that when "thus thinned," the flower "stock" will survive. The essence of vitality, then, is the secret of inspiration that is the source of poetry and poets. Cut off from that source of life, neither poet nor poem may flourish.

R. Scott LaMascus

I BRING AN UNACCUSTOMED WINE

Author: Emily Dickinson (1830-1886)
Type of poem: Meditation
First published: 1891, in *Poems: Second Series*; collected in *The Poems of Emily Dickinson*, 1955

The Poem

Typical of Emily Dickinson's terse, succinct poems that have a way of exploding with meaning, "I bring an unaccustomed wine" delivers its impact in twenty-two lines divided into seven stanzas, the first of four lines, the subsequent ones of three lines each. Dickinson frequently uses alcoholic metaphors—wine, beer, liquor—in her poems, not to celebrate drinking but to convey cryptic messages to her readers. In her poem "I taste a liquor never brewed," for example, the liquor she refers to is honey, liquor to the bees that gather the pollen to make honey.

In "I bring an unaccustomed wine," the wine referred to is an elixir of sorts, a potion to wet dry, unkissed lips. The "lips long parching," however, are not her own but are next to hers, giving a passionate overtone to the first verse. She summons the lips to drink, which can be taken to mean that she longs for them to kiss her lips. This poem is among Dickinson's "I/eye" poems. In letters that she wrote during this period in her poetic development, Dickinson revealed that she was experimenting with these words. Note that not only does the poem begin with the word "I" but that also in the first two lines alone the letter "i" appears in "bring," "wine," "lips," and "parching." Save for her letters indicating her conscious experimentation with "I," one might think simply that many two-line segments of poetry or prose could contain the letter five times. The evidence gleaned from her letters is that Dickinson's incorporation of this single letter was calculated and deliberate.

As the poem proceeds, the "I" in the poem turns "my brimming eyes away," suggesting tears and a denial of love. But although her eyes are turned away, the speaker returns the next hour to look. By stanza 3, the speaker is hugging the glass that holds the wine. She calls the glass "tardy," meaning that the salvation that the wine would have brought—metaphorically a kiss and, even more broadly, love—has been delayed to the point that it is no longer likely to occur. The final line of this stanza suggests that the lips are cold, that either the object of the speaker's love or the love itself is now dead.

The following verse reveals clearly that it is the love rather than the object of that love that is dead, because the speaker asserts that she cannot hope to "warm/ The bosoms where the frost has lain/ Ages beneath the mould—." Here the word "mould" suggests "mound," although it serves a dual purpose in invoking images of the disintegration of organic matter as well as that of a form that is used to shape pliable materials.

The speaker goes on to imply that the possibility of some other love entering her life might have existed but that this has not happened. During her lifetime, Dickinson lived through the painful losses of many people she loved dearly; from the isolation of her secluded room, she loved many people who were unavailable to her. But in the next to last stanza, she implies that her love is still available, her thirst still unslaked, leading into the last stanza in which she proffers the hope, but not the guarantee, of an eternity, of final salvation.

Forms and Devices

Emily Dickinson's poems are usually less than a page long and consist most frequently of short stanzas, often no more than three or four lines long. This poem is typical in this respect. It is also typical in that just as the poet has achieved the conventional rhyme of "wine" and "mine" in the first stanza, she departs from conventional rhyme by introducing the word "drink," which certainly does not rhyme either with "parching" (line 2) or with the last word in the second stanza, "look," although here the *k* sound gives Dickinson the poetic link she requires.

The last words of stanzas 3 and 4, "Cold" and "mould," rhyme perfectly. Dickinson again uses rhyme whimsically with her choice of the final words in stanzas 5, 6, and 7, where she suggests rhyme by choosing "speak" and "slake" but then returns to conventional rhyme with "slake" and "awake."

An examination of Dickinson's poetic manuscripts, presented in striking detail in Thomas H. Johnson's edition, *The Poems of Emily Dickinson, Including Variant Readings Critically Compared with All Known Manuscripts*, published by the Harvard University Press in a three-volume edition in 1955, reveals that the poet often obliterated a word that rhymed perfectly, preferring another word that suggested only the slightest similarity, as seen in the linking *k* sounds of "drink" and "look" in stanzas 1 and 2, of "warm" and "lain" in stanza four, and of "cup" and "drop" in stanza 6. She selected her words with the conscious intent, as both her revisions and her letters indicate, to heighten her reader's attention, of keeping her writing from becoming pedestrianly sing-songy.

For the same reasons, she also frequently disturbed regular meter, as she does in the last line of stanza 3 in this poem, which reads, "Are so superfluous Cold—." A more regular and conventional meter would have been achieved by using "superfluously" rather than "superfluous," a much more usual choice because the word in question is an adverb of manner and such words often end in "-ly."

The imagery in "I bring an unaccustomed wine" is highly visual, with words that overlap other words, such as the lips that are "crackling with fever" in the second stanza. Not only do readers receive the impression of lips that are hot and dry, but the work "crackling" also is so similar to "cracking" that one involuntarily concocts a double visual image upon reading it. Although she wrote under the Victorian constraints that characterized her day, Dickinson was a highly passionate, albeit sexually frustrated, woman. Her use of the word "bosoms" in the fourth stanza ties in with her choice of "cup" in the sixth stanza rather than "glass," as used previously in the third stanza. In her refined and indirect way, she here expresses the unfulfilled passion that dogged her solitary, puritanical existence.

The "drink/thirst" metaphor in this poem extends far beyond its literal meaning, although the literal meaning is credible, as the meaning of any successful metaphor must be. The thirst Dickinson refers to is a longing, a restrained passion; on a metaphysical level it may be seen as a thirst for the eternal life that many religions promise. Dickinson did not dogmatically regard eternal life as a certainty but only as a possibility, as she makes clear in her last stanza. The wine to which she refers is clearly the wine of salvation, but it exists as a hope, a mere possibility.

Themes and Meanings

In "I bring an unaccustomed wine," Emily Dickinson is concerned both with unfulfilled love and with questions of eternity. The first concern is exemplified well in the early stanzas of this poem, but as Dickinson moves into the poem, beginning as early as the fourth stanza, she begins to consider questions regarding death and immortality, subjects with which she deals extensively throughout the corpus of her writing.

Despite having been raised in a conventionally Christian home as a member of a socially prominent New England family, Dickinson was far from a blind follower of Christian theology. Throughout her life she harbored a profound skepticism. She hoped that the Christian promises with which she had been raised were valid, but she did not presume to assert categorically that they were. The poem also deals with unrequited love and with loss, but just as Dickinson has not foreclosed the possibility of an eternal existence, neither has she foreclosed the possibility that love may still come.

The "I" in Emily Dickinson's poems is more often a universalized "I" than a first-person reference to the poet herself. Her natural modesty would have forbidden her to use the personal "I" to the extent that she uses that pronoun in her poems. In most of the poems, a universal voice interacts with the reader, which is one of the distinguishing traits of Emily Dickinson's poetry.

In this respect, although her poems are far removed stylistically from those of Walt Whitman, she bears a similarity to him. In both poets, some inexperienced readers may be irritated by the seeming egoism of the poet, but in neither poet is the surface egoism a personalized egoism. Rather, this seeming egoism is a device used thematically to develop a relationship among the poet, the reader, and the substance of what is being written about.

This is not to suggest that the poems of either Dickinson or Whitman are not informed by their personal experiences. Such experiences are basic to most writing. The competent writer, as in the case of these two significant American poets, moves from the specifically personal to the universal.

R. Baird Shuman

I CANNOT LIVE WITH YOU—

Author: Emily Dickinson (1830-1886)
Type of poem: Lyric
First published: 1890, as "In Vain," in *Poems*; collected in *The Poems of Emily Dickinson*, 1955

The Poem

"I cannot live with You—" (the title is not Emily Dickinson's, since she did not title her poems) is a poem of fifty lines divided into eleven four-line stanzas and a concluding twelfth stanza of six lines. The poem is an unusually long poem for Dickinson. It is written in the first person from the point of view of a speaker addressing a lover.

Structurally, the poem is a list of things the speaker and her lover cannot do together and the reasons why they cannot. In the first three stanzas, the speaker announces to her beloved that she cannot "live" with the person because of the nature of "Life" itself. Life as it is ordinarily conceived of by those who deal with it daily on its most basic levels—the "Housewife" and the "Sexton" who locks up and unlocks ("keeps the Key to") both earthly possessions and the graveyard—is something subject to decay: It can "crack" and be "Discarded."

The speaker goes on to assert in the fourth and fifth stanzas that neither could she "die" with her beloved, because one of them would have to remain alive in order to close the other's eyes ("For One must wait/ To shut the Other's Gaze down"). The speaker asserts further that logically it would be impossible for her both to "see" the beloved die ("freeze") and to be dead at the same time (to have her "Right of Frost").

In the sixth and seventh stanzas, the speaker explains why she could not "rise," or be resurrected, with her beloved. Her reason is that resurrection to the "New Grace" of Jesus requires placing Jesus at the center of one's life, acknowledging him to be, metaphorically, the brightest sun. The speaker's "homesick Eye," however, is focused on her beloved: "Because Your Face/ Would put out Jesus'." The beloved not only is more central than Jesus to the speaker's life but also entirely blots out the face of Jesus. The eighth and ninth stanzas then predict the inevitable judgment that would be brought about by the speaker's blasphemy. The speaker's only defense, however, is a reiteration of her blasphemy: Her beloved "saturated" her "Sight" so completely that she could no longer see ("had no more Eyes/ For") more shadowy, "sordid" types of "excellence" such as God's "Paradise."

In the tenth and eleventh stanzas, the speaker cites further difficulties that could arise should the two lovers be resurrected and judged together: One of them could be damned and the other saved. Regardless, the speaker insists, her own "self" would be a "Hell" to her if she were separated from her lover. It is these reasons that lead to the conclusion of the final and longest stanza: "So We must meet apart." Since the two lovers cannot be together, they can only be with each other by being apart and sustaining themselves with the only things they share: distance and "Despair."

Forms and Devices

One of the most important devices used in the poem is metaphor, a figure of speech in which one thing is seen in terms of something else. The speaker of the poem uses the language of love—specifically, that of the renunciation of love—as a way of both denouncing and renouncing the traditional paradigm for human life set forth by Christianity.

The poem is structured according to the stages of human life as defined by this traditional Christian paradigm: life, death, resurrection, judgment, damnation/salvation, eternity. Rather than overtly criticize the adequacy of this model for human life, however, the speaker considers the value and "Sustenance" afforded by this paradigm through an examination of its implications for a love relationship.

Within this larger metaphorical structure, the poem incorporates a parallel metaphor of sensory experiences that underscores the speaker's rejection of both traditional definitions of "Life" and conventional modes of experiencing and perceiving "Life"; the speaker invokes images of eating, seeing, hearing, physical proximity, and again, at the end, eating. The first three stanzas employ images associated with eating in order to develop a metaphor for human life as it is traditionally viewed: "Life" is a piece of "Porcelain" or a "Cup" that contains the human spirit for a while until it cracks, breaks, or becomes outmoded ("Quaint") and needs to be "Discarded." The speaker implies that she and her lover require "A newer Sevres," a finer piece of porcelain—in other words a newer, more elaborate metaphor for "Life."

The fourth through the ninth stanzas focus on the process of seeing in order to critique traditional notions about death, resurrection, and judgment. In the traditional Christian paradigm, death is not subject to human intervention, resurrection is contingent on the "New Grace" of God, and judgment is solely the province of God. Through metaphors of sight, however, the speaker undermines God's authority and power in all of these realms. In stanzas 4 and 5, death is redefined as the freezing of sight, and only the lovers have the power "To shut the Other's Gaze down." Similarly, in stanzas 6 and 7, it is the vision of the beloved's face—not Christ's—in the "Eye" of the lover that shines brighter and "closer" and that, therefore, makes possible resurrection.

Finally, in stanzas 8 and 9, the implications of this metaphor of the sun (with a pun on "son of God") are fully developed. The speaker—in a dazzling metaphor of blindness—discounts conventional judgment and defends herself: She has been so ecstatically blinded ("You saturated Sight") by the beloved that she no longer has "Eyes" and can no longer see such "sordid" things as traditional "Paradise." In the final stanza, the speaker returns to the metaphor of eating to assert the lack of nourishment provided by the traditional model for human life; she and her lover have created a new form of "Sustenance"—"Despair."

Themes and Meanings

This poem is a critique of the traditional paradigm for human life set forth by Christianity. By means of the metaphor of a love relationship, the speaker delineates the inadequacy of this paradigm as a model for human existence and affirms a superior, individual definition of "Life." What first appears in the poem to be a renunciation of love becomes, in fact, a renunciation of those ways of viewing life that interfere with the higher vision of the lovers.

The speaker renounces those definitions of life which do not provide "Sustenance." "Life" that is susceptible to decay, mutability, and—more important—the authority of others (the "Sexton," the "Housewife," "They," or God Himself) is life that can be and needs to be "Discarded." The speaker, from the beginning, implies that the two lovers can create a different kind of life that is not perishable—an eternal life: "A newer Sevres pleases." Similarly, power over death is appropriated by the lovers. If, as the speaker metaphorically asserts, to die is to have one's sight "freeze," then the lovers will be looking at each other so steadfastly that only they can stop the gaze of each other, only they can bring about death.

The speaker goes on to eradicate the possibility of traditional resurrection when she says, in effect, that her beloved is brighter, more enlightening, and more of a "sun" to her "Eye" than Jesus: Her lover, in other words, is the source of true vision. Furthermore, the speaker argues, trying to fit into this traditional paradigm only makes the lovers vulnerable to the judgments of others. Once her beloved becomes vision itself—"You saturated Sight"—she is blinded and unable to perceive lesser, "sordid" things such as "Paradise." Both lovers thus are freed to develop their own criteria for damnation and salvation: To be together is to be "saved," to be apart is "Hell."

In the final stanza, the speaker arrives at the conclusion that the poem has been building up to: Because the traditional paradigm available to the lovers for expressing life, love, salvation, vision, and eternity does not work, they "must meet apart." Because the lovers now create the terms of their own life, death, and salvation, they are free enough and powerful enough to redefine, too, both the traditional love relationship and the conventional meanings of language.

In this way, the poem can be viewed as a critique of God's divine plan for human life, in which Christ will be "that bread of life," "the light of the world," and "the resurrection, and the life" (John 6:48, 9:5, 11:25). In accordance with God's plan, Christ asserts in John 14:6: "I am the way, the truth, and the life: no man cometh unto the Father, but by me." By means of the poem, however—which is disguised as a renunciation of love—the speaker creates a "Life" to rival God's traditional plan for life; by developing their rival definitions of life, death, and salvation, the lovers arrive at their self-determined "judgment" and "Paradise." They become their own saviors. Christ as the sustaining "bread" of life has been supplanted by the lovers' self-derived source of nourishment: "that White Sustenance—/ Despair." Finally, the last stanza of the poem—with its additional two lines—literally and metaphorically adds one more stage to the traditional Christian paradigm for human life—an augmentation that is both a further act of blasphemy and a final assertion of the speaker's ultimate power and triumph.

Angela M. Estes

I DREAMED THAT IN A CITY DARK AS PARIS

Author: Louis Simpson (1923-   )
Type of poem: Lyric
First published: 1959, in *A Dream of Governors*

The Poem

In Louis Simpson's "I Dreamed That in a City Dark as Paris," the speaker imagines himself a soldier in Paris during World War I witnessing the bombardment of the city and reflecting upon his relationship to his imaginary soldier, with whom he ultimately feels a shared identity. The poem unfolds as though the reader is viewing a drama filled with the colorful flash of cannons and airplanes buzzing overhead. The speaker describes the scene in details that convey his solitary condition—"I stood alone in a deserted square," he says—and his emotions are reflected in his description of this night, "trembling with a violet/ Expectancy."

The second stanza shifts to the speaker's feelings of forlorn abandonment, highlighted by the "empty city and the empty square.." He feels even more alien to this world because of his uniform, which consists of a "helmet with its vestige of a crest," along with an overcoat and hobnail boots. The heavy, oversized uniform is a metaphor for the burden of a war that is exploding around him.

The poem develops on two levels at once. It offers itself as the speaker's dream, which frames the wartime scene in Paris, which in turn becomes the central focus through most of the poem. Although readers see what the speaker describes, they are constantly made aware of the speaker himself: the first two lines of the poem begin, "I dreamed" and "I stood alone," and in the next stanza, the speaker continues, "I was lonely," "I wore," "I was the man."

The final two stanzas turn to the speaker's reflections on the nature of dreams and the truths they can reveal. Near the end, the speaker addresses the imaginary soldier as "My confrere" and asks him whether he is "amazed/ To wander through my brain four decades later/ As I have wandered in a dream through yours?" In this way, Simpson distances the speaker from the soldier, who is a fiction of the speaker's imagination, and reflects on all wars, on history, and on "waking life" itself, whose violence "disrupts/ The order of our death." The speaker realizes that ultimately peace is achieved only in death and that life is a dream, a strange dream in which war is the prevailing condition that creates disorder.

The somber mood of the beginning never dissipates entirely, but by the end of the poem the speaker's attention has turned from feelings of loneliness to a sense of brotherhood with the soldier he has imagined. In stanza 2, the speaker declares, "I was the man," that is, he was the soldier; by the end, the speaker and his fictional companion have become one: "My confrere/ In whose thick boots I stood." The speaker has also discovered something positive about himself and about human history: Brotherhood is possible. At the beginning of the dream-poem, he has been "Left behind, abandoned by the army," but at the end, he has found companionship through an act of imagination and insight.

Forms and Devices

The poem consists of five stanzas, totaling twenty-nine lines. The second and fourth stanzas are of equal length, six lines each, and the others are irregular in length. One pair of lines in the second stanza and the poem's final two lines rhyme. The poem's rhythms are sustained by metrical stresses, essentially five in each of the lines. The absence of a regular rhyme scheme or uniform stanzaic pattern shifts the reader's focus from these traditional devices to more subtle uses of sound and design, and when rhyme does occur, especially in the final stanza, its effect is enhanced. Simpson also uses repetitive structures generously to give his poem unity and force. The opening repetition of the personal pronoun "I," for example, places the focus on the central figure, and similar structures in the second stanza add weight to the soldier's catalog: "The helmet," "The rifle," "The belt," "the trailing overcoat." The accentual pattern, too, is so subtle that, without end rhymes, the soldier's narrative has the quality of conversation, as when he reports, "The German *Taube* and the *Nieuport Scout*,/ They chased each other tumbling through the sky,/ Till one streamed down on fire to the earth."

Simpson's use of stanzaic length also subtly guides the reader's response. The poem's central drama, Paris under fire, occupies almost three quarters of the poem, running through the three longest stanzas. Of these, the second stanza focuses on the soldier's appearance and feelings. The poem's emotional center is the soldier's sense of isolation, abandonment, and alienation, and Simpson devotes his longest stanza to this subject. The six-line opening stanza sets both mood and scene, which the second stanza elaborates, making the soldier central to both; the third stanza directs attention to the airplanes and concludes appropriately with the ending of the aerial dogfight. Stanza length works like a spotlight on a stage, moving attention from place to place, thereby controlling emphasis and pace.

Simpson also uses specific details, run-on lines, and striking language to highlight the poem's drama and underscore its meaning. The poem's third line, for example, develops an attractive image—"The night was trembling with a violet"—which runs grammatically into the next line, where the image is abruptly transformed into something very unpleasant, a violet "Expectancy." One of the poem's themes is that war yokes together beauty and ugliness, as when guns pump "color in the sky" and beautiful airplanes destroy each other.

The rhythms of lines also helps control the emotional effect of the soldier's narrative, as when he describes his predicament: "There was the Front. But I was lonely here,/ Left behind, abandoned by the army." Pauses and full stops here reflect the soldier's mental state, which is matter-of-fact yet consistent with his reference to his "unrest" two lines later. When he describes aerial flight, however, the line moves with unsettling swiftness: "They chased each other tumbling through the sky." His use of "inhabitation" to describe his place in the empty square forecasts in its awkwardness his later statement: "I was the man, as awkward as a bear."

To suggest the soldier's static alienation from the battle, Simpson surrounds him with words that express vivid images of motion: "trembling," "flickering," and "pumping." To suggest the soldier's alienation further, Simpson gives a sprinkling of foreign words, such as *"poilu"* to describe his shaggy appearance, and the names of the airplanes, *"Nieuport Scout"* and *"Taube"* (which, ironically, means "dove").

Themes and Meanings

If imagination gives the poet power to relive history, it can bring insight. The poem begins with a dark picture of loneliness and abandonment and ends with a realization that something positive can be wrested from the "violence of waking life" that spans human history from the Egyptian dynasties to World War I and beyond. Despite the poem's focus on war's violence and the soldier's lonely isolation, the mood is neither very dark nor despairing. One might even feel that a note of nostalgia runs through some of the descriptions, guns rumbling and "pumping color in the sky." The soldier's helmet, "with its vestige of a crest," is reminiscent of the Great War and its ornate trappings. The cathedrals of Paris "loomed/ In speaking majesty" as the airplanes "chased each other tumbling through the sky." The poem lacks the bitter indictment of war's devastation and maiming. Simpson focuses, rather, on sounds that only hint at destruction and on scenes that evoke sadness rather than horror—the two airplanes, for example, are "Forlorn as birds" and, if one can imagine them, are as beautiful in design and color as birds. Even the soldier is compared to a shaggy bear, more cuddly perhaps than ferocious.

When Simpson turns from the scene of war, in the penultimate stanza, to a reflection on the passage of time, the nostalgic undertone continues: "These wars have been so great, they are forgotten/ Like the Egyptian dynasts." The poet's imagination can save one from despair by discovering not only a shared identity with one of war's victims but also an understanding of one's relation to war, history, and the "violence of waking life."

The poem's final irony is expressed in the last sentence: "Strange dreams occur,/ For dreams are licensed as they never were." The dream, this poem, brings understanding but is after all only a dream. The paradox is that the dream can capture a seeming truth about life and a mitigating perspective. Simpson's subject is not war's horror but the power of the dream to discover the fraternity of those who are lonely and abandoned. Even great wars are ultimately forgotten, and other wars continue to occur. If one seeks order, death offers it. Those who choose life have their strange dreams, which can lead to an understanding that people are never really alone as long as they can dream.

Bernard E. Morris

I FELT A FUNERAL, IN MY BRAIN

Author: Emily Dickinson (1830-1886)
Type of poem: Lyric
First published: 1896, in *Poems: Third Series*; collected in *The Poems of Emily Dickinson*, 1955

The Poem

Like all Emily Dickinson's poems, this one bears no title. The usual way of referring to a Dickinson poem is therefore through either its first line or its assigned number in Thomas Johnson's definitive edition. "I felt a Funeral, in my Brain" is vintage Dickinson in both form and theme, given to homely illustration from life—here a funeral—simplicity of construction, irregular rhyme, and a preoccupation with death in a context of somber meditation. Outwardly a simple poem, it is one of several that Dickinson wrote not only to note the pervasiveness of death as ending, but also to explore the very nature of death itself.

The initial stanza commences with what is fundamentally a conceit through which the persona, or speaker in the poem, attempts to articulate what death is like through an unusual analogy—that of a "Funeral in [the] Brain." Intriguingly, and not an uncommon stance in Dickinson, the viewpoint is that of one who has already died. In recall, the funeral is sufficiently vivid nearly to transport the persona back to the realm of sense—or, as the speaker says, "it seemed/ That Sense was breaking through."

Stanza 2 continues the poem's emphasis on the ritual of death with a movement from sense to numbing, as if underscoring death's inexorable onslaught on life. The analogy is to the funeral service. As in the opening stanza, the third line reinforces death's macabre finality in its repetitive insistence, here by using the participle "berating."

Stanza 3 moves toward burial with the lifting of the coffin "across [the] soul," a way of suggesting not merely the disembodiment of the soul, or psyche, the coffin passing through its immaterial substance, but also an obliteration of human and immortal significance. This fact lies behind the stanza's mournful clarion, "Then space began to toll," depicting both the resonance of the church bells and the thunderous fact of the grave as the ultimate separator from the senses.

Unusual here is Dickinson's use of a run-on stanza, leading into the penultimate fourth stanza, in which the persona is metonymized as an "Ear" forced to take in this overwhelming proclamation of the bells—"As [though] all the Heavens were a bell." Death empties one of personhood, and one is joined to an eternal silence, countermanding that of the world of sense above. Thus, the persona suggests the analogy of shipwreck in "Wrecked solitary" to depict the disintegration and isolation of the dead.

In the final stanza, the persona recalls her interment in the ground, and here the true crisis of the poem is waged with the breaking of "a plank in reason." Death represents a fall from rationality into nothingness—hence, into nonbeing. Cryptically, the persona speaks of the consequence of this fall as one of "hit[ting] a world at every plunge," perhaps suggesting the hellish worlds of mythological and biblical import and their traditional association with the earth's interior. Death is thus the legacy of man's first fall and its own hell, in which humankind has "finished knowing."

Forms and Devices

Noteworthy in the poem is the employment of near rhyme in lines 2 and 4 of the initial stanza to suggest disintegration. In the ceremonial observances of the next three stanzas, regularity asserts itself in the rhyming of the second and fourth lines, as if the poet were suggesting that it is in human rite that humans attempt to assign meaning to death. The final stanza, however, is ominous in its breaking of the "plank of reason," as if implying the folly of such attempts to bridge, or transcend, death's chasm through the imposition of a rationale upon the cosmic scheme of things. Accordingly, there is not even near rhyme, for death is the ultimate cessation of any kind of knowing, the consummate disintegration of sense.

Repetition is pervasive in the first three stanzas to underscore both the solemnity of the occasion and the ominous truth that death represents. There are "mourners to and fro" who keep "treading, treading"; there is a service that is like a drum that is "Kept beating, beating," while in stanza 3, the persona hears "those same boots of lead again." Behind this repetition lies the implication of death as an inexorable process undoing everyone. Thus, while the time aspect of the poem is ostensibly one of past tense, the persona reminiscing, one finds the irony of a repetition affirming time's slow but inevitable movement toward human dissolution in which time itself will die. It is a theme similar to that of Dickinson's more familiar poem "Because I could not stop for Death."

As always in a Dickinson poem, the imagery of the poem is arresting, both for its sources in the commonality of everyday life and for its assigned function in the poem as the weave of a conceit, or extended analogy. Here the real event is inner, not outer. The poem deals not with what death means to mourners, but with what death means for its victim: the loss of that which makes life possible, the senses. That loss is referred to in the poem as a "funeral in [the] brain" or a "mind . . . going numb," or "a plank in reason" that breaks.

This last image is the most striking of all. In the context, the plank suggests a means of passage over a chasm. It breaks, hurling the persona into the depths below. Dickinson may be suggesting the insufficiency of rationality to prepare one for the "fall" into death. Quite certainly, death marks the ending of all rationality and, hence, of all knowing. Strikingly, it is with the breaking of the plank of reason that the reader returns full circle to the poem's startling opening, "I felt a Funeral, in my Brain."

Themes and Meanings

Dickinson often objectifies death through a narrator who recalls her own death. This occurs, for example, in poems 449, 465, and 712. Along with God, nature, and love, death is a favorite theme. At times Dickinson's position toward death seems contradictory. On one hand, she seems nearly to celebrate it as an anodyne to life, as in "Because I could not stop for Death," where death appears in the guise of a suitor and the grave is a "House" in the ground. On the other hand, death is that stain upon the cosmos, an act of a "burglar" deity. In one of her letters, she exclaimed, "I can't stay any longer in a world of death."

The poem is notable for its lack of a consolatory element, a departure from the custom of the time. Indeed, it offers no message of any kind, either about how to live or how to prepare for Eternity. The emphasis is upon death, its stark reality as a divorcer from the senses and as life's ultimate ritual. A person has no source of promptings for its content. Clearly the poem is not Christian in its depiction of death as ultimate extinction rather than as passage into glory.

It is possible that the poem deals with a psychical death—that is, with the desperate attempt of the mind to ward off pain through repression, or the forgoing of consciousness. In this vein, the analogy of burial is an appropriate one. Elsewhere (poem 777), Dickinson writes of "The Horror not to be surveyed—/ But skirted in the Dark—/ With Consciousness suspended—/ And Being under Lock." In poem 341, Dickinson writes that "After great pain, a formal feeling comes—/ The Nerves sit ceremonious, like Tombs." In the same poem, she writes, "This is the hour of Lead," which may be compared with the "boots of lead" in the present poem.

It is also conceivable that the poem depicts the mind's downward journey into madness or psychological dislocation. In this connection, poem 435 speaks of "Madness" as the "divinest Sense" and of "Much Sense—the starkest Madness." Indeed, some critics have argued for a psychotic disturbance in Emily Dickinson or for some kind of severe loss in her life that created a devastating emotional aftermath.

Ralph Robert Joly

I HAVE A RENDEZVOUS WITH DEATH

Author: Alan Seeger (1888-1916)
Type of poem: Elegy
First published: 1916, in *Poems*

The Poem

A short elegy in iambic pentameter, "I Have a Rendezvous with Death" has three stanzas of six, eight, and ten lines that employ irregular rhyme. Elegy is a lyric poetic form that traditionally takes as its subject a meditation on death or other similarly grave theme. In its classical form, in both Latin and Greek poetry, the elegy was distinguished more for its use of the elegiac meter, the dactylic hexameter—an accented syllable followed by two unaccented syllables—than for its subject matter. The elegy has been a popular form throughout the English poetic tradition. Geoffrey Chaucer, John Donne, Thomas Gray, and Alfred, Lord Tennyson all wrote in the conventional form. Elizabethan poets often used the elegy for love poems which they called "complaints." A typical example in American poetry can be found in Walt Whitman's "When Lilacs Last in the Dooryard Bloom'd."

In "I Have a Rendezvous with Death," the American poet Alan Seeger modernized the elegy by employing an iambic meter that gives his poem a more regular, even cadence and by emphasizing the theme of impending death. Not occasioned by the death of someone else, as elegies generally are, Seeger's poem meditates on his own possible death during World War I, when he was serving on the Western Front. In fact, Seeger was killed in action in the war at the Battle of the Somme.

An atypical lyric on the war, "I Have a Rendezvous with Death" alludes to the realities of the war only sparingly in phrases such as "disputed barricade," "some scarred slope," and "some flaming town." The poem's title announces its theme of death, while suggesting, through its use of the word "rendezvous," that the poet is heading toward his meeting with death involuntarily. "Rendezvous" suggests a prearranged coming together at a particular time and place. In this context it implies a deliberate or willed connection with death, which reinforces the root meaning of the word, derived from Old French for "presenting oneself." Seeger's use of the word also echoes his reasons for joining the army in the first place: He wished to stand up and be counted in the struggle against the cultural darkness that German military expansion represented to him and the Allies during the early years of the conflict.

The poem opens with Seeger contemplating his death in the springtime—a particularly jarring note because spring is normally associated with the renewal of life after the "death" of winter. The second stanza reverses this disjunctive note as the poet hints that his journey into death's "dark land" with the "closing of his eyes" and quenching of his breath might be avoided and that he may yet once again experience the seasonal return of life and "meadow-flowers."

The third stanza begins with a conventional comparison between death and sleep by contrasting "blissful sleep" with its dear "hushed awakenings" to the finality of death from which no one awakens. However, the elegy concludes with the poet's reiteration that his death comes, not unexpectedly, but as a result of his "pledged word," the word of a soldier who has volunteered to embrace death as a part of his profession. It is a rendezvous that the poet-soldier will not fail to keep: As spring "trips north again this year," at midnight in some burning town he may meet his end.

Forms and Devices

The presence of death in the poem is softened by the recurring references in each stanza to springtime and the life-giving urges that spring evokes. The poet says that the season will bring back "blue days and fair" with "rustling shade," "apple-blossoms," and "meadow flowers." Reminiscent of Geoffrey Chaucer's description of spring in his prologue to *The Canterbury Tales* (1387-1400), Seeger's poem also "throbs," pulses, and breathes with the reawakening of life's urges. Its references to spring—a time the poet may well not live to see—add an especially poignant note to the possibility of his dying.

The poem's personification of death also contributes to its touching mood by emphasizing both the acceptance and tenderness of death. Its second stanza describes meeting death in terms almost of friendship. Death will take the poet by the hand and lead him into his "dark land." It is an image suggesting a gentle, coaxing death, not one that arrives violently or unannounced. Such imagery evokes Seeger's traditional grounding in the classics. This poem reminds one of the cicerone, or guide, in Dante's *Inferno* (c. 1320) who shepherds his charge through the mazes of the underworld, instructing him at every turn. In Seeger's poem, however, the guide will not lead him safely through the pitfalls of Hell and out again but will close the poet's eyes and quench his breath. Here death is gentle but also insistent, and the journey he presages is terminal.

In the third stanza, Seeger introduces sleep imagery—using a traditional trope of death as a "little" sleep, comparing and contrasting to the finality of death. He does this by employing a seductive and inviting sexual imagery. Sleep is described as "deep/ Pillowed in silk" and "scented down." In this "sleep," "Love throbs" and pulse is "nigh to pulse, and breath to breath," and awakenings are "hushed" and "dear." The Association of love with death is deeply rooted in the traditions of poetry. With its conceit of a "rendezvous," which also has overtones of a meeting of lovers, this poem's connection of love and death becomes all the more suggestive. Such comparisons join with the final couplet of the poem in which the poet uses the term "pledge," another word often applied to meetings between lovers, which additionally expands the meaning of the poem.

Themes and Meanings

"I Have a Rendezvous with Death" is a young soldier's poem about facing the very real possibility of his own death. To any soldier who fought during World War I the possibility of dying in combat was especially real. The casualty figures for combatants in that war were staggering. Alan Seeger happened to be living in London at the outbreak of the war in August, 1914. During the late summer of that year the realities of the conflict were perhaps more urgent for him than for most Americans. He enlisted in the Foreign Legion of France because of an urgent sense of duty to the cultural values and traditions he had learned to embrace. In this respect he truly represented the idealism that motivated so many to volunteer for the war effort. His enlistment in the Foreign Legion was also necessary because the United States was not yet an active participant in the conflict. His eager involvement in the war further illuminates the pledge he mentions in the last couplet of the poem and to which he wished to remain true.

Seeger's idealism contributes to the tone of the poem, in which the poet does not shrink from his rendezvous with death but actually welcomes it. His idealism also may account for the absence of the more unpleasant aspects of the war's horrors in the poem, the grisly details of which characterize the better known war poetry of such British poets as Rupert Brooke, Wilfred Owen, and Sigfried Sassoon. Furthermore, Seeger's idealism helps to explain his place as the most famous of America's war poets. Wealthy, young, and full of promise, he became a symbol for the United States of the selfless sacrifice that the war called forth in the name of all that was thought worthy in the Western civilization which was being destroyed by German military aggression. In contrast to the later American writings about war by such authors as Ernest Hemingway, John Dos Passos, E. E. Cummings, and Laurence Stallings, Seeger's patriotism appears as an anomaly.

The equanimity with which Alan Seeger could write about his own mortality and the haunting gentleness of his most famous poem have made "I Have a Rendezvous with Death" one of the more telling literary expressions from what was then known as the Great War. It also assured this young and sensitive poet a small but secure place among the writers of elegies in the English language.

Charles L. P. Silet

I HAVE A TERRIBLE FEAR OF BEING AN ANIMAL

Author: César Vallejo (1892-1938)
Type of poem: Narrative
First published: 1939, as "Tengo un miedo de ser un animal," in *Poemas humanos*; English translation collected in *Human Poems*, 1968

The Poem

"I have a terrible fear of being an animal" is a poem of twenty-seven lines that is divided into four stanzas. It is in free verse and makes ample use of internal rhyme and assonance in the original Spanish. One of the dated poems in *Poemas humanos*, this poem bears the date of October 22, 1937.

The poem is actually untitled; using its first line as its title is a convenience for scholars, critics, translators, and students, not the wish of the poet. The first line, however, does reveal more about the poem and the poet in what it does not say than in what it does. It is not "becoming" an animal that the persona/poet fears, but "being" one. With that acknowledgment, he gives credibility to his grosser animal self, the more profoundly sensual self that he carries within. Although the animal exists, it is one of "white snow."

The first stanza also expresses the idea that each positive natural element has its negative aspect; each object of strength has its implied weakness. The animal has power, but that power is ameliorated by its snowy substance. The same is true of the other elements of nature. The splendid and supremely sunny day, because of its brilliance, has implicit within it the equally supreme and pervasive night.

The second stanza explores the absurdity of humanity—its fragmentation, its emptiness, and its implicit and unfulfilled dual nature. In the third stanza, César Vallejo seems to appeal more to the senses than to the mind. In nostalgic reminiscence of the early Symbolist poets' perfume concerts, he seeks "aromatic logic." The unusual juxtaposition of aroma and logic serves to infuse each with the qualities of the other, thus negating the pure quality of both.

The fourth stanza centers on the essential struggle in which each person is engaged: the basic struggle to bring together the elements of the transcendent and the prosaic, the physical and the ephemeral, the mind and the senses. The poet exhorts one to act, to remain within and without at the same time. For Vallejo, the intangibility of existence can be seen in the consistent verbal destablization of concept and sensation. Therefore, "to thrash, to exist, to cough, to secure oneself" is to be in constant flux, but the function of existence is to try to capture the essential reality that exists somewhere between all oppositions.

Forms and Devices

When reading Vallejo, and particularly the poems in *Poemas humanos*, it is useful to be aware of the figure of speech called synecdoche. Synecdoche is the use of a part of something to represent the whole—an individual for a class, a material for a thing—or vice versa. In "I have a terrible fear of being an animal," Vallejo makes extensive use of synecdoche. The purpose of using this device is to expand the evocative power of language by calling up all of the associations and consequent allusions that each fragment contains, and in so doing to build the levels of meaning of the poem. Another reason, especially noteworthy in Vallejo, is to confuse the reader.

In the first stanza, for example, there are several synecdochic fragments accenting light and darkness; day and night are obvious. "Archepiscopal" is less obvious but no less germane. This metonymic device relating to the church hierarchy may imply both light and darkness depending on the needs of poet and poem.

There are repeated allusions to power or powerlessness in the references to the "animal," to "snow," to earthly and unearthly forces, as in the ecclesiastical reference, to the animal's "veiny circulation," to his ability to "breathe" and transform himself, and finally in the terrestrial but significant emblem of "money," which leads both power and powerlessness to the man/animal.

The story that the poet tells by linking all these elements is neither direct nor easy to follow. It is almost like a series of verbal mirrors, each of which reflects and absorbs the light of the others in order to create a more rich and varied impression. In the second stanza, Vallejo refers to the human as an "absurd" creature, a "premise" rather than a person. By using synecdoche, placing a hinge at his waist, separating his neck from the rest of his body, and giving him a snout rather than a nose, Vallejo shows just how fragmented and perhaps even puppetlike the animal/man is.

By including a reference to the "tabla of [John] Locke," Vallejo at once calls up the philosophical notion of the human entity born as a blank table, an empty slate, without heavenly gifts, and its author, who claimed that logic could be obtained through the association of ideas. The reference to "Bacon" is to Francis Bacon, the English philosopher who established the technique of scientific inquiry based on what is observable and, therefore, deducible. By means of those various synecdochic juxtapositions, Vallejo underscores how absurd any creature—even a "premise" who is a man—actually is.

When Vallejo calls upon aromatic logic in the third stanza, the reader knows that he is drawing on the earlier mentioned technique of sensory stimulation of literary efforts by perfume, but he is also alluding to what foolishness the animal, man, has made of the idea as well as the operation of logic. There is further use of the sense of smell, but in a reality in which day is night—"lunar day"—and life is equal to death: "the alive absurdity and the dead absurdity." The pervasive scent there is putrid.

The last stanza compounds synecdochic and metonymic confusion, and the poet now can be seen thrashing about within the existence of the poem, using numbers as a further abstraction of the illusory power of words.

Themes and Meanings

"I have a terrible fear of being an animal" encapsulates the multiple spiritual, social, and aesthetic struggles of Vallejo the man and Vallejo the poet. From his earliest days, Vallejo struggled with the traditional and acceptable forms of spirituality. He rebelled against the imposition of the moral and ethical values of his family and society by listening to the promptings of his interior life. He tried to make sense of the disparate nature of theory and practice whether at work in theology, life, or literature.

Vallejo uses this poem to explore the conflicts between art and life, the earth and beyond, humankind and God. The poem itself becomes an analogue, a reflection of these various systems and bodies.

Vallejo says in "Los dados eternos" ("The Eternal Dice"), for example, that God is dead, at least in his supremacy over humankind, but he acknowledges the existence of God in a diminished form. In that work, he elevates humankind, but in this poem, he reduces humankind by exposing his frailty and his invincibility simultaneously. In his theoretical writing on the avante-garde, Vallejo deplores the capitalist intelligentsia's control of the ostensibly new in poetry. In this poem, however, he laments the animal's inability "to change itself and have money." Vallejo also repeatedly uses many of the techniques of the movements he reviles.

Vallejo says in his essay on "New Poetry" that new poetry that is based on new words or new metaphors is new only in the sense of novelty or complication, but new poetry that is based on "new sensibility is . . . simple and human and . . . might be taken for old." Nevertheless, his own poetry retains all the conventions of the modern.

The poem, then, can be seen as a duel between Vallejo and himself. Essentially, he fulfills Arthur Rimbaud's idea that his self is an "other." The poem is his battleground, and rather than drawing the reader into the fray, the poet further distances and alienates his audience. He uses numbers at the end, when words have lost their meaning. They become cheap, valueless in their ability to communicate. Ultimately, the poem is left open to as many possibilities as humankind is. As Vallejo has said, one must be careful of the human substance in poetry.

Heather Rosario-Sievert

I HAVE FORGOTTEN THE WORD I WANTED TO SAY

Author: Osip Mandelstam (1891-1938)
Type of poem: Lyric
First published: 1922, as "Ia slovo pozabyl, chto ia khotel skazat'," in *Tristia*; English translation collected in *The Eyesight of Wasps*, 1989

The Poem

"I Have Forgotten the Word I Wanted to Say" is a poem of six stanzas, each composed of four lines. Its rhythm is created by the placement of a regular number of accented syllables before and after the caesura, the pause in the middle of the line. This style of tonic verse is called *dolniki* in Russian and was the verse form preferred by some innovative Russian poets of the early twentieth century.

The poem, as is frequently the case in Russian lyric poetry, depends very much on its form to convey the poetic content. By writing in *dolniki* instead of a stricter accentual-syllabic meter, Osip Mandelstam enjoyed greater flexibility in the number of unaccented syllables he could use in a line. As a result, the lines vary in length from nine to thirteen syllables while echoing consistently in four beats. This irregularity in the line length allows the poem to assume a more individual nature where shorter lines add tension and longer lines develop the thought. The caesura, while helping to organize the sound pattern by dividing the lines into two sound groups with two accents each, also inserts a pause into the often rather long line. Since the poem is philosophical and laden with profuse symbolism, the caesura gives the reader/listener some extra time to visualize or reflect on the poem's meaning.

The persona begins relating his experience using a phrase very much like one used by everyone at some time: "I have forgotten the word I wanted to say." In this first line (which serves as the title), in Russian, the "word" is emphasized. This emphasis at the very beginning hints that it is not only that the persona has forgotten what to say, but also that there is a special importance to the word, that the word is invested with a special value. Resounding throughout the remainder of the poem is the frustration and anguish this experience causes the persona.

For the poet, the loss of a word is catastrophic, since the dominant force in his life is communicated in words. Thus, in the second stanza, as "the word swoons," life itself seems to cease: "No birds are heard. No blossom on the immortelle." Similar images of the void and bleakness echo this one—for example, "An empty boat floats on an arid estuary."

Nor can the persona find that word for all his searching. It takes on varying attitudes, becoming a "tent or shrine," acting like the mourning Antigone, or falling "like a dead swallow." He bemoans his predicament and wishes for a return to a former state of being, in which he was able to command his words and never let down the creative expectations of the muses. Having forgotten what he wanted to say, he has become lifeless. He associates only with death, and can only articulate a sense of muteness and loss.

Forms and Devices

Mandelstam wrote during a period very heavily influenced by Russian Symbolism, a type of writing in which profuse images that take on the aspect of symbols are greatly instrumental in conveying the artistic designs of the poet. Some of Mandelstam's images may appear strange, and their sheer density with respect to the content of the poem makes for difficult reading. To the reader uninitiated in classical poetry, the repeated evocation of swallows and shadows may seem quite foreign, but other images may be more akin to the reader's experience, such as singing absentmindedly, which conveys the mental destitution the poet feels at his powerlessness.

The entire poem revolves around an extended metaphor laden with symbolic imagery. "The word" represents expression, which, particularly to a poet but also to every mortal, is life itself. When the persona says he has "forgotten the word," he is saying figuratively that he has lost his ability to create or express and, thus, the power to live in a human sense.

The word in this metaphorical sense is symbolized by the swallow. Thus, either the word (in stanza 5) or the swallow (in stanza 1) must "fly back" to the "palace of shadows"; the symbol for "the word" becomes interchangeable with what it symbolizes.

Flying would seem to be a mixed metaphor used with "the word," but since "the word" has been clearly identified with the swallow, the figure transfers successfully without any confusion. Moreover, many romantic notions of creativity involve the metaphor of flying to achieve inspiration. Among these, Plato's chariot of winged steeds (in *Phaedrus*, fourth century B.C.E.) is very important to Mandelstam. On this chariot, the artist can be drawn above the mundane, everyday world into the heavens, where the ideal from which to model one's artistic vision can be found. The swallow naturally embodies an experience outside everyday human life, the ability to fly, and thus symbolically represents the poet's power of inspiration, which must also draw on experience outside daily human existence. The blind swallow, however, has no power; indeed, her wings are clipped. Similarly, Mandelstam's persona is powerless, and his position is much like death.

The "shadows" and the "transparent ones" represent the insubstantial remains of the dead in Hades, the place where Mandelstam's word is detained. The "palace of shadows" is thus the edifice of the realm of the dead. "Stygian affection" (stanza 3) and "Stygian clamour" (stanza 6)—from the river Styx, in Hades—repeat the motif of the realm of the dead.

The profusion of symbols throughout the poem does not obscure its pure, lyric beauty. "Oh to bring back the shyness of clairvoyant fingers,/ Recognition's rounded happiness!" Somehow, the numbness that has overtaken the persona cannot obliterate the former state of grace in which even his fingers could see and memory connected properly with its original sensation.

Themes and Meanings

"I Have Forgotten the Word I Wanted to Say" is a poem about creation, about the act and paramount importance of creating. "The Word made flesh" is the biblical metonymy for God's most unique creation, His son, Jesus. Also in the Bible, "the Word" was the first, and thus arguably the greatest, thing created by God. In the Russian Symbolist world view, to which Mandelstam ascribed in many respects, the poet is like a god. Although, like any human, the poet is forced to exist in the domain of everyday life, during the act of poetic creation, he or she is lifted above the crowd (as though by the chariot of Plato's *Phaedrus*) to the lofty heights usually accessible only to deities. Losing the ability to create, then, condemns the poet to an earthbound existence with the gray masses, symbolized by the shadows of Hades. There is something godlike in creating with words. There were special reasons, however, that creation was important to Mandelstam—not only because he aspired to attain some exalted status as a god-man.

Expression in the Soviet Union after the Bolshevik Revolution of 1917 was becoming less and less free. Schools of writing were initiated to teach the proper social class, the so-called proletariat, which was often constituted more of agrarian types, the proper production of a new type of literature that was really mythologized propaganda. People were writing panegyrics to Lenin, to socialism, to factories, hydroelectric stations, tractors, combines, collectivization, and the most pedestrian of topics imaginable, which the authorities claimed fulfilled the real mission of literature: to inculcate "correct" culture into the masses. Some poets joined the bandwagon and began writing propagandistic verse, most notably Vladimir Mayakovsky ("Eat your pineapple and chew your veal/ Your end is coming soon, you bourgeois!"). Poets such as Mandelstam were under pressure to conform to this unaesthetic, institutionalized norm. Thus, the symbols of the world of the dead—the shadows or shades of Hades, the river Styx—really symbolize the fate of all expression, the death of the ability to create. Mandelstam's earliest fears were, unfortunately, well-founded. Twelve years after the writing of this poem, he would be arrested for the first time, and four years after that he would die in a transit camp in Siberia.

Creativity is the very essence of life, but it is a latent human talent; creation is its active principle and supplies the necessary vessel for the embodiment of that creativity. The word left unembodied is not a part of a creation; if forgotten, perhaps the word does not exist at all. If kept from writing, perhaps the poet is not alive at all. Mandelstam conveys this damnation poetically: "I have forgotten what I wanted to say/ And a thought without flesh flies back to its palace of shadows."

Christine D. Tomei

I HEARD A FLY BUZZ—WHEN I DIED—

Author: Emily Dickinson (1830-1886)
Type of poem: Dramatic monologue
First published: 1896, as "Dying," in *Poems: Third Series*; collected in *The Poems of Emily Dickinson*, 1955

The Poem

Emily Dickinson did not give titles to most of her poems. They are usually labeled by their first lines, and her modern editor, Thomas H. Johnson, has numbered them according to his conclusions about their order of composition (this poem is numbered 465). Publications of the poem before Johnson's *The Poems of Emily Dickinson* (1955) are usually of the text as it was altered by Mabel Loomis Todd when she published *Poems: Third Series* (1896).

"I heard a Fly buzz—when I died—" consists of four stanzas, with Dickinson's characteristic slant- or near-rhymes in the second and fourth lines of each quatrain. The first-person speaker of the poem is at some remove from Dickinson's lyric voice; these words come from beyond the grave. Dickinson wrote a number of poems from this point of view; perhaps the most famous is "Because I could not stop for Death—" (poem 712). This subject held a particular fascination for Dickinson, in part because she was interested in resolving religious doubts about life continuing after death. In this poem, the dead speaker looks back at the moment of death.

After announcing that she heard a fly buzz when she died, the speaker describes the moments that led up to this event. The first stanza describes the silence of the room before she died as like the quiet between two phases of a storm. The second stanza describes the people present at the deathbed. They are also quiet, exhausted from their watch and preparing now for the final loss. In the third stanza, she says she had just made her last wishes known when the fly "interposed." The last two lines of this stanza begin the long sentence that continues through the final stanza. This sentence describes how the fly seemed to blot out the light, and then all light ceased, leaving her conscious but utterly blinded.

The poem announces at the outset that sound will be important. The middle of the poem emphasizes the silence as temporary, as a fragile period between storms of suffering and weeping. The end of the poem returns to the sound of the fly's buzz, seemingly quiet and inconsequential, not a storm at all and yet marking indelibly the momentous instant of transition.

Forms and Devices

Dickinson's stanza form is not remarkable in itself; indeed, students of her poetry take delight in finding comically inappropriate melodies for singing her poems, the majority of which follow the rhythms of familiar hymn tunes. (This poem, for example, works equally well with "Oh God Our Help in Ages Past" and "The Yellow Rose of Texas.") What makes her stanzas remarkable is the contrast between their conventional rhythms and the striking metaphors, symbols, and points of view they contain. Two complexes of comparison are especially interesting in this work: those conveying the silence before the fly appears and those characterizing the fly.

When Dickinson compares the stillness in the room to the "Stillness in the Air—/ Between the Heaves of Storm," she conveys at least three interesting things about this quiet moment. First, it is a temporary lull that follows violence and is expected to precede more violence. That violence, being associated with a storm, seems to exceed the capacity of a mere room to hold it. By giving the storm "heaves," she begins a second comparison between the storm and weeping. This comparison is taken up in the second stanza by means of synecdoche, in which a part of something is used to signify the whole. She says "The Eyes around—had wrung them dry." Eyes signify the mourners as do the breaths in the following line. Just as the mourners have been heaving in their weeping, their eyes have been wringing themselves dry, like wet cloths, or like clouds in a storm. By this means, Dickinson asks readers to imagine both the room and each individual mourner as filled with a storm of grief that is beyond encompassing. Finally, she reveals that the mourners are awaiting "the last Onset," the image of the storm is extended to the speaker herself, for there is a storm taking place in her as well, a storm of suffering that might also be compared to a battle, in which this lull signals the final, fatal onset.

What is expected next, then, is momentous sound, the climax of mourning, grief, and suffering. When the expectation of painful climax is clear, the poem turns to the idea of compensation or comfort. The second stanza says that when the last onset comes, the "King" will manifest himself. In the conventional view of death in nineteenth century America, that "King" (capitalized for emphasis and to indicate divinity) would be Christ, come to reap the soul of the dying Christian. By not naming this "King" however, Dickinson creates an ambiguity that reverberates through the whole experience of the poem. The figure might just as well be Death as Christ. Furthermore, what actually appears to the dying woman is not any recognizable king at all but a fly.

When the fly appears, a double reversal takes place. The storm metaphor and the expectation of a king lead the reader to anticipate something momentous at the end of the poem. This expectation is answered by the fly. These reversals invite the reader to explore the connections between the fly and the king. Such explorations lead into further shocking violations of expectation regarding meaning in the poem.

By exploring the metaphor of fly as king, one comes to the realization of the fly as a symbol. The best-known "fly king" is Beelzebub, lord of the flies and prince of devils. There is nothing in the poem to suggest that the woman should expect eternal damnation, yet Dickinson seems to have made this connection with its surprising connotations. Furthermore, flies are conventionally associated with death; they swarm on carrion, and their larvae thrive there. The most terrifying possible meaning for a religious person in the substitution of a fly for a king is that death is final, that the soul dies with the body and there is no afterlife.

Dickinson's technique emphasizes the violation of expectations. In addition to the primary substitution (of fly for king), she enacts a similar violation when she rhymes "me" and "fly" in the third stanza, reintroducing the fly with a near-rhyme. Finally, she repeats this pattern by shifting from sound to sight at the end of the poem, when the buzz of the fly seems to blot out the speaker's light so that the windows fail to let light into her room, and her consciousness, still apparently operational, loses its connections by means of sight and sound to the familiar physical world.

Themes and Meanings

Dickinson, like many of her contemporaries in the middle of the nineteenth century, was deeply concerned about the truth of the conventional Christianity taught and generally believed in her culture. Like that of Ralph Waldo Emerson, Nathaniel Hawthorne, and Herman Melville, her religious questioning resulted in part from the general decline of the authority of Christianity in Western civilization. This decline had begun most visibly perhaps with the rise of rivals to the Roman Catholic Church's secular power in nation-states and had continued through the splintering of that church in the Reformation, the intellectual and scientific critique of Christianity's traditional interpretations of history and nature during the Enlightenment, the challenges to Christianity's moral and political power in the American and French revolutions, and the spread of knowledge about powerful rival religious systems partly as a result of advancing world trade and communication.

Many of Dickinson's poems are about the various problems of faith and doubt that would occur to a brilliant and imaginative mind in her culture. This poem is an attempt to pierce through the absolute barrier that stands between the poet and the life beyond death. It attempts to answer the question: What comes in the moment that follows death?

Dickinson places herself in the mind of a woman who has died. She relives the moment of death, trying to imagine it and the hoped-for illumination that should follow. She finds at the instant of death a clarity of perception that she tries to extend through that instant. Yet what her imagination provides at that crucial instant is the fly, which ends illumination and leaves the consciousness in utter darkness.

Nevertheless, consciousness remains. The voice speaks from beyond the grave, but all it can reveal is what its senses could apprehend before death, that instant when the senses ceased to operate. Beyond that is a blank, toward which the fly as a symbol points but about which it reveals nothing but questions: Who is the King? Is it death? Is it Christ? Is it something unimaginably terrifying, like Beelzebub? The fly ushers the poet across the threshold suggested by its "Blue—uncertain stumbling buzz." The fly points the way, but the living cannot interpret its buzz, and her voice stops.

Terry Heller

I KNEW A WOMAN

Author: Theodore Roethke (1908-1963)
Type of poem: Lyric
First published: 1954; collected in *Words for the Wind*, 1958

The Poem

"I Knew a Woman" (along with fifteen other short lyrics) appeared in a section of *Words for the Wind* entitled "Love Poems." This poem was apparently written about the time of Theodore Roethke's marriage to Beatrice O'Connell (a former student of his), and its speaker is a man very much in love and awed by the beauty of the woman he admires so profoundly. The poem concentrates on the erotic and physical but deals also with larger philosophical issues. Its tone is a subtle mix of the comic and the serious.

The poem's metrical pattern is consistently iambic pentameter, but its stanza form is somewhat unusual. Each of the four stanzas consists of seven lines, and the typical rhyme scheme is *ababccc*. Actually the first four lines contain no rhyme at all, but later lines (except for line 21) follow this scheme precisely. This movement from complete lack of rhyme to a very regular rhyme scheme parallels the growing harmony between the two lovers.

Since the poem's first line uses a past-tense verb and refers to bones, some readers have assumed that the central female character is now dead. Such a conclusion is questionable. In this case the verb "knew" surely alludes (in the biblical sense) to specific episodes of sexual intimacy and not necessarily to a relationship that has ended completely. Furthermore, the assertion that the woman was "lovely in her bones" may actually be extravagant praise of her enduring beauty. Such beauty is not only skin deep, and it will abide even if she is, in due time, reduced to a skeleton. Thus the poem is a grand eulogy rather than an elegy.

In its high praise of a beloved woman, the poem recalls numerous English sonnets in the Petrarchan tradition by such authors as Sir Thomas Wyatt, Henry Howard (the earl of Surrey), and Sir Philip Sidney. (In fact, according to lines 5-6 these "English poets who grew up on Greek" might be worthy of singing the "choice virtues" of Roethke's lady.) Just as those poems cataloged the physical traits attributed to the ideal woman (eyes bright as the sun, lips red as rubies, hair shining like gold, cheeks like roses, and so on), Roethke's speaker lists comparable qualities in the one he loves. In stanza 1, for example, this woman's voice is as harmonious as the song of birds, and she moves about with dazzling grace.

Even so, the woman's beauty and erotic allure are not the only subjects of the poem. In stanzas 2 and 3 she becomes also a skilled teacher, schooling the speaker in the ways of love. These lessons in worldly love lead, in stanza 4, to cosmic insights. Through his relationship with this remarkable woman, who lives in total harmony with the natural world, he acquires more profound knowledge about the cycles of life and his own role in a mysterious universe.

Forms and Devices

Roethke's metaphors are rapidly changing and, in some cases, subject to diverse interpretations. In their complexity and extravagance they are akin to the conceits of John Donne and other metaphysical poets. In stanza 2, for example, several capitalized terms ("Turn," "Counter-turn," "Stand," and "Touch") establish a sustained comparison. These terms describe the content of the speaker's lessons in love, and figuratively they suggest movements or positions in a carefully choreographed dance. Dancing is a recurring image in many of Roethke's poems (see, for example, "Four for Sir John Davies"). Here the various stages of the dance imply a graceful movement through seduction to lovemaking.

While Roethke compares lovemaking to dancing, he simultaneously suggests another conceit. The capitalized words denoting dance positions are also technical terms from the sport of coursing, or hunting with hounds. In Roethke's complex metaphor the seductive woman is both the dog trainer and the object of the hunt. She strokes the speaker's chin as the keeper of the hounds might pet a favorite dog. She coyly orchestrates the chase by indicating changes in the direction ("Turn" and "Counter-turn") taken by the hound. In hunting, the term "Stand" denotes the rigid posture of the hound as it locates and points out the quarry, and here the term is also a humorous indication of the speaker's readiness for lovemaking. The term "Touch" denotes the initial contact between hound and quarry, and Roethke uses it to suggest the imminent union of the two lovers. Finally, the speaker nibbles meekly from the woman's hand. Just as a faithful dog might gain a treat from its trainer, the man receives the rewards of love. At several points Roethke's hunting metaphor is sexually suggestive, but its ingenuity prevents it from becoming especially bawdy.

To describe the actual lovemaking, Roethke abandons the hunting conceit and shifts abruptly to an earthy agricultural metaphor. Figuratively the two lovers are now engaged in making hay. The sickle is frequently a grim image associated with death, but here it suggests exuberant life—the woman's erotic power over everything in her path and also perhaps the enticing curves of her body. "Coming behind," the speaker enthusiastically rakes the mown grass. Here the term "rake" is a triple pun—agricultural implement, dissolute male, and (recalling the earlier coursing metaphor) a dog's action of following a trail by keeping its nose to the ground. Mowing, especially in Scottish dialect, is a slang term for sexual intercourse, and Roethke slyly reinforces this double meaning in a later poem entitled "Reply to a Lady Editor." That poem is a comic response to the literary editor of *Harper's Bazaar* who had liked "I Knew a Woman" but apparently failed to comprehend its sexual implications. In the later poem Roethke incorporates more Scottish dialect by calling Cupid a "braw laddie-buck."

Along with extravagant metaphors Roethke uses a number of paradoxical statements. Amid energetic sexual activity he observes in the "several parts" of his partner "a pure repose." Indeed, in line 21 ("She moved in circles, and those circles moved") he suggests that she is like the *primum mobile*. In the old Ptolemaic astronomy the *primum mobile* was the outermost sphere of the universe, which contained all lesser orbits of heavenly bodies and whose revolution was the source of all other celestial movement. By implication then, the woman in the poem is the powerful cause of dramatic action but at the same time she remains the basis of order and stability.

Themes and Meanings

The paradox of the *primum mobile* prepares for a more solemn consideration of the poem's themes in stanza 4. The speaker's union with a remarkable woman is both the means to and a symbol of a higher union. Ultimately carnal knowledge becomes elevated to philosophic insight.

Several of Roethke's love poems portray women as instruments of illumination and salvation. For example, in "The Voice" (placed immediately after "I Knew a Woman" in the *Words for the Wind* collection) the woman is not even present physically. Nevertheless, simply hearing her voice lifts the poet above the level of awareness afforded to most mortals. In "Light Listened" the female character is again a teacher, and when she sings, even the light pays careful attention. In this exaggerated claim that the woman controls light, Roethke implies that she is a crucial source of illumination.

In "I Knew a Woman," just as the act of love fuses the physical and the spiritual, it leads the speaker on to other important harmonies. Well taught by the woman, he is now able to reconcile the temporal and the eternal, tyranny and freedom. By referring to seed, grass, and hay in line 22, the speaker acknowledges the inevitable cycle of birth, life, and death. He is a slave to this grand movement through time just as he is a "martyr" to the alluring motion of the woman who acts as a sickle. In this realization his mood is not mere resignation but eager acquiescence. In slavishly following behind another person, he sacrifices autonomy but gains a larger freedom. In accepting his mortality, he acquires the power to live more fully.

In his newly enlightened state the speaker measures "time by how a body sways." Presumably this body is that of the woman he loves rather than a clock pendulum or a planet in orbit. In short, the woman has completely displaced traditional methods of measuring time. All such conventional guides seem trivial compared to his new source of order and direction.

Two more paradoxical statements in the final stanza reinforce the speaker's bold assertions. In line 25 he affirms that the woman "cast a shadow white as stone." Ordinarily shadows are dark and insubstantial, but this one is strangely bathed in light and solid as a rock. In line 27 he speaks of "old bones" that are alive to continue learning. Though skeletons usually suggest death, these bones are vital and energetic. Having made his peace with mortality, the speaker is now animated by the energy of love.

Albert E. Wilhelm

I KNOW A MAN

Author: Robert Creeley (1926-   )
Type of poem: Lyric
First published: 1957, in *The Whip*

The Poem

There is a deceptive simplicity to many of Robert Creeley's poems which tends to camouflage the power the poet brings to his subject and temporarily delay a full apprehension of the work's psychological penetration. A typical example is "I Know a Man," one of Creeley's most anthologized early lyrics, which is written in the discursive and reflective voice Creeley often uses. Its four stanzas are essentially a continuous expression in which nearly every word is a unit of meaning, its position and location amid punctuation, space, and other words crucial to its purpose.

This poem is an example of "open verse" or "composition by field," which Creeley developed through his friendship and correspondence with Charles Olson; it is employed throughout the poems collected in *For Love* (1962) to permit Creeley an "obsessive confrontation with solipsism" (as Charles Altieri identified it) and an occasion for close scrutiny of the psychological mood of the speaker.

The opening lines, beginning "As I sd to my/ friend," plunge into what appears to be an ongoing dialogue. Although there is a suggestion that the poem is part of a conversation, it is also a version of an inner dialogue in which dual components of the poet's psyche are involved. The ambiguity is introduced in the second stanza when the speaker observes, after what seems like a direct address to his friend—the person called "John"—that it "was not his/ name." When the second stanza asserts that "the darkness sur-/ rounds us," it is evident that this is as much a statement of psychic perception as a literal account of a specific occurrence.

When the poet asks, "what/ can we do against/ it," the second stanza joined to the third by the query, a mood of resignation begins to develop, but it is immediately challenged by a reversal that pivots around the phrase "or else" and abruptly moves toward direct action in the proposal to "buy a goddamn big car." This assertion links the philosophical with the physical, and the bold proposition to do something is both a specific possibility and a figure for choosing to take action. After the word "car," the third stanza concludes with a comma, a more significant pause than the previous connections between stanzas, which lack any punctuation; this sets off the last stanza, making it almost a response to the previous ones.

Once again, the opening line, "drive, he sd," maintains a dual focus, referring both to the "I" who speaks first and the "he" who is the other part of the dialogue. There is a momentary agreement that action is necessary, but this is fractured almost immediately when it become evident that the word "drive" more properly belongs to the "I" who suggests buying the car, while "he" is warning "look/ out where yr going." This admonition to retain an awareness of direction while acting reinforces the initial division in consciousness, but from an altered position.

Forms and Devices

The spare and urgent lyricism, as Charles Molesworth described it, which is the essence of Creeley's style in "I Know a Man," is developed through the employment of a vernacular mode of speech, by the arrangement of this language into tightly controlled rhythmic patterns, and by the organization of these rhythms into a structural frame that permits abrupt changes in psychic mood.

One of Creeley's governing poetic principles is the precept that a poem cannot be arranged in any previously anticipated form, but that its shape develops from the circumstances of its composition. In "I Know a Man," the concise, monosyllabic terseness of the first line establishes a clipped form of utterance in which the weight of each unit of meaning is important. Creeley is particularly attentive to nuances of stress, so that the opening statement moves toward completion in the second line, underscoring the importance of the "friend" who is addressed. The line then continues toward the phrase "I am," intensifying the personal nature of the declaration, a point pushed further by the third use of the word "I" to conclude the stanza. At the same time, the thought is carried directly to the next stanza by the power of the third "I" reaching across the space to the second use of "sd."

This firm control of perspective culminates in the brilliant ambiguity of the last stanza, where, as Creeley has described it, "the poem protects itself" through syntax which compels a reflective consideration of the conclusion:

> why not, buy a goddamn big car,
> drive, he sd, for
> christ's sake, look
> out where yr going.

While it is a legitimate interpretation to regard the directive "drive" as a part of the proposal that "he" has made, as some critics have done, Creeley's explanation that "[i]t's the 'I' of the poem who is saying 'why don't we get out of here' . . . it's the friend who comes into it, who says 'take it easy, look out where you're going,'" shows how concerned he is about carefully controlling meaning. Creeley further observes that he could have placed a period after "drive," but he believed that the "actual impulse" of the poem would eventually make the same point. His constant alertness to the complexity of language is also expressed in his choice of such abbreviations as "sd," "yr," and "&," which help to carry the tension of the speaker's voice throughout the poem, and which are in consonance with the compact nature of the speech as it moves from an arresting hesitancy to impulsive action. The division of the word "sur-/ rounds," with its use of a hyphen, conveys not only the tentativeness of the speaker but also the sense of enclosure from which he is trying to escape.

The third stanza moves toward this escape as the poet considers possibilities. The rapid change of mood is captured by the positioning of the threatening "it, or else," (suggesting unknown danger), followed by the sudden proposal, "shall we," which includes both members of the dialogue. This moves toward the almost manic assurance of "&/ why not," which is followed by the plunge into the specific, "buy a goddamn big car." The success of the poem depends on the relationship of words and on Creeley's sensitivity to the subtlest nuances of pitch, timbre, and sound duration. The absence of metaphor, metrical form, rhyme, figurative language, and other familiar technical devices places the total burden of meaning on word placement.

Themes and Meanings

Robert Hass has described "I Know a Man" as "the poem of the decade about a world gone out of control," while Creeley has spoken of the "senses of confusion and muddiness and opaqueness that people obviously feel in their lives" and which he tried to express in the poem. These insights together represent the dual focus of the poem—it is a reaction to chaos surrounding the poet and a response to the uncertainty that he regards as a prime component of his own psychic makeup. As Charles Altieri has observed, one of Creeley's goals is to construct "an aesthetic space for the multiple facets of the self," and in "I Know a Man," the conversational exchange is both a dialogue with another person and a reflective interior monologue in which alternative courses of action are debated. The friend called "John" is a representative of what Creeley sees as a fixture of friendship, a quality he values, and the phrase "I know a man" is used as a form of compliment that implies the friend's usefulness for both support and caution. In other words, the poet is describing an intimate encounter in which he feels close enough to the "other"—whether an aspect of his mind or an actual person—to share some of his deepest concerns.

The poem approaches the problem of stasis, a condition of dread that requires a bold stroke summoning energy from any available source. The "goddamn big car" is both a literal means of escape and a figure for seizing and using whatever power is accessible. The admonition to "look/ out where yr going" is part of a recognition by the "friend" (or inner voice of conscience) that the impulse to act is very human and must be respected, but that this type of spasmodic action does not really accomplish much.

The uncertainty (as well as the necessity) of the proposed solution is also an aspect of one of Creeley's most crucial aesthetic considerations: the relationship of the poet to his primary instrument, his language. It is through words that the poet attempts to reconcile the conflicting impulses of the self, but the words he uses carry their own inherent ambiguities, their implications of uncertainty. Therefore, just as it is sometimes necessary to "drive" without direction, it is also necessary to begin a poem without any assurance about its conclusion. The driver (or poet) may discover his destination (the poem) in the course of the act of driving (writing). The poet knows that merely getting into a "big car" is not sufficient; it is also crucial to watch "where yr going," and the admonition from the useful "friend" is as much a part of the poet's practice as the commitment to begin the poem to overcome the surrounding darkness. The parallel between writing and driving—an instant-by-instant awareness of where one is, a process requiring constant attention—is part of Creeley's desire to exercise his craft as "an immediate relationship with the experience at hand," as Robert Kern has put it.

The poet is aware that he is "always talking" to combat the darkness, whether his voice is inner or externally directed, but he also knows that he is committed to an ultimately inexact solution. Language itself, the words of the poem, may be a barrier as well as an entrance, and the compulsive speech, replete with self-reflection, may be a kind of overcompensation for this limitation. When the poet says that John "was not his/ name," the poem shifts into a realm composed of words beyond direct connection to the outer world—a form of reality, but one with the potential for further abstraction. In this sense, the closing "look/ out where yr going" has implications for psychic stability that are almost as ominous as encouraging. This is why the friend prefaces it with "for/ christ's sake" and why the entire vehicle seems dangerously close to the edge of disaster.

Leon Lewis

I LIE HERE IN A STRANGE GIRL'S APARTMENT

Author: Richard Brautigan (1935-1984)
Type of poem: Meditation
First published: 1968, in *The Pill versus the Springhill Mine Disaster*

The Poem

Like almost all of Richard Brautigan's poems, "I Lie Here in a Strange Girl's Apartment" is short (three stanzas, fourteen lines) and written in free verse. The title, which is also the first line, not only provides the setting of the poem but also suggests the dynamic that is the subject of the narrator's meditation: the narrator as he sees himself in uncomfortable relation to this "strange" woman. The language of the poem, characteristic of Brautigan's style, is colloquial and deceptively direct—though the final stanza makes it clear that the author's appreciation of the abstract and surreal should not be underestimated, as it tends to vastly complicate otherwise simple images.

The structure of the poem appeals to a kind of minimalism that introduces only what is necessary in order for the payload of the poet's meaning to be delivered to the reader in the most direct, significant, and unburdened fashion. In the first stanza, the narrator presents himself as a man lying (presumably in bed) in the apartment of a woman who is "unhappy." As he watches her move "about the place," he reveals that she has both a sunburn and a poison oak rash. The curious similarity between these two ailments makes it unclear whether she is unhappy because she is afflicted with this double irritation or whether her unhappiness is being characterized by Brautigan's use of the metaphor of the skin conditions. She is clearly uncomfortable. Her unease, Brautigan seems to be suggesting, is akin to the itching experienced with a sunburn or poison oak. She is, as the saying goes, uncomfortable in her own skin. This unease is given greater specificity by the final, more explicit metaphor that closes the first stanza and points to the emotional and psychological breach between the narrator and the woman, who appears to him "distant" and "solemn."

The second stanza implicates the very language of the poem in the ambiguity that characterizes the relationship between the narrator and the woman. The woman's actions are described in both ambiguous terms ("She opens and closes things") and specific terms ("She turns the water on"). But these rather quotidian images give way to the broad and almost overwhelming metaphor of the final stanza, wherein the sounds the woman is making as she moves around the apartment are likened to a distant city populated with people of its own. The enormity of the metaphor for what are the relatively minor sounds of movement in a small apartment suggests that the narrator is at once fixated on the movements of the woman (thus their seeming huge) yet inevitably alienated from them (thus their seeming distant). Indeed, the final metaphor seems to take on a life of its own, dominating the reader's memory of the poem by the vastness of its scope. Readers are left, finally, with not simply the narrator's fixation with this woman but with the image of an entire city of people whose "eyes are filled with the sounds/ of what she is doing."

Forms and Devices

As with many of his contemporaries, Brautigan playfully explores the disparity between poetic devices (such as metaphor) and minimalist description (which eschews such poetic devices) by abutting the two in the same poem. The colorless second stanza avoids poetic imagery altogether, refusing to make the woman's actions any more vivid to the reader. Brautigan resists poeticizing his subject, employing a dull repetition to reinforce the quotidian aspect of the scene: "She turns the water on,/ and she turns the water off." The metaphor of the third stanza, however, achieves an almost absurd extreme of poetic artifice—especially in comparison to the previous stanza. Here Brautigan employs a metaphor that is so broad, so indulgent in its poetic license, that the reader is apt to forget what, exactly, the metaphor refers to by the end of the stanza. Indeed, the final line has the air of a reminder, returning readers to the woman whom they may have let slip from their focus: "Their eyes are filled with the sounds/ of what she is doing." By presenting the reader with two distinct reading experiences—one completely unqualified by metaphor, and the other overwhelmed by it—Brautigan calls into question the uses of the poetic device itself.

Even if the final stanza were to stand on its own, one could not help but notice that Brautigan exerts an extreme degree of pressure on the final metaphorical device. Whereas a metaphor is meant to qualify or elucidate the less obvious layers of significance behind any given object, Brautigan's metaphor goes beyond its object. The metaphor of the city, by employing much more specific and vivid imagery than any found elsewhere in the poem, usurps and dwarfs the significance of the woman's movements by drawing all poetic attention to itself. At first, readers are told simply that the sounds are so far away that they could be in a different city—a simple enough statement, mildly evoking the unprepossessing image of a city. Many poets would end the metaphor here. However, Brautigan goes on to populate and describe the city, telling readers that it is dusk and that people are staring out of their windows in the city. This image removes readers from the initial image of the woman moving around the apartment because they are hard-pressed to understand just exactly how her sounds are *similar* to a city filled with people at dusk. Furthermore, when the connection between the metaphor and its subject is so abstract as to be lost, then the metaphor breaks free of its subject and becomes a subject of its own.

This self-conscious use of poetic devices is characteristic of Brautigan's literary era, the eve of postmodernism, in which writers were less interested in using literary devices invisibly to draw in a reader than they were in focusing the reader's attention on the *process* of the writing itself. A poem that is seemingly "about" a woman in a room turns out, at the end, to be "about" the poetic device of metaphor, its uses, and its abuses.

Themes and Meanings

As with many instances of postmodern literature, this poem blurs the distinction between its "devices" and its "themes." By the end of the poem, the devices *become* the theme; the metaphor, its function, its purpose, its value as a mode of expression, and its effect when taken to its extreme—all of these issues become relevant to Brautigan as a theme of metaphoricity. By giving an example of how a metaphor can get out of control if not used with care, he gives readers both an invitation and an admonition. They are invited to revel in the free-form playground of poetic language and succumb to the temptation of poetry's extremes—and they are warned that if they do so they may lose sight of perhaps more "real" concerns. These other usurped concerns in the poem involve the narrator's relationship with the woman in the apartment.

Brautigan uses language and metaphoricity to emphasize the strained relation between the concrete specificities of the apartment around him and the ambiguous distance he feels between himself and the woman. The narrator feels at once intimate with this woman—even if by simple proximity, one human being to another—yet he is also anxious about the alienation he feels from this "strange girl." He seems, on the one hand, infatuated by the absolute particulars he can glean from the situation: her movements, her discomfort, her sounds, the fact that he is given the opportunity to observe it all so closely. Even though the repetition of her turning the water on and off reinforces the movement's rote plainness (as discussed above), the simple fact of such a mundane action being afforded two whole lines in a short fourteen-line poem validates the action and gives it an magnitude it would not otherwise have. The focus of two lines on her turning the faucet on and off reveals the (appreciative) scrutiny with which he observes her.

On the other hand, the narrator is forced to reconcile the fact that he is a stranger in her daily life; he must come to grips with the fact that as close as he may be in proximity to the movements he so reveres, they are nonetheless foreign to him. Although in intimate quarters, he is so alienated from the sounds of her daily movements that they seem far off. The final image of the poem is a melancholy but reconciled one, as the narrator determines to observe her affectionately even if he must do so from a great distance. Her actions may belong to a different world than his own, they may be so far away as to be in a different city, but whatever city she lives in, all the eyes of that city are fixed on "what she is doing."

Joshua Alden Gaylord

I LIKE TO SEE IT LAP THE MILES—

Author: Emily Dickinson (1830-1886)
Type of poem: Lyric
First published: 1891, as "The Railway Train," in *Poems: Second Series*; collected in *The Poems of Emily Dickinson*, 1955

The Poem

As the title given to it by the first editors of Emily Dickinson's poem suggests, "I like to see it lap the Miles—" is about a train. It was not unusual for Emily Dickinson to write short descriptive poems of this kind, although she more often wrote about natural objects than mechanical ones. In this poem, she uses natural images to describe a thing which is only nearly named in a pun.

Dickinson first describes the thing as if it were like a cat, lapping and licking so many miles like so much milk. When it stops "to feed itself at tanks," however, one must adjust one's image from a household pet to something much larger. The next line reinforces this impression, as this thing is something "prodigious." It is big enough to go around not only one but many mountains in a single "step." When in the second stanza the reader is told that it looks into the windows of houses, one might even imagine a giant leaning down with his eye to a window. In line 8, however, the poem shifts focus from size to power: This thing can "pare" or carve a "quarry" out of rock.

In the first line of the third stanza, one's impression of the largeness of the thing shifts from height to length: It is something that "crawl[s]" and is noisy. In lines 10 and 11, the reader is told that its "complaint[s]" are "horrid" and "hooting," but because its noise is referred to as a "stanza," it is known somehow also to have a poetic or musical quality.

In the last line of the third stanza, the thing once again takes on a kittenish, playful quality—it "chase[s] itself down hill" like a kitten chasing its tail—but then, in the fourth stanza, it takes shape as a horse that "neigh[s]" and returns to its "stable." Here, Dickinson makes a pun: In the nineteenth century, because the railroad had only recently replaced transport by cart horse, the railroad was referred to as the "Iron Horse" and its storage buildings as "car barns." Rather than being a reference to horses, "Boanerges" in the fourth stanza is a name applied to the disciples James and John, who were called "sons of thunder" when they cursed the Samaritans for not believing in the mission of Jesus. Presumably this reference in the poem is to the fearfulness of the thunderous "neigh" of the "Iron Horse."

The movement of the train is like clockwork. A natural image serves to communicate a sense of the mechanical: The train's movements are as regular as those of stars. The image of the shining star also suggests the metallic shininess of the train. At the end of the poem, the train abruptly ends its headlong journey with a "Stop—." When it is still, it seems "docile" and without aggression, but its force is only dormant, because it is still "omnipotent."

Forms and Devices

The poem's four stanzas are quatrains (they are four lines each). The pattern of beats, syllables, and rhymes in each stanza is called ballad meter, because this form is found in most traditional musical ballads: four iambic feet in the first and third line, three iambic feet in the second and fourth line, and a rhyme scheme of *abcb*.

It is difficult to analyze exactly what causes Dickinson's poems to have what one of her editors called a "strange cadence of inner rhythmical music," but one way to approach the matter is to trace the pattern of sounds in her poetry. For example, the consonance that begins with the repetition of certain letters in the first line carries through the entire poem. The repeating *l* of "like," "lap," and "miles" continues through the stanza with "valleys" and "itself"; one also finds it in "pile" and "supercilious" in the second stanza, in "crawl," "all," "while," and "downhill" in the third, and in "punctual," "docile," and "stable" in the fourth.

In each stanza, the words that have approximately the same sound at the end of the second and fourth lines—up/step, peer/pare, while/hill, star/door—are called near-rhymes; they are characteristic of Dickinson's poetry. Moreover, the pair of near-rhymes in the second stanza forms a near-rhyme with the pair in the fourth stanza: Both pairs end with *r* but have different vowel sounds.

Both of these consonants, *l* and *r*, are also part of internal near-rhymes in the second and third stanzas. In line 6, one finds a near-rhyme formed by the second syllable of "supercilious" (*per*) in the middle of the line and "peer" at the end of the line, and in line 5, by the first syllable of "quarry" (*quar*) with "pare." In line 10, there is an internal near-rhyme of "all" with "while," and in line 12, of "-self" with "Hill." The internal rhyme of "lap" in line 1 with the end rhyme of the stanza, "up"/"step," is repeated again with "stop" in line 15. The end consonant of those words also appears at the beginning of the end rhymes of stanza 2.

One finds this same kind of extended repetition with certain vowel sounds (that is, assonance), particularly with the long *i* that appears with the first word in line 1, "I." This sound reappears throughout the poem, with "like" and "miles" in line 1, "pile" in line 5, "sides" in line 9, "while" in line 10, "like" again in line 13, and depending upon how one pronounces it, possibly "docile" in line 15.

The question of how a word is to be pronounced is behind the elusive musiclike quality of the poem. Following a certain sound pattern may call for words to be pronounced one way, while another calls for the same words to be pronounced differently. These various sound patterns pull at individual words—for example, the word "docile": The *i* sound begun in line 1 calls for the second syllable to be pronounced with a long *i*, but the nearer sound of "Hill" calls for the *i* to be short. At the same time, the end sound of "punctual" in the preceding line presses for a *schwa* sound for the vowel.

Themes and Meanings

This economical single-sentence poem manages to propose various images for the locomotive. Some of them are natural, playful, and benign, while others are threatening or overwhelming. Between these two very different representations arises an ambiguity that is one of the themes of the poem.

In one sense, this ambiguity is a question of perspective. Seen from afar, perhaps, the train is a small, toylike thing, but at close range, it is gigantic. To step around piles of mountains is to pass beyond boundaries, which is in a sense to dislocate the horizon. To peer in windows is to intrude past other kinds of boundaries, to cause private life to become public, which is to violate the border between interior and exterior realms. A star is a thing which looks tiny but which science states is in fact huge almost beyond comprehension, so that comparing the locomotive to a star is to make a thing that appeared small and yet became huge seem infinitely small again. The poem, by playing with perspective, reveals the ambiguity that is intrinsic to the seen world.

In another sense, the ambiguity is one of attitude. The beast described does much consuming—it laps, licks, feeds, and pares rocks like vegetables. "Prodigious" is only one step away from prodigality, or excessive consumption. In addition, at the end of its breathless ride, like a horse, it arrives at the stable door, inside which it will presumably be fed. Meanwhile, it is "supercilious," or haughty, and "complain[s]" throughout its journey. The impression created by this series of images is that of a demanding, arrogant taskmaster.

Yet, ironically, the locomotive was invented to serve humanity, not to be served by humanity. So the poem, without explicitly saying so, questions the relationship between humankind and machine. This representation of the railroad as something of potential runaway power is strengthened by the references to the Boagernes, the star, and omnipotence. These images cast the locomotive in the role of a god. It resembles the disciples of Christ; its coincidence with a star associates it with the arrival of a messiah; its all-powerfulness is like God's. Nevertheless, the train is a thing made by humans, not by God, as the many natural objects which represent it are. The problems of perspective which the poem raises call into question humankind's ability to see accurately at all and thus to know enough to undertake such creations.

The poem exaggerates this uncertainty by expressing itself in metaphors—images which are understood to portray a subject not explicitly but by suggestion. At the same time that the poem questions the wisdom of such creations as locomotives, however, it is itself a creation. Therefore, the subtle monstrosity of the poem—its shifting, protean metaphors—comes to mirror the possible monstrosity of its subject, and the presumption of divinity on the part of the inventors of the railroad is the same presumption claimed by the poet.

Laurie Glover

I MARRIED

Author: Lorine Niedecker (1903-1970)
Type of poem: Lyric
First published: 1976, in *Blue Chicory*

The Poem

"I married" is short and untitled; by convention, it is referred to by its first line. The simple declaration of the opening line is followed by a stanza break, and then by twenty short lines arranged in four stanzas. Though this is a free-verse lyric, the third and fourth lines of each stanza are linked by a rhyme or near-rhyme. Sometimes the focus of the poet's attention shifts dramatically within a given stanza, as well as from one stanza to the next.

In the first stanza, Lorine Niedecker speaks of her motivation for marrying—she sought a refuge of human kindness in a world whose deplorable condition she characterizes as a state of "black night." She next says that she expected "warmth" from her marriage but could not realistically hope for "repose." In this context, "warmth" is also something one desperately seeks in the face of a society that is "cold" like nighttime, and "repose" is something that is difficult to come by in a world that seems organized for the benefit of evildoers, just as nightfall is the time when criminals gain advantage and malevolent supernatural spirits are thought to stir. Niedecker concludes the stanza by noting that "at the close" she has found a companion. She was indeed sixty years old in 1963, when the marriage she speaks of took place.

In the second stanza, one gains a clearer sense of "the world's black night." Here Niedecker speaks of herself and her husband seeking shelter from "the long range guns." This phrase is packed with menacing significance. It suggests the deadly trajectory of a long-range nuclear missile launched at a target from somewhere far across the planet. It also evokes the wounding of concerned and knowledgeable persons by their awareness of armed conflicts occurring in other parts of the globe. Finally, the poet may be thinking of the electronic mass media: the television and radio stations that send their signals across long distances in every direction, seeking to addict as many people as possible to their inane offerings. The conclusion of the stanza turns from this evocation of violence and manipulation to another matter—it comments, amusingly, on the cramped condition of the apartment shared by the poet and her husband.

The opening of the third stanza speaks of "A slit of light/ at no bird dawn—." The first line evokes the stripe of brightness visible on the horizon at daybreak, but this dawn, presumably in winter, is unaccompanied by the delight offered by a chorus of birds. This suggests a moment when one feels a sense of spiritual renewal that is not as sweet as one had anticipated such a moment might be. Niedecker is telling readers that such vivifying, if not totally radiant, moments are typical of her marriage. The stanza then veers toward another consideration—the poet discusses the history of her attitude toward her husband's drinking habits.

In the final stanza, Niedecker builds on the poem's opening declaration to state that "I married/ and lived unburied." That is to say, the marriage has helped her to avoid sinking into a demoralized state of half-deadness. The poem ends not with this conclusive-sounding sentence, but rather with the enigma of the broken-off statement, "I thought—."

Forms and Devices

"I married" is a challenging poem—it forces one constantly to maintain one's interpretive alertness, and one may be puzzled or even exasperated by its sometimes quirky movement from subject to subject. If one listens well to Niedecker's tone, one finds that it is also an engagingly friendly poem, for it radiates a feeling of candid and calm personal revelation, in which there is self-assurance without a trace of pompous self-importance, and meditation without brooding or abstraction.

Avoiding any theatrical outcries or effusions, the poet speaks quietly of the renewal she gained from her marriage and displays unembittered acceptance of the inherent limitations of human relationships and lives. Even wrenching societal horror is addressed in a calm manner. The poem's tone of amiable stillness and strength can be seen in the following lines:

> for warmth
> if not repose
> At the close—
> someone.

The phrase "at the close" speaks of a potentially devastating fact: not having many more years to live. Yet these lines are arranged for the word "close" to be lightened by fitting into a cheerful rhyme. If one pronounces the lines aloud, one rushes eagerly to this rhyme once one has spoken the word "repose," for "at" and "the" are not syllables the tongue lingers over. One feels that Niedecker is facing her advanced age without terror.

There are odd shifts of attention in "I married" and sections that seem only loosely connected to the themes of the whole. Listening to the rhythms and other sonic aspects of the poem is relevant to this concern also; one perceives that, as in an excellent piece of music in which each passage grows logically from the notes that precede it, each moment of the poem sounds as if it fits exactly where it is. This tends to wear down any resistance one might have to the way the poem is constructed.

If one shifts one's attention from sound to meaning, resistance is also challenged by the vibrant nature of each portion of the poem. The passage about living in unroomy lodgings charms with its comical exaggeration, and when Niedecker writes

> Untaught
> I thought
> he drank
>
> too much,

the phrase "too much," isolated after the pause of a skipped line, links with the previous words of the sentence in two different ways. The sentence can mean, "Inexperienced, I thought he drank excessively," and, less obviously, "Inexperienced, I thought too much about his drinking." Both meanings are intended. The double duty performed by the simple words "too much" is an example of the condensed nature of Niedecker's poetry. She saw the compression of much meaning into few words as central to her poetic activity.

From beginning to end, "I married" is terse in its expression. One may note especially, however, the way in which the phrase "long range guns" encapsulates various frightening realities, and the curious manner in which the compact phrase "no bird dawn" is crafted by wrenching the noun "bird" into adjectival usage.

Themes and Meanings

"I married" sets its love story against the backdrop of a tragically unenlightened human race whose actions allow the "long range guns" to gather strength. Reference has already been made to the phrase "long range guns" as pointing both to warfare and to the broadcasts of the mass media. This interpretation may seem far-fetched; however, turning to other works of Niedecker, one finds that she often takes note of radio and television, sometimes quite negatively. In "Alone," for example, she celebrates being without a television set with the statement, "At last no (TV) gun." The gun metaphor in "Alone" refers to the way in which the public uses electronic entertainment as a weapon against meditation, anxieties, and other things it wishes to avoid.

Niedecker states in "I married" that her relationship to her husband has brought her much of the comfort she had sought. She speaks of the somewhat disappointing but still invigorating "dawn" moments and states near the end of the poem about eluding, through her marriage, a "buried" feeling of death in life.

In the latter passage, there is also another possible meaning: When Niedecker states, "I married/ and lived unburied," she can be seen as expressing thanks that the marriage itself has not crushed her spirit. The tangles and perils that must accompany the attempt to mingle two human lives are an important concern of this poem. The passage about drinking can be viewed as relevantly exhibiting one of the tangles of Niedecker's married life.

This leads, finally, to a possible added significance of the passage about "a slit of light." In addition to the meaning already discussed, Niedecker indicates in these lines that her dawnlike moments of spiritual renewal, and her experiences of literal sunrises, cannot be characterized as "bird dawn[s]," because she cannot feel the simple elation one imagines a bird to experience when it senses sunlight or otherwise feels invigorated. Her happiness, like her other emotions, can only be human and complex, intertwined with intellectual conceptions and the details of a complicated life.

Stephen M. Baraban

I, MENCIUS, PUPIL OF THE MASTER . . .

Author: Charles Olson (1910-1970)
Type of poem: Dramatic monologue
First published: 1954; collected in *The Distances*, 1960

The Poem

"I, Mencius, Pupil of the Master . . ." is a long, open-form poem in three major sections containing twenty-five stanzas. The entire poem comprises eighty-four lines of various length. Understanding the title is crucial in detecting the voice, theme, and tone of this challenging poem. Assuming the persona of an earlier poet is a technique that Charles Olson, one of contemporary America's first postmodernist poets, used throughout his controversial career. In this poem, he speaks through the persona of Mencius (372-289 B.C.E.), a devoted follower of the great Chinese philosopher Confucius (551-479 B.C.E.) and author of *The Book of History*, in which he set out the Confucian rules for a "benevolent government." First and foremost, great rulers must be men of virtue.

In the voice of Mencius, Olson scolds his poetic master, Ezra Pound. The occasion for Olson's outrage was the publication of Pound's translation of one of the most venerated books of Chinese poetry, *The Book of Odes* (poetry written between 1000 and 700 B.C.E.). Confucius himself had gathered the 305 poems that made up *The Book of Odes*. What provoked Olson's anger was that Pound translated them into ballads, an archaic form of English poetry in regular meter, rhyme, and stanzaic form. Ironically, it had been Ezra Pound himself who helped formulate the rules for a fresh kind of poetry called Imagism, rejecting what he considered the worn-out poetic tradition of Victorian and early twentieth century English poetry.

One of the tenets of Imagism required that a poem's rhythm be based "in the sequence of the musical phrase, not in the sequence of the metronome." Pound also laid down directives for using rhythm: "Don't chop your stuff into separate iambs. Don't make each line stop dead at the end, and then begin every next line with a heave." Pound had derived the clarity of Imagist poetry from Chinese and Japanese art and poetry, and when his translation of ancient Chinese poetry into the rigid structures of traditional English ballads appeared, Olson was incredulous. Olson embodied that rigidity in the image of Pittsburgh, the seat of the American steel industry and, more specifically, in the rails of the railroads which covered and violated the American landscape. Olson compares the "clank" of the locomotives' wheels to the "clank" of the regular rhythms, rhymes, and couplets of an exhausted literary tradition: "We do not see/ ballads."

Forms and Devices

The major structural device Olson uses throughout the poem is juxtaposition. In all three parts he juxtaposes the fallen world of technological violation (such as the steel

mills of Pittsburgh and the Bremerton Shipyards) to the clarity of the world of James
Whistler, whose paintings had been affected by Japanese and Chinese art and whose
influence had spread to Pound himself: "Whistler, be with America/ at this hour."
Olson also juxtaposes the image of the whorehouse (the product of an inhumane industrial system) to the palace, representing the innocent world of Mencius. Pound's
balladizing of *The Chinese Odes* was mere "decoration" rather than "presenting the
image accurately," which was the chief aim of the Imagist poets. Olson also juxtaposes the open structure of part 3, with images positioned all over the page, to some of
the closed, clotted stanzas of parts 1 and 2.

In the seventh stanza of part 1, Olson replaces the word "clank" with "Noise!" and
then scolds his master Pound for betraying his original project:

> . . . he
> who taught us all
> that no line must sleep,
> that as the line goes so goes
> the Nation! that the Master
> should now be embraced by the demon
> he drove off! O Ruler.

Olson puns on the word "lines," referring to the poetic line, which pound had emanci-
pated from traditional restrictions and then returned to its former constraints in his
translation of *The Odes of Confucius*. Olson demonstrates the power of presenting the
image accurately in the second half of part 1: "that what the eye sees,/ that in the East
the sun untangles itself/ from among branches." Olson had learned from Pound, his
master, that the greatest accomplishment of Imagist poetry was to give the reader a direct and sensuous experience of reality.

Olson also used the poetic device of apostrophe to address Walt Whitman, the great
American bard who broke all the rules:

> o Whitman,
> let us keep our trade with you when
> the Distributor
> who couldn't go beyond wood,
> apparently,
> has gone out of business.

Olson criticizes Pound for forgetting what he had learned from Whitman's use of free
verse and for not being able to move beyond the Sacred Wood, the central metaphor of
Pound's early book of literary essays, *The Spirit of Romance* (1910). That book
placed the beginning of European civilization in the pastoral works of ancient Greece
and Rome, a view Olson found too limited in scope.

Part 3 begins with the pronoun "we," referring to those poets of Olson's circle who
refused to revert to the regressive pastoralism of romantic ballads: "We'll to these
woods/ no more, where we were used/ to get so much." Olson then brings in the image

of the dance, a favorite of Pound's, and refers to his former master as "Old Bones." "[D]o not try to dance," he advises, "the Charleston/ is still for us." In other words, the old traditional dances are no longer relevant (they are literally "still") for the genuinely new poetry and its practitioners. Pound had become an "Old Bones" or mere observer of the emerging poetics of process which he began and to which he had led Olson: "we are the process/ and our feet," feet here meaning an open-form poetry that does not confine poetic feet to the rules of regular rhyme and rhythm. Olson separates himself and his fellow poets from old forms: "We do not march"—"march" referring both to rigid rhythms and to moving in lockstep without imagination. Words such as "roads," "rails," "march," "clank," "noise," "ruler," and "ballads" become cumulative metaphors for an overindustrialized, life-denying culture built on dead traditions that impede the growth of new poetry.

Themes and Meanings

"I, Mencius, Pupil of the Master . . ." is from *The Distances* (1960), Charles Olson's first major collection of poems. Many of the poems in this collection deal with one of Olson's major themes throughout his writing career; the distance or alienation of human beings from anything that comes between them and their direct experience of reality. Olson's most beloved quotation was from Heraclitus, the pre-Socratic Greek philosopher: "Man is estranged from that with which he is most familiar." That is the major theme of "I, Mencius, Pupil of the Master. . . " Furthermore, Olson's greatest inspiration was Ezra Pound, whose early poetry cleansed the English language of empty abstractions. Pound's dictum "Go in fear of abstractions!" helped formulate the rules for Imagism which, when followed, would give modern poetry the clear, revelatory quality of Chinese and Japanese poetry and art. "Images in verse are not mere decoration, but the very essence of an intuitive language," asserted one of the other founders of Imagism, T. E. Hulme. Hulme also wrote that the best poetry "endeavors to arrest you, and to make you continuously see a physical thing, to prevent you gliding through an abstract process."

This poem expresses Olson's outrage that his old mentor had rejected the very rules that he helped formulate and violated the clarity and simplicity of the venerable *Odes of Confucius* by reducing them to "coolie verse." That, for Olson, was a sacrilegious act and returned poetry to the "clank" and "noise" of old, depleted forms. Olson's use of the persona and voice of Mencius gives the poem even greater thematic impact and underscores Olson's sense of betrayal.

According to Olson, Pound, by joining with the reactionary enemies of art and poetry, shared the same mentality that created the dark satanic mills (to echo William Blake's phrase) of Pittsburgh Steel and the Bremerton Shipyards. Pound had produced "the dross of verse." In returning to an enervated tradition, Pound had betrayed his original definition of virtue: to restore human beings to that with which they are most familiar, their own sense of themselves responding to the vividness of a life of the senses and, thus, an intensification of objective reality. The second word in the poem, and the most important, is "dross," which literally means the waste product on the surface of molten steel but also echoes Pound's use of it in his most famous poem, *Pisan Canto 81:* "What thou lovest well remains, the rest is dross/ What thou lovest well shall not be reft from thee/ What thou lovest well is thy true heritage." By alluding to one of Pound's most famous lines, Olson shows how far he had fallen from his earlier position as the major defender and practitioner of a new kind of poetry intended to restore poetry to the freshness of original perception, unencumbered by the useless "decoration" of dead forms.

Patrick Meanor

I REMEMBER GALILEO

Author: Gerald Stern (1925-   )
Type of poem: Meditation
First published: 1981, in *The Red Coal*

The Poem

Gerald Stern's poem "I Remember Galileo" is composed of two twelve-line free-verse stanzas in which Stern contrasts Galileo's image of the mind as a "piece of paper blown around by the wind" with his own preferred image of the mind as a squirrel narrowly escaping death on the highway. The poem exhibits Stern's characteristic expansiveness (he is often compared to the nineteenth century American poet Walt Whitman) and humor, but in the end his point is serious as he applauds the squirrel's insistent race to save his life (Stern appoints a masculine gender to the animal) instead of the paper's random blowing.

Stern begins the poem by describing the piece of paper as Galileo saw it, "blown around by the wind," an image he once found appealing, evidently in part because of its randomness. The implications of the metaphor for the mind are suggestive. Galileo says that the mind, like the paper, is subject to random forces outside itself, forces that take it into unpredictable places. That unpredictability is evident in the places Stern once imagined the paper—against a tree, in a car, in various cities. (Although the speaker of a poem should not necessarily be confused with the poet, in Stern's work his voice is often so personal, as here, that the idea of a persona widely removed from the poet himself seems unnecessarily artificial.) Stern says he was satisfied with the comparison for years, but he has come to prefer another metaphor instead.

His new preference is for a squirrel like one he saw "crossing/ Route 80 between the wheels of a giant truck." The squirrel escaped death under the truck's wheels, though Stern describes the way the animal's life must surely have been shortened "by all that terror." In the second stanza Stern amplifies the significance of the squirrel as an image for the mind, noting especially his speed, "his lowness to the ground,/ his great purpose and the alertness of his dancing" as the qualities that distinguished the squirrel from the paper. The paper, Stern says, "will do in theory," but the living animal is what is needed "for this life." At the poem's end, Stern leaves his usual conversational voice briefly to apostrophize "O philosophical mind, O mind of paper" and then explains to that mind his need for the squirrel and his "wild dash."

Throughout the poem Stern moves easily from serious commentary to a sort of humorous exaggeration (as in the description of the squirrel's fear at his narrow escape) and finally, as in the last three lines, to a higher level of lyricism as he praises the squirrel's intensity. That intensity is what makes the squirrel an appealing image for what Stern admires in the mind; it chooses where it will go instead of being blown randomly into cars and trees.

Forms and Devices

Stern is a free-verse poet; he does not use conventional forms, and his use of traditional figures of speech is sparse. In this poem he creates a stanza break, not so much to contrast the idea of the paper with the squirrel but instead to use the second stanza to define and amplify exactly what about the squirrel resembles the mind.

The conversational tone with which Stern begins is typical of his work; he sounds as if he is continuing a conversation he has already begun with the reader. Throughout most of the poem his diction is colloquial, the ordinary language of conversation among educated people, thus supporting the conversational tone. Even the first figure of speech, the simile of mind and paper, is introduced quite matter-of-factly. Stern recalls what Galileo said about mind being like "a piece of paper blown around by the wind," asserts that he "loved the sight of it," and imagines the places the paper might blow—a tree, "the backseat of a car." At last, with an air of exaggeration, he claims that for years the paper would "leap" through his cities.

The next simile is Stern's own, the comparison of the mind to a squirrel. Stern locates the squirrel precisely; it is on Route 80 and caught "between the wheels of a giant truck." Stern compares the squirrel's indecisive darting to "a thin leaf,/ or a frightened string," but in fact the scene is one that almost everyone has seen—a squirrel wavering in his own misjudgment about the speed of oncoming traffic, darting now in one direction, now another.

Although Stern is present as observer and recorder through most of this poem, at this point he views the situation from the squirrel's point of view, imagining how terror has shortened his life, has even caused "his yellow teeth" to be "ground down to dust" (perhaps another exaggeration).

The second stanza explains why the animal seems a more satisfactory mind-model than the paper. Paper, Stern says, is for theory, "when there is time/ to sit back in a metal chair and study shadows." Yet life is not carried out in the metal office chairs of theory; the squirrel's speed and intensity at this crucial moment of his life are what move Stern, "his great purpose and the alertness of his dancing." Stern goes on to describe how the threat of death electrifies the squirrel and makes his life somehow more vivid. At that point Stern indents a line and, in the last three rather Whitmanesque lines, addresses the "philosophical mind" of paper, telling it that he needs not it but the squirrel, which seems now to represent raw energy as he makes the dash which saves his life and lets him run "up his green ungoverned hillside," a free being who has gambled for his own fate.

Themes and Meanings

A Zen parable tells of a man who has fallen off a cliff; he clings to the side of a steep precipice by holding onto a single root. If he lets go, he will fall to his death. If he scrambles back up to the top, a ferocious tiger waits to devour him. Suddenly he notices a single strawberry growing from the cliffside near his face. Cautiously he uses one hand to pick and eat the berry: How sweet it tastes!

The speaker of the parable uses it to suggest how intense life and its experiences can seem when one is in mortal danger. Because, as philosophers have often noted, no one leaves this world alive, there is a sense that all people are in mortal danger. Like Stern's squirrel, each person may sense that at any moment he or she could be flattened by huge truck wheels. This seems to be what Stern is suggesting when he says that he wants the squirrel-mind, not the paper-mind.

Significantly, the squirrel's experience is not a pleasant one. Trapped in terror on the highway, he braces for death or escape with "his clawed feet spread, his whole soul quivering." The effects of the truck are not simply philosophical, perhaps not philosophical at all; they are thoroughly physical. The little animal's hair is blown by the engine's hot wind; its loud noise shakes his entire being. This is the sort of engagement Stern prefers to the passivity of the paper, which is blown around the landscape with no sense of itself. Like the paper, the squirrel is subject to forces outside himself, forces beyond control, but unlike the paper, the squirrel can recognize his own dangerous situation and make a bid to save himself. The danger calls into action all his "great purpose and the alertness of his dancing." This is the significance of the poem's last three lines in which the poet uses a bardic voice to say that he needs the squirrel whose "wild dash" ends with his "rushing up his green ungoverned hillside," a hillside that is the color of life and which, like life itself, Stern implies, cannot be governed.

The twentieth century American novelist and philosopher Walker Percy explored the implications of a common phenomenon—in times of great crisis people often seem to rise above their ordinary dull concerns to new heights of understanding and experience. They may treat each other with generosity, even with heroism. In the aftermath of hurricanes, in the midst of life-threatening disease, people may suddenly recognize that their own actions can give meaning to life even if they cannot extend it. That is the existential crisis in which the squirrel finds himself, and the green field to which he escapes is like the strawberry of the Zen parable, all the sweeter for being snatched out of peril.

Ann D. Garbett

I SAW IN LOUISIANA A LIVE-OAK GROWING

Author: Walt Whitman (1819-1892)
Type of poem: Lyric
First published: 1860, as "Calamus.20," in *Leaves of Grass*, 3d ed.; 1867, as "I Saw in Louisiana a Live-Oak Growing," in *Leaves of Grass*, 4th ed.

The Poem
"I Saw in Louisiana a Live-Oak Growing" is a short lyric poem made up of thirteen lines of free verse (verse written in no traditional meter). The speaker of the poem may be identified with the poet or at least with "Walt Whitman," as the reader comes to know him in *Leaves of Grass*, the book in which this poem appears. The poem begins with a memory: The poet remembers the live oak tree he saw standing by itself in Louisiana, whose "rude" and "lusty" look reminded the poet of himself. In one important respect, however, the tree was very different from the poet, for the tree was "uttering joyous leaves" even though it stood without another of its kind (a "companion") nearby, and this is something that the poet knew he could never do. That the tree was in Louisiana may have some autobiographical significance: Whitman, who lived most of his life in New York and New Jersey, spent some time in Louisiana. In any case, the live oak flourishes in Louisiana, and the geographical reference grounds the poem in fact. The poet is speaking of a real tree he actually saw rather than of a metaphor for his feelings.

In speaking of the tree as "uttering" its leaves, Whitman uses a word that is perfectly appropriate on a literal level. In this context, "utter" can simply mean to "put forth" or "sprout." However, since the word is more commonly used to describe human speech and since Whitman habitually refers to his poems as "leaves" (as in the title *Leaves of Grass*), the word implies more. The tree that "utters . . . leaves" is an image not only of the man but also of the poet. The poet tells the reader that he broke a twig from the tree and that he now keeps the twig, with a little moss tied around it, in his room, where it remains a curious token. Its purpose is not to remind him of his friends because, he reveals, he thinks of little else. Rather, it stands for manly love or the love of man for man. Yet the phrase is ambiguous. A reader might take "manly love" to mean the love a man may feel for a woman. Whitman probably accepted, even intended, the ambiguity.

The poem's last lines return to the theme of the opening. In this restatement, the live oak's isolation is still more strongly emphasized: "solitary/ in a wide flat space." The phrase "friends and lovers," uniting two forms of human relationship in one grammatical unit, appears for the first time. Furthermore, the poet is again in awe at the memory of the tree "uttering joyous leaves" in its isolation. The poet's response is reaffirmed in the last line of the poem: "I know very well I could not." For the poet, then, it is in the presence of companions, friends, and lovers that he finds the inspiration to utter his leaves; for the man, to be isolated from those he loves would cause him pain beyond his powers of expression.

Forms and Devices

Whitman was a pioneer in the development of free verse, but, as any experienced reader knows, successful free verse is never really free. Free of meter (the regular distribution of stresses across a line that dominated English verse from the Renaissance to Whitman's time and beyond), free verse must find its own principles of rhythm. A number of qualities contribute to the overall rhythm of Whitman's verse. Two of these are line length and syntax. Using the syllable as the unit of measurement, the reader can find in the poem a rhythm of expansion and contraction. The first line is shorter than any other line except for the last. The longest lines, the fifth and sixth, are followed by three relatively short lines of fifteen syllables each. Line 10 expands to twenty syllables, line 11 to twenty-five. Line 12 contracts to seventeen syllables, leading to the eight syllables of the eloquently concise last line.

Syntax also contributes to rhythm. Each line is capable of standing alone as at least a complete sentence, and line 11 could be written as two sentences. Yet only line 11 ends with a full stop of any kind, and the first period appears only at the end of the poem. The result is a rhythmically significant tension between sense and sound as the punctuation forbids the major pause at the end of the line that the sense would seem to call for. Syntactical subtleties also produce effects beyond the rhythmic. An air of straightforward simplicity is suggested by the repeated use of the simple past tense in the early lines of the poem. Yet the subjects of these verbs shift from "it," a pronoun whose antecedent is "live-oak," through "moss" and "its look" to "I," defining the progression of the poet's thought. Furthermore, while the last lines restate the theme of the opening, what had been in the past ("stood") is now in the present ("glistens"). An experience of the past transcends temporal categories to live in the present of the poet's, as well as the reader's, imagination.

Themes and Meanings

What one takes to be the meaning of this poem depends, in part, on context. To a reader not otherwise familiar with Whitman's work, it seems to be a reflection on the relation of the natural and human, with a special bearing on the artistic. While the tree utters its leaves regardless of the absence of companions, the human consciousness requires human companionship to inspire it to creativity. Readers who are familiar with *Leaves of Grass*, however, and specifically with "Calamus," the section (or "cluster") of the book in which the poem is found, will be aware of further implications. "Calamus" immediately follows "Children of Adam," a cluster dealing with what Whitman calls "amativeness" or the love between men and women. The organizing theme of "Calamus" is "adhesiveness" or male comradeship. Readers are increasingly inclined to read "Calamus" as an expression of the poet's homoerotic inclinations, but it seems that few of Whitman's contemporaries read it that way. To most of its nineteenth century readers, "Calamus" moved beyond the sexual concerns of "Children of Adam." In fact, some readers were scandalized by "Children of Adam," but "Calamus" seems to have raised scarcely an eyebrow during Whitman's lifetime. While later critics are prepared to ridicule the naïveté and bad faith of nineteen century readers, those are the readers Whitman knew. If one attempts to read these poems as one of Whitman's contemporaries might have, the emphasis on relationships between men is not necessarily homosexual. For these readers, relationships between men are simply not sexual. Thus, these poems are about the spiritual dimensions of human experience, taking the reader beyond the physical and implying the judgment that the spiritual is "higher" than the physical.

Any interpretation of poetry reflects the worldview of the interpreter. More than a century has passed since Whitman's death, and in that time American culture has come to question hierarchies such as the one valuing the spiritual over the physical; it has also come to place the sexual much closer to the center of human experience than Whitman's contemporaries would have. Whether this has been, on the whole, for better or worse, it may have brought readers closer to the personal feelings and values of Whitman. For more recent readers, the poems of "Calamus" derive much of their emotional energy from the sexual longings of the poet, which seem to have been toward members of his own sex.

The "manly love" of "I Saw in Louisiana a Live-Oak Growing" is thus the love (including, even if not limited to, the sexual) of man for man. No reading that denies that is likely to be accepted today by sophisticated readers. Does this mean that the poem affirms that poetry is based on homosexual love? It seems, rather, to suggest that poetry is inspired by the poet's deepest and most authentic feelings, whatever value the surrounding society may place on those feelings. For Whitman, these are the feelings of a homosexual man, and it is not difficult to see a symbol of male sexuality in the twig around which a little moss is twined. Yet the poem is not, in any reductive sense, about sex; the longing that drives the poem is linked to the artistic creativity of which the poem is an emblem. Further, the authentic feelings of a heterosexual man or of a heterosexual or homosexual woman are equally powerful sources of inspiration. What kills creativity, the poem suggests, is inauthenticity, the denial of oneself and of one's feelings. This, rather than mere physical separation from other people—there is no lover present as the poet speaks—is perhaps, at the deepest level, what would prevent the poet from uttering his leaves.

W. P. Kenney

I SING OF OLAF GLAD AND BIG

Author: E. E. Cummings (1894-1962)
Type of poem: Elegy
First published: 1931, in *W: Seventy New Poems*

The Poem

According to Richard S. Kennedy's biography of E. E. Cummings, *Dreams in the Mirror* (1982), "i sing of Olaf glad and big" grew out of Cummings's experience at Camp Devens, Massachussetts, shortly after he was drafted into the Army in July of 1918. Cummings's memories of the camp remained vivid until he composed a collection of poetry entitled *W* for "ViVa," meaning "long live," which was published in October, 1931. The book began darkly, dealing satirically with the sordidness of the world, and ended more happily, with an emphasis on the earth and lyrical love poems.

This poem, one of the satires, is number 30 in the series; it has a strongly negative emphasis. Usually considered the most hard-hitting antimilitary piece written by Cummings, it is based on his brief acquaintance with one soldier at Camp Devens who shared his disgust for violence and his unwillingness to participate in war or to use a gun. After a confrontation with the commanding officer, Olaf (not his real name) was seen no more, but rumor persisted that he had been transferred to the Army prison at Fort Leavenworth and would be brutalized for his pacifistic stance.

The poem consists of seven stanzas of inconsistent length, and it praises those individuals whose conscience compelled them to resist war and its destruction. The poem's beginning parallels the *Aeneid* (c. 29-19 B.C.E.), in which Vergil sings of arms and the man. Olaf is a new kind of personal and private hero who refuses to merge his will with the gods and persists in maintaining a gentle and patient rather than warlike attitude. Nevertheless, Olaf cannot be classified as passive, since he combats his ignoble humility with brutal obscenities, invectives that his tormentors will understand. The poem offers an alternative to violence: the heroic value of moral strength. This strength allows Olaf to achieve epic stature even when his torturers try to strip him of the last vestige of human dignity. These attempts to destroy him are countered by Olaf's love and courage, traits which are misinterpreted by the masses as weakness or cowardice.

The poem closes by forcing the reader into more intense involvement with Olaf and a recognition that Olaf's plight is a universal dilemma. If the qualities that society prizes are epitomized in the poem's officers and noncoms, readers will no doubt see more value in Olaf's renunciation of renown, reputation, and life in the face of their repressive actions. His courage allows him to die not for a cause, but because of a cause, not for his country but because of his country. The value of individualism and integrity is stressed, and Cummings's humorous contempt for the military establishment reiterates his approval of nonconformity, both in life and on the printed page.

Forms and Devices

E. E. Cummings's work is characterized by unorthodoxy, invention, and especially by experimentation with language. Some of the unusual writing techniques normally present in Cummings include pun, paradox, inversion of cliché, grammatical turning, and typographical experiments. The purpose of these techniques is their immediacy of effect: Cummings wishes to surprise the reader into a new and unique vision about the topic under discussion.

Several evidences of Cummings's unorthodoxy are evident in "i sing of Olaf glad and big." Cummings avoids traditional capitalization. The narrative "i" is in lower case to indicate his own humility, while the importance of Olaf is indicated by the fact that each "I" referring to him is capitalized.

Word choice is yet another indicator of Cummings's refusal to follow the norm. For example, there is formal speech ("being of which/ assertions duly notified," lines 34-35) which is appropriate for legal documents, while there are also colloquialisms such as "yellowsonofabitch." Obscenities seem to be included for shock value, yet there are also archaisms which seem out of place in a modern poem.

Syntactical changes exemplify Cummings's unique approach to poetry. The most obvious is the reversal of the common "noun, verb, direct object" pattern to noun, direct object, verb, or direct object, noun, verb. Examples of such inversions include "officers// their passive prey did kick and curse" (lines 22-24) and "Christ . . ./ i pray to see" (lines 38-39). Cummings also uses redundancies, "bayonets roasted hot with heat" (line 30); shift in parts of speech by adding adverbial suffixes, "preponderatingly" (line 40); and words broken into component parts, "object-or" (line 3) to draw attention to his message. Typographically, he removes spacing to increase speed and indicate mood. The technique appears in line 5, "westpointer"; line 27, "firstclassprivates"; and line 36, "yellowsonofabitch."

Several puns appear in this poem as well, including "grave" (line 20) and "firstclassprivates" (line 27). In addition to their regular definitions of "serious" and "military rank," the words also suggest death and sexual organs, respectively, expanding their potential meanings.

Finally, Cummings's unusual use of punctuation—semicolons, commas, and colons—allows him to control where his readers pause and how long they meditate on a certain idea. Yet despite these nonconformist features, the poem utilizes a traditional rhythm (iambic tetrameter) and a traditional rhyme scheme.

Cummings thus combines experimentation with traditionalism, exploring new uses of typography, syntax, ellipses, and visual arrangements while retaining relatively normal rhythm and rhyme. The resulting tension in form and style parallels the situation depicted in the text, pitting the individual against society, peace against violence, and nonconformity against conformity. This merger of methodology and meaning is at the heart of Cummings's accomplishments.

Themes and Meanings

This poem presents a strong antiwar statement as Cummings lauds a conscientious objector for his resistance and eventual refusal to participate in battle. Although Olaf's actions eventually result in his death by torture, the narrator believes that he will see Olaf in heaven: Olaf has chosen a Christ-centered path and will be forgiven for his lack of "patriotism," since in this case patriotism is evil.

The poem begins with a positive picture of Olaf—his massive physical frame, his joyful attitude, and his warm heart—but in line 3, Cummings hyphenates the word objector ("object-or"). This hyphenation establishes a new mood in the poem by suggesting that Olaf is merely an object, manipulated by society to meet its own ends. Cummings sarcastically describes Olaf's colonel as "well beloved" and "succinctly bred"; these two back-handed compliments play against the word "erring," used to describe Olaf. The real intent is to evoke pity for the nonconformist and to portray the military figures as inhumane and cruel. This purpose continues with the sarcastic description of the noncoms employed to convince Olaf of the war's correctness as "overjoyed" (line 7) and "kindred intellects" (line 13): These men are happy being brutal. Olaf, in contrast, is calm and controlled. He recognizes that he is "a corpse"; these men will eventually kill him, but he coolly (without annoyance) replies to their abuse with defiant words.

Eventually, Olaf's case is referred to the commander-in-chief of the Army, the president, who sadly agrees about the "yellowsonofabitch" and decides on imprisonment—no doubt solitary confinement—in a dungeonlike prison, reiterating both the medieval/war images and the tactics of torture used in the Dark Ages. Line 42 associates Christ, also punished and killed for his nonconformity, with Olaf. Despite the fact that Christ faced opposition to His actions, Cummings implies that he attained heaven and conquered both torture and death; similarly, Olaf will gain this reward for his fortitude and perseverance. The poem maintains that the American ideal of patriotism has been perverted to depraved cruelty as the war machine grinds any opposition to pulp. On the other hand, Olaf is portrayed as a heroic example of true perfection, a perfection which defies warlike society and advocates peace and pacifism.

Michael J. Meyer

I SING THE BODY ELECTRIC

Author: Walt Whitman (1819-1892)
Type of poem: Lyric
First published: 1860, in *Leaves of Grass*

The Poem

"I Sing the Body Electric" appeared in the 1860 third edition of Walt Whitman's revolutionary volume of poetry, *Leaves of Grass*, as poem 3 of the "Enfans d'Adam" (later Anglicized to "Children of Adam") sequence. It is a celebration of the beauty of the human body, both male and female, that dwells on its physicality, its many forms, its sexuality, and its divinity. The poem—in the final, 1892 edition of *Leaves of Grass* discussed here—is composed of nine numbered sections of free verse.

The title, joyously proclaiming the poet's intent, is also the first line of section 1, which introduces the poem. The first four lines speak of the connectedness of everyone the poet loves; the next four are a series of rhetorical questions that stress the evils of corrupting the body and proclaim a direct link between the body and the soul: "And if the body were not the soul, what is the soul?"

Section 2 states that the body of the male and of the female is "perfect" and that the expression of the human face "balks account"—its beauty simply cannot be explained. Whitman proceeds from the face to other parts of the body, describing movement and grace as seen in people of all ages and walks of life: grown men, babies, women, girls, swimmers, wrestlers, laborers, the "farmer's daughter," "two apprentice-boys." He concludes by again proclaiming his unity with them all: "I loosen myself . . . am at the mother's breast with the little child,/ Swim with the swimmers, wrestle with wrestlers."

In section 3, Whitman reminisces about an old farmer he knew who was the father of five sons. He describes him as vigorous, calm, beautiful, and handsome; he was a man that anyone would want to be with—and would want to touch. Section 4, one of the shortest in the poem, speaks of the delight of being among those that one likes, of being "surrounded by beautiful, curious, breathing, laughing flesh." Again, the soul is mentioned; physical things, Whitman states—the touch and the odor of the body—"please the soul well."

Section 5 describes the female form, and it contains explicitly sexual imagery. The female has a "fierce" attraction, Whitman declares, then goes on to describe the activities resulting from that attraction—the "love-flesh swelling and deliciously aching," ejaculation, and the "night of love working surely and softly into the prostrate dawn." The sexual imagery is also tied to birth, to the creation of the new generations of the future. Section 6, depicting the male, ascribes action, power, passions, and pride to the male. Both male and female have their places in the procession of the universe. At the end of the section, Whitman asks another series of rhetorical questions, arguing forcefully for the equality of all humans.

Sections 7 and 8 begin by picturing a man's body and a woman's body, respectively, "at auction." The mention of a slave auction in this hymn of praise to the human form is jarring (and, to modern sensibilities, repugnant), but Whitman uses the setting as another avenue for observing the body's perfection, musing on the basic equality of all people, and imagining future generations: "How do you know who shall come from the offspring of his offspring through the centuries?"

The final section, one of the poem's two longest, consists mostly of a long catalog of parts of the body, with descriptions of the activities and movements they can perform. It both begins and ends by linking, once again, the body and the soul. More than that, however, the body and soul are united as one, and they are united with the poem itself: Bodies "are the soul," and "they are my poems," which are also everyone's poems. The soul, Whitman concludes, can be nothing but the body and the parts of the body.

Forms and Devices

Whitman's poetic style in the poems of *Leaves of Grass* (the first edition appeared in 1855) stood nineteenth century poetic convention on its ear. In order to approximate the rhythms of oratorical speech, he wrote in long lines that do not fit on one line on the page. He generally avoided the use of regular stanzas and rhyme. He wove together vocabularies from many walks of life, speaking in a voice larger than life, a bardic voice he meant to represent both himself and all of America.

In a series of vignettes, "I Sing the Body Electric" presents image after image of the body and its movements, portraying swimmers, rowers, laborers, wrestlers, and firemen. They seem almost Olympian figures, and the figures are nearly always in motion; the swimmer, naked, "rolls silently with the heave of the water," apprentices wrestle after work, and firemen march. The female figure, too, is idealized, as woman soothes a child or "moves with perfect balance." Whitman is observing acutely throughout the poem—he worked for a time as a newspaper reporter and editor—and he reports his observations one after another with emotion and immediacy. He views scenes of the body from a distance, then moves to small parts of the body, both seen and unseen, such as "eye-fringes," "tongue, lips, teeth," "scapula," "arm-pit," and "heart-valves." The small and the large are united, none seemingly more important than the other, as no one person is more "equal" than any other.

Whitman uses the technique of the catalog to great effect in this and other poems. The technique goes back to the lengthy catalog of ships in Homer's *Iliad* (c. 800 B.C.E.) and was used effectively by John Milton in the seventeenth century, yet Whitman makes it his own. In the poem's ninth and final section, he creates an apparently endless list of parts of the body, and the cumulative effect is to emphasize the wonder of the body—in its totality and in all of its parts.

Leaves of Grass was intended by Whitman to be a poetic text that he would expand and revise throughout his life; he published numerous editions of the work between 1855 and 1892, with most of the revision occurring prior to the 1881 edition. There are therefore differing versions of many of the poems, and critics have disagreed as to which edition represents Whitman's finest achievement. "I Sing the Body Electric" first appeared in the book's third edition and was subsequently revised. The 1860 version, in fact, was untitled, and it did not begin with that incantatory phrase. Instead, it directly addressed readers immediately—"O my children! O my mates!"—and, instead of the 1867 version's reference to "armies of those I love" (line 2), addressed the "bodies of you, and of all men and women."

Themes and Meanings

Whitman was not reticent about proclaiming his beliefs (or his own talents). "I celebrate myself, and sing myself," he wrote in "Song of Myself," yet that self was always seen as a part of all humanity and particularly of the people of the United States. Sexuality was not something to be left unspoken or concealed; it was one of the most vital aspects of life. Again in "Song of Myself," he described himself as "hankering, gross, mystical, nude" and said that, like a hawk, he would sound his "barbaric yawp."

The celebration of the physical and the sexual in "I Sing the Body Electric" was indeed too barbaric for the sensibilities of many people in the nineteenth century. Even Whitman supporter Ralph Waldo Emerson supposedly advised him not to include the poem (or the sexual and homoerotic "Calamus" poems) in the 1860 edition, but Whitman held to his artistic vision. Many readers were outraged. A few years later, Whitman was fired from a government post after a superior read the sexual poems.

Whitman presents his glimpses of the body almost as quick snapshots, and he is both observer and participant in the scenes and experiences. The poem is not concerned with the intellectual question "What is beauty?" but observes beauty at the physical and sensual level—one recalls John Keats's description of a life of sensation rather than thought.

Whitman's responses are immediate, bold, and unapologetic. They almost swoon with the joy of the human form—both the joys of living in his own body and of being surrounded by others: "I do not ask any more delight," he says, "I swim in it as in a sea."

The body transcends the mundane; it leads to artistic experiences and even mystical understanding. Whitman's sort of transcendence differs from that of Transcendentalists such as Emerson, however, in that Whitman is not concerned with a dualism of matter and spirit: "the parts and poems of the body," he concludes, "these are the soul." They are one. Like nineteenth century English poet Gerard Manley Hopkins, Whitman sees the body as a wonder, as sacred; unlike Hopkins, he does not see that divinity as explicitly Christian.

Whitman frequently meditated on future generations and on the future of the United States, and the sexuality of "I Sing the Body Electric" and the other "Children of Adam" poems is seen as part of the cycle of procreation; the poems reflect his projections into the future. When he looks at the man or the woman standing before him, he sees "countless immortal lives" and "the start of populous states and rich republics"; he sees "the teeming mother of mothers." Whitman celebrated the joy of the moment and the ecstasies of the physical, but the present was united with the future and the physical was one with the spiritual.

Clarence McClanahan

I TASTE A LIQUOR NEVER BREWED—

Author: Emily Dickinson (1830-1886)
Type of poem: Lyric
First published: 1861, as "The May Wine"; collected in *The Poems of Emily Dickinson*, 1955

The Poem

Emily Dickinson did not give titles to most of her poems, so they are generally referred to by their first lines. The editor of the 1955 edition of her poems, Thomas H. Johnson, attempted to number them according to the order of their composition; "I taste a liquor never brewed—" is listed as number 214. Dickinson sometimes left alternate versions of her poems, and the version discussed here is what Johnson believed to be her final one.

"I taste a liquor never brewed—" consists of four stanzas, the second and fourth lines rhyming in each quatrain. This is a poem of visionary experience in which the richness of a natural setting in summer is the cause. Speaking in her own lyric voice, Dickinson describes the exhilaration of going outdoors in summer in terms of getting drunk in a tavern.

In the first stanza, she asserts that she is drinking an unusual kind of liquor, one that has not been brewed but that is superior to the finest Rhine wine. In the second stanza, she says that she has become drunk by consuming the air and the dew of summer days. This consumption has taken place in "inns of Molten Blue," or under the hot summer sky. In the third stanza, she claims that her capacity for this liquor exceeds that of the most dedicated of summer's drinkers, the bees and the butterflies: When they have ceased drinking, she will continue. In the final quatrain, she affirms that she will drink until seraphs—the six-winged angels that stand in the presence of God—and saints as well run to Heaven's windows to see her, "the little Tippler/ Leaning against the—Sun—."

The last image of the poem, which grows out of the central comparison between drunkenness and her experiences of the summer day, humorously conveys a spiritual expansion of the self. Through this expansion, she comes to the notice of divine spirits, calling them away from their usual adoration of God in order to see this smaller god who, though perhaps a little unruly, has grown momentarily toward her true stature and importance.

Forms and Devices

Dickinson employs careful placement of pauses and an implied phrase repetition to break up what would otherwise be a steady marching rhythm. By this means, she conveys a dual sense of staggering, of the drunk losing physical control and the mystic stumbling into the presence of divinity. She makes her conventional stanza serve the unconventional, even the daring juxtaposition of drinking alcohol with nature as an inspiration of sublime perceptions.

Dickinson's central device is the metaphor that brings together drunkenness with visionary perception. She establishes that, for her, the air and dew of summer constitute a liquor and that she is a drunkard, reeling through days that are like streets, after drinking in the inn of the sky. Therefore, she has prepared the reader for the whimsical and surprising development of this comparison in the final two stanzas.

In the third quatrain, the foxglove flower becomes the tavern of the bee. Dickinson produces fanciful humor in this comparison by inventing "landlords"—placing the word in quotation marks—who will turn the bees out of the foxgloves when they have become too drunk. She continues in this vein by speaking of butterflies that, after drinking deep, "renounce their 'drams.'" The language of these comparisons evokes one of the many popular crusades of Dickinson's lifetime, the temperance movement. Often, the temperance movement called for total abstinence from alcohol, and it temporarily succeeded in legally enforced abstinence with the passage of national prohibition within forty years after Dickinson's death. By playing at opposing both abstinence and temperance, Dickinson pokes fun at the seriousness of the predominantly Protestant and conservative culture in her native Amherst, Massachusetts, where the rhetoric of temperance was familiar. This seeming irreverence extends to serious religious ideas as well.

A playful irreverence appears in the final stanza. Here, her drunken antics call to their windows not the upright citizens of the town, who might observe disdainfully the loud drunkard leaning against a lamppost in a sorry state. Instead, the observers are the angels and saints, and the tippler who they see is not leaning against something stabilizing in the street. Rather, she leans against the sun itself (capitalized for emphasis and to suggest divinity), the blazing source of summer and of the wine of the air and dew, the visible symbol of the God from whom these divine beings presumably have turned their attention in order to watch her. There is implied irreverence in making a spectacle of oneself and disturbing the heavens, but the final comparison between a mere lamppost and the sun seems to resolve this irreverence by asserting that the one who becomes drunk on summer comes ultimately to lean upon God.

The final stanza exhibits fairly clearly a technique that Dickinson used often in her poems: the implied repetition of a line or phrase. The last line of the second stanza may be implicitly the first line of the third stanza, but it is much clearer that the last line of the third stanza is implicitly repeated at the beginning of the fourth. Repeating "I shall but drink the more!" grammatically completes the lines that follow. In this way, one reads the line once to complete the third stanza and then must think it again in order to understand the beginning of the following stanza. One of the more striking uses of this technique in Dickinson's work is at the beginning of the fourth stanza of "A Bird came down the Walk—" (poem 328), where the first line both completes the previous sentence and begins the next one.

The repeatable lines and the placement of dashes in this poem give it a spasmodic gait which parallels the drunkard's staggering and thereby underlines the poem's central comparison.

Themes and Meanings

One of the main themes of Dickinson's poetry is the religious quest. She wanted to know with some certainty true answers to the questions that human beings repeatedly ask about the meaning of life: How did we come to be? Why are we here? What is our ultimate destiny? In her poems, she uses the poet's tools, a powerful imagination and a command of language, to seek in her own experience the answers to these questions. In this way, she associates herself with the Romantic poets, giving primary authority to personal experience, especially in nature, rather than to that of previously written words in scriptures and commentaries. Her work as a whole suggests that she was not comfortable with having to depend on nature and personal experience as sources of knowledge about God and religious truth, but that she was less comfortable with simply accepting what others believed because they had lived before her or occupied positions of authority. Among the more revealing poems about this quest are "I had not minded—Walls—" (398), "Me prove it now—Whoever doubt" (poem 537), and "Those—dying then" (1551).

Her humorous irreverence in this poem regarding her culture's attitudes toward alcohol and the seriousness of religious subjects reflects her rebellion against authority. Her presentation of the experience of nature as uniting her with divinity illustrates her hope that, through personal experience, she might gain true religious knowledge.

Although Dickinson wrote often about the power that she found in nature to heal and reveal, her discoveries were not unambiguously positive. Indeed, poems such as this one about the possibility of joyous vision in the contemplation of nature are roughly balanced by those about its more dangerous and unsettling mysteries, not the least of which are those questions evoked by the presence of death.

A poem closely related to "I taste a liquor never brewed—" is "The Soul has Bandaged moments—" (poem 512), in which Dickinson illustrates the contrast between moments of paradise, "When bursting all the doors—/ She dances like a Bomb," and "retaken moments—/ When, Felon led along,/ With shackles on the plumed feet,/ And staples, in the Song." "I taste a liquor never brewed—" captures a moment of paradise, when Dickinson believes that she is at home in the world and is certain that this world is a sure route to heaven. In many other poems, Dickinson tells of the "retaken moments," when she seems to be a prisoner in the world, with impenetrable, dragon-guarded walls between herself and what she wants most to know.

In this poem, Dickinson's blend of joy and humor in her controlling metaphor of drinking to excess conveys vividly her perception of a benevolent deity in the natural beauty of a summer day.

Terry Heller

I THINK CONTINUALLY OF THOSE
WHO WERE TRULY GREAT

Author: Stephen Spender (1909-1995)
Type of poem: Elegy
First published: 1932; collected in *Poems*, 1933

The Poem

"I think continually of those who were truly great" is an untitled poem that first appeared in *New Signatures*, a collection of poetry selected by Michael Roberts to offer an imaginative and intellectual blend that would deal positively with the problems of the twentieth century. This popular collection also represented the works of emerging poets such as W. H. Auden, C. Day Lewis, William Empson, John Lehmann, and Richard Eberhart, who collectively became known, for a time, as *New Signatures* poets. Spender contributed more poems than any of the others, and his seven poems promptly became part of his collected canon.

"I think continually of those who were truly great" is written in free verse with three stanzas containing eight, seven, and eight lines, respectively. The meter of the poem is highly varied, containing fine examples of most meters used in English poetry. While this poem settles into no regular meter, line length, or rhyme scheme, it is, nonetheless, highly musical with its syncopated rhythms and sharp images.

The opening line of the poem, which is typically used in place of its omitted title, sets a tone of reminiscing about the great; the verb "were" signals that those the poet admires are already dead. The second line declares that these noteworthy souls were born to greatness, having existed before birth and having had a history of the greatness they would realize in life on earth. The language is almost Neoplatonic as the poet discusses how these individuals have come from the light and are going back to the light or "Spirit." Plato's philosophy of learning maintained that education was a process of remembering what one already knows. Great people, as described in this poem, are those whose recollection of the lofty state from which they have come is fresh and vital like spring blossoms.

The second stanza continues this definition of greatness as a process of remembering not only human ancestry but also the spiritual ancestry dating before the creation of the Earth as humans know it. In one sense, the poem seems to be advocating a kind of reincarnation, but, in another sense, the poem is discussing the power of getting in touch with the ancient roots of culture that form the lifeblood of most great poetry. To continue this tradition introduced by great people, the poet encourages people to never forget these individuals and "Never to allow gradually the traffic to smother/ With noise and fog, the flowering of the Spirit."

The final stanza declares that creation itself celebrates the names of the great. This creation is alive and well aware of the noteworthy souls. The final four lines of the poem state elegantly how the great are "those who in their lives fought for life." Such souls who keep the value and purpose of life in their hearts leave their signature across the sky like a vivid sunset that one can never forget. Those who have been true to the best in life are destined to be remembered well.

Forms and Devices

"I think continually of those who were truly great" is a fine example of the *New Signatures* era of poetry. The style of the poem shows the influence of T. S. Eliot (whom Spender respected and admired), especially in its use of a highly imagistic, free-verse form. Those of Spender's own generation, such as Auden and Lewis, also influenced Spender to hold a very optimistic view of what humanity could accomplish in life. While the *New Signatures* poets often, in keeping with Marxist ideals, railed against capitalism and championed the common laborer, Spender seems to set aside this agenda for a moment. What remains of this cultural development among the poets is a sense of enthusiasm about the potential of individuals for achieving greatness.

The images in this poem are primarily tied to life and inspiration. In the ancient Greek tradition, inspiration was the product of the gods breathing new life into the writer, performer, or speaker. The phrase "lips, still touched with fire" reminds one of Isaiah 6, in which the prophet's lips are cleansed by the touch of a coal from the altar, leaving the prophet with inspiration to go forth and speak purely for God. Images of light and singing are also connected with inspiration. For the ancient Greeks, from which this elegiac form is derived, all forms of poetry and most parts of their plays were to be sung. Singing was considered the natural medium of inspiration, especially for the poet.

The images in the second stanza contrast with those in the first and third stanzas by being more visceral and earthy. Images such as "blood," "rocks," "grave evening," "noise," and "fog" are reminders of the frailty and struggle of life against impending death. Great people are those who face great challenges well. The images in the third stanza are also earthy, but they move one's view upward toward the sun. The elements of these bodily souls dissolve into light as they leave their honorable signature on the very air other people breathe. The phrase "vivid air" in the last line is another reminder that creation itself is vitally alive to the greatness of humanity and can be played like a harp humming with the song of life. The motifs of travel in the closing lines also remind readers that life is a pilgrimage. While this journey through life is terribly brief, it does tell much about one's basic inclinations and sets an angle of travel into eternity. The great not only aim high, they aim truly at their point of origin, which is also their point of destiny.

Themes and Meanings

"I think continually of those who were truly great" springs from an era of great enthusiasm for the potential of people to change their world. The Marxist dogmas that many of the idealistic upper-middle-class English people adopted were, in many ways, a well-intentioned effort to improve the state of the poor and underprivileged.

Spender gave up his affiliation to Marxist ideologies after seeing the inconsistencies of the communist leaders in the Spanish Civil War. Spender was also to lose some of his naïve optimism about life after he witnessed the protracted suffering and death of his sister Margaret, who died of cancer on Christmas day, 1945. His "Elegy for Margaret" is much more somber than this earlier elegy, yet the sense of triumph is still evident, and the sense that this life is only a phase of one's total existence is still very strong.

The exact philosophy that undergirds this poem is ambiguous. One can find evidence of strong Christian convictions as well as views that are more Eastern or Hindu in their mystical view of life. As critic Sanford Sternlicht has noted, throughout his life, Spender remained "unsure of, and ambivalent toward, philosophy, aesthetics, religion, politics, and sexuality." This ambivalence helps explain why this poem does not fit firmly into any given philosophical or religious agenda. Spender is speaking of the universal yearnings of the soul and of the sense that all of humanity is connected to the past in some profound way, whether spiritually, genetically, or psychologically.

Regardless of how one assesses the religious and philosophical dimensions of this poem, Spender has achieved an extraordinary statement of hope about the potential of human beings to live significant, great lives. Such a statement is all the more surprising when one realizes that it came out of the era of the Great Depression and not long before Europeans knew they would soon be engulfed in another world war. Somehow, Spender has been able to take the images that have often been used in elegies and employ them with a fresh turn of phrasing that makes of these images a brilliant statement against death, which often seems to dwarf the value and significance of life. The poet seems to understand that the spiritual dimension of who people are is more significant than the mortal body. This view strongly contrasts with the Marxist view of life as being materialistic and existing exclusively on this side of death.

Compared to Spender's other poems from this era, "I think continually of those who were truly great" stands out as one of his best works. Some of his early poems, such as "Beethoven's Death Mask" and "The Express," also achieve a degree of aptness in phrasing and imagery, but most are very romantic and sometimes sentimental, the product of seeing the trials of life from a distance. These early successes show that Spender was a fine poet in the making who was moving toward the sun of his greatness. In 1971, he was awarded the Queen's Gold Medal for Poetry; in 1979, he was made an honorary fellow of University College, Oxford; and, in 1982, he was knighted—a fitting crown to his own noble career as a poet and critic.

Daven M. Kari

I WANDERED LONELY AS A CLOUD

Author: William Wordsworth (1770-1850)
Type of poem: Lyric
First published: 1807, in *Poems in Two Vols.*; expanded in *Poems*, 1815

The Poem

"I Wandered Lonely as a Cloud" resulted from an experience of William Wordsworth and his sister Dorothy while on a walking tour of the Ullswater region in April, 1802. Dorothy wrote of it at length in her journal; when the poet began to compose the present poem two years later, his wife Mary Hutchinson Wordsworth contributed what are now lines 21-22, which William correctly identified as the best two in the poem. While rearranging his works for an 1815 publication, Wordsworth added the second stanza. As it presently stands, this poem is reputed to be the most anthologized poem in the world.

The "I" of the poem is explicitly a poet (line 15); the implied "you" is therefore explicitly a reader of a poem. Such clear roles doubtless add to the poem's illusion of simplicity.

The final stanza confers poetic meaning upon the experience of the previous three descriptive and narrative stanzas. In his famous preface to the second edition of *Lyrical Ballads* (1800), Wordsworth said that poetry results from "emotion recollected in tranquillity," and in the fourth stanza the poet, in tranquillity, recollects an earlier experience and sees more deeply into it. Suddenly the poem's simplicity is complicated by the addition of an explicit program: Wordsworth is exemplifying his contention that the events and emotions of the first three stanzas must recur in an altered mode of existence, neither in nature nor in history but in memory, if they are to occasion a poem.

Returning to the beginning of the poem, one finds the poet hiking on a windy day. He has no set destination. Happening upon innumerable wild daffodils, he compares them to a crowd of people and to an army ("host" implies that the flowers are the heavenly army of the divinity). He compares the densely packed flowers to the stars in the Milky Way and to a multitude of dancers engaged in a spirited dance. This stanza, added in 1815, balances the original event more evenly between isolated subject ("I") and communal object (daffodils) by concentrating on the external scene. The other three stanzas rely heavily on the first-person singular.

The poet had enjoyed the event even while he experienced it, but in later years, when he is more mature, he comments that at the earlier time he had not recognized its full value. In the final six lines, the poet moves into the present tense, using the key Wordsworthian word "oft" to generalize about the reiterated and enduring effects of recollection. The word "vacant" usually connotes for Wordsworth positive things such as vacations. "Pensive," by contrast, implies melancholy, the serious, gloomy, earthbound humor among the four humors; but it mainly serves as a dark foil to set off the bright and joyful conclusion.

Forms and Devices

The poem contains four six-line stanzas of iambic tetrameter, rhyming *ababcc*. The usual metrical substitutions (trochee or anapest for iamb) are very sparingly used. Wind characterized the original experience. Dorothy Wordsworth made it a strong unifying motif of her journal entry. It endured while her brother deleted and altered other particulars, and it continues to unify the reader's experience of the poem.

The wind enhances almost every visual aspect of this highly visual poem. The visual words that imply movement—"fluttering," "dancing," "shine," and "sparkling"— all imply the motion imparted by the wind. The Milky Way stars even "twinkle" because of the instability of the upper air. The one visual image that suggests no motion, "golden," perhaps devalues literal material wealth in favor of the aesthetic wealth of the last eight lines.

The wind also occasions the poem's powerful kinesthetic images—images of the tactile sensation of one's own motion or empathy with another's. The first three forms of a key word—"dancing," "dance," and "danced"—literally name the wind's past effects, and the fourth, "dances," names the continuing effect of remembering the past wind; "flash" does the same. Even more important, the wind unites the many individual flowers, waves, or stars by making them perform together some single action; they are not a multitude of separate and isolated beings, for although they are originally perceived merely as "a crowd,/ A host," they soon form a community.

As such they can be company for the lonely poet: Since he was a cloud at the beginning of the poem, he was also subject to the wind's motion. The wind has brought him to the destined meeting. His condition at the end of the poem involves no literal wind but, instead, the psychological results of the original experience: Emotion-charged memory is the psychic wind that often blows the poet and the daffodils together again. Moreover, the poet relives the experience so much more deeply in later years that this psychic wind sets his heart dancing with his old friends the daffodils, even though he had not danced with them during the original encounter.

The three main groups—daffodils, waves, and stars—both as they were and as they are remembered, create some correlatives that make the poem applicable to vast ranges of space and time: as below (daffodils), so above (stars); as on sea (waves), so on land (daffodils); as in day (waves and daffodils), so at night (stars); as in the past (daffodils, waves, and stars), so in the present (they and their associated emotions when recollected in tranquillity).

Themes and Meanings

One can conjecture that the earthbound melancholy of the poet's pensive mood (line 20) is transformed into its opposite, the sensual, cheerful sanguine humor which is associated with the element air. As fire and choler are the opposites of water and the phlegmatic humor, so air and the sanguine humor are the opposites of earth and melancholy. Since air (wind) and water (waves) are so prominent in the poem, one finds oneself with another Garden of Eden built of the same two elements that John Milton used to build his doomed Eden in *Paradise Lost* (1667, 1674). It is no accident that five lines near the start of the 1805 version of Wordsworth's *The Prelude* (1850), written within a few months of "I Wandered Lonely as a Cloud," subtly echo the final five lines of Milton's *Paradise Lost*. At the end of *Paradise Lost*, Adam and Eve leave the Garden of Eden with the world "all before them"; providence is their guide as they take their "solitary way." In *The Prelude*, Wordsworth writes that the "earth is all before me"; even if his guide is only "a wandering cloud," he says, "I cannot miss my way."

Wordsworth plainly anoints himself as the new Adam; two Eves, Dorothy and Mary, saunter with him into the new postlapsarian world of Romanticism. Not the Judaeo-Christian providence but Nature—or more precisely, the wind, as the holiest spirit remaining—will bring the poet who abandons himself to it to his daffodils, his destiny, for their sprightly (spirited, inspired) dance. During hours of apparently aimless sauntering, the wind will lead him away from melancholy into the sensual and sanguine Eden of a post-Christian, nearly pantheistic cosmos.

The reader might suspect "I Wandered Lonely as a Cloud" to be guilty of the "pathetic fallacy"—of attributing human emotions to subhuman things. Wordsworth's pantheistic Nature, however, is poles apart from the totally demythologized nature of late nineteenth century naturalism, which has no traits of consciousness. Instead, it is an all-inclusive cosmic entity of which the attributes of any of its parts may be affirmed.

David Hartley, an influential British psychologist and philosopher in the eighteenth century, had a major impact on Wordsworth. In Hartley's psychology (empirical associationalism), sensory data begin to associate and synthesize themselves within a passive and unreflective mind; the poet's initial aimlessness in this poem probably reflects that childish condition. Wordsworth, who was no systematic thinker, supplemented Hartley with some transcendental intuitive idealism. The resulting self-contradictory jumble makes some sense in practice if one sees passivity as a program, aimless wandering as a conscious discipline, and memory as being extremely important to Wordsworth. Once Nature has impressed itself on the poet's senses, especially by eliciting pleasure or pain, his memory and intuition continue to associate, unify, and refine the impressions long after the sensory objects that caused them have disappeared. In the sensitive mind, these products eventually flower into ideal forms, poetic ideas, and aesthetic emotions.

In "I Wandered Lonely as a Cloud," then, a holy wind brings the poet to the place of meeting that Nature has appointed, Nature reveals itself to him through the daffodil host (as if the flowers are a multitude of angelic messengers of the divine), and the wind of Nature finally empowers the poet to utter his enduring inner experience.

Thomas J. Steele

I WASH THE SHIRT

Author: Anna Świr (Anna Świrszczyñîska; 1909-1984)
Type of poem: Lyric
First published: 1985, as "Piorąò koszuląò," in *Cierpienie i rad oñóã*; English transla-
tion collected in *Talking to My Body*, 1996

The Poem
    "I Wash the Shirt" is a prose poem composed of nineteen lines that vary greatly in
length. It is a very short work, but, like many of Anna Świr's poems, it is rooted deeply
in her private life. The author describes washing the shirt of her recently deceased father, a task so personal that Świr kept the poem to herself for several years; it was only
published posthumously by her daughter. Although it can be appreciated on its own,
the reader who understands something of Świr's life and circumstances will see more
meaning in it than others will. In many of her poems, Świr depicts her father as a
strong, gentle man who took pride in his people's culture and who labored continually
to depict that heritage in his art despite the lifetime of poverty and struggle he endured
to do so. This image is continued in "I Wash the Shirt." He was a painter who specialized in religious and historical themes, and the title refers to Świr washing the shirt he
wore while working in his studio. Since he did not wear the shirt outside, he merely
asked his daughter to dry it on the wood-burning stove that heated his workshop rather
than iron it. For Świr, the shirt has strong associations with her father's daily toil as
well as with his passion and pride; even its scent, as she puts it into the wash water, reminds her of him.
    Świr compares washing the shirt with the other times she washed her father's cloth-
ing, which always smelled of his perspiration. She has performed the same task since
girlhood, but while she previously laid the shirt for him to find on the stove, now she
simply prepares to put it away. Once it is washed, it no longer conveys the familiar
sense of her father's presence, and she realizes that in one more small way she has lost
another aspect of him. His paintings will be left, but they are a public and sterile (if
beautiful) side of his activity. The living, breathing, perspiring man whose love and
effort brought that beauty into existence is gone forever and so is his scent. She also
suggests elsewhere that although he labored intensely on his paintings, they could
never adequately convey his feelings. In "I Wash the Shirt," death has removed the devoted artist and father, leaving only a shirt and some oil paintings. What could easily
be a grotesque meditation on soiled laundry, seemingly inappropriate in the face of
death, becomes instead a musing on how irreplaceable Świr's father was, not because
of his paintings but because of his unique presence and personality.

Forms and Devices
    As in most of her poetry, Świr makes no attempt in "I Wash the Shirt" to sound "po-
etic." Her translator, Czesław Miłosz, discusses Świr's desire to write poetry in which

the ideas would show through clearly, unimpeded by any noticeable attempt at style or verbal sophistication. She specialized in very short works, often termed "miniatures" by critics. These poems, by concentrating the reader's attention on one or two images in only a few lines, strengthen the impact of those images. In "I Wash the Shirt," as in many of her works, Świr succeeds particularly well. Her language is purely conversational, as in the third and fourth lines: "The shirt smells of sweat. I remember/ that sweat from my childhood." Just as the image of a sweaty shirt is neither traditionally poetic nor even aesthetically pleasing, the language also avoids ornamentation and communicates its forceful emotion through simple, almost blunt wording. Because of Świr's approach, the image of the woman washing a shirt as she recalls more than six decades of her father's presence, now lost forever, is haunting.

Such writing depends upon its thought and subject matter (in this case loss and death) for its poetic power, and this strength is particularly found in the novelty of finding the smell of stale clothing a powerful reminder of a beloved parent, the sort of reminder most people are not likely to prize or even to think about until the loved one is gone. In keeping with her concept of poetry, Świr transforms a mundane chore into a moment of profound insight and grief. She smells the scent of the almost obsessive effort that he put into his work rather than the scent of the paintings themselves, which only smell like oil paint. What survives—the paintings—are only artifacts, not part of life. The sweat recalls his spirit, his concentration and patience, and his compulsion to keep the Polish heritage alive. In washing the shirt, she realizes she has lost not only a physical smell but also the sense of her father's presence, the body that produced the perspiration. The simple three- and four-syllable lines ("I destroy it/ forever") evoke the finality of loss more powerfully than most traditionally written laments would. The alteration of her father from living man to mere memory is complete: Although his paintings remain, the sense of his active and moving body, the passion and feeling of the man who sweated while he worked, the influence he had in his daughter's life, and his love are all gone forever.

Themes and Meanings

Świr was affected all her life by the death and destruction she witnessed as a young woman during World War II. For her, life itself, with all its processes, attractive and otherwise, became compelling. Her poetry generally reflects an intense interest in the physical, simple acts of existence such as breathing and walking and in the everyday sights, sounds, and smells of urban streets and crowded apartment buildings. For such a poet, the scent of a deceased man's perspiration can evoke a strong sense of his identity. Świr sometimes uses breathing as a symbol of life, strength, and joy in her poems. In "I Wash the Shirt," however, breathing, coupled with a simple task performed for the last time, evokes grief. For Świr, that scent, so familiar to her from almost seven decades with her father, identifies only one body in the world. Since that body is gone, she feels she destroys a remnant of the man by washing his shirt. Breathing and perspiring are essential functions of human life and are thus tokens of continued living; the poet's father, who no longer lives, neither breathes nor works. Only relatively odorless and inanimate paintings remain of his vision and the struggle he underwent to express it. However much these paintings reflect his love of beauty and of his homeland, they do not have the physical, animal presence his missing body once had, and the poet will never have the comfort of his presence again. In other poems, she writes about how he painted, working painstakingly and correcting himself as he went. This process, with its great self-discipline and perseverance, was the true mark of her father's personality and feelings. It is thus her father's process of painting rather than the paintings themselves that she loves and misses.

Such a theme is typical of Świr's work, and it is true to the experience of many people who lose loved ones. Those who grieve often find that mundane tasks and ordinary objects trigger the deepest feelings of sorrow. In the case of "I Wash the Shirt," Świr's grief is caused by doing a very familiar task that she will never perform again. There will be no point to laying the shirt on top of the wood-burning stove for her father because he will not wear it to work anymore. Just as small, commonplace realizations often evoke the profoundest sadness, a short poem in everyday language suggests Świr's deep loneliness and sadness for her father and the stunning finality of death, which can make even the act of doing laundry seem like another instance of destruction and loss.

Paul James Buczkowski

ICE

Author: Ai (1947-   )
Type of poem: Narrative/dramatic monologue
First published: 1978; collected in *Killing Floor,* 1979

The Poem

The free-verse poem "Ice" is a monologue that dramatically narrates the speaker's experiences as a cast-off teenager, her killing of her child and her man, and the warm memory she has for this man as she comes to reconcile her adolescent confusion. The poem consists of four stanzas, the first three having thirteen lines each and the last, twelve. The title word proceeds into the first line, with the thought that will compare the conditions on a river as a harsh winter ends with the chilly and irresolute emotions she felt toward her new family.

The speaker is a young woman. Throughout the poem she addresses her lover, beside whose grave she stands. She had strangled their first child, which the reader discovers only after being confronted with the oddly juxtaposed images of the sunrise surrounding her man and the baby's skull in the box. Despite having violently attacked and killed him, she finds that her affection for him strengthens. In this monologue, Ai creates an effect similar to that achieved by Robert Browning in "My Last Duchess," except that Ai dramatically relates the specific details of the speaker's actions.

The opening stanza establishes the fact that, as an adolescent Choctaw, she is far from home, living in Minnesota. The Choctaws were called one of the "Five Civilized Tribes" of the southeastern United States; however, taking up European ways did not exempt them from being forcibly removed from their original homelands in northern Alabama and Mississippi and relocated to the Indian Territory, which later became the state of Oklahoma, in the 1830's. The speaker resents her father for considering her already "a burden" at twelve, and her feelings of resentment at his giving her away during her menses are powerful.

At fourteen, the speaker, literally a child-woman, is ill-disposed to the roles of mate and mother (nowhere in the poem is marriage explicitly stated or implied). She describes her man's warmth and disposition as he enters their abode, hugged by the sun, in stanza 2. The rocking horse he made for her is subtly placed in that stanza; it introduces details such as "the ebony box/ with the baby's skull inside," the husband combing his hair with a casual gesture, and the dramatic action in stanza 3 that may shock the reader. She dismounts from the rocking horse, which is essentially a toy, to attack, maim, and slay him.

Reopening her eyes in the last stanza, she recalls how "I wanted you then and now/ and I never let you know." Together—he in death, and she vibrant and filled with mixed emotions about their past—they will "slide forward" into an eventual and eternal realm of the spirit.

Forms and Devices

When using first-person points of view, poets often adopt a persona or mask in order to create a character that seems mentally and physically active and real. Creating this persona does not mean that the poet intends to veil autobiographical details. The figurative devices in "Ice" may be drawn from oral history, readings, historical documents, and the like. Ai may feel close to the images she creates, and her Native American, Asian American, and mixed black and white ancestry makes her imagery, details, and emotions more profound.

Images of remembrance, retribution, distrust of males, and killing abound in "Ice." The ice on the river breaks into "obelisks," which as tapered monolithic structures bear a phallic significance. Ice metaphorically reflects the speaker's attitude toward her man, her distrust of him, just as its breakage results from the onset of warm conditions.

Juxtaposed to the poem's bittersweet memory and dramatic violence are images of soft materials such as "that shawl of cotton wool," the "white smock," the piece of velvet, and "the pony-skin rug," all of which convey nonthreatening surroundings. Ai balances this set of images, however, by introducing early in the poem the material central to the speaker's rage—"the roll of green gingham" she had to use to absorb the blood of her menstrual flow, a flow that confirms that she is ready for childbearing. This bloody roll of gingham embodies her child-woman's humiliation over being disposed of for being a burden to her father. In the second stanza, the horse she rides has a "black mane cut from my own hair," a mane she strokes, but which, because it is her hair, fills her with mixed emotions. The clashing of these images corresponds to the speaker's inner turmoil over what are also natural and utilitarian events and practices. Ai's perceptions of serenity balanced by physical acts of rage characterize other poems in her books *Cruelty* (1974) and *The Killing Floor* (1979).

Ai gives "Ice" a cyclical narrative structure. A poet achieves a cyclical structure by connecting historical events with present emotions in a fashion that is neither chronological nor linear. Reminiscence, flashback, and an organic sense of the relationship of events across or despite temporal realities distinguishes such a poetic structure. T. S. Eliot's lengthy sequence, *The Waste Land* (1922), is one example of this kind of circular construction. The cyclical character of "Ice" may derive from Ai's heritage, in that this nonlinear form is common is storytelling narratives among indigenous peoples, and is particularly important to Native American and certain Indonesian groups. The expressionist does not attempt a deliberate shaping of the form to meet a cultural demand. The form results from the people's nonlinear and nonchronological perception and understanding of time.

Early in "Ice," the speaker by the graveside holds back her head and remembers, then closes her eyes, taking the reader to the second stanza's memory of being a mate and the mother of a dead child. Closing this stanza, the speaker blocks out the cries of the new infant, cries that provoke finally her rage against her man. The "row of bear teeth" image seems less clear regarding her intentions than the closing of her eyes and the covering of her ears, both of which are avoidance gestures. Thus one may infer that these bear teeth are part of a rug or a pelt similar to the pony skin. As the speaker manipulates these teeth, she parallels the masticating imagery of the previous lines, and completes the image of attempting to crush the gingham roll, her man nailing shut the black box, and the strangulation imagery in the third stanza as a whole. When she opens her eyes in stanza 4, she completes a cycle of memory and physical position. In the two closing lines, she affirms her feelings of growing warmth toward him "without bitterness," emotions she grasps more keenly and can better articulate. "Everlasting," the poem's final word, reaffirms the seasonal breaking up of river ice, and her perpetual reminiscence.

The number of stanzas and lines is probably not arbitrary. The four stanzas reflect the seasons and the cardinal directions. That stanzas one through three have thirteen lines each seems to suggest not ill luck but the thirteen moons in a year as understood by the Choctaw girl. Each menstrual period is called a "moon." The twelve lines of the last stanza suggest that she has jettisoned the hurt and humiliation she recalled earlier in the poem.

Themes and Meanings

This poem might be misinterpreted if the reader finds its violent imagery gratuitous. Ai's juxtaposition of the soft materials and the man, who is low-key and caring, with verbs of force and destruction actually reveals the speaker's adolescent confusion and hurt.

The onset of adolescence brings forth a variety of conflicting emotions that teenagers cannot articulate or understand. Male readers of "Ice" can become sensitive to the fact that preteen and adolescent girls find the onset of menstruation a dynamic physical change and an emotionally terrifying experience. The speaker resents her father for having no need for her, and for casually giving her away to a man who seems to be gentle to her, but toward whom she enacts a displaced violence.

She resents the blood-producing menses, and her anger compels acts of crushing and squeezing. Curiously, the first infant was a girl; the second, a boy, she does not harm. Like the bear's teeth, this is an intangible detail in the poem. A child herself at twelve or thirteen, the speaker can be interpreted as saving her daughter from "the curse" and the boy for a later vindication.

The sexuality suggested by the obelisks evolves to a less threatening aspect as the speaker's attitude toward the man softens. The core of distress and anger from stanza 1 through stanza 3 is nevertheless framed by the serenity of stanza 4 and the opening of the poem. Even her mate's ".45 you call *Grace of God* that keeps you alive," which enables him to survive and provide for his family is, after all, empty, making him defenseless and vulnerable.

Ron Welburn

THE IDEA OF ANCESTRY

Author: Etheridge Knight (1933-1991)
Type of poem: Dramatic monologue
First published: 1968, in *Poems from Prison*

The Poem

"The Idea of Ancestry" is a forty-two-line poem in free verse divided into two parts of three and two stanzas, respectively. The title names the subject of the poem—the poet's connection to his family, his birthplace, and his culture. The poem is written in the autobiographical, first-person voice of Knight. In stanza 1 of part 1, the poet describes his cell in prison, the walls covered with "47" photographs of his relatives. He reclines on his bunk and contemplates the pictures, imagining they are alive and looking at him. Pointedly, he reflects that he shares identities with them: "I am all of them, they are all of me." He ends the reflection and the stanza with a statement that presents a radical shift in point of view: "They are thee." "Thee" addresses all the poem's readers, indeed all of humanity.

In stanza 2, the poet inventories the twelve relatives he has been "in love" with, starting with his mother and ending with a seven-year-old niece who sends him letters in prison. One of the aunts he loved went into an asylum. It is not clear if all these relatives are female. In stanza 3, the poet gives an inventory of his male relatives, especially those with whom he shares the same name. He considers, in particular, a fugitive uncle who has, since age fifteen, been conspicuous by his absence. This uncle is missed each year by the family at its reunions, particularly by the poet's ninety-three-year-old grandmother ("my father's mother") who keeps track of everybody's birth and death dates in the "Family Bible."

In the first stanza of part 2, the poet's attention turns from the members of his family to himself as he recalls his beginnings in Mississippi, his grandfathers' graves there, and his return visit the previous year. He says his visit from Los Angeles was almost strengthening enough to allow him to break his drug habit—but not quite. He therefore takes drugs ("caps") and walks barefoot in his grandmother's backyard, flirts with the local women, and has fun until he runs out of narcotics, experiences withdrawal pain, and ends up stealing drugs from a doctor's house ("cracked a croaker's crib for a fix"). In the second stanza of part 2—the poem's final stanza—the poet describes himself again in his prison cell. It is "Fall," the poem's dominant season. He repeats his reference to his forty-seven photographs of "black faces." In stanza 1, "they stare" at him. In this final stanza, he stares back at them. He repeats that he is "all of them, they are all of [him]." Climactically, he also repeats that "they are thee," addressing the reader and perhaps himself, as if talking to himself as people in solitary environments such as prison might. Finally, the poet announces that he has "no sons" to take a place in the world that he shares with the reader ("thee").

Forms and Devices

Knight's poetry is essentially oral. His own voice was a baritone warble, full of water and passion, exactly right for the poetic diction he created. His poems are rich with single-syllable words, and "The Idea of Ancestry" is no exception. Monosyllabic words outnumber polysyllabic words by over four to one through the first four stanzas, an effect that is multiplied until the proportion is ten to one in the final stanza. Monosyllabic words arrest rhythm and are the discourse of the arrested time of the imprisoned poet who is forbidden participation in the flow of his "birthstream"—and thus in history, wherein "ancestry" occurs. The poem's grammar and punctuation are resolutely simple: The poem's lines do not begin with capitalized words; integer numbers—1, 2, and 3, for example—are not spelled out; and words such as "yr," "1st," and "2nd" are adopted, though "year" is also used. Notably, after its use as the principal word in the title, "ancestry" is not among the words used in the poem. Meanwhile, additional oral characteristics of the poem are in keeping with its elemental and emotionally simple meaning. For example, memorized inventories of the contents of one's life are typical of oral culture, and certain kinds of oral poetry are designed to collect and remember the personalities of family members. The poem also inventories the poet's personal experience. He has forty-seven photographs of forty-seven relatives, indexed as "father, mother, grandmothers (1 dead), grand/ fathers (both dead), brothers, sisters, uncles, aunts, cousins (1st & 2nd), nieces, and nephews." He reports having been "in love" with twelve relatives, whom he enumerates. Next he inventories his male relative namesakes—eight of them. In part 2 of the poem, an inventory of ten declarative sentences enumerates the events of his trip to his Mississippi birthplace.

Significantly, the poem's most important figurative language occurs in part 2 of the poem. The first example is its central metaphor, "like a salmon quitting/ the cold ocean—leaping and bucking up his birthstream," which is completed in the last stanza, "a gray stone wall damming my stream, . . . [I] flop on my bunk and stare" (like a fish). The second example employs an oddly esoteric diction in the "electric/ messages" from his home in Mississippi that are "galvanizing" his "genes." The third example is a sampling of a drug addict's jargon: "a monkey on my back" and "I cracked a croaker's crib for a fix." Otherwise, the poem's diction is literal. These details of the poet's simple personal culture are nevertheless divided in the diptych structure of the poem's two parts, hinged like a tabletop photograph frame. The parts are pictures, respectively, of Knight's relatives and of Knight himself. A final feature worth noting about the poem is the average number of syllables in its lines. The first forty-one lines have an average of thirteen syllables. The last line, "to float in the space between," is emphatically truncated, one is tempted to say decapitated, at seven, followed by the endless space beyond the end of the poem, an emptiness in place of the "sons" the poet does not have.

Themes and Meanings

The main meaning of the title "The Idea of Ancestry" can be expressed as an interrogative one: Is there an ancestry—an actual relationship to a prior human family—or is it just an idea, a construct of language, photography, and Scripture? The Bible is an ambivalent referent for African Americans, used as it was to help them cope with slavery and other difficulties. Even so, it presents, with its enumeration of the tribes and families of the Hebrew people, the most famous of all Western civilization's rubrics of homage to ancestry. Meanwhile, it is interesting that Knight does not name the dynastic ancestry celebrated in the Egyptian culture that paralleled the Hebraic one. People of African ancestry can claim an authentic and august pedigree in Egyptian terms, but Knight eschews this. He is without pretension. Instead, he mentions his grandmother five times: She is old, and she has survived long enough to become an ancestor. His grandfathers are both dead. The poem does answer these questions about ancestry, however. Ancestry does exist. The stone wall of the prison dams the poet's "stream," his "birthstream." When it separates him from society, it erases him from history, and therefore he cannot have sons and thus become an ancestor.

The idea of ancestry, therefore, works both ways: The society that put the poet in prison enjoys an ancestry, a historical identity that nourishes and "galvanizes" it. Society denies the dignity of ancestry to the imprisoned poet, whose identity in history is thereby interrupted. Ancestry, however, is collective: "I am all of them" and "they are thee." Therefore, when society erases the poet's identity in history by extinguishing his power to have sons, it diminishes the numbers, of which the poet is one, of its ancestral generation and thereby flaws its unanimity. Thus, the space left by the poet's lost uncle, the space of the prison cell, and "the space between" with which the poem ends represent the loss of personhood, the extinction of freedom, and the end of connection to family, people, and history.

John R. Pfeiffer

THE IDEA OF ORDER AT KEY WEST

Author: Wallace Stevens (1879-1955)
Type of poem: Meditation
First published: 1934; collected in *Ideas of Order,* 1935

The Poem
"The Idea of Order at Key West" is a meditative poem in a relaxed iambic pentameter. Its fifty-six lines are broken into groups of uneven length that define the major points of its argument. The poem examines the interaction between imagination and reality through the figure of a woman who sings beside the sea and whose voice neither violates the reality of the sea nor simply reproduces it. She is the creator or "maker," not merely a mirror. She puts the sea's "dark voice" into human words, drawing it into the realm of human experience: "When she sang, the sea/ Whatever self it had, became the self/ That was her song, for she was the maker." Her song is not an exact reproduction of nature's own utterances. If it were it would not be meaningful to the human listener, but "would have been the heaving speech of air." Nor could it be simply her own voice; "it was more than that." The woman's voice is a translation of the natural into the human, which allows her listeners to perceive their world anew. It is her song of nature that heightens the listeners' sense both of the world itself and of their uncertain position in it: "It was her voice that made/ The sky acutest at its vanishing."

The listeners find that at the conclusion of her song, the world has been re-ordered for them: The lights in the fishing boats at the harbor have created a new arrangement of the natural. These lights have "mastered the night and portioned out the sea,/ . . . Arranging, deepening, enchanting night." The speaker of the poem, after hearing the woman's song, asks "Ramon Fernandez" to explain, if he can, why this reordering has taken place. Ramon Fernandez was an actual French critic, but when Wallace Stevens was asked about the allusion he claimed that he chose the name at random. (Since Stevens was acquainted with Fernandez's work, the disclaimer may be suspect.) One can think of the Fernandez in the poem as "the critic" or simply as an intelligent listener. In the last five-line section, the speaker, still addressing Fernandez, answers his own question by referring to the "blessed rage for order" which is responsible for the transformation. This "maker's rage to order words of the sea" causes humans to search for more precise definitions of their points of arrival and departure. In studying the obscure hints of the nature of humanity, humans seek more exact and intense poetry: "In ghostlier demarcations, keener sounds."

The poem's title is reflected in the title of the collection, *Ideas of Order* (1935). At this point in his work, Stevens had turned from the Florida images of fecund nature that dominated his earlier poems to more active poems exploring and defining the act of creative perception.

Forms and Devices

The iambic pentameter of this poem is not, strictly speaking, blank verse, but irregular rhyme. The use and abandonment of rhyme seems appropriate to the poem's portrayal of the creative act as an attempt to impose order—the system of language—on chaos, the reality of the sea. The rhymes themselves, often identical rhymes, suggest the motion of the waves.

The poem begins with two seven-line segments containing rhyme; the second is the most tightly structured, its lines concluding with the words "she," "sound," "heard," "word," "stirred," "wind," and "heard." As the reader believes that a pattern has been established, however, the sections become more irregular and the vocabulary more varied. The flow of the poem becomes less artificial, more subtle, as it changes from rhyming iambic pentameter in the direction of more flexible blank verse. The last five lines, which make up the exalted address to the critic, conclude with the words "Ramon," "sea," "starred," "origins," and "sounds."

The overall form of the first part suggests the subject: the sea put into words. The images and metaphors in this description of sea and singer emphasize their difference through imaginative combinations of them: "The water never formed to mind or voice,/ Like a body wholly body, fluttering/ Its empty sleeves." The comparison is both physical and intellectual, and it illustrates Stevens's agility in embodying aesthetic concepts in poetry. The sea's inhumanness is ironically demonstrated by comparing it with the human, giving it attributes of "body" and clothing—"empty sleeves." Lines such as "The grinding water and the gasping wind" bring the sea graphically into the poem as the backdrop and source of the woman's song.

When the poem describes the song's ending and the listeners turning "toward the town," the tone and imagery "turn" too, in the direction of the final affirmation of poetry and humanity both. As the rhymes diminish, the images change from the sea's repetitions to the ordering power of the lights on the boats—lights (and flames) tending to represent consciousness. From the disordered sea of reality one moves to geometric structures of light, "emblazoned zones and fiery poles," which art has created by changing the way the real is envisioned.

Themes and Meanings

In 1954, the year before his death, Wallace Stevens was asked to define his major theme for a contributor's column. His clear, direct statement might have been taken from almost any of his earlier critics' analyses. His work, he said,

> suggests the possibility of a supreme fiction, recognized as a fiction, in which men could propose to themselves a fulfillment. In the creation of any such fiction, poetry would have a vital significance. There are many poems relating to the interactions between reality and the imagination, which are to be regarded as marginal to this central theme.

This summary statement encapsulates the general thrust of Stevens's poetry and the motivation behind "The Idea of Order at Key West," a relatively early poem.

One of the characteristics that establishes Stevens's modernism is the self-reflexiveness of his work. His poems are all about writing poetry; they reflect themselves. This poem explores three questions, all relating to the creative act. It asks, What is the relationship between the imagination and reality in art? What does art do for, or to, its perceiver? Where does art originate?

The relationship between sea and song, as described in the first part of the poem, illustrates that ideally art puts reality into a human structure without violating the nature of that reality—that is, without falsification. The speaker emphasizes the role of the imagination as "maker" but suggests that the "she" who is the singer of the poem is being as true as she can to what she observes, considering the limitation that she must express her vision in the human vehicle of words. (That the imagined world must be bound by the real is suggested in other of Stevens's poems, such as "The Ordinary Women.")

The question of what art does for its perceiver is given a double answer. Art provides an understanding of what would otherwise be the alien language of nature. Moreover, art increases one's sense of one's place in this world, although this position may be one of isolation and filled with uncertainties. In other words, art gives a heightened sense of both one's world and oneself.

Finally, the source of art is represented as desire, as a human need that transcends logic. The source of art is a desire for truth and poetry at once. The poetic impulse is a furious need (a "rage") to "order words of the sea," or create order from the chaos of the world. Yet it is also a need to explore human origins and points of departure, "fragrant portals" barely perceived and shrouded in mystery. The pursuit of such understanding leads to both greater knowledge and more acute poetry ("In ghostlier demarcations, keener sounds"). The poet alters how he or she and others perceive reality, and the source of this change is the "blessed rage" that is the poet's curse and gift.

Janet McCann

IF YOU ASK ME

Author: Gunnar Ekelöf (1907-1968)
Type of poem: Dramatic monologue
First published: 1955, as "Frågar du mig var jag finns," in *Strountes*; English transla-
tion collected in *Selected Poems of Gunnar Ekelöf*, 1967

The Poem
　"If You Ask Me" is a short dramatic monologue in free verse. The speaker seems to
be identical with Gunnar Ekelöf himself. In the opening lines he anticipates—and answers—a question posed by his unidentified interlocutor about where he exists–*finns*,
the Swedish verb Ekelöf uses, means something between "abide" and "reside." As the
monologue continues, the reader becomes closely identified with the silent friend to
whom the poet is speaking. Using the familiar *du* form of address (which in 1955 still
implied a certain degree of intimacy), the poet explains that he lives beyond the mountains in a world that is at once far away and nearby. He admits that he inhabits another
world but insists that the friend—perhaps without knowing it—lives there too. Like
the earth's atmosphere, this other world is everywhere; but, like helium, it only exists
in minute quantities in relation to some of the other permanent constituents of the atmosphere like nitrogen, carbon dioxide, and hydrogen.
　The poet's friend has apparently believed this other world to be some sort of mystical, transcendent realm; therefore he has asked for an airship (a helium-filled dirigi-
ble) to take him there. The poet tells him that what he really needs for the journey is a
filter—that is, some sort of gas mask that will eliminate noxious gases. He tells him to
ask for a filter that will take out everything that separates people from each other, a filter that will even separate them from "life," in other words, from the mundane concerns that prevent them from entering the other world. The meaning of this metaphoric filter becomes one of the cruxes of the poem.
　Having apparently received and donned the requisite filtering mask, the friend next
blames it for the fact that he finds it difficult to breathe. The poet reproves him by
pointing out that everyone who uses the filter to attain the purer air of the other world
has difficulty breathing, though most of the time they tolerate this condition without
complaint. As a final reproof to his friend, the poet implicitly—and ironically—compares him to a certain "wise" man who blamed the darkness for the difficulty he had in
seeing the stars. Whether or not the friend feels the sting of the poet's irony and understands that darkness is the necessary precondition for seeing stars the reader never
learns.

Forms and Devices
　Strountes, the curious title of the collection in which "If You Ask Me" appeared,
points to one of the most striking stylistic aspects of this poem: its plain, unpoetic diction. The word *Strountes* appears to be a French transliteration of the Swedish word

strunt, which means "rubbish" or "nonsense." One of the epigraphs Ekelöf chose for this collection was a statement by the great Swedish Romantic poet and novelist, C. J. L. Almqvist, that it is unbelievably—almost insuperably—difficult to write *strunt*. Göran Printz-Påhlson has observed that in this volume of poems, Ekelöf is "attempting to make poetry by counterposing completely uncorrelated styles and in that way to find out his own 'style'" (*Solen i spegeln*, 1958). Leif Sjöberg's rendering of *Strountes* as "Tryflings" captures something of the Joycean wit Ekelöf doubtless intended the title to convey to his Swedish readers (introduction to *Selected Poems of Gunnar Ekelöf*). The casual, freewheeling style of the *Strountes* poems allows Ekelöf to steer a course that moves between the cosmic and the comic. "If You Ask Me," which was also translated by Robert Bly in his anthology *Friends, You Drank Some Darkness: Three Swedish Poets* (1975), lies closer to the comic pole. Like most of the forty-eight poems in this collection, it has no title, no punctuation, and no identifiable form.

What, then, makes it a poem? Poetry, according to Ekelöf, arises not from the contents of the poem, but from the counterpoint of its words. In one of his most important essays, "En outsiders väg" ("An Outsider's Way," 1941), he explains this principle: "Seen in one light a group of words means something that was clear as day, seen in another the meaning of the same words is uncertain—as night. And poetry is this very tension-filled relationship *between* the words, *between* the lines, *between* the meanings." An example of Ekelöf's ability to create such tensions is evident in the way in which we glide by association from "helium" to "airship" (which is usually filled with helium). His skill at creating the kind of counterpoint he requires in a true poem is much more evident in the original Swedish text, however, in which the first syllable of "helium" may suggest *hel* ("whole")—and consequently the kind of *helhet* (wholeness) that can only be found in the "other" world. Similarly, the banal Swedish phrase he attributes to the "wise" man, *nätt och jämnt* ("barely"), interacts with *natt* ("night") and *jämnmod* ("equanimity") in a way that highlights the significance of these two key words in the poem.

Themes and Meanings

A first reading of this poem about the other world inhabited by the isolated poet might tempt the reader to see it as a restatement of the Nature-Art dichotomy, a traditional theme that is perhaps best known to readers of modern poetry in "Sailing to Byzantium" (1928) by William Butler Yeats. But Ekelöf is not seeking to replace mutability with the permanence of art. Indeed, he appears to reject the idea that one can sail away by airship to a world that might be filled with "monuments of unageing intellect." He is isolated, not because he is old or because he is a poet, but because isolation is the human condition. What he is saying in this poem is that though he is daily in close, but superficial, contact with other people, he is really totally isolated, deeply confined within his own self. Quite satisfied with his shallow relations with other people, the addressee fails to realize that he has no real self. What Ekelöf says to his reader in "Tag och skriv" ("Open it, Write") applies equally to the friend in "If You Ask Me":

In reality you are no one.
Your suit; a place, a name—
all else is merely your wish,
your 'I' a wish, your lostness one, your savedness another:
you have taken it all out in advance!

In "If You Ask Me," breathing (or difficulty in breathing), a common theme in Ekelöf, vividly concretizes the desperate inadequacy of the atmosphere ("sphere of breath")—that is, of reality. Merely living in this atmosphere fragments one; not only does it separate people from one another, it also keeps them from themselves. This is why he recommends the filter with which to isolate the helium that is diffused among the other components of the air. This "helium," this "other world," is Ekelöf's metaphor for the self. What one can hope to find after filtering out everything that keeps people from entering this pure self is best stated in "An Outsider's Way":

A writer's first task is to resemble himself, to become a person. His duty, or rather, his best way of attaining this, is to acknowledge his incurable loneliness and the futility of his wandering on Earth. It is only then that he can strip away all the stage scenery, decorations, and disguises from reality. And it is only in that capacity that he can be useful to others—by placing himself in the predicaments of others—of everyone! It is futility that gives life its meaning.

This short dramatic monologue is a concise poetic restatement of that credo. It involves a paradox that, as Printz-Påhlson has pointed out, recurs in many of Ekelöf's poems: Only in the depths of the self does one find what is common to all. Because the poet has found this kind of wholeness in his self, he urges a "filter" upon his friend. Even though the quest for wholeness involves considerable discomfort, the potential reward should encourage the reader to undertake the filtering process with equanimity. The final fillip in the poem comes when he discredits the "wise" man who blames the darkness for the fact that he can barely see the stars, traditional symbols of aspiration and of direction. Implicit in the last word in the poem, "night," is the idea, frequently expressed in Ekelöf's poetry, that all of the familiar polarities—day and night, good and evil, life and death, meaning and meaninglessness—are complementary concepts that only acquire meaning when considered in relation to each other.

Barry Jacobs

IL PENSEROSO

Author: John Milton (1608-1674)
Type of poem: Pastoral
First published: 1645, in *Poems of Mr. John Milton*

The Poem

The poem stands as the companion piece to "L'Allegro," using the same non-stanzaic tetrameter form; at 176 lines, it is twenty-four lines longer than its companion. The title, meaning "the thinker" or "the contemplative man," suggests its opposition to its companion piece. The poem expresses the joys of the solitary man walking abroad during the evening, sitting studying at night in the midst of quiet woodlands, or finding pleasure in tragic and heroic literature and in mystic churches.

The poem's opening rejects mirth as delusion and triviality. Instead, the poet welcomes the goddess Melancholy. He gives her a more original and much older genealogy than that given to Euphrosyne in "L'Allegro," seeing her as daughter of the pre-Olympian deity Hestia (John Milton uses the Roman form of Vesta), goddess of sacred and domestic fire, whom he makes wife and daughter of Saturn. Hesiod had made her the eternally virgin daughter of Chronos and Rhea; Milton transfers her virginity to her daughter. As at her conception, Melancholy remains associated with evening and "secret shades." Her traditional blackness is, paradoxically, her intense brightness and is as beautiful as that of Cassiopeia, the Ethiopian queen who was transformed into a constellation.

He invites her to come to him, together with Peace and Quiet, rather vague personifications, and especially with "the cherub Contemplation," in a silence broken only by the nightingale's song. None of the country's sounds or society is for him; he would prefer to wander solitary in the moonlight through woods and meadows or walk near the seashore. If the weather is inclement, he would happily study through the night. His chosen reading is either ancient volumes of hermetic (or secret) wisdom, Greek and more recent tragedy, or epic poetry. He mentions Geoffrey Chaucer, Torquato Tasso, and Edmund Spenser in particular. Unlike the persona of "L'Allegro," he is not interested in seeing the drama live: He wants it to inspire him imaginatively, to transport him as if Orpheus himself were to sing to him.

Eventually he sees the morning come, and—unlike the morning of the companion piece—it conforms to his mood: It is cloudy, with blustery showers. If the sun breaks through, he would prefer to walk in the forest, listening to the murmuring of the streams, perhaps falling asleep on their banks. On waking, he wishes to hear the mysterious music of the nature spirits of the woodland. Finally, as he looks forward in his life, he would like to retire to "the studious Cloysters pale" of a college or church and be overwhelmed with the beauty of the ritual and the music of the organ. Eventually, through such study and perception of beauty, he would wish to become a prophetic figure. If Melancholy can give all this to him, he will follow her.

Forms and Devices

Most readers will read this poem after reading "L'Allegro." Attention is thus focused necessarily on the two poems' parallel structures and on the differences to be found at each level. Clearly, one of the parallel structures is the opening: ten lines of alternating iambic trimeter and pentameter. In rejecting Mirth, he sets up a parody figure, just as in "L'Allegro" a parody figure of Melancholy is set up only to be mocked and rejected.

The verse form also uses a parallel structure, with rhyming couplets of iambic tetrameter; however, the rhythm of the poem is completely different. In the difference, one may see a clear indication of the young Milton's very mature poetic technique and control (already seen in the even earlier "On the Morning of Christ's Nativity"). The rhythmic differences are established by a slightly longer line; by more clustering of stressed syllables and consonants, as in "Thy rapt soul sitting in thine eyes"; and by a preference for long vowel sounds, especially those with a darker coloring. Apart from these differences, the overall sense and tone determine the rhythm. Milton has taken a verse form which, in couplets especially, can sound very trivial, and given it a solemn and stately movement that becomes almost trance-like toward the end.

At the level of content, the structures reverse those of "L'Allegro." That poem goes from morning until late evening, this from the late evening until morning. The invocation to the goddess, together with her companions, closely parallels the other poem, although Milton expands this section considerably. He seems much more interested in the figure of Melancholy than in that of Euphrosyne. The nightingale's song is evoked rather than the lark's; the moon, rather than the sun, is "riding neer her highest noon"; and instead of the "Towers and Battlements" of the idyllic landscape, he prefers "some high lonely Towr" as a place of study. Types of literature are contrasted, as are types of music; the story of Orpheus is noble, a source of tragic beauty that moves one to tears. The morning must not be "trickt and frounc't" for good hunting weather but should suit his melancholy. References continue throughout to shade—as "comly Cloud," "twilight groves," "close covert," and "hide"—in language that John Keats was later to make his own.

The final twenty lines, however, go beyond the structure of "L'Allegro," as the speaker sees himself listening to the church service. The poem expands toward its conclusion and finishes with the climactic "To something like Prophetic strain." The poet's real engagement with his subject matter is perhaps sensed here; the earlier desire for the unfolding worlds of philosophy becomes a total sensory and spiritual experience of rapture to "bring all heav'n before mine eyes."

Themes and Meanings

Any attempt to understand "L'Allegro" and "Il Penseroso" as a pair does not exhaust the readings that "Il Penseroso" is able to generate in itself. This is largely attributable to the thematic complexity surrounding the idea of melancholy, a complexity not found in discussing mirth. Renaissance literature was profoundly interested in the subject: *The Anatomy of Melancholy* (1621) by Robert Burton had recently been published; William Shakespeare's *Hamlet* (1602) and *Timon of Athens* (c. 1607-1608) are both dramatic studies in the subject, as were many Jacobean plays. The melancholic person was seen ambiguously as a killjoy (in comedy), a depressive, and a scholar, and as having a source of wisdom denied to others. The interest in melancholy was partly an extension of medieval psychology and physiology, based on the notion of the humors, but it partly arose from a cultural mood of confusion and insecurity.

Modern readers are tempted to read into the poem the Romantic delineation of melancholy, expressed by such poets as Samuel Taylor Coleridge, Keats, and Alfred, Lord Tennyson. Keats's version seems the closest to that of "Il Penseroso," with its depiction of moonlit night, woods, streams, cloud, shade, and visions of the sublime. Thus, the poem could be read (somewhat anachronistically) as a Romantic mood poem: searching for intensity of experience, reaching beyond normative states of consciousness into ecstasy or sublimity, and thus grasping truths and revelation not available otherwise. Yet "mood" seems too weak a word here (although it would do for "L'Allegro"); one is driven to a deeper reading that, while retaining such Romantic elements, does so by virtue of its Neoplatonism.

The "spirit of Plato" is invoked in line 89 to unfold the regions forsaken by the soul in its descent into the human body at birth. The "extasies" aroused by the organ music can be seen as a parallel attempt to reach back into this Platonic state of original perfection. The hermetic wisdom to which he refers can be loosely linked to Neoplatonic philosophy. The tower that he mentions is a Neoplatonic symbol of the soul seeking divine wisdom—a symbol that the Irish poet William Butler Yeats was later to use literally. Renaissance literature in England, as elsewhere, tended to embrace Plato as part of its rejection of medieval Aristotelianism. John Milton's poetry, like Andrew Marvell's, is explicitly Platonic at times, especially in the masque *Comus* (1637). It is this tradition that Romanticism continued.

The way of melancholy is thus the only way possible to reach that higher and older wisdom denied most humans, for it is the way of contemplation. The genealogy of Melancholy also suggests this: It is a much more ancient genealogy than that given to Mirth, who must content herself with a post-Olympian birth. Saturn is the presiding star for the melancholic. Saturn is the oldest divinity, predating Zeus and the Olympians, and thus he enshrines the most ancient knowledge—a point that Keats struggled to make in *Hyperion* (1820). Thus the poet, in choosing melancholy, chooses to be the poet-philosopher of Platonic tradition and, even more powerfully, the poet-prophet, a role (already envisaged in "On the Morning of Christ's Nativity") which would give Milton's religious faith full expression.

David Barratt

I'M HERE

Author: David Ignatow (1914-1997)
Type of poem: Narrative/verse essay
First published: 1975, in *Facing the Tree: New Poems*

The Poem

David Ignatow's "I'm Here" qualifies as an Armageddon poem, a poem of utter destruction, presumably resulting from nuclear holocaust. A forewarning broadcasts the onset of this dire event: "The radio said, Go to your shelters." However, this message is delivered in such a low voice that the unnamed participants fail to heed it. They do not want to heed it; they do not want to face the reality that the end may be near. Standing paralyzed before the set, they are powerless to act and can take no steps to delay the inevitable.

The blast erupts with colorful drama. They (the "we" in the poem) watch as it colors the horizon, knowing that they are about to be killed. They cannot embrace the reality of their encroaching nonexistence. In the first stanza, the participants continue to be physical realities, people with faces, bodies, bones, flesh. In the following stanza, however, they begin as physical entities but soon lose their corporeal identities. In the poem's most visual passage, they run, having their bodies drop away as they proceed, attempting futilely to beat the odds.

They gradually become parts of nature, the faceless, nonhuman nature that constitutes much of the physical world: "We could be the wind rushing/ through the trees or the stars moving out/ to the perimeter." In the great chaos unleashed by the detonation of a powerful destructive force, identities disappear as the physical bodies vanish, melt down into what is left of the surrounding physical world:

> We know we felt ourselves
> vanishing in flame and wind
> and it seemed as though we were becoming
> one or the other.

These lines project a feeling of primordial chaos. The self, now appearing to give way, is being amalgamated into some greater whole, apparently becoming one with nature, one with the flame and the wind.

In the third stanza, the speaker considers what life is and what it is to live. His physical being now gone, the speaker asks, "How then can we still speak to you/ without body or voice?" It is unclear who is being addressed. Perhaps the disembodied voice is crying out into a wilderness in which no human receptors remain. This stanza poses questions about nonexistence, leaving the reader to ponder whether people can imagine their own ceasing to be.

In the poem's final and longest stanza, the disembodied voice wonders what has become of the "you" it is addressing, in some cave at rest, waiting for the enemy to arrive, or with its family. The speaker, reflecting on having once been human, presumes "nothing for you has changed in form, body/ or mind." He longs for a voice to fill the "emptiness in [his] speech."

The voice, desperate to communicate, copes with its own invisibility. It can communicate only subliminally, assuring the "you," the hoped-for recipient, that "You can speak to me by standing perfectly still/ where you are and breathing regularly." This rudimentary communication will assure the disembodied speaker "that all is well/ for the human" and will enable the speaker to depart in peace.

Forms and Devices

The four stanzas of "I'm Here" build gradually. They contain seven, eight, ten, and fifteen lines, respectively. In the revised version printed in *New and Collected Poems, 1970-1985* (1986), however, the last stanza is sonnet-length, fourteen lines. Other small changes occur in this later version.

The poem is written in blank verse, most of its lines iambic, most in pentameter with a few in hexameter, both of which resemble the rhythms of human speech. Although none of its lines rhymes, Ignatow in the first stanza engages in subtle wordplay. Line 2 reads in part "that we stood there," and the following line ends with "wanting to understand." One might find a suggestion of wordplay in the correlation between "stood" and "understand," especially after reading to the end of that stanza, where "still unable to realize" is followed by "being killed, for real." If, indeed, the poet consciously employs this technique, he abandons it as the poem becomes increasingly philosophical.

Beginning as a physical entity, the speaker loses his physicality by the last stanza and becomes invisible. In the final lines of the early version of the poem, Ignatow writes, "Then I'll understand that all is well/ for the human and leave,/ content." In the later version, however, the poet consolidates the last two lines into one that reads, "for the human to vanish, content." "Vanish" is a more decisive word in this context than "leave." To leave can imply a return. To vanish is to slip into invisibility, to disappear, presumably forever, a fear the speaker expresses forcefully in the final stanza.

The other alteration between the two versions of the poem occurs in the third stanza, where the original text reads, "you hear every word I speak but do not see/ or feel me anywhere at all. I have no sight." The second line has six iambic feet, whereas the later version omits the words "at all," resulting in a line of five iambic feet. The shorter, later line is stronger and more effective. The earlier version overstates, and, in doing so, violates the cardinal rule that good poetry be economical in its use of words.

Very early versions of "I'm Here" appeared in periodicals under the titles "Here I Am" and "In a Dream." The choice of the final title "I'm Here" captures the essence of what the poem is about better than these two titles because "I'm Here" conveys a sort of calling out, a cry for recognition that the other two titles lack. Also, the contracted "I'm" adds a desired informality and colloquialism to the poem.

Themes and Meanings

The pervasive theme in "I'm Here" is one of annihilation, although the title suggests, as does the last stanza, that the speaker is not fully gone. The poem does not offer hope of the kinds of afterlife that many of the world's religions promise. Rather, the speaker, quickly losing his physical attributes, seeks only to connect with an anonymous "you," who is addressed in the last two stanzas.

Early in the poem, the speaker communicates in a single voice but uses the first-person plural, the royal "we," rather than the first-person singular in referring to itself. Not until the third stanza is the pronoun "I" employed, and it recurs in the final stanza. Although the speaker addresses the "you" in the poem, in the lines "I hunger for a voice to fill/ an emptiness in my speech," the pronoun "your" is not used before "voice," indicating that the speaker wants his own voice back. The speaker, once he loses his corporeal being, is invisible but, much worse in some ways, is also without a voice, without the power to communicate.

The very fact that the being that has lost its body in the violent event that generates the poem suggests annihilation, but this suggestion is subverted by the fact that the incorporeal stranger is still communicating, often, quite ironically, about his own inability to communicate. Although the speaker is invisible, he is present creating the poem and posing questions about what happens when one dies. The lines that begin the third stanza, "How then can we still speak to you/ without body or voice?," are followed by another question and suggest that the world of the dead "penetrates this one you're in."

Certainly the speaker, now dead, continues to be concerned about the "you," which can be read as singular or plural, although Ignatow seems to imply that the "you" is a mother figure, one concerned with family, one who is "comforting them with food," as mothers tend to do. This is the poem's sole hint of gender. From it, however, readers cannot categorically presume that a mother figure is being portrayed. The hint is tormentingly subtle.

The author moves beyond the "ashes to ashes, dust to dust" theology of conventional Christianity to a theology that reminds one of Robert Frost's question about whether the world ends in fire or in ice. In "I'm Here," the world ends in flames and wind. Those who try to outrun the devastation lose their corporeal forms, becoming part of the very elements that consume them, "vanishing in flame and wind," and lead to their vanishing. The fact that there remains a speaker, however, combined with the poem's title, offers hope, however slight, that humankind will endure.

R. Baird Shuman

THE IMAGE IN LAVA

Author: Felicia Hemans (1793-1835)
Type of poem: Lyric
First published: 1828, in *Records of Woman*

The Poem

"The Image in Lava" is a short poem of eleven four-line stanzas. The title refers to an impression, in volcanic ash and lava, of a woman clasping a baby to her breast that was discovered during the excavation of the ruins of the ancient city of Herculaneum (buried with Pompeii by an eruption of the volcano Mount Vesuvius in 79 C.E.). In the first stanza, the speaker of the poem addresses the image directly, asking "What ages have gone by" since the moment when the mother and infant were killed ("the mournful seal was set" in "love and agony"). The next stanza comments on all the empires, with their temples and towers (places of power), that have come and gone since that moment. The speaker thus establishes, early in the poem, one of its central themes—that the human love between mother and child is more lasting than all the powerful institutions humans may build. This contrast is continued in the third stanza with the idea that the image of childhood, despite its fragility, has outlasted the "proud memorials" of the "conquerors of mankind."

The next five stanzas address the infant directly, first asking if it was sleeping when the moment of death came, then setting up the idea that though the fiery death was a "strange, dark fate," it was better to end life at that moment of love than to live to know the pain of separation. That thought leads the speaker to speculate about the mother while still speaking to the child. She asks the child if it was the only "treasure" left to the mother, whether she had been forsaken by all others on whom she had "lavished" her love in vain. The speaker wonders, in the seventh stanza, if all the others the mother had loved and trusted had left her only "thorns on which to lean." If so, the speaker suggests in the eighth stanza, it was better for her also to die clasping her remaining loved one than to continue to live and perhaps lose this last object of her love.

The last three stanzas return to the theme established in the second stanza—the contrast between the love of mother and child and all the power of "cities of renown" that have not lasted as the impression in lava has. The speaker says, in stanza 9, that she would bypass all the relics and ruins of all the impressive buildings left from the "pomps of old" to look at the image of the mother and child; though a "rude" (simple, not magnificent) "monument," it is cast in "affection's mould," that is, created by a mother's love. The tenth stanza addresses "Love, human love!" directly, asking it what allows it to leave its imprint to be preserved when all that the mighty have erected has turned to dust. The speaker answers the question in the concluding stanza, saying that human love is the "earthly glow" of holy love, a representation or a shining through into human existence, of the light of immortal love. Though the mother and child have perished, the imprint left by their love has outlasted all the monuments of power and "given these ashes holiness." "It must, it *must* be so," the poem concludes.

Forms and Devices

The eleven stanzas of the poem are in ballad stanza; that is, the second and fourth lines rhyme, while the first and third do not. Ballad stanza was repopularized in Hemans's time; her contemporaries William Wordsworth and Samuel Taylor Coleridge revived the form, which had been in disuse for some time, in their joint volume of poems *Lyrical Ballads* (1798).

"The Image in Lava" also resembles, in its three-part structure, a form that Wordsworth and Coleridge employed and called a "conversation poem": a description of the scene, a meditation upon the scene, and then a return to the scene. The scene in this case would be the impression of the woman and the infant in lava, described in the first three stanzas; the meditation on the scene would be the middle five stanzas in which the speaker of the poem addresses the infant; and the return to the scene would be the final three stanzas, in which the speaker returns to the image in lava to compare it once again to the relics of the mighty and conclude that it is an earthly image of immortal love. As is traditional with ballads, the meter of the poem is predominantly iambic (an unstressed syllable followed by a stressed syllable); it has three iambic feet in a line (trimeter) except for the third line in each stanza, which has four iambic feet (tetrameter).

The imagery of the poem arises primarily from the contrast between the love of the mother and child and the proud buildings and monuments raised by the mighty as evidence of their earthly power. The poet refers to these structures of "empires" and "mighty cities" as "temple" (church) and "tower" (government) and describes them with words such as "pomp" and "pride," using alliteration in both instances. Childhood, in contrast, is described as "fragile," but the words and images used to describe the child and mother and their love for each other suggest permanence—"image," "print," "monument," and "enshrined." These words suggest the iconic and the representational, especially of holy things, of things that are immortal, so that the impression of the mother and child in the volcanic dust, representing a "woman's heart" and "human love," are icons of divine, immortal love.

This ironic use of the imagery of an image is related to another subtle irony: Though the bodies of mother and child have turned to dust and disappeared while the buildings still stand, the image in dust survives because it is a semblance of divine love, while the buildings, symbols of earthly power, are in ruins, and no trace remains of the mighty who built them. This ironic contrast is also embedded in the imagery of dark and light: The sudden, early death of the mother and child was a "strange, dark fate," but their love was an "earthly glow," an image of the divine brightness.

Themes and Meanings

In "The Image in Lava," Hemans explores, as she does frequently in her work, the conflict between fame, which she sought and succeeded in obtaining in large measure, and the quieter, domestic virtues of family and motherhood. This conflict was especially real to a woman writer in her time, since middle- and upper-class women were discouraged from working outside the home and taught that their proper sphere was caring for a household and a family. Women who sought nondomestic careers were thought of as unwomanly, even when financial necessity forced them to earn money, as was the case with Hemans, a mother of five sons and their sole financial support (her husband separated from the family, never to return). The great nurse Florence Nightingale, who knew Hemans's work and copied one of her poems for a cousin, detailed, in her book *Cassandra* (1852-59), the obstacles faced by women similar to herself who sought self-expression outside the home.

In "The Image in Lava," as elsewhere in her poetry, Hemans supports the cultural expectations of her time by suggesting that motherhood is finer than any of the other achievements to which humans can aspire and more lasting than the monuments they build to their own power and fame. Yet the poem also hints at the price women pay for this sacrifice. When the poem explores the possibility that all the others the mother had lavished her love upon had abandoned her, she acknowledges the sad reality, experienced by both herself and her beloved mother, that women were often left to sustain a household and rear the children alone. Hemans was also aware of the grim reality that many women died early from childbirth and the rigors of child-rearing, and that the infant mortality rate in her time was very high; though the mother and child in the poem die in a volcanic eruption, they image the early death of many nineteenth century women and children.

Indeed, much of the poetry of British (and American) women in the nineteenth century is preoccupied with the early death of women; often, the speaker of the poem is a voice from the grave, and often, too, the concern of the speaker is with remembrance of her after death, as in Emily Brontë's "Remembrance" and Christina Rossetti's "Remember." Hemans, whose poetry predates that of Brontë and Rossetti, helps to establish this motif in women's poetry when she contrasts the enduring impression of the love between mother and child to the ephemeral quality of fame in the world. Also like Rossetti, she finds consolation for womanly suffering in the belief in a divine power; "The Image in Lava" concludes with the insistence ("It must, it *must* be so!") that the sacrificial love of the mother for her child is an image of the divine love, an evidence of eternal love.

June M. Frazer

THE IMPALPABILITIES

Author: Charles Tomlinson (1927-   )
Type of poem: Lyric
First published: 1963, in *A Peopled Landscape*

The Poem
"The Impalpabilities" is a short lyric in one stanza of twenty-two lines, written in free verse. It does not have a traditional lyric subject, such as a person, place, or object. Instead, it is concerned with the subtleties involved in the way what is outside oneself is perceived.

The poem is written in an impersonal mode. It uses the first-person plural "we" in order to include the reader in the statements it makes about the nature of experience. By describing shades and tones of his perceptions in as detailed a manner as possible, the poet hopes to remind readers of moments in their own experience that are similar to his.

The poem starts by directing readers to the "things we must include/ because we do not understand them." It is the impalpable things that cannot immediately be grasped and molded into shape by humanity that will concern the poet. Not being able to understand impalpable things with the ease and readiness with which one knows the palpable, does not mean that the impalpable can merely be passed by. That which is beyond one's knowledge is still encountered, and its mystery is tempting rather than daunting.

The impalpabilities, as one would expect, never take final form in the poem, but the poet finds suggestions of them in various half-realized events or objects. In the fifth line of the poem, the impalpabilities linger in the "marine dark" like an uncanny sea creature. In the nine lines that follow, there is a sustained evocation of musical chords. These chords do not end in a harmonious closure. Instead, they remain suspended in a kind of frozen, perpetual dissolution. This dissolution does not mean, however, that the chords vanish into nothingness. They may be impalpable, but they are still there, exacting and requiring one's attention.

The next image in the poem is unfolded in the succeeding four lines: It is a wood which "advances before the evening takes it"—a forest glimpsed at twilight. After the sun has set, the wood is no longer illuminated as an independent and palpable phenomenon. Yet, as long as the dark has not fully advanced, it retains a distinct atmosphere of identity. This identity is not merely a vestige of its daylight one, but possesses shadowy, fascinating meanings of its own.

In the final lines, the branches of the trees in the forest are compared to "extended fingers" dipped in water that seem to become detached from the rest of the body, supporting "the cool immensity" of the external shadows and not the human form of which they were originally a part. They have passed into a distant and foreign sphere of perception, yet they are never completely separated from the human.

Forms and Devices

Much of the poem's formal effects are embodied in its appearance on the page. This is a poem whose visual aspect is not only in the images within the poem but in the poem's external shape. It is composed of short lines that are organized in groups of three apiece. In each group of three, the first line is fixed in the standard left-hand margin, while the next two lines each begin with a sharp indentation to the right. This form mirrors the subject matter of the poem, where the possibility of different perceptual shapes for different varieties of experience is acknowledged. The poet uses another device as a counterpoint to the formal organization of the lines. By varying the length of each line (from as short as only two syllables to as long as nine), he supports the poem's assertion of the whirling patterns of experience.

The poem is recognizable as a product of modern free verse, yet its agenda is not as much to depict chaos or disorder as to show ideas of order existing where one ordinarily would not suspect them to be. The poem filters its impalpable content through a tightly organized network of form. The two parentheses that appear in the eleventh and nineteenth lines remind one of the author's presence and display a layer of conscious awareness against the inchoate areas that the poem chronicles. The potential for chaos is also held in by the eloquence and reserve of the poet's language. His language is exact while being austere and reflective. Words are displayed in a way that maximizes their force. When, for example, the poem speaks of the chords that "hang/ in an orchestral undertow," the position of the word "hang" at the end of a two-word line is subtly suggestive of the action of hanging performed by the chords themselves.

Charles Tomlinson, a musician and an artist as well as a poet, skillfully combines different sense and sensory processes. Although the dominant motif in the poem is a visual one, much space is also given to hearing and to touch. The idea of the impalpable refers to something not amenable to touch, yet the powerful concluding image of the fingerlike branches implies that there is as much of a tangible sensation in failing to grasp something as in fully seizing it. The tableau of the wood standing in near darkness is a visual one, as is the previous image of the marine dark. The central orchestral metaphor brings in the element of sound. Yet these senses often seem to merge into each other, as in the previously quoted image of the "orchestral undertow." Here sound and touch are gathered together, yoked with one another in meaning, yet never merged or dissolved into a shapeless mass. By holding different senses in poised juxtaposition, the poet creates the impression of complexity and ambiguity without collapsing into confusion. Ironically, the language of sensory perception is used to convey a quantity—the impalpable—that is inherently beyond the senses. The sensory language can never hope to convey fully what is beyond us, yet it can depict this very effort at understanding.

Themes and Meanings

In his early poetry, Tomlinson concentrated on a meticulous observation of the external world. The subjects of nature and of art were especially prominent. In poems such as "On the Hall at Stowey" and "Farewell to Van Gogh," Tomlinson combined a gorgeously exact scenic vividness with a declared poetic goal. This goal was to take the lead from the masters of the Modernist movement, Ezra Pound and T. S. Eliot, who were prominent influences on Tomlinson, in rejecting a purely subjective view of experience. Tomlinson was far more sensitive to nature and to visual detail than the earlier poets, yet their influence combined with his own distinct personality to create an unusual and fascinating way of approaching the world. Instead of placing the self at the center of the universe, Tomlinson wished to direct his attention to objects whose appeal lay in the fact that they were external to the self. Tomlinson rejected what he saw as the Romantic self-indulgence of painters such as Vincent van Gogh. Instead of advertising himself, Tomlinson sought to enter into a proper relation with the world, one that would not simply subjugate all phenomena to an egoistic self-infatuation. This does not mean the self is renounced. For the poet to humble himself before the outside world is still a gesture of the poetic self. It is Tomlinson's dedicated poetic mission to move readers closer to the world as it is.

In this poem, though, Tomlinson is not depicting tangible objects, such as houses, trees, or paintings. Instead, he concentrates on their very opposites: the impalpabilities. He regards the impalpabilities in a cool, discriminating light, not with an excess of emotional energy. They do not reside in a distinct landscape, the way objects would ordinarily, yet they are placed in a sharply contoured landscape, not in a free-floating void. The poet's aim here is to break down the barrier between the opposites of the knowable and the unknowable. Tomlinson does not celebrate the impalpable because it cannot be fully known, nor does he resign himself to looking merely at what is apparent because it is all that can be fully understood. Tomlinson makes a distinction between what can be approached and what can be explained, and insists that the latter should not be mistaken for the former. To retrench from the orchestral undertow or from the looming wood at twilight would be shallow; to fantasize about it as something dark and inexplicable would be overly heated and melodramatic. Tomlinson takes the middle course, but he does not achieve a simple reconciliation between extremes. The tension and liveliness in the poem convey the strange paradox that what may be most gripping are those very phenomena on which the readers find it hardest to maintain a stable grip. In a sense, things are most palpable when they are impalpable.

Nicholas Birns

THE IMPERFECT PARADISE

Author: Linda Pastan (1932-   )
Type of poem: Sonnet sequence
First published: 1988, in *The Imperfect Paradise*

The Poem

"The Imperfect Paradise" is a sequence of six Shakespearean sonnets meditating on aspects of the story of Adam and Eve and the Fall of Man. The sonnets, in order, are titled "Seasonal," "In the Garden," "Deep in These Woods," "Thief," "The Imperfect Paradise," and "Somewhere in the Euphrates."

"Seasonal" presents a contrast between the pessimistic perspective of the speaker and the more optimistic perspective of a second person, whom the speaker addresses as "you," perhaps the speaker's husband: "you" is also referred to as "My Adam." The speaker asks this second person which season he considers the loveliest. He unhesitatingly chooses spring, while the speaker chooses winter, and the rest of the sonnet contrasts these perspectives and examines the evidence that each perspective considers decisive.

"In the Garden" opens with the question, "How do we tell the flowers from the weeds" and extends this botanical discrimination to how one chooses among people, such as Jacob—the chosen brother in Genesis 25-27—and Esau. The sonnet ends by noting how roses are dying while "dandelions and chokeweed multiply," implying that the good and the beautiful is more fragile and ephemeral, while the base increases.

"Deep in These Woods" depicts a somewhat ambiguous dialogue between the speaker and a gardener. The speaker questions how a garden can be made to grow deep within the woods, and supposes that the gardener is concealing an axe and must be cutting down oaks in order to create room and light for the garden to grow. The speaker wonders if Adam also hid certain things from Eve.

"Thief" imagines a thieving squirrel, caught in the garden, who is removed five miles away, but then returns to where it was originally trapped. The squirrel is then compared to people's fluctuating states of mind: doubts and alternating boredom and passion, which appear to be as uncontrollable as the thieving squirrel.

"The Imperfect Paradise" asks what would have happened if God had stopped creating after the fifth day, before humans were created. The speaker wonders if the wind could have adequately supplied the sound of lamentation and asks if God would have been satisfied or would have hungered for a "human crowd." The speaker contrasts the "green hosannas of a budding leaf" with "the strict contract between love and grief." The unthinking praise implied by the beauty of the natural world is thus contrasted with the bittersweet result of creating human life.

"Somewhere in the Euphrates," the final sonnet in the sequence, contrasts two ways in which the modern person might relate to the Eden stories. In the first eight lines the poet speaks of "the rusted gates of Eden" still existing, buried somewhere in the Euphrates River. She imagines archaeologists "at awful cost" trying to find "a snakeskin or an apple stain," searching out of the need to either prove the existence of these ancient legends or disprove and discard them. The poet calls such seekers "fools of science," who must either have something literally in hand or not believe in it. On the other hand, the poet sees a value in "Geographies of what we only feel," implying that legendary or not, the Eden story helps make humans what they are and is to that extent "true" and valuable. In the last six lines the poet looks outside at a gardener, on his knees planting flowers. This, she says, is as close as the gardener comes to prayer, and in a final line she conceives his actions as "Digging up Eden with a single hoe."

Forms and Devices

Almost all of Linda Pastan's published poetry is free verse, so this sonnet sequence is quite unusual for her. As Shakespearean or English sonnets, each of the six poems that make up "The Imperfect Paradise" is composed of fourteen pentameter lines, arranged in a rhyme scheme of *ababcdcdefefgg*. In the tradition of the sonnet sequence, much like Sir Philip Sidney's *Astrophel and Stella* (1591), Edmund Spenser's *Amoretti* (1595), or Elizabeth Barrett Browning's *Sonnets from the Portuguese* (1850), each of Pastan's sonnets is tied to a central theme, in this case the Eden story.

Pastan furthers the allusion to Eden, in four of the sonnets, by conceiving a dialogue between the speaker and another character who is a sort of Adam in the garden to Pastan's Eve. Indeed, Pastan's husband Ira was a gardener, and the poems, while clearly works of art, have some biographical resonance.

The first five sonnets are each formed around a question: Which is the loveliest season? How does one tell the flowers from the weeds? How does a garden grow in the middle of a deep and dark woods? Is the thieving squirrel like human moods? What if humans had not been created? In that sense the sonnets are meditations, speculations about basic questions raised by the story of Eden and the Fall, Adam and Eve's sin and humanity's banishment from the garden. The speaker does not give direct answers to these questions. Rather, she ends each sonnet with a somewhat ambiguous but richly suggestive image. A look at the first sonnet will illustrate this.

"Seasonal" asks the question, "Which season is the loveliest of all?" At first this seems to be an innocent and easy question, similar to whether one prefers chocolate or vanilla ice cream. However, from the answers given to the question, one can see that the issue at stake is no less than the essential nature of the world, and which season best represents this nature. "My Adam," the person being spoken to, finds the world "a warm and charming place," and his choice of spring as the loveliest season matches his basic optimism. The speaker, in contrast, finds the world "a garden of conspicuous waste" and thinks the "chaos of the snow" better represents this world.

The final image, in lines 13-14, illustrates a sort of synthesis but also a remaining tension between these perspectives: "Still, at your touch my house warms to the eaves/ As autumn torches all the fragile leaves." The use of the word "still" suggests that the speaker is being convinced by the warmth of "Adam's" touch that the world may be a good place after all; yet when this touch is compared, in the next line, to the torch autumn applies to the leaves, the speaker seems to be confirming her original idea even more strongly than at first. The apparent beauty of this world, it would seem, serves only to confirm and make more poignant an even deeper meaninglessness. The alliteration between "touches" and "torches" adds beauty and force to this conclusion.

Themes and Meanings

Pastan chose two epigraphs to open her book *The Imperfect Paradise*. The first, from Stanley Kunitz, reads, "We have all been expelled from the Garden, but the ones who suffer most in exile are those who are still permitted to dream of perfection." The second, from Wallace Stevens, reads, "The imperfect is our paradise." The Stevens quote emphasizes Pastan's focus on the deeply flawed nature of the world, while the Kunitz lines point to Pastan's yearning for something better than what this world offers, a beauty that does not fade, a vitality that does not grow old and die.

The questioning format of the first five sonnets implies that, although tending to a strong pessimism, the speaker still has an open mind about essential questions, still hopes for better answers than she currently has. The last sonnet asks no questions. Rather, in the first eight lines, it scoffs at archaeologists who take the Eden story too literally and must either have it proved historical or throw it out altogether. The speaker (and presumably Pastan as well) disagrees with this stance, implying that the "Geographies of what we only feel" are important and valuable, even if based on legend. For Pastan, it seems, the Eden story is a vital vehicle for raising essential questions about the world. Were humans created by God? Was there a "Fall" in the garden, resulting in all the imperfection that one sees in the current world? Why do humans have such a love for beauty if they are so flawed? The Eden story, true or not, allows one to talk about all these questions, to talk about humankind's essential identity as a species, its origin and nature, as well as the nature of the world humans inhabit.

However, after all the discussion—in this case five and a half sonnets—there are no clear answers. The poet ends by looking out the window at "Adam" in the garden, "Digging up Eden with a single hoe." This is a richly suggestive and appropriate image with which to end the sequence. The "single hoe" in the immensity of the garden suggests something of the difficulty in understanding the world. Human tools—historical, scientific, theological, literary—are disproportionate to the task. Nevertheless, one picks away at the remains of this Eden, creating what moments of beauty one can, through such activities as planting flowers and writing poetry.

Scott E. Moncrieff

IMPERIAL ADAM

Author: A. D. Hope (1907-2000)
Type of poem: Narrative
First published: 1955, in *The Wandering Islands*

The Poem

"Imperial Adam" consists of eleven quatrains. The quatrain is a traditional English verse form of four lines with various rhyme schemes. A. D. Hope has chosen to rhyme the first and third lines, then the second and fourth. The lilting rhythm is altogether appropriate for the erotic subject matter, and the poem derives a pervasive sensuality from its voluptuous diction and imagery.

"Imperial Adam" starts out by retelling the story from the second chapter of Genesis in which Eve emerges from Adam's rib so that Adam will no longer be alone. The poem dwells, however, on what the Old Testament writer fails to record in the blunt statement, "Adam knew Eve," and it offers a vivid account of the initial sexual encounter enjoyed by the father and mother of humankind. Once extracted from Adam's rib, Eve sighs and smiles at her male counterpart as she lies on the grass of paradise with "the honey of her flesh" shining in the sunlight and her "place of love" beckoning to him. Understanding what he should do through watching the animals copulate, he takes Eve into his arms and "like the clean beasts, embracing from behind," begins the joyful work of founding "the breed of men." He plants his seed in the woman that "Jahweh" (Jehovah) had given him, then watches her breasts ripen and her "belly" swell and grow.

The final stanza records the birth of their child, and it contrasts sharply with what has gone before. Vanished are the eroticism, the paradisaical aura, the bliss. In their place emerges the ugly reality that accompanies loss of innocence: The child who crawls from between Eve's legs is a pygmy and is named "the first murderer."

"Imperial Adam" stands as the best of Hope's series of erotic poems written in the 1950's. On one level, the poet is celebrating—much in the way earlier English writers such as Andrew Marvell (1621-1678) and John Donne (1572-1631) did—female beauty and sexuality. Hope's attraction to such poetry and his imitation of it in his own fashion are typical of his art because he is thoroughly schooled in the English tradition and often relies on it as a source.

Had "Imperial Adam" not contained that final, jarring revelation, it could be considered an imaginative re-creation of Adam and Eve's first sexual encounter and might be placed in the earlier English tradition of erotic poetry. The horror of the final quatrain, however, destroys the sense of pleasure generated by the sensual imagery in the preceding stanzas, and the poem becomes a distinctively modern one.

Forms and Devices

The main device lending "Imperial Adam" its erotic quality in the first ten stanzas is diction. Loaded phrases such as "naked in the dew," "brown flanks," "virile root," and "spurt of seed" distill Adam's masculinity. The major part of the poem, however, focuses on Eve, who has skin like honey—even richer in texture than the "golden breasts" of the papaw, a fruit noted for its fleshiness. She lies on the grass like a "plump gourd," loosens "her sinuous thighs," and reveals breasts rising "softly." Even her "place of love," its dark hairs covered with dew, "winked crisp and fresh."

Another method Hope employs to imbue the poem with an air of sexual abandon is the use of animal imagery. As Adam and Eve "Began in joy" their sexual union, the animals in the Garden of Eden watch. The elephant is "gravid"—that is, pregnant—or distended and enlarged by pregnancy, which this rare word connotes. The "hind"—a red deer—is calving, the "bitch" breeding, the "she-ape big with young." As Eve lies on the grass after the "lightning stroke" of sexual pleasure, she enjoys the licking of "The teeming lioness"—teeming used in the archaic manner to mean breeding and producing young. Then the exotic vicuña, an animal famous for its fine, silky fleece, "nuzzled" Eve as she slept.

The poet has conjured up a fecund and fruitful place in his narrative, using the only devices he has at his command: words formed into images. They are exactly the right formations to extend and give life to the scant details Genesis provides. It does appear that the writer of "Imperial Adam" took his cue not from Genesis but from another book of the Old Testament, the Song of Solomon, which exults in the female body and sensuality. Biblical imagery and allusions abound in Hope's poetry.

The abrupt juxtaposition in the final stanza of "Imperial Adam" devastates the mood the poet worked so hard to create, and the question arises in the mind of the reader: Why does Hope seemingly defile the pleasure-filled garden? In the last quatrain, even the soft sounds disappear, and Adam sees Eve's "water break," then watches her "quaking muscles" as she gives birth to a monster destined to become a murderer. This sudden switch in mood effectively places side by side beauty and ugliness, light and dark, good and evil, pleasure and pain—in essence, all those contrasting elements that make up the mosaic of human experience.

Themes and Meanings

The poem's title is problematic. Why should Adam be called "imperial"? The word most often denotes an emperor or the empire itself—for example, an imperial nation, led by the emperor, wields power over scattered colonies. To interpret the poem as a protest against imperialism seems far-fetched, however, considering the time in which it was written and Hope's own attitude toward colonialism. On the other hand, an obsolete meaning of imperial is "sovereign," and it could describe someone, emperor or not, who exercises supreme authority. A feminist reading, with this definition in mind, might see Adam as guilty of subjecting and corrupting Eve and Adam as the agent of authority. While such an approach is possible, it too, appears unlikely to be Hope's intent. Finally, imperial means "outstanding in size or quality." Perhaps this last definition is the right one to apply in order to approach the poem best.

Adam and Eve are considered in Christian mythology to be the father and mother of the human race, so this rather literal definition of imperial seems appropriate. Once they, in their supposed superiority, give themselves over to animal pleasure, they awaken to the terrible knowledge of evil, thus being reduced from their imperial status to that of ordinary humans. The animals gained no similar awareness as the result of their coupling; to possess such knowledge is the curse of humankind.

The final stanza raises significant questions: Why should their child have "a pygmy face"? What is notable about an undersized face? In addition to delineating physical smallness, when capitalized, pygmy describes African and Asian people four to five feet tall; in Greek mythology, the Pygmies were a tiny race noted for their warlike and barbaric ways. Right or not, the word does carry the connotation of ferocity, barbarism, abnormality, or physical aberration. This meaning comes not only from the mythological source, but also from the early explorers who encountered the real Pygmies during their forays into Africa and Asia. The explorers found these small people distasteful, seeing them as ugly, fierce, and uncivilized. Pygmy also contrasts with the "imperial stature" of Adam—and of Eve by implication.

Because the word pygmy immediately creates revulsion in the reader, it works splendidly as a metaphor that unfolds without effort. The effect is then compounded by the final line: "And the first murderer lay upon the earth." According to the fourth chapter of Genesis, the eldest son—not a pygmy—of Adam and Eve was called Cain, and he killed his brother Abel out of jealousy. Hope obviously expects his reader to know the rest of the story and to extend its meaning. Cain has evolved into the personification of evil, containing in his person the seed of destruction, of war and enmity, of hostility and rancor among humans. The poem's conclusion brings to mind the final lines of William Butler Yeats's (1865-1939) "The Second Coming": "And what rough beast, its hour come round at last,/ Slouches towards Bethlehem to be born?" Hope is obviously an admirer of Yeats, whose "noble, candid speech" he praises in his poem "William Butler Yeats." Because Hope draws constantly from earlier sources for his inspiration, he may well have had the famous lines from "The Second Coming" in mind when he concluded his own poem. Not consciously imitating, Hope more likely wanted his reader to be aware of the connection. Certainly, when the haunting Yeats lines echo in the background, the conclusion of "Imperial Adam" gains resonance.

What begins, then, as a joyful amplification of Adam and Eve's first encounter evolves into the history of the human race. In one respect, "Imperial Adam" recounts in an economic and suggestive way the whole story told in Genesis—moving from innocence to awareness, from ignorance to knowledge, from good to evil.

Robert L. Ross

IN A DARK TIME

Author: Theodore Roethke (1908-1963)
Type of poem: Lyric
First published: 1960; collected in *The Far Field,* 1964

The Poem

In this confessional poem, Theodore Roethke describes a passage through a "dark time" in his life and his emergence from this episode, not into peace and quietude, but at least into wholeness. The journey to and out of the psychic pit described in the poem may be a metaphor for personal tragedy, spiritual emptiness, or, more likely, because it is known that Roethke suffered from periods of psychosis, a poetic attempt to deal with a mental breakdown.

The poet insists that a plunge to the bottom of the abyss of psychological disorientation and dislocation of identity is necessary to achieve clarity: "In a dark time, the eye begins to see." There must be painful struggle, though, before this end is reached. In the first stanza, the poet has glimpses of his personality, but he finds only fragments and pieces, meeting not himself but his shadow, hearing not his voice but his echo. As he says later in the poem, "The edge is what I have." He also finds that he is not sure of his place in the larger scheme of life because he "live[s] between the heron" (a stately, beautiful creature) "and the wren" (an ordinary bird), between "beasts of the hill" (highly placed, but brutal animals) "and serpents of the den" (associated with evil and danger, but also with knowledge).

In the second stanza, the poet specifically identifies his problem as mental illness but implies that it is not he but the world which is out of joint: "What's madness but nobility of soul/ At odds with circumstance?" In fact, madness may not necessarily be "a cave" in which one is lost, but may be "a winding path" to a new awareness. Despair experienced completely may lead to "purity."

Meanwhile, there is the chaos described in the third stanza, in which daytime is suddenly replaced by midnight, ordinary objects blaze as if lit from within, and images are thrown one upon another at such a dizzying pace that the experience is described as "a steady storm of correspondences." Nevertheless, the confusion is necessary because the old personality must be destroyed before a new one can be born: "Death of the self in a long, tearless night."

Although the paradoxes ("dark, dark my light") and the unanswered questions ("Which I is *I*?") continue in the final stanza, there is an apparently unexpected resolution of the conflict, as the poet touches the bottom and then begins to rise: "A fallen man, I climb out of my fear." At last, there comes a mystic union with God and the poet feels a part of everything ("one is One"), but there is no safe haven. The poet has been born again into a violent world, but this time he is able to face it "free in the tearing wind."

Forms and Devices

Although, at first glance, "In a Dark Time" seems to be a collection of outbursts and slapped-together images which is less a description of madness than an example of it, the poem is really a carefully crafted work in which its conclusion is implicit in all of its elements, beginning with the rhyme pattern of the poem. Roethke uses a six-line stanza, the rhyme scheme of which is *abcadd*. This pattern, which appears at first glance to be no rhyme scheme at all until the stanza's last three lines, reinforces the point of the poem, which is that disintegration may be necessary to achieve unity. There appears to be no rhyme after the first three lines, but with the end of the fourth comes a resonance of the first—the suggestion that there is order where there had appeared to be none. The last two lines of the stanza, a strongly rhymed couplet, imply that the poet is drawing his world together again into a type of order.

The *a* rhyme of the first stanza ("see" and "tree") is strong and definite, but the same element of the second stanza ("soul" and "wall") is only a near rhyme, as is that of the third ("correspondences" and "what he is—") and fourth ("desire" and "fear"). These near rhymes reinforce the idea that the poet is only barely in control of himself and the poem, but the strongly rhyming last couplet of each stanza pulls the poem and the reader away from formlessness. As a final seal on the idea that to endure this kind of psychic torment is to break through into a new kind of reality, the last two lines of the poem, the ones which in each stanza had borne a strong rhyme, themselves yield to near rhyme ("mind" and "wind"). It is as if the poet is telling his readers that they thought they had his poem figured out, but that they do not. To experience fully the reality that the poet is describing, it is necessary to see things in a totally new way.

The imagery of the poem, at first confusing, also reinforces the idea that from apparent paradox and nonsense come new knowledge. Some of the images embody contradiction, such as the serpent with its double meaning in Western culture. Others lose their paradoxical quality when seen in the terms of the poem's entire statement. It seems impossible that a "light" could be "dark," but Roethke means that one must embrace all elements of one's personality in order to integrate them, even those parts which one does not regard as admirable ("beasts of the hill") and even if the process is confusing ("Which I is *I*?"). Confusion and disorientation are necessary, Roethke says, for only by asking the question and admitting ignorance can one begin to find new ways of learning.

Themes and Meanings

In "In a Dark Time," Theodore Roethke uses one of his own major themes—the renewal of the human spirit through contact with the natural world (a theme which unites him with the Romantic poets of the early nineteenth century)—in company with a major theme of modern literature—the theory that it is necessary not merely to test limits but also to break past limits in order to become fully oneself.

In many of his other poems, Roethke comes to the creatures and the milieu of the physical world to renew himself and give his life meaning during a time of crisis. Roethke is primarily a poet of small nature, reveling in the existence of little creatures such as sparrows, snails (as in "Elegy for Jane"), tiny fish, and even amoeba ("The Minimal"), and feeling a sense of kinship and brotherhood with them. In "In a Dark Time," however, the representatives of the natural world are threatening beasts and serpents, and the poet is unsure of his place in the scheme of things, as he lives "between" the various living things that he mentions. Furthermore, the natural world is no longer an ordered, understandable place: The moon is "ragged," and midnight descends during day. The creature with which the poet finally chooses to identify "my soul" is the not only despised but also wretched "heat-maddened summer fly" which, "buzzing at the sill," can see the world that it wants to enter but is unable to do so.

One of the points made by the poem is that the world is not understandable, not only by logical means, but also by any kind of ordinary human perception or judgment. Perhaps the path of insanity or psychic disintegration, feared and shunned by most people with good reason can, instead of leading to destruction, provide a gateway to a new kind of reality. At the end of the poem, Roethke says that he "climb[s] out of [his] fear" and becomes "free in the tearing wind" but does not offer the reason that this change has occurred because the process is incomprehensible by the usual methods of evaluation. The poet has not arrived at a quiet place, such as the eye of a storm, but is still in the midst of the tearing wind which unsettles and jumbles everything. At least he himself is whole—"one"—and can endure what he had previously feared. It is also unclear just who or what is the "God" which the poet encounters at the end of the poem. Roethke was neither conventionally religious nor consistently mystical; in his other poems in which he speaks of union with all life, he does not maintain that he is thereby always contacting a divine spirit, as did one of his poetic heroes and ancestors, William Blake.

"In a Dark Time" is, after all, not a philosophical treatise but a highly charged description of an emotional storm. As Roethke states in another poem: "We think by feeling. What is there to know?" ("The Waking"). Roethke would also say that poetry is not read for answers but for experiences. Even as the only way to find the world that lies beyond ordinary human consciousness is to push sanity past its limits, so the only way to understand a lyric poem such as "In a Dark Time" is to push reason past its limits and *feel* the poem.

Jim Baird

IN CALIFORNIA

Author: Louis Simpson (1923-   )
Type of poem: Lyric
First published: 1963, in *At the End of the Open Road*

The Poem

"In California" consists of six unrhymed stanzas of four lines each, with irregular line lengths, in which the speaker reflects on his geographical and historical situation. Louis Simpson, though born in Jamaica, settled in New York City in 1940—hence, the reference to his protagonist's "New York face" in line 2 of the poem. He begins the poem on the California coast ("the dream coast"), having come from New York and finding himself among business and outdoor types ("realtors/ And tennis-players"). He feels out of place on this western edge of the nation. What he has seen, and how he feels, has left him with a "dark preoccupation."

The second stanza recalls the westward movement, the "epical clatter" (line 5) of the pioneers making their way through Tennessee and Ohio, toward where the speaker stands, reflecting on the music and spirit ("Voices and banjos") of their quest to settle the new land. Then, heaven regarded this westward advance favorably. Now, the "angel in the gate" (line 8) above the Western coast witnesses the "dream" unfolding, not becoming involved in human affairs.

Stanza 3 opens with an address to Walt Whitman, who celebrated the American pioneering spirit in the nineteenth century and wrote exuberantly of the westward expansion. The "King and the Duke" (line 10) are characters in Mark Twain's novel *The Adventures of Huckleberry Finn* (1884); these clownish charlatans call themselves the Duke of Bilgewater and King Looy the Seventeen of France. The poet tells Whitman to step down from his poetic promontory overlooking the march west and join the fictional King and Duke on their journey down the Mississippi with Huck Finn and the escaped black, Jim. Placing the great poet of the American dream with two charlatans suggests that the speaker sees the epic voice mocked by the reality of what the dream has become: a collection of realtors and tennis players and rows of sailboats in a marina facing Alcatraz Island with its notorious (but defunct) federal penitentiary. Here, he says, the pioneers should turn back.

Still addressing Whitman, the speaker in the fourth stanza continues to explain why he believes the pioneer spirit of early America has vanished: "We" have lost the capacity—courage, intellectual scope, vision—to "bear/ The stars . . . those infinite spaces" (line 14). Capitulate, he tells Whitman; give up the mountain from which the American dream was envisioned. It will be parceled up and sold for tract homes as the valley has been. This thought reminds the poet of past civilizations that have died: Babylon and Tenochtitlan. Those cities were but precursors to what the poet sees around him, a dying empire.

In the final stanza, the poet realizes that the human spirit can neither "turn" nor "stay"; it must be ever in motion. The American pioneer has been stopped at the western gate, has fallen into a materialistic sleep, and has lost the spirit to surge onward. The poet's final lines separate the somnolent populace from the pioneering spirit itself, which the poet sees in a final vision as a train of "great cloud-wagons" advancing beyond the Rock, the Marina, and the subdivided valley. Its spiritual pioneers continue "dreaming of a Pacific."

Forms and Devices

The poem's structure combines convention with free form. A quick glance reveals evenly spaced and numbered stanzas, each line begun with a capital letter, each stanza consisting of exactly four lines. On closer examination, however, the form opens: The lines do not rhyme, have no regular length, and lack conventional metric form. The poet clearly wants phrasing to determine line length and keeps the rhythms near natural speech. The regular stanzaic structures provide secure parameters in which the reflective spirit can move back and forth geographically and historically. Visually, the poem advances evenly and surely, while the emotions stir in phrasal eddies.

Attention is thereby divided between conventional structure and the poet's voice and mood, between ideas and conventional techniques. By fencing the open linear form with regular stanzas, the poet exactly suits his mood and theme, which dwell on the abandonment of an ideal, of a defunct dream that could not—or did not—hold up under the advance of the pioneer spirit.

The poem's allusions give symbolic weight to the poet's argument. California, its realtors, yacht clubs, and subdivisions, all symbolize the failure of the dream, a vulgar distortion of the epic vision of which Walt Whitman sang and which he symbolizes here. The poet's vision sweeps over thousands of years of history, with specific allusions to Babylon and the ancient Aztec city. In this way, the poet's ideas do not fade in a welter of abstract concepts. Despite the generalized diction—phrases such as "the fabulous raft" and "those infinite spaces" are characteristic of the poem as a whole— the pictures that emerge from the language and the allusions are sufficiently clear. The poet's ideas are sustained by suggestion rather than by graphic detail, by allusion rather than by vivid imagery. Though "epical clatter" (line 5) is alluded to, one does not hear it in the "Voices and banjos," nor does one smell the "incense" or see very distinctly the "angel in the gate." If Babylon "astonished Herodotus," one does not see his astonishment, but one feels the weight of the ideas nevertheless, because the voice of the poet brings the reader into his vision with his allusions, moods, and rhythms.

One feels from the start that one is hearing the reflections of a somewhat demoralized witness to a sad reality—that one is overhearing him. He assumes that someone is listening, absorbing his mood as his phrases carry the poem along: "Here I am, troubling the dream coast." His mysterious voice awakens a desire to know, to follow along, listening to the echoes of his despair reverberate through history as he sweeps the reader along toward his final apotheosis. His commanding tone reinforces this march forward: "Turn round the wagons here," he says, then, "We cannot turn or stay," and if the poem tells more than it shows, the final vision nevertheless leaves the reader with a majestic image of "great cloud-wagons" floating beyond the dying land where the poet is left with his "dark preoccupation."

Themes and Meanings

The poet speaks through visions as he reflects on the remnants of a dream that inspired a nation before it dwindled into subdivisions, tennis games, and sailboats. The failure represented by the realtors and tennis players may be attributable in part to a hard reality: Whenever the human spirit is brought to material considerations, its death is assured. Looking back, he sees the pioneers, hears their voices and banjos, and sees their spirit rising to heaven; now he sees it stopped by a great barrier, the Pacific. It appears to be time to surrender the dream and settle into comfort, to acquiesce to the inevitable: decay and death. The great singer of this dream, Walt Whitman, should "Lie back," for the pioneer voice is quieted. In the silence, one hears the speaker's "dark preoccupation," dark because he is reminded of other civilizations, once astonishing, now only names.

The "I" in the first stanza represents the poet's sense of alienation from his surroundings. He has a specific identity, a "New York face," but by the end of his grand sweep through history, foreign and domestic, the solitary figure has become the "we" that is possessed of a spirit that "cannot turn or stay." The poet sees a separation of physical manifestations from the human spirit itself. People, things, places—these objectify the spirit, but they eventually die and are sloughed away, like dead skin. The elevated spirit moves onward, drawn by another dream, another Pacific. Irony tempers the poet's voice in this final vision without deflating the grand vision entirely, for the Pacific has become a symbol of a physical barrier that stops people, nations, and dreams. Humankind, the poet seems to be saying, will always surge outward, following the lofty dream that spirit forever discovers in its quest for perfection, but as long as it finds physical expression, it will be halted by the great imponderables of reality, such as the Pacific Ocean. Material forms die; the spirit survives.

The final vision seems to revive the poet's spirit; he rejects the death of spirit while accepting the death of the dream that Whitman celebrated. The poet's final mood is plaintive. Uplifted by the vision of the "great cloud-wagons" moving outward, he is also aware that "we" are not in them. A twinge of regret and a bit of irony remain: As the pioneers sleep and surrender to the great reality before them (represented by the Rock, Alcatraz Island), the human spirit moves on, a dream itself, a dreamer still. Though elevated by the final vision, the poet is also doubtful. He seems to be asking what good all that pioneer effort is if it comes to this—a dead place that is abandoned finally by a spirit that surges toward another dream coast, which will eventually meet the same fate.

Bernard E. Morris

IN COLD HELL, IN THICKET

Author: Charles Olson (1910-1970)
Type of poem: Meditation
First published: 1951; collected in *In Cold Hell, in Thicket*, 1953

The Poem

"In Cold Hell, in Thicket" is a sequential poem in two parts: Each part is subdivided into numbered sections that work like the movements in a musical score, each developing an aspect of the theme of the whole poem. The title of the poem is taken from images used in the *Inferno*, the first book of Dante's epic poem *The Divine Comedy* (c. 1320), in which Dante describes his descent into the Christian underworld by entering a dense thicket covering the gate of hell. The "cold" hell refers to the winter day of the poem and to the snow that is falling on the fields.

The situation of the poem is of a speaker walking across the frozen ground of a fort, most likely the battlefield at Manassas, Virginia, now the Manassas National Battlefield Park, where the battles of Bull Run in the Civil War (1861-1865) had been fought. Manassas is near Washington, D.C., where Charles Olson was living at the time he wrote this poem in August, 1950. A letter to his friend, Edward Dahlberg, reports his car trips out to various Civil War sites.

The most striking characteristic of the poem is its visual appearance on the page, what the French call the *mise en page*, or layout of a poem. It is marked by strophes, long stanzas in open form, some beginning at the left margin of the page, others beginning at indented margins. Every section has a different spatial order in which the thinking process is given a typographical signature or formal design. Indenting in Olson's poetry means the thought has drifted inward toward memory or dreamy reverie. The sum of his techniques is explained in his essay "Projective Verse," written in 1950, in which he discusses his metrical strategies and his use of a "breath" unit for the line, a nonmetrical unit of speech based on the length of breath needed to utter a phrase or completed thought.

The tone of the poem is one of heightened oratory, a formal discourse marked by stately rhetorical assertions and questions, complex syntactical structures in which long dependent clauses intersect direct questions. This form of oratory, notable in other poems Olson wrote in the early 1950's, was partly influenced by his brief career in politics (1940-1946), when he served in various offices under Franklin D. Roosevelt's administration. One may detect some of Roosevelt's eloquent style of delivery in this language; Olson was himself a talented orator in youth, and he won several state and national awards for public speech.

Part I of the poem opens on the subject of war, a frequent theme of Olson's poetry. His keen sensitivity to history makes him reexperience the bloodshed of the Civil War battles fought on the snowy ground over which he trudges. The poet is middle-aged, forty years old, and he compares his situation to that of Dante, who wrote his epic poem "in the middle way" of life. The "cold hell" of the title is the confusion and directionlessness the poet feels as he meditates on the subject of bloodshed and death. At the back of his mind is the imminent death of his mother, who died several months later, on Christmas, 1950.

The first numbered section sketches in a new theme: the speaker as Osiris, the Egyptian god who was murdered and dismembered, his limbs scattered over the Nile river. Osiris's mother, Nut, is the night sky, whose breasts are the stars. His sister, Isis, gathers up the limbs and brings her brother-husband back to life. The poet, however, looks up into the night sky and cannot organize his perceptions to see the form of a god overhead. He is fractured within and cannot sort out the meaning of his own surroundings or his experience. Like Osiris, he is dismembered body from soul in his grief.

In section 2, Olson's major theme emerges: the role of imagination as builder of forms out of the fragments of nature and lived experience. The snowy grounds of the fort are a vast array of unassorted particles that he must shape and invest with understanding. After the first stanza, the language is indented to suggest a deepening thought process, as the poet asks himself directly how he will regain control of his emotions and overcome his grief. He feels that he must do so without the aid of his figurative sister, Isis.

Section 3 goes to the heart of the problem by asking, "Who am I?" He notes that the "scene" before him is organized by its own inherent principle; all but himself seems to participate in natural form. Only he is isolated, set apart from the form nature assumes in any landscape. The word "abstract" comes to him in this passage and suggests not only the root meaning of things dragged from their context, but the human tendency to remove the self from its surroundings, to contemplate its own subjectivity in isolation of other events and influences. One must take a "fix," or reading of the self within the natural landscape, he argues, to enter the order of natural events and to take one's place among them.

The second half of the poem, part II, is divided into two movements. The first, unnumbered, part opens with a phrase from the *Inferno*: "*selva oscura*," or dark wood. Olson, however, puns on the *selva* to suggest "self," or dark self. He asserts that the darkness of the self is psychological; all grief comes from within the self and not from the world. Nature is a perfectly ordered system, a paradise in which individual human beings suffer privately from their gross illusions and selfish concerns.

Section 2 formulates the rest of the argument by noting that hell and paradise are functions of human subjectivity, attitudes formed from cultural and psychological factors having little or no bearing on the actual state of the world. Hell is a projection of personal despair that distorts the appearance of the world. Accordingly, he can begin to resolve his despair and confusion by accepting that his remorse is purely subjective, a form of self-grieving. This leads to the final section of the poem in which he remarks that men "are now their own wood," an image taken from Ezra Pound's poem "A Pact," in which Pound pays homage to the poet Walt Whitman by acknowledging him as having cleared a path through the American wilderness, and that the fallen trees may now be carved, shaped by the poets who follow. The "wood" in Olson's poem is also figurative, a material of mind and imagination to be "wrought, to be shaped, to be carved, for use, for/ others."

The speaker overcomes his remorse after having reasoned that his depair is a product of selfish emotions and that the "world" remains the same despite an individual's personal mood or attitude. The way forward is to recognize that emotion is a vague generality and that reality is always a tissue of detailed and precise elements woven together in a pattern enclosing the world. Thus death has its place, even his mother's coming death and the son's anticipatory grief; they are not isolated events but part of the unity of nature. The speaker can now move again and begin his further pilgrimage through the "wilderness" toward greater understanding of the unity of life. The reader is again reminded of Dante's *The Divine Comedy* as the speaker moves out of the field to the next stage of his journey: The way forward out of hell is toward purgatory, and finally, into paradise.

Forms and Devices

Olson is skillful in balancing his use of images in the poem. On the one hand, the fort mentioned in the second stanza of the poem is literal, identified by a number of facts about its location and structure on the landscape; but almost immediately after, the description of the setting widens into allegory, characterizing the scene as "unclear," a "hell." The landscape on which the figure meditates is both exterior and interior at once, an actual place and a metaphorical setting in which the speaker explores his own inner psychological terrain. The language moves back and forth between the two poles of reference and sustains the dual nature of the setting throughout the poem.

The thicket mentioned in section 3 of the first half of the poem is simultaneously the trees on the battlefield and the state of the poet's own consciousness as he looks out over the setting. The black branches in the winter sky are like nerves "laid open"; they strike the poet and generate the words that form his language in the poem, line by line. Thus, each image of the poem is the result of an impinging datum from the surrounding fields; the poet stands mutely in the center of a landscape that acts upon him detail by detail, which he then composes as language in the poem. The poem, therefore, is the reenactment of the scene. Somewhere in the abstract ordering of the words is the ghost of the actual trees and their wiry branches, "these black and silvered knivings."

It is this device of turning each objective item into its subjective equilavent that makes the poem a meditation. The word itself describes that act of internalizing an object until it fills the mind with its influences. The restless self-exploring that goes on in the poem worries each datum until it is elevated to a complex psychological issue, as in the final resolution of the poem in part II, stanza 2, where even the field becomes a "choice," a "prayer."

Themes and Meanings

"In Cold Hell, in Thicket" is about the process of understanding. The poem begins in a state of utter desolation brought on by the adverse circumstances in which the poet finds himself. These feelings have nothing to do with the actual setting he confronts, but his perception or misperception of what he sees is an indication of how far removed he is from the world. As the poem unfolds, one watches the procedure by which the landscape comes to represent the speaker's inner turmoil. The second half of the poem, however, reverses the flow of Romantic meditation by refusing to accept this view of the world as real. Instead, the speaker renounces his despair and searches to discover how the world is not only different from himself, but of a form that remains perfect and inalterable in its integrity.

By accepting the primacy of the natural order of things as the true picture of the world, Olson's persona decides he must rediscover the order within himself, beneath the emotional chaos of his feelings. As he remarks to himself near the close of part I, only by exact and precise attention can the real underlying form of self be discovered. The poem is a lesson in self-analysis, a way of confronting the pains of experience without ending in pity and remorse. The meditation demands of the speaker a clear, open attention to the details of feeling, and when properly traced, will reveal that the single self, the isolated human in the landscape, is a fiction. The truth of human nature is that it belongs within the matrix of other life, and that its responsibilities are to others, not only to the isolated individual. The poem renounces that aspect of individuality in which selfish desires are primary. Instead, the concept of the individual is redefined in the poem to mean an originality of attention focused on a world of connected life and its system of relations. The poem ends with the speaker reentering the world as an imaginative participant, no longer the grieving outsider.

Paul Christensen

IN DISTRUST OF MERITS

Author: Marianne Moore (1887-1972)
Type of poem: Lyric
First published: 1944, in *Nevertheless*

The Poem

Marianne Moore's "In Distrust of Merits" is a poem so artfully constructed that although it seems to read like prose, it actually follows a consistent pattern that contains many conventional poetic forms. Each of the eight stanzas comprises ten lines. The first four lines of each stanza form a quatrain in which the second and fourth lines rhyme, while the next two lines are decasyllabic (ten syllables to a line). These lines are followed by another quatrain that differs from the first one in that both alternating lines rhyme. Although Moore imposes this formal pattern of syllabic grouping and internal as well as end rhyme, the rhymes are muted and the lines remain flexible.

The first line of the first stanza immediately sets up a thematic paradox by asking whether those who are prepared ("strengthened") to fight or to die are adequately compensated by the "medals and positioned victories" of war. The paradox continues in the next four lines: The soldiers are fighting a "blind/ man who thinks he sees" and who, because of his moral blindness, is "enslaved" and "harmed." The questioner appeals to nature ("firm stars"—perhaps truth) to guide humankind. This apostrophe includes the need for the individual to "know/ depth": In order to understand what motivates humankind to the violence of war, the speaker must plumb the depths of history and of herself.

The second stanza alludes to the possible causes of war: religious differences (the "star of David" of Judaism and the "star of Bethlehem" of Christianity) and racial differences (the "black imperial lion," a title given to Haile Selassie, Emperor of Ethiopia and one of the first victims of Italian dictator Benito Mussolini's fascist aggression). The third stanza describes the ongoing fighting in terms of a disease that will kill some and not others; however, the paradox "we devour ourselves" moves the guilt from the external enemy to an internal one.

The fourth stanza continues to express the need for people to see themselves and not be like the hypocritical "false comforters" who placed blame on a guiltless Job in the Bible. However, the fifth stanza explains the difficulty of trying to make promises not to discriminate when the speaker is not sure whether or not she is the enemy herself. Because of this quandary, the sixth stanza points out the easier decision to fight the foreign enemy as opposed to the more difficult choice of being patient (fighting oneself?) as a form of defense. Finally, the seventh stanza galvanizes the internal dialogue of the persona by describing the results that war always produces: the pain of the survivors ("The world's an orphans' home"). The speaker must learn the lessons that so many dead and suffering people have paid for. In conclusion, the speaker addresses her own "Hate-hardened heart." The merits of fighting are to be distrusted be-

cause battles are not directed against the real problem: the inability of people to acknowledge their own guilt.

Forms and Devices

One of Moore's favorite poetic devices is the paradox. This device of presenting an
apparent contradiction that proves to be true after some reflection works well to express the thesis of "In Distrust of Merits." Even the title suggests the author is questioning some concept that the rest of society not only accepts without question but
also rewards. For example, the first two lines of the first stanza ("Strengthened to live,
strengthened to die for/ medals and positioned victories?") immediately set up a thematic paradox by repeating the same action ("Strengthened") with opposite purposes
(to live and to die). Yet the meaning is not contradictory, for soldiers are trained both
to fight ("live") and to die in combat. The feeling of contradiction provokes continued
dialogue as the speaker tries to make sense of a senseless situation. Some other examples of paradoxes in the poem are "a blind man who/ can see," the "enslaver" who is
"enslaved," and the "alive who are dead." Most of these paradoxes are based on the
gap between material and spiritual perception. People are more impressed when their
senses experience success in battle and war; unfortunately, these tangible senses can
veil intangible spiritual truth. In spite of witnessing turmoil, fighting, and death, the
persona in this dialogue with self must uncover, chiefly by means of unraveling the
paradox, the truth that lies beneath the external causes of war: the guilt of the individual conscience that does not express the ideals in which it intuitively believes.

Moore uses some rather traditional metaphors: "hate's crown," "dust of the earth,"
"heart of iron," the world as "an orphans' home," and Iscariot's "crime." Critics debate
whether frequent use has turned these phrases into trite clichés or whether they are being used because they express certain universal feelings and experiences. Like the
apostrophe that expresses hope that the "star of David, star of Bethlehem" and "the
black imperial lion/ of the Lord" be "joined at last," the well-known phrases point to
thousands of years of conflict that preceded the anti-Semitic attacks and claims of
Aryan superiority that provoked World War II, which was in progress at the time of
the poem's composition. By using these conventional phrases, the author is perhaps
saying that war and suffering will continue until individuals in each generation face
their moral responsibility and end the underlying causes of war. Like the use of recognizable symbolic phrases, the repetition of certain words such as "fighting" and "patience" provides both a feeling of intensity and a feeling of longevity. The persona is
asking, "When will people see themselves as the solution to the horrors of war?"

Themes and Meanings

Although a photograph of a slain soldier in *Life* magazine sparked the immediate
compassion and the reaction Moore expressed in "In Distrust of Merits," the poet,
throughout her later years, frequently expressed her concern with moral issues in her
poetry. When she was asked how she felt about this frequently anthologized poem,
she responded that she believed that it expressed her deep and sincere emotion but that

it was perhaps somewhat disjointed in form. However, it seems tenable that the form reflects the speaker's feelings: When personal feelings do not conform with those of people with whom one usually agrees, the normal reaction is to feel cut off or disjointed.

The title expresses the feeling the persona explores in the poem. The word "distrust" sets up a rejection of trust in what is usually considered to have merit. The poem attempts to penetrate the positive veneer of society's merits by looking beneath the surface to the reality. In World War II, for example, leaders such as Adolf Hitler and Mussolini were successful in their bids for power; however, beneath the merit of success lay the suffering Jews and the conquered Ethiopians. Such a "successful" leader is "the blind/ man who thinks he sees." The same description is used in reference to those who give "false comfort" to a "disheartened" Job. These comforters suggest the apparent moral uprightness of those who are more concerned about external rectitude than spiritual integrity. They believe that if Job is suffering, he must have deserved it. The poem suggests such merits also are suspect.

The final expression of distrust is directed at the speaker: "I must/ fight till I have conquered in myself what/ causes war, but I would not believe it." The speaker explicitly identifies her inability to accept personal responsibility. Therefore, she does nothing and betrays herself and humanity ("O Iscariot-like crime!"). The final two lines complete the circle from distrust to trust by affirming the perspective at which the speaker has arrived: "Beauty is everlasting/ and dust is for a time." The merits that the world supports are but transient dust; however, true merit will always last. The word "everlasting" also affirms a central theme of the poem: The situations that are usually identified as leading to war may vary, but the underlying cause, a "Hate-hardened heart," remains constant. Recognition of this cause must precede and support the vow "We'll/ never hate black, white, red, yellow, Jew,/ Gentile, Untouchable."

Throughout the poem, the author points to the need for the individual to make hard personal choices and then to express those choices so that others will feel supported in the choices their consciences make. One way the author expresses this movement from one individual toward other individuals (but not toward the collective society that supports the distrusted merits) is simply to use the first-person singular pronoun ("I"), the third-person singular pronoun ("he"), and the first-person plural pronoun ("we"). The syntax supports Moore's concern that the individuals must announce their beliefs publicly, unlike the cowardly Judas Iscariot who betrayed his friend Jesus.

Agnes A. Shields

1942

IN GOYA'S GREATEST SCENES WE SEEM TO SEE

Author: Lawrence Ferlinghetti (1919-   )
Type of poem: Lyric
First published: 1957; collected in *A Coney Island of the Mind*, 1958

The Poem

Within a few months in 1956, Lawrence Ferlinghetti wrote twenty-nine poems that he envisioned as a unit. In his second book of poetry, *A Coney Island of the Mind*, they appear numbered, without titles. Number 1, "In Goya's greatest scenes we seem to see," is a lyric written in open form, having no regular rhyme, meter, or line length. Placed on the page so as to have a visual effect, the poem has six sections of varying length, ranging from twenty lines to three words. (Anthologies vary in the way they present the poem, not always retaining the original spacing between lines and thereby varying the number of sections.)

The title, taken from the first line of the poem, immediately introduces the first of two topics: works by the Spanish artist Francisco de Goya. The poet directs readers first to Goya's works, which present "suffering humanity." Ferlinghetti then suggests scenes of war through words such as "writhe," "veritable rage," and "adversity." Specifically, the poem alludes to Goya's *Disasters of War*, created in 1810 but not published until 1863, years after his death. This series of sketches depicts the brutality, on the part of both the French and the Spanish, in the Peninsular War (1808-1814). Although Ferlinghetti never names the *Disasters of War*, he uses words to bring Goya's images from those sketches to mind: "bayonets," "landscape of blasted trees," "wings and beaks," "carnivorous cocks," "gibbets," and "cadavers."

The grammar and syntax of the first twenty lines (section 1) reveal three sentences, although the lack of straight margins and terminal punctuation suggests fragmentation rather than grammatical units. (Ferlinghetti uses no punctuation in the poem except for quotation marks and an apostrophe, but capital letters help locate new grammatical units.) The open form and line design contribute to a tone of confusion and isolation that matches the tone of Goya's sketches. The next two sections of the poem, each one line long, provide transition to the second topic: The poet maintains that the suffering humanity of Goya's sketches is still alive more than a century later but is now living in another "landscape" and, as the reader soon learns, on another continent: America. The last three sections of the poem describe these new sufferers and this new landscape.

As with Goya's sufferers, these people are "ranged along the roads" instead of being pictured in their homes or communities; again the landscape is bleak, and again the people are seen as victims of a senseless, predatory power. Yet the images of suffering are very different. Goya's sketches focus on the people, often with no background buildings, objects, or vegetation. When buildings or vegetation are included, their presentation adds to the plight of the people instead of taking the focus away from them. In Ferlinghetti's poem, however, the landscape is central and the people are in the background. They are not physically depicted as in the Goya prints; rather, they are described only as "maimed citizens." The landscape is now bleak, not because it is barren, gray, or war torn, but because it is morally vacuous—"freeways fifty lanes wide" are crowded with "bland billboards" and automobiles. The people are trapped in a world built for machinery and advertising.

Forms and Devices

The poem depends, for its power, on the connection Ferlinghetti makes between the people in Goya's sketches and those of twentieth century America. The allusion to art is not unusual for Ferlinghetti. A painter and art critic himself, he is influenced not only by great works of art but also by painters' techniques. Just as he calls up Goya's sketches through words, Ferlinghetti presents his poem, in part, as a picture. The page is a canvas, and his words and lines are placed for visual effect. The design on the page suggests an unexpected or brutal separation of parts that reinforces his theme. Goya's prints graphically show dismemberment; the poem envisions American culture as an isolating force. What is physical brutality in the Goya section becomes spiritual brutality in the section on America. Even Ferlinghetti's alliteration signals the difference: Goya's sketches link "babies and bayonets" and "cadavers and carnivorous cocks," while the section on America speaks of "bland billboards/ illustrating imbecile illusions" and "a concrete continent." The physical destruction gives way to a spiritual nothingness. Yet despite the move from blood to banality, the poem highlights the continuity between the Spanish and the American scenes through the lack of terminal punctuation; one flows into the other. America has discovered its own form of brutality.

Ferlinghetti repeats key images and grammatical structures from the Goya section of the poem in the America section in order to draw a parallel between the sufferers of early nineteenth century warring Spain and those of twentieth century America. In the Goya section, the sufferers "writhe upon the page"; in the second section, they are "ranged along the roads." First they are "under cement skies," then they are "on a concrete continent." The Spanish scenes include "slippery gibbets,/ cadavers and carnivorous cocks"; the American sufferers see "legionaires/ false windmills and demented roosters." A powerful image in the Goya sketches that Ferlinghetti alludes to is the predatory nature of grotesque birds as a symbol of the death and destruction of war. In the America section of the poem, however, the bird is not "carnivorous" but "demented." Instead of predatory birds, car "engines/ . . . devour America." A poet who enjoys puns and wordplay, Ferlinghetti suggests the irony of the word "freeway." Instead of "tumbrils" (carts carrying revolutionaries to the gallows), "painted cars" on "freeways fifty lanes wide" lead Americans to a barren existence. The poet indicts a society that foregrounds technology and privileges merchandising rather than people. In the second half of the poem, Ferlinghetti indicts the American way of life as being every bit as deadly as war.

Themes and Meanings

"In Goya's greatest scenes we seem to see" alludes to powerful sketches of predatory death in order to highlight the dangers of American society. The poem moves from recalling Goya's well-known and influential criticism of war to the poet's view of what is destroying American society. In linking the two, Ferlinghetti takes a risk. Will the reader accept the view that American life is as destructive as war? Is American society so predatory? The reader must decide whether Ferlinghetti has made his case. By beginning with such powerful images of suffering, the poet must, to be credible, establish the reality of the danger he sees in American society. Ferlinghetti seeks to convince the reader that internal destruction is taking place in America on the same scale as the overt destruction that Goya witnessed in Spain. The brutality of Goya's sketches illustrate a lack of humanity. Likewise, the American culture depicted in the poem suggests a lack of human warmth and contact. The people are far "from home," and they are amassed on "freeways fifty lanes wide." As Goya's sketches downplay any natural growth in the landscape, the Americans live "on a concrete continent." The suggestion is that America is being eaten away from the inside by a dearth of humanity. Materialism and mechanism have replaced human interaction. Ferlinghetti admits the America scene has "fewer tumbrils": The death and destruction are not graphic or immediate or physical. However, the poet claims Americans are being devoured just the same.

Goya's war sketches are all the more powerful because of the frankness about the horrors of war. Goya rejected the conventional view of his time; the sketches refuse to glorify the combatants or the cause but instead zoom in on the brutal acts of war—destruction, rape, death, dismemberment of corpses. The Goya section of the poem builds in intensity with the penultimate line asserting that the suffering is "so bloody real." Like Goya, the poet refuses to take the conventional view: He does not extol the wealth and freedom of America but focuses on the destruction. The climax in the second section depends not so much on building to intensity but on withholding, until the last word of the poem, the new landscape of suffering. It is not until the last word that Ferlinghetti tells his readers, predominantly Americans, that he is speaking of them as the new suffering humanity.

Marion Petrillo

IN JUST-

Author: E. E. Cummings (1894-1962)
Type of poem: Lyric
First published: 1920; collected in *Tulips and Chimneys*, 1923

The Poem

In only twenty-four lines, E. E. Cummings captures both the feeling and the meaning of spring. Only in spring, or "just" in spring, is the world a kind of wonderful mud bath for children. Spring rains make puddles in which children love to play. Spring is a carnival season—a time to celebrate nature—which accounts for the appearance of the "balloonman," who adds a festive air to the season.

The first stanza and the next line also suggest that adults spring to life "in just," or precisely in, spring. The balloonman may be little and lame, but he is whistling and apparently happy to be out and about. Cummings suggests the enthusiasm of children and the childlike enthusiasms of adults in his first use of the word "wee" in line 5. The word "wide" is expected after "far and," but Cummings changes this clichéd expression to convey the "wee" of the fun that spring represents.

In the second stanza, the childlike speaker of the poem revels in playmates and their games. Playing marbles and pretending to be pirates are examples of the energy and imagination that spring stimulates. The poem itself is a manifestation of vigor; it is at once a description, celebration, and evocation of what spring feels like.

Line 10 suggests that spring turns the world into a splendid playground. The balloonman enters the poem again—this time described as "queer" and "old" but still whistling, as if in spring he forgets his age and his difference from others. In spring, everyone shares the same feelings about being alive and enjoying it. Just as the boys play marbles and pirate games, the girls play hopscotch and jump-rope, and the poem—mimicking their animation—proclaims once again that it is spring.

The innocent games of the children are followed in line 20 and in the last stanza by the antics of the "goat-footed/ balloonMan," who is still whistling "far and wee." In this third appearance, he is no longer lame or old, but spry, having come back to life. The image of the goat suggests nimbleness—one thinks of goats threading their way along mountain passes and rocky cliffs. But goat is also a term that connotes a horny or lecherous man. In other words, in spring the lame old man is aroused sexually, and he recovers some of the same spirit and drive that the children channel into their games.

Forms and Devices

Cummings has been justly praised for his innovative use of typography. Beginning with the poem's title, "in Just-," which begins in the lower case and ends with a hyphen, the poet is evoking a fresh way of rendering the freshness of spring. The season is a part of the unending cycle of nature, and the poem's title is an expression of that ongoing cycle. Spring is both a season and an action (a noun and a verb), and to capitalize it—or to capitalize the first word of the title "in"—would be to make spring as a season and a state of mind conform to typography. Cummings takes the opposite approach, making typography conform to the feeling of being in the season of spring.

Similarly, by ending the title with a hyphen (a punctuation mark that usually connects two words) Cummings is emphasizing that spring is connected not to one word or idea but to many—to a sense of the wide world, of its possibilities. Spring makes people feel expansive and connected to each other and to the rest of the world, the poem implies. Finally, "Just" is capitalized because of the poem's insistence that it is "just" in spring that people feel so in touch with everything.

Note also that there are gaps or spaces between words in lines 2, 5, 13, and 21. These intervals between words are filled, so to speak, with the actions and feelings of the poem, with its springing words that imitate the jumping and playing of the children and the balloonman. The gaps also provide a kind of imaginative ground on which the balloonman is whistling and going about and of the children playing. Giving the words more room also makes the words on the page more prominent, so that the multiple value of each word is more easily recognizable. The spaces between the words make each word more important.

The excitement of spring is also conveyed in the way the poet runs words and names together ("eddieandbill") and in words that the poet coins such as "puddle-wonderful." Spring is the season of creation, so the inventiveness of the human imagination also springs to life.

The poem's form and meaning are built on subtle repetitions. The phrase "far and wee," for example, is spaced differently each time it appears (lines 5, 13, and 22-24). The variations suggest individuality. The "wee" which expresses balloonman's excitement is never quite the same; each time it is seen on the page and heard in the imagination a little differently. The horizontal placement of the phrase "far and wee" also changes to the vertical at the end of the poem, so that each word forms a column that is the embodiment of spring's vitality. Cummings was a painter as well as a poet, and the look of his poem is obviously as important to him as what the words say. Finally, notice that at line 21 balloonman changes to "balloonMan," emphasizing his sexuality and the idea that he has been aroused by spring.

Themes and Meanings

A nature poet, Cummings wrote poems that celebrate nature as a cycle of experience. The changes of the seasons provoke changes in human moods. In this poem, spring is presented as a miraculous event. An old, lame balloonman comes to life, whistling and nimbly moving about. It is as if he has discovered his second childhood. But spring also makes him more fully a man—as the last reference to him suggests.

Balloons are associated with parties, carnivals, birthdays, and other special events. Balloons are attractive playthings because they float through the air so effortlessly. They express the human desire to fly, and they lift the spirits. They soar through space just as human feelings do in this poem. That a lame, queer old man should be associated with balloons suggests how powerful the need to play and to imagine is for every-one—not just for the children who play games and splash in mud puddles. Whatever is old, or lame, or queer about human beings is cured "in Just-" spring.

The images of nature in the poem—mud and water—suggest the basic elements of life. Without water, life perishes. Moreover, water mixed with earth—mud—becomes a human construction. It is not only a material children play with but also the stuff from which human beings construct their games and build life for themselves. With the word "mud-luscious" the poet mimics the inventiveness of human beings playing in mud. "Luscious" suggests the sensuality of the mud. Children like it because it can be shaped to their desires, and they enjoy the touch and the feel of it. But so do adult sculptors and artists, who use clay or mud for the material of art. In some creation myths, human beings are made out of mud—from the stuff of the earth and of spring. Given the way Cummings coins words, alters punctuation, and invents his own typography, it would seem that the poem is not only about spring but also about creativity itself and how it springs from the earth.

Line by line, "in Just-" is a feast for the eye and the imagination. Read too quickly, the poem seems simplistic, repeating the same message over and over. But if the poem's rhythm is respected, it becomes a complex of intellect and emotion. The first line, for example, seems to gird itself to spring in the poem's third word—spring. The poem jumps just like "bettyandisbel" do in their games of hopscotch and jump rope. These games arise out of spring, the poem implies, just as the poem's unique use of vocabulary and typography does.

The second part of the second line, "when the world is mud-," sets up the rest of the poem, which suggests what happens when the world turns to mud in spring. The hyphen after mud also connects the physical element to the human imagination, which comes up with the word luscious in the next line. Indeed, much of the poem moves from the physical world to the human imagination, making the poem and what it describes part of an indivisible whole.

Carl Rollyson

1948

IN MEMORY OF MAJOR ROBERT GREGORY

Author: William Butler Yeats (1865-1939)
Type of poem: Elegy
First published: 1918, as "In Memory of Robert Gregory"; collected as "In Memory of Major Robert Gregory" in *The Wild Swans at Coole*, 1919

The Poem

"In Memory of Major Robert Gregory" is William Butler Yeats's elegy to Robert Gregory, an Irish airman who died in battle during World War I. Written in the first person, it is a poem of twelve stanzas, in octets, which is primarily composed in iambic pentameter but which also includes iambic tetrameter. Gregory was the only son of Lady Augusta Gregory, Yeats's close colleague for two decades. They worked together as pivotal figures in the Irish Literary Revival and were among the founders of Dublin's Abbey Theatre. Over the years, Yeats had relied upon Lady Gregory for financial, intellectual, and emotional support. Coole Park, her country estate in the west of Ireland, had been a second home to Yeats.

Robert Gregory's death in January, 1918, occurred on the eve of the move of Yeats and his wife into their new home, Thoor Ballylee, an old Norman tower not far from the Gregory estate. The death of "my dear friend's dear son" leads the author to reflect upon friends from his past, who, because they are dead, cannot dine and talk together before going up the tower stairs to bed.

The first dead friend he mentions is Lionel Johnson, whom Yeats had known from his earliest days as a writer and who had come to love "learning better than mankind." Another absentee is John Synge, among the greatest of the Irish playwrights; his *Playboy of the Western World* had inflamed literary Dublin when first performed at the Abbey Theatre in 1907. Rather than catering to a romanticized or politically acceptable subject, Synge had chosen "the living world for text," modeling *Playboy of the Western World* from the actual lives of peasants in Ireland's western islands. George Pollexfen, Yeats's uncle and a tie to his own Protestant Irish past, is the third who "cannot sup with us." A horseman when young, Pollexfen had later "grown sluggish and contemplative."

Johnson, Synge, and Pollexfen were significant figures in Yeats's life, but all had been dead for many years, and their "breathless faces seem to look/ Out of some old picture-book." Gregory's death, however, was different, and, coming so suddenly, it was impossible to believe that he "Could share in that discourtesy of death." Gregory would have been the "heartiest welcomer" of Yeats and his wife to their new home because, better than the rest, he knew the tower and its stream, the bridge, the broken trees, the drinking cattle, and the water-hen.

In a reference to the sixteenth century Renaissance figure Philip Sidney, a poet who also died in war and who was elegized by Edmund Spenser, Yeats's Gregory personified the Renaissance man. Like Pollexfen, Gregory, too, was an athletic horseman. He was also a scholar and a soldier; in the poem, however, he is mainly the artist—a painter and a craftsman—who died in his youthful prime, an event that Yeats indicates should have been no surprise when he asks, "What made us dream that he could comb grey hair?" The poem closes with Yeats reflecting that he had intended to describe some of their dreams and accomplishments, but, in the end, he cannot do so, for Gregory's death has stilled the poet's voice.

Forms and Devices

"In Memory of Major Robert Gregory" has frequently been praised as being among Yeats's greatest poems; some critics claim that it is the first of his poems that exhibits the full range of his poetic voice, a voice that later received the Nobel Prize in Literature. Although the poem's meter varies slightly, the rhyme scheme is regular, with an *ababcddc* pattern throughout. On one level, the poem exhibits a straightforward literalness grounded in the actual lands of western Ireland. When the poet describes Thoor Ballylee, "The tower set on the stream's edge" with its "narrow winding stair" and the "old storm-broken trees/ That cast their shadows upon road and bridge," it is a faithful rendering of the landscape. Gregory was a physical product of those Irish counties, "born/ To cold Clare rock and Galway rock and thorn."

In opposition to the poem's solid physicality, however, is the element of dream, of melancholy memory that infuses the poem and raises it beyond mere description. The opening stanza describes the poet reflecting on the past, remembering those gone—both long gone and recently gone—who cannot join him in the tower for talk and drink: "All, all are in my thoughts to-night being dead." Reflecting on Gregory's promise as an artist, the poet states that "We dreamed that a great painter had been born." Continuing with these dreamlike qualities, Gregory's hair is used in a synecdoche to represent the impossibility of his ever attaining a ripe old age when Yeats asks, "What made us dream that he could comb grey hair?"

In one of the central stanzas of the poem, Yeats divides humankind into two categories: Some plod along over the many years, doing what they must do, while others make their contributions and quickly pass on. In a metaphor, he compares those who "burn damp faggots" to others, such as Gregory, who died in Italian skies at thirty-seven and who "may consume/ The entire combustible world . . ./ As though dried straw, and if we turn about/ The bare chimney is gone black out/ Because the work had finished in that flare." The intensity of their lives is both the compensation for and the cause of its brevity.

Themes and Meanings

As in so much of Yeats's work, one of the themes of "In Memory of Major Robert Gregory" is Yeats himself, the self-reflective artist and the Irishman. The tensions between Yeats (a Protestant Irishman) and the Catholic majority, and between his art and that of those who merely pandered to sentimental and patriotic feelings, existed throughout Yeats's career. The tower of Thoor Ballylee, where he lived beginning in 1918, became a symbol for the artist's isolation and for what might be called high culture in many of his later poems. However, if the tower is the symbol of the artist and his retreat from the mundane world in pursuit of his craft, what does it mean to be an artist in the complete sense, to "Climb up the narrow winding stair"?

His choice of absent associates is revealing. All four—Johnson, Synge, Pollexfen, and Gregory—had been important in his life, but in the poem they also signify something other than their human realities. Johnson, an influence upon Yeats in the 1890's, symbolizes the writer who renounces the real world for what Yeats called "the twilight world," seeking the isolation supposedly required by the true artist. Synge, on the other hand, in his portrayal of the Aran islanders in *The Playboy of the Western World*, reached out and "chose the living world for text// . . . a race/ Passionate and simple like his heart." Yeats's uncle Pollexfen was not primarily a writer, but, in representing the Yeats and Pollexfen families, he symbolizes the passing Protestant Ascendancy which, "Having grown sluggish and contemplative," is giving way to the Catholic majority.

Gregory's portrayal in the elegy is something more and something less than the historical Gregory: He becomes a Platonic figure who reconciles, in the poem, the incomplete personages of Johnson, Synge, and Pollexfen. Gregory, Yeats's Renaissance man, is "Our Sidney," another Philip Sidney, the statesman-diplomat, author of the epic prose romance *Arcadia* (c.1580) and a collection of love sonnets, *Astrophel and Stella* (1591), who also died in his thirties of a fatal battle wound. However, while Gregory exhibited all the qualities of "Soldier, scholar, horseman," in the poet's thoughts it is Gregory as the artist who is worthy of being memorialized, though he died as a soldier and a man of action.

The younger Yeats had been active in radical political movements in Ireland, but over time he had distanced himself from those involvements, coming to defend the contributions that the Protestant Ascendancy were making to Ireland's lasting culture. Yeats was not a soldier, and his life was not "finished in that flare" as was Gregory's. Perhaps this was a cause for regret by Yeats when he wrote his elegy to Gregory, given the bloody sacrifices so many (such as Gregory in World War I and the Irish rebels in the Easter Rising of 1916) had made.

The concluding stanza presents a somber world, "seeing how bitter is that wind/ That shakes the shutter." In nostalgic loss, the poet looks back again to comment on his dead friends and their deeds. However, there is nothing he can say, for "that late death took all my heart for speech." The historical Major Robert Gregory was, perhaps, less of a Renaissance man than the one portrayed in Yeats's eloquent elegy, but the poem is also an elegy to the poet himself, alive but now alone in his tower in the emptier present, "For all that come into my mind are dead."

Eugene Larson

IN MEMORY OF MY FEELINGS

Author: Frank O'Hara (1926-1966)
Type of poem: Elegy
First published: 1958; collected in *In Memory of My Feelings: A Selection of Poems,*
1967

The Poem

The manuscript of Frank O'Hara's poem "In Memory of My Feelings" indicates the time of composition as having occurred between June 27 and July 1, 1956, ostensibly to mark the poet's thirtieth birthday, and, incidentally, the midpoint of his poetic career—the threshold of maturity, by any counts. At the time of the writing, O'Hara believed he had been born on June 27, 1926, but, in fact, it was later discovered, after the poet's death, he had been born three months earlier, on March 27.

Totaling 194 lines, the poem is subdivided into five fairly balanced and numbered sections of, respectively, 41, 33, 41, 44, and 35 lines grouped in rather irregular verse paragraphs, which often begin in midpage, following a third, a half, or even three-quarters of the preceding line. This accounts for the jagged, prose-like aspect of the poem, which highlights its rhetorical stance—described by the poet some months later in "Poem Read at Joan Mitchell's" as "post-anti-esthetic, bland, unpicturesque and William Carlos Williamsian! [...] Not nineteenth century . . . not even Partisan Review . . . new . . . vanguard."

The poem is dedicated to Grace Hartigan, an artist who at the time was the poet's lover and chief muse. Her name is gracefully punned in the heart of the fourth section: "Grace/ to be born and live as variously as possible." The line was fated to become one of the best known in O'Hara's poetry, since ten years later it was chiseled as an apt and terse epitaph on his tombstone. At 3 A.M. on July 25, 1966, the poet was struck on a Long Island beach by a truck and mortally wounded.

There is no need to stress further the clearly autobiographical nature of the poem. However, instead of being prospective and confident, as behooves a person on the brink of manhood, the tone of the poem is wistful and retrospective. Remembering the past means, in this case, dealing with absences in the wake of numerous deaths of close relatives and friends. It likewise boils down to meditating on the plurality of one's own inner selves, which grow out of the various feelings elicited by the events evoked by memory. The poet sadly realizes that his former transparent selves have one by one shriveled and melted into thin air. History with its pageantry of civilizations, the landscapes and climates of remote parts of the globe, wars and revolutions, and works of art crop up in memory, and thus the feel of formerly lived experiences can be recaptured fleetingly.

Ultimately, according to the O'Hara poem, one seeks to avoid being pinned down by simply adding up one's former selves. The Proteus-like selfhood of O'Hara is at its shrewdest when it defies stasis. Hence the poem itself shuns closure and a final commitment, whether intellectual, moral, or spiritual.

Forms and Devices

"In Memory of My Feelings" is a medium-length poem generally employed by O'Hara as a vehicle for weightier, quasi-philosophical statements, which by their nature require an accumulation of facts or evidence in support of a thesis, however vague or elusive at a first reading that might appear to be. His main concern is the marshaling of instances, rather than the musicality of his utterances. There is an absence of clearcut, clean tunefulness in this poem. Its lyricism is subdued, in spite of the conspicuous part the poet's ego plays throughout. Rhythm too is achieved not by means of regular metrical beats or evenly distributed stresses, but—as in Walt Whitman, Vladimir Mayakovsky, or William Carlos Williams—by syntactical parallelisms or the cavalcade of catalogues of alternative actions, as in part 4 (lines 26-36), which originally was an independent poem cast as a regular sequence of four quatrains. However, when it was incorporated into the larger structure, it had to obey its dominant formal principle. That required the redistribution of words or syllables as well as the relaxation of the grip of the regular metrical pattern.

Furthermore, if one looks at the poem as a whole, one cannot fail noticing the fivefold structure of the grand Romantic symphony (which may have a fifth part added to the usual classical four). Indeed, the poem makes much structural sense when it is viewed from this compositional perspective. The opening is solemn and evenly measured in stately fourteen- to fifteen-syllable lines—the highest number in this poem reaching twenty-one, which almost blurs the boundary separating verse from prose: "My quietness has a man in it, he is transparent/ and he carries me quietly, like a gondola, through the streets." Throughout part 1, the poem puts forth compendious, explanatory moves, ending with the presentation of the motif of the serpent. The tempo is moderately slow.

Part 2 is lighter, with shorter lines and a profusion of first-person-singular possessive adjectives. The natural background contrasts with the mainly urban environment of part 1, as well. It is the shortest and most rapidly unfolding movement, and the pace is slightly faster. Part 3, the median or central part, is devoted to history and its blind alleys. Narrative in character, with overtures to the reader in order to involve him or her, this section's pace picks up.

Part 4—the longest—brings, in its first half, the poem back to the United States just to recycle its foreign materials so far, under the pretext of a masque or pageantry that the poet dismisses as a series of "sordid identifications." Finally, in part 5 the poem comes full circle, returning to the serpent motif: "since to move is to love/ and the scrutiny of all things is syllogistic." Another memorable statement is "To bend the ear to the outer world," which tries to bring in a more objective and witnessing stance. The lament goes on with "I have forgotten my loves"—the pace slowing, the elegy of one's own selfhood dying down on its failure to sustain its "ruses," but with a lastditch attempt to spare the viable, almost sacred, serpent from their midst. The poem thus seemingly comes to a rest, only to urge its readers to tackle once more the obscure spots for further scrutiny and communion with the poem's newly yielded insights.

Themes and Meanings

The lexicon of the poem makes the reader aware of several thematic concerns: time and space, history and geography, languages, the arts, and the animal kingdom. The protagonist measures himself against historical or cultural heroes and their roles. He is by turns Manfred—a well-known Byronic solitary, roaming the Alps, torn by remorse and obsessed by suicide on account of an unnamable cardinal sin, presumably of an incestuous nature, committed in his youth. Other people and places, whose chief characteristics or features he briefly shares, succeed one another: He is by turns witnessing an invasion of Australians, of restless Arabs, of a Chinese climbing a mountain, of Greeks rebuffing Persians, or of Romans making copies. He actually feels like being a Hittite in love with a horse, an African prince, an American Indian asleep over his enemy's scalp. He even knows what it feels like to be French, German, Norwegian, a man of the world, a sailor, a prisoner, a dictator, a painter, a physician, and a journalist. Consequently words in such languages as Italian, French, Spanish, German, Russian, and Arabic are sprinkled all over the poem.

All sorts of ideologies and forms of government are hinted at: humanism and democracy, dictatorships and guerilla warfare, American Indian wars, and Arabian, Greek and French love of ideas. Also mentioned are such places as Borneo, Venice, Paris, and Chicago; a wedding (*sposalizio*); Lord Nelson's death and its aftermath; the *Firebird Suite* by Igor Stravinsky; a painting by Gustave Courbet; Medusa's head, teeming with vipers instead of locks; and above all the search for the most coveted energy resource—crude oil.

The reader of "In Memory of My Feelings" will by the end of the analytical process feel exhilarated to realize that taxonomy, knowledge, and scholarship are stages required to establish a grammar of relationships among phenomena by means of which the horizons of understanding of the world's challenging meaningfulness may be expanded, even though the free, surrealistic associations subvert syllogistic logic and rely on the sudden, surprising metamorphoses encountered in dreams. The reader abandons herself or himself to the flux of images and partakes in the sensuousness and delight of drifting along in the company of a self remarkable in its capacity of integrating experiences and impersonating so many roles, reminding one of John Keats's "negative capability"—the empathetic abnegation of the Romantics.

Reality can be varied and beautiful, provided one approach it with the superbly educated sensibility of O'Hara's writing self and poetic imagination. Darker, then, becomes the poem's underlying melancholy, because of its seeming inability to transmute its intense, fleeting states into the permanence of history or art.

Stefan Stoenescu

1954

IN MEMORY OF SIGMUND FREUD

Author: W. H. Auden (1907-1973)
Type of poem: Elegy
First published: 1940, in *Another Time*

The Poem
"In Memory of Sigmund Freud" is an elegy to the famous psychologist written in twenty-eight alcaic stanzas. W. H. Auden read works by Sigmund Freud when he was very young, and Freudian theories played an important part in Auden's poetry throughout his life. Although the poem is a fitting tribute to the creator of psychoanalysis, it is better studied as a description of Freud's importance to Auden and his influence on Auden's own psychological, political, and aesthetic theories than as a precise description of Freud's character or theories.

The first two stanzas remind the reader that Freud died during World War II, when many others were dying, and strike the moral note that will dominate the poem. Stanza 6 records Freud's death in England, where he had fled when the Nazis occupied his native Austria in 1938. The remaining stanzas shift back and forth among metaphoric descriptions of Freud's theories, Auden's evaluation of those theories, and his discussion of his contemporary world. The "problems" of stanza 4 anticipate the complexity of Freud's theories and Auden's description of them.

Freud's psychoanalysis rests upon the belief that psychological problems are provoked by emotions repressed in the unconscious. Stanza 3 concerns the lack of control of the unconscious and its determining effects upon individual lives. In stanzas 5 and 25, the unconscious is compared to "shades" and the "night." Patients are cured through uncovering repressed emotions by probing their pasts through free association. Stanzas 8 through 11 describe this process of "looking back . . . to recite the past" in order to heal the "unhappy present" and the well-known "Freudian slip," by which the unconscious inadvertently betrays itself in describing the past "falter[ing] . . . at the line where/ long ago the accusations had begun." This illumination frees one to be less inhibited and to accept many facets of oneself, which Auden illustrates in stanzas 20-22.

Freud also identified certain instincts that govern conscious and unconscious behavior. Central to his theories—and to the tremendous controversy that they incited—is Eros, or the sex/love instinct, which (like the Greek god for which it is named) is both creative and destructive. Eros is implicit in many details of the poem, such as the jealousy portrayed in stanza 4 and the appeal of the unconscious' "creatures" in stanza 26. It appears explicitly in the last two lines of the poem, which also invoke Aphrodite, the goddess of love and mother of Eros. Auden believed that Eros, together with the release of unconscious emotions, allows one to reconcile internal conflicts, including the tension between the reason and the emotions. He describes this in stanzas 23 through 27.

Auden celebrates these theories because he believes that they enable people to live more virtuous lives; he makes this claim in stanza 2 and elaborates upon it throughout the poem. They allow one to escape involuntary behavior and make self-conscious, moral decisions. Because Freudian theory reconciles warring contraries and makes a person whole, the synthesis that Auden describes in the last six stanzas of the poem is, to him, inherently moral.

Forms and Devices

"In Memory of Sigmund Freud" is an elegy in alcaic stanzas. Auden uses Freud's death not only to commemorate him, but also to meditate upon good and evil and to comment upon the malignity that infested the Fascist powers in World War II. This is typical of elegies, which traditionally reach beyond their immediate subjects to broader, often social, concerns. Usually this comment is in the form of protest. John Milton, for example, took the occasion of the death of Edward King to attack the corrupted clergy (as well as materialism and the aspiration for fame) in "Lycidas."

The poem also resembles other elegies in that it offers consolation for Freud's death: His theories, like art and literature in earlier elegies, survive him. It elaborates upon this consolation in much less detail than most elegies do, however, and it observes very few other elegiac conventions. Most elegies, for example, are really meditations upon death and upon human effort to deal with life's transience. Auden spends very little time reflecting upon death itself. Nor does he use pastoral elegiac conventions, such as the pathetic fallacy or the procession of mourners. This nonconformity marks the difference between earlier, traditional, coherent cultures and the troubled modern world.

Auden was one of the most brilliant and innovative prosodists among modern poets. No other twentieth century poet uses as many old and new verse forms. An alcaic stanza has four lines: The first two have eleven syllables; the third, nine; and the fourth, ten. Auden and Marianne Moore are two of the very few poets in English successfully to employ syllabic meter rather than accentual-syllabic meter. Determined by the number of syllables per line rather than the number of syllables and number of accents, syllabic meter is common in languages such as Italian and Japanese but is rare in English.

The verse of "In Memory of Sigmund Freud" is also technically unusual because of its heavy use of enjambment or run-over lines, in which the sense of a line and its punctuation do not pause at the end. The enjambment is so extreme that many stanzas are not even end-stopped. This creates a ruminating, meditative effect, which is reinforced by the fact that—contrary to normal practice—the first words of most lines are not capitalized. This enjambment means that, in spite of its contrived form, the poem lacks strict demarcations, and its ideas are fluidly connected.

The importance of connection can also be seen in many of the poem's metaphors, the most distinctive of which are topographical. These geographic metaphors are typical of Freud, who often explained the psyche by dividing it into different territories. The most sustained use of these metaphors describes Freud's pervasive influence by comparing him to a "climate of opinion" or a "weather" which "extends" everywhere and penetrates "even the remotest miserable duchy" (stanzas 17 through 21). This metaphor and its enjambment create an impression of expansion, dispersal, and flow.

Themes and Meanings

The expansion and connection characteristic of the poem's images and its verse are central to the meaning of "In Memory of Sigmund Freud." The poem is in large part about modern alienation and fragmentation and how to overcome them. The isolation and disjunction of modern lives are highlighted by Freud's having been a Jew in exile, the unconscious' "delectable creatures" being "exiles," freedom's loneliness (stanza 23), and the description of "unequal moieties fractured" (stanzas 23 and following). These themes preoccupy many modernist writers, including T. S. Eliot, Virginia Woolf, and James Joyce, whose works imitate their subjects through subjective, unconnected voices and disjointed syntax and structure. Auden resembles these and many other modernists in blaming rationality—and the elevation of reason—for these modern malaises. Auden, however, has chosen to imitate the connection he recommends instead of the fractured world around him.

Alienation and fragmentation can be cured through recognizing repressed problems. This acknowledgment results in free choice, a virtue which threatens evil because it empowers the individual to determine his or her own fate. His contemporary world gave relevance, even urgency, to Auden's message. Implicit in the capitalization of the "monolith[ic] State" (stanzas 13 and 20), for example, is a criticism of World War II's autocratic, Fascist countries, such as Germany and Italy. The reminder in stanza 6 that Freud was Jewish and the comparison in stanza 7 of Hate's repression of emotions to killing and burning call up the Nazis' slaughter and burning of the Jews.

Generosity contrasts with evil's tyranny and grounds the recognition that frees humankind. If one is generous to oneself by accepting one's acts and stopping the "accusations," one will be made whole: "long-forgotten" parts of oneself will be restored. If one is generous to others, then modern ills will be cured. One also needs to be open and generous to the surrounding world in order to have the sense of wonder acclaimed in stanza 25. Such unselfishness results in the love personified in Eros and recommended in stanza 26. By reaching out to others, we can rescue "the future that lies in our power"—in other words, save civilization.

Freud is an example of the magnanimity that Auden describes. He is one of those who "hoped to improve" and help humankind in spite of his own persecution. By underlining Freud's persecution, Auden stresses modern humanity's alienation and protects Freud against the charge that his methods were too authoritative. This also reminds the reader that it is often very difficult to be forgiving and altruistic, but that people must love and forgive one another even when fact and reason seem to justify hate and resentment. Auden's praise of and appreciation for Freud is itself an example of the love and generosity he promotes.

Laura Cowan

IN MEMORY OF W. B. YEATS

Author: W. H. Auden (1907-1973)
Type of poem: Ode
First published: 1939; collected in *Another Time*, 1940; revised in *Collected Shorter Poems, 1927-1957*, 1966

The Poem

The Irishman William Butler Yeats was the most famous and important poet writing in English at the time of his death in January, 1939, and W. H. Auden sought to make a living memorial to Yeats through this ode. The ode form is traditionally reserved for important and serious subjects and is written in an elevated style, so Auden gave Yeats great value and dignity by using this genre. The poem was written within one month of Yeats's death and published shortly thereafter. It has three distinct parts; Auden radically revised the third part by eliminating three entire stanzas which were part of the original when he included it twenty-seven years later in his *Collected Shorter Poems, 1927-1957* in 1966.

In part 1, Auden paints a dark, frozen, wintry landscape as the backdrop for Yeats's death; it is almost as if the earth mourns his loss. The animals in the forest and rivers, however, run their usual courses unaware of the magnitude of the loss. Yeats's poems are treated as being human, like part of his family; the news of his death is withheld from his poems, which live on. On his last afternoon, his whole being, like a city under siege, is invaded by death. His body revolts, his mind is emptied, silence overcomes him, and he is stilled. After he is physically dead, Yeats's poems still live and are scattered across the world; the dead poet loses control over their meanings and over the kinds of affection they will excite. The poems are "the words of a dead man," which, after his death, are reinterpreted "in the guts of the living." Auden repeats that one might try to measure the loss of Yeats with scientific "instruments," but they only can tell one that "the day of his death was a dark cold day." He implies that Yeats had a value much greater than any "instrument" can measure.

In part 2 of the ode, Auden switches to Yeats's life and contrasts the man to his work: The man dies, but his poetry lives forever. Yeats's poetry survives Yeats's silliness and mysticism, his own physical decay, his insane country of Ireland, and even the damp and sometimes miserable Irish weather. Auden claims that poetry "makes nothing happen" in a practical sense but that it survives in the human imagination, far from the control of business executives. The poetry flows through imagination and unites humankind, which may be isolated, grief-stricken, and living in crude towns. Even though Yeats dies physically, he lives on in the imagination through his poetry.

Part 3 is beautifully formal and rhetorical. Auden begins by directly addressing the earth, into which Yeats will be placed. He instructs the earth to accept an "honored guest," not a dead man; the section is decidedly celebratory rather than grim. In the later (1966) version of the poem, Auden eliminated three entire stanzas, which in the original followed the first stanza. In these stanzas, Auden explains that time, meaning history and chronological time, pardons poets and does not fully claim them, since it "worships language" and those who write it. Yeats was therefore to be pardoned any personal idiosyncrasy, and such a pardon by time presumably would make him one of the immortal poets. Auden's speaker then compares the nightmarish days of 1939 immediately before World War II broke out with the ability of Yeats to create art and poetry out of disastrous times.

Yeats is looked up to as a role model for other poets, because he had an unconstrained voice which would tell the truth even during times of "intellectual disgrace" when nations were barking at each other like threatening curs. Even in dark times such as those of 1939, when human pity seems "frozen," Auden asks the spirit of Yeats to "Still persuade us to rejoice." He wants the "poet," either Yeats or himself, to make something fruitful (a "vineyard") from the distressing period by "farming" it in his poetry. In the last stanza, he wants poets to help start the "healing fountain" which will teach free men to endure even in hateful and evil days and will teach them again "how to praise." Poetry needs to give life and hope even in the darkest days.

Forms and Devices

Auden begins this ode with an archetypal image cluster that links winter and death. The setting is desolate and filled with winter, death, and negative words, which often are linked by alliteration of *d* sounds. Alliterating negative words and phrases include: "disappeared" and "dead" (line 1), "deserted" (line 2), "disfigured" (line 3), "dying day" (line 4), and "day," "death," and "dark," (line 6). This repetitive cluster of alliterating negative words in conjunction with the frozen, wintry words creates a powerful scene of desolation in which the world's dead time seems to mirror the poet Yeats's death. In an extended form of personification, the wintering earth itself seems to mourn the loss of the poet.

In addition, Auden makes good use of other extended metaphors by establishing a different central metaphor for almost each stanza in part 1. He compares death to an invading army that takes over Yeats's whole being in stanza 4. The "invasion" is preceded by "rumours," then "revolt" in the provinces of his body; then the "squares of his mind" are emptied, silence pervades the "suburbs" of his existence, and lights go out when the "current of his feeling failed." Auden uses a cluster of geographic terms (provinces, squares, and suburbs) to illustrate the personal world of Yeats being shut down. These linked geographical comparisons metaphorically make Yeats a whole country unto himself, which magnifies the gravity of the loss.

Auden also uses individual metaphors with great cleverness. One example is his use of "mouth" at the end of part 2 to talk about poetry and the poet simultaneously. Poetry is a "mouth" in that it metaphorically speaks to the reader. Since the "mouth" is also the organ of speech, the word is used as a form of metonomy to refer to the poet himself. Like a mouth, poetry is an open potential from which words can issue. Mouths, like poems, are eternal features of humankind—one, the mouth, is a permanent physical feature, while the other, the poem, is an imaginative creation that endures beyond the poet's death.

Themes and Meanings

Auden seeks to immortalize W. B. Yeats by writing a poem about his memory and its value. He celebrates the immortality of Yeats's great poetry instead of mourning the man's demise. One of Auden's main points is that once an artist creates his art, the art develops its own autonomy and life and is not limited by the artist or his intentions. To Auden, as he makes clear in part 3 of the poem, poetry needs to teach humankind to rejoice and to endure the hideous times of life. Poets, following Yeats's example, must create great eternal art from the disasters of their times as they "farm" and perfect their verse. Writing poetry about painful experiences can be healing both for the poet who writes and for the reader who reads. Yeats presumably did write painful and healing verse in his own "unconstraining voice." He transmuted disasters in Ireland, such as the violently repressed Irish rebellion against the British during Easter, 1916, into poems of great beauty and dignity. Auden seeks to follow that example in this ode. The disaster that Auden comes to "celebrate" is the death of the greatest living English poet, W. B. Yeats. In his memorial ode, Auden tries to transform the "curse" of Yeats's physical death into an occasion for rejoicing. Yeats's personal death ends his production of new poems and permanently closes his "mouth," but, paradoxically, the poet does not die. Yeats lives through his monumental poems and takes his place with the other immortals. By reminding readers of the paradox of death not being final for a poet, Auden implies that one should not be sad at Yeats's passing. The poet lives forever in and through his poetry. Art is eternal, and that is an encouraging thought even in the darkest of day.

David J. Amante

IN MOURNING WISE SINCE DAILY I INCREASE

Author: Sir Thomas Wyatt (1503-1542)
Type of poem: Ballad
First published: 1816, in *The Works of Henry Howard, Earl of Surrey, and of Sir Thomas Wyatt the Elder* (vol. 2)

The Poem

"In mourning wise since daily I increase" is a ballad composed of eight stanzas, with each stanza consisting of two quatrains of generally regular iambic pentameter. Based on a historical incident at the court of the English monarch King Henry VIII, the poem is Sir Thomas Wyatt's meditation on the execution of five men of the court for their alleged adultery with Queen Anne Boleyn.

According to Kenneth Muir's *Sir Thomas Wyatt, Life and Letters* (1963), the five men addressed in the poem were executed on May 17, 1536, for improper sexual relations with Queen Anne. They were Lord Rochford, the queen's brother, who was charged with incest; Sir Henry Norris, Sir Francis Weston, and Sir William Bereton, three court officials charged with adultery with the queen; and Mark Smeaton, a court musician who appears to have confessed under torture and who may have implicated the four others.

The poem is divided into three sections: an opening of two stanzas that establishes the specific situation that has saddened the poet; a central portion of five stanzas in which the executed individuals are directly addressed by the poet, who comments on their virtues and weaknesses; and a concluding single stanza that again returns the poem to consider the general implications of this specific tragedy. Each of the people the poet addresses is given some touch of individuality, which, generally, is the immediate reason to mourn his loss. Rochford had great wit, Norris would be missed by his friends at court, Weston was unmatched "in active things," and Bereton, of whom the poet knows the least, at least had a good reputation. Only Smeaton seems to have been without individual virtue, but he is to be pitied, for he has climbed above his station and "A rotten twig upon so high a tree/ Hath slipped [his] hold."

At the time of the executions, Wyatt was himself imprisoned in the Tower of London, perhaps under suspicion of adultery with the queen but more likely as possibly having knowledge of the alleged crimes. It is possible that while in the tower, Wyatt witnessed the deaths of the five men and, on May 19, the execution of Anne herself. It is certain that the impact of the events is registered in his poem. At the same time, however, while this is a poem triggered by a specific historical event, it is also a meditation on the sense of loss and sadness caused by any human death.

Forms and Devices

The poetic form for "In mourning wise" is that of the ballad, which usually tells a story but, in this case, presents a situation and comments upon it. The traditional ballad is typically presented in a four-line stanza, rhyming *abab.* Wyatt combines two of these stanzas into a single eight-line stanza. The ballad's relatively casual, informal style, which allows the poet to address both the participants in the poem and the reader directly, is especially suitable for the meaning and purpose of "In mourning wise."

The underlying logical scheme for "In mourning wise" is that of classical rhetoric. Specifically, Wyatt has taken the rhetorical tradition of addressing absent individuals as if they were actually present. In this case, these individuals are the reader, to whom Wyatt speaks in the opening and closing of the poem, and the guilty dead, each of whom he addresses in turn. This sort of formal patterning was a tradition from the classical world, and educated courtiers such as Wyatt and his readers would have been intimately familiar with it. It permits him to go from a specific personal and historic situation (the execution of five men while he himself was imprisoned in the Tower of London) to a larger, more embracing consideration: how the death of any human being deprives the world of unique talents and personalities and so is a cause for sorrow.

Over this logical framework, the poet has fashioned a linguistic surface to express both his meanings and his feelings. Wyatt, who was known among his contemporaries for improving and regularizing the form of English verse, uses a consistent structure for his poem, with the regularity of the rhyme scheme (*ababcdcd*) matched by the rhythmic pattern of the iambic pentameter lines. Wyatt uses this regularity both to link his work together and as a vehicle to present his narration and description: This is who these men were, and this is why the poet is sad they are gone. Moving beyond that, Wyatt's steady, methodical form can be seen as imposing a sense of inevitability about the events described in the poem.

The poem is further knit together by its use of repetition, especially the phrase "dead and gone," which ends the last line of each stanza except the second, where it is only slightly varied as "bewail the death of some be gone." Since the poem is about a group of executed men, the phrase is tellingly apt, and its repetition should heighten the reader's sense of a series of executions happening one after the other and leaving each victim, in turn, inexorably "dead and gone." By the eighth and final stanza, the hammer strokes of the three short words have impressed more than their literal meaning on the reader. In addition to the repeated use of the phrase, its final word, "gone," is invariably linked by rhyme with either "moan" or "bemoan," thus driving home the mournful, elegiac tone of the work. No matter how any stanza opens, its end always draws the reader back to a sense of sadness and loss because of the inescapable fact of death. Such simplicity and repetition are important sources of the poem's powerful impact on the attentive reader.

Themes and Meanings

The underlying theme of "In mourning wise" is a sense of loss in the face of the death of human beings. Such death may be through official execution, as in the case of the characters in this poem, but, ultimately, all human death is a cause for solemn reflection. Rochford and the others have been executed, Wyatt reflects, but the death they endure through judicial violence is the fate that all human beings inevitably experience as part of the course of nature. Death is death, the poem implies, and while these men have been justly punished for their crimes, still their deaths and the loss that they bring are an occasion for sorrow.

A second, interlocking theme is that the deaths of Rochford and the others were unnecessary, since they were caused by bad judgment on the part of the condemned or perhaps, the poem suggests, through the conspiracies of the Tudor court. In either event, death has come sooner than it would normally. The underlying theme of the poem refers to the wheel of fortune, a commonplace of English Renaissance literature that carries individuals into prominence, fame, and power only to cast them down into obscurity, shame, and impotence. Such has been the fate of the characters in Wyatt's poem and such, the poet well knows from personal experience, could be the fate of any attendant of the Tudor dynasty. The ancient biblical adage "trust not in princes" was never more true than at the court of Henry VIII.

Throughout the poem, Wyatt assumes the role of speaker, first to the reader (or perhaps to himself) and then to each of the condemned men in turn. In doing this, he can examine the impact of each man's particular death upon himself. Some he knows well; others, notably Bereton, he knows less well. Still, the sense of loss seems as keen for the unfamiliar as for the well known. This theme is reinforced by the way that the poem presents it to the reader. Having first announced that he has grown deeper (and perhaps more knowing, given the first line's underlying play on words) in mourning, Wyatt next examines the cause of his sorrow by addressing each of the executed men and praising them for some virtue or gift that has been undone and lost by their crime. He is careful to make no excuses for them. Smeaton, the court musician and commoner who dared sleep with a queen, is addressed with brutal directness: "thy death thou hast deserved best." Yet even so, the poet will "moan thee with the rest" because Smeaton too is dead and gone. Indeed, as the final stanza makes clear, it is the loss by death of any individual, just as much as the specific situation of these executions of a few members of court, that evokes the pity and sorrow of the poet and his poem: "Leave sobs therefore, and every Christian heart/ Pray for the souls of those be dead and gone."

Michael Witkoski

IN PARENTHESIS

Author: David Jones (1895-1974)
Type of poem: Epic
First published: 1937

The Poem

The 187-page poem *In Parenthesis* is in seven sections, and it tells the story of a group of British soldiers of all ranks as they proceed from England to the trench warfare at the battle of the Somme. The action, therefore, is set during World War I but extends only from December, 1915, to July, 1916.

The preface and the thirty-five pages of footnotes, both written by David Jones, should be considered a part of the poem. In the preface, David Jones explains that the title refers, first, to the war itself as a "space between," a turning aside from the regularity of one's ordinary business. Second, he implies that life itself, "our curious type of existence here," is a space between nonexistence and the future.

T. S. Eliot's "A Note of Introduction" was added in 1961 and suggests that readers will have to "get used to" this unusual poem. Eliot puts his literary mantle over Jones by including him in a quartet of modern writers (Eliot himself, James Joyce, and Ezra Pound being the other three) whose lives were altered by the war, but he singles Jones out as the only one of the four who had actually been a soldier.

The first section introduces the reader to the principal characters: Major Lillywhite, Captain Gwynn, Lieutenant Piers Jenkins, Sergeant Snell, Corporal Quilter, Lance-Corporal Aneirin Lewis, and Private John Ball. They, and others, are members of the Royal Welsh Regiment, 55th Battalion, "B" Company, No. 7 Platoon. They are somewhat clumsy and apprehensive of the new role that has been thrust upon them, as they move across the Channel and disembark from "cattle trucks" on French soil.

In section 2, the platoon sees its first, impersonal, action, coming with an explosion of "some stinking physicist's destroying toy." This literal explosion interrupts a personal "explosion" by Sergeant Snell, who is caught in mid-sentence in a diatribe against Private Ball. The explosion rips up the dirt and plants, covering in disorder the invading "order" of the soldiers' camp.

Section 3 is a nightwatch. Little happens, and very little can be seen. The men cannot see one another clearly enough to recognize their companions. Private Ball, who has by now become the principal figure in the poem, particularly feels a sense of isolation. In section 4, the soldiers are in the midst of the waiting for something to happen. Even as the rain falls miserably down, Lance-Corporal Lewis stands up and offers a paean to all the war heroes in Western history. His speech is somewhat surrealistic in its grandeur and scope, as if he were temporarily possessed by the valor of so many who died in catastrophes similar to World War I.

In section 5, several soldiers get promotions (Quilter, Watcyn, and Jenkins, though Watcyn soon loses his for drunkenness). The troops see more action, and the platoon has its first death. Meanwhile, the focus of each individual becomes increasingly narrow: Each day becomes more important; each minor celebration, like a food parcel from home, seems more significant. Tension increases beneath the "ordinariness" of it all.

Section 6 is the final preparation of the battalion for its turn on the front line. Private Ball sees his friends from back in England, from back before this parenthetical war, one final time. The battalion moves forward and sees, along the road, dead mules "sunk in their servility." The soldiers cannot help but think of themselves in similar terms.

In the concluding section, characters from the opening of the poem are killed. The killing seems arbitrary, not for any didactic or balancing purpose. Lance-Corporal Lewis dies anonymously, unobserved. Jenkins leads the platoon into battle and is quickly mowed down. Next to die is Sergeant Quilter, who had assumed temporary command. Lillywhite also dies. Private John Ball survives, however, having been wounded in the leg. In the end he discards his rifle and lies down by a fallen oak, hoping the stretcher-bearers will find him and noticing in a cloudy way the many other soldiers who surge past him.

Forms and Devices

From the time of its publication there has been controversy over the genre of this "writing," as Jones himself called it. Large portions read very much like narrative prose, and at least as many read like lyric poetry. In his preface, Jones describes his work in terms that seem to refer to sculpture rather than song, and he suggests he has carved out a new "shape in words" from an otherwise amorphous welter of experience. The emphasis on physical description is not surprising, since Jones was a painter before he wrote any poetry.

The materials he uses for this new shape derive from "the complex of sights, sounds, fears, hopes, apprehensions, smells, things exterior and interior, the landscape and paraphernalia of that singular time and of those particular men." This is clearly, therefore, a poem of mixed styles, some imitative of colloquial speech, as though the poet were standing in the field of battle with a tape recorder, surrounded by the welter of British accents and vocabularies. At other points in the poem, however, Jones's style becomes highly crafted and careful, far more dense and lyrical than common speech. This poem, he writes, "has to do with some things I saw, felt, and was part of." Therefore, it might be described as autobiography, though it is impersonal and not confessional writing; it shares much, as well, with the genres of historical writing, philosophy, and even theology.

It is significant, however, that Eliot in 1961 added his introduction to the poem, since, in doing so, he put his imprimatur on the "Eliotic" stitching together of allusions, myth, history, snatches of conversation, songs, and the other elements that had come to be associated with his own poetry, and especially with *The Waste Land* (1922). It is unlikely that Jones's poem would have been recognized at all before the experimentation of Eliot and James Joyce: Since it is even less obviously generic than their creations, it would have been too apparently shapeless even for discerning readers. Following the lead of these modernists, Jones seems consciously to be expanding the generic poetic tradition he has inherited, allowing a topic as brutal as World War I to explode old categories and to reflect in the lines of *In Parenthesis* the slippery, arbitrary, and confusing experience of modern warfare, as well as its eclectic mix of conflicting emotions.

The topic itself and the time in which the poem was written both contribute to its form, but there are other significant factors in Jones's biography that shape the poem's allusions and voice. These, in a more traditional way, break out of the limited setting of one man's experience of a specific war and let the poem address all such "parenthetical" human experiences. Jones was a Londoner of Welsh and English descent, and a convert to Roman Catholicism. He draws on historical and ritualistic elements from all these sources and lets them influence the form of the telling.

Jones never mastered the Welsh language but hoped he might use this poem and his later *The Anathemata* (1952) as vessels to preserve a portion of the vast Welsh literary heritage. The most intimidating aspects of this poem often can be clarified with reference to the notes Jones provides. These indicate the Welsh allusions, the early epic *Y Gododdin, The Mabinogion, Kulhwch ac Olwen* (the Welsh version of the Waste Land myth), and others.

There are Latin references as well, to the Roman invasion of Britain, the battles and heroism of that early period, and the language used to express that heroism. There are Elizabethan allusions and quotations from Shakespeare's iambic pentameter, Victorian ditties such as Lewis Carroll's *The Hunting of the Snark: Or, An Agony in Eight Fits* (1876), and contemporary slang. The result is an amalgam of the historic languages of Great Britain—a human voice, timebound and amorphous, but expressive of the grandeur and pain common to all, regardless of the age.

Jones's Roman Catholicism also influenced the form of the poem. (He converted in 1921, three years after leaving the army and seven years before beginning writing *In Parenthesis*.) This is particularly true in section 3, with its liturgical references to the service for Good Friday and frequent allusions to a battle between light and dark. Section 7, with its early reference to the canonical hours of prime, terce, sext, and none, sets a ritualistic context for the slaughter soon to follow, suggesting participation in a larger mystery beyond the confusion of human violence.

Themes and Meanings

The title page of section 7 quotes from a sixth century Welsh poem: "Gododdin I demand thy support. It is our duty to sing: a meeting place has been found." This suggests the complex theme running through the "shape" of this poem and the war it records: As horrible as war is, there is something here to celebrate. This is not a classic antiwar poem in the same vein as that of a Rupert Brooke or a Wilfred Owen. *In Parenthesis* is graphic in its depiction of the horrors of war, of the mindlessness of much of the violence resulting from nationalistic pride, but it also speaks with an aesthetic voice and wonders if some beauty can be found even in the very instruments of human destruction. Jones is skeptical that this will be possible but sees the attempt as part of his responsibility as a poet in the twentieth century, an age that now must live with "increasingly exacting mechanical devices; some fascinating and compelling, others sinister in the extreme."

Jones's poem speaks with a profoundly humanistic voice, transcending the grotesque suddenness of individual deaths in battle and finding in history a common thread connecting all soldiers to the nobility of being a man or a woman. *In Parenthesis* deals with powers that tap into the life force itself, the incomprehensible energies that bring humans into existence and dispatch them just as quickly. The poem might be said to be basically religious, using the war as a metaphor for life itself—to Jones, each is a parenthesis. His poem suggests that war helps people become more aware of that larger parenthetical condition called life, a condition ultimately as sudden and individually crafted as the war would have been for each soldier.

"It is our duty to sing," as the Welsh poem states, because "a meeting place has been found." It is a sad and grim meeting place, but there, at the bloody battle of the Somme, humanity meets its past, and in some sense its future. In the search for this meeting place and in the preparations for this bloody battle, Jones's characters take their place in an oddly liturgical procession, each rank knowing its proper place. This arbitrary, human-imposed order finally becomes ineffectual in the face of the war's blind aggression.

The new level of alienation forced upon soldiers by modern weaponry is, on one level, imitated by Jones's insistence, like Eliot's, on stitching together a tapestry from the colored threads of many unfamiliar cultures. The need for footnotes in major works by both poets emphasizes this growing ignorance. Most readers, after all, will know few of the details of the Arthurian legend, let alone the lesser known Welsh myths and the ramifications of other literary and liturgical allusions.

Use of theological language reminds the reader of a sacrament, and reading the poem becomes something of a ritual of remembrance. Common humanity is certainly a thematic strain running throughout this poem; the increasing difficulty modern men and women have in maintaining this sense in the face of cultural disintegration necessitates the poem's melancholy tension.

The poem produces a sense that history, as well as the individual, is slipping through the cracks even as Western civilization concentrates its attention on "toys" of destruction. In such a porous world, simple goodness becomes heroic, and salvific. This seems to be what Private John Ball learns as he observes the various sorts of British fighter. Wounded and waiting for rescue, watching an endless stream of fresh-faced soldiers streaming by, he remembers past Welsh heroes and the *Song of Roland* (c. 1100).

Jones seems finally to offer up to God the entire poem and all it represents: the history of the British Isles and much of Western civilization. The formal poem is followed by footnotes (and the cultural history they embody), and then Jones offers a concluding frame: a final page of scriptural quotations, equating the soldiers throughout history with sacrificial victims and with the Sacrificial Lamb of Christianity, Jesus. *In Parenthesis* is, finally, a poem about the "mystical body of Christ."

John C. Hawley

IN SANTA MARIA DEL POPOLO

Author: Thom Gunn (1929-   )
Type of poem: Lyric
First published: 1958; collected in *My Sad Captains, and Other Poems*, 1961

The Poem

"In Santa Maria del Popolo" is composed of four stanzas, each containing eight lines of iambic pentameter, with the rhyme scheme *ababcdcd*. The title refers to a famous church in Rome, Italy, which houses the painting *The Conversion of Saint Paul* by Caravaggio (1573-1610). The painting depicts the moment in the biblical story (Acts 9) in which Saul of Tarsus is blinded by a heavenly light and falls to the ground. Later, Saul is cured of his blindness by Ananías and converted, eventually to become Saint Paul. The poem's title, however, focuses on the painting's location and, therefore, on the poet's experience of viewing the painting.

"In Santa Maria del Popolo" opens with the narrator waiting in the dim church for the light to strike the painting in just the right way. His knowledge of the artist makes it clear that he has sought out the painting in a kind of pilgrimage. The dim light is fortuitous because it shows something essential about the painting: "how shadow in the painting brims/ With a real shadow, drowning all shapes out." Only the horse's backside and the "various limbs" of the fallen rider are highlighted. These dominant physical details seem to put in doubt "the very subject" of the painting, supposedly the conversion of Saint Paul.

The second stanza completes the description of the painting. Then the narrator begins to interpret the painting by asking the "wily" painter what he means by "limiting the scene" to the "one convulsion" of Saul lifting his arms "in that wide gesture" toward the horse.

The third stanza's mention of Ananías reminds the reader that Saul's sight has not yet been restored, nor has he been converted. The painter sees not what is to be, but only "what was," including "an alternate/ Candor and secrecy inside the skin." This enigma is somewhat clarified when the second half of the stanza mentions Caravaggio's models, "pudgy cheats" and "sharpers," who may have led to the artist's death in a brawl.

The poem concludes with the narrator turning away from the painting, "hardly enlightened." In the "dim interior" of the church, he sees old women praying, their arms "too tired" to make the "large gesture of the solitary man." Unlike Saul, or perhaps the narrator, they cannot make the heroic act of "Resisting . . . nothingness" by "embracing" it.

Forms and Devices

The practice of writing poems about paintings is common, especially in the twentieth century. Examples of the practice are W. H. Auden's "Musée des Beaux Arts,"

William Carlos Williams's "The Dance," and John Ashbery's "Self-Portrait in a Convex Mirror." Poets often use such poems to state their affinity with the artist's sensibility or aesthetic. A poet will approach a painting in a way different from that of a scholar, yet if his poem is to be more than impressionistic description, he must know some of what the scholar knows.

Thom Gunn, who has done his homework, translates the artist's pictorial effects into poetic devices. The poem, for example, sets the painting within a narrative frame: The poet enters the church, waits for the good "oblique" light, views the painting, and then, upon leaving, considers how he has been "enlightened."

This play of light and dark is echoed in other dualities, such as the identity of "Saul becoming Paul" and the stanzas' two-part structure. Caravaggio is known for his manipulation of light and dark, a device called tenebrism, or the "dark manner." He creates highly dramatic, realistic effects by highlighting physical forms that seem to lurch out of the darkness toward the viewer, often at unusual angles. Gunn re-creates this angular effect first by describing the light in the church with an unusual syntax: "the sun an hour or less/ Conveniently oblique makes visible/ the painting." He then highlights the physical forms of the "dim horse's haunch and various limbs" of Paul.

Paul's figure is "Foreshortened from the head, with hidden face." Caravaggio uses this over-the-shoulder point of view to encourage the viewer to identify with Paul, just as Gunn allows the reader to see the painting through his eyes, never putting himself in the foreground of the poem.

Caravaggio was also known for his disregard of convention. His figures, composition, and color were pictorial heresy to his contemporaries. His depiction of Paul beneath his horse lacks the decorum of most treatments of scripture. His composition can be defended by pointing out that in the moment depicted, Saul has not yet become Paul. Unconverted, Saul is still in the realm of the profane. His future conversion is unavailable to the artist, whose subject is the visible world: "The painter saw what was."

Gunn notices that Caravaggio's emphasis on the horse's backside detracts from the supposed focus on Paul, whose "various limbs" hardly identify him as the saint of the painting's title. It is this compositional decision to shift the focus away from Paul that intrigues Gunn, however, and becomes the center for his own interpretive re-creation of the painting.

Themes and Meanings

"In Santa Maria del Popolo" is a poem about blindness and revelation and the relative abilities of religion and art to enlighten human experience. Gunn wrote in "My Life Up to Now" (1977) that he was "forever grateful" that he was "brought up in no religion at all." Attracted to existentialism for its philosophy that each person makes his or her own meaning in an absurd universe, and to poetry as his chosen vehicle for creating that meaning, Gunn confronts the relative power of religion, art, and poetry.

Gunn undoubtedly identified with Caravaggio, a violent, sensual, risk-taking individualist known for his homoerotic renderings of traditional motifs. Gunn addresses the painter as one artist to another ("O wily painter"), complimenting him on his daring artistry: "limiting the scene/ From a cacophony of dusty forms/ To the one convulsion." The word "cacophony" is the poet's word of sound, not the painter's of sight, and it seals their artistic fraternity. What Gunn wants to know, though, is "what is it you mean/ In that wide gesture of the lifting arms?"

The focus of the painting for Gunn is the "Candor and secrecy inside the skin" that leads to Saul's conversion. But what secret? The second half of the stanza seems to suggest that Saul's secret may have something to do with Caravaggio's homoerotic paintings, specifically "that firm insolent/ Young whore in Venus's clothes" and the "pudgy cheats" and "sharpers" of such paintings as *Concert, Lute Player*, and *Bacchus*. Accounts of Caravaggio's death disagree, but Gunn accepts the account of violent death at the hands of one of these male prostitutes "picked off the streets." The suggestion is that Saul (a famous misogynist) harbored a sensual secret, perhaps not unlike the homoerotic tendencies of Caravaggio and Gunn himself.

It is not Paul's specific erotic preference that is important, however, but the "alternate/ Candor and secrecy" that caused him to be an outsider. Paul is representative of the "solitary man" of existential philosophy who resists "nothingness" by "embracing" it. Unlike the women in the church who keep their secrets "closeted" in their heads, as in the confessional, the artist confesses the "Candor and secrecy inside his skin." The saint, too, admits his fallen state. Finally, the poem's narrator, who leaves the church "hardly enlightened," also admits his failure to achieve revelation through religion. This may only mean, however, that he leaves with the dark burden of what Caravaggio's painting has shown him and that what enlightenment it has inspired in the creation of his own poem has not been easy.

Richard Collins

IN TENEBRIS

Author: Thomas Hardy (1840-1928)
Type of poem: Lyric
First published: 1901, in *Poems of the Past and the Present*

The Poem
"In Tenebris" is a sequence of three meditative poems, divided into six quatrains in poem I, four in poem II, and five in poem III. Each poem is headed by a Latin epigraph or motto from the Psalms that expresses alienation and despair. The title is Latin for "in the darkness," anticipating the light and dark imagery in all three poems. The original title in *Poems of the Past and the Present*, "De Profundis," or "Out of the Depths," also reflects the speaker's gloomy vision and his preoccupation with physical and spiritual death.

"In Tenebris" is an intensely personal expression of grief and isolation written in the first person. It was written in 1895-1896, when Thomas Hardy was despondent about the decline of love in his marriage and the public's rejection of *Jude the Obscure* (1895), his last novel before he gave up fiction and devoted himself to poetry. Biographers and critics disagree about the extent to which this poem expresses Hardy's bitterness about his own experience and conveys an attitude of unrelieved pessimism, "pessimistic" being a label Hardy himself rejected. Although the speaker claims to be emotionally dead in poem I, the energy with which he mocks the optimistic majority in poem II and questions his own fate in poem III suggests that he is exploring alternative responses to the harsh realities of life that he faces unflinchingly.

The motto of the first poem, which translates as "my heart is smitten and withered like grass," introduces a series of terse poetic statements comparing the cruel catastrophes of nature as winter approaches with the speaker's stoic assertions that he cannot be hurt by these signs of approaching death; he is already dead, having lost friendship, love, and hope.

The mottoes of poems II and III place the speaker and his woe in the context of a society in which he has no place. Poem II is headed by lines which translate as "I looked on my right hand and beheld, but there was no man that would know me. . . . no man cared for my soul." The tone of derision throughout this poem is obvious from its opening lines, as the clouds echo the shouts of the "stout upstanders" who assume all is for the best. Each stanza begins by mocking the masses, with their "lusty joys" and smug Victorian belief in progress, and ends with the speaker's denigration of himself as one born at the wrong time. This contrast climaxes as the entire last stanza mimics the crowd's rejection of the speaker's insistence on facing "the Worst" to find a "way to the Better." He imagines them casting him out as one who is deformed, who "disturbs the order here."

Poem III's opening Latin reference to warlike ancient tribes in distant places reinforces the speaker's sense of alienation: "Woe is me that I sojourn in Mesech, that I dwell in the tents of Kedar. My soul hath long dwelt with him that hateth peace." The first and last stanzas repeat his notion that his life might as well have ended before his disillusioning realization that "the world was a welter of futile doing." The middle stanzas recall three different moments in his youth that might have been more fitting times for him to die, while he was welcoming spring, feeling secure with his mother on Egdon Heath, or suffering a childhood illness. Thus "In Tenebris" concludes with the speaker daring to question even the divine law that determines when life begins and ends.

Forms and Devices

The three poems of "In Tenebris" combine a number of the poetic techniques that distinguish the large and diverse body of poetry written throughout Hardy's life. His adaptions of traditional meters can be seen in the contrast between the short lines of poem I, with its heavy use of spondees and trochees in the first and last lines accenting the funereal theme, and the much longer lines of poems II and III that imitate heroic and alliterative verse as the speaker mocks society and questions fate. The poem's diction, in addition to blending colloquial, formal, and archaic words, includes original coinages such as "unhope" and "upstanders." The biblical quotations and the images from the events and landscape of Hardy's childhood show the influences of his past in relation to the modern social and philosophical themes of the poem.

The structure of each poem of "In Tenebris" is regular and repetitive, reflecting, perhaps, the speaker's entrapment in his own vision of despair and alienation, but also his persistent assertion of that vision in defiance of all opposing forces. The common patterns of language and imagery that unite the three poems follow the movement of the speaker's thoughts as he views himself in the context of nature, society, and the universal laws of time and fate.

Every stanza of poem I begins with an image from nature showing the harm done to flowers, birds, and leaves by the cold and tempests of winter, except that the last stanza uses the black of night to introduce another symbol of death that reappears later. Every second line (all except one beginning with "But") stresses the speaker's immunity to these rhythms of nature, since he is permanently enervated, heartless, and hopeless—past the stages of grieving or doubting for a season. The occurrence of one or two phrases of negation in every stanza further emphasizes the speaker's insistence that he is beyond the reach of the horror and dread that winter, night, and death usually evoke.

Poem II also contains a number of negative statements and images from nature in every stanza, but they have become part of a more expansive and energetic outcry against society. Statements such as "the clouds' swoln bosoms echo," "breezily go they, breezily come," and "their dawns bring lusty joys, it seems" add a mock-heroic flavor to this exposure of the easy optimism of the masses. The speaker's more sensitive view that "delight is a delicate growth cramped by crookedness, custom, and fear" relates to the other images of deformity he attributes to himself. The fact that this poem not only uses the same rhyme in the second half of every quatrain, but repeats the same word—"here"—at the end of every stanza, however, suggests that the speaker is determined to stand his ground with his unpopular but honest compulsion to face "the Worst."

In poem III, the images of nature are associated with specific memories of home near Egdon Heath. The heavy use of alliteration, along with some archaic language, gives this poem a more dignified and ponderous tone, as the speaker turns from his satire of contemporary society in poem II to question universal laws of time and death. The images of light and dark culminate in the realization that, since true vision and knowledge bring pain and frustration, it would be better to have been overtaken by the darkness of death earlier in life. This idea is repeated throughout the first and last stanzas, with three occurrences of the same phrase indicating the persistent desire to consider a better time when "the ending [might] have come," creating an especially emphatic ending for a series of poems that explores various dimensions of spiritual and physical death.

Themes and Meanings

In a poem with so many images from nature and biblical references, it may seem ironic to find no suggestion that nature or religion offers comfort to one as lonely and dejected as the speaker of "In Tenebris." Although the indifference of God or nature is not discussed as explicitly as it is in many other poems by Hardy, this speaker's view that he is isolated from the cycles of nature, from society, and from the entire world of darkness and chaos shows that he rejects all conventional sources of support. Nevertheless, this poem demonstrates that Hardy never stopped seeing in the Bible and in nature powerful sources of inspiration and reflections of the human condition.

Hardy's vision of human life in this poem seems to be one of unrelieved gloom and hopelessness. He asserts that life is not worth living once childhood innocence is replaced by the disillusionment that comes from experiencing pain and futility. It is important to recognize, however, that this despair is just one of many moods expressed in Hardy's poetry. He stated in his preface to *Poems of the Past and the Present* (1901) that this collection "comprises a series of feelings and fancies written down in widely differing moods and circumstances, and at various dates. . . . the road to a true philosophy of life seems to lie in humbly recording diverse readings of its phenomena as they are forced upon us by chance and change."

Twenty-five years later, in the "Apology" that prefaced his new volume, *Late Lyrics and Earlier* (1922), Hardy again stressed the mixed character of his collections of poems. He responded to criticisms that he was too pessimistic by quoting a line from "In Tenebris," reminding his readers that facing "the Worst" was a necessary preliminary to seeking a "way to the Better." In spite of the predominance of negative statements in this poem and its preoccupation with death, it contains implicit revelations of much that Hardy did value in life. His isolation from the cycles of nature in poem I is overshadowed by the strength of his own independence and assertion of individual will. His alienation from society is balanced by his skill at satirizing its smug optimism with wit and irony in poem II. His questioning of his own fate in poem III is accompanied by reminders of the value of memory and individual life. Although he is unable to see any fulfilling order in society or the world, the poem itself demonstrates that he is able to create a meaningful artistic order out of his frustration and despair.

Tina Hanlon

1974

IN THE BLUE DISTANCE

Author: Nelly Sachs (1891-1970)
Type of poem: Lyric
First published: 1957, as "In der blauen Ferne," in *Und niemand weiss weiter*; English
translation collected in *O the Chimneys*, 1967

The Poem

"In the Blue Distance" is a haunting meditative lyric. Its intense images are presented in free verse. Like most of Nelly Sachs's painfully beautiful poems, it is a variation on her basic theme, the Holocaust. This poem searches for a way to go on afterward, reflecting the theme of the book's title, translated as "and no one knows how to
go on." The poem's travelers look toward "the blue distance" where "longing is dis-
tilled" or where one can recognize and find deliverance from longing. Exactly what
one longs for (peace, forgiveness, love, death?) is not determined by the poem, but its
mood is one of acceptance. This mood of quiet reconciliation, in the last stanza, offers
the possibility of transcendence from hate and bitterness. That offer is perhaps made
with reference to the suffering of the Holocaust, if only implicitly.

The first stanza presents a vista—a metaphorical view from a valley. Those who
live below can see far away a row of apple trees with "rooted feet climbing the sky." In
this image, the juxtaposition of "rooted" and "climbing" suggests a tension between
two longings, perhaps. One is to remain earthbound, and the other looks toward the
blue distance, skyward. In Nelly Sachs's vocabulary, flying—one way to interpret
"climbing the sky"—often signifies transcendence or re-creation. "Those who live in
the valley" might feel some comfort knowing that another higher realm exists.

The apple trees in one sense signify the hope and abundance of such a spiritual
place. Perhaps it can be as simple as those on earth wishing to see heaven, or simply to
know one exists. Thus the poem in stanza 1 seems to consider another way (among all
the ways in Sachs's poetry) for those hurt by the insanity of the war to expiate their terrors, and to relieve longings intensified by the losses they suffered.

One could also say that "rooted" and "climbing" allude to the magic of organic
growth—the magic that all plants possess. Such organic growth, or regeneration,
would mean, in human terms, spiritual healing. Apple trees also are heavily laden
with mythology: They are the forbidden fruit of the tree of knowledge, but they also
bring blossoms in spring, and thus hope. Thus, stanza 1 suggests the necessity for
those who are suffering from their pasts to find some way to regenerate their spiritual balance and inner peace, the way plants are able to come back after being cut
back. There seems to be a yearning for some way to grow toward the sky, out of the
low valley.

"The sun, lying by the roadside" is, on the one hand, a descriptive image of the sun
lying low on the horizon, at sunset: It appears to lie by the road. Yet on the other hand,
the image is frightening. For if the sun really lay by the roadside, like some suffering

or ambushed traveler, such eerie displacement would suggest the worst kind of chaos. The "magic wands" could suggest that this sun is an impostor, a prankster, or a sorcerer. If so, perhaps the travelers are being deceived. Perhaps even nature is not to be trusted in a world so prone to chaos and pain.

In a lighter and more positive interpretation, these magic wands could simply suggest the regenerative magic of the natural world, of which the sun is a part. It provides light, so basic to life, and in a figurative sense, knowledge. Perhaps the stanza reflects the wrenching uncertainty of life during the Holocaust—the command "to halt" could come at any time, from any quarter. Life during the Holocaust had become so unpredictable, so unnatural, one might not be surprised to see the sun collapse, and become earthbound.

In stanza 3, the travelers have halted, although they seem alone "in the glassy nightmare." One cannot be sure why or for whom they have stopped. This lack of certainty compounds the eeriness that arose in the second stanza. "Glassy" lends an apt sense of distortion and again, uncertainty, to the poem's increasingly nightmarish atmosphere.

An image from the natural world characteristically rescues people from the nightmare and barely breaks the silence of this poem. A cricket "scratches softly at the invisible"—a beautiful and redeeming, although practically inexplicable, image. The mystical quality of Sachs's work is exemplified here in that the relief this profound image bestows upon the reader must be felt, rather than understood. No easy explanations exist for "the invisible" (eternity? the unknown? the deity?). These attempts at explanation dilute the power of the image itself, which is effective primarily in its emotional impact.

The poem ends with a second such image, which again, characteristic of Sachs's poetry, relies on emotion to complete what it communicates. "Stone" and "dust" reverberate in their earthboundness back to the tension in stanza 1 between being rooted and "climbing the sky." In Sachs's poetry, images of earth, dust and sand often signify the past, specifically here, the human suffering of years past. In the transcendent spirit-filled final lines of this poem, the stone does fly—it dances and "changes its dust to music." The transformation signifies that out of suffering, upheaval, or even death can come a spiritual insistence on life and beauty, only two ideas that "music" might suggest here. The stone thus dances a dance of renewal and life, not of death.

Forms and Devices

"In the Blue Distance" is highly imagistic. Its impact comes from the visual intensity of its metaphors, as well as their eerie, mystical reverberations. In this sense it compares to most of Sachs's work.

Known for its enigmatic quality, Sachs's poetry is not "easy" to read. Whatever difficulty the reader confronts, however, is not attributable to the technical devices of her poems. They are not written in encoded language, nor are they riddles to be solved. Readers may experience difficulty laying aside their demands to have the poem's "meaning" made easily comprehensible. Her concentrated and emotional language, its allusions and metaphors, unfold only slowly, and the reader must be prepared not to rely on a need for explicit meaning, but to experience the mystery of the poem. That is, as with the cricket image, one feels her poetry better than one can hope to understand it in the analytical sense.

Yet Sachs uses masterful craftsmanship in her poems. The earthy images in this poem manage to root the poem itself in good warm soil. Its movement from section to section seems almost, again inexplicably, like natural growth. Each stanza has an image central to its movement and the "narrative" movement of the poem. The climbing apple trees, the "lying" sun, the cricket scratching and the dancing stone are simple pictures yet profoundly intriguing and suggestive. These images, one to a stanza, move the poem forward with sure quiet steps, as if the delicate thread of emotion spun stronger by each new line is being handed carefully along.

Personification is also used; it lends an eerie yet somehow friendly quality to otherwise mysterious images—the cricket scratching "at the invisible" and the stone dancing. Since the stanzas are not regular in number of lines or line length, the images that reside within the poem provide its form. The interplay between them unifies the poem.

Sachs speaks in simple language, and the rhythm of "In the Blue Distance" is relaxed and unassuming. In fact, the low-key conversational tone the poem has is amazing, given the otherworldly intensity of the images. That it breaks down into three relatively simple sentences shows Sachs's ability to comb away the wool surrounding an emotion she wishes to convey and to find a beautifully simple correlation in the imagery. Her concrete images are the key to this fertile simplicity.

Themes and Meanings

"Death gave me my language," Sachs said. "My metaphors are my wounds." Such a statement implies an intensely private poetry, and there is perhaps a sort of arrogant folly in searching for "meanings" in images whose very strength comes from their wildly errant suggestiveness. Her images suggest many directions, many meanings. Yet Sachs's statement also simplifies a discussion of meaning. Her basic theme, the Holocaust, leads her to explore all avenues of thought and emotion in terms of the great mystery, death.

One could read this poem as a meditation on arriving at the edge of death. The stillness, approaching silence, at the heart of this poem certainly suggests that the travelers teeter between worlds—where language becomes unnecessary. The momentary yet strong break in movement after stanza 2 ("The sun . . . commands the travelers to halt") suggests an interface between the worlds of life and death. In the "glassy nightmare," the travelers are fairly on the edge of a world. The "invisible" at which the cricket scratches suggests an entrance point, if one follows this theme, into the next world.

Yet death in this poem is neither fearsome nor terrible. In a sense, it has already happened, for there is no escape from the sun. The poem is really a reckoning, an acceptance of the inevitable event of death, which seems to approach almost tenderly in this poem—as softly as the cricket scratches at the door. Sachs has written harshly accusatory poems about the Holocaust, but this is not one of them. Her work has been called forgiving, and the calm lyricism of this poem certainly demonstrates that quality. In it, even death seems forgiving. The stone is cold and hard, but "dancing," transforming dust, and the past with all its anguish, to music.

JoAnn Balingit

IN THE CREVICE OF TIME

Author: Josephine Jacobsen (1908-   )
Type of poem: Lyric
First published: 1968; collected in *The Shade-Seller: New and Selected Poems*, 1974

The Poem

"In the Crevice of Time" is a brief meditative lyric consisting of four stanzas of six lines each. The first stanza makes clear the subject of the poem: poet Josephine Jacobsen's reaction to cave paintings in Spain. Unlike many poems that respond to or are influenced by works of art, this poem provides very little sense of what the cave painting looks like. The first three lines identify an ambiguous prey—"The bison, or tiger, or whatever beast"—and "the twiggy hunter/ with legs and spear." The rest of the poem speculates on the artist who created the painting that has endured so long, preserved "in the crevice of time."

The artist is introduced in the last line of the first stanza as "the hunter-priest" since, in an era so primitive, artistry could hardly have been his main occupation. The second stanza shows that the poet imagines this cave painter as the original artist, the first (or one of the first) to act on an impulse to represent reality. She imagines him struck, in the act of hunting, by the spatial arrangement of animals and hunters; the hunter becomes an observer and art is born as "an offering strange as some new kind of death." The puzzling comparison of art to death grows clearer in the third stanza, where the poet relates the beginning of cave painting to the beginning of the practice of burial—both behaviors said to distinguish humans from their more animalistic ancestors. The death that is related to art, then, is not simply the ending of life but "the knowledge of death." With that knowledge comes a different awareness of time and the beginnings of a new emotion: grief. The poet argues, by imaginative extrapolation, that art, like funeral customs, is a way of preserving human experience against the forces of time and mortality that threaten to turn everything to dust.

The last stanza imagines the cave painter in the act of creation, "scraping the wall." However, the great temporal distance has been bridged: The early human is a "confrère" or brother, and, most importantly, "he is close." The final lines of the poem conclude the meditation on the relationship of funeral customs and art by asserting their common purpose as acts of faith; art is celebrated as a force that can cross "the crevice of time," even providing a bridge between the contemporary and the prehistoric.

Forms and Devices

This poem reads prosaically at first. That is, the diction is simple and speechlike, and, in the first two stanzas, most of the lines are enjambed, which tends to disguise the metrical pattern and rhyme. However, like most modern rhymed poetry, a careful structure undergirds the graceful surface of the poem. The rhyme scheme seems more pronounced in the third stanza, with its end-stopped lines and one extra rhyme. The first and last lines of each stanza rhyme, as do the second and fourth. More importantly, the first/last rhyming words outline significant contrasts that reveal some of the poem's meaning: "beast" and "priest"; "breath" and "death"; "grave" and "gave"; and "wall" and "burial." The contrast between "beast" and "priest" highlights the contrast between primitive and civilized organizations of the human species. "Breath" and "death" suggest the awareness of mortality that shapes human consciousness. "Grave" and "gave" remind the reader that the burial customs of prehistoric people ironically give the contemporary world information about how they lived. The "wall" that is the prehistoric canvas is also part of a tomb or "burial."

Most of the lines in the poem are four-stress lines with ten or eleven syllables, indicating a mix of iambic and anapestic feet. In stanzas 1, 2, and 4, the fifth line is a shorter, three-stress line. The point is that the poem, while not adhering to a rigorously strict metrical pattern, is carved out in roughly regular units of four-stress lines— a loose but recognizable meter. The figurative language stands out against the speechlike or ordinary diction, as in the synecdoches "the million rains of summer" and "the mean mists of winter," both signifying the passing of time. "Blood" and "breath" in line 7 also create a synecdoche for the killing of the hunt. When that same device is carried over into the next line—referring to the hunted animals as "shank," "horn," or "hide"—the figurative language becomes literal. That is, the reader knows that the slain prey will be converted into its parts and used by the hunters as food, tools, and clothing. However, the hunter-priest-cum-artist no longer perceives the prey in that way but as an artistic whole—"the terrible functionless whole." The term "functionless," a surprisingly abstract word in the midst of a concrete stanza, reminds the reader that art is often viewed (and even celebrated) as useless, as not having a practical or survival-oriented function.

The third stanza presents two vivid personifications: "time the wicked thief" and "the prompt monster of foreseeable grief." The first is more familiar, even close to clichéd in its association of time with theft of life and memory. The incarnation of grief as a monster is more original, and the words "prompt" and "foreseeable" stress the immediacy of the mental transformation and its consequences in the moment in which art and awareness of mortality are born as twins.

Alliteration, assonance, and word repetition provide further shape to the poem. The second line packs in three versions of "hunt"; the next line alliterates "spear," "still," and "Spain." The second half of the first stanza repeats *m* sounds prominently and sharpens them with the short *i* assonance of "mists" and "winter." Similar examples appear throughout the poem and testify to how carefully Jacobsen chooses her words. The language is chiseled like the lines of an ancient sculpture. In the third stanza, for example, "grave" echoes "gross," while "gesture" is repeated; "neither," "nor," "news," "no," "need," and "knowledge" alliterate in the space of three lines; and assonance is accented in adjacent words (the short *o* in "prompt monster" and the long *e* in "foreseeable grief").

Themes and Meanings

The encounter with a prehistoric cave painting raises questions in the poet's mind. What inspired the first efforts to record experience in human-created, artificial forms? How did the creation of art change the animal that created it? In using poetry to answer these questions, the writer is responding to one art form with another. Ancient paintings offer a way for the poet to speak about poetry. The painter's tools are visual images—line and shape and color—while the poet's tools are words.

Two words that strain with double meanings help illuminate the poet's purposes. In the last stanza, she remarks that the prehistoric artist is "close." The primary meaning here is "near": Paradoxically, the poet-observer feels a kinship with the long-deceased human artist who painted the cave. However, "close" also suggests "shut" or even "dark and stuffy," secondary meanings that remind the reader that a cave is shut off from outside reality and protected from the erosion of the centuries. In the first stanza, the poet describes the Spanish caves as "still." The primary meaning is "quiet and unmoving," but the meaning of "remaining" or "yet" haunts the poem, since part of the point is that the paintings are "still" there. This double meaning of "still" harks back to the English Romantic poet John Keats, who described an ancient vase as a "still unravished bride of quietness" in "Ode on a Grecian Urn." The line identifies the artifact not only as a bride as yet unravished but also as an unmoving and unchanging work of art that endures the ages. It is hard for a modern poet to reflect on the endurance of a work of art across the ages without evoking Keats's famous poem. Keats, too, saw the endurance of the ancient artifact as a triumph against mortality and as an emblem for his own poetry. Where Jacobsen's poem differs is in reaching back to primitive humankind rather than the highly refined civilization of the Greeks. Keats evokes a distant kinship with the artists and people of ancient Greece. Jacobsen, in reaching further to the cave paintings, is able to raise questions about the very origins of art.

Answering those questions, or at least providing an imaginative hypothesis in response to them, Jacobsen sees the artistic impulse as a desire to communicate beyond the grave. The work of art becomes a monument, something that outlives the artist and thus reflects a conscious awareness of mortality. She suggests that such an awareness of death is cause for celebration, an artistic force that gives birth to history out of the prehistoric. In this grand context, the poet's own work has a place, her own equivalent of the stick figures and hunted bison—the record of feelings, thoughts, and images of a living creature that knows it is going to die and leaves a poem behind.

Christopher Ames

IN THE EVENING

Author: Anna Akhmatova (Anna Andreyevna Gorenko, 1889-1966)
Type of poem: Lyric
First published: 1914, as "Vecherom," in *Chetki*; English translation collected in *The Complete Poems of Anna Akhmatova*, 1990

The Poem

Opening with a reference to music, a garden, and grief, the first of the poem's sixteen lines places a man and a woman in a romantic setting, as seen from the woman's point of view. She is recollecting a meeting with a friend, and the mood is sorrowful, perhaps because of the music, which provides an emotional context as well. By mentioning the music, the poet hints at unspoken suffering. It is suggested by the music, or the music prompts sad memories, here unexpressed, in her own past. Abruptly, another detail is remembered. The second pair of lines uses the image of "oysters in ice," whose smell reminded the poet of the sea. The couple is at dinner at a seaside restaurant—the title suggests a romantic time of day—and the memory is rich in sensory detail: the sound of sad music, the smell of the sea brought in by the oysters. The mood is bittersweet.

The second stanza continues the romantic moment, the poet recalling what her friend said and his simple gesture of touching her dress. The next two lines dwell on the peculiar quality of his touch, which the poet remembers as "unlike a caress." The negative comparison interrupts the romantic mood that has so far been sustained. Its significance captures her attention for the moment as she begins stanza three. She compares the man's touch to stroking a small, delicate creature—a cat, for example, or even a bird. Leaping further in an imaginative comparison, the next line compares the gesture to watching young ladies ride horses. A distance between the two people is suggested. His avowal—"I am your true friend"—is not that of an ardent lover. Love is not mentioned or hinted at, and his gesture, "unlike a caress," is like the kind one uses on other creatures—a cat, a bird—not a lover. It reminds her of watching slender women ride, not of the passionate gaze of a lover. She remembers the smallest details, the slightest movement, subtle shades of expression and color, as the next two lines demonstrate, describing "the light gold lashes" and "the laughter in his tranquil eyes." A true friend he may be, but his eyes are tranquil, not lovesick or fiery with passion.

The final stanza returns to the music, which is still dolorous, but now the violins "sing," and their "voices" are remembered through a visual image—that of drifting smoke. Perhaps they are expressing the poet's own sorrow. The vision prompts her to express sudden emotion, gratitude for the time when "You're alone with the man you love." The poem ends on an ambiguous note: The poet may be addressing heaven on the reader's behalf or she may be inviting the reader to join her in thanking heaven. The poem addresses the reader throughout in standard lyrical fashion, but the final address, "You're alone with the man you love," suggests that the poet, knowing what it is like not to enjoy such moments, is telling the reader to praise heaven for such time as the reader will have.

Forms and Devices

The primary devices of the poem are somewhat unconventional to the lyric. As the poem opens, it appears to be a love poem focusing on a fond recollection of a meeting between two lovers, but after the speaker mentions "Oysters in ice," music ringing out with "inexpressible grief," she focuses on the man's seemingly casual gesture for five of the poem's sixteen lines. The man's comment that he is the poet's "true friend" suggests that something other than love is in question or on his mind, perhaps only loyalty, not the passion of a lover. The poem's drama, then, unfolds in a series of details that hint at something other than what is directly expressed in the poem. Juxtaposing images, the poem invites inference while seeming to deliver a simple recollection of a meeting between two friends, if not lovers. The poet remembers signs of emotions— sorrowful music, tranquil eyes—without appearing to feel any herself. Her attention seems to be deflected from any direct recognition of her own emotions toward more distant elements, letting the reader surmise rather than see.

The poem develops in a way that is reminiscent of the haiku, using juxtaposed images that create, by means of their interaction, a significant perception. The poem surprises the reader with its placement of detail and imaginative leaps. The third stanza illustrates these effects most clearly as the poet associates the man's touch with stroking a cat, or a bird, or—making a dramatic leap to a sensory image of a very different kind—the act of watching slender horseback riders. The poet seems to be searching for an objective correlative to that momentous gesture, a trifle that merits unusual attention because it seems to have extraordinary meaning. To find the right evocative correlative is to discover and reveal the significance of a poem. The image also suggests the nature of the poem itself—a performance watched by the poet as she recollects; as she performs, the reader watches her, a slender equestrienne.

The weight given to minute matters in this poem is evident in the little that happens between the beginning and ending references to sad music: The man says he is a true friend and touches her dress. The moment is fixed in a nest of details, the way one remembers a first kiss, a birth, a death. The poem challenges the reader to find that significant event—is it the man's remark, the peculiar gesture, the music, or all together? The whole may be greater than the aggregate of parts, or else the parts do not make a significant whole. The colon setting off the poet's final words in line 14 suggests a summary comment, perhaps an ironic moral: Thank heaven for a time like this one—or unlike it. The instability at which the ambiguities hint corresponds to a changing rhyming pattern in the final stanza. In the original, the first three stanzas rhyme *abba, cddc, effe*, but the final stanza rhymes *ghgh*. It may be that the final alteration in rhyme scheme parallels the poet's own changing attitude toward the preceding situation.

Themes and Meanings

Undeniably, the poem is about a meeting between two people. Loyalty appears to be an issue, and the mood is not cheerful. It is difficult to know the source of the sorrowful emotions the poet mentions at the start and returns to in the final stanza. The lines say that the music is sad—the violins are "mournful"—and without commentary, the poet lets the reader associate the sadness with the speaker's mood, as though she recalls those details that reflected her own feelings. The poem is intriguing because it appears to develop a romantic meeting without providing enough confirmation for the reader to be certain. The speaker's attention to subtleties and her sensory awareness contrasts with the poem's understated quality. Rich with detail, the poem lacks emotional commitment to any single statement or point of view other than that of the poet, whose attitude is noncommittal. For all the reader knows, the poem may be about a profound disappointment. The man's avowal speaks of friendship, not love. His gesture is not that of a lover. Rather, it reminds the speaker of a spectator watching others. The man's apparent emotional distance from her—he is a "true friend," not a lover—may be a response to her own detachment. The poem seems to contradict itself, appearing to describe a romantic moment while creating ambivalence, doubt.

The poem's meaning, then, may be inferred not from what the poet says but from what she does with a handful of details. The poem's true subject is not the remembered meeting between two friends but how the poet remembers the meeting, how she felt then and how she feels as she remembers. Since she gives more attention to the setting and to the associations a gesture causes than to her male companion, the reader loses sight of him, sees the hands gesturing and the slender equestriennes riding, hears the mournful music, sees the drifting smoke, and hears the poet's voice praising heaven, or telling the reader to praise heaven. The man's one remark—"I am your true friend!"—stands out because it lacks motivation and has no definite relationship to the rest of the poem. The reader is not told what prompted it or what the speaker thinks of it. It is a non sequitur, like watching young women riding on horseback—like the final two lines, in fact. The poet has managed to express her own ambivalence toward the male friend by collecting disparate images in a poem that refuses to focus on any one meaning. The poem is about what was or what could have been. Anna Akhmatova might also be advising the reader, based on her own disappointments, about the value of time alone "with the man you love."

Bernard E. Morris

IN THE NAKED BED, IN PLATO'S CAVE

Author: Delmore Schwartz (1913-1966)
Type of poem: Lyric
First published: 1938, in *In Dreams Begin Responsibilities*

The Poem

Like many other poems by Delmore Schwartz, this—the author's most frequently anthologized piece—takes its title from its first line, which provides the work with an intriguing and memorable opening. This is matched by an equally powerful, if dispiriting, concluding statement. The poem is thus securely framed.

Structurally, the poem is made up of two compact blocks of text, each about fourteen lines long. Hence, one might regard it as a rhymeless double sonnet. It would be perhaps more accurate to say that each half of the poem behaves like a double octave and like a double sestet, as considerable tension and interaction is going on between the two parts.

Indeed, the first half can be seen to break further into two verse paragraphs in the middle of line eight. In this way, the author points out a slight departure from the main thrust of the preceding seven and a half lines. Similarly, in the poem's very last line, a break occurs that marks off the concluding statement or capstone of the work. A more decisive turning point is indicated by the continuous break separating the two halves of the piece.

Although the poem is written in the first person, the speaker keeps himself in the background as much as possible. The poem's chief concern is not so much to give an account of a unique personal experience as to focus on what binds humanity together. Thus the "I" in the first half of the poem is referred to as "son of man" in the latter. In spite of this generalizing impulse, however, the author is at pains to fill in with a wealth of particulars the state he is trying to define, evoke, and describe: that is, insomnia or sleeplessness by night, followed by the drowsiness attending pulling himself together in the waking hours of morning.

The title of the poem provides a good entry into the poem. Its first half, "In the Naked Bed," conveys the feeling of an insomniac's futile tossing. This is suggested by the rather unexpected and seemingly superfluous attribute "naked." The other phrase, "in Plato's Cave," reminds the reader of the famous myth of human consciousness depicted by Plato in the *Republic* (388-368 B.C.E.). In its early stages of becoming, humanity but dimly realizes its condition. Perceptions are like shadows projected onto the wall of a cave. Only later, according to the ancient Greek philosopher, is humanity capable of escaping its delusions and getting out of the cave to confront reality as it really is, in broad daylight, by dint of the tools of abstract reasoning. Schwartz seems to require one to regard his poem as dealing alternately with the delusional and obsessional aspects of both insomnia and waking. The twin phrases making up the title are thus complementary and, up to a point, synonymous. The two stages—sleeplessness and drowsiness—are consecutive and therefore separable, each being dealt with analytically and at length. One cannot, however, draw the dividing line so neatly, for as early as the middle of the first part, the figure of the milkman might be taken to herald the break of day, providing a transitional moment in the poem.

Forms and Devices

The poem is characterized by a sustained unidirectional movement with a break between its two parts that stands for a brief interlude of sleep. The continuous string of verbs—all in the past tense—ensures the even pace of the unfolding narrative. Many realistic details are touched upon in passing, each contributing to the density of the text. The accumulation of tangible facts provides the poem's momentum and its self-transcending transformation toward the end: the conversion of past into present, and the abandonment of the sequential development. Instead, the speaker points now to a pattern of recurrences and cyclicity that define human history.

Both parts are replete with visual and auditory images. Alone in his room, the insomniac is aware of the amplified noises of the street below, as well as of the flitting shadows chasing themselves along the ceiling and down the wall until the milkman's sound makes him aware of the impending dawn. Drawn to the window, the speaker is struck by the eerie emptiness of the cityscape whose atmosphere seems to descend from the early metaphysical paintings of Giorgio di Chirico.

This effect is further matched and enhanced in the second part by such compelling metaphors as the waterfalls of hooves and the coughing of a car's engine. Further, the image of the half-awakened bird tentatively testing the reality of the dawn by means of its song recalls poetic moments in Alfred, Lord Tennyson ("Tears, Idle Tears") and Wallace Stevens ("Sunday Morning"). Finally, the sensation of one's self as being "still wet with sleep" creates a singular graphic moment in which the reader is, so to speak, invited to recognize the poetic as the chief constitutive feature of the work in hand. By contrast, the concluding sentence restricts the figurative tendency of the language to a minimum. "So, so"—the very first words of this section—show the reluctance of the speaker to indulge in the figurative game again. The time has come to conclude. Such epithets as "ignorant" qualifying "night" and "the travail of early morning" aptly sum up and contrast the oppositions developed in the poem. Then, in a totalizing gesture, they are blended into a formula of recurrence, "the mystery of beginning/ Again and again," which is an attempt to define historical time as a sequence of half-realized moments.

Themes and Meanings

"In the Naked Bed, in Plato's Cave" is a poem about the workings of the half-conscious mind in its strivings to extinguish itself in sleep and in its trials to refocus while awakening. Out of this twofold struggle humankind emerges "perplexed," sleepy, "affectionate, hungry, and cold." It is in this sense that history, in the end, remains "unforgiven" or unredeemed—an ever-renewable mystery. While in the making, history can be neither comprehensible nor controllable, the poet seems to intimate.

It is sheer activity, somehow escaping humankind's moral aspirations toward truth, order, and justice.

"Plato's cave" is reenacted (ontology repeats philogeny) in the insomniac's "naked-bed" struggle to obliterate the stubborn or obssessional contours of the hard material facts of outer reality. Likewise, it still provides a valid analogy to the exhausted mind's attempts to regather itself and its sense of identity (in terms of reconstituting familiar surroundings) while trying hard to wake up.

This dramatization of the mental ebb and flow provides the forcefulness of the work. The reader is bound to leave it with a heightened awareness of her or his own subjectivity—the first essential step toward the light of reason and out of the chimeras of one's cave. This daily struggle to regain and reconquer one's mind's sovereign control is aptly introduced by the figure of the milkman, who, like an unobtrusive minister, enables one to connect again to the source of innocence and well-being. The milk of human kindness is there, in Delmore Schwartz's poem, ready to bestow its miraculously redeeming vitality—but for how long? Its promise seems to loom there only for history to "dismember and disremember" it in its eagerness to tarnish and undo.

Stefan Stoenescu

IN THE RUINS OF AN ANCIENT TEMPLE

Author: Yannis Ritsos (1909-1990)
Type of poem: Lyric
First published: 1979, as "Sta ereipia archaiou naou," in *Ritsos in Parentheses* (includes English translation)

The Poem

"In the Ruins of an Ancient Temple" is a free-verse poem in two stanzas of nine and six lines. The title shows a concern shared by much modern Greek poetry with its ancient inheritance, although here that concern is ironic and unromanticized.

The first stanza presents a series of short, declarative sentences, almost one per line, describing the life of common people in a modern Greek rural setting. These straightforward statements set the tone of the down-to-earth life depicted. Each subject has its own verb, just as each worker has his or her own distinctive action to perform. The museum guard observes, the women wash, the blacksmith hammers, the shepherd whistles.

When the animal and mineral worlds are introduced, the lines are longer, enjambed, and colored with metaphor. Responding to the shepherd's whistle, "The sheep ran to him/ as though the marble ruins were running." The water of the river is personified, its "thick nape/ shone with coolness."

The final sentence of the first stanza is more than two lines long and focuses on a woman hanging clothes to dry. She spreads them on "shrubs and statues," her husband's underpants hung from the shoulders of a statue of the goddess Hera. Her action might appear satirical (imagine someone hanging their underwear from a crucifix), except that it is an action, not a gesture.

The second stanza consists of only two sentences. The first is a fragment: "Foreign, peaceful, silent intimacy—years on years." Like the ruins, the fragment has no verb to animate it. Time is stopped, spanned, to suggest the long years that have gone into the easy relationship between these people and their ancient landscape. The Greeks go about their business, as they have for thousands of years, without undue respect for the archaeological and artistic ruins around them.

The final sentence's complex structure fits the complexity of the poem's conclusion. Fishermen carry on their heads "broad baskets full of fish," but it is "as though" they are "long and narrow flashes of light:/ gold, rose, and violet." These are the same colors as the "richly embroidered veil of the goddess" carried in a procession, which the communal "we" have cut up "to arrange as curtains, and tablecloths in our emptied houses."

As in many of Yannis Ritsos's poems, the simplicity of the description is deceptive. Each of the actions carries symbolic cargo made more substantial by the reality of the activity being described. In the end, a texture of meaning has accrued, so that one understands, however vaguely, that something of importance has taken place before one's eyes, even in the simplest of scenes.

Forms and Devices

The poem's thematic tension between ancient and modern is developed through a series of contrasts. From the very beginning, the tension between dead stone and living flesh is established. Yet their identity is suggested in the off rhyme of the lines' endings: *marmara* (marbles) and *mantra* (sheepfold). This contrast is fused, if not erased, when the sheep's movement makes the marbles appear to be moving also. The image is a simple metaphor on the surface, but the optical illusion has the surrealistic effect of making the ordinary landscape magical.

The dualities the poem addresses are embodied in the two-part structure. In the first stanza, ancient and modern collide and merge, like overlapping transparencies: the museum guard "in front of" the sheepfold; the sheep "among" the marbles; the water's sculptural nape and marmoreal coolness "behind" the oleanders. In the second stanza, the duality is less visual than temporal (years "on" years). Spatial positioning gives way to symbolic layering: fishermen "on" the shore with baskets "on" their heads; the procession "bearing" the veil; the curtains and tablecloths "in" our houses.

In the first stanza, Ritsos uses sound and movement to contrast the ancient-contemporary scene. The present is animate with the sound and motion of work: the plash of washing in the river, the beat of the hammer, the whistle of the shepherd. Even the museum guard, whose job is to protect by observing, moves, though minimally. Silence and stillness dominate the second stanza.

In both stanzas, however, color is used to contrast the vibrancy of the present with the colorlessness of the temple ruins. The oleanders give color to the statuesque water, while the underpants give color back to the statue of Hera. The fish in the baskets illuminate the landscape with "flashes of light," and the veil of the goddess, like the fish of "gold, rose, and violet," illuminate the interiors of the houses.

Ritsos never uses imagery or metaphor for mere decoration. Each stanza's symbolic significance turns on a metaphor: "as though" the marble and the sheep were the same; "as though" the fish and the goddess' veil were identical. These are finely observed details, but they are also optical illusions, symbolic sleight of hand, which turn one thing into another, alluding to traditional religious symbolism, both pagan and Christian.

Ritsos avoids using these symbols for didactic purposes. His technique is to suggest an ambiguity inherent in the thing itself. By working up a visual and symbolic texture, he allows readers to draw their own conclusions about the poem's meanings.

Themes and Meanings

"In the Ruins of an Ancient Temple" is a poem about the role of the gods in the modern world, and the role of humans in their creation or perpetuation. It can be read as an ironic expression of how the gods—both pagan and Christian—have lost all color, life, and vibrancy in the modern world. Such a reading, however, turns the poem into a satire instead of an exploration of the role (even the responsibility) the imagination has in giving life to gods, statues, and poems.

Statues appear in many of Ritsos's poems, almost always as a life-affirming reminder. "The Statues in the Cemeteries," for example, "don't copy us; they are alone too; they suffer; they contradict nonexistence." One should keep in mind that the marbles in the landscape are not the gods themselves, but only works of art, sharing in the imaginative project that the poet himself is working on. If they have no life of their own, they remind readers that they are the ones who are alive.

The careless way the woman spreads her husband's underpants on Hera's shoulder is designedly comic. Far from showing a lack of respect, however, this easy familiarity is more in line with the ancients' view of the gods than the modern-day museum mentality of reverence for anything classical. (The gods had no amnesty from the barbs of Aristophanes' comedy, and Greek statuary was painted to make it appear more lifelike.) As the sheep animate the marbles, the cloth gives back to the statues some of their original coloring.

In the ancient fertility ritual of *sparagmos*, the god was "cut up" and distributed among the fields to ensure a bountiful harvest. Ritsos evokes the ritual of *sparagmos* in a political sense when the communal "we" cuts up the "richly embroidered" veil of the goddess and redistributes this aesthetic wealth to the people for "our emptied houses."

The word "emptied" instead of "empty" is a political, or economic, choice. "Empty" would signify a simple lack, perhaps an ascetic renunciation of the material world, consonant with Christian orthodoxy, while "emptied" signifies a fullness that has been taken away. It is an indictment of those who have "emptied" our houses in the name of the gods to fill the coffers of the church or state.

In examining the museum guard, an employee of the state, standing as sentry at the beginning of the poem, one may ask What is he guarding? His casual attitude shows that there is nothing really to protect. It is not as though the sheep or the washer women are going to run off with the statues, which are, if not meaningless, valueless to them, except as mannequin drying racks.

The real riches are highlighted by the colorful patches in the poem. "The water's thick nape" concealed "behind the oleanders" is more valuable to the people, both for its utility in their work and for its intrinsic aesthetic qualities. The fishermen bearing "flashes of light" have more power of religion, like Christ's fishers of men, than the dead formalities and useless processions of the church.

These riches need no museum guard. These are the flashes of perception that Ritsos considered the job of the poet—living among the things of the world in a "Foreign, peaceful, silent intimacy . . . years on years"—to cut from the cloth of the "long, richly embroidered veil" of culture and to redistribute to the people to brighten their emptied houses.

Richard Collins

IN THE THIRTIETH YEAR

Author: J. V. Cunningham (1911-1985)
Type of poem: Satire
First published: 1960, in *The Exclusions of a Rhyme*

The Poem

The title of "In the Thirtieth Year" is clearly significant. It points to the time and moment of choice when the speaker elects to take his "heart to be his wife." It also indicates that the normal search for someone to give his heart to has been ended. It is a choice, instead, of solitariness and self-sufficiency. The reason this choice comes at the "thirtieth year" is not explained, but it suggests a deliberate choice after earlier failures in love, failures to find someone to whom his heart may be given.

The speaker of the poem is not the poet, J. V. Cunningham. He is an ironic speaker who seems not only to explain but also to justify his choice of separateness. Cunningham is usually a straightforward poet who despises the fashionable use of irony. Here, however, he uses a mask to represent a way of thinking and living that is quite different from his own. He is satirizing the type of man who would make such a choice to protect himself from the pain and risk of human relationships.

Only eight lines long, "In the Thirtieth Year" is a very precise poem. It begins by describing an unusual wedding of the speaker to his heart; this substitute for a "wife" is announced as a reasonable and viable option. Yet a person who keeps his "heart" to himself, who actually weds it, is an egoist who feeds upon himself rather than risk the effort involved in developing a relationship with another person.

The second couplet clarifies this solipsistic union: "and as I turn in bed by night/ I have my heart for my delight." The "heart" has not been given away to another, a situation about which many poets have written. Instead, his "heart" is there at his call and command and gives him the only delight he will receive. Indeed, there is a parody of a sexual relationship as the speaker turns to meet not his beloved but his own heart.

The "heart" in the third stanza remains a part of the speaker. There is, at least, the assurance of fidelity. "No other heart may mine estrange" since it is a part of him. It alters as he alters, forming a perfect union. The "heart" is an echo of its solitary possessor, changing and mirroring its owner and sole proprietor.

The last section of the poem produces an interesting disjunction: "and it is bound, and I am free." The "heart" cannot wander to another; it cannot leave the speaker. The speaker, however, has attained his freedom by excluding all other possibilities, a very illusory freedom based on the imprisonment of his heart.

The last line brings the poem and the relationship to an appropriate close: "and with my death it dies with me." They are joined together in life in an exclusive relationship, so it is only appropriate that they perish together at death.

Forms and Devices

"In the Thirtieth Year" is written in rhyming couplets that are appropriate for the balance and antithesis that Cunningham uses to trace the relationship between self and heart. The union is complete and will allow no one else to intrude. The heart has been joined to the self in alternating lines of verse in nearly every couplet. For example, in the second couplet the first line has the speaker touch on his turning in bed and the closing line of the couplet has the heart turn to the speaker.

The meter is iambic tetrameter, but there are a few significant variations. The first line of the poem, for example, has slack syllables at the beginning of the line, and the sixth line ("For my heart changes as I change") violates the iambic pattern in the first and second feet. The regular meter is quickly reestablished, however, in the next line ("And it is bound, and I am free"). The poem is also divided into stanzas of two lines in which the first runs on and the second is end-stopped, making each couplet a separate and complete unit.

The rhymes of the poem are also interesting. For the most part, they provide effective contrasts. For example, "estrange" is rhymed with the very different "change." Change suggests freedom and estrange a fracturing. Best of all, perhaps, in the last couplet "free" is rhymed with "me." The supposed freedom is only the result of a relentless concentration on the self by excluding all others.

The language of the poem is the language of love; "wife," "delight," and "estrange" all suggest a close love relationship, although the relationship that is established in the poem is very different from usual. It is protective self-love that will not risk itself by reaching out to another.

Of the few poetic devices used, the metaphor of taking "my heart to be my wife" frames the whole self-contained parody of a relationship. The images of turning in bed to meet not a loved one but one's own heart for "delight" is appropriately derisive. The image of the heart being "bound" is also interesting, especially since that binding is the means to the speaker's freedom, which would be impossible in a true relationship.

The most important device, however, is the personification of the speaker's heart. It assumes the characteristics of a person as it substitutes for a wife in its fidelity and companionship; it also provides the only delight that is possible for the speaker.

Themes and Meanings

The primary theme of "In the Thirtieth Year" is that of the egoism and isolation of a man who would close in on himself because of the pain a struggle for love would involve. He escapes the struggle into a smug self-satisfaction.

Cunningham powerfully portrays the seemingly reasonable choice of the speaker. The tone of the poem is also noteworthy, as Cunningham does not reveal the satiric nature of the poem directly; he describes the choice of heart for wife as if it were commonplace. It is only when the reader begins to look beyond the choice into its consequences that the poem can be seen in a very different light.

The poem as a whole portrays a complete relationship, bizarre as it is. It begins at the moment of the choice of the beloved. It develops into the closeness of an intimate relationship, swears fidelity, and finally completes itself with a mutual death.

The poem is a satirical exposure of a certain way of life. Cunningham does not satirize a specific individual but a more general type. The type that is represented here is one that seems to interest him frequently as a satirical subject. For example, in an earlier poem, "The Solipsist," he writes of the type of person who recognizes no "others." Everyone is subsumed into the demanding self. It is a position of absolute certainty that is achieved by the exclusion of the very existence of others.

It is interesting that in the same group of poems, Cunningham has written a poem on a very different relationship. "To my Wife" speaks of the difficulties and joys of love. In this poem, love is not a static relationship as it is in "In the Thirtieth Year"; it changes as "affections alter" the two partners. Even though there is constant change, the creation of a real relationship is impressive.

> So love by love we come at last,
> As through the exclusions of a rhyme,
> Or the exactions of a past,
> To the simplicity of time,

This achieved love is both "quiet as regret" and "like anger in the night." It is a complex love that can include opposites and still sustain itself.

Cunningham is best known for his epigrams, and all of his poems are terse and compressed. In this poem, the reader will not find any of the witty turns and surprises found in the epigrams. To understand it, the reader must see it as the encapsulation of a life in very few lines. Such economy is appropriate because it is a life that rigidly excludes the possibility of anything other than the self. So the unity of the poem is the unity of a deliberately reduced and restricted life. Cunningham does not intrude his own voice into the poem. The "I" of the poem tells his own story and condemns himself with his own words.

James Sullivan

IN THE WAITING ROOM

Author: Elizabeth Bishop (1911-1979)
Type of poem: Lyric
First published: 1976, in *Geography III*

The Poem
"In the Waiting Room" describes a child's sudden awareness—frightening and even terrifying—that she is both a separate person and one who belongs to the strange world of grown-ups. The poet locates the experience in a specific time and place, yet every human being must awaken to multiple identities in the process of growing up and becoming a self-aware individual.

Elizabeth Bishop wrote about this experience as it had happened to her many years before she wrote the poem. Published in her final collection, it is considered one of her most important poems. The speaker in the poem is Elizabeth, a young girl "almost seven," who is waiting in a dentist's waiting room for her Aunt Consuelo who is inside having her teeth fixed. In the manner of a dramatic monologue or a soliloquy in a play, the reader overhears or listens to the child talking to herself about her astonishment and surprise. She tries to reason with herself about the upwelling feelings she can hardly understand. The result is a convincing account of a universal experience of access to greater consciousness.

In the long first stanza of fifty-three lines, the girl begins her story in a matter-of-fact tone. The place is Worcester, Massachusetts. On a cold and dark February afternoon in the year 1918, she finds herself in a dentist's waiting room. In plain words, she says that the room is full of grown-ups in their winter boots and coats. She picks up an issue of the *National Geographic* because the wait is so long. She is proud that she can read as the other people in the room are doing.

She looks at the photographs: a volcano spilling fire, the famous explorers Osa and Martin Johnson in their African safari clothes. Then scenes from African villages amaze and horrify her. A dead man (called "Long Pig") hangs from a pole; babies have intentionally deformed heads; women stretch their necks with rounds of wire. Their bare breasts shock the little girl, too shy to put the magazine away under the eyes of the grown-ups in the room.

To recover from her fright, she checks the date on the cover of the magazine and notes the familiar yellow color. Suddenly, a voice cries out in pain—it must be Aunt Consuelo: "even then I knew she was/ a foolish, timid woman." The voice, however, is Elizabeth's own, and she and her aunt are falling together, looking fixedly at the cover of the *National Geographic*. One infers that Elizabeth might have slipped off her chair—or feared that she might—and tried to keep her balance.

In the second long stanza of the poem (thirty-six lines), Elizabeth attempts to stop the sensation of falling into a void, a panic that threatens oblivion in "cold, blue-black space." She reminds herself that she is nearly seven years old, that she is an "I," with a name, "*Elizabeth*," and is the same as those other people sitting around her. She does not dare to look any higher than the "shadowy" knees and hands of the grown-ups. She understands that a singularly strange event has happened. Questions arise in her mind. Why is she who she is? Why should she be like those people, or like her Aunt Consuelo, or those women with hanging breasts in the magazine? She heard the cry of pain, but it did not get louder—the world sets some limit to the panic.

Two short stanzas close the monologue. The first, in only four lines, reverts to a feeling of vertigo. The hot and brightly lit waiting room is drowned in a monstrous, black wave; more waves follow. Then, in the six-line coda, her everyday consciousness returns. It is wartime (World War I lasted from 1914 to 1918) on a cold winter afternoon in Worcester, Massachusetts, February 5, 1918. The experience that disoriented her is over. Here, at the end of the poem, the reader understands that Elizabeth Bishop, a mature and experienced poet, has fashioned the essence of an unforgotten childhood experience into a memorable poem.

Forms and Devices

For the voice of Elizabeth, the speaker of "In the Waiting Room," the poet needed a sentence style and vocabulary appropriate to a seven-year-old girl. Bishop relied on the many possibilities of diction and syntax to create a plausible narrator's tone.

The words spoken by Elizabeth in the poem reveal a very bright young girl (she is proud of the fact that she reads). Almost all the words come from Anglo-Saxon roots, with few of the longer, Latin-root forms. The plain verbs—I went, I sat, I read, I knew, I felt—are surrounded by the most common verb, to be: "I was." The last two stanzas, for example, use "was" and "were" six times in ten lines. A beginner in language relies on the "to be" verb as a means of naming and identifying her situation among objects, people, and places. "What is that?" comes early to a one-year-old with a vocabulary of very few words. In her reliance on the verb "to be," Bishop shows an exact ear for children's speech.

The nouns and adjectives indicate a child who is eager to learn. She names the articles of clothing: "boots" appear in the waiting room and in the picture of Osa and Martin Johnson in the *National Geographic*. Perhaps the most "poetic" word she speaks is "rivulet," in describing the volcano. She could be quoting from the article she is reading—the caption under the picture. Similarly, "pith helmets" may come from the writer of the article. In the next line, Elizabeth does specify that the words "Long Pig" for the dead man on a pole comes directly from the page.

Along with a restricted vocabulary, sentence style helps Bishop convey the tone of a child's speech. Most of the sentences begin with the subject and verb ("I said to myself . . .") in a style called "right-branching"—subordinate descriptive phrases come after the subject and verb. Short sentences of three to six words are frequent: "It was winter"; "I was too shy to stop."

Bishop's skill in creating an authentic child's voice may be compared with the work of other modern authors. Henry James created a novel in a child's voice, *What Maisie Knew* (1897). The child Maisie learns that even if adults often tell her "I love you," the real truth may be just the opposite. Another modern author, Joyce Carol Oates, has written a novel in a child's voice, *Expensive People* (1968). Ideas of violence and antagonism to adults are examined in a child's experience.

Themes and Meanings

"In the Waiting Room" asks eternal questions: Who am I in the world? Where do I fit in? Like a kaleidoscope, life presents fractured levels of existence in a single moment. The individual feels divided and yet united to each level. The experience can be frightening. Poets and philosophers from Socrates to William Butler Yeats, in all religious traditions, have expressed the paradox of the person being at one time individuals and members of a whole society.

The religious overtones of the poem begin in the title; the visible world is often seen as a vestibule or waiting room in which one gradually comes to understand the larger dimensions of one's dwelling place. While one is in "the waiting room," one is, in a sense, an exile, away from home, a child among grown-ups.

As children, people begin their understanding with homely, familiar objects—the boots and coats of the people in the dentist's office on a wintry afternoon. Like Elizabeth in the poem, people feel that they know securely when they exist. "Now" is Worcester, Massachusetts, February, 1918.

Soon the larger world comes in, as one learns about other places and times. Strange and alien events disturb one's serenity: Those "others" are not like me. The child's world is invaded by violent scenes—to Elizabeth, a dead man being carried on a pole, women's breasts exposed. The world begins to swing as her experience of the "far" finds an echo in the "near." Her Aunt Consuelo's voice is *her* voice. Between these poles of the far and near, where does an individual belong? Vertigo sets in, the angst of modern life, Søren Kierkegaard's "fear and trembling," and, further back, the Fall of Adam. Only an effort of the conscious will can stop the descent.

The poet as child conquers the experience and arrests the fall by asserting her uniqueness. The three levels of "otherness" suggested by Aunt Consuelo (the intimate family), those sharing the waiting room (those in boots seated around Elizabeth), and the far-off people (those in boots in the *National Geographic* picture) must be pushed away. The access to adult ego-consciousness comes with the lines, "you are an *I*,/ you are an *Elizabeth*,/ you are one of *them*." The idea is similar to the Hindu phrase, *om tot sat om*, "I am that I am"—both an individual and one with the other.

Yet people continually want to trace that boundary of the self and society. In the poem, vertigo again assails the poet. Like a hell, the waiting room of this world is too hot, too bright. Uncomfortable waves of emotion roll over it. The poem ends on another religious analogy about the question of existence in the world, life as a battle: "The War was on." Everyone, like a soldier, faces unknown and alien forces from the many levels of the real and imaginary world. Everyone continues to orient themselves with all the power they can muster in the "night and slush and cold."

Doris Earnshaw

IN THE WINTER OF MY THIRTY-EIGHTH YEAR

Author: W. S. Merwin (1927-   )
Type of poem: Lyric
First published: 1967, in *The Lice*

The Poem

"In the Winter of My Thirty-Eighth Year" is a free-verse, unpunctuated, twenty-two line meditative lyric, divided into five unequal sections. The speaking "I" is clearly the author. The title of the poem calls to mind the famous opening line of Dante's *Divine Comedy* (c. 1320), "At midpoint of the journey of our life." The Florentine poet meant by that midpoint the age of thirty-five, regarded—in biblical terms—as the apex of manhood and creativity. Viewed in this light, the poem might be said to hold that central place in W. S. Merwin's *Selected Poems* (1988).

The first section of the poem makes the reader feel at ease by adopting from the very beginning a familiar tone. The feeling is further strengthened by the ordinariness of the situation. It is indeed true that the border between young adulthood and middle age is a blurred one, and consequently one does not experience it as something actually dividing or cutting one off from younger days.

The poet has made the first section, which belongs to the past, *"when I was young,"* spill over into the second—dealing with his present condition, in which the speaker can still afford to toy with the idea of appointing his own age in spite of what the calendar says. He is still not showing his age; his understanding seems to have been both affected and untouched by the passage of time.

There is a more clearly marked break after the second section. Each of the remaining three sections deals with an isolated aspect of biography: age (youth), speech, and stars (fate). These sections, though discrete, are constructed in keeping with the same rhetorical pattern. Each is meant to be reassuring by dismissing a negative assessment. Eventually they add up to an odd, undefinable feeling that leaves the poem open-ended and ambivalent.

Forms and Devices

The poet muses in a relaxed tone of voice. The object of his meditation is the nature of experienced inner or subjective time and its relation to chronological or mechanical time. To emphasize this imaginative effort of grasping the twofold nature of time, the poet makes sparse use of imagery. The first section is conspicuously devoid of concreteness. The aim of the speaker is to establish temporal relationships with which to capture his sense of his own selfhood. Yet he feels remote and disoriented, "As far from [himself] as ever."

The same dearth of figurative material (there can be no metaphorical activity in the absence of tangible imagery) can be encountered in the third and fourth sections. Both rely on an impeccable logic by means of which the speaker hopes to achieve a clearer and more stable view of his whereabouts.

This is even more true of the second section, which contains a more elaborate design of hypothetical and guarded statements in which time is shown to be both relative and elusive. Its functions or effects are no less difficult to evaluate. This rather artificial and contrived textual space—a kind of hall lined with reflecting mirrors—is introduced by two lines that carry the whole weight of poetic figuration available in the first half of the poem: "Waking in fog and rain and seeing nothing" describes the speaker's condition now that middle age has overtaken him. The only certainty available is that there is practically nothing to grasp or to lean on. Hence, the speaker goes on, "I imagine all the clocks have died in the night." This is perhaps the most compelling statement in the whole poem, creating a sense that time has come to a stop and has ceased to matter.

The concluding, fifth section rounds off the picture by contributing its powerful description of stars as drifting "farther away in the invisible morning." The concluding image—if it can bear that name—"the invisible morning," is arguably more pregnant than that of the waking self "seeing nothing" and that of the imagined death of all clocks "in the night." "Invisible morning" is but another way of naming the ungraspable. Yet "morning" is morning, and it sounds a kind of a hopeful note at the end of the tunnel.

The poem is therefore quite telling by the very way in which is eschews direct perception by one's senses. On the other hand, the figures of thinking—or the way temporality is hurried or arrested, hypothetically juggled and surveyed—make up for the rarefied concreteness of the text. This in itself is a remarkable achievement: To be simultaneously in and out of time, forgetful of its flow and yet mindful of its consequences, is not an easy task for neutral, transparent syntax to accomplish.

Themes and Meanings

"In the Winter of My Thirty-Eighth Year" is a poem about manhood and its problems. The sense of achievement is definitely there, for "speech"—the most precious tool of the poet—has already "lent itself to [the speaker's] uses." There is also a sense of impending crisis in spite of the disclaimer: "There is nothing wrong with my age now." The speaker feels at odds, as the reader has seen, with his present condition. Moreover, his "emptiness" is freely floating among the receding stars. This levitation and boundlessness is what ultimately prevails.

The difficulty the speaker faces is one of definition. The speaker's age has been imagined, anticipated, and, like his youth, indefinitely deferred. The perplexity and confusion results from the fact that the observer's vantage point does not lie outside the moving system of reference (Albert Einstein's theory of relativity comes to mind here) but is a part of it. One cannot experience directly both the river of time and its relative speed with respect to stationary objects along the banks.

On the other hand, the thirty-eighth year in the life of an American poet, as a critic of Merwin's oeuvre has pointed out, is an important landmark. At that very age, Walt

Whitman completed his first edition of *Leaves of Grass* (1855). Consequently, later poets of the self—and Merwin is one of them—may be tempted to measure their own achievement against Whitman's time scale.

Many poems in *The Lice* are concerned with Merwin's own maturity and its problems: "Looking East at Night," "December Night," "After the Solstice," "December Among the Vanished," "Glimpse of the Ice," "The Cold Before the Moonrise," "Early January," "Dusk in Winter," and "For the Anniversary of My Death." (Indeed, Merwin "must have the mind of winter," as Wallace Stevens might say.) Read as a sequence, these poems provide an illuminating context for a deeper grasping of this poem. What seems to be missing from it is a direct reference to death. The tone of "In the Winter of My Thirty-Eighth Year" is, or seems to be, free of metaphysical anxiety: "Of course there is nothing the matter with the stars." Nor is it fraught with longing or hope, as is Dylan Thomas's "Poem in October," its most kindred forerunner. Merwin's sense of his own individual destiny seems to bask suspended in a relativity of his own making: "Now no one is looking I could choose my age/ It would be younger I suppose so I am older." The arbitrariness of the gesture is supported by the fluidity of the syntax, unmonitored as it is by any punctuation markers.

In giving his 1967 volume the title *The Lice*, Merwin believed he should unravel for the benefit of his public the context from which he had lifted this rather unusual reference. He printed an epigraph from the pre-Socratic philosopher Heraclitus on the left-hand side of that volume's title page:

> All men are deceived by appearances of things, even Homer himself, who was the wisest man in Greece; for he was deceived by boys catching lice: they said to him, "What we have caught and what we have killed we have left behind, but what has escaped us we bring with us."

No better illustration of this observation could be provided than Merwin's meditation on his own mid-term balance of gains and losses. Yet in Merwin's poem there can be no easy discrimination between such opposites, for the reason that his losses and his gains are on the move themselves, continually shifting and changing their own significances.

Stefan Stoenescu

INCANTATA

Author: Paul Muldoon (1951-   )
Type of poem: Elegy
First published: 1994, in *The Annals of Chile*

The Poem

"Incantata," written in memory of the artist Mary Farl Powers, is a nearly perfect synthesis of formal construction and emotional content. Spoken directly to the poet's former lover, the poem is both elegy and celebration. Each of the forty-five eight-line stanzas has the rhyme scheme *aabbcddc*, called a "stadium stanza"—a form invented by Abraham Cowley for elegiac purposes and later adopted by William Butler Yeats. Because of its length (360 lines), "Incantata" can sustain some variation; the lines range from four to seventeen syllables, and there is no regular underlying rhythm.

The first twenty-two stanzas tell the story of the accidental fortunes of a friendship, the shared history, the ways one life enriches another and the ways in which they differ. The poet begins thinking of his dead friend when he is cutting into a potato to make an Incan glyph in the shape of a mouth, and this, in turn, reminds him of the first time he saw her works of art. The mouth itself is significant because the poet is attempting to speak across the boundary of death. The title suggests that this is a kind of incantation, as though he could call her back through verbal ritual. It also suggests a "non-song" (in-cantata), and this association, too, is appropriate, since he cannot seem to find the proper words to express his feelings.

As the poet rushes through specific memories of what appears to have been a stimulating and challenging relationship, he is forced to face again the fact that Mary Powers had refused an operation for her breast cancer, believing that everything in life is predetermined, including her own death. There are moments of humor and moments of poignant loss, the most moving of which is a metaphorical sense that something good must be built from such pain, as when a bird plucks a straw to build a nest in the aftermath of a battle.

The central stanza serves as a hinge; poet and poem alike balk at the visual artist's fierce determination to die because her death is part of the natural "order." It ends in a breakdown of speech itself: "with its '*quaquaqua*,' with its 'Quoiquoi-quoiquoiquoiquoiquoiquioq.'" The nonsensical quotations are direct references to the plays of Samuel Beckett, several of whose characters are mentioned throughout the poem.

The last half of the poem transforms grief into celebration—of life, art, history, and especially the power of friendship to transcend death. In Powers's own theological terms, memory is all that is left of the friendship. The last twenty-two stanzas pick up the idea of memory itself, creating one long list of their shared experiences—all that is left. "That's all that's left of the voice of Enrico Caruso" and "of Sunday afternoons in the Botanic Gardens" and of the sight of a particular road between Leiden and The Hague, and of particular pieces of music and specific places and people, and so on. The incantatory list accelerates, extending for pages as the memories flood over the poet, culminating with, if not an acceptance of his friend's "fate," an imaginative union of the life and the art.

Forms and Devices

Because "Incantata" employs a regular rhyme scheme, it demonstrates how what is sometimes called the "pressure of form" can help give shape to its subject matter. Muldoon is a master of "slant rhyme" or "half-rhyme," so the sounds are often subtle, even clever. Muldoon's poems are characteristically clever—playing on words, making puns, referring to the works of other writers and even to his own earlier poems. He often rhymes one language with another. This approach is somewhat true of "Incantata," but the tendency to play with words (and with the facts) is somewhat muted because of the passionate and autobiographical nature of his material. The poem was written in a rush of emotion over a period of five days, Muldoon has said, and the feelings are all the more compressed and shaped by the use of the regular, rhymed stanzas.

In the first half of the poem, the rhymes are noticeable but do not dominate; the intimate voice of the writer is so urgent that the reader is more involved in the unfolding narrative of Mary Powers's death. In the second half, however, the reader becomes more and more aware of rhyme and how Muldoon is orchestrating his material. The mixture of philosophy, theology, comedy, literary allusion, pop culture, history, and personal memory creates a collage of unrelated images, thereby making the reader doubly conscious of the way the poet is choosing his words. Sometimes the sounds are compressed:

> of the early-ripening jardonelle, the tumorous jardon,
>   the jargon
> of jays, the jars
> of tomato relish and the jars
> of Victoria plums . . .

Sometimes they are deceptive:

> Of the great big dishes of chicken lo mein and beef chow mein,
> of what's mine is yours and what's yours mine,
> of the oxlips and cowslips
> on the banks of the Liffey at Leixlip
> where the salmon breaks through the either/or neither/nor
>   nether
> reaches despite the temple-veil
> of itself being rent and the penny left out overnight on the rail
> is a sheet of copper when the mail-train has passed over.

The slant rhymes (mein/mine, cowslips/Leixlip, nether/over, and veil/rail) are so surprising that the reader must pause to make sense of it all. Even the clichés are given new contexts: the transformation of the sharing of Chinese food into "what's mine is yours" is comic; the salmon could be expected to break through anything but the "nether reaches"; the penny is returned to its original state by the train. The result is a melding of the literal and the figurative as well as of the private and the actively communal.

The use of private material is also characteristic of Muldoon. Some of his material is merely unfamiliar—foreign words, Irish history, references to specific works of art—but remains in the public domain. Some is intensely private, and Muldoon is willing to keep things secret, hardly minding if his audience does not understand many of his references. Because the poem has many of the "overheard" qualities of a lyric, the reader eavesdrops on a very personal grief—with all the specifics of individual loss. And because the poem consistently employs the device of direct address, referring to Mary as "you" throughout, the poet can be confidential without revealing the private references. One could argue that the poem's stance toward the reader is one of profound indifference. Still, in *Paul Muldoon* (1996), the critic Tim Kendall has suggested that, through the use of this device, "even though the particular significance of these references is never explained, 'Incantata' does convey a shared intimacy which incorporates the reader."

Themes and Meanings

To employ a musical metaphor, "Incantata" is the concerto for which Muldoon had been practicing the scales of form. The poet's considerable technical skill keeps the poem afloat as it makes a space for the grief it embodies. The question that emerges in "Incantata" is what to make of an individual life. If the poet can begin to make sense of the death of his friend, he may be able to come to terms with her philosophy of life. The tension in the poem is enhanced by its form—by the quirky rhymes and the way it seems to slip out from under its own overarching questions—but its source is philosophical, maybe even theological. Mary's philosophy is described as Thomism—that "the things of this world sing out in a great oratorio"—but a Thomism "tempered by" Jean-Paul Sartre and Samuel Beckett. So even as Muldoon tries to honor her sense that death is preordained, he is angry at it (and her?), saddened by loss, and frustrated by his failure to find a meaning in the void.

The result is a tacit resistance; even as Muldoon pays lip service to Mary Powers's assertions that nothing is random, he provides a seemingly random set of memories. In the first half, he announces his desire to "body out your disembodied *vox/ clamantis in deserto*," to let his potato-mouth speak "unencumbered." In the second half, he abandons the potato-mouth (reduced to "quaquaqua") in favor of his own embodied voice. In doing so, he illuminates Powers's life in rich detail.

The final three stanzas are not end-stopped, but spill into each other in a frenzy, a furious desire to pull her back from her beliefs, to find buried in the Irish language and folklore the one herb that would cure her, to speak across the barrier of death and have her respond. Because these stanzas are syntactically complex, framed in the negative, the final image is actually positive; the reader watches Powers reach out her ink-stained hands to take Muldoon's "hands stained with ink." The power of the written word has transcended death, however briefly. Finally, "Incantata" is life affirming. It makes of personal grief an "oratorio."

Judith Kitchen

THE INDIAN BURYING GROUND

Author: Philip Freneau (1752-1832)
Type of poem: Lyric
First published: 1788, in *The Miscellaneous Works of Mr. Philip Freneau Containing His Essays and Additional Poems*

The Poem

"The Indian Burying Ground" is a short lyric poem of forty lines celebrating the spirits of Native Americans haunting their sequestered graves in the North American wilderness. It is an early American example of the Romantic movement in Western literature. Although its elegiac subject matter harks back to the eighteenth century British school of "graveyard" poetry, Philip Freneau adds a Romantic twist to the sepulchral theme of human mortality. This writer displays a Gothic fascination with supernatural phenomena and moonlit scenes of fancy, a primitivistic attention to unspoiled natives and pristine nature, a nostalgia for a legendary past, and an interest in the spellbinding powers of the imagination (or "fancy") as superior to the reason of the European Enlightenment. In lyric form and fanciful poetic theme, Freneau bears close comparison to William Collins in eighteenth century England.

The poem opens with a primitivistic speaker in the guise of a common man challenging civilized burial customs, which betray what a culture thinks of the state of death. When civilized culture demands burying a corpse in a prone position, death is seen as an eternal sleep for the soul.

If readers consider not the European past but the antiquity of the New World, however, they contemplate America's primordial race of Indians, whose sitting posture in their graves suggests that their souls actively continue the simple pursuits of their former mortal lives, as depicted on their pottery and as indicated by their weapons. For example, an Indian arrowhead, or "head of stone," symbolizes the opposite of a European headstone—namely, the enduring vitality of the dead person's spirit, unlike the cold, engraved memorial for a dead white man.

Almost midway through the poem, there is a shift from commentary about burial rites to an exhortation to an unnamed stranger forbidding any violation of a secluded Indian grave site where the dead were buried sitting, not sleeping, and whose corpses therefore left a noticeable swelling in the grass-covered landscape. This Indian graveyard lay in a setting of Romantic sublimity, set off grandly by a boulder of native carvings and sheltered by a venerable elm tree that once witnessed Indian pastimes.

Let the passerby and local farmer ("the shepherd") beware of disturbing the ghosts of these departed Indians, who haunt their burial site and ward off injuries done to the hallowed place. One such spirit is the ghost of an Indian maiden as beautiful as the darker-skinned Queen of Sheba in the Bible.

At the haunting time of midnight in a dewy moonlit setting, the passerby will let reason be overpowered by imagination, or "fancy," so as to be able to see a frightening supernatural vision of deer hunters and an Indian chief wearing war paint and riding perpetually in night's shadows.

Forms and Devices

"The Indian Burying Ground" is a lyric poem consisting of ten quatrains with alternating end rhymes. The prevailing meter is iambic tetrameter with variations. A lyric poem tends to be a simple evocation of a single, simple experience and/or emotion, and such is this poem's aim and achievement. Freneau's lyric poetry, though minor, is often haunting in its beauty. Using contemporary themes of nature, evanescence, interest in an unspoiled humanity and solitude, primitivism, and the supernatural, he evoked a real charm that is at odds with the harsh satire for which he was best known in his own time.

His lyric poems are rooted in the eighteenth century seedbed of British "graveyard" poetry, and especially in William Collins's more formally ornate Romantic poems that pay homage to the new European interest in fancy, fantasy, Gothic supernaturalism, and nostalgia for remote national history. Freneau's accomplishment was to naturalize these English literary trends and European artistic impulses to help give impetus to a national literature for the burgeoning United States of America.

As Freneau lamented in his "Advice to Authors" (published in the same year, 1788, as the poem under discussion), the United States was as yet a very thin, rocky soil for cultivating the fine arts and for nurturing starving poets. It was a miracle that any literature emerged at all in a nation that was too young and too rude to have developed a fully civilized culture sustaining poetic creation:

> In a country, which two hundred years ago was peopled only by savages, and where the government has ever, in effect, since the first establishment of the white men in these parts, been no other than republican, it is really wonderful there should be any polite original authors at all in any line, especially when it is considered, that according to the common course of things, any particular nation or people must have arrived to, or rather passed, their meridian of opulence and refinement, before they consider the professors of the fine arts in any other light than a nuisance to the community.

Even outside the context of an uncultured United States, "The Indian Burying Ground" should be considered a good performance, if not a great poem; it is a lovely piece, of European inspiration and idealistic American sensibility.

Themes and Meanings

"The Indian Burying Ground" is a poem about the admirable ways of Native Americans, here viewed essentially as "noble savages," a fairly common eighteenth century idea, as exemplified in their custom of burying the dead in a sitting position symbolic of their pristine vitality in life and for eternity.

The poem indulges in a nostalgia for the primitive, the past, and the fantastic as envisaged through the poet's and the reader's imagination, which is deemed more powerful than the faculty of reason in the human mind. Freneau begins his poem with a declaration of independence from received notions of European civilization respecting burial rites, and ends, appropriately, with a declaration of allegiance not to fact-based reason but to the new Romantic imagination: fancy-bound and therefore capable of conjuring up Indian spirits that are shown to be forever alive in the sublime realm of mist, moonlight, and shadow. The growing interest of Americans such as Freneau in their own past and in the original natives of the country may be seen as the result of an impulse similar to the one that made the Germanic and Celtic past an important topic of English Romanticism. Veneration of the "noble savage" was also widespread in England and on the Continent in the eighteenth century.

It must be pointed out, however, that Freneau's worship of the noble American savage is unconsciously compromised by large doses of implicit condescension toward Indians. Compared to white people of European background, the Indians are written off as "a ruder race" (line 24) and as the "children of the forest" (line 28) who in death produce "many a barbarous form" (line 31) to haunt their graveyard and punish unwary intruders. Hence, critics and readers alike must be cautious about ascribing an enlightened primitivism to Philip Freneau and his poetry.

Thomas M. Curley

INNOCENCE

Author: Thomas Traherne (c. 1637-1674)
Type of poem: Lyric
First published: 1903, in *The Poetical Works of Thomas Traherne*

The Poem

"Innocence" is a medium-length poem with sixty lines divided into five parts, each containing three rhyming four-line stanzas (quatrains). It follows an intricate metrical pattern and rhyme scheme. The first three lines of the beginning stanza of each part are in iambic pentameter, while the shorter fourth line is in iambic tetrameter. These first stanzas rhyme *aabb*. The second stanzas in each of the five parts of the poem are entirely in iambic tetrameter and rhyme *abab* (words such as "love" and "remove," which occur in the second stanza of part 2, were pronounced so that they rhymed in the seventeenth century). The first, third, and fourth lines of the third stanzas of each part of "Innocence" are in iambic tetrameter, with the second lines being in iambic trimeter. They also rhyme *abab*.

"Innocence" is the fourth poem in a sequence of thirty-seven, known as the Dobell poems in honor of the man who first published the manuscript containing them. In the preceding three poems, Traherne describes how new and marvelous everything seemed in infancy and childhood, in the Eden-like world that God had prepared for him. In "Innocence" he elaborates upon what most thrilled him as a child—as he states in part 1, that "I felt no Stain, nor Spot of Sin." The title thus refers to the state of innocence that the speaker enjoyed then and to which he desires to return now as an adult. Speaking from the authority of personal experience, the poet expresses wonder at the completely natural and spontaneous state of joy he experienced in his childhood. All he can remember of that blessed state is its sweet simplicity and light, "A Joyfull Sence and Puritie."

In part 2 Traherne goes on to explain that even though he was only a child, he recognized that this pure joy originated within himself, not outside from material things. His inner joy was so complete and full that he was able to appreciate the objects that surrounded him entirely in themselves without becoming dependent upon them for his happiness: "that which takes [Objects] from the Ey/ Of others, offerd them to me." To him alone they seemed perpetually fresh and new.

In part 3 Traherne adds a moral dimension to this experience. He asserts that it was characterized by an immunity to polluting influences such as greed, anger, and pride: "No Fraud nor Anger in me movd/ No Malice Jealousie or Spite;/ All that I saw I truly lovd./ Contentment only and Delight." His sense of his own natural goodness and the delight it engendered inspires him to "daily Kneel" for a return to that blessed state of life.

He then declares, in part 4, that whether his powerful childhood experience was the product of pure nature uncorrupted by human "Custom," or a miracle whereby God removed the stain of original sin from his soul, or the fortuitous experience of one shining day, its beauty and meaning still thrill him. He concludes, in part 5, that his innocence was akin to Adam's experience in Eden before the Fall. He envisions his childhood self, in fact, as "A little Adam in a Sphere/ of Joys!" This innocence is, he exclaims, a foretaste of heaven. It is important to note, however, that this Edenic state, which is "beyond all Bound and Price," is characterized by both a self-sufficient inner happiness and by sensory delights. Traherne's paradise does not deny the senses but rather encompasses both the inner and outer faculties.

That Traherne was orphaned at an early age adds poignancy to the poem. "Innocence," however, does not sentimentalize childhood as some fleetingly charming state of life. It rather argues that the same pure inner awareness which sparkles in childhood is available to adults as well. All in all, the poem serves as a compelling illustration of Christ's teaching that "Whosoever shall not receive the kingdom of God as a little child shall in no wise enter therein" (Luke 18:17).

Forms and Devices

Traherne is one of the so-called Metaphysical poets, a loose grouping of seventeenth century poets who imitated the dazzling poetic innovations of John Donne. Donne's poetry, a poetry of aspiration, was noted for its exuberant rhythms, striking verbal displays, surprising imagery, and artistic intelligence. For Donne, a poem was "a naked thinking heart"—it was an expression of an intense fusion of thought and feeling. Traherne's poem exhibits the energy and flair of Metaphysical poetry generally. It makes a convincing presentation, through universal light/dark metaphors, penetrating paradoxes, and bold imagery, of a more holistic state of being.

Light imagery is present in parts 1, 4, and 5 and is associated with the felicitous state of childhood innocence. Light is both the literal light that shone in Eden and the symbolic light of pure goodness, in contrast to the darkness of guilt and evil. Paradoxically, this benign light filled even the nighttime, for Traherne says that "the very Night to me was bright." It is as if his mind was fully enlivened by blissful awareness even when sleeping. Perhaps the most stunning image in the poem is that of the boy in the bubble, the "Adam in a Sphere/ Of Joys." The picture of a little Adam floating joyously in a soap bubble conveys memorably the sense of wonder and freedom that epitomize Traherne's conception of childhood.

An underlying paradox in the poem is parallel with an idea expressed by a later poet, William Wordsworth, namely that "The Child is father of the Man." The belief that childhood is spiritually superior to adulthood is recurrent in Traherne's poetry and prose. That Traherne, an Anglican clergyman (he was the private chaplain to the Lord High Keeper of the Royal Seal, Sir Orlando Bridgeman), yearns with all his heart to "becom a Child again" may sound at first illogical, but Traherne makes a convincing imaginative case for the sublimity of childhood innocence.

One of Traherne's most characteristic techniques, the cataloging device, is apparent in part 3. Here he enumerates the bad inclinations that he did not feel as a child— avarice, pride, lust, strife, fraud, anger, malice, jealousy, and spite. Traherne's catalog suggests an encyclopedic approach to experience, not unlike that of a scientist drawing up a comprehensive list of observed phenomena. Traherne was knowledgeable about the science of his day and was particularly interested in the writings of Francis Bacon, the leading English empiricist of the early seventeenth century. His frequent use in his poetry and prose of such catalogs reflects Bacon's influence.

Traherne's signature exclamation points are not extravagantly sprinkled throughout this poem; rather, they appear only twice in part 3 and once in part 5. In the hands of a lesser poet, they could come across as gimmicky overdramatization, but Traherne's sparing and appropriate use of them at just the right moments in "Innocence"—when he is full of the memory of the original joy of his childhood and when he concludes that this innocence was an "Antepast" (or foretaste) of the heaven to come—lends an infectious quality to the poem.

Themes and Meanings

The poem argues that the innocence which typifies childhood is an actual state of pure awareness that is recoverable in adulthood. It is, according to Traherne, the basis of both a full inner spiritual life and of a glorious and free enjoyment of the world. The mind in this state of felicity is fully awake, self-sufficient, and naturally tending to good. It is, in short, a state of awareness having primordial Edenic overtones.

In addition to the felicity theme, the concept known as the "pre-existence doctrine" is strongly implied by Traherne's poem. This idea, that children may recall their previous unclouded existence in heaven, also occurs in "The Retreate," a poem by another Metaphysical poet, Henry Vaughan. Vaughan, interestingly, was initially thought to be the author of the first anonymous Traherne poetry manuscript that was found in the late nineteenth century, but Dobell corrected this misattribution. Traherne, like Vaughan, reflects the stress that Anglicanism placed on an idealized childhood characterized by original innocence. This concept stands in contrast to the view of the Puritans of the time that children were wicked creatures who inherited original sin, though they could be morally transformed.

James J. Balakier

INSOMNIA. HOMER. TAUT SAILS

Author: Osip Mandelstam (1891-1938)
Type of poem: Lyric
First published: 1916, as "Bessonnitsa. Gomer. Tugie parusa," in *Kamen*, second edition; English translation collected in *Modern Russian Poetry*, 1967

The Poem

"Insomnia. Homer. Taut Sails" is a short poem of only three stanzas, told in the first person. It is untitled, like many of Osip Mandelstam's poems, although the very first word, "Insomnia," fits the mood of the entire poem. It is one of his early poems and one of many poems in which he used classical motifs. The lines are six-foot iambic, rhymed regularly *abba*.

The poem opens with three noun sentences, setting the stage in a most concise manner. The persona is suffering from insomnia and is reading the list of the ships of Homer's *Iliad* (c. 800 B.C.E.), most likely hoping that it will help him fall asleep. He has read half of it when, in his imagination, the sails of the ships on the list turn into white cranes, which are now flying high above Hellas. The connection between the first words of the poem becomes clear: Insomnia leads to Homer, and Homer leads to white sails and the ships.

In his imagination, the poet sees the ships as a flock of cranes and follows them as they fly off in wedge formation to distant lands. They are compared, parenthetically, to royalties whose heads are covered with the foam of gods. The poet then unexpectedly asks where they are flying, even though he gave a hint in stanza 1. He immediately gives another hint, after suddenly shifting the perspective, by asking the Achaeans another unexpected question: What would Troy be to them without Helen?

In the third stanza, the poet provides further elucidation about the mystery by shifting his focus again to the sea and Homer. He flatly states that both the sea and Homer are governed by love, but now he is faced with a dilemma: Should he listen to the sea or to Homer? The dilemma resolves itself when Homer falls silent and only the majestic roar of the sea is audible.

By now, sleep is taking over as the sea inundates the persona's pillow: He has sunk into drowsiness after the dilemma has been resolved. The perspective shifts back to the persona and the bed, where it all began.

Forms and Devices

In this poem, as in most of Mandelstam's poems, metaphors and images reign supreme, beginning with the opening metaphor of Homer. Homer serves not only as the provider of reading material (the catalog of ships), but also, in a much more important role, as a guide toward the revelation that the persona (poet) is seeking. This metaphor also opens the door for other metaphors, all of which are closely connected with Homer.

The sea is the second important metaphor. At first, it is a beautiful, calm sea on which the ships/white cranes sail majestically. Toward the end, it turns into "the dark sea" that roars and crashes heavily, the dominant sound before the persona sleeps. The sea metaphor also contains a clue to the central message of the poem.

The third important metaphor is that of the cranes, which clearly stand for the ships. They are seen as beautiful white creatures sailing gracefully through space. They are not used here merely for description, however—nor is their geographical destination particularly important, or else the poet would have told the reader about it immediately. By sailing to Troy, as the poet hints by mentioning the Achaeans, the cranes direct the reader's attention toward the focal point of the poem.

Helen is used as the fourth metaphor, in which the three previous metaphors converge. Although she is mentioned only once, she provides the all-important clue to the rationale of the poem.

Thus the four main metaphors work in harmony not only to bring sleep to the persona of the poem but also to provide the answer he is seeking. All four are therefore indispensable; remove one and the whole edifice collapses.

There are several striking images in the poem. The description of the long-extended flock of cranes and their wedge formation adds grace to the significant role of the birds. The white vision of their graceful sailing amid the blue sky and the sea lends them a touch of royalty. The crane image is reinforced by the image of the kings, who are sailing on and guiding the ships. The kings' heads are covered with foam produced either by the swift sailing of the ships or by clouds descending upon their heads. Moreover, the foam is modified by "divine"—no doubt a reference to Aphrodite, the goddess of love, who was born out of sea foam. (Mandelstam has used this motif in another poem, "Silentium.")

The poem concludes with the image of a dark, roaring sea that crashes and thunders against the pillow, providing a fitting climax to the search and to the solution. It is interesting that the whiteness of the cranes contrasts with the darkness of the sea, as if to underscore the change of focus of both the persona and the reader from the lightness of the pre-sleep condition to the heaviness immediately preceding the sleep.

Themes and Meanings

"Insomnia. Homer. Taut Sails" is a poem about love. It takes an unconventional approach to the subject, to be sure, as Mandelstam's poems often do.

It is not easy to determine that the poem deals with love, since the reader's attention is captivated by the beauty of the metaphors and the images of Homer and the white ships/cranes. The reader is also puzzled by the seemingly incongruous association of insomnia and Homer (although the association between Homer and ships is quite apparent).

The first hint that love is the main theme occurs in the reference to the "divine foam," which immediately conjures up the vision of Aphrodite, the goddess of love. The next hint is contained in the innocent and apparently pointless question about where the ships are sailing. Certainly, the royal sailors—that is, those who command the ships—know their destination. The poet does not wait to provide the answer, even though it is a cryptic one. By acknowledging the fact that the sailors are Achaeans sailing toward Troy, and by asking rhetorically what Troy would mean to them without Helen, Mandelstam supplies a one-word answer, love, as Nils Ake Nilsson points out in his book *Osip Mandelstam: Five Poems* (1974). After all, did not the Achaeans fight a battle at Troy primarily to liberate Helen? Was not Helen the symbol of love, worth going to war and fighting for?

After providing the simple, if cryptic, answer, the poet further complicates his own answer by stating in the first half of the next line, very forthrightly, that "both sea and Homer" are moved by love, a statement requiring further elucidation. The aphorism used to complete the verse, "all is moved by love," may be seen as a lame truism or as a safety valve. The fact that he shifted his attention in the closing lines away from the issue altogether may indicate that Mandelstam thought that he had made the point clear, but additional explanation is necessary.

Aside from the euphonic similarity, perhaps relatedness, in Russian of the two words, sea and Homer (*more* and *Gomer*), there are other possible explanations. Victor Terras, in his article "Classical Motives in the Poetry of Osip Mandelstam" (1966), finds examples in classical literature that express the belief that the entire universe (including sea) is governed by love. Nilsson quotes additional examples from other literatures, including the work of Dante. Certainly, the primary moving force of poetry is love. Homer, the epitome of a poet, composed some of the best passages of his works, especially those concerning Helen, on love. The logic of the juxtaposition of sea and Homer becomes clear now. By deciding in the final lines of his poem to "listen" to the sea rather than to Homer, Mandelstam opts for the stronger of the two, having used Homer metaphorically to proclaim the divine force of love.

Vasa D. Mihailovich

INSPIRATION

Author: Henry David Thoreau (1817-1862)
Type of poem: Lyric
First published: 1863; collected in *Poems of Nature*, 1895

The Poem

Henry David Thoreau's "Inspiration" consists of twenty-one four-line stanzas that declare that only through a humility of spirit can one find communion with the god-like "ancient harmony" that is the basis of truth and that lies at the heart of human experience. This humility of spirit is necessary to purge the mind from the artificial distractions of what the poet calls "the general show of things." The poem signals this humility in the second stanza, when the poet declares that if he sings with a "light head erect" his verse will remain "weak and shallow" despite even the efforts of the "muses." The muses here are not the true sources of inspiration, as they may have been to traditional, classical poets, but merely conduits through which the poet's verse may take shape. The "light head erect" refers to the presumptuous, unthinking attitudes and conventions that make the poet complacent and thus unable to receive the truth.

To receive such truth the poet must make his soul an "accomplice" to his heart's yearnings. He must grope "with bended neck" and listen—as in an act of faith—to the timeless "line" that God has written. This act of faith is superior to the intellect—Thoreau calls it "wit"—and the hope that naturally springs from it. The poet must learn to surrender to the prompting of his heart and realize first that his "love and reverence" for the external beauty of things has blinded him to the truth of a deeper reality.

Stanzas 6-10 form the heart of the poem, containing the central idea of the philosophy that became known as Transcendentalism. After the poet has gained the necessary humility in the face of the natural world, accepting, by an act of faith, the prompting of his heart, he suddenly feels—"unsought, unseen"—the divine power residing within him. In an instant—"More swift its bolt than lightning is"—the poet becomes more keenly aware of the life around and within him. Like God, he becomes an all-absorbing mind, seeing and hearing beyond sight and sound, living years within the span of moments. He comprehends the truth, not as knowledge gained from books but as a "clear and ancient harmony" that expands his "privacies" and unites him to the eternal. It is at this very moment that the poet feels both newly born and at the prime of life.

Unfortunately, this experience of unity with all of nature is not gained without conflict. Though it gives the poet a sense of "manhood's strength," it also comes at an "unseasoned time" and "vexe[s] the day with its presuming face." The poet, then, must rely on his undying faith in the validity of the experience, on that moment of inspiration that "shows where life's true kernel's laid."

Forms and Devices

Thoreau wrote more than two hundred poems during his early career, but only a few were published during his lifetime. Some critics consider his poetry as mere glosses to his more significant prose works such as *A Week on the Concord and Merrimack Rivers* (1849) and his masterpiece, *Walden: Or, Life in the Woods* (1854). However, his poems often provide insight into certain characteristics of Thoreau's writing style. "Inspiration" is a good example of the clarity of expression that has often been attributed to his work.

This clarity of expression has been achieved despite the restraints imposed on the poem by the poet's use of the traditional verse form of the quatrain and the even more limiting use of rhyming tetrameters. In four beats to each line and with every other line in the quatrain rhyming, Thoreau still manages to convey exactly what he means. As a direct statement of the principles of Transcendentalism, the poem contains few images. Its diction relies more on the use of aphoristic wit than the traditional devices of metaphor or simile. The very first quatrain contains a didactic statement which, in its concise, aphoristic form, suggests the style of such eighteenth century poets as Alexander Pope: "The work we choose should be our own,/ God lets alone."

Like Pope, Thoreau enjoys clever wordplay. In the sixth quatrain, for instance, in which the poet explains the presence of the divine force within him, he plays with the words "sensual" and "sensible," thereby making a distinction between the physical world and the internal world of the mind. It is this disciplined approach to diction that saves the poem from becoming simply a bald, direct statement or an abstruse philosophical exposition.

One charge that may rightly be leveled on the poem, however, is its lack of brevity. The poet makes his point by the end of the twelfth quatrain (line 48). The last nine quatrains merely elaborate on the effect of that "ancient harmony" which he has experienced. Yet this elaboration highlights another aspect of Thoreau's creative process.

We know that for most of his adult life Thoreau kept a journal, and that it provided him, in effect, with the working notes that were to form the basis of his published works. In one entry, for instance, Thoreau observes that only a superficial "acquaintance" with external reality is not "sufficient to make it completely the subject of [one's] muse." This idea is clearly seen and more cogently presented in the opening sections of "Inspiration."

Themes and Meanings

"Inspiration" is the clearest expression in verse of the principles of the American philosophy of Transcendentalism. As such, it is important not only for what it says, but also for the way in which it says it. Part of what the poet says is about the intriguing nature of inspiration itself. On one hand, it is a force by which the creative artist communes with the spiritual reality signaled in nature and which resides in corresponding form in the mind. On the other, it is a divine "electuary," as Thoreau calls it in the fifth quatrain of the poem, which, while it attunes one to the "ancient harmony," also leaves the poet "single in the crowd" and alone with eternity. This idea of the poet being both joined and isolated is one of the basic contradictions of a philosophy that glorifies the personal and the intuitive. Thoreau would insist, however, as did his mentor and friend Ralph Waldo Emerson, that the separation is not so much an alienation as it is a form of elevation to a higher level of awareness. Any man or woman, properly attuned, is capable of achieving such an intuitive grasp of the divinity that is at once a part of nature and of his or her own soul. Inspiration, in other words, is open to all humanity.

Inspiration for the poet, however, is another matter. As Thoreau declares in the last stanza of the poem, the poet—untempted by fame, unmoved by the prospect of earthly rewards—becomes a kind of interpreter, a priest in the service of inspiration, who reconciles all contradictions. The poet is a kind of intermediary between the unthinking mass of humanity, those with "light head erect," and the force of inspiration which "with one breath attunes the spheres." The role of poet as priest, in fact, was a popular and influential idea in the first half of the nineteenth century.

Finally, the poem is interesting as an illustration of the very contradictions it seeks to resolve. The poet, for example, insists on the primacy of an intuitive grasp of reality. The intellectual perception of the truth is, in the poet's phrase, "but learning's lore." Yet the poem is not composed intuitively, in a kind of associative method whereby the work takes the shape organically demanded of it by its subject. Romantic literary theory, for example, often supported the idea of a work taking its own shape, like a living organism. By this theory, form was secondary to content. Yet "Inspiration" clearly shows a deliberate, intellectual approach to its composition. The four-line rhyming units, for example, and the tight, rhythmical cadence show the poem's indebtedness, at least structurally, to an older, more classical tradition.

Edward Fiorelli

INSTINCT

Author: Cesare Pavese (1908-1950)
Type of poem: Narrative
First published: 1936, as "L'istinto," in *Lavorare stanca*; English translation collected in *Hard Labor*, 1976

The Poem

Cesare Pavese's "Instinct" portrays the power of instinct and its complexities, especially as seen by the poem's central character, an old, nameless man. Written in five loose, unrhyming stanzas of free verse, the poem follows the consciousness of the old man as he negotiates between the role of instinct in his past and in the present moment of the poem while he watches two mating dogs "satisfy their instinct."

The poem begins with a clarity that is typical of Pavese: It is almost as if he is providing a stage direction for a play when he announces the gender, age, and mental state of his central character, as well as the location and time of day for the action taking place. The three-line first sentence (and stanza) of the poem provides the answers to the journalistic equivalent of the who-what-when-where-why questions.

The second stanza provides the background to the action. The action of the dogs mating is not as important as the reaction of the viewer, the consciousness that is revealed. Readers enter the old man's mind and discover his relationship with instinct: In the past, when he still had teeth and no flies settled on his gums, he was able to "satisfy his instinct" at night with his wife. Then, the English translation suggests, instinct was "fine," but the Italian is even more robust: Instinct "*era bello*," was beautiful.

The third stanza provides a meditation by the old man on dogs. What is interesting here is the gender identification given by the man; this is not about dogs in general, but about male dogs in particular. When he announces that what is good about dogs is their "great freedom," the reader needs to insert the words "male dogs" in place of "dogs." The Italian language makes this distinction clearer with its word endings based on gender. The male dog, unlike the man and his wife, does not wait until night to mount the female, the bitch; the old man admires the male dog's enthusiasm, its freedom from clocks and customs.

The old man conjures up one particular memory of unbridled instinct in the next stanza: Here he identifies with the male dog's freedom from ritual and recalls his own youthful exuberance when, in full daylight, he "did it in a wheatfield, just like a dog" with a woman whose name he cannot recall. The stanza ends with the meditation's final words: If he were young again, he'd like to do it in a wheat field forever.

The entire reverie ends when the man is interrupted by others watching the scene; he is no longer alone with his memories and yearnings. Now the social world enters. A priest turns away from the "action," a woman watches, and a boy ruins the moment by throwing stones at the coupling dogs. The old man "is indignant," not because of his concern for the dogs, but because his own link to the world of instinct and sexuality—his only link now that he is old—has been severed.

Forms and Devices

Typically, poets who write without rhyme or meter in irregular stanzas attract readers with their verbal inventiveness—either metaphorical leaps or musical cadences. Pavese is an exception to this principle. The music of the poem is flat, colloquial, without flourish. In addition, the poem is not in the least metaphorical; in fact, only two similes occur: The old man "did it in a wheatfield, just like a dog," and doing it in the wheat field was like doing it "in bed." Pavese's draw is his point of view. By the 1930's he had as a central character in a poem an old man whose mind is less than stereotypically poetic, and he offers the reader a voyage into the mind of a man in tune with the most basic elements of life, the animalistic underbelly of civilized decorum. Not many other poets of the time wrote about old men with flies on their gums watching dogs coupling. Pavese attracts because of his honesty, his directness, his ability to create poetry out of the essential—but often neglected—aspects of life.

Also, Pavese uses a cinematic device in his poems to create and enhance this realistic surface. It is almost as if a camera shot is used for each stanza: The reader moves from the old man in the doorway watching the dogs in the piazza, to the memories of the man making love with his wife in their bed at night, to the man in the wheat field having sex "like a dog," to the man again watching the dogs in the piazza getting separated by the stone-throwing boy. If some poems lose readers because of the convolutions in plot or direction, the avant-garde slipperiness of the poem's meaning, this is not one of them. Pavese's writing is winning because of, to use his own words, the "solid honesty of the objective style" of his poems.

One place where Pavese may lose some of his audience is with his word choice. His character of the old man conflates *la cagna*—a female dog—with women, calling them both *le cagne*. Perhaps in Italian this conflation does not call attention to itself, but in the English translation Pavese sounds a little rough when his old man thinks that his woman was "like all bitches," or when he cannot remember "who the bitch was" with whom he had sex in the wheat field. The purpose of this conflation is clear: The old man yearns for the simplicity and naturalness of the animal kingdom and remembers with fondness the moments he shared in that holy unity with the natural world. However, this substitution of the word "bitch" for "woman" may exceed some readers' threshold of acceptability for a poem's literary devices.

Themes and Meanings

In *Lavorare stanca*, "Instinct" is the third-from-last poem in the collection, in a section entitled "Paternity." The poems that precede it and follow it begin with these words: *L'uomo solo, Uomo solo,* and *L'uomo solo* (the man alone, a man alone, and the man alone). Although *Instinct* begins differently, with *L'uomo vecchio* (the old man), the result is the same. This poem and the collection as a whole ends with a man alone, cut off from the natural world and, by extension, the world of sexual intimacy.

If this poem fits into a section of the book called "Paternity," it is only ironically. This old man is as removed as possible from the world of paternity, of sexual coupling. His teeth are removed from his gums, his memories are removed from the present reality of his solitude, and so he is, as the poem announces in the first line, "disappointed in everything."

One could offer perhaps a more optimistic reading of the poem's meaning by suggesting that no one can take away the man's memories, or that time's power to decimate is counteracted by the power of human memory to re-create scenes from the past. Yet this reading takes away from the poem's overwhelming sense of loss and displacement. The old man is no longer a participant in life's feast; he is now relegated to the status of voyeur, and what he sees is an instinctual world that he has lost completely. Even his life as a voyeur is interrupted by the stone-throwing boy who cannot tolerate the scary, foreboding world of instinct and sexuality.

Pavese wrote this poem in Italy during the Fascist reign of Benito Mussolini, when citizens were encouraged to raise their voices in praise of the accomplishments of their leaders or their "race." Pavese chose another route; rather than blinding himself to the realities of his world, he chose to speak honestly in a plain voice about the suffering and "disappointments" of himself and his people through direct, unembellished, realistic poems.

Kevin Boyle

THE INVITATION TO THE VOYAGE

Author: Charles Baudelaire (1821-1867)
Type of poem: Lyric
First published: 1857, as "L'Invitation au Voyage," in *Les Fleurs du mal*; English translation collected in *Flowers of Evil*, 1963

The Poem

"The Invitation to the Voyage" is number 53 in *Les Fleurs du mal* (*Flowers of Evil*, 1909), part of the book's "Spleen and Ideal" section. Written in direct address, the poem uses the familiar forms of pronouns and verbs, which the French language reserves for children, close family, lovers and long-term friends, and prayer.

Charles Baudelaire was a master of traditional French verse form. In this poem, he chose to employ stanzas of twelve lines, alternating with a repeating two-line refrain. Each stanza is divided into distinct halves built on an *aabccb, ddeffe* rhyme pattern. An initial pair of rhyming five-syllable lines is followed by a seven-syllable line, another rhyming couplet of five-syllable lines, then a seven-syllable line which rhymes with the preceding seven-syllable line. The pattern of five-and seven-syllable lines is repeated with new rhymes then followed by the refrain couplet of seven-syllable lines. The regular alternation of long and short lines produces a gently syncopated rhythm, difficult to duplicate in translation.

The poem opens gently, addressing the beloved as "My child, my sister." She is invited to dream of the sweetness of another place, to live, to love, and to die in a land which resembles her. The tone is intimate, the outlines gently blurred. The lady and the destination are described with ambiguity: The suns there are damp and veiled in mist; the lady's eyes are treacherous and shine through tears. The refrain promises order, beauty, luxury, calm, and voluptuous pleasure in the indefinite "there."

In the second stanza, the poet describes an interior scene, a luxurious bedroom where time, light and color, and scent and exoticism combine to speak the secret language of the soul. The description is made in the conditional form; this dream interior has not yet been realized. Again, the refrain returns with its promise of order and beauty, now in reference to the room which has just been described.

The last stanza presents a landscape, an ideal scene of ships at anchor in canals, ships which have traveled from the ends of the earth to satisfy the whims of the lady. Although vagabond by nature, they are gathered to sleep on canals which, unlike the untamed sea, are waters controlled and directed by human agency. As in the first stanza, the tone is generalized; the poet speaks of sunsets in the plural. The light of the sunsets, which dresses the fields, canals, and town, is described in terms of precious stones ("hyacinth," as a color, may be the blue-purple of a sapphire or the reddish orange of a dark topaz) and gold, recalling the luxury of the second stanza. The stanza ends in warm light and sleep as the refrain returns with its promise of order, beauty, and calm.

Forms and Devices

"The Invitation to the Voyage" makes full use of the music of language as its carefully measured lines paint one glowing picture after another. A successful translation must approximate as much as possible the verbal harmony produced in the original language, with its gentle rhythm and rich rhymes. Equally important appeals are made to the senses of sight and smell in the images employed by the poet.

The three stanzas of "The Invitation to the Voyage" correspond to three visual images, three landscapes. The first is vague and hazy, a "somewhere" where the poet emphasizes the qualities of misty indistinctness and moisture. There is sunlight, but it is diffuse. The "suns" of the imaginary landscape are doubled by the lady's eyes. The beloved and the imaginary landscape are alike mysterious and indistinct.

In the second stanza, the interior scene is also distinguished by its light, reflected from age-polished furniture and profound mirrors. It is also distinguished by the rare perfume of flowers mixed with amber. As with the light, the amber scent is "vague." The emphasis is on complexity of stimuli: many-layered scents and elaborate decoration enhanced by time and exotic origin. The intimate tone of the first stanza is preserved through this descriptive passage; it is "our" room which is pictured, and the last line of the stanza echoes the "sweetness" of the beginning of the "Invitation" by describing the native language of the soul as "sweet."

In the third stanza, a second exterior landscape is presented, with many elements of a Dutch genre painting: ships, with their implied voyages behind them, slumbering on orderly canals, the hint of a town in the background, the whole warmed by the golden light of the setting sun. The eye is invited to enjoy this picture, a glowing visual image painted with words. The environment is not the enclosed, hothouse atmosphere of the second stanza. The light is wider, more expanded, the poignant hyacinth and gold of sunset. Still, the gem quality of the "hyacinth" light recalls the opulence of the second stanza, as the "sunsets" of the third stanza echo the "suns" of the first.

The three visual images presented by the main stanzas of the poem are connected in many ways. The most obvious is the repeated refrain, with its indefinite "There," which refers simultaneously to each separate scene and to the imaginary whole. With each return of the refrain, the poet tightens the embrace that holds the poem together in an intimate unity.

The complex pattern of rhyme in the original version is also an instrument of the poetic unity, especially since it is doubled by an interior structure of repetition and assonance. The fourth and fifth lines begin with the same word, *aimer* ("to love"). No less than nine lines begin with *d* and fourteen with *l*. Moreover, there is a striking incidence of *l, s,* and *r* sounds throughout the poem, forming a whispering undercurrent of sound. Even when this effect is lost in translation, the formal structure of the poem and the strength of its images ensure that the reader will be struck by its unified construction.

Themes and Meanings

In *Flowers of Evil*, and most particularly in the "Spleen and Ideal" section, Baudelaire explored self-destruction and exaltation, beauty in its most sordid and ethereal forms, and the place of the poet in interpreting human sensation and knowledge. "The Invitation to the Voyage" is one of the most beautiful of his "ideal" poems, a tour-de-force of seductive appeal, a love poem which offers the beloved a world of beauty. The more beautiful and desirable the world of the poem, the greater the compliment to the lady, since the poet declares them to be alike. The complexity and richness of the formal structure of rhyme and rhythm are echoed in the thematic structures of the interior and exterior landscapes, where ornament and exotic luxury are highly valued. Adventure and the outer world are at a distance, exotic themes which perfume the dream without troubling it. The wandering boats are still and asleep on canals, not the wild ocean. The "ends of the earth" send their treasures, but they are to be protected in a closed space, not diffused.

The "voyage" to which the beloved is invited is an imaginary and interior one. The qualities of warmth, diffused light, vague perfume, order, and luxurious and exotic ornamentation are cultivated beauties, neither wild nor natural. Everything within this enclosed paradise is united by an intimate harmony and communicates in the intimate and secret language of the soul.

The beloved must be convinced to enter this ideal world, where every desire is fulfilled. The first stanza presents the invitation in gentle terms, addressing the beloved as "my child" and "my sister." Yet, in contrast to the later stanzas, suffused in light and warmth, the first stanza speaks of ambiguities: love coupled with death, sunshine with dampness, misty skies. The beloved herself is the prototype of the imaginary world—charming but mysterious and treacherous. She is also the "sister" of the speaker, intimately known and like him. Readers meet her especially through the image of her eyes, shining through their tears.

Eyes are a frequent image in Baudelaire's poems. In "Autumn Sonnet" (number 64 of *Flowers of Evil*), the eyes of the beloved are "clear like crystal." In "The Cat" (number 51 of *Flowers of Evil*), the poet gazes into a cat's eyes with astonishment and sees fire, clear lights, living opals—which stare back at him. In "Beauty" (number 17 of *Flowers of Evil*), Baudelaire ends the sonnet with the image of the eyes of the goddess Beauty, pure mirrors which fascinate poets. In many of these poems, the eyes are inscrutable sources of light or living mirrors and a means by which the poet's gaze is turned back upon himself. In gazing at the Other, be it cat or goddess, the poet is thrown back on his own yearning soul.

The diffuse light and misty eyes of "The Invitation to the Voyage" conceal the pain implicit in the bond of poet and lady, the betrayal and tears present in the formation of the imaginary world of the poem. The beloved, the speaker, and their world are intimately bound in a unity where luxury, calm, order, and sensual beauty are a means of control over the ambiguous mystery and sorrow of life. The poetic text itself is emblematic of the promised paradise. The beauty, formal order, and musical appeal to the senses fulfill that promise and build that world.

Anne W. Sienkewicz

AN IRISH AIRMAN FORESEES HIS DEATH

Author: William Butler Yeats (1865-1939)
Type of poem: Dramatic monologue
First published: 1919, in *The Wild Swans at Coole*

The Poem

"An Irish Airman Foresees His Death" is a short dramatic monologue, originally one of four poems written by William Butler Yeats to commemorate the death of Major Robert Gregory, son of Lady Augusta Gregory (Yeats's onetime patron and later his colleague). Gregory, never a close personal friend of Yeats, was a multitalented Renaissance man, titled Irish gentry, athlete, aviator, scholar, and artist who, even though over the age for compulsory military service, enlisted in World War I. He did so because it was a magnificent avenue for adventure.

The poem is equally divided into two eight-line sentences with four iambic tetrameter quatrains. Yeats writes in the first person, donning the persona of the airman as he prepares to go into battle in the sky. In the first quatrain, Yeats shows the airman's ambiguous feelings about fighting in the war; he has no strong emotions concerning either those he is fighting against or those he is fighting to protect. Even with these mixed sentiments, however, he is sure that he will die in this adventure. Not only is death from enemy contact possible but also, with aviation in its infancy, the chances for mechanical error multiply the dangers he faces.

The second quatrain continues this ambiguity as the airman realizes the fruitlessness of his participation in the war. He knows that no matter what the outcome of his personal battles, they will not affect the overall war effort—nor will the outcome of the war affect the lives of the Irish peasants with whom he identifies.

The third quatrain indicates the selfish desire for adventure that was the airman's reason for enlisting to fight. His rugged individualism made his choice preordained; only his method of fighting was open. True to a romantic tradition, the airman chose the imagined "chivalry" of single combat in the rarefied heavens over the anonymity of the wholesale slaughter which the ground soldier confronted on the battlefield when faced with the advancements of modern warfare. Gone were the traditional concepts of bravery and honor; the arbitrariness of artillery, machine-gun fire, and poison gas killed randomly.

In the final line of the last quatrain, Yeats leaves the first person when he says, "In balance with this life, this death." Particular attention should be paid to Yeats's shift to "this" life, "this" death as opposed to using "my." He is universalizing the airman's experiences, transcending the politics of World War I and moving to the realization of the futility of all wars, all waste of human life.

Throughout the poem, the airman feels no sense of disappointment, no misgivings about his fate, no disillusionment about his outcome. He has accepted the challenge in the tradition of the romantic hero and will continue on toward his preordained end.

Forms and Devices

At first glance, the structure of the poem seems awkward, almost as if Yeats made punctuation errors by omitting periods. There are also two locations where he has used semicolons rather than commas (after "clouds above" in line 2 and after "clouds" in line 12). Yeats uses these semicolons to provide positive links with the thoughts immediately following. He links (and contrasts) the serenity in the line ending "clouds above" with the agitation among the populace, figuratively "below" him both in space and temperament. In line 12, he uses the semicolon to link (and contrast) the "tumult in the clouds" with the clear, rational balancing of his mind.

Yeats, always the quintessential Irish nationalist, uses this poem as a vehicle to allude ironically to the part that the Irish played in World War I. When the airman states, "Those that I fight I do not hate,/ Those that I guard I do not love," he is showing implicitly that the Irish, who were constantly at odds with British domination, were forced into the war on the Allied side with ambivalent feelings. They had no more sympathy for the British than they had for the Germans.

Voluntarily fighting as a British ally, the airman may be grouped with the "Byronic heroes," the literary epitome of Romantic individuality. True to this metaphor, the airman comes to realize his own self-destruction and embraces it with composure and aristocratic nonchalance. He did not have to fight, but when "A lonely impulse of delight/ Drove to this tumult in the clouds," he joins the legions of Byronic heroes (Robert Browning's Childe Roland, Alfred, Lord Tennyson's Ulysses, and Lord Byron's Manfred, to name a few) who are a combination of boundless energy and fatalistic recklessness.

The airman knew that his death was predestined; it can be compared to the death of Icarus from Greek mythology. Icarus, ignoring his father's (Daedalus's) warnings as they were escaping from Minos in Crete, flew too near the sun on the wax and feather wings that he and his father had constructed. The heat from the sun melted the wax, and Icarus fell to his death. The airman knows that as he continues to be driven to the "tumult in the clouds" he, too, will eventually meet his death.

This foreknowledge of fate is effectively used, as is the juxtaposition of contrasting thoughts throughout the poem. Two prevalent examples are the airman not hating the enemy and not loving the Allies. The airman is placing himself above such emotions and continuing on his personal "quest" for adventure. In the age of technologically advanced weaponry, it would be impossible for the Byronic hero to pursue his adventures on the ground; it was left to the Yeatsian hero to turn to the skies.

Themes and Meanings

In "An Irish Airman Foresees His Death," Yeats uses the dramatic monologue to accomplish a dual purpose. Yeats is using the death of an Irish hero to further the prestige of Irish nationalism; Gregory was well-suited for the purpose. He was of the nobility; he was a volunteer in the truest sense of the word; he was a worldly, sophisticated Renaissance man; he was a war hero (recipient of the Military Cross); and he was an Irish patriot. No matter what the true reason Gregory chose to fight in World War I, he was an ideal vehicle for Yeats's propaganda.

Several ironic facts may be noted about Gregory's death and about the possible influence that he may have had (if his life had continued) on both the public and private sphere. Gregory was accidentally shot down by an Allied war plane, a fact that Yeats did not know at the time he composed this poem. Gregory also had been active in Irish politics prior to his enlistment. After the war, England sent in the hated Black and Tans to enforce order in Ireland. Because of Gregory's prestige and power, he may have been able to exert some mollifying control over the chain of events that immediately followed the armistice. His death also led his impoverished wife to sell his ancestral home, Coole, because she was unable to manage the estate.

Yeats's second purpose is to explore the futility of war and the waste of human life that results. The airman balances his past life and his future, and decides that they are equally wasteful. War will have no effect either on him or on the populace for whom the war is supposedly being fought. The banality of the situation is that the airman is able to see this and is able to ignore the emotional pleas that are normally used to entice men to fight. Yeats was confronted with a complex problem. The traditional language of poetry was of no use in conveying the ghastly horrors of modern trench warfare. Many poets, such as Siegfried Sassoon, Wilfred Owen, and Edward Thomas, developed a new language and form to meet these new demands. For Yeats, an escape back to the traditional romantic hero allowed him to voice his own poignant protest in a world gone mad.

Stephen H. Crane

IRREPRESSIBLY BRONZE, BEAUTIFUL AND MINE

Author: Ntozake Shange (Paulette Williams, 1948-   )
Type of poem: Lyric
First published: 1987, in *Ridin' the Moon in Texas: Word Paintings*

The Poem

Ridin' the Moon in Texas, the collection of poems containing "irrepressibly bronze, beautiful and mine," responds to particular works of art. The artwork to which "irrepressibly bronze" specifically responds is an untitled photograph of a man's back by acclaimed and controversial photographer Robert Mapplethorpe. The poem, occupying four and one-half pages, is not an extended description of the photograph; rather, it is a poem on a topic—black men—inspired by it.

The poem is divided into three sections, all written in free verse. The first section, written in the first person, itself seems to break up into two parts. The first part provides a history of the speaker's sexual awakening. It begins with a childhood crush on a friend of her father who used to arrive in St. Louis each summer with different white women. The speaker thought of this man as hers because he was black, as she is. This memory triggers another, of laughing and playing with young boys who would grow up into black men "if they lived so long." She remembers the sexual excitement and mild sense of danger of dancing with black men as a young woman.

This leads into a part of the poem, written in the present tense—a portion that reads like a seduction. "Look at me pretty niggah," she says, and "bring it on baby." The language in this part of the poem is explicitly sensuous, clearly sexual, and full of images of "holding your heart" and other representations of love. When the speaker says, "you rode off & left/ your heart in the palm/ of my child hand," it seems that person she is addressing is still the friend of her father who used to visit in the summer.

In section 2, the poem begins a transformation. Grammatically, this section expands outward, from the first-person singular to the first-person plural. By the end, the narrator is talking about "our beauty" and "our heroes." Similarly, the personal tone of the first section becomes political when she identifies the man who used to arrive each summer as "of course george jackson," referring to the black militant and writer who died in prison. The line *"soledad, soledad"* is at once a reference to the Soledad Prison, where George Jackson served time; to his book, *Soledad Brother* (1971), written in prison; and to the literal translation of this Spanish word, "solitude." Ntozake Shange pictures Jackson fighting for air in prison and associates him with two other slain black activists, Malcolm X and Martin Luther King, Jr. This triggers a chain of associations of black men whom she considers beautiful for their courage, including Bob Marley, the legendary reggae performer, and Jackie Wilson, the popular soul singer of the 1960's and 1970's who died in the 1980's. The closing line of this section, *"soledad mi amor soledad,"* seems to be a meditation not only about George

Jackson and his imprisonment but also about the solitude of assassination, or simply neglect, visited upon many of the strongest black men of her youth.

Section 3 is a brief description of lovers making love under palm trees. Against the mournful, almost elegiac background of the second section, this description of petticoats and panties being pulled down, of the music of muscles, of shoulders and bodies in motion, and of jaguars prowling "when their/ eyes meet" is presented as a life-affirming image. Under these trees, young black women make love with young black men whose lives are threatened and often cut short by the violence of a racist society.

Forms and Devices

Ntozake Shange is perhaps best known as a playwright who infuses her plays with poetry. It should come as no surprise, then, that her poetry has its own theatricality; that is, it is poetry which is best read aloud.

In "irrepressibly bronze, beautiful and mine," she does not use standard punctuation. The only punctuation she allows herself is a slash mark (/), which she uses to indicate a slight pause but not specifically to replace other forms of punctuation. These slash marks can be seen as analogous to the marks of a conductor's sheet that indicate the pace of the music. The effect is that some of Shange's lines of poetry seem to contain several lines within them.

The shift in person the poem undergoes, from first-person singular in section 1 to first-person plural in section 2 to third person in section 3, indicates a similar shift in the perspective of the poem. In the first section, Shange speaks from the point of view of a woman recalling her own sexual awakening and excitement with black men. Thus, the tone is personal. In section 2, she remembers the struggles and deaths that black men have faced in her lifetime. The identification of the man about whom she was specifically speaking in section 1 as George Jackson should not be taken too literally. Rather, she is painting a collective picture of the black man: The black man is Jackson, Malcolm X, Martin Luther King, Jr., Jackie Wilson, and many others. Thus, she speaks in a plural voice. The third section tries to put the erotic excitement of young black men and women in perspective. Following the descriptions of men who have had to struggle for life, this section looks approvingly on young men and women taking pleasure in life. The metaphors she uses in this section—of tongues wrapping around each other, of "dew like honey" slipping from lips, and of jaguars prowling when eyes meet—makes it clear not only that making love is a life-affirming act but also that it is an act that can productively express the ferocity of the lives of black youths.

Themes and Meanings

The reader of "irrepressibly bronze, beautiful and mine" should recall that the late 1980's, when the poem was written, was a period of raging political and literary debate about the depiction of black men in novels by black women—and in the media at large—as brutal rapists and victimizers. This debate frequently centered on Alice

Masterplots II

Walker's novel (and the film adaptation of) *The Color Purple* (1982). Shange often found herself in the middle of the debate because of her widely popular play, *for colored girls who have considered suicide/ when the rainbow is enuf* (1976), which depicted black men as potential rapists and killers of black women. Against this backdrop, "irrepressibly bronze, beautiful and mine" can be seen for what it is—a political love poem to black men.

The basic message of the poem is that the speaker has for all of her life felt intimately connected to black men. The black man she is addressing toward the end of section 1 is literally the friend of her father, who used to appear every summer, but is also an image of black men she has known throughout her life. All of her life, she says to him, she has been holding his heart in her hand. This is a turn on the cliché of holding *"my* heart in my hand" and implies not that she has always wanted to give herself to him but that she has always felt that she had a part of *him* she wanted to give to him. It also implies that the man in question, who is a stand-in for black men in general, has a lot of heart, so much that he could leave some with her.

The list of black male heroes in section 2 is a tribute to the hearts of these men and an appreciation of the way they have defined the black spirit of which she feels a part. It is to the struggle and pain of defining this spirit that she pays tribute.

The third section of this poem should also be read historically. A widely expressed belief of the time held that the lack of moral values within the black community was responsible for the ongoing economic subjugation of blacks and that sexuality in young people was best repressed. Opposed to this, Shange stresses the sense of vitality, excitement, and completion in sexuality.

The title of this poem provides a good clue to understanding the poem itself. That the person is "irrepressible" implies a vitality of spirit that cannot be contained. The element of sensuality implicit in describing him as "bronze, beautiful and mine" conveys not only the deep intimacy the speaker feels for her subject but also contains in language the sensuousness of spirit celebrated and infused by the poem.

Thomas J. Cassidy

ISOLATION. TO MARGUERITE

Author: Matthew Arnold (1822-1888)
Type of poem: Lyric
First published: 1857, in *Poems* (revised edition)

The Poem

Matthew Arnold's "Isolation. To Marguerite" is—as its title suggests—a poem about a lover's keen awareness of human isolation. Each of the work's seven stanzas intensifies both the lover's feelings of separation and his increasing devotion to his beloved. Indeed, in order to experience his love more deeply, the lover commands his heart to "keep the world away." As he begins to feel that he has stood the test of loyalty to his love, he declares (in the first stanza) his belief that his beloved has "likewise" grown in her love for him. Love is dramatized at the beginning of the poem as a daily discipline, a rededication of the heart to the beloved that demands a single focus undistracted by the world at large. He strives for a "more constant" love that will create a "home" exclusively for Marguerite.

The strong sense of a bond between the lovers is challenged in the second stanza, which develops an image of the heart as a great sea ebbing and swelling with feeling. Fixated on his own feelings, the lover declares that the "heart can bind itself alone." His fear (a word first mentioned in the first stanza) is that the heart is "self-swayed"; that is, the more acutely he feels his love, the more isolated he becomes. He is prone to misgivings that turn to panic: "Thou lov'st no more;—Farewell! Farewell!"

In the third stanza, the lover's feelings of isolation concentrate on an image of the "lonely heart" that inhabits a separate, remote universe revolving around its own passions. Addressing this conception of the heart's "sphered course" the lover exclaims: "Back to thy solitude again!" This last line suggests a view of love as an eternal return to feelings that isolate the lover.

The fourth and fifth stanzas return to the image of the ebbing and flowing sea—its tides controlled by the moon. The lover invokes the classical myth of Luna and Endymion, the story of how the moon fell in love with a man. Such is the pull of love that even a "chaste queen" can feel the "conscious thrill of shame" excited by love. Yet the heaven of such a god is "far removed" from the lover's conviction that the human heart has "long had place to prove/ This truth—to prove, and make thine own:/ 'Thou hast been, shalt be, art, alone.'" The history of humanity, in other words, is a perennial record of isolation.

In the sixth and seventh stanzas, the lover feels so bereft, so alienated from the rest of the world, by his own passions that he can hardly admit the heart is "not quite alone." Yet his proximity is to "unmating things" such as the "Ocean and clouds and night and day." If this world includes love, it is the love of "happier men" who have "*dreamed* two human hearts might blend/ In one." These men experience a sense of "faith released/ From isolation." The emphasis on the word "dreamed" implies that in fact human isolation persists even among those who believe they have overcome it. In fact, they do not know they are no "less/ Alone than thou" in their "loneliness."

Forms and Devices

The fervor of Arnold's poem is enhanced by his tightly controlled eight-syllable lines built upon repetition of key words, rhythms, and rhymes:

> We were apart; yet day by day,
> I bade my heart more constant be.
> I bade it keep the world away,
> And grow a home for only thee;

Thus the poem begins with the announcement of a separation and the evocation of what it is like all the time to be alone and to make a world only out of feelings for the beloved.

Several stanzas begin with terse statements and exclamations that terminate in midline or stop the line short after only one word: "We were apart" (stanza 1); "The fault was grave!" (stanza 2); "Farewell!" (stanza 3); "Back!" (stanza 4). These abrupt announcements reflect the speaker's unsettled mood, the very ebb and flow of feeling he describes in stanza 2. He swings between extreme feelings, almost angry at his turbulent emotions, which begin to subside and give way to a more resigned, philosophical tone only in the last three stanzas, which brood on the nature of human feelings and how they tend to isolate human beings, except for those "happier men" who seem able to sustain the illusions of being united with their loves.

Arnold also uses the repetition of key words as a pattern of overlapping echoes from stanza to stanza. Thus in stanza 2, just after he has compared the heart's rhythms to the "ebb and swell" of the sea, he exclaims "Farewell! Farewell!"—a dramatic portrayal of swaying feelings that is carried into the next stanza, which begins with the repetition of "Farewell!" Similarly, the end of stanza 3, which declares, "Back to thy solitude again!," is immediately followed in stanza 4 by "Back!" In other words, the poem develops a vocabulary of key words that reinforce the rocking of feeling that moves the lover.

The nexus between truth, faith, feeling, and knowledge—the words and concepts that bind together the beginning and ending of the poem—is intensified in the poem's final stanza, in which Arnold contrasts the illusions of men who feel they have found love and union with his own awareness that they are "alone" in "their loneliness." The lover brings an awareness of what he acknowledges in the first stanza: "I might have known,/ What far too soon, alas! I learned" that "faith may oft be unreturned" and what he wryly concludes in the fifth stanza "This truth—to prove, and make thine own:/ 'Thou has been, shalt be, art, alone.'"

The poem's circular structure, then, imitates the lover's image in stanza 3 of the heart's "remote and sphered course." The poem comes back to the same key words because human emotions tend to revolve in the same circuits or orbits from which they can find no release, except in the illusory "faith released/ From isolation" described in the work's conclusion.

Themes and Meanings

On the most obvious level, "Isolation. To Marguerite" seems self-explanatory: It is an evocation of human isolation that is intensified by the lover's yearning to unite with his beloved. Although he bravely begins by envisioning a world that is made out of his love for Marguerite, and out of her love for him, the element of doubt is already raised by his use of the word "fear." The world is not one in which love is readily reciprocated. On the contrary, it is a world in which human feelings are in flux and where human hearts are separate and can only yearn for fusion. The self is alone, the lover announces in the middle of the poem. Indeed, solitude is proclaimed as though it were a judgment on human behavior: "Thou has been, shalt be, art, alone." The finality of the phrasing is a crushing blow barely mitigated by the final stanzas, which acknowledge that not all people have found happiness and apparent communion with their lovers.

The poet expresses a bleak message that is tempered by his recognition that human beings will continue to search for love and to express their faith in love. It is a faith he seems to have lost by acquiring knowledge. What he knows of the world and its history prevents him from sharing the faith of others and overcoming his sense of isolation. He also suggests, however, that this faith he cannot share blinds others to the true nature of the world, which is one that includes an awareness of how utterly alone the human heart is.

Arnold's poem takes its place in a body of work that mourns the loss of faith. There is, for example, his great image of the ebbing sea of faith in "Dover Beach" (1867). Like that great poem, "Isolation. To Marguerite" is a love poem that meditates on a world that is no longer, in the poet's view, united by religion or any coherent body of beliefs. Individuals are thus thrown back upon themselves, probing their feelings without the support of a comforting worldview. They still desire faith but feel they know too much to surrender the bitter truths they have learned through experience. What remains for people, and for the poem, is a heroic struggle with the consciousness of a fragmented world. Arnold renews the themes of "Isolation. To Marguerite" in "To Marguerite—Continued," in which he observes "we mortal millions live *alone*" and yet are plagued by a feelings that "we were/ Parts of a single continent!"

Carl Rollyson

ISRAFEL

Author: Edgar Allan Poe (1809-1849)
Type of poem: Lyric
First published: 1831, in *Poems*; revised in *The Raven and Other Poems*, 1845

The Poem

"Israfel" is a lyrical poem of eight uneven stanzas, each stanza ranging from five to eight lines in length. The title is the name of an angel mentioned in the Koran, the sacred book of the Muslims. Edgar Allan Poe appended a note to this poem to make sure that his readers understood Israfel's significance; the note read: "And the angel Israfel, whose heartstrings are a lute, and who has the sweetest voice of all God's creatures—KORAN." Israfel's importance as a singer or artist is central to the poem, and Poe's consideration here of creativity—singing and music making—reflects a typical concern of other Romantic poets such as George Gordon, Lord Byron, Percy Bysshe Shelley, and John Keats. The poem is written in the first person from the point of view of someone—perhaps Poe himself—who is also a singer or creator of some sort, but readers do not discover this important information until the last stanza of the poem. The poem begins by stating that an angel lives in heaven and that his name is Israfel. Israfel, who is so creative that his very heart is a musical instrument, is such a wonderful singer that, according to legend, the stars even stop their own "hymns" to listen to him. The moon is, moreover, in love with him, while the lightning and constellations such as the "Pleiads" listen as well.

In the third stanza, Poe begins to explain what makes Israfel's music so lovely that even the heavens take notice: His singing is exquisite and passionate because of the instrument he plays—his own heart ("The trembling living wire"). In this stanza, Poe refers to this instrument as a "lyre" (a stringed instrument like a harp), but in the first stanza he calls it a "lute" (a stringed instrument more like a guitar or mandolin). In the fourth stanza, Poe explains that where Israfel lives ("the skies that angel trod") is extraordinary ("deep thoughts are a duty") and beautiful (the Houri, beautiful women who wait in heaven for the devout Muslim, are as lovely as stars here).

For these reasons (because his surroundings are so lovely and because he plays his music from his heart), Israfel is not wrong to despise inferior art ("An unimpassioned song"); he deserves the reward of being called "Best bard" (the greatest singer), and he deserves to wear the honorary crown of the most skillful—the laurels. Here the poem shifts slightly in that Poe addresses Israfel directly; he writes, "thou art not wrong." In the last two stanzas, the tone of the poem changes dramatically, and we see the speaker emerging more forcefully and somewhat bitterly. Poe tells Israfel that all that is in Heaven is there for Israfel while people on earth live with both pain and pleasure: in "a world of sweets and sours,/ Our flowers are merely—flowers." The poem concludes with the somewhat angry observation that if the speaker of the poem could live in heaven and Israfel on earth, Israfel might not be such a wonderful singer, and he—the speaker or Poe—might be much better.

Forms and Devices

At the center of "Israfel" is the figure of the angel, Israfel. Since Israfel sings and plays music, since he is referred to as a "bard," and since—by the end of the poem— he is compared to the speaker of the poem who is himself a poet, one can safely assume that Israfel serves as a representative for the artist or the creative spirit. As such, one might refer to Israfel as a metaphor for the artist, as a stand-in which allows Poe to develop his ideas about art, writing, and creativity. Involved in this metaphorical framework are other important aspects of the poem. First, Israfel's instrument—or his means to create—is represented variously by a lute, a lyre, and his human heart. The fruits of Israfel's creativity are rendered as singing and as music so that these two creative efforts become emblematic for all creative efforts. Finally, those who listen to Israfel's music are the heavens; his audience includes the highest and most unreachable elements in the physical world—stars, lightning, the moon, constellations.

Although the rhymes in "Israfel" are unpredictable, conforming to no particular formal pattern, each stanza is intricately and skillfully set to rhyme. Most stanzas have only two distinct end rhymes (the first stanza rhymes "dwell," "well," "Israfel," "tell," and "spell" as the first rhyme and "lute" and "mute" as the second), but occasionally a stanza has three different rhymes (the second stanza rhymes "above" and "love," "noon" and "moon," and "levin," "even," "seven," and "heaven"). Sometimes Poe uses near rhymes, words which do not quite repeat the same sounds (in the last stanza, "I" and "melody"); and sometimes he uses visual rhymes, words which look alike but sound different (in the second stanza, "even" and "seven").

Like the rhymes in "Israfel," the meters and the stanza structures are uneven and refuse to conform to a particular pattern. Occasionally, the poem establishes a regular rhythm only to interrupt the pattern it sets up. In the first stanza, for example, the opening four lines have three beats each, while the next two lines carry on and increase the momentum with four beats per line. Suddenly, however, the stanza ends with an abrupt line of only two beats. Sometimes readers feel a little disrupted and surprised by such techniques.

Several sets of polarities or oppositions are set up in "Israfel," and these become central to Poe's focus in the poem. There is, first, the distinction between heaven and earth: Israfel, an angel, lives in heaven, and the speaker of the poem is an inhabitant of earth. Israfel's world is so far superior to the speaker's that what is "shadow" for Israfel becomes "sunshine" in the earthly realm. Israfel is, moreover, a "spirit" while the speaker, again, is flesh and blood. There is also the opposition between singing and silence, since those who are most moved by the artistry of Israfel are moved to listen and to remain "mute." Finally, there is the beauty of the heavens, the "deep thoughts," the lovely Houris, and the sense of love as mature and fully developed ("Where Love's a grown-up god"). This excellence is set against the real world of "sweets and sours" where even beautiful things are limited: "Our flowers are merely—flowers."

Themes and Meanings

During the Romantic period in both British and American literature the attention of many writers—especially poets—turned to the issue of creativity itself. By the end of the eighteenth century an emphasis on individualism prevailed, and creativity was seen as an expression of the imaginative spirit of an intensely feeling and expressive soul. In "Israfel," Poe displays many of these attitudes about creativity, creative genius, and art. In his very concern with what makes a superior artist, he finds himself in harmony with other poets and writers of the Romantic age.

Israfel represents the ideal Romantic artist for many reasons, the first of which is that his very heart is his instrument. He plays and sings, in other words, "from the heart," from his passions and his emotions. The Romantic writer trusted emotions; he had turned from the eighteenth century's emphasis on the mind, on logic and reason, to a veneration of feeling, sensitivity, and even sensation. Thus, not only does Israfel play with passion, but he also sings "wildly" with "fire." He is not held back by decorum or inhibition; he sings what he feels.

Like the consummate artist that he represents, Israfel commands respect from the rest of the universe; somehow, what he does when he sings causes all of creation to take notice. Even the inhabitants of the heavens take notice, for Israfel's art is so perfectly an expression of his singing heart that all acknowledge his gift. Finally, Israfel's art is enhanced by his closeness to perfection; he lives, after all, in heaven. He is an angel. The Platonic notion that the world is an inferior representation of some ultimate, perfect ideal informed the thought of many Romantic writers, and Poe reveals himself to be no exception. Heaven and perfection belong to Israfel, so he can sing beautifully.

What of the earthbound artist, however—what of the writer who is not an angel and who does not own heaven and all of heaven's glories? This is the question that the poem seems to raise, for the poem is spoken by just such an artist. The speaker of the poem—probably Poe—reminds Israfel that writing poetry on earth is more difficult than writing poetry in heaven, and he asserts that Israfel would himself not be such a great artist were he "mortal." Even more significantly, the speaker boasts that if he were in Israfel's place, he might sing "a bolder note," a more beautiful song.

Since the speaker, who also is the creator of the poem, is only mortal, his work—this very poem—must be flawed. It will not be the perfect song that Israfel sings. In fact, this might even explain some of the oddities of this poem. Perhaps Poe's use of unmatched stanzas, his irregular patterns of meter and rhyme, and his use of two different words for Israfel's musical instrument ("lute" and "lyre") are simply his evidence of imperfection. Perhaps he indicates, with these reminders of his mortality, that he is still far from the ideal that an artist should seek. His poem is merely—a poem.

Kathleen Margaret Lant

ISSEI STRAWBERRY

Author: David Mura (1952-   )
Type of poem: Meditation
First published: 1995, in *The Colors of Desire*

The Poem

David Mura's "Issei Strawberry" begins with an invitation to an unspecified audience: "Taste this strawberry." The next phrases indicate swift action—the reader is not only to "taste" but also to "spin" and "whirl" the flavor on the tongue. The narrator guides readers through the literal savoring of the fruit in their mouths and also guides them through quite a different panorama, a sweep of the mundane and repetitive gestures of migrant laborers, workers on the Pacific coast, whose job it is to pick and process the strawberries. The narrator invites readers to turn their eyes "west" toward "some. . ./ sleepy California town" and to imagine workers there bending down and up picking the berries. The narrator specifies that the scene is set in the autumn of the 1930's, before World War II.

The poem indicates hardships that the Japanese immigrants have to cope with, including intolerable working conditions, which generate complaints, misery, and eventually labor strikes. Even more deplorable is a situation touched on briefly in the poem and then tossed off: the sad reality that such nonnative people are ignored in the present because they have traditionally been "written out of history" in the past. This situation makes the prosperity that some of the immigrants have been able to achieve even more laudable and significant. In spite of the grueling odds, if they do succeed, that success is miraculous.

Industrious workers of any ethnic background have a right to expect their hard work to pay off; if they are immigrants, they are on the way to realizing the American Dream. For some, the poem suggests, this immigrant dream does, in fact, become reality. For unfortunate others, however, the dream either gets shelved or vanishes. Although, because of government regulations, the immigrants can never own the land that they sweat over, they work it as if it were their own. The poem also suggests that the immigrants' lack of fluency in the English language is a barrier that can cause them to be duped and swindled.

In any case, the harvest is the important thing, and they are motivated by empty purses and by empty promises that spur them to give it their all. They believe that in working hard they are "gaining a harvest, a country, a future." The poem makes plain the posture of servitude that the immigrants are compelled to assume. Rather than presume to talk back to a "tart and trickier" foreman if he is unreasonable, for example, they are told to "bit[e] your tongue." This action produces blood in the mouth of the laborer, which literally and figuratively becomes mixed with the blood-red strawberry juice in the mouth of the reader. The poem ends with a plea for "memory" that connects both worker and reader.

Forms and Devices

One of the reasons that "Issei Strawberry" is an unusual poem is that it is a full page long and yet is written in a single sentence. For all its length, its grammar is impeccable. The poem is composed of thirty lines of varying lengths. It is unrhymed and has no discernible meter. The four shortest lines, which are notably much shorter than the other lines, all mention gestures of loss or anger in some way: Line 4 ends in "spit," line 10 ends in "declines," line 19 says "you're no one here," and line 24 ends in "losing." These words and phrases signify that the immigrants are shut out in important ways from the American society that they live and labor in.

The poem is a declarative invitation couched in simple, neutral language that belies its complex and subjective meanings. The only word that a non-Japanese reader might not be familiar with is "Issei," which refers to a first-generation immigrant, someone born in Japan who moves to the United States. Poet Mura is a Sansei, a third-generation Japanese American, the offspring of a Nisei, who is offspring of an Issei.

The only cultural reference in the poem that may require some glossing is "Capra" in line 11. This reference is to the filmmaker Frank Capra, whose 1930's films both relate to the Great Depression and are gently satiric situation comedies. These include *Platinum Blonde* (1931), *Lady for a Day* (1933), *It Happened One Night* (1934), *Mr. Smith Goes to Washington* (1939), and *It's a Wonderful Life* (1946). In general, Capra's films have a naïve, idealistic hero who triumphs because of his essential optimism. Two departures from this essential optimism are notable: the fantasy *Lost Horizon* (1937) and *Meet John Doe* (1941), an exposé of fascist elements in American society. Capra, according to the poem, "redefine[s] an American dream." A filmmaker can mirror the culture around him and, if he is taken seriously, his vision then suggests or prescribes what that culture will be in the future. If Capra is redefining an American dream, it is one that largely ignores the nonnative immigrants and their plights, except for the lucky few who make it in American society. The fact that these Issei are not "preferred," that they do not figure into Capra's films in any meaningful way, is a subtle but real statement of prejudice.

"Issei Strawberry" is an aggressive and passionate poem. It compares the immigrant laborer to a "piston," to "fire," to "a swirling dervish," to "a lover ready to ravish." In contrast to this personal energy, everyone else, the poem says, "declines around you." This is a poem of celebration of the immigrant spirit, one that will ultimately endure and prosper, even if there are roadblocks and setbacks in the present: "you have managed your own/ prosperity, a smacking ripeness on the vine." It is the children who will carry forward this spirit and heritage in the new world.

Themes and Meanings

Strawberries in the poem become symbols of something desired and prized, of sweetness and beauty, but they are gotten at a price. Put another way, they symbolize something that is sought after but that can never be fully possessed. The narrator compares the motions of chewing and savoring strawberries with the bodily motions of the workers as they pick this fruit in the fields. The reader is thus reminded of origins, first principles, getting in touch with essential, undeniable truths.

As the first poem in *The Colors of Desire*, Mura's second volume of poetry, "Issei Strawberry" emphasizes a particular color and a particular desire. This color is red, the color of love, of fire, of blood, and of the strawberry, which all figure in the poem. This red is a passionate color, full of life. The poem uses it to voice a desire for all immigrant groups to succeed and to make a mark for themselves and their descendants in a new culture.

The "desire" in the poem is one of focus and drive and motivation. "Issei Strawberry" forms an appropriate introduction to the other poems in the volume, which are all expressions of strong desire: Some of these desires are productive, and some others—most, in fact—are forbidden. These include racism in the form of a lynching, verbal taunting, and abuse; meditations on the internment camps; pornography and voyeurism; sexual love and transgression; and the miracle of first pregnancy. It is notable that the poems spring directly from Mura's life and the lives of his friends and relatives. To read these poems is to become familiar with important influences, deviations, sorrows, and joys in his personal life. As a Japanese youth who grew up in Chicago to parents who downplayed and repressed their ethnicity, Mura preferred "American" foods and identified with Caucasian film heroes. As a result, he struggled with first denying and then, ultimately, after agonizing suffering and a great deal of destructive behavior, embracing his Japanese ethnicity.

"Issei Strawberry" is important for a number of reasons. First, the poem is relatively brief and its language is accessible; many provocative ideas are compressed into a short space. Second, it raises issues of allegiance to one's ethnic heritage and the difficulties of assimilation. Finally, it touches on important aspects of American culture and history.

Jill B. Gidmark

IT IS A BEAUTEOUS EVENING

Author: William Wordsworth (1770-1850)
Type of poem: Sonnet
First published: 1807, in *Poems in Two Volumes*

The Poem

In William Wordsworth's poem "It Is a Beauteous Evening" the poet is watching the sun set over the ocean; the evening is beautiful and calm, inspiring a mood of religious awe, like "a Nun/ Breathless with adoration." Amid the tranquility, the poet's attention shifts, and he suddenly takes note of the sound of the waves. The noise, "like thunder," shows that the ocean is awake. Its unceasing motion brings to the poet's mind thoughts of eternity.

The reader first realizes that the poet is not alone as he addresses a young girl, who is walking by his side. The scene does not seem to inspire lofty, "solemn" thoughts in her, as it has done in the poet, but her nature is not "less divine" for that reason. On the contrary, she is always close to the divine: She lies "in Abraham's bosom all the year." God is with her, and she is worshiping even when that is not apparent to an observer.

Forms and Devices

The most striking structural feature of the sonnet are the two sudden shifts, each of which adds an important complication to the situation described in the poem's opening lines. The first five lines emphasize the quietness and tranquility of the evening. This natural scene is given a specifically religious dimension when the time is called "holy" in line 2. The epithet blossoms into the metaphor of "a Nun/ Breathless with adoration." The metaphor suggests a tense alertness to the presence of something higher, as opposed to a passive letting go.

The same tension appears in the next lines. The sun is "sinking down in its tranquility." (When Wordsworth calls the sun "broad," he refers very precisely to the well-known visual phenomenon that the sun and moon appear larger as they get close to the horizon.) Yet the heaven "broods"—actively, though gently—"o'er the Sea." The phrase echoes John Milton's rephrasing in *Paradise Lost* (1667, 1674) of Genesis 1:2, in which the "Spirit of God was moving over the face of the waters" just before God creates light. There may be a slight irony to this evocation of creation just as the day is sinking into night. However, the main effect of the metaphor and the allusion in these lines is to underscore the paradoxical fusion of tranquility and alertness while also suggesting a deeper, even religious dimension to the experience of natural beauty.

Line 6 begins with an imperative "Listen!" Shifting from vision to sound and motion, the tranquil scene is paradoxically and unexpectedly loud with "A sound like thunder." By calling the ocean "the mighty Being," Wordsworth evokes God. The ocean "is awake," just as God never sleeps; its waves are in "eternal motion" and make their thunder "everlastingly," just as God is eternal. Thus, in the very tranquility of the scene, as well as in the brooding of the heaven and the motion and sound of the waves, Wordsworth suggests the presence of a higher power.

The poem suddenly shifts again in line 9, when the poet addresses the companion of his walk: "Dear Child! dear Girl!" The imperative "Listen!" in line 6 becomes retrospectively ambiguous: Is it addressed to the reader or to the girl? In lines 1-8, the poet has described the scene in language that evokes the thought of an eternal divine presence. Yet another paradox emerges: The child does not see the scene in this way. Wordsworth puts it negatively that she seems "untouched by solemn thought," apparently feeling she needs some defense for this unawareness. Her nature, he says, "is not therefore less divine." Presumably he does not mean to say, tactlessly, that her nature is less divine than his, but rather to imply that her nature may well be divine, even though she does not show that fact in the way he does, by sensing a higher presence in this natural scene. The child, he suggests, bears divinity within her and does not need to draw it from observing the external world.

This may explain the shift from sensory description of the scene to a biblical language used metaphorically to characterize the girl. She lies "in Abraham's bosom" at all times (Luke 16:22; John 1:18), and she worships "at the Temple's inner shrine" (referring to the Jerusalem Temple, where the Ark of the Covenant was kept in an inner shrine). The meaning of these phrases is made explicit in the final line: God is with the girl constantly, even "when we know it not." The biblical phrases seem to connect with the nun in line 2, thus rounding out the religious dimension the poet is stressing.

The sonnet's rhyme scheme is Italianate (*abbaaccadefdfe*), following the example of Milton. Reading Milton inspired Wordsworth to begin writing sonnets, and eventually he composed many. The first eight lines, or octave, build a strong unit of thought and feeling, in this case with two unsymmetrical components: five mainly visual lines and three lines presenting sound and motion. With the final six lines, or sestet, the thought turns in a way that qualifies the octave. Italianate sonnets usually take care not to end in a couplet, which might give the final two lines too much autonomy. Rather, the main contrast is between the octave and the sestet.

Themes and Meanings

It is characteristic of Wordsworth's poetry to describe nature in a way that evokes some spirit infused in what lies open to sensory observation. As he says in a famous passage from "Lines Composed a Few Miles Above Tintern Abbey,"

> . . . . And I have felt
> A presence that disturbs me with the joy
> Of elevated thoughts; a sense sublime
> Of something far more deeply interfused,
> Whose dwelling is the light of setting suns,
> And the round ocean and the living air,
> And the blue sky, and in the mind of man:

The octave in particular exemplifies this outlook. Yet the metaphor of the nun is surprising. Early in his poetic career, Wordsworth is rarely so explicitly Christian, and a Catholic term is most unusual, since Wordsworth was Anglican and even sympathetic with Methodism.

Even more surprising is the child. Usually, for Wordsworth, adults have been worn down by life's difficulties and demands and have become insensitive to the beauty and healing spirit of nature. Children are much closer to this spirit, and it is the "natural piety," as he calls it elsewhere, that binds the adult through memory to childhood, which provides a nurturing recollection of a higher presence. This child seems indifferent to nature, yet she does not lack a relation to the divine. To describe her religious sensibility, Wordsworth turns to a more biblical and orthodox language than is usual for him and makes her relation to God a matter of inward, spiritual proximity rather than conscious awareness.

Thanks to letters and a journal kept by his sister Dorothy, there is a record of the specific occasion that inspired this sonnet. While traveling in France in the years just after the French Revolution, Wordsworth met Annette Vallon. They fell passionately in love and had a daughter, Caroline, in 1792. Although Vallon was French, Catholic, and from a reasonably prosperous family, whereas Wordsworth was English, Anglican, and penniless, they intended to get married. Her family was strongly opposed and kept them apart. Out of money and with an impending war between France and England, Wordsworth was forced to return to England at the end of 1792.

A few letters from Annette may have reached Wordsworth, but the couple were out of touch until a brief peace in 1801-1802. By then, Wordsworth was about to marry Mary Hutchinson. However, first he needed to settle his relations with Annette. He and his sister traveled to France to meet her and Caroline at Calais. It was one of many walks on the beach that led to the sonnet. Annette was no lover of nature, and the whole Vallon family was deeply Catholic. This may explain Caroline's indifference to the beauty of the scene, and the nun in line 2 may be a quiet allusion to the family religion. Wordsworth did not conceal this story from his friends and family, but he probably judged it inappropriate for public disclosure and in any case distracting from the fundamental contrast the sonnet explores—namely, in contrast to his earlier thinking, that even someone not responsive to the higher power that can be felt in nature might nevertheless have a close spiritual relation to the divine, in a specifically Christian way.

Donald G. Marshall

IT IS DEEP

Author: Carolyn M. Rodgers (1945-   )
Type of poem: Lyric
First published: 1969, in *Songs of a Black Bird*

The Poem

"It Is Deep" is a short dramatic monologue of free verse divided into five stanzas of irregular length. The title, beginning with the indefinite pronoun "it," suggests the slang meaning of "deep": a highly abstract, intellectually profound idea lying beneath layers of superficial meanings. In Carolyn M. Rodgers's poem, the superficial layers stem from the conflicting realities that typically exist between a mother and her adult daughter as the daughter asserts her independence and individuality.

The poet, commenting on her mother's recent visit, notes how different her and her mother's views are on issues of religion, politics, and lifestyle. This difference is particularly noted in their attitudes toward racism. The poet regards her mother, "religiously girdled in her god," as having endured racial oppression by a delusion of heavenly deliverance and meek acquiescence. The poet, however, rebels against racism by stripping the "god" myth away and engaging in revolutionary rejection of the political ideology and lifestyles of white America. The opening of the poem makes the point that the mother, in her dogged role of "religious-negro," cannot appreciate the daughter's racial progress. Thus, when the daughter refuses to use the "witch cord" and gets her telephone disconnected, the mother can only suppose "that her 'baby' was starving" for lack of money to pay bills and buy food. The mother, "gruff and tight-lipped/ and scared," comes to the rescue—uninvited and barely tolerated by the daughter.

The mother's presence only reminds the daughter how little attention her mother pays to things important to her daughter. The mother does not know who "the grand le-roi (al)" is, and she has not seen her daughter's book of poems, which the speaker interprets as a denial of the relevance of black liberation and concludes how much, in "any impression," her mother "would not be/ considered 'relevant' or 'Black.'" However, upon recalling the painful memories of her mother's humiliating encounters with racism, the daughter begins to empathize with her mother's perspective and feels compassion rather than contempt for her mother who is, nonetheless, "here now, not able to understand, what she had/ been forced to deny, still—."

The poet tells of her mother's visit in the first person. With this point of view, the poet/narrator requires only that the reader listen to her complaint about her mother's intrusion. As the conversation recounts this visit, the reader inevitably shares in the poet's discovery of the more profound meaning of the event. "It Is Deep" begins as a simple retelling of the mother's visit, and, as the daughter tells the story, the reader hears not only the details of the visit but also the poet's self-righteous judgment of her mother. Initially, the daughter regards her mother as out of sync with the times. However, by the time she arrives at the end of the conversation, she realizes that there is a connection, after all, between her mother's world and her own. The last stanza and the subtitle, "(don't ever forget the bridge/ that you crossed over on)," express that connection.

Forms and Devices

The language of Rodgers's poem is rich in its imagery and use of black speech forms. The poet's use of rhythmic speech lends cultural authority to her voice as she speaks the language of black culture with all of its irony, humor, and depth. Characteristic of black speech are its complex linguistic forms, the repetition of which create a musical, polyrhythmic style much like that of rap music. Several of Rodgers's descriptions hinge on long phrases consisting of heavily subordinated and embedded sentence elements. For example, the first stanza consists of two long, complex phrases that introduce the main clause, which begins in the next stanza. Rodgers frequently violates conventional syntax to push the rhythm of her words forward. In the line "blew through my door warm wind from the south/ concern making her gruff and tight-lipped," Rodgers juxtaposes the sentence's obvious subject, "My mother," with the "warm wind from the south," leaving the reader to judge whether the mother or the wind blew through the door. Rodgers's irony is that the southern wind intruding through the door is both a real breeze and her mother, who represents the passé lifestyle of the old South with its stereotypically submissive "religious-negro." The inconsistency of conventional punctuation between these complex sentences creates an ambiguity of subject and action, oddly resulting in the poem's structural coherence. This coherence justifies the narrative pattern as the poet develops and reveals a perspective that, in the end, allows her to resolve the ideological conflict with her mother through love.

Along with the rhythm created by carefully crafted sentences, Rodgers uses the conventional devices of alliterative and figurative language. Many of her phrases depend on the colorful imagery of slang for their simple, yet vividly concrete, images: The telephone is a "witch cord" and a "talk box"; "the cheap j-boss" is her mother's Jewish employer; and her mother "slip[s] on some love" and "[lays] on [her] bell like a truck," while the mother gets upset when the daughter talks "about Black as anything/ other than something ugly to kill it befo it grows." The reference to contemporary poet LeRoi Jones (Amiri Baraka) as "the grand le-roi (al) cat on the wall" plays with both the French term *le roi* ("the king") and the jive word "cat" from the Beat generation. The ultimate wordplay, however, is on the word "disconnected," which is explained as being the result of "non-payment of bills." The mother presses fifty dollars into her daughter's hand to pay for her daughter's food and utilities—to get her nourished and reconnected. Likewise, the daughter, seemingly disconnected from her mother's past, gets reconnected to her in the end: Through the mother's past struggles, the daughter receives spiritual nourishment and pays the necessary dues to get reconnected to her cultural past.

Themes and Meanings

Rodgers, a member of the Black Arts movement of the 1960's, often writes about black women seeking their cultural identity. "It Is Deep" is about identity and appreciation for one's roots, a sense of self deeply rooted in family history, loyalty, and circumstance. This is a theme that can be found in Rodgers's companion poem, "Jesus Was Crucified or, It Must Be Deep," which also mentions the persona of the "religious-negro," her mother's arduously long hours in the "white mans factori," and her mother's belief that her daughter is influenced by communists.

The mother in "Jesus Was Crucified," like the mother of "It Is Deep," is a woman who has lived a hard and disappointing life. She is a mother who has no time for causes other than survival and seeing to it that her child gets a better chance. This is a mother who holds tenaciously to her past for all that it was and was not, who, despite her own financial struggles, can find fifty dollars to give to her daughter, and who has invested all the struggles and tears of her past into a better future for her child. Though the mother fails to recognize that the daughter does, in fact, have a better future, the daughter does not fail to recognize that her "better chance" is derived from her mother's life struggles.

The central symbol of that connection to the past is the "sturdy Black bridge" mentioned at the poem's end. Despite the daughter's caustic remarks about her mother's religious delusions ("girdled in/ her god") and her mother's submission to oppression ("what she had/ been forced to deny"), the poet can still admire her mother's pride in having "waded through a storm." The mother shows a comparable contempt for her daughter's lifestyle. She disapproves of her daughter's racially biased politics, her rejection of religion, and her poor management of household and finances. However, none of these differences, including a disconnected telephone, could keep the mother from making the trip down "the stretch of thirty-three blocks," standing in the daughter's room "not loudly condemning that day," and pushing into the daughter's kitchen to check on the food supply. Remembering her mother's tears, the daughter recalls her love and emphatically proclaims that her mother is "obviously/ a sturdy Black bridge that I/ crossed over, on." The comma before the ending preposition emphasizes the daughter's realization that her own passage was made only on her mother's back.

Rodgers's poetic narrative about the conflict between a mother and her adult child was especially timely at its initial publication. The 1960's were a time of great generational conflict and misunderstanding. Rodgers's eloquent use of imagery and language, however, evokes a timeless truth of reconciliation through love and respect for one's roots.

Betty L. Hart

IT WAS MY CHOICE, IT WAS NO CHANCE

Author: Sir Thomas Wyatt (1503-1542)
Type of poem: Ode
First published: 1911, in *A Study of Wyatt's Poems*, by A. K. Foxwell; collected in *Collected Poems of Sir Thomas Wyatt*, 1969

The Poem

Composed of five stanzas with seven lines each, "It was my choice, it was no chance" is one of Sir Thomas Wyatt's poems that was probably written as a song to be accompanied by lute. In many ways a companion piece to the more familiar song "Blame not my lute," "It was my choice, it was no chance" plays on the conventional themes of early Renaissance poetry in England. The persona, a young lover wooing a reluctant mistress, faces the specter of rejection. He carries out his attempts to persuade her to favor his suit with varying degrees of logic and fancy.

In the traditional scenario, the lover usually sees his mistress as a cruel temptress who simultaneously lures and ignores her courtier despite the fact that she has no intentions of returning his affections; furthermore, any dalliance in which she might engage with him will be fraught with inconstancy and infidelity. Wyatt supplies a twist on the usual theme, however, by having fate, rather than the woman herself, present the only real possibility of rejecting his love and, even more significantly, by seeing truth and trust as the only way to achieve a lasting love. In this way, the persona, though he affirms the role of the mistress in his unrequited bondage, softens the "attack" on the mistress and thereby places her at a disadvantage by denying her the possibility of a defensive reaction.

The poem begins with the persona's admission that he has willingly given his heart to his lady. He therefore rationalizes that she will accept his love, which has been patiently waiting in her "hold" for so long. He cannot fathom how she could reject a love so freely given and now, paradoxically, so closely "bound" to her. Only "Fortune," he feels, has the ability to reject his rightful love. This is true only because, as the ancients believed, Fortune becomes jealous of the lovers since their love, no matter how brief, is more powerful than either "right or might." He wonders then what benefit can exist in the rightness of their love if Fortune chooses to frown on them: It will be to no avail.

Questioning this situation, he examines what happens if lovers simply "trust to chance and go by guess" and finds that, if chance does not smile on this kind of lover, his only recourse is to petition "Uncertain hope" for reparation. Others, more skeptical or more naïve, may, on the contrary, assure the lover that he can take his suit to the "higher court" of fantasy where he may make an appeal for his release. Neither of these options is very promising.

However, fantasy, to the persona, indicates the possibility of choice. He can say this with some certainty as he has had personal experience with it: Fantasy stimulated him to fall in love in the first place. He also knows, though, that fantasy breeds a love that is unstable and quickly lost, having no "faster knot." Attempting to maintain a love that must please both changeable "Fancy" and weak "Fortune" is too constraining and unnatural, and it is virtually impossible, so he seeks a surer way, a way that is not doomed to fail. He finds the right way in truth and trust.

Forms and Devices

Composed of plain words and no visual imagery, "It was my choice, it was no chance" definitely fits C. S. Lewis's often quoted description of Wyatt's poetry as "lean and sinewy." While the poem does not contain sensuous imagery, Wyatt does not altogether abandon conventional poetic technique in the poem. He relies on metaphor to carry much of its meaning. The pervasive metaphor of the poem turns on the idea of an imprisoned, "bound" lover who seeks justice: the acceptance of his love that has patiently endured bondage. Wyatt continues this legal metaphor in the third stanza when he speaks of the lover who, having trusted chance, now "may well go sue/ Uncertain hope for his redress" or perhaps "mayst appeal for" his "release/ To fantasy." A brief metaphor, connected with the binding of the lover but unrelated to the legal metaphor, is the slipknot of fanciful love found only in stanza 4. Other words in the poem, such as "choice," "just," "sufferance," "right or might," "power," "abuse," "vaileth," and "prevail," though they are not specifically connected to the metaphor, serve to reinforce the atmosphere of litigation and deliberation. Even the final search for truth echoes the legal terms, since the purpose of every trial supposedly is to find the truth. Here, the truth is what ultimately will free the imprisoned lover. This legal metaphor is particularly apt for a poet who uses logic and rhetorical methods of persuasion to convince his lady: Justice demands that she should love him and thus free him from his state of imprisonment. The metaphor is also particularly appropriate if one considers that the word "court" can mean the court of law in which trials are held, and it can also mean to woo.

Several clues lead scholars to believe that this poem was originally written to be set to music. Frequently anthologized next to a song that has an extant melody, "Blame not my lute," "It was my choice, it was no chance" is structured in much the same way, with the final line of each stanza repeated as the first two or three words of the first line of the next stanza, very much like a refrain. The emphasis on rhyme, as well as the inverted syntax necessitated by that emphasis, may also point to a musical setting for this poem.

The meter, on the other hand, though it does not negate the possibility that the poem was written as a song, is not highly regular as might be expected of a song. This poem appears to be written in what C. S. Lewis called the "native meter" that he felt to be the prevailing meter of fifteenth century poetry rather than the smoother iambic pentameter. Composed predominantly of four stresses per line despite the number of syllables in the line, this type of meter, like verse written during the alliterative revival of the fourteenth century, uses alliteration to mark the stresses and a caesura (a break in the middle of the line) to form word groups. These features are perhaps most clear in the first line of the poem ("It was my choice, it was no chance") with its eight syllables and four stresses: The obvious caesura is indicated by the comma that breaks the line into two repetitive clauses, the only difference between them being the final word of each clause ("choice" and "chance"), which repeat the initial consonant sound.

Themes and Meanings

"It was my choice, it was no chance" is a deceptively simple poem. Perhaps the only certainty about the poem is that it is about a man courting a woman who has not yet returned his advances. Whether the tone of the poem is playful, serious, or cynical, however, is open to debate. The picture the persona draws of the woman he loves is the merest outline. The reader knows that she has held his heart—whether she intended to do so or not is not made clear—for some time without either freeing it or accepting it. The picture the persona draws of himself is, likewise, superficial. Rather than plumbing the depths of his feelings, he makes a relatively objective case before the court of his love.

The real difficulty in interpreting this poem comes with the fourth stanza, in which the persona admits that fantasy first caused him to love. The problem lies in his firm assertion that a love based on fantasy will end as quickly and easily as it began because it has "no faster knot." From this realization, he moves to the further revelation that a love that maintains itself "by change" (a paradox in that maintenance and change are diametrically opposed) cannot endure and that only a love based on truth that leads to trust will triumph. The relationship of these statements to the opening situation is unclear: If he sees his love as based on fantasy (he makes this connection explicit through the use of the word "choice" in the first stanza and "choose" in the fourth), the reader must wonder why he persists in pressing for a love that he knows cannot last. On the other hand, he may see his love as having found a stronger foundation despite the fact that it was founded on such tenuous grounds.

Any interpretation of a Wyatt love poem must mention his purported relationship with Anne Boleyn, the second wife of King Henry VIII. Certain aspects of the poem suggest, but certainly do not confirm, the possibility of such a connection. The references to "one happy hour" that can "prevail" more than "right or might," the power that only "Fortune" has to quash his love, and the legal framing of the entire poem could conceivably allude to this liaison.

Jaquelyn W. Walsh

IT WEEPS IN MY HEART

Author: Paul Verlaine (1844-1896)
Type of poem: Lyric
First published: 1874, in *Romances sans paroles*; English translation collected in *Romances Without Words*, 1921

The Poem

"It weeps in my heart" is actually the first line of an untitled work in the group of poems called "Ariettes oubliées" ("Forgotten Melodies"). This sixteen-line poem, composed of hexasyllabic quatrains in the original French, contains a very musical rhyme scheme known as *rimes croisées*, or what might be noted as the following pattern: *abaa, cdcc, eaee, fdff.* The epigraph, "It rains gently on the town," attributed to Arthur Rimbaud, Paul Verlaine's companion and literary confrere, is not found among Rimbaud's known body of work, and the tribute's origin, therefore, remains a mystery. Many critics have made suppositions as to its source, but nothing has been verified positively.

Many of Verlaine's poems have musical titles, as his artistic credo (from his poem "Art poétique") was "De la musique avant toute chose" ("Music first and foremost"), and his emphasis on the musicality of the poem is evident throughout his career. The title of this collection, "Romances," connotes sentimentality, and the echoes of such sounds as "heart" and "rain" (in French, *coeur* and *pluie*) are reminiscent of the simple medieval ballads and troubadour songs.

The poem is written in the first person and is a lyric poem in the classical tradition that expresses the intensely personal feelings of the narrator. The first quatrain sets the mood, explaining that the poet's weeping heart is mirrored by the exterior world as it rains on the town. He asks, "What languorous hurt/ thus pierces my heart?" He cannot locate the source of his suffering.

The second stanza demonstrates how the falling rain provides music: "a sweet sound," "the song of the rain," but his heart remains "dulled with pain." Both sentences that compose the quatrain are exclamatory, demonstrating the relief that the poet hopes the rain will bring to his aching heart. He cries out to the rain that he hears, grateful that its music offers him diversion.

The third quatrain reveals the poet's agony: Although he is longing to find the cause for his suffering, the heart will not betray itself to him. He seeks a rational answer to an emotional problem that is not forthcoming. This causes greater agitation.

The fourth quatrain confirms the poet's anxiety that the worst pain "is not to know why." He suffers neither from "love" nor "disdain." The exterior world may possess music, but his "heart has such pain." The mood at the end of the poem is consistent with the state of being that was expressed at the beginning. There is no relief provided by outside forces nor is the poet's own understanding of his situation ameliorated. The ache is overpowering and lingers. His song is a lonely, single melody, a lament that bemoans unhappy solitude.

Forms and Devices

In its original French, the poem's rhyme scheme ends in mostly soft feminine vowel sounds. The tonality is a light one; the poet tries to emulate the sound of softly falling rain. Such consonants as *pl* and *t* that echo throughout the original French poem are also reminiscent of the "song" of the rain that drops onto the roofs and the ground–*tois* and *terre*.

Verlaine uses metonymy: The heart is given the function of representing the whole human being filled with pain. Although the exterior rain falls gently, the weeping in his heart is certainly not as pleasant; therefore, his use of the simile comparing the tears of the heart with the rain on the town really serves to show a dissimilarity rather than an equation. The alliterative devices of the "sweet sound" contrast with his pervasive unhappiness.

The poem's only resolution is the declarative statement that "It's far the worst pain/ not to know why." The poet expresses no newfound knowledge during the poem. He continually questions: What is the cause of my pain? There is no answer. The questions merely echo the pain and his ponderings provide no relief. This device of using rhetorical questions shows the poet's attempt at blending rationality with emotion. Because there is no transformation, it is clear that the poet is stating that logical answers cannot be applied to unnameable feelings. His "grief's without reason."

In his quest to examine the possible reasons behind his state of sadness, the poet tries to distance himself from the emotions and expresses this through his poetic imagery. "It weeps" is as impersonal as "it rains," displaying an analytic posturing on the part of the narrator. The oxymoron "disheartened heart" and the use of "love or disdain" as a paradox to explain the extremes of sensation by the heart further demonstrate a scientific stance by the poet, who is trying to study the source of his pain. As his experiment is failing, so too his metaphors reveal an evaporation through words such as *pénètre* (the translated word "pierce" is deceptive—*pénètre* means to penetrate, not to prick); a heart *qui s'ennuie* (the translated world "dulled" is also inappropriate, because *s'ennuie* means to lapse into boredom, which clearly demonstrates the passivity of this person); and, again, the *coeur qui s'écoeure* (the heart that simply languishes).

The poem's sensorial imagery reveals how sight ("weeps in my heart/ as it rains on the town"), touch ("pierces my heart"), hearing ("song of the rain"), taste, and smell paralyze the poet from actively and methodically tempering these strong perceptions that conquer his mind and taunt him by flaunting their power.

Themes and Meanings

An aria is an elaborate melody for a single voice with accompaniment. Verlaine placed this poem in a group of poems called "little arias" that lie within the framework of the larger group called "ballads." The importance of music in "It weeps in my heart" is unquestionable. The solo is sung by the narrator whose melody—one of sadness—is in disharmony with the sweet sounds of life around him. The epigraph attributed to Rimbaud that appears as the introduction to the poem, "It rains gently on the town," portrays a simple and almost peacefully somnambulant scene that, the reader discovers, is a counterpoint or descant to the woeful tune that measures discord within the man. As there is no satisfactory resolution for the narrator because the heart will not betray the cause of its melancholy, so, too, the two melodies never assonate. Although the ballad and the aria are both traditional vehicles to express unrequited love, the homophonic structure of the ballad and the labeling of the poem a "little aria" are ironic, as the poet seeks to empty generic norms with this theme of pervasive depression attributable to unknown causes: There is no grand passion *d'amour* here, simply a lack of comprehension. This particular "arietta" is a psychological portrait and not at all a sentimental one, despite the fact that structurally the poem is composed like a ballad.

One reason that Verlaine's poetry does not translate well is his emphasis on musicality. It is possible to translate the metaphors, the imagery, and themes, but his technical ability to create music of the French language is out of reach to English-language readers. The French language has masculine and feminine rhymes and other sounds that cannot be duplicated. To read Verlaine in French is to understand what made him not only a writer but a symphonic composer as well. Generations of readers can recite "Il pleure dans mon coeur/ Comme il pleut sur la ville" almost as if it were a song and not a poem.

"It weeps in my heart" reveals a state of ennui that Verlaine chose to treat in many of his poems. This portrayal of the passive intellectual is a unifying thread among the French Symbolist poets of his day. Here, Verlaine does not attempt to confuse the senses as was typical of the Symbolist craft, but rather he presents a perplexed human being who aches for clarity. It is the spirit of the narrator more than anything else that allows this poem to be characterized as Symbolist. Verlaine, here, is certainly a less radical alchemist than his friend Rimbaud, whose uncharacteristically simple and charming quote serves as the inspiration for the poem.

The explosive relationship between Verlaine and Rimbaud (at one point, Verlaine shot Rimbaud and was imprisoned in Belgium) and its effect on Verlaine's sanity is not, despite some critics' claims, depicted in content or form in this poem, regardless of the selected epigraph. "It weeps in my heart" reveals impeccable and methodical craftsmanship by a writer who is in command and in control.

Susan Nagel

JABBERWOCKY

Author: Lewis Carroll (Charles Lutwidge Dodgson, 1832-1898)
Type of poem: Lyric
First published: 1871, in *Through the Looking-Glass and What Alice Found There*

The Poem

"Jabberwocky," possibly the most famous of all nonsense poems, consists of seven stanzas, each of four lines, each line having eight syllables. The orthodox form and the fixed rhythm provide a framework whose rigidity further emphasizes the nonsensical quality of each individual line. Because the final stanza is an exact repetition of the first, these two units, unrelated in content to the remainder, perform a parenthetical function. The five stanzas thus bracketed contain a consecutive narrative in which a young man, having received a series of warnings, rides away to find and kill the monstrous Jabberwock and then returns to his delighted father.

When the first stanza appeared separately it was represented as a "Stanza of Anglo-Saxon Poetry," and all the unfamiliar words were footnoted as if they were medieval terms whose meanings had been rendered obsolete or lost. In the interests of maintaining this parodic imposture, three of the key words were rendered "bryllyg," "slythy," and "gymble," but Carroll reverted to more orthodox spellings when he introduced the lines into a different context.

Forms and Devices

The original version of the first stanza is a humorous pastiche of scholarly versions of Old English poems such as *Beowulf* (sixth century). Carroll's notes are an exercise in etymological slapstick, according to which "bryllyg" is derived from the verb "to bryl or broil" and thus refers to the time of broiling dinner, or the late afternoon. "Slythy" is a compound of slimy and lithe, meaning "smooth and active"; "tove" is a species of badger with horns like a stag, which lived chiefly on cheese. "Gyre" is derived from "giaour"—here said to mean "dog," although it actually means "infidel" and had acquired more sinister implications by way of George Gordon, Lord Byron's poem "The Giaour"—and means "to scratch like a dog."

"Gymble" means "to screw holes" and is the alleged origin of "gimblet" (gimlet); "wabe" is derived from the verb "to swab or soak" and refers, by casually mysterious means, to the side of a hill; "mimsy" means unhappy, and thus provides the root, via "mimserable," of "miserable." "Borogove" is an extinct species of parrot, which was wingless, possessed of an upturned beak, nested under sundials and lived on veal; "mome"—from which evolved "solemome," "solemone," and ultimately "solemn"— means "grave." "Rath" is a species of land turtle that had a mouth like a shark, walked on its knees, and lived on swallows and oysters; "outgrabe," the past tense of the verb "to outgribe," is related to several words, including "grike," "shrike," "shriek," and "creak," and thus means "squeaked."

Some of these meanings are retained when the version of the stanza used in *Through the Looking-Glass and What Alice Found There* is explained in chapter 6 by Humpty Dumpty, although he claims that toves are only "something like badgers," also having affinities with lizards and corkscrews. According to Humpty Dumpty it is they, rather than borogoves, that nest under sundials, although their propensity for cheese is retained. He scrupulously gives the correct meaning of "gyre," which is "to go round and round like a gyroscope," but claims that a rath is a green pig. It is, however, Alice who suggests—sarcastically, although Humpty Dumpty endorses the conclusion—that a wabe must be a grass plot around a sundial. Gyre is not the only word used in the stanza that had a real meaning, but it seems unlikely that Carroll expected his readers to know—even if he knew himself—that "slithy" was a variant of an obsolete term meaning "slovenly," that "gimble" is a variant of "gimbal," that "mome" had several obsolete meanings, or that "rath" is an Irish word for a fortified enclosure.

The invented words distributed in a slightly more economical fashion through the five enclosed stanzas mostly went unannotated by Carroll, although he did comment further on some of the eight that he used again in *The Hunting of the Snark: An Agony in Eight Fits* (1876). In a preface to the later poem he explains that "frumious" is a slurred compound of "fuming" and "furious," while a letter written in 1877 declares that "uffish" is "a state of mind when the voice is gruffish, the manner roughish, and the temper huffish." Another letter, replying to some Boston schoolgirls who wanted to call a magazine *The Jabberwock*, obligingly deciphered this term as a compound of "jabber" and the allegedly Anglo-Saxon "wocer" or "wocor," meaning "offspring" or "fruit," thus making the whole "the result of much excited discussion."

In response to queries regarding the meanings of "vorpal" and "tulgey," however, he confessed his ignorance. Although no evidence survives of his derivation of "frabjous" the example of frumious suggests that it might be an amalgam of "rejoice" and "fabulous," and the *Oxford English Dictionary* speculates, similarly, that "galumph" is an amalgam of "gallop" and "triumphant."

Many of the words deployed for the first time in these verses have entered common usage, "chortle" being the most popular. Paradoxically, the real words used in the enclosed stanzas seem to have fallen out of fashion despite their citation; few people nowadays refer to a "burbling brook," describe happy expressions as "beamish," or employ "whiffling" in any of its actual or metaphorical senses. Humpty Dumpty's explanations have, however, inspired one further term; his judgment that the formation of "slithy" by packing two meanings into a single word is "like a portmanteau" originated the useful concept of a portmanteau word. There is no firmer evidence than this poem of the potential that well-crafted nonsense has to enrich both thought and oratory.

Themes and Meanings

Deliberate nonsense claims, by definition, to be devoid of meaning. Although Carroll's satirical annotation of the original version of the first stanza produces a painstaking word-by-word analysis, the result is calculatedly silly. Because the five enclosed stanzas constitute a story of sorts, however, it is perfectly reasonable to discuss the theme of the narrative. The tale offers a conventional account of a young man's quest; like any knight errant—whether of Anglo-Norman romance or modern genre fantasy—he sets out, forearmed by the warnings of his worldly-wise father, to confront a draconian threat, which he despatches with casual ease before returning home to a hero's welcome. The net effect of the rhythmically interpolated nonsense words is, however, to make the adventure seem utterly absurd.

The implicit meaninglessness and perverse interpretation of the poem's neologisms are extremely contagious, overspilling the words to call into question both the conventionality of the knightly quest as a generic device and the formality of lyric poetry as a vehicle for conveying that kind of content. It is not surprising that Carroll went on to produce a much more elaborate and more carefully satirical account of a vaingloriously futile quest in the mock epic *Hunting of the Snark*, nor is it surprising that he should take the trouble to acknowledge the contribution of "Jabberwocky" to the longer poem's inspiration by reusing several of its key terms, intermingled with new coinages. It is necessary to observe, however, that the flow of contagion is not unidirectional. While the nonsensical vocabulary infects the tale in which it is embedded, the narrative force and energy of the tale infuses the words themselves, casting shadows of meaning where none really exist.

So powerful is this process of infusion that some of the words acquire indelibly clear connotations bestowed upon them by context, and even those that remain the most stubbornly opaque acquire a certain propriety. Even though one cannot say what "vorpal" means, the story links it so inextricably with the "snicker-snackering" sword that it is forever trapped as an adjective applicable to blades. Any claim of meaninglessness, no matter how definitive, is bound to falter when nonsense words are built into sentences, and the sentences into stories.

Only the bracketing stanza of "Jabberwocky," which scrupulously avoids juxtaposing its nonsense terms with everyday nouns, adjectives, and verbs, can hope to pass muster as authentic nonsense, and even those four lines cannot entirely overcome the handicaps imposed by grammar and rhythm. Meaning springs unbidden from the information that toves can be slithy, that they gyre and gimble together, that borogoves are prone to mimsiness, and that raths—perhaps especially when mome—are liable to grabe exceedingly.

Alice comments, after discovering the poem inscribed in mirror-writing, that "it seems to fill my head with ideas—only I don't exactly know what they are!" She is reproducing the response of any child (or adult) confronted with a text replete with as-yet-unfamiliar jargon, whose confusion is ameliorated—if only slightly—by the enthusiasm of discovery. Having found "Jabberwocky," Alice wants to know what it means, and she is understandably distressed when the explanation she eventually demands from Humpty Dumpty is no help at all.

People are not born with language; it confronts everyone, in the first instance, as nonsense, but within its organization there is always hope of finding meaning. More important is hope of finding the real meaning not merely of the world and its story but also of each person's hopefully heroic part in the narrative of life. The other side of the coin is, however, the anxiety that even when people have done their utmost to comprehend it, the world will remain stubbornly nonsensical, and the awful certainty that when the "frabjous" day is done people shall again encounter, for a second and final time, the confusion that reigned before they learned to be themselves—and after that, silence.

Brian Stableford

JAIL POEMS

Author: Bob Kaufman (1925-1986)
Type of poem: Lyric
First published: 1965, in *Solitudes Crowded with Loneliness*

The Poem
"Jail Poems" is a collection of thirty-four numbered lyric strophes (irregular stanzas) that vary in length from one to fourteen lines and function together to convey a series of related though disparate images for the reader. The title of this poem not only sets the mood but also reveals the setting in which the poem is reported to have been written and serves as a recurrent theme throughout. From his perspective inside the jail, the narrator describes the various sensory and reflective perceptions of an inmate, variously turning his eye toward his surroundings, his fellow inmates, the society that put him in jail, and himself.

The first section of the poem describes the narrator's immediate surroundings: what he sees, what he hears, and how he interprets the situations of the other occupants of the jail. The second section is more oriented toward the senses, concentrating on visual imagery at first, then moving toward the auditory. The third section takes a philosophical approach, asking "who is not in jail?" and theorizing about the degree to which human beings can "know" things that are outside their own experience. In the fourth section, the narrator speculates about the perceptions of others and questions his own motivations. Thus the poem proceeds, asking difficult questions and then answering them not from the perspective of a "universal truth" but from the unique position of one person in a particular context, the salient feature of which is the jail cell in which the narrator is incarcerated while pondering these issues.

The various sections follow one another as if the reader was following along with the wandering thoughts of the narrator's stream of consciousness. Thus the narrator's discomfort at the death of a "wino" in an adjacent cell (section 5) is followed by focused introspection about the turns of his own life (section 6). Questions about the nature of existence (section 7) are answered with the certainty of sensory perception (sections 8 and 9). As the poem proceeds, the narrator's thoughts become more diffuse and more fragmented until, at the end, they become surreal as the narrator entreats, "Come, help flatten a raindrop." Taken individually, the sections and the lines within them offer a montage of sensory images interspersed with philosophical questions and angry invective. Together, however, the poem paints not just an image of jail life but also an image of a narrator who is separated from society by more than the iron bars that imprison him.

Like many lyric poets, the narrator draws his power from the vividness of personal description. In "Jail Poems," however, there is a tension between the personal nature of the experiences and the necessarily public sphere in which they occur. Perhaps it is because of this tension that the poem vacillates between personal observations specifically made by the narrator and more casual observations that might have been made by a passerby. The former are more numerous, but the narrator seems to be reminding readers that part of the reality of being imprisoned is that one is, at all times, exposed to public view. As the poem progresses, the casual commentary decreases and the observations become more personal and more cryptic until, at the end, the narrator seems to have shut out the outside world altogether and retreated into himself.

Forms and Devices

"Jail Poems," like much of Bob Kaufman's poetry, exemplifies the oral tradition associated with the Beat poets of the 1950's and 1960's, many of whom were influenced by the music of their era, especially jazz. Rhythmic lines such as "Here—me—now—hear—me—now—always here somehow" allow the reader to hear—even feel—the cadence that is present when the words are spoken aloud. Additionally, the nonuniformity of the poem's sections mimics the irregular measures of jazz music, varying between long, drawn-out wailings and short, intense, angry bursts, all of which are held together by the commonality of the unwavering depth of the feelings that inspire them. The Beat poets were reacting against rigid stylistic conventions, eschewing not only regulated rhyme schemes and uniform meter but also formulaic stanzas and consistency of perspective and case. By rejecting the rules of their predecessors, the Beat poets created a style that was fluid and resembled spoken discourse or even thought processes. In fact, Kaufman, who preferred to deliver his poems orally, is said to have resisted their publication, preferring to recite his own poetry (and that of others) from memory whenever the opportunity presented itself.

The Beat poets rejected common formulaic constructions as well, avoiding the binary relationships that are found in other styles of poetry and rejecting simple themes such as male versus female, us versus them, and now versus then in favor of more obscure or complicated depictions that, they asserted, more accurately portray the human condition. Although "Jail Poems" represents the judicial system in a negative way, for instance, it does not portray it as a singular structure, solely responsible for the narrator's misery, that can be readily identified, confronted, and overcome. Rather, Kaufman implies that there are multiple causes of the wretchedness he describes, ranging from the police who "batten down hatches of human souls" to the Muscatel that contributes to "wine-diluted blood."

Surrealist imagery is a third characteristic that "Jail Poems" shares with other examples of Beat poetry. Exemplifying this feature are lines such as "One more day to hell, filled with floating glands," which abuts two or more contrasting, concrete images in such a way that meaning is accentuated by the difficulty of picturing the image itself. Many of the shorter sections (10, 12, 13, and 23, for example) consist entirely of these contrasting images, which heighten the reader's sense of the absurdity of anyone who would condemn the likes of Socrates or turn the American Dream into something that mocks a group of people rather than empowering them. Surrealist imagery expresses visually the same dissonances that loose structure expresses in terms of form.

Themes and Meanings

Everything about "Jail Poems," from its irregular sections, each numbered and kept separate from the other, to the way that the narrator increasingly withdraws into himself, contributes to the overall theme of disfranchisement, a theme that Kaufman addresses often. The collection in which "Jail Poems" appears, *Solitudes Crowded with Loneliness*, begins with a poem entitled "I Have Folded My Sorrows" and proceeds to explore both loneliness and disfranchisement from a number of different angles: from the quiet, solitary isolation of an individual to the collective grief felt by a community when one of its icons passes away. Each of the poems touches a nerve as Kaufman explores grief, disillusionment, and the acute sense of betrayal felt by people whom society excludes or marginalizes. "Jail Poems" contributes to this collage by dramatizing the plight of the disfranchised through a combination of rhythm and imagery; however, because of the complexity with which Kaufman treats his subject even on a thematic level, there are no absolutes.

At random intervals throughout the poem, there are causes for hope such as the "Three long strings of light/ Braided into a ray." Moreover, the poem itself represents an act of expression, an affirmation of self that exists against all odds. Even if, as the narrator asserts, he is writing the poem "For fear of seeing what's outside [his] head," he still admits a desire to eat "a wild poetic loaf of bread," a longing that confirms that even at his worst, the narrator continues to hold on to his artistic desires. The most conspicuous meaning of the poem, however, is much less positive. The final two images are of a man, fumbling on the floor, who was once much more than he is now and a raindrop that will be flattened not by gravity but by a conspiratorial act. Together, these images convey a profound sense of regret that some people are prevented from living up to their potential not because of random happenstance but because forces conspire to limit them. It is these purposeful limitations that Kaufman rails against because, like his contemporaries, he cannot abide rules that make virtual prisoners of those held within their sway. Ultimately, "Jail Poems" is about the need to protest violations of the human spirit. As Kaufman reminds readers, these violations occur not only through physical incarceration but also through sensory deprivation and social isolation.

T. A. Fishman

JANET WAKING

Author: John Crowe Ransom (1888-1974)
Type of poem: Lyric
First published: 1926; collected in *Two Gentlemen in Bonds*, 1927

The Poem

"Janet Waking" is in seven stanzas, four lines each, with the first and fourth lines rhymed and the second and third lines rhymed (*abba* rhyme scheme). The title suggests the coming of age theme that is evident in the poem. As is true of any moment of understanding in the works of John Crowe Ransom, the formal constraint of the tight form reinforces the recognition of people's position in the larger universe: operating within a strict schema and perceiving the abstraction and formlessness of the universe ("far beyond the daughters of men"). The poem is written from the point of view of the father, "Who would have kissed each curl of his shining baby." He is the only adult whose thoughts the reader is given. Beginning as an observation of a beloved child and including the first-person perspective in the final verse paragraph ("Janet implored us"), the poem moves from the intensely personal to the universal.

"Janet Waking" begins with a scene familiar to any parent. Ransom's poem follows the child through her morning rituals. The complication is suggested in the opening lines when the child, thinking of her pet hen, wants "To see how it had kept." The end of the third stanza informs the reader that the hen had died. The centerpiece of the poem is the fourth stanza, in which the bee sting is described, a stanza in which Ransom juxtaposes a "transmogrifying bee" and "Chucky's old bald head," foreshadowing the final change in the poem: The parents' change from seeming all-powerful to being all too weak.

The structure of the poem suggests a brief play in which the opening scene shows the protagonist waking and thinking "about her dainty-feathered hen." The second scene introduces the rest of the characters—the father, mother, and brother. Then, as the setting shifts outside the house to the farmyard, death and danger are revealed in the death of the pet, the tragic force in this brief drama. In drama, the "catastrophe" marks the tragic failure and comes as a natural consequence of the death. In this case the child's innocence and belief die. She no longer believes that her parents are all-powerful because they cannot bring her pet back to life.

The poem's narrative structure leads the reader to experience the frustration and powerlessness of the parent watching the child and being unable to help. The father and child in this small drama are at the mercy of larger forces—forces that they begin to understand through experience.

Forms and Devices

Throughout "Janet Waking," language and situation bespeak the fairy-tale quality of the work. One important device in the poem is allusion. "Beautifully Janet slept" recalls the innocent sleep of Snow White and Rose Red. The child wakes not merely to full sun but to a time that is "deeply morning." "Beautifully" and "deeply" suggest the rhythm and the tone of fairy tales. The fairy-tale motif continues as the father notes that he "would have kissed each curl of his shining baby." Just as the sun sets out on a new day, so does the child of this fairy-tale farm world. The phrase "Running across the world upon the grass" also locates the child in the land of fairy tales. That which intrudes upon her world is "the forgetful kingdom of death." The archaic term "alas" also suggests a past time, a fairy-tale world.

Another important device is juxtaposition. The poem juxtaposes realism with innocence and idealism. To the little girl, the pet is "her dainty-feathered hen." In the father's description, the chicken has an "old bald head." "Janet Waking" also juxtaposes formal diction with simple and direct Anglo-Saxon English. Ransom's choice of "transmogrifying" to describe the bee forces a reader—even a casual reader—to recognize unwitting power. Just as the venom of the bee communicates its rigor, so does the word "transmogrify" communicate the status of the event. The pathos of the unsuspecting victim is heightened by the description of the bee "droning down on Chucky's old bald head." Chucky, bald, is unprotected, vulnerable to the remorseless and methodical bee.

A juxtaposition that further exemplifies the duality of this poem appears in the final two lines of the fifth stanza: "Now the poor comb stood up straight/ But Chucky did not." With humor, Ransom balances the tension and sadness of the poem, again with realism intruding on any romantic description. Ransom shelters the reader from the harshness of death and destruction with his naming the pet "Chucky" and with these final lines of the fifth stanza.

A third device is enclosure. Each of the stanzas rhymes in an *abba* pattern, implying a close relationship between each of the rhymed words, with the closest relationships being those that function as internal couplets. For instance, when in the second stanza Ransom introduces the family in rhyme, lines five and eight rhyme "mother" and "brother"; lines six and seven less exactly rhyme "daddy" and "baby." The mother and brother complete the family, but in this poem they serve merely to enclose what is the closest relationship: the father and daughter. The final stanza serves as another readily accessible example of the relationship between rhyme and meaning. Ransom rhymes "breath" and "death" in the opening and closing of the concluding stanza, enclosing rhymes of "sleep" and "deep." The child's breath itself is ragged and painful, breath with the rhythm of weeping, because she has seen death. The child wants death to be sleep, so the pet will awaken, but the death sleep is too deep. The knowledge that some sleep is not beautiful, that some sleep is deep, the sleep of death, is reflected in the rhyme.

Ransom provides another fine enclosure for the poem itself: "deeply" in line 2 and "deep" in the penultimate line of the poem. Ransom describes a circumstance in which the truth is beyond a reader's understanding, too deep. As Ransom notes, the brown hen has been "translated far beyond the daughters of men" and is therefore beyond the understanding of the child and ultimately of any observer.

Themes and Meanings

Ransom explores change and initiation, drawing attention to the theme in his diction. The first instance appears in the title itself. "Waking" deliberately invokes a time of change, a dawning of consciousness. Rather than a simple return to consciousness, the child awakens to the world, very much as the child in "Jack and the Beanstalk" awakens to full sun and the shadow of the beanstalk, which symbolizes the changed world for Jack. Another word that draws the reader toward change, "transmogrifying," appears in the middle stanza of the poem, centering the poem on transformation. The bee-sting knot itself "Swell[s] with the venom," changing an appearance, realistic once more.

This poem suggests several layers of meaning in the word "waking." At the first level, the child wakes to the meaning of death: Her pet will no longer be in the world with her. At another level the parent wakes to the recognition of helplessness that accompanies all moments of watching a child grow through pain. The child, in fact, cannot "be instructed" but learns on her own; the feeling of uselessness is extremely difficult for many parents to accept. At another level, the speaker recognizes his own similarity to Chucky. If the little girl sees "her dainty-feathered hen" while the father sees "Chucky's old bald head," the reader can be assured that the speaker is aware of who in fact is old and bald. The child, the "shining baby" with curly hair, is analogous to the "dainty-feathered hen" of imagination and innocence. The speaker, helpless at this moment of learning for the child, recognizes that his own bald head is likely to communicate the rigor of mortality.

The poem moves beyond the caring parent and toward existential contemplation in a final transformation, erasure to nothingness: "the forgetful kingdom of death." The word "forgetful" itself suggests the short memory and attention span of a child (realism, once again) as well as the essence of loss and the possibility that all experience and knowledge is ultimately forgotten. The existential question is clearly secondary within "Janet Waking," however, a poem in which family drama provides the framework for Ransom's representation of transformation and growth, making visceral a moment of loving and anguished understanding.

Janet Taylor Palmer

THE JEWELS

Author: Charles Baudelaire (1821-1867)
Type of poem: Narrative
First published: 1857, as "Les Bijoux," in *Les Fleurs du mal*; English translation collected in *Baudelaire: Selected Verse*, 1961

The Poem

In "The Jewels," a poem composed of eight quatrains in regular Alexandrine lines, Charles Baudelaire records a portrait of his mulatto mistress dressed only in her jewelry. While the description will not seem excessively graphic to the modern reader, this poem was one of the ones responsible for the censure and withdrawal from sale of the first edition of *Les Fleurs du mal* (1857; *Flowers of Evil*, 1909).

The principal development of the poem follows a seduction scene in which the woman seduces, and thus psychologically dominates, the poet. The stage is set during the first two quatrains while the woman remains relatively passive. The poet is attracted to her, but his attention remains focused on her jewels. The only indication that the woman already controls the situation comes in the first line, where she is said to wear the jewels because she knows the poet's heart. Yet rather than conveying a form of manipulation, this phrase may also be read as her desire to please him.

The description of the jewels contains elements that will fascinate the poet through a simultaneous appeal to his various senses. By the third quatrain, this fascination begins to have its effect. The poet appears below the woman, in a position suggesting adoration, while she smiles at him from the "height of the sofa." Still, she remains passive, merely accepting his love that "rises up" to her.

In the fourth quatrain, the woman becomes active. Her eyes are still those of a "subdued tiger," but they contain all the implicit danger of the beast. As she moves in an increasingly sensual manner, the poet notes her "metamorphoses." These movements continue through the ensuing quatrains until the poet must admit that she can "trouble the repose" of his soul.

Although the poet must see the danger the woman presents when he describes her breasts as more seductive than "the Angels of evil," he does not heed the warning implicit in this insight. His admiration continues in the seventh quatrain, where he is still fascinated by the contradictory elements, combining feminine and masculine allusions, that make up her beauty.

Thus the final image of the lamp "resigned to its death" figures both the passage of time and the final disposition of the poet. The ebbing lamplight signals an end to the love scene, but a fire in the hearth, also dying to embers, continues to flare up periodically with a "flaming sigh." The sigh may echo the poet's satisfaction or his resignation. If it contains elements of the latter, he has accepted the troubles to his soul as the price of pleasure. Danger and beauty remain inextricably linked in the last line, where the firelight "inundated with blood [the woman's] amber-colored skin." The blood, a clearly symbolic application of the red color imparted by the dying fire, suggests the threat of violence, but the poet's attention remains fixed on the beauty of the mingling colors.

Forms and Devices

The poet's fascination with the woman's "sonorous jewels" reflects the importance Baudelaire accorded to synesthesia as a source of poetic inspiration. In his sonnet "Correspondences," he defined this fusion of appeals to various senses, specifically the harmony of perfumes, colors, and sounds, as "having the expansion of infinite things." Thus objects capable of producing synesthesia offered a special opportunity to the poet to grasp those transcendent ideas that should be expressed in poetry.

The poet desires the woman in "The Jewels" both for her own beauty and for her potential role in his inspiration. He reminds the reader in language reminiscent of "Correspondences" that he loves "things where sound is mixed with light." The light caught by the "radiant world" of the gems is joined by sound as the woman moves. The jewels striking against one another "throw off while dancing a lively, mocking sound." Characterizing the jewelry as a "world" and its sound as "lively" emphasizes its importance. It seems to be alive, but it depends on the movements of the woman to animate it.

With the adjective "mocking," however, Baudelaire introduces an element of uncertainty. Why would the sound of the jewels mock the poet? If the poet desires inspiration from them, would these living jewels somehow foresee that his creative desire would be frustrated? The mockery Baudelaire perceives in the jewels reflects his failure to find his increasingly elusive poetic vision.

Although Jeanne Duval had come to Paris from the Caribbean, a source of her appeal to Baudelaire could have been that she reminded him of a trip he had taken around Africa to the islands of Mauritius and Reunion in 1841-1842. Baudelaire first met his mistress some three months after his return to France. As he suffered from the cold of cloudy, northern Paris, Baudelaire increasingly saw the sunny, tropical climate he had known only briefly as an emblem of the vision that he sought.

A consistent theme of exoticism in *Flowers of Evil* links Baudelaire's desire to distant lands. Thus the jewels give the woman "the triumphant air that the slaves of the Moors have on their happy days." Not only does this phrase draw on the concept of exotic locales, but it also contains very conflicting suggestions concerning the role of the woman. She is cast as a slave but at the same time is triumphant. The ambiguity can be resolved if one realizes that by submitting to the poet's desires, the woman is actually controlling him.

Exoticism continues in the use of animal imagery to describe the woman. She is, in a sense, the poet's pet. Yet the animals that represent her, a tiger and a swan, are far from domesticated: the one dangerous and the other silent and enigmatic. The animals' strength is echoed in the allusion to Antiope, sister of the queen of the Amazons in Greek legend, who further shares the element of exoticism as part of a temporally remote and foreign culture. The images combine to convey the woman's strength and her potential fascination to the poet.

Themes and Meanings

Baudelaire's hero in *Flowers of Evil* strives for a poetic vision that parallels Christian salvation. Just as the Fall resulted from the temptation of Eve, woman becomes the agent of the poet's separation from his vision of the ideal. Immediately before "The Jewels" in the first edition of *Flowers of Evil*—the only edition where it was to appear in Baudelaire's lifetime—a series of three sonnets, "Beauty," "The Ideal," and "The Giantess," defines an ideal of beauty presented in female form. Following "The Jewels," "Exotic Perfume" continues the association of synesthesia with the woman saying that her perfume causes the poet to "see happy shores spread out" before him.

The vision the woman offers, however, is one of a false paradise. Only ten poems later in the 1857 edition, the poet both literally and figuratively awakens. In "One night when I was with a frightful Jewess . . . ," Baudelaire sees the act of love linked with death and dreams of "the sad beauty of which my desire is depriving itself." The vision of beauty, represented in the earlier sonnets by a statue or a giantess, cannot be translated into a living woman.

Because various elements of female beauty cause Baudelaire to believe, for a time, that he can regain transcendent vision through love, he is drawn into distractions that cause him to waste his life in this false pursuit. The central attraction of woman in this regard is her eyes—eyes that often reflect the light of heaven and thus become confused with it. Consequently, in "The Jewels," it is especially significant that the woman dominates the poet through her hypnotic eyes.

In the same way, the choice of the jewels themselves as the focal point of this poem underlines the deceptive elements that, from the first, have impeded the poet's vision. The poet's only direct access to celestial light occurs at the beginning of *Flowers of Evil*, when "Benediction" offers him a glimpse of his "mystic crown." Poetry, however, which is incapable of portraying this pure light, must fall back on images of the crown and the jewels that compose it, translating the celestial into earthly images.

The light reflected by the gems in "The Jewels" thus recalls to the poet images, though false ones, of his initial vision. Yet the gems in this poem are not confined to the ones worn by the woman. As the poet compares her charms to evil angels, he says they remove his soul from its solitary "crystal rock." The contrast between the purity of this single crystal and the multiplicity of the woman's jewels parallels the concentration of transcendent experience compared with the fragmentation echoed in the numerous and contrasting images used to describe the woman.

Dorothy M. Betz

THE JEWISH CEMETERY AT NEWPORT

Author: Henry Wadsworth Longfellow (1807-1882)
Type of poem: Meditation
First published: 1854; collected in *The Courtship of Miles Standish and Other Poems*, 1858

The Poem

"The Jewish Cemetery at Newport" is a lyric meditation in fifteen rhymed quatrains. The title indicates the location where Henry Wadsworth Longfellow focuses his reverie on time, history, and death. As in the tradition of English meditative poetry of the eighteenth century, the poem at once paints a visual portrait of the cemetery yet also uses the place as a way to explore the poet's own reflections.

The poem is set in Newport, Rhode Island, at the oldest Jewish burial ground in America, one long since abandoned. It is written from the perspective of a solitary observer basically identical with the poet himself. In the first two stanzas, the poet regards the cemetery, muses over its desertion, and thinks not only of the desolate present but also of its hallowed past.

In the fourth stanza, reading the names chiseled on the gravestones, the poet is caught by the incongruity between the biblical first names of the deceased and their Spanish and Portuguese surnames. This leads him to imagine the people behind the names, initiating the central movement in the poem, from the fourth to the eleventh stanzas. In this part of the poem, the poet conjures up a vivid spectacle as he contemplates the story of those now dead. He envisions the people worshiping in the synagogue, chanting Psalms, and mourning for their dead. He asked what prompted the Jews to emigrate, what "burst of Christian hate" led them to undertake the perilous voyage to America. The poet is eloquently aware of the oppression and suffering they had undergone in their lives, "The life of anguish and the death of fire," as well as the pathos of their deaths. With a historical sensitivity rare for his time, he mentions the many persecutions Jews had suffered at the hands of Christians who had accused the Jews of killing Christ.

In the final four stanzas, the poet takes a more detached point of view. Shifting from his imaginative vision of the experiences of those buried in the cemetery, he reflects on the implications of their fate. The poet feels pity for them, but he also admires their ability to persist through such obstacles. The persistence of their faith through the centuries moves him deeply. Because of their persecution, however, the Jews have had to bury themselves in their past. They read the "mystic volume" of the world "backward, like a Hebrew book." Instead of investing their hopes in the American promise offered to others who have made a similar journey, the Jews focus on the study of their religion and their laws. The poet sees this immersion in the past as grim and deathlike, yet he respects the learning and commitment this past inspired and is even astonished at its determination to endure in a new and strange land. Death, though, overtakes even the most determined of human traditions. The poem ends with the realization that, despite the sympathy and regret of the poet, "the dead nations never rise again."

Forms and Devices

Longfellow adapts his stanzaic form from poems in the English tradition, such as Thomas Gray's "Elegy Written in a Country Churchyard." These poems, like "The Jewish Cemetery at Newport," are concerned with the presence of death in the midst of a human landscape. The first and third lines of each four-line stanza rhyme, as do the second and fourth. This variety of stanza gives the impression of ceremony and dignity. The rhyming words are usually of one or two syllables and often contain very sharply defined vowels and consonants. This effect contributes to the sense of enclosure and reflective weight to be found in the poem. Longfellow departs from the tradition by his own highly individual stress and meter, which do not always follow the largely iambic patterns expected in English prosody since the Renaissance, and the poem's forms convey a sense of familiarity and ease. This ease assists in transmitting the very specific subject matter of the poem to an achieved poetic level.

The poem is filled with many strong visual images. These images do not point to the physical reality of the cemetery before the poet's eyes as much as to the scenes in the life that the poet imagines for the dead who are buried there. Much of the imagery is, either implicitly or explicitly, biblical. Longfellow, who was not Jewish himself, drew upon the knowledge of the Old Testament he possessed by virtue of his Christian background to supply the detail for his picture of the Jews buried in Newport. Longfellow assumes that the reader is educated and shares this knowledge. By comparing the lives of the Newport Jews with those of their biblical forebears, Longfellow lends the poem an aura of emotion and reverence. There is a sense that the cycle of life and death related in the poem has occurred not once but many times since biblical days. Longfellow's skillful choice of words (for example, when he rhymes "Synagogue" with "Decalogue," the Latin phrase for the Ten Commandments) combines specifically Jewish and biblical images with more universal poetic ones. An instance of this practice occurs when he speaks of the Jews living in "Ghetto and Judenstrass, in mirk and mire."

When specifically biblical terms are not being employed, Longfellow uses a diction that aspires to rhetorical heights. Longfellow's words express feeling, yet also decorum and gravity. By using words that even at the time seemed old-fashioned, such as "climes" and "spake," the poem exudes a sense of respect for the importance and venerability of its subject, and also of the tragic, somber level of its theme.

Although the poem is basically a monologue by the poet-observer, at times the poet seems to be speaking not only to himself but also to a more general reader. This is especially true when exclamation points are used in the first and final stanzas. The punctuation in both cases seeks to arouse the reader into responding intellectually and emotionally to the subject.

Themes and Meanings

"The Jewish Cemetery at Newport" is about death and about the past. These are themes to which Longfellow was unusually sensitive among poets of his age. Although Longfellow's reputation has never recovered from the drastic fall it took during the era of modernism, it should be recognized that the concern about history and memory this poem shows is rare during a period in which literature was often more concerned with an examination of the American present. Longfellow looks into the neglected odds and ends of history and finds meanings there that others overlook.

The poem contains well-researched, accurate information. It is true, for example, that the first Jews in America were Sephardim from Southern Europe. Longfellow, though, does not passively rely on this knowledge, but incorporates it into his own imaginative meditation. The story that the poet sees and finds in the cemetery in the end seems far more noteworthy than more contemporary ones that are more immediately attractive. The sensitivity of the poet is all the more impressive in that his positive regard for the Jews is notable at a time when anti-Semitism was unfortunately still not totally unrespectable.

The poem is not sentimental about the Jews of Newport. It does not try to pretend that their lives were ideal, nor does the poet become overly optimistic about what he can learn from them. There is no sense of breakthrough to a greater or inner truth at the end of the poem. His experience of the cemetery does not teach the poet about the nature of life. What he contemplates enriches his imagination, yet also warns it of the reality of suffering and of loss that has occurred in the past. Longfellow is vitally interested in the past, but he does not think this interest can save or redeem the present.

Although the poem is immersed in the details, real and imagined, of the Jewish cemetery, it is not exclusively about the place where it is set. In the final stanza, the poet makes the more universal point that "The groaning earth in travail and in pain/ Brings forth its races, but does not restore." Though one may learn from history, one finds that it is not full of endless creativity, but instead, of loss and sorrow. The final reference to the "dead nations" does not mean the poet sees the extinction of the Jewish people. He is referring more broadly to the impossibility of bringing the past into the present. The poet's empathy with the people buried at Newport can only go so far. They and he in the end are separated by the most crucial boundary of all: that between life and death.

Nicholas Birns

JOURNEY OF THE MAGI

Author: T. S. Eliot (1888-1965)
Type of poem: Dramatic monologue
First published: 1927; collected in *Collected Poems, 1909-1935*, 1936

The Poem

From the time that he prepared "The Hollow Men" for publication in 1925 until he wrote "Journey of the Magi" in July, 1927, T. S. Eliot wrote virtually no poetry at all. His personal convictions underwent enormous upheaval during that two-year hiatus, culminating in his baptism into the Church of England on June 29, 1927. Shortly thereafter, the editor at Faber & Gwyer publishers, for whom Eliot worked as an editor, asked Eliot to write a Christmas poem as one in a series of short, illustrated poems called the Ariel Poems. The result was "Journey of the Magi," published on August 25, 1927. It was, as Eliot said in an interview published in *The New York Times Book Review* (November 29, 1953), the poem that released the stream for all his future work. Thus the poem bears personal as well as artistic significance for Eliot.

"Journey of the Magi" is a first-person recollection of a Magus, one of the Persian Magi who came to visit the Christ child as recorded in the second chapter of Matthew. The poem is narrated, however, from the perspective of many years later, after the Magus has returned to his home country. He is an elderly man, reflecting on events that occurred many years prior.

The recollection is divided into three parts. The first stanza recalls the journey itself, the long and demanding ordeal of the caravan to Judaea. The weather was very cold and sharp; the camels had sores and often balked; the camel drivers were unhappy at their deprivations and ran away. There was little shelter, and the people they met were unfriendly: "A hard time we had of it." The second stanza describes their arrival, at dawn, at the Judaean valley, where they at last find a hospitable landscape with water and vegetation. In the stanza's last two lines, they arrive at Bethlehem, "not a moment too soon," and find the infant Christ.

The third stanza consists of a reflection on the meaning of the event. Here the Magus struggles with the significance of birth and death. He is aware of the prophecy that the Christ was born to die as an atonement, but he also reflects on his own approaching death.

It is helpful while reading the poem to remember that the Magi were king-priests of the royal tribe of Medes and that their primary tasks were to understand astronomical signs, to interpret dreams, and to understand prophecy. Their entire knowledge of the Christ derived from the Hebrew kingdom during its exile in Babylon beginning in 605 B.C.E., when Nebuchadnezzar conquered Judah. The most influential figure of that period was the Hebrew Daniel, who lived for sixty-six years in Persia and who prophesied the Messiah (Daniel 7:14).

Forms and Devices

This relatively simple story of the Magi is tightly packed with significance, particularly in Eliot's use of allusion and symbolism.

The poem bears echoes of authors who influenced Eliot's own spiritual journey, most notably Lancelot Andrewes. The poem opens with a quotation taken from Lancelot Andrewes's Nativity sermon, preached in 1622 to the Jacobean court. As he pointed out in his essay "Lancelot Andrewes" (*Selected Essays*, 1934), Eliot admired Andrewes's intellectual achievement, his ability to hold both intellectual idea and emotional sensibility in harmony, and his leadership in the church of seventeenth century England. Andrewes seemed to validate church membership for Eliot at a time when he was contemplating his own baptism into the church.

Furthermore, the staccato-like lines of the last section of the poem—the hesitation, repetition, and acceleration—were all techniques that Eliot admired in Andrewes's prose style. Eliot's lines in stanza 3, "but set down/ This set down/ This" also derive from patterns that Andrewes used in his Nativity sermons of 1616, 1622, and 1623.

"Journey of the Magi" creates more interest, however, by its complex pattern of biblical symbolism, which intensifies in stanza 2 as the Magi approach Bethlehem and the birth of the Christ. The symbolism seems to accelerate, as does the journey itself, toward its fulfillment.

The valley they enter is cut by a flowing stream, suggesting Jesus' claim to be the Living Water in John 4:10-14, and this living stream powers a mill that seems to beat away the darkness, further suggesting Jesus' claim in John 8:12 to be the Light of the World. With the dawning of this light, however, the Magi see first of all a symbol of death—"three trees on the low sky," or on the western horizon.

As they enter the valley, an old white horse gallops away. The reference here cannot be to the white horse of Revelation 19:11, as some have assumed, since that horse bears the Christ at his second coming. Rather, it refers to the white horse of Zechariah 6:5, whose task it was to announce the coming of the Messiah. That task now completed, the horse gallops away.

The Magi arrive at the first outpost of civilization and see, at a tavern, vine leaves over the lintel, suggesting the Old Testament Passover and Christ's fulfillment of it in his claim that he is the True Vine (John 15:1, 5). The next two lines were recorded earlier than the drafting of the poem in a notebook that Eliot kept, but they do fit the biblical pattern. The hands dicing for silver suggest the bartering for Christ (Matthew 26:14-16), and the feet kicking the empty wine-skins suggest Jesus' parable of the new wine in Matthew 9:17.

Led by such signs, the Magi arrive at the Christ child, finding the place and deeming it "satisfactory." The adjective satisfactory has troubled some readers, since it seems to understate the event, or to show some disappointment. That may be so. After all, the Magi were kingly priests seeking a king, and they found instead a rude stable. It may also be that Eliot employs the term "satisfactory" based on his study in philosophy, drawing upon the philosophical definition as a necessary and sufficient fulfillment of the signs given. As such, it is a statement of resolute conviction.

The Magus who tells the poem is, in any event, so powerfully taken by the event that years later it still disturbs him profoundly. The disturbance arises from the paradox of birth and death, the fact that this Messiah was also the one destined to die on one of the "three trees on the low sky." In fact, the Crucifixion may already have occurred and come to the Magus's knowledge. Thus he puzzles over the paradox: The Christ was born to die, and believers are dying to an old way of life, to be born again. He does not fully understand the puzzle, but he takes considerable solace from it, claiming that he would now be glad of his own physical death.

Themes and Meanings

Two important themes of Eliot emerge, and they link the poem to both his earlier and his later work. Like so many of Eliot's patterns, they are themselves in tension: light and dark, water and aridity.

Eliot's earlier poems are full of hot sunlight blasting across arid landscapes. It is a destructive light, seeming to drive people inward toward a spiritual isolation and darkness. "Journey of the Magi" begins in such a darkness. In fact, the Magi, after their guides desert them and they meet hostilities along the way, prefer to travel in darkness. The pattern signifies a lack of spiritual direction, a mere wandering, but it is only by the traveling itself that one can hope to apprehend the light. Moreover, their seeking is reciprocated. The power of the stream drives a water mill that drives away the night. Light does come, and with it comes revelation. A way is given; an end to the seeking is arrived at.

Concomitantly with the dawning of light comes the presence of renewing water. Although the travel of the Magi is not through the parched landscape of *The Waste Land* (1922), it is through an equally sterile and arid landscape of the cold winter. With the dawning, however, they meet the stream of running water. The two patterns work synchronously: The light signifies illumination; the water, renewal. Light and water are both notably absent in Eliot's earlier poems; they appear in significant ways, however, in the poetry he wrote following "Journey of the Magi." The poem represented a crossroads in Eliot's poetic career, providing a direction for his work to follow.

John H. Timmerman

JUNK

Author: Richard Wilbur (1921-   )
Type of poem: Lyric
First published: 1961, in *Advice to a Prophet and Other Poems*

The Poem

"Junk" is a thirty-line poem written in Anglo-Saxon strong-stress meter. Each line is alliterated and broken into two halves, the second of which is indented, making each full line two-tiered. In a note to the poem, Richard Wilbur provides a rough translation of the epigraph, which is excerpted from an Anglo-Saxon fragment: "Truly, Wayland's handiwork—the sword Mimming which he made—will never fail any man who knows how to use it bravely." The epigraph gives an example of the alliterative, accentual meter of the original.

The poem begins with the narrator's detailed description of a neighbor's trash, viewed with a frown of disapproval. It is a critic's notice: "hell's handiwork," inferior wood, the grain not followed in its construction, broken tumblers, warped boards. The cool appraisal is interrupted by an exclamation in line 11: "Haul them off! Hide them!" The speaker can hardly stand to look at this deplorable "junk and gimcrack," or to think of those responsible for the shoddiness, "men who make them/ for a little money." He likens these craftspeople to dishonest boxers and jockeys, but he thinks more favorably of the things themselves. Somehow they retain their honor, their composure, since they are not to blame for their sorry condition. They are prisoners whose consignment to the dump is a release, a purgatory in which they shed their junkiness and become like new again, unspoiled, ready to be used properly.

The elements will gradually transform these objects back to something close to their original states. The dump is a compost heap, a place where time and depth can pressurize the materials into diamondlike purity. The poem ends by referring to the mythic smiths Hephaestus and Wayland, immortal craftspeople as opposed to the immoral tricksters responsible for the junk. "Junk" describes a return to origins and proclaims a faith in something good and creative in the "making dark" of the human psyche.

Forms and Devices

Each line of Anglo-Saxon strong-stress meter contains four stresses, or accents, three of which are usually alliterated. The number of unstressed syllables is not counted. There is a strong caesura (pause or break) in the middle of each line. This caesura can be indicated by space between the two hemistiches (half-lines), but Wilbur chooses to drop the second half down so that each full line has a two-step arrangement. As Wilbur's first line shows, assonance (vowel repetition) can be used instead of consonant repetition: "axe angles," "ashcan." His second line, as well as the remaining twenty-eight, repeats consonants: "hell's handiwork," "hickory." Any three of a line's four stresses can alliterate. Sometimes all four do, as in the fifth line ("plastic playthings," "paper plates") and the nineteenth ("Talk," "torture," "tossed," "tailgate"). Lines 22 and 30 repeat the *w* sound in all four stresses. No adjacent lines alliterate on the same sound.

On the framework of the poem's thirty lines, Wilbur winds a series of ten sentences. A reader can chart the poem's tone and temper by noting how full and steady or how brief and fragmentary those sentences are. The poem begins with three long sentences, each three or four full lines long. Then two exclamations burst out in a single half-line and are followed by the longest sentence of the poem, which runs five and one-half lines. The next two sentences also include half-lines, but the poem ends with the steadiness of two sentences that are both four full lines in length. On a seismograph, the poem would begin calmly, register tremors in the middle, and end calmly after a gradual return to regularity. That structure supports the dramatic or emotional "plot" of the poem, which begins with detached observation, erupts with disgust, then comes to reassurance, to a recognition of good after all.

Rhetorically, the poem turns on the word "Yet" in line 17, slightly after the halfway point. After that, Wilbur emphasizes the passivity of the objects, which are unable to speak on their own behalf. They are tortured, "tossed," and will "waste in the weather/ toward what they were." They need an advocate, just as they need an honest craftsperson to bring out the lasting beauty latent within them, the "good grain" that can be rediscovered.

Wilbur, as advocate of these things, uses similes to describe their construction and quick disposal, presenting a little morality play: the villainous makers, "like the bought boxer" or the "paid-off jockey," versus the things themselves, "like captives who would not/ Talk under torture." The poem describes dishonesty countered by honor, but it is not especially comforting that the heroes are inanimate, simply able to withstand or outlast punishment, better off buried than out in the open.

The alliteration tends to cluster words that are palpable, words that have heft and flavor, even when they refer to the deplorable junk: "shivered shaft," "shattered tumblers," a "cast-off cabinet/ Of wavily-warped/ unseasoned wood." In describing ugliness, the poem rises to beauty. It is an illustration of how this ordinary junk really does have the potential to be more than "jerrybuilt things." Wilbur himself shows how.

Themes and Meanings

"Junk" is a poem about renewal. On a literal level, it envisions the recycling of shoddy goods into good raw materials. By extension, however, it also foresees the regeneration of the human soul. It is a paean to biodegradability as well as a meditation on culture, both a lament for American planned obsolescence and a hymn to natural process and artistic dedication.

Although the poem begins with an ironic, detached view of a banal, commercialized hell, a scene of wastefulness on an ordinary sidewalk, it ends with a lofty, impassioned vision of a different underworld, the "making dark." Between the dull, discarded objects and the "depth of diamonds" there is an all-important illumination, the sun glorying "in the glitter of glass-chips." This sunlight will act literally and figuratively like a paint stripper, a purging light in which both object and spirit can be cleansed.

The image of an axe at the poem's opening represents a means of breaking into pieces, chopping down, and gathering materials, yet it too is simply junk headed for the dump. The axe also echoes the sword mentioned in the epigraph, a weapon for a hero, an instrument of deliverance. Knowing how to use a sword bravely is analogous to the poet's task of cutting through the appearances of things to the truth they embody—or could embody.

A number of words in the poem suggest Anglo-Saxon culture: "axe," "angles," "shaft," "shellheap," "dolmens," "barrows." As in most of Wilbur's poems, the vocabulary is rich, precise, and evocative. The Anglo-Saxon form reflects a rough culture; the alliterative line clangs noisily. It is physical, hefty, pushy, combative, primitive, almost berserk on words, almost incantatory and hypnotic. It brings Beowulf to suburbia. One of the marvels of the poem is the blending of this tough, hardy, oar-splashing, sword-wielding form with the characteristic elegance of Wilbur's argument, his steady pacing of sentences interrupted in line 11 by two exclamations that are the dramatic heart of the poem: "Haul them off! Hide them!"

One of the twentieth century's poetic dilemmas has been the difficulty of bringing the industrialized world into poems without losing the poetry. Poetry that ignores its actual surroundings is merely escapist, yet poetry that uncritically embraces cultural trash might not be poetry at all. Wilbur presents the junk of mass production directly as evidence of industrial degradation, but he also imagines a way out, a way that is not merely a nostalgic return to a buried vitality but also a vigorous recapturing of it.

The poem is about discarding and recovering—and the transformation that time, earth, and the decay of the compost heap can bring about. One of the things recovered here is the poetic form itself, the Anglo-Saxon meter, revived from obsolescence into something contemporary and American. Other twentieth century English and American poets used the form, notably W. H. Auden in his long poem, *The Age of Anxiety* (1947). As if to demonstrate that writing in the form was more than a tour de force, Wilbur began his next collection, *Walking to Sleep: New Poems and Translations* (1969), with "The Lilacs," another poem in Anglo-Saxon meter.

"Junk" is a kind of *ars poetica*, suggesting a view of the art of poetry, which similarly begins anew in the "making dark." The Scots call a poet a *makar*, or "maker," and Robert Graves has likened the craft of poetry to smithcraft. The two deities allied in this restorative enterprise are the Germanic Wayland and the Greek Hephaestus, both smiths. The poem begins (in the epigraph, a recovered fragment) and ends with Wayland, who gives a sense of mythic transformation, which is the goal and reward of honest craftsmanship.

John Drury

THE K

Author: Charles Olson (1910-1970)
Type of poem: Lyric
First published: 1948, in *Y and X*

The Poem

"The K" is a lyric poem of twenty-six lines written in free verse. It interprets the let-ter *K* as a physical symbol of the fully realized human being who, in harmony with the moon's gravitational force, moves beyond conventional limitations conditioned by Western civilization and bridges the gap between the subjective and the objective and between the self and the natural realm of total reality.

The escape from the partitioning of reality characteristic of the modern Western mind to the attainment of a wholeness of being marked the principal aim of Charles Olson's art and thought. As he stated about ultimate human aspirations in *The Special View of History* (1956), "each one of us has the desire for the good (Love), we move to beauty (Aphrodite), we care for the Real (Truth or Idea), and we have to do something about it, whatever we do (we Will)." Poetry is meant to assist humanity in the process of such self-realization by reimagining the world, reorienting readers, and thereby dissolving the separation between the delimited self and the outer, total reality.

The poem begins with an energetic and upbeat interpretation of "The K" as, liter-ally, an alphabetical symbol of the "tumescent I" that is the fully realized self in har-mony with the external natural force of the moon acting on the tidal energies and po-tentialities of a human being. The upward linear stroke of the letter *K* represents the flowing out of the self in response to the moon's gravitational pull. The K's downward linear stroke signifies the ebbing of the self under relaxation of the lunar force. The "tumescent I" is a vital, ever-expanding and contracting flowering of one's identity.

Such self-actualization is a revolutionary new goal for humanity ("The affairs of men remain a chief concern"). Reaching the goal brings harmony ("We have come full circle") and promises a millennial victory for the liberation of the self, provided one transcends boundaries, such as delimiting gender identity ("the fatal male small span"), and integrates opposites, like male and female, into a wholeness of being ("I shall not see the year 2000/ unless I stem straight from my father's mother"). If that in-tegration is humanity's fate ("what the tarot pack proposed"), then the speaker will sing a fitting song integrating opposites: He sings "as she" does and weds silence and sound in "one unheard liturgy."

Self-actualization is not a prophecy for the future: It is happening now, as inner tidal energies inherently reach out to bond with the lunar-driven forces of the outer natural world. Such harmony of being ("Full circle") is attainable. Therefore, discard the delimiting culture of Western civilization, and end all rule-mongering derived from Roman, Greek, and Christian systems of thought. Put a stop to "romans" (mean-ing "Romans" as well as restrictive conventions signified by "roman types, letters, and print"). Rid the world of "hippocrats" (the conflation of "hypocrites" and of "Hippocratic" followers of stifling Western codes embodied in the medical oath). Finally, go beyond the stifling Western creed of "christians" imitating ("ecco" for "echo") their misery-loving Christ crucified ("Ecce homo!" for "Behold the man!")

Genuine self-realization requires rejecting the lessons of the civilized past and pursuing a "simpler" route to oneness with the natural world's lunar forces ("The salts and minerals of the earth return"). The speaker's final advice is for humanity to embrace the moon, its shadows and its night, as the way of reaching wholeness of being ("a bridge, a horse") and as the way of ending ("the gun, a grave") the old conventional life of the circumscribed self of society's making.

Forms and Devices

"The K" has an exuberantly affirmative mood that bears comparison with the hortatory tone of Walt Whitman's *Song of Myself* (1855) and Friedrich Nietzsche's *Also sprach Zarathustra* (1883-1885; *Thus Spake Zarathustra*, 1896).

Olson's poetry was directly influenced by the poetic techniques of Ezra Pound. Pound had helped spearhead the modernist revolution in early twentieth century poetry of the Western world, and Olson was perhaps the most prominent, if critical, follower of the methods practiced in Ezra Pound's *Cantos* (1917-1970). Both men shared an abhorrence of vague abstractions (Olson considered them the major obstacle preventing the attainment of a totality of being).

Both poets strove for the exact word (*le mot juste*) and the precise image and discarded discursive poetic statement. Both favored intense compression and ellipsis—the deletion of all unnecessary words—to achieve a complex suggestiveness of meaning with an absolute economy of language (for example, "Assume I shall not" or "Our attention is simpler"). Both had a flair for neologism and created new words out of familiar ones. Olson invents "hippocrats" by conflating "hypocrites" and adherents to "Hippocratic" oaths, and he invents "ecco" by conflating the verb "to echo" in English with the Latin adverb "ecce" as in the phrase "ecce homo!" or "behold the crucified Christ!" in the Gospel passage.

Both Pound and Olson indulged heavily in allusions to literary and historical figures and events to lend a mythic richness and universality of meaning to their poems (for example, Olson's "romans, hippocrats and christians" and "the cross/ ecco men and dull copernican sun").

Olson imitated Pound's penchant for the literal and pictorial character of words that reached its zenith with the use of ideograms (word signs capturing a physical actuality, in place of detested abstractions). Hence, Olson's poem focuses on the letter *K* to signify the gravitational ebb and flow of the fulfilled human spirit (the "tumescent I") in harmony with the lunar force of nature. Word signs of moving toward integration ("a bridge, a horse") and of ending old habits ("the gun, a grave") conclude the poem.

The major symbol of the poem is the moon. With its gravitational effect on tides, it is used to express the harmony between the self and the totality of the natural world of being and becoming.

Themes and Meanings

"The K" is about remaking oneself into a "tumescent I" by moving into a wider world of being and becoming, beyond the conventional boundaries of Western civilization and in harmony with nature's lunar force.

Olson's influential essay "Projective Verse" (1950) rejected the partitioning of reality separating the human from the natural world. Poetry is to assist readers in breaking down conventional boundaries and in experiencing the totality of things: "A poem is energy transferred from where the poet got it, . . . by way of the poem itself to, all the way over to, the reader. Okay. Then the poem itself must, at all points, be a high energy-construct and, at all points, an energy discharge." Thus, the poem must go beyond the representation of meaning and seek a presentation of reality to end the estrangement between the socially conditioned self and the totality of the objective world of nature.

In another of Olson's experimental essays, *"Human Universe"* (1965), there is an attack against Socrates for fathering the delimiting Western system of education: "We have lived long in a generalizing time, at least since 450 B.C.E. And it has had its effects on the best of men, on the best of things. Logos, or discourse, for example, has, in that time, so worked its abstractions into our concept and use of language that language's other function, speech, seems so in need of restoration that several of us go back to hieroglyphs or to ideograms to right the balance. (The distinction here is between language as the act of the instant and language as the act of thought about the instant.)" Olson's poetry, indulging in a regular use of ideograms influenced by Pound, aimed to retrieve language's supposedly lost function of speech for a vivid communication of actuality ("the act of the instant") transcending the cognitive detachment of abstraction and generalization. "Art does not seek to describe but to enact": "The K" attempts to fulfill this artistic imperative.

Thomas M. Curley

KADDISH

Author: Allen Ginsberg (1926-1997)
Type of poem: Elegy
First published: 1961, in *Kaddish and Other Poems, 1958-1960*

The Poem

"Kaddish" is a long elegy infused with stream of consciousness; it is divided into six parts with long poetic lines and passages of prose. The title comes from the Judaic prayer, recited in daily services, in praise of God and in memory of the dead. The term itself sets the elegiac tone of the poem, announcing principally that the poem is in memory of the poet's mother, Naomi Ginsberg, who had died three years earlier.

The title also anticipates the poem's first-person point of view and suggests a confessional tone. To say that the poem is confessional is to suggest that the poet directly addresses the reader (or, in this case, his mother, as a posthumous reader) without the mediation of a persona. More important than the confessional stance, which could imply simply an autobiographical approach, is that Allen Ginsberg is revealing intensely private experiences that have not only shaped his life but also formed the muse of his poetic sensibilities. Thus, he claims early in the poem that "Death is that remedy all singers dream of." Singer here represents the poet, whose historic duty has been to sing the truth. This concept of the singer brings to mind the beginning of Vergil's *Aeneid* (c. 29-19 B.C.E.), which begins "Arma virumque cano" (I sing of arms and the man). "Kaddish" becomes a song for the dead, begun, as the first six words indicate, in present tense, but with the distance of recollection: "Strange now to think of you."

The first section of the poem, called "Proem," acts as a prelude for what follows in the other five sections. It has the aura of a musical overture, highlighting the themes and motifs that will come forth in their full complexities later. The first two lines announce the poem's modus operandi, as the following words suggest: strange, think, you, eyes, walk, village, winter, night, Kaddish, blues. The poet is in a singularly peculiar state. He believes that it is strange to think of his mother while walking on a sunny day in New York City's Greenwich Village; he has been up the night before reading the Kaddish aloud and listening to the blues. In these two images, Ginsberg unites the larger backdrops of this elegy: his Jewish heritage and the private suffering, as depicted in blues music, of living painfully and in isolation. Readers familiar with Ginsberg's poetry will recognize that these two ideas create the foundation of his canon.

What follows is a recollection of his mother's immigration and early life in America, ending with the invented prayer, written in prose lines, that he sings to the "Nameless, One Faced, Forever beyond me, beginningless, endless, Father." The second section, called "Narrative," recounts his mother's bouts with insanity, from the time the poet was twelve until her death in 1956, three years before the poem was written. The story of her paranoia ends at the moment of her final sickness and ultimate death. Infused in these final passages about her life is the poet's sudden dramatic address to her, where he writes: "O glorious muse that bore me from the womb, gave suck first mystic life & taught me talk and music, from whose pained head I first took Vision." Here Ginsberg reveals what he only implied in the poem's first few lines—that his mother's life, and death, constitute the source of his poetic energy.

The third section, called "Hymmnn," is a complete and invented prayer, a return to the song motif, recited both to "He who builds Heaven in Darkness" and to the mother-muse Naomi. The fourth section, "Lament," is a list of regrets. The poet wishes he could have understood his mother's painful, paranoiac visions better and not have resisted the uncontrollable way that she brought pain on him and his family. The fifth, called "Litany," reiterates the poem's major episodes of his mother's illnesses and relapses into an incantatory prayer which begins "O mother/ what have I left out" and ends with a list of the various "eyes" of her life, from the "eyes of Russia and the "eyes of Czechoslovakia attacked by robots" to the "eyes of lobotomy" and the "eyes of stroke." The final section, "Fugue," ends in an utter rending of emotion with the poet unable to articulate anything more than "Lord Lord Lord caw caw caw."

Forms and Devices

Ginsberg's two principal formal devices in "Kaddish" bring about the poem's impression of sadness and remorse. The first is what could best be called stream-of-consciousness writing—that is, the unending and unyielding movement of thoughts and emotions. One can see this stream of consciousness most obviously in the poem's punctuation, in particular the dash. The use of the dash is relentless; in each use, it announces an associative and subsequent thought or emotional condition. For example, in the second section, "Narrative," a prose stanza reads: "Once locked herself in with razor or iodine—could hear her cough in tears at sink—Lou broke through glass greenpainted door, we pulled her out to the bedroom."

Lou is the poet's father. What is typical of this passage is that the dash separates images into categories that resemble the pattern in which the poet remembers them. By not relying on traditional syntactic constructions or regular sentence patterns, Ginsberg heightens the tension between memory and experience. He intensifies the severity and the unswerving nature of the narrative itself. Because he leaves out the expected punctuation of periods, for example, thoughts never end but keep moving, the way the poet himself keeps moving by walking on the streets of New York City, as announced at the beginning of the poem.

A second device is the poet's simultaneous juxtaposition and linkage of song and prayer. Both song and prayer are expressions of celebration, be they joyous or sorrowful. If one thinks of song as the more secular and prayer as the more religious, one can see how Ginsberg uses these two forms to mediate the pathos of the poem. Ultimately, as the title of the poem predicts, prayer wins out—as the final sections of the poem give way to an outpouring of emotion and recitation of mourning.

Still, the poet is constantly trying to use the motif of song as a remedy for his grief. Thus, as he says at the beginning of section 2, images "run thru the mind—like the saxophone chorus of houses and years." By returning to the texture and sound of blues, the poet can resist his sorrow. Yet in a moment of self-blame and self-guilt later in the same section, the poet breaks from the narrative to recite a line in Hebrew from the Kaddish itself: "Yisborach, v'yistabach, v'yispoar, v'yisroman, v'yisnaseh, v'yishador, v'yishalleh, v'yishallol, sh'meh d'kudsho, b'rich hu." Here, the recitation of the Kaddish perhaps eases his suffering; or, if not that, since the song of the poem is not the remedy he had sought, the recitation of the actual Kaddish—rather than the poem as a form of Kaddish—reminds him of his sorrow, and in that he finds a kind of solace.

Themes and Meanings

Ultimately, a prayer for the dead is recited to cleanse the pain of the speaker. Yet it appears in "Kaddish" that Ginsberg only makes things worse for himself. One theme of the poem is the double nature of remembrance: how it both heals and hurts. This juxtaposition is typical for the elegy. For the speaker, remembering his mother is a method for praising her life—except that here, her life is revealed as one that incurred such immense pain that remembering and retelling the horror of it becomes another form of pain, a reiteration of past sorrows, a recapitulation of the poet's loss.

In one moment, Ginsberg describes his whole poem as a lament. If one thinks of lament less as regret or mourning and more as wailing—and in that sound it is a song of grief—one comes closer to the poem's overriding theme of calling out, of moaning. This crying is articulated at the end of the "Proem": "Death, stay thy phantoms!" Ginsberg suggests that living is painful enough, full of psychological adversities such as those experienced by Naomi, that death would be helpful if it simply did not unleash its gestures of remorse. In a larger context, her suffering embodies the fear of the unknown, everyone's fear of the unaccountable. Perhaps that fear in and of itself is a reason people say prayers for the dead.

In that, one finds another theme of "Kaddish": the poet's need to write poems. Ginsberg has always filled the role of the prophet-poet, and those familiar with his work will recognize the bardic nature of "Kaddish." In this sense, the poem is an act of primordial utterance, spoken to the dead out of respect for the dead.

David Biespiel

KALEIDOSCOPE

Author: Paul Verlaine (1844-1896)
Type of poem: Lyric
First published: 1883, as "Kaléidoscope"; collected in *Jadis et naguère*, 1884; English translation collected in *Selected Poems*, 1948

The Poem

The twenty-eight lines of "Kaleidoscope" are divided into seven four-line stanzas of Alexandrine verse (twelve-syllable lines). The rhyme scheme (*abba, cddc,* and so on), with alternating masculine and feminine end rhymes, is traditional in French poetry. In these seven quatrains, fragments of diverse sensory impressions of the past are presented to the reader in juxtaposed images that change like bits of colored glass in a kaleidoscope.

Paul Verlaine composed the poem during his incarceration in Brussels, after being arrested for firing at and wounding his lover, the young poet Arthur Rimbaud. The two poets had returned from London, where they had spent several months. The poem recollects images from this period spent wandering the streets of London with Rimbaud, reality obscured by alcohol, time rendered timeless by love and pleasure.

In the first stanza, the locale of the poem is established: a city street. Neither the street nor the city is real, though: It is a dream city, yet one that evokes a sensation of past experience, of déjà vu characterized by vagueness and clarity at the same time. A single image, "sun shining through a fog," appears in the first stanza and confirms the inspiration for the poem: The sun suggests physical desire, the fog suggests London.

The second stanza opens with two auditory images. There is a "voice in the woods" and a "cry on the sea." These sounds are surprising, for they seem contradictory to the city street locale of the first stanza. The contradiction is resolved when one wakes up from these "metempsychoses" (transmigrations of the soul, used here in the sense of altered states, or dreams) only to find that things have not changed. Reality is, then, in a woods, near the sea. The city is the dream.

The third stanza plunges the reader back into the dream city streets where organ grinders and marching bands are heard, where cats sleep on tavern countertops. Two of these three images are musical ones and show the importance of music in Verlaine's poetry. "Music above all," he would write later in his "Art poétique."

In the fourth stanza, a polarity of human emotions—joy and sadness, laughter and tears—are "invocations to death." In the dream city, one experiences emotional extremes that are viewed as inevitable and fatal. Such was indeed the case of Verlaine's relationship with Rimbaud. Verlaine claimed to have been born under the malignant influence of a dark star. His escapade with Rimbaud was both agony and ecstasy. Verlaine considered it his ineluctable fate.

The next two stanzas continue to present colorful sights, sounds, and smells of the city: Widows, peasant women, and prostitutes mingle with soldiers and dandruff-laden old men; dance-hall music and firecrackers are heard; the odor of urine is in the air.

The final quatrain is a return to the states of dreaming and waking mentioned in the second stanza. One wakes up and falls asleep again into the same dream, but this time the dream is not the city. It is the summer, the grass, and the buzz of a bee—the bucolic decor of woods and seashore in stanza 2. Reality and dream have changed places.

Forms and Devices

The poem is an example of poetic impressionism: Verlaine suggests with verbal imagery the same way Debussy suggests with music and Monet suggests with pastels. Verlaine veils his meaning, deliberately obscuring contours in order to create an enchanting vagueness in which there are elements of both the unknown and the familiar. "Kaleidoscope" is written in accordance with Verlaine's personal system, which he developed around the time the poem was written (1873, ten years before publication). In this system, Verlaine sought to eliminate entirely the first person, the poet, the "moi," from poetry. In this poem, the "I" is replaced by the more nebulous, nonspecific pronoun "one."

Although the poem is set visually in quatrains, it is knit together verbally. Three stanzas are joined by the continuation of a sentence from the last line of one to the first line of the next without a syntactical pause. Others are joined by repeating first words (lines 4 and 5 begin "Oh this . . . !"), which allows Verlaine to blur the traditional boundaries of the poetic stanza.

Except for the word "metempsychoses," the vocabulary of the poem is simple, almost childlike. The phrase "It will be as if . . ." ("Ce sera comme quand on . . .") is a colloquialism Verlaine often used. In keeping with this puerile simplicity, he uses much repetition, especially at line beginnings (in French, "Où" begins lines 10 and 11 and "Des" opens lines 14, 15, 16, and 17). There are alliterations (a *v* sound in the first stanza and an *f* sound in the fifth); internal rhyme (the "on" and "or" of line 26: "Et que l'on se rendort et que l'on rêve encor"); consonances; and weak end rhymes that function primarily as assonance with a preponderance of "open" vowels. These devices create sonorities that enhance the suggestivity and musicality of the work.

Of all the figurative language in "Kaleidoscope," the most striking are the two oxymorons in the fourth stanza. In line 14, the tears rolling down his cheeks are qualified in French as "douces" ("sweet"), the opposite of "salty." The oxymoron in the next line is easily translated as "laughter sobbed." The apparent contradiction in terms serves to heighten the degree of each emotion and, simultaneously, to cloud the reader's perception of the causes for the extreme joy or sorrow. After all, "It will be as if one had forgotten the causes" (line 6).

Since music was extremely important to Verlaine, the rhythm of his verse is particularly interesting. His favorite rhythmic innovation was the displacement of the caesura. (In French poetry, this mid-line pause is after the sixth syllable.) It is displaced in most of the lines of "Kaleidoscope." In several lines, there is no place at all for the caesura (notably in those lines beginning "It will be as if one . . ."). As the poem progresses, the number of pauses increases. By the final stanza, there is a caesura in the first three lines and two caesuras (reinforced by commas) in the last line. The effect is that of a musical ritardando, a slowing down of the rhythm for the conclusion.

Themes and Meanings

Verlaine was a Parnassian poet (that is, believing in art for art's sake) in the sense that he was horrified at the idea of using poetry as a vehicle for preaching ideas or indulging in self-pity, as was often the case with the Romantics. He wrote to the poet Stéphane Mallarmé that his poetry was an effort to render sensations drawn from a personal world of memory and illusion. It is helpful to keep this purpose in mind when interpreting Verlaine's work.

Many poets through the ages have dealt with the theme of the passage of time. "Kaleidoscope" looks to the future in using the repeated line "It will be . . ." ("Ce sera . . .") and by the predominance of the future tense throughout the poem in French. Yet the dream is about the past "as if one had lived there." The verbs "wakes" and "falls asleep" are in the present tense. By obscuring the division of time into past, present, and future, the poem presents time as an illusion, irrelevant, because it is subject to distortion by the senses.

Like Charles Baudelaire (1821-1867), a poet of the preceding generation, Verlaine chose as his primary subject modern man, who must cope physically with the refinements of an excessive civilization, more specifically, the sentient creature confronted with the lure of the city, the vices of the social underworld. In "Kaleidoscope," the city is London, but it is also Paris, Brussels, any city. The reader enters the poet's personal world of sensation, which immediately becomes the reader's personal world, "one's" own experience. It suffices merely to hint at, to suggest, meaning in muted tones and minor keys.

"Kaleidoscope" is a poem about the dichotomy of the human condition, the contrasts and contradictions inherent in human beings. There are dream states and waking states, both of which seem to be reality at the time. There are experiences of great joy and extreme sadness. There are moments of clarity ("this sun") and moments of dim perception ("a fog"). There is a longing for the purity of nature and a fascination with the corruption of the city. There is the will to live and the will to die. In the poem, lines distinguishing one from its opposite have been obscured; it is impossible to differentiate reality from dreams, pleasure from pain, past from present or present from future, or, by extension, good from bad and right from wrong. One is no more than the reflected image of the other. Viewed in this light, the poem is truly a kaleidoscope in which the mirror of poetry creates symmetrical patterns out of random pieces of sensation.

Judith Barban

KICKING THE HABIT

Author: Lawson Fusao Inada (1938-   )
Type of poem: Lyric
First published: 1993; collected in *Drawing the Line*, 1997

The Poem
"Kicking the Habit" is a poem of slightly fewer than one hundred lines written in free verse. Most of the lines are relatively short, averaging three to five words. The stanzas are irregular and break every few lines where the voice would normally pause or reach a full stop. Lawson Fusao Inada also indents several sections to indicate vocal emphasis in this poem, which, given its conversational language, was obviously intended to be read aloud. It is also obvious that the poem is meant to be read aloud specifically by the poet himself, who uses the first-person "I" to tell of his experience and frustration with the English language.

The title of the poem suggests a resolution that a person makes to get rid of some annoying, obsessive, or destructive behavior. The phrase is commonly used in connection with smoking cigarettes or consuming alcohol, the goal being to "kick" or overcome a bad habit. Surprisingly, Inada applies the phrase to his habit of speaking English, which readers are to assume has become a bad habit for him: "I was exhausted,/ burned out,/ by the habit./ And I decided to/ kick the habit,/ cold turkey." One of the methods of any poet is to use surprising, even arresting verbal juxtapositions to shape new and memorable images in proving his point, and Inada does that here. He upsets his readers' expectations because he is upset.

From the beginning, Inada brings his readers into the immediacy and frustration that he feels on the particular morning that his poem is set. He has made an urgent and irreversible promise to himself "Late last night" to give up on the English language. This resolve was reached, as a series of seven progressive verbs specifies, after the poet had immersed himself in English thoroughly by "talking," "listening," "thinking," "reading," "remembering," "feeling," and "even driving" in English. He therefore decides to go on an unusual, symbolic journey, pulling himself "off the main highway." After arriving at a place that is completely new, he simply stops. The poet then digresses for several lines to reassure readers and himself that he does not mean to complain; after all, the language that he is intent on giving up is his own "native tongue," and, until last night, he had been "addicted to it" all his life.

After kicking English out of his life, the poet "kicked/ open the door of a cage/ and stepped out from confinement/ into the greater world." It is that greater, larger, and therefore better world that he spends the last half of the poem describing. It is a world of liberation in which nature and humanity of all races are in harmony, and real communication, awareness, and empathy are possible. Having happened onto such a new place, having experienced such an elevated realm of sharpened senses and appreciation, the poet is then able to retain some essence of that world and take it with him "on the road of life,/ in the code of life" back to his own place in the universe.

Forms and Devices

The central symbol in Inada's poem is that of a profoundly important journey. This is a significant symbol for a Japanese American writer such as Inada to use. A journey can be undertaken in hope, in the belief that the place of arrival holds the promise of a better life than the life one leaves behind. This was the dream that many Asian immigrants held as they boarded boats bound to America, the Gold Mountain. Though Inada and his parents were born in California—he is thus not a first-generation immigrant but a Sansei, or third-generation resident—some of his writing concerns the history of Japanese people in general and of his grandparents in particular, people who crossed the Pacific Ocean in search of a new life in America. The "greater world" that the narrator perceives and the " 'Clackamas, Siskiyou'" that the pine trees utter resonate with the hope and beauty at the end of such a journey, specifically the beauty and peace that Inada found in the landscape of Oregon, where he has made his home since the mid-1960's.

Inada's journey motif is also significant in the sense that some journeys are not willingly undertaken but imposed, and these can be difficult and even harsh. Inada's family undertook this type of relocation three times during the World War II internment of the Japanese living in the United States. "Each camp was different, and the same," Inada says of the three camps in which his family was detained: Fresno Assembly Center (the county fairgrounds), Jerome Camp (an Arkansas swamp in the Mississippi Delta), and Amache Camp (in the Colorado desert). Inada's second collection of poetry, *Legends from Camp* (1992), is loosely based on his childhood impressions of his years in the camps recollected in the adult perceptions of a poet who is also a lover of jazz. The collection in which "Kicking the Habit" appears is Inada's third book of poetry, *Drawing the Line*, which continues the thread of those camp recollections. The title of the book refers to a group of Japanese men in the Heart Mountain internment camp who "drew the line" by resisting the government's order to be drafted into the military and who were thus sent to federal prison. "Kicking the Habit," along with the other poems in this collection, is Inada's way of drawing a personal and ethnic line of his own. It is a statement about what he loves, what he remembers, what place and landscape mean to him, and what it is that has given him hope and has made him wise. Though a journey may be fraught with complexities and surprises, the poem suggests, both the traveling and the arrival significantly shape the poet's identity.

Themes and Meanings

"Kicking the Habit" is protest literature voiced in the most effective way that a poet can utter it. It is a serious statement for a poet, whose business involves writing words, to insist on giving up those words "cold turkey," refusing to use the language anymore. Inada wants readers to think about just how serious the implications are: Poets without words have given up their essences and their identities. Inada knows that this is a metaphor for giving up anything precious and essential, which is basically what the Japanese Americans were forced to do during the internment years of World War II. They were ordered to relinquish possessions, homes, neighborhoods, and businesses and relocate to barracks in fairgrounds and deserted racetracks. Though Inada's recollections of his camp life in *Legends from Camp* and *Drawing the Line* are told with nostalgia and even warmth rather than overt bitterness or anger, the message is obvious nonetheless: Japanese Americans, Inada and his family among them, were victimized by the U.S. government. He, the poet, will protest this atrocity with an atrocity of his own: giving up his use of the English language.

The poet knows that the problem is that he is a member of a minority race rather than part of the American mainstream: "I pulled off the main highway/ onto a dark country road." He knows he must justify his existence by showing his "passport" to "insects" and his "baggage" to "frogs": "After all, I was a foreigner,/ and had to comply." However, the continual deferring and explaining, the apology for using English, is wearing him out. Therefore, he goes on his own internal journey to get in touch with himself, which results in becoming attuned to a universe of all races and creatures: "Ah, the exquisite seasonings/ of syllables, the consummate consonants, the vigorous/ vowels of varied vocabularies."

The poet's passive method of resistance is to give up his language and then to take it up again after he has been renewed. It is a statement not only of threat and revenge but also of promise because readers find out that the revenge does not last: Having satisfied his need for revenge, having visited that place for a while, the poet has worked through his problem, has been avenged, and has come to a greater, more benevolent, more forgiving place. "Kicking the Habit" is thus a poem of reconciliation and redemption ending with a blessing by the morning sun, which, being "yellow" (usually a derogatory term when applied to Asians and cowards) is also the color of his race, a color he can now acknowledge with pride. The poet has, in effect, turned a negative vision, one that he has harbored and that others have harbored about him and his race, into a positive one.

Jill B. Gidmark

KILLING FLOOR

Author: Ai (Florence Anthony; 1947-   )
Type of poem: Dramatic monologue
First published: 1978; collected in *Killing Floor,* 1979

The Poem

"Killing Floor" is a free-verse monologue that dramatizes three moments in the life of Leon Trotsky. Born Lev Davidovich Bronstein, Trotsky—one of the most important figures of the Bolshevik Revolution of 1917—was assassinated in Mexico in 1940 after being exiled from the Soviet Union. Using violent imagery to establish a context of spiritual and political crisis, Ai constructs a poetic autobiography of Trotsky that exposes the spiritual and psychological dimensions underlying historical fact. Related by Ai's imagined version of Trotsky, the poem's series of nightmares and awakenings leads gradually to the scene of Trotsky's assassination with an ax. Within this context of nightmare, politics, and butchery, "Killing Floor" explores the effects that political and personal sacrifices have on the human soul.

Section 1, entitled "Russia, 1927," introduces the atmosphere of anxiety and violence that gradually permeates the poem. Trotsky, the speaker of the poem, is both Bronstein the private individual and Trotsky the political figure. He awakens "ninety-three million miles" (the distance from the Earth to the Sun) from himself to a swim not in the "azure water of Jordan" but in the "darkened" waters of the Volga. Just as the river Jordan is displaced upon waking by the Volga, the deathlike man with the "spade-shaped hands" is replaced upon waking by Joseph Stalin, the man who exiled Trotsky. Ten years after the revolution, with Communist leader Vladimir Ilich Lenin dead, the Soviet Union is at a crossroads, a choice between the totalitarian road Stalin proposed or the more democratic path advocated by Trotsky. The depredation and violence Stalin would bring to the Soviet Union is foreshadowed in Trotsky's vision:

> but I hear the hosts of a man drowning in water and holiness,
> the castrati voices I can't recognize,
> skating on knives, from trees, from air
> on the thin ice of my last night in Russia.

Stalin whispers in Trotsky's ear the conditions of his exile. The section ends with Trotsky's answer: *"I have only myself. Put me on the train./ I won't look back."*

In the poem's second section, "Mexico, 1940," the submerged violence of section 1 erupts into Trotsky's dreams. Trotsky awakens from a nightmare vision; this awakening amplifies rather than dispels the reader's sense of impending disaster. Ai heightens the dramatic tension of this section by breaking it into two halves. The first half relates the fact that Trotsky has had a dream of murder; the second half depicts in striking imagery the details of this dream. Between the two halves of the section, Ai wedges an expression of calm and serenity: "A marigold in winter." She then closes the section by obliterating this sense of calm removal, returning to the nightmare: "my head fell to one side, hanging only by skin."

"Mexico, August 20, 1940," the third section of the poem, opens with another nightmare but quickly moves the violence into Trotsky's reality. In his nightmare, bullets zigzag up the body of his wife. Trotsky cuts open her gown and attempts to stop the bleeding with his own body. This final nightmare emerges into the reality of the poem. As Trotsky rouges his cheeks and lips at his wife's vanity, he feels "lined and empty." The toll of exile and of continual threat has exhausted him. As he looks into the mirror, he is attacked—not in dream, but in fact:

> He moves from the doorway,
> lifts the pickax
> and strikes the top of my head.
> My brain splits.
> The pickax keeps going
> and when it hits the tile floor,
> it flies from his hands,
> a black dove on whose back I ride

The killing floor of the poem's title resounds with the violence of the fatal blow and the exhilaration of Trotsky's release from the myriad uncertainties of his existence. In the closing lines, the oppositions of identity and perspective that haunt Ai's version of Trotsky are not so much resolved as recognized: "a black dove on whose back I ride,/ two men, one cursing,/ the other blessing all things." In an ambiguous ending, the personal figure (Bronstein) separates from the political one (Trotsky). Ironically, this killing becomes a liberation from duality that frees Trotsky from the burden of nightmarish anxiety. The split between the two halves of himself resolves in a unifying act of purification in the holy river of Trotsky's Jewish ancestors: "*Lev Davidovich Bronstein,/ I step from Jordan without you.*"

Forms and Devices

Ai adopts Trotsky as a poetic persona through which she narrates this first-person, three-act drama about the human costs of revolutionary commitment. Emphasizing oppositions between the political and the personal, the public and the private, and dream and reality, this poem portrays the personal crises behind the historical facts of Trotsky's life. The three sections of the poem lead the reader through three stages in Trotsky's journey from exile to assassination. Imparting to history a surrealistic, cinematic context, the poem provides the reader with a narrative of striking images and compelling oppositions. These images and contrasting oppositions, in turn, offer the reader a means to evaluate and appreciate the personal implications of political action.

"Killing Floor" is dominated by the power of Ai's startling images of violence. Recognized and reviled by critics for the visceral power of its imagery, Ai's poetry depicts suffering and survival in sometimes lurid, bloody detail. In very ordinary, very straightforward language, Ai constructs images of violence that capture the reader's attention. Images such as "skating on knives," a head hanging only by a sliver of skin, a bullet-riddled body, and a pickax splitting a brain reflect the unfortunately gruesome facts of life in a violent and cruel society. It would be a mistake, though, to read the violence of "Killing Floor" without also reading its images of beauty. In phrases such as "easing me down into the azure water of Jordan," "water caught in my lashes," and "A river of sighs poured from the cut," Ai offers the reader a respite from the force of blood and violence. She juxtaposes these images of spirituality (baptism, Jordan, dove) and beauty with violent imagery in order to communicate the complex connection between violence and beauty. The alternating rhythm of violence and beauty, nightmare and wakefulness is crucial to the poem's depiction of the divided and hounded life of Trotsky.

Restricted by the historical fact of Trotsky's assassination, the poem's oppositions of imagery and tone serve to enrich the reader's appreciation of the psychological and personal costs Trotsky paid for his commitment to his political beliefs. Juxtapositions of violent and beautiful images—paired with the narration of dream and waking—create a surrealistic atmosphere in which Ai reimagines history. In this atmosphere, the sections of the poem describe the prelude, crisis, and culmination of Trotsky's political and personal drama. By setting up oppositions within the poem (Jordan/Volga, Russia/Mexico, Bronstein/Trotsky, dream/waking, and marmot/dove), Ai renders history tangible and universal in its human implications.

Themes and Meanings

"Killing Floor" is the title poem of Ai's second collection of poems and represents a departure from the poems of her first collection, *Cruelty* (1973). Published in 1978 and a winner of the Lamont Poetry Selection Award for the best second book by an American poet, *Killing Floor* moves the violent themes of *Cruelty* (monologues delivered by unnamed, ordinary people) into contexts of historical and cultural significance. Ai's straightforward, unadorned language can lead readers to evaluate her poems as merely sensational documents of bloodshed without further meaning. With poems about Trotsky, Mexican revolutionary Emiliano Zapata, film star Marilyn Monroe, and Japanese author Yukio Mishima, *Killing Floor* establishes a larger social context through which readers can interpret Ai's work. Violence in Ai's poetry must be unadorned and direct in order to shock the reader with the bloody contexts of history and of society. "Killing Floor" places the details of Trotsky's life among such imagery in order to situate his life into a more universal dilemma between personal and political choices.

In this process of emotional and psychological reinterpretation of Trotsky, some suggestions of the poet's life arise. For example, the focus on the multiplicity and fluidity of identities of Bronstein/Trotsky connects to the multiplicity of identities Ai herself encompasses. Born Florence Anthony, Ai's poetry reflects the multiple ethnicities of her heritage (Japanese, African American, Choctaw, and Irish) and the anxieties that the world's demand for static identity creates. In this light, one can read the poem as an expression of anxiety over the stricture of social definitions. Identity is too multiple and too persistent to limit itself to rules, even self-imposed ones.

Ai's use of historical and ordinary personas to give voice to her monologues invites comparisons with the monologues of Robert Browning, A. E. Housman, and Sterling Brown. The starkness of her violent imagery, however, is particular to her work. In "Killing Floor," the political life of Trotsky emerges from the Volga and returns, transformed, to the Jordan. Arranged within the concentric boxes of dream and waking, history in "Killing Floor" is fraught with crisis, longing, and violence. Ai ironically humanizes history by her persistent attention to emotional and spiritual identity. By presenting to the reader a rich blend of violence, beauty, nightmare, spirituality, history, and poetry, Ai creates a unique vision of the struggle that rages in life to define and be oneself.

Daniel M. Scott III

THE KING OF HARLEM

Author: Federico García Lorca (1898-1936)
Type of poem: Ode
First published: 1940, as "El rey de Harlem," in *Poeta en Nueva York*; English translation collected in *Poet in New York and Other Poems*, 1940

The Poem
    In his "Lecture on New York," Federico García Lorca said that he wanted to write a poem about black people in North America that would emphasize the pain that they experience for being black in a contrary world. García Lorca accomplishes his goal in his long poem entitled "The King of Harlem," collected in the volume *Poet in New York and Other Poems*. This long poem (119 lines) is an ode (an elaborate lyric directed to a fixed purpose and theme); its twenty-four stanzas are divided into three sections, and it is written in free verse.
    The title of the poem is ironic. The black man, who was respected as a king in his ancestral land and who was the master of his own destiny, is now the "king" of an alien land and culture: New York City's Harlem.
    Section 1 of the poem contains seven stanzas. The first stanza opens with a violent image: The black man uses the white man's ineffectual tool, a wooden spoon, to overcome crocodiles—symbols of evil. The black man dares to gouge out the "eyes of crocodiles" with a wooden spoon.
    In the next two stanzas, the natural world (exemplified by fire and water) that the black man once inhabited either lies dormant ("age-old fire slept in the flints") or putrefies ("vats of putrid water arrived"). In the fourth stanza, the loss of feeling and identity with nature continues. Instead of children being initiated into the hunt of majestic beasts, they perversely "flattened tiny squirrels."
    In the fifth stanza of the poem, a bridge appears. The whites are exhorted to "cross the bridge" to the world of the blacks in order to understand what they have lost in the process of civilization. The descent into the underworld (classically symbolized in the works of Dante and Vergil by the crossing of a bridge) progresses in the next stanza; however, the powers to be fought and conquered in the wasteland of New York are not typical forces of evil but a "blood vendor of firewater" or "Jewesses" in their bubble baths. Among the absurd visions that are encountered in the descent is "the infinite beauty/ of feather dusters, graters, copper pans, and kitchen/ casseroles."
    In the final stanza of the first section, the black man is hopelessly enslaved in a doorman's uniform by the millionaires of New York. His suppressed energy has become pent-up anguish as a result of his "red" oppression. This stanza relies heavily on red imagery to convey its mood of suppressed violence; for example, the black man's blood shudders with rage, and his violence is "garnet."
    Section 2 of the poem contains nine stanzas. The first two stanzas describe American girls and boys in Harlem who "stretched their limbs and fainted on the cross,"

Christlike sacrificial victims of white civilization. The third stanza echoes a stanza in section 1 of the poem. The king of Harlem once again digs out the crocodiles' eyes, not with a wooden spoon this time but with "an unbreakable spoon," a tool even more unnatural than wood.

The blood motif dominates the next six stanzas of the poem's second section. The rage in the blood that rushes through the black man cannot be seen because of the darkness of his skin; it surges beneath the surface. Yet "There must be some way out of here," the ninth stanza begins.

The third and last section of the poem is even more emphatic in its denial of escape from the situation and in its affirmation of an ultimate victory of sorts by the primitivism of the black man over the rational. In the first stanza of the section, blacks seek their king in the streets. In the fourth stanza, however, a wall rises in the black man's path, blocking any creature's escape. The poet exhorts the black man not to look to its cracks for escape but to "the great central sun" for the answer. The black man must wait in his "king's jungle" until the tide turns against the forces that contain him and the highest rooftops are devoured by the primeval forest. Then, blacks will be able to return to their natural order and dance free of doubt. The white man's Moses will be engulfed by flowers and put to rest before reaching the supposed promised land. The instruments of science will be relegated to the caves of squirrels, and the wheel, symbol of industry and progress, will no longer be an object of fear.

Forms and Devices

García Lorca's strongly negative feelings about New York—its chaos, materialism, harshness, and brutality—necessitated a form or vehicle of expression that would lend itself to those feelings. García Lorca chose the vehicle of surrealism to express his strong reaction to the city and its inhabitants. Strongly within the surrealist tradition (surrealism is a movement in art and literature emphasizing the expression of the imagination as realized in dreams and presented without conscious control), "The King of Harlem," as well as the rest of the poems in the collection *Poet in New York*, relies almost exclusively on jarring rhythms, unexpected juxtapositions, and stark imagery and symbolism to convey its meaning.

The poem's imagery clusters around two focal points that are continually juxtaposed in García Lorca's poem: the "civilized" world of the white man and the natural world of the black man. For example, animals of Africa—such as crocodiles, monkeys, serpents, and zebras—are contrasted with animals of the city—such as squirrels and salamanders. García Lorca also contrasts the natural beauty of the African forest, with its "tattooed sun that descends the river" and "bristling flowers," to the "civilized" ugliness of the Harlem landscape, with its "putrid water," "rigid, descending skies in which the colonies of planets/ can wheel with the litter on the beaches," "chemical rose," and "black mire." The interior landscape of Harlem is also repulsive; apartments are cluttered with "feather dusters, graters, copper pans, and kitchen/ casseroles," "tarnished mirrors," and "elevator shafts."

The blood motif in the poem is connected not only with the black man's nature, his life and vitality, but also with his rage. In the course of the poem, the primitive vitality of the blacks is symbolized by gushing, pervasive blood imagery—"blood raging under the skin"; however, phrases such as "blood shuddering with rage" and "blood wrung from hemp and subway nectars," and the description of blood flowing "everywhere,/ and burn the blond women's chlorophyll" are images of the blood of anger that the black man carries within him, ready to explode at any time.

Themes and Meanings

Critics have pointed out that *Poet in New York and Other Poems* in general, and "The King of Harlem" in particular, is as much about the poet's own psychological state while he was visiting the city as it is about New York and the alienation of the black man from that city. García Lorca had come to New York hoping that the journey would distract him from a severe emotional crisis. Once he arrived, however, he slowly began not to recognize himself. Coming to New York immersed García Lorca in a culture that was as different from his native Andalusia (southern Spain) as any place could possibly be. In his personal alienation from the mechanized and dehumanized city, he identified with the black man in the poem; they were going through an identity crisis together.

Thus, the theme of alienation from one's roots is the dominant theme of García Lorca's poem. Harlem represents the extreme domination of culture over nature; like the poet, the city—as well as the black man—is divorced from an origin that, unlike humankind, it cannot even acknowledge. In the poem, civilization is repeatedly equated with barbarism and technological progress with physical violence and moral and spiritual regression. A general decadence, which the poet characteristically renders in imagery of violent fragmentation, disintegration, and decomposition, abounds. For García Lorca, these circumstances must be the accumulated effects of a cause; the dismembered bodies and disembodied emotions are the debris of some catastrophe or series of catastrophes. The black man is a slave to the white man; the white man is a slave to his own technological progress.

Of those of New York's citizens still endowed with vitality, the blacks, although geographically distant from their homeland, are pictured as being the least removed from their spiritual origin. These citizens, having incorporated potentially explosive tendencies, are dormant volcanoes waiting to erupt.

Genevieve Slomski

KING SAUL AND I

Author: Yehuda Amichai (1924-2000)
Type of poem: Lyric
First published: 1958, as "Hapelekh Sha'ūl va'ănī," in *Be-merhak shete tikvot*; English translation collected in *Selected Poems*, 1968

The Poem
Written in the first person, "King Saul and I" is a poem of fifty-five lines divided into three sections. As the title suggests, the poem is based on a comparison of the lives of the legendary King Saul and the author. The tone of the poem indicates that the poet is speaking directly to the reader, undisguised, in the classic tradition of lyric poetry.

Section 1 has three stanzas. The first stanza emphasizes the difference between king and poet in the opening two lines: "They gave him a finger, but he took the whole hand." By contrast, the poet has been offered "the whole hand" but did not "even take the little finger." This is followed by a reference to King Saul's "tearing of oxen," which refers to the king's action when he needed to raise an army to defend the Israelites against the Ammonites. He cut up a yoke of oxen and sent the pieces throughout Israel, threatening to do the same to the oxen of the men who would not join him. The second stanza has four lines which again emphasize the difference: The poet's pulse was like "drips from a tap"; the king's, like hammers pounding. The third stanza states the relationship between the two in a slightly different way. "He was my big brother," the poet says, and in a homey, familiar image, adds that he got the king's used clothes.

King Saul is the subject of the second section. The first two-line stanza is a simile, comparing the king's head to a compass that will always bring him to the "sure north of his future." The "sure north" refers to the north pole, necessary for navigating precisely. This section ends with a reference to the asses in the story of King Saul in the first book of Samuel from the Old Testament. It is typical of Yehuda Amichai to juxtapose images from modern life with biblical images, defining the cultural heritage from which he creates literature. The ass image is continued into the third section of the poem. When King Saul was looking for his father's lost asses, he inquired of King Samuel, the prophet, which way he should go. Samuel recognized and embraced him as a prince of Israel, and Saul gave up his search for the asses. In a bold leap of time from the Old Testament to the modern era, Amichai writes that he, the poet, has now found the asses, "But I don't know how to handle them./ They kick me."

Other references to the story of King Saul abound. The third section of the poem tells of the anointing of Saul, of the people who were below his shoulders when he came among them, and of his triumph. Yet the poem ends in a series of couplets that create a mood of resigned weariness, ending with "He is a dead king. I am a tired man." Glory, power, and victory are associated with Old Testament time, while in contemporary time the poet leads a weary, diminished life.

Forms and Devices

Amichai's career is the longest and most productive in the history of modern Hebrew literature, and he is the most widely read Israeli poet, both in the original Hebrew and in English translation. Although something is always lost in poetic translation, Amichai has a formidable reputation among American readers. He grew up in an Orthodox household but abandoned formal religious practice in his adolescence. He retained his love for the poetry of the Jewish liturgy, which he exploits in his work. "Words are a new beginning with the stones of the past," he said in an address to a writers convention in Jerusalem in 1968: "No matter how small these stones are or how broken they are the new building will be stronger."

Many early biblical documents, such as the Song of Deborah, the Song of Moses, and the Song of Songs, are couched in rhythmic verse, and even the historical prose in the Pentateuch and the stories of Esther and Ruth are close to poetry in their cadenced sentences. The ethical ideas that contribute to Western civilization made their impact because they were written in poetic language. Instead of developing a symmetry of poetic feet, which is the unifying principle of Western poetry, Hebrew poetry developed a symmetry of units called parallelism. There are essentially three types of parallelism: sameness, antithesis (or opposition), and complement. A good example of sameness in the poem is the couplet "My sleep is just/ My dream is my verdict." A solemn sense of justice is suggested in the first line, and the second line, in parallel syntax, reinforces the judgmental quality of his life.

Antithesis is the main device used to organize the poem and create tension. The two opening lines are based on antithesis, and the poem ends with a series of parallel oppositions: "My arms are short, like string too short/ to tie a parcel./ His arms are like the chains in a harbor/ For cargo to be carried across time./ He is a dead king./ I am a tired man." Another interesting use of antithesis describes the poet's life: "I was raised with the straw,/ I fell with heavy seeds." This couplet is also complementary, for although the verbs "raised" and "fell" are antonyms, the second line extends the metaphor in which the poet is a crop growing from the land.

Themes and Meanings

The Israeli writers of Amichai's generation were born between 1915 and 1930. They were either born in Palestine or had immigrated there when very young. They were the first generation to speak Hebrew as their mother tongue, and they were the first to have grown up in the Israeli landscape with its biblical references. Amichai's personality as a poet is a reflection and distillation of this generation, typified by his identification with Israel's historic processes, his argument with Jewish Orthodoxy, and his perspective on contemporary society. He declared that all poetry is to an extent autobiographical, meaning that it allows insight into the mind and heart of the writer. The lyric "I" that pervades his poetry is a poetic myth of himself, derived not only from his life events but also from biblical motifs, including victories of ancient heroes such as King Saul. The characteristic long runs of metaphors and similes are linked by the spokesman who is at the core of the described experience.

A sense of loss in contemporary life is the mood that dominates "King Saul and I." In addition to individual sets of antithetical lines, the poem as a whole is built on the antithesis between the biblical Saul and "I"; "I" refers to a generalized speaker rather than to a totally individualized one. In every comparison between King Saul and the modern speaker, the speaker is timid, derivative ("I got his used clothes"), and diminished. In this way the poem typifies the social and political disillusionment of Amichai's generation with a state of Israel that had failed to create the agrarian, utopian community for which they had fought.

Amichai's poetry is not strictly chronological. His verse rests on the processes of remembering and forgetting, and through the procedures of memory time becomes an individual, existential, nonhistorical time. The poet is not remembering past events but incorporating them into the desires and disappointments of his present. Time is important in this poem; King Saul's heart is set "like an alarm clock," and "Dead prophets turned time-wheels." Significantly, the asses that King Saul was seeking at the beginning of his own story are still present and have been found by the speaker, although he does not know how to handle them. A bridge is thus created between the past and present.

The dualism so prominent in this poem is characteristic of the body of Amichai's work and points to conflicts in the poet's own autobiography. Personal oppositions are a model for oppositions in the poetry and provide a method of perception which allows a thing and its opposite to be perceived at the same time. The "I" of the poetry speaks from the tension between incompatible poles of his life: past and present, orthodoxy and apostasy; love and death; and two different languages, German and Hebrew. The reference to sleeping and dreaming in "King Saul and I" introduces one more opposition; that of the real and the illusory. In another of Amichai's poems, "This Is the Story of Dust," the poet tells readers that "between my going out in the morning/ and my return in the evening half of what is to happen happens/ and in my sleep, the other half." Amichai's precise imagery is designed to force awareness of the vital contradictions that shape both his life and that of his nation.

Sheila Golburgh Johnson

THE KINGFISHER

Author: Amy Clampitt (1920-1994)
Type of poem: Narrative
First published: 1982; collected in *The Kingfisher,* 1983

The Poem

"The Kingfisher" is divided into seven stanzas, each made up of six lines of approximately the same length. Although it is written in free verse, not in a metrical form, the poem looks more conventional than many other free-verse works, including some in the same collection by Amy Clampitt. It appears even more traditional because each of the first three stanzas is a definite unit, ending with a period; the remainder of the poem consists of double-stanza units, but again, the first stanza in each pair ends with a punctuated pause and the second with a period. Thus the poem is made up of five segments, each distinct in setting, which are arranged chronologically.

Clampitt emphasizes her narrative intent in her notes to "The Kingfisher" when she describes the poem as a "novel trying to work itself into a piece of cloisonné." The subject of this poem, she says, is "an episodic love affair that begins in England and is taken up again in New York City." Although the story is related in the third person, the point of view is that of limited omniscience, for while the author reports the thoughts and feelings of the woman, the reactions of the man are presented as his lover's guesses or assumptions.

The setting of the first stanza and thus of the first episode in this love affair is rural England. In the late spring or the summer of a year marked by especially vociferous nightingales, the two lovers spend an evening going from pub to pub. At some point, too, they walk by the ruins of a convent and see peacocks displaying their feathers. "Months later," the lovers are in a Manhattan pub. They have been attending a symphony concert, and during intermission they have rushed out for refreshments and a discussion of what they have heard. They do not agree, but it does not seem to matter.

The next scene takes place in the Bronx Zoo. Through the headphones provided for visitors, the lovers hear the "bellbird." The man makes a comment that seems to his lover to imply much more than the mere words would indicate. There seems to be increasing tension in the relationship, and the answer on this day is to drink "yet another fifth" of liquor.

In the fourth and fifth stanzas, the lovers are still in New York. On a Sunday morning in November, they stroll through a churchyard in lower Manhattan, near Wall Street, listening to the choirs from nearby churches and looking at a thrush, which has paused there on its way south. Some time later that month the love affair ends. No details are given, only that the breakup was a "cataclysm."

Unfortunately, the relationship did not end neatly. During the years that followed, readers are told in the sixth stanza, there was a great deal of "muted recrimination," until at last the lovers ceased communicating altogether. Long afterward, again in En-

gland, the woman is looking back over the affair, trying to identify the signs of disharmony in every ecstatic encounter. In the last stanza, as urgent as a kingfisher diving
upon its prey, the persona summons up her memories. However, she cannot capture
her old passion. Her plunge into the past ends in an almost unbearable unhappiness.

Forms and Devices

Like most of Clampitt's work, "The Kingfisher" is crowded with nature imagery,
especially references to birds. The poet mentions nightingales and peacocks twice,
once in the initial stanza and again when she is summing up the failure of the affair.
She also writes about tropical birds in the zoo, including the bellbird, describes a
thrush in detail, and concludes by comparing her emotional experiences to the dive of
a kingfisher.

Moreover, the symphonic selection about which the lovers disagree is Igor Stravinsky's composition entitled *The Firebird*. In an obvious play on words, the performance is compared to a bird of prey, a "kite." However, since the persona almost immediately refers to her partner's "hauling down" the musical work by his ridicule, it is
evident that the poet has switched to another kind of kite, that which is made by human hands and flown for as long as the wind is favorable. Both meanings are applicable to the poem. The bird is linked to the subject of the musical composition and, more
subtly, as a bird of prey suggests the developing destructiveness in the relationship;
the frailty of the paper creation, its dependence on external forces, including the skill
and the will of the person flying it, reminds the reader of the conditional nature of human love.

It has been pointed out that although there are fine examples of visual imagery in
her poems, Clampitt draws upon the other senses with equal skill. In "The Kingfisher," she comments on the pheasants' display of feathers and describes both the
thrush and the kingfisher in detail. However, there are also many references to sound
in the poem, and they are particularly significant in relation to theme. For example,
though ordinarily one thinks of nightingales as producing songs of great beauty,
Clampitt uses the adjective "loud" in her first mention of them and later seems to
blame their noisiness for keeping the lovers awake and for the "frantic" episode which
in retrospect has produced more pain than pleasure. Similarly, the sounds made by
both the peacocks and the bellbird are characterized as screams, and, again in retrospect, the poet wonders how many sexual encounters have "gone down screaming."
Although the birds who seemed to her to be screaming were not indeed suffering, that
unusual wording is now more than appropriate as a symbol of human pain.

Themes and Meanings

The notes Amy Clampitt appended to "The Kingfisher" are probably the best starting point for a discussion of the poem's themes. On the face of it, her comparison of
the work to a novel, episodic in form, and her mention of a "piece of cloisonné" would
appear to be at odds, for one implies narrative movement, the other a static form.
(Cloisonné is a technique for applying enamel to metal, as for jewelry.) However,

while the poem is organized chronologically, the love affair itself does not go anywhere. As the persona points out in the sixth stanza, every meeting had the same pattern. However well it began, each encounter went wrong. Thus the love affair and the poem describing it are both more like cloisonné, with its repetition of colors and forms, than like a narrative that moves to a conclusion.

In the notes, Clampitt also amplifies her parenthetical comment on the poet Dylan Thomas, thus stressing one of the themes that is repeated in each of the episodes, that of destruction, decay, and death. For example, the lovers walk near a convent that is in ruins and later meet in a cemetery. The male lover makes a "wreck" of Stravinsky's music and of the evening. Later, he is said to have "mourned" as one would a death, evidently over the loss of "poetry" and because he sees himself aging. The death of Thomas, which is mentioned parenthetically, occurred the same week and in the same city as the lovers' Sunday morning meeting. His death could certainly, in a sense, be considered another death of poetry.

These symbolic references reinforce what is evident throughout the poem: that however "dazzled" the lovers were, the relationship was doomed. Even that first "gaudy" evening evidently became "frantic," and the second evening depicted was wrecked by a quarrel which revealed not only dissimilarities in taste but also insensitivity or downright malice on the part of the male lover. At the zoo, the two were isolated because they used different headphones; moreover, the male lover seemed focused only on his own feelings, not hers.

The use of the kingfisher in the title and in the final stanza is therefore highly ironic. As the poet explains in her notes, the bird has long been a symbol for marital devotion and for serenity. In the story told by the Roman poet Ovid, a human couple, Ceyx and Alcyon, were so devoted that when Ceyx was drowned, his wife Alcyon plunged into the waves to join him. The sympathetic gods changed the two into kingfishers and made them immortal. Ever since, Ovid continues, there has been a period of seven successive days each year when the seas are calm, for that is the period when Alcyon is brooding over her nest as it floats on the surface of the water. From this story comes the term "halcyon days," or, in Clampitt's definition, a time of "general peace and serenity." Clampitt uses mythology not to indicate a parallel but to underline the ironic difference between what one hopes for in love and what one generally gets. With their "halcyon" hue, the peacocks seemed to forecast a happy outcome for the lovers, and even now the kingfisher looks like "felicity afire," but the reality is that there has been a death of love. The kingfisher, then, is not a symbol of serenity but of the persona's plunge through incomprehension into "uninhabitable sorrow."

Rosemary M. Canfield Reisman

THE KINGFISHERS

Author: Charles Olson (1910-1970)
Type of poem: Meditation
First published: 1950; collected in *In Cold Hell, in Thicket*, 1953

The Poem

"The Kingfishers," a lyrical meditation on the ruins of an Aztec burial ground, is written in a bold style invented for this poem, which Charles Olson explained shortly after in his essay of 1950, "Projective Verse." The poem does away with such formalities as rhyme and regular meters, symmetrical stanzas, and the normal pattern of argument in which particulars move toward universals or vice versa. Instead, it proceeds through a succession of widely varying stanzaic units as information is brought into the discourse and a unifying perception is drawn from the array of accumulated facts and ideas.

The poem opens with a paradox taken from the early Greek philosopher Heraclitus, which states that only change itself is unchanging. Olson's rendering of the phrase emphasizes the *will* of change, which gives pretext to what follows. The poem cuts abruptly to a party in its last hour somewhere in Mexico, near the ruins of an Aztec city, perhaps Tenochtitlán, the old Aztec capital that is now Mexico City. A man is addressing a stunned audience of guests with remarks about the deterioration of Mexican culture, the downward path of change toward entropy. "The pool is slime," he concludes, and disappears into the ruins.

So begins part 1 of a three-part meditation on change and the poet's responsibility to heed the shiftings of reality in his calling as writer. Part 1, the longest of the sections, is divided into four smaller movements, each with its own set of relations to be worked out. Various principles are at work in the building up of the poem's content. In the first movement of part 1, the juxtaposition of elements is cinematic, a "jump-cut" technique of butting events together without transition markers.

The second movement combines elements of three different topics, each separate and sequential in the poem's exposition but increasingly part of some deeper unifying chord tying all three topics together. The *E* on the stone, the first topic, is an allusion to the description by Plutarch, the second century C.E. Roman writer, of a navel stone (*omphalos*) found at the temple of Delphi, site of the ancient Greek oracles. The second is snippets of Mao Tse-tung's speech before the Chinese Communist Party in 1948, on the eve of the revolution that drove out the regime of Chiang Kai-shek from mainland China, bringing to an abrupt end the long hold of Western imperialism there. The third is a technical description of the kingfisher bird, much of which is lifted directly from the eleventh edition of the *Encyclopædia Britannica*. All three mark points of change in time, with the kingfisher as the principle of unity in change. The ancient *E* is the last remnant of a great civilization; Mao's speech is the turning point of another civilization. The bird's mortal existence transcends the rise and fall of human civilization by means of some other agency of nature, which balances change with structural constancy of form.

The third movement is a commentary on human violence and aggression, in particular the conquest of Mexico by Hernán Cortés in 1517. Olson quotes from William H. Prescott's *History of The Conquest of Mexico* (1843), which itemizes some of the loot taken from the temples by Cortés's army, including two gold embroideries of birds, possibly quetzal birds, whose feathers were important in Aztec mythology and rituals. The Mexican quetzal is equivalent to the kingfisher in Amerindian cultures. "And all now is war," Olson remarks at the close of the movement, as he draws a line from the Spanish Conquest to the Korean conflict of his own time.

The fourth and final movement of part 1 raises the discussion of change to a principle: Nothing remains the same; everything is driven to the next stage of development or mutation. Change is the pervasive force running throughout nature, yet it cannot be abstracted or directed by human means.

Part 2 is a fugue that combines the information gathered in the opening part. It begins in the middle of a guided tour of an Aztec burial ground that has been partially excavated. The mounds contain the remains of Aztecs who had lived prior to Cortés's conquest; the figure in the grave recalls the young in the kingfisher's nest, the first connection. Mao's exhortation to rise and act is woven in. The discussion points up the frailty and haplessness of human notions of order against the lasting, vital orders of nature. The Mexican guide turns from the ruins to admire a yellow rose, the setting sun, the mystical figure of unity, spirit, and transcendent permanence within a realm of violent upheaval and chaos.

Part 3 is a coda in which the various themes of the poem are resolved in the form of a decision reached by the poet. He renounces the violence and errors of Western tradition, stemming from Greek and Roman civilization, and finds his true heritage among such rebel poets as Arthur Rimbaud, who left his own country to live in the deserts of the Middle East. Olson quotes a passage from Rimbaud's *Une Saison en enfer* (1873; *A Season in Hell*, 1932), which he translates immediately below, and closes the poem with a similar commitment to renounce Western culture and adopt the New World as his proper heritage.

Forms and Devices

One must "look" at an Olson poem as well as read it. Visually, it is an arrangement of words intended to convey the motion of thought itself. The term "projective" literally means to project the thinking process of composition onto paper and to reenact—a strategic term for Olson—the subtle motions of memory and association as they feed into the main discourse of imaginative activity. The poem is therefore "kinetic," even cinematic in its abrupt shift from scene to scene, in the "framing" that ensues as discourse contracts into a perception or lengthens out into narrative or description. Olson, like many other innovative American poets, based the new prosody of the poem on the techniques of filmmaking and emphasized motility and dramatic shift as the rhetoric of thought and articulation.

As many critics have noted in describing this poem, it is structured as an extended "ideogram," Ezra Pound's term for the elemental relations that constitute a poem's unity and force as language. The many separate parts of the poem are the clustered details that form a single structure of thought, the way a snowflake's radiations and delicate latticework constitute a single flake of snow. The challenge to the reader is to discern the connections and integrity of these many pieces as they cohere within a single flash of understanding.

Olson's poem runs the gamut of open forms, from the proselike strophes of the opening section, to the stepped lines showing the rhythm of Mao's words, to the steep descent of other passages in which the rhythm accelerates. The sprawling shapes of many of the paragraphs are indicators that the thought is labored or resistant, or that it emerges under conflict. It is not until the coda that one sees the resolution of opposites visually projected, the "balance" of the quatrains as they direct the reader to the declaration, "I hunt among stones."

Stylistically, the poem observes many of the conventions of verse discourse. Certain tropes predominate, especially the image of the kingfisher, which appears in every section of part 1 as its principal motif; another is the sun marking east and west, dawn and sunset, decay and renewal. The language is clean and spare, written in a stately tempo partly achieved through the use of pithy aphorisms and formal parallels, and partly by means of a series of stark assertions in tones ranging from scientific formality to the emotional declaration of his changed allegiance at the end.

Themes and Meanings

The poem is an analysis of the failures of Western expansion over the centuries, of the desire of one civilization to take possession of and exploit others. This vast subject provides the means by which the poet reaches his decision to change his cultural allegiance away from Europe to the New World. The poem's elaborate procedure of argument and analysis begins with the corruptions of modern Mexico, where a figure announces that the civilization that began with the achievements of the Mayas and Aztecs has been brought by Spanish conquerors to its present degradation.

Though Olson had not yet visited Mexico, he was becoming interested in modern archaeological diggings at some of the principal Aztec temple grounds, and had conceived this scene purely from his reading. Several months after writing the poem, he undertook an expedition to Mexico's Yucatán peninsula, where he resided for six months and wrote vigorous letters home about his own findings and speculations, later collected by Robert Creeley and published in 1953 under the title *Mayan Letters*. An important part of his ideas as a poet and cultural historian was derived from his studies of Mayan civilization. In "The Kingfishers," however, his interest lies principally in his view of modern Mexico as the victim of Spanish invasion and colonialism.

That focus on one victim of empire opens into a vision of the frailties of all human civilizations, their vulnerability to the decay of time or to the instinct of human violence to crush them. Hence, the *E* cut on the stone marks the last mysterious expression of a lost civilization marking one boundary of time, a point of origin along a continuum of growth and decay known as the Western tradition. The kingfisher, who flies into the sun to meet the westering light and warm its breast against it, is thus a figure of enduring vitality that stands in vivid contrast to the tragedy of human history.

By the end of part 1, Olson has wrested a valuable lesson from his musings on history: Time is "not accumulation but change." Little endures of human nature but a few ruins; nature's vast backdrop is the stage on which human life plays out its tragedy. The Mongolian louse inherits the few possessions that were heaped in the Aztec burial mounds. Olson scorns the Western attitude that would destroy a civilization that lived close to nature. He senses in his own time a decay in social ideals and reads in the Korean conflict that had broken out in 1949 a continuation of Western violence against other cultures.

Arriving at the coda in part 3, the reader observes Olson's own ritual rebirth as a poet as he proclaims his new heritage and birthright as an heir to the New World, a descendant of Aztec roots. He sides with the victims of imperialism and claims them as his true ancestors. It is Olson's way of protesting against the nature of war and the aggressions of his own civilization. "The Kingfishers" is the first anti-imperialist poem written in an era that saw the end of many colonial states and the breakup of the major European empires.

Though "The Kingfishers" belongs to a long tradition of landscape and graveyard meditations, it turns this tradition around by meditating over the burial mounds of an ancient people who become, through the urgency of the poet's musings, his own ancestors and bloodline. With this poem, Olson may be said to have invented postmodernism, with its array of anti-imperialist arguments and its desire to reconcile contemporary Western art with ancient myth and ritual.

Paul Christensen

. KITTENS

Author: Robert Peters (1924-   )
Type of poem: Lyric/elegy
First published: 1967, in *Songs for a Son*

The Poem

"Kittens" is a long poem written in free verse; its short lines are grouped into ten stanzas. It is an elegy, a poem written in grief or mourning. This poem is also a song, a lyric lament for Robert Peters's son Richard, who died suddenly in childhood. It laments unfulfilled wishes and lost promise. The poem is generated by the boy's wish to have kittens and his father's wish that his son had lived to experience more of the world.

The poem begins with the kittens that finally did come to fulfill the child's wish—after his death. They are filled with energy and life: "plump dark woolly cats/ with eyes like olives/ . . . tumbling/ on the floor . . ./ lapping up blue milk." Only "death-day/ morning" and perhaps the milk's tinge suggest an elegy. In addition, the stanza that follows, a finely paced account of the birth of the kittens, celebrates abundance and beginnings. The kittens, "fur wet like licorice," "fell/ into a land of honey." The description of the births, although precisely detailed, conveys the mystery of the event.

In stanzas 3 and 4, however, the poem moves with fortitude and resignation into the body of another mystery: death. The poet describes the breakfast conversation during which the boy expressed his wish for kittens. His last wish, however, was rejected that "wish-day/ death-day" by his father, who tried to explain about pets:

> "they die.
> Their little toes
> curl up like leaves,
> their waxy eyes go shut,
> their tails hang limp
> their whiskers droop."

Stanza 4 reveals a central admission. As if death itself were communicable (and parents are good at imagining that it is), the poet observes, "Dreading each death's/ advent, I sought to/ spare you." A fear of invasion emerges: "Each lost/ pet might break deep,/ deep within your heart" —in almost the same way that an infestation might "crystallize" inside the boy "into long beads of rice/ to feed the worm." One senses the father's realization that he feared becoming a helpless witness to his son's death almost more than he feared the death itself. The stanza ends with a surprising tactile image—each pet's death might be "a buzz," like an eel's tail delivering "a fatal jolt!"

The following two stanzas document the deaths of Snake and Mouse, and their elaborate funerals. The father retells these tales to the boy in "proof" of the folly of keeping pets. Mouse, for example, left "sprinkling mortality/ like ivy-juice/ all over you that day." Again, the theme of contagion arises, as if mortality were a condition that one might carefully avoid, but death is one of the inescapable consequences of being born. Stanza 6 ends with a rumination on transformation; the bones of the mouse and the boy are imagined as ash slipping down between layers of rock in the "earthy crypt." These lines introduce a mood of calm acceptance.

The boy was not swayed by the scare tactics, his father's tales of "deep-felled nightmare," and although already carrying (invisible in his brain) "the hung smoke of the/ sleeping fatal fever," the delighted child snapped the wishbone to "free [his] wish." The poet looks back at this moment and confronts joy and loss simultaneously; as the bone breaks in the poem, one is aware of an instant of innocent yet fervent hope coupled with the father's sudden snap of agony over the boy's absence. Tenderness is accompanied by pain. The finality of the last line in stanza 8 echoes the suddenness and finality of the child's death.

The last two stanzas return to the present, a house filled with tumbling kittens, like tiny reincarnations of the boy's delight and movements. The kittens "do all the acts,/ make all the gestures that/ you knew live kittens make." These facts, the knowledge the boy took "into the night," are better than the "shouts of passion,/ war; the violence of cars," which he was spared. Sorrow is both relieved and rekindled in the end, as it has been throughout the poem. The poet mourns "the poetry that never/ broke itself against/ your ears," and although he struggles to accept Richard's loss, still wishes "that there had been more."

Forms and Devices

"My poems to my son were meant to give the illusion that a five-year-old child could understand them" says Peters. His language in "Kittens" is therefore direct, his rhythm plain, and his diction simple. Although the poem is not really written for a five-year-old (the metaphors and allusions are grown-up, and some of the vocabulary is too hard), the poem nevertheless is simple. This surface plainness allows a clear-eyed rumination on the boy's death, on life and death, which does not fall prey to gross sentimentality or overlush expressions of sorrow. The poet/speaker simply talks; on the surface, he shares what happened.

The poems in *Songs for a Son* grew out of an emotionally charged situation and thus are blessed with a sudden abundance of energy that peaks, seemingly paradoxically, and turns into musical celebration at precisely the moments of greatest sorrow and pain. A good example in "Kittens" is the indented final lines of the seventh stanza, which lead to the jumbling, joyful liveliness of the next stanza. The short lines help sustain this energetic movement; the poem moves quickly through thoughts and memories.

In "Kittens," the stanzas vary in length. Their form is loose enough to accommodate the varying needs and depths of the scenes. The poem's temporal movement from scene to scene (stanza to stanza) gives the poem a narrative shape. It has chronology and various settings, both of which are familiar components of storytelling. The narrative begins in the speaker's present, moves back in time to the death-day, moves further back in time to the funerals of Snake and Mouse, comes back to the death-day, and finally returns the reader to the present and the new kittens. Thus the poem is a cycle that examines, celebrates, and reveres, by means of the child's death, the basic cycle of birth, life, and death. The sections of the poem represent eras in the boy's short life.

What lends the poem further unity is that, like a talisman, *the wish*, which is directly referred to in four stanzas and is implicitly there in the rest, becomes almost an entity, a being with its own life that must be protected. An abstraction somehow concretized, it becomes an energy source in the poem, especially when it is fulfilled by the birth of the kittens.

Themes and Meanings

In this poem about things dying, the death of the boy's wish for kittens is mourned as heavily as the death of the boy. In fact, the poem seems almost to be, with its catalog of pets that die, an elegy for small pleasures. Pleasures often die or are lost to those who believe their daily routines are all-important. Possibilities for joy are also sometimes forsaken by those who fear taking risks—even small ones.

Thus one theme of the poem is to question the illusion of "safety" from life's horrors; there really was no way his father could have spared the boy from suffering, or even suffering only over each lost pet. The "blue, fatal jolt" can happen again and again in anyone's life. The poem suggests that only when one accepts life openly, with all of its risks, can one truly begin to live. Another suggestion is made about risks: that the boy, had he lived, would have dealt with the risks and dangers of his own life capably, and as a child, with a childlike openness that a wise adult might envy. Richard did not really need to be and could not have been protected from life. He "seized the dish," he was so eager.

As if to prove how futile it was for the father to refuse the boy his kittens, the kittens arrive anyway. They resurrect the boy's wish; in fact, they return the boy to the father in the vehicle of this poem. The kittens represent the acceptance of death, and therefore the acceptance of life.

JoAnn Balingit

THE KNIGHT, DEATH, AND THE DEVIL

Author: Randall Jarrell (1914-1965)
Type of poem: Lyric
First published: 1951, in *The Seven-League Crutches*

The Poem

"The Knight, Death, and the Devil" by Randall Jarrell is a carefully organized forty-line free-verse poem inspired by an engraving from the sixteenth century German artist Albrecht Dürer. The poem's title is the same as the traditional title given to the engraving, but in German it is simply called "Der Reuter," "The Rider," making reference to the knight, its central figure.

In anthologies, the two works, one verbal, one visual, are often presented together. Thus the poem is an example of ekphrasis (Greek for "to speak out"), the verbal representation of a visual work of art. Its technique of alternating description and interpretation can be compared with the pure ekphrasis of John Keats's "Ode on a Grecian Urn," in which the art object exists solely and wholly in words, and with W. H. Auden's "Musée des Beaux Arts," which uses several paintings but centers finally upon Pieter Brueghel the Elder's *Landscape with Fall of Icarus.*

In an ekphrastic poem such as Jarrell's, description of the art object complements interpretation. Indeed, the very choice of what to describe, and in what order and in how much detail, itself constitutes an element of interpretation. Each choice suggests a thematic priority. The titles for the poem and the engraving suggest that first the knight, then Death, and finally the devil will be described, but Jarrell begins with Death (lines 1-8), moves next to the devil (lines 9-20), and concludes with the knight (lines 21-40). Ultimately the poem is about the resolute knight, symbol of all humanity, journeying with Death ever nearby while beset with trials and tribulations from the devil.

Forms and Devices

Jarrell opens with a description of Death "cowhorn-crowned, shockheaded, cornshuck-bearded," compound adjectives that seek to capture the way Dürer has drawn him. Participles and strings of adjectives throughout the poem mimic a German extended adjective construction, appropriate diction since the inspiration for the poem is a German work of art. As Jarrell likens Death's scraggly beard to cornshucks, he decides Death is but a "scarecrow" such as one might find in a cornfield, but his head "trimmed with adders," poisonous snakes, is sinister nevertheless.

The artist has placed Death upon a pale horse that, Jarrell notes, "crops herbs beside a skull," evidence of Death's work. The pale horse is dictated by a biblical passage, Revelation 6:8. The skull and other imagery in the engraving suggest to the poet metaphors for the brevity of life. For example, in the engraving, Death holds up "the crossed cones of time," an hourglass filled with sand. Death is "warning" the knight that his time is running out. Indeed, the sands of time "narrowing into now, the Past and Future/ Are quicksand" that will trap the knight, symbol of all humanity.

With a line break, Jarrell shifts his attention to the devil, but he does not name him until line 19. He is "the hoofed pikeman [who] trots behind," for as the Book of Revelation says, "There was Death on a pale horse, and Hades [the devil] followed close behind." In the engraving, the devil's hoof might easily be mistaken for a horse's hoof, but Jarrell carefully notes its owner.

Unmentioned in the poem but clearly visible in the engraving is a salamander that the artist has drawn near the devil's hoof. Fabled for its ability to survive flames, the creature is an emblem of the virtuous soul shunning hellfire. Jarrell's attention, however, is focused not on the salamander but on the hideousness of the devil's appearance, his horn which is a "soaring crescent," his "great limp ears," the dangling "dewlap bunched at his breast," and something like "a ram's horn wound/ Beneath each ear." The devil "leers up" at the knight, "joyless, vile, in meek obscenity." Jarrell takes the poem beyond the picture as he says of the devil "Flesh to flesh, he bleats/ The herd back to the pit of being." The phrase "flesh to flesh" suggests that the body is most vulnerable to the devil's attack. Sins of the flesh are his delight. Like some diabolical ram he leads his sheep, docile humanity, into sin. Thus he is the antithesis of Christ, who leads his sheep away from hell, "the pit of being," and who perhaps is symbolized by the "sheep-dog."

Themes and Meanings

The phrase "the pit of being" is the first clue to the poem's theme. Jarrell will return to the word "being" in his description of the knight, which concludes the poem. The poem is progressively about what it means to be human. The last words of the poem, "I am," are formed from the verb "to be." By placing such emphasis on these words, Jarrell suggests an existential reading of his poem would be appropriate. Similarly, Hamlet's famous "To be or not to be" soliloquy has led critics to offer existentialist interpretations of William Shakespeare's tragedy. Jarrell's career paralleled a time when existentialism was a popular topic for discussion and poetic analysis.

A central point of existentialism is that existence, "being," precedes the determination of one's essence. This was true in the atheistic existentialism of Jean-Paul Sartre as well as in the Christian existentialism of Søren Kierkegaard. This view is the opposite of a more traditional Christian position known as Original Sin or, as the Bay Psalm Book of American Puritans expressed it, "In Adam's fall/ We sinned all." Original Sin is a subject central to John Milton's *Paradise Lost* (1667, 1674). In Milton's view, after the fall of Adam and Eve, essence, in this case sinfulness, forever precedes existence. One is born sinning and sinful; sin defines humanity. The existentialists, however, believed that one's essence, or being, is the result of a life lived and choices made. An archetypal symbol for a life of choices is the journey, such as one finds in the picture of the knight upon his horse.

Jarrell asks of the knight, "The death of his own flesh, set up outside him;/ The flesh of his own soul, set up outside him—/ Death and the devil, what are these to him?"

The painting invites the same question. Are the two figures opponents of the knight, against whom he may struggle as he makes choices along life's journey? Are they mirrors of the knight, who is himself, by his vocation, an instrument of death and the devil? Though "outside of him," Jarrell suggests they represent the choices that define his "being." Of the knight, Jarrell says, "His being accuses him." Good existentialist that he is, the knight abides by the choices he has made—"his face is firm/ In resolution, in absolute persistence." His face and body language say "a man does what he must." Humanity can do no more than define itself, assert its humanness in the face of Death and the devil.

In the engraving, Jarrell finds an emblem of what it means to be human and translates the picture into words that describe and interpret the human situation. The knight's journey is the human journey. If the knight in the engraving is meant to represent someone specific, as some art critics suggest, there are few clues. In his poem, Jarrell takes a more universal view. Even the landscape is universalized. In the background, "His castle—some man's castle—set on every crag" is either the knight's goal or his point of departure. The knight "moves through this world," and that is geography enough.

On the knight's lance is "the bush/ Of that old fox." Jarrell's adjectives point to the fox as being more than just "any" fox. Traditionally, he symbolizes the devil; the fox brush, or tail, suggests the knight has encountered the devil before and bested him. Accompanying the knight is a dog that Jarrell makes "a sheep-dog bounding at his stirrup." Looking at the dog, Jarrell sees "In its eyes the cast of faithfulness (our help,/ Our foolish help)." Faithfulness, like a dog at one's feet, is "foolish help" because it is from outside, less than one's pure inner being.

"So, companioned so," by dog and horse, by Death and devil, each person journeys despite the certainty of death, despite the temptations of evil. A true knight "listens in assurance, has no glance/ To spare for them [Death and the devil], but looks past steadily." It is not so much at what one looks as the very fact that "a man's look completes [defines] itself." No matter who the knight is, an adulterous Lancelot or a saintly Joan of Arc, he or she is not defined but defines.

Thus the poem concludes with the triumphant existentialist manifesto: "I am."

R. Parks Lanier, Jr.

THE KNIGHT'S TALE

Author: Geoffrey Chaucer (c. 1343-1400)
Type of poem: Narrative
First transcribed: 1387-1400, in *The Canterbury Tales*

The Poem

Geoffrey Chaucer's "The Knight's Tale" is the first actual tale in the unfinished *Canterbury Tales*, a sequence of stories told by different members of a pilgrimage to Canterbury Cathedral in the Middle Ages. It is a structured, formal, 2,249-line poem told in four parts, which follows immediately after the "General Prologue"—an introductory poem describing each of the pilgrims.

Essentially, it is the story of a love triangle. Two Theban warriors, the cousins Palamon and Arcite, are thrown into prison by their captor, the Greek king Theseus. There, first Palamon, then Arcite, espy the king's sister-in-law Emily and are immediately smitten with love. After a period of time, Arcite is released from Theseus's prison through the intervention of a friend, and Palamon escapes. By chance they find each other and arrange to fight for Emily. Theseus discovers them, however, and decrees that a trial by arms in fifty weeks' time will settle the matter.

On the day of battle, Emily prays to Diana that she might remain a maid, but that, if that cannot be, then the man who loves her most might win her; Arcite vows service to Mars if he might prove victorious; Palamon begs Venus that he might win his beloved. Diana appears to Emily, saying it is decreed she must be wed, but both men receive signs that their prayers will be answered. While there is some consternation in Olympus over this seeming irreconcilable set of promises, Saturn assures everyone that no deity's word will be broken. Arcite indeed wins, but at the moment of his triumph, his horse shies, throwing him down in what turns out to be a mortal injury. After a period of mourning, Theseus hands Emily to Palamon, and they live a life of bliss.

Forms and Devices

"The Knight's Tale" is a story within a story. On one level, the whole of *The Canterbury Tales* is the story of the thirty-two pilgrims as they wend their way to Canterbury, entertaining each other by telling stories. At this level, each tale serves to amplify and confirm the characterization of the teller given in the "General Prologue." In the very mixed company of pilgrims, the Knight is one of the few not treated satirically or ironically. He is, in fact, "a parfit gentil knyght," and his tale substantiates this.

By luck of the draw, the Knight becomes the first pilgrim to fulfill host Harry Bailly's request that each member of the company enliven the journey to Canterbury by storytelling. This was a fortunate chance for the others: The Knight understands his social obligation and is happy to comply. He reaches back to classical times for his courtly tale, which Chaucer adapted from Giovanni Boccaccio's *Teseida* (1340-1341; *The Book of Theseus*, 1974). Immediately this bespeaks his sophistication and sets a certain tone and standard. The matter itself, with its artful conundrum, is suitable entertainment for his audience—unlike some of the ruder, coarser tales told by other pilgrims—and is applauded roundly at its conclusion. Set in ancient Greece, it speaks of high matters: the Roman gods, Theseus's court, the knightly world of honor and chivalry. By flattering the taste of the audience, it reveals the courtliness of the teller. The selection and narration show the Knight to be a confident, experienced, and indeed elegant member of society, one entirely at ease in his role of first storyteller.

On this level, Chaucer's hand in shaping *The Canterbury Tales* is evident. It is no accident, although it is presented as such, that the Knight is the first pilgrim to tell a tale. He was also, by design, the first one introduced in the "General Prologue." His prominence elevates the entire work; by leading off with his star player, Chaucer positions his poem in a way which would have been very different if the short straw had fallen to the drunken Miller or the sleazy Pardoner.

On a second level, "The Knight's Tale" has a literary life of its own. Written in pentameter, using rhyming couplets, it is basically a warning to watch what one asks for. It pivots around the seeming paradox that both Palamon and Arcite have been promised by different gods that they will emerge victorious as the suitor for Emily. The puzzle is solved by the simple solution that each man gets his exact wish. Arcite's mistake is that he asks for a secondary goal—military victory—which he deems will win him his primary desire, Emily. Palamon is intent on winning his lady, and addresses his prayers to the goddess of love. Arcite gets his victory but does not live to enjoy his prize; Palamon gets the girl. In a delicate irony, it is Arcite himself who articulates the confusion that is the lot of humankind, "We witen nat what thing we preyen heere."

"The Knight's Tale" is a leisurely one, which uses some of the conventions of the epic. Descriptions are lavish and are given to matters that may seem tangential to the main story. Readers are treated to the circumstances of Theseus's marriage, the splendid oratories built for the deities, and the noble retainers who fight with Palamon and Arcite. To the Knight, all of this is integral to the telling; he even interjects that people would think it a "necligence" if he omitted it. Likewise, the action is diffuse, shifting from one character to another. The focus is first on Palamon in prison, then Arcite in Thebes, then Emily, then Theseus. Yet the tale is never divorced from its teller; the Knight speaks frequently in his own voice, thus keeping the framing story of the Canterbury pilgrimage at the forefront.

Themes and Meanings

One of the things the Knight talks about is philosophy, and philosophical reflections abound in the poem. After Arcite is released from prison but banished from Greece, the Knight poses the question, which lover has it worse? The imprisoned Palamon, who can daily see Emily, or the freed Arcite, separated from his beloved? Later he reminds the company, "The purveiaunce that God hath seyn biforn" rules over all that befalls humankind. All the principal characters have philosophical moments, when they reflect on fate, destiny, and love. It is, possibly, these observations which initially recommended this story to the Knight—or he may be the one who has infused them into it. In the Knight's telling, Theseus considers the omnipotence of the Prime Mover in a way very reminiscent of the Knight's own musings. At another point in the poem Theseus has recourse to the old proverb that it is wisdom to make a virtue of necessity.

It is part of the multilayered complexity of *The Canterbury Tales* that the real voice behind these reflections is impossible to determine: Perhaps Theseus is the original speaker; perhaps the Knight attributes his own thoughts to the Athenian king; perhaps Chaucer uses them both to articulate his own perspective. Chaucer himself is not even a stable entity, as he has created a clownish counterpart to himself, Chaucer the pilgrim, who is a member of the company on the pilgrimage and who also speaks with his own distinct voice.

The most prominent theme of this tale is the recognition that it is the lot of humankind to be unable to recognize the true circumstances of one's own position. When Arcite finds out that he is to be released from captivity through the intercession of his friend Perotheus, he laments the day he met his friend, since freedom now means severance from Emily. His prison, once a torment, is now a paradise. He wonders why people complain of the "purveiaunce of God, or of Fortune," which frequently blesses them with a better situation than they themselves could devise. A man might wish for riches, he thinks, and those same riches might be the cause of his murder.

Closely connected with this is the role destiny plays in human affairs. Inasmuch as mortals cannot recognize the value of the fortunes meted out to them, likewise they cannot alter the fate decreed for them. Diana informs Emily that she must marry Arcite or Palamon; her prayer that she might remain unwed will not be granted, since it is predetermined otherwise. This omnipotence is called by various names, "purveiaunce of God," "Fortune," "Firste Moevere." Its workings may be a mystery to mortal men and women, and they might be powerless against it, yet in the realm of "The Knight's Tale" it is their ultimate safeguard.

Linda Turzynski

KUBLA KHAN

Author: Samuel Taylor Coleridge (1772-1834)
Type of poem: Lyric
First published: 1816, in *Christabel*

The Poem

"Kubla Khan," one of the most famous and most analyzed English poems, is a fifty-four-line lyric in three verse paragraphs. In the opening paragraph, the title character decrees that a "stately pleasure-dome" be built in Xanadu. Although numerous commentators have striven to find sources for the place names used here by Samuel Taylor Coleridge, there is no critical consensus about the origins or meanings of these names. The real-life Kubla Khan, a thirteenth century Mongolian general and statesman who conquered and unified China, lived in an elaborate residence known as K'ai-p'ing, or Shang-tu, in southeastern Mongolia. Coleridge's Kubla has his palace constructed where Alph, "the sacred river," begins its journey to the sea. The construction of the palace on "twice five miles of fertile ground" is described. It is surrounded by walls and towers within which are ancient forests and ornate gardens "bright with sinuous rills."

Xanadu is described more romantically in the second stanza. It becomes "A savage place! as holy and enchanted/ As e'er beneath a waning moon was haunted/ By woman wailing for her demon-lover!" It is inhabited not by Kubla's family and followers, but by images from Coleridge's imagination. His Xanadu is a magical place where the unusual is to be expected, as when a "mighty fountain" bursts from the earth, sending "dancing rocks" into the air, followed by the sacred river itself. The poem has thus progressed from the creations of Kubla Khan to the even more magical actions of nature. The river meanders for five miles until it reaches "caverns measureless to man" and sinks "in tumult to a lifeless ocean."

This intricate description is interrupted briefly when Kubla hears "from far/ Ancestral voices prophesying war!" This may be an allusion to the opposition of the real Khan by his younger brother, Arigböge, which led eventually to a military victory for Kubla. Coleridge then shifts the focus back to the pleasure-dome, with its shadow floating on the waves of the river: "It was a miracle of rare device,/ A sunny pleasure-dome with caves of ice!"

The final paragraph presents a first-person narrator who recounts a vision he once had of an Abyssinian maid playing a dulcimer and singing of Mount Abora. The narrator says that if he could revive her music within himself, he would build a pleasure-dome, and all who would see it would be frightened of "his flashing eyes, his floating hair!" His observers would close their eyes "with holy dread,/ For he on honey-dew hath fed,/ And drunk the milk of Paradise."

Coleridge prefaces the poem with an explanation of how what he calls a "psychological curiosity" came to be published. According to Coleridge, he was living in ill health during the summer of 1797 in a "lonely farm-house between Porlock and Lin-

ton, on the Exmoor confines of Somerset and Devonshire." Having taken an "anodyne," he fell asleep immediately upon reading in a seventeenth century travel book
by Samuel Purchas: "Here the Khan Kubla commanded a palace to be built, and a
stately garden thereunto. And thus ten miles of fertile ground were inclosed with a
wall." He claims that while sleeping for three hours he composed two-hundred to
three-hundred lines, "if that indeed can be called composition in which all the images
rose up before him as *things*, with a parallel production of the correspondent expressions, without any sensation or consciousness of effort."

When Coleridge awoke, he remembered the entire poem and set about copying it
down, only to be interrupted for an hour "by a person on business from Porlock." Returning to the poem, Coleridge could recall only "some eight or ten scattered lines and
images." He claims he has since intended to finish "Kubla Khan" but has not yet been
able to.

Forms and Devices

The most striking of the many poetic devices in "Kubla Khan" are its sounds and
images. One of the most musical of poems, it is full of assonance and alliteration, as
can be seen in the opening five lines:

> In Xanadu did Kubla Khan
> A stately pleasure-dome decree:
> Where Alph, the sacred river, ran
> Through caverns measureless to man
> Down to a sunless sea.

This repetition of *a, e*, and *u* sounds continues throughout the poem with the *a* sounds
dominating, creating a vivid yet mournful song appropriate for one intended to inspire
its listeners to cry "Beware! Beware!" in their awe of the poet. The halting assonance
in the line "As if this earth in fast thick pants were breathing" creates the effect of
breathing.

The alliteration is especially prevalent in the opening lines, as each line closes with
it: "Kubla Khan," "pleasure-dome decree," "river, ran," "measureless to man," and
"sunless sea." The effect is almost to hypnotize the reader or listener into being receptive to the marvelous visions about to appear. Other notable uses of alliteration include the juxtaposition of "waning" and "woman wailing" to create a wailing sound.
"Five miles meandering with a mazy motion" sounds like the movement it describes.
The repetition of the initial *h* and *d* sounds in the closing lines creates an image of the
narrator as haunted and doomed:

> His flashing eyes, his floating hair!
> Weave a circle round him thrice,
> And close your eyes with holy dread,
> For he on honey-dew hath fed,
> And drunk the milk of Paradise.

The assonance and alliteration soften the impact of the terminal rhyme and establish a sensation of movement to reinforce the image of the flowing river with the shadow of the pleasure dome floating upon it.

The imagery of "Kubla Khan" is evocative without being so specific that it negates the magical, dreamlike effect for which Coleridge is striving. The "gardens bright with sinuous rills," "incense-bearing tree," "forests ancient as the hills," and "sunny spots of greenery" are deliberately vague, as if recalled from a dream. Such images stimulate a vision of Xanadu bound only by the reader's imagination.

Themes and Meanings

Much of the commentary on "Kubla Khan" has focused on the influence of Coleridge's addiction to opium, on its dreamlike qualities, the "anodyne" he refers to in his preface, but no conclusive connection between the two can be proved. Considerable criticism has also dealt with whether the poem is truly, as Coleridge claimed, a fragment of a spontaneous creation. The poet's account of the unusual origin of his poem is probably only one of numerous instances in which one of the Romantic poets proclaimed the spontaneity or naturalness of their art. Most critics of "Kubla Khan" believe that its language and meter are too intricate for it to have been created by the fevered mind of a sleeping poet. Others say that its ending is too fitting for the poem to be a fragment.

Other contentions about "Kubla Khan" revolve around its meanings (or lack thereof). Some critics, including T. S. Eliot in *The Use of Poetry and the Use of Criticism* (1933), have claimed the poem has no veritable meaning. Such analysts say its method and meaning are inseparable: The poem's form is its only meaning. For other commentators, "Kubla Khan" is clearly an allegory about the creation of art. As the artist decided to create his work of art, so does Kubla Khan decide to have his pleasure-dome constructed. The poem's structure refutes Coleridge's claim about its origins, since the first thirty-six lines describe what Kubla has ordered built, and the last eighteen lines deal with the narrator's desire to approximate the creation of the pleasure-dome.

Xanadu is an example of humanity imposing its will upon nature to create a vision of paradise, since the palace is surrounded by an elaborate park. That the forests are "ancient as the hills" makes the imposing of order upon them more of a challenge. Like a work of art, Xanadu results from an act of inspiration and is a "holy and enchanted" place. Within this man-decreed creation are natural creations such as the river that bursts from the earth. The origin of Alph is depicted almost in sexual terms, with the earth breathing "in fast thick pants" before ejaculating the river, a "mighty fountain," in an explosion of rocks. The sexual imagery helps reinforce the creation theme of "Kubla Khan."

Like Kubla's pleasure-dome, a work of art is a "miracle of rare device," and the last paragraph of the poem depicts the narrator's desire to emulate Kubla's act through music. As with Kubla, the narrator wants to impose order on a tumultuous world. Like Xanadu, art offers a refuge from the chaos. The narrator, as with a poet, is inspired by a muse, the Abyssinian maid, and wants to re-create her song. The resulting music would be the equivalent "in air" of the pleasure-dome. As an artist, the narrator would then stand apart from a society that fears those who create, those who have "drunk the milk of Paradise."

Michael Adams

LA BELLE DAME SANS MERCI

Author: John Keats (1795-1821)
Type of poem: Ballad
First published: 1820; collected in *Life, Letters, and Literary Remains of John Keats,* 1848

The Poem

"La Belle Dame sans Merci" is a remarkably evocative poem attaining subtle effects of mood and music in the short space of forty-eight lines. The twelve stanzas consist of three tetrameter lines followed by a concluding line of only two stresses. The title is taken from a medieval French poem by Alain Chartier in which the speaker is mourning his dead mistress. Other than the title, John Keats's poem has nothing in common with Chartier's.

The poem opens with an unnamed speaker asking a knight at arms what ails him, since he is all alone, pale, and wandering about aimlessly in a barren, desolate landscape. For the first twelve lines the speaker pointedly and persistently questions the knight, describes the landscape, and comments on the knight's physical appearance in a brutally frank and tactless manner. The melancholy tone is created immediately by the speaker's opening words: "O what can ail thee, . . .// The sedge has wither'd from the lake/ And no birds sing."

Beginning with stanza 4 and continuing to the end, the knight tells his strange story, one unlike any other in English poetry. In the flowering fields he met a young woman of supernal beauty, "a fairy's child" who in reality is a femme fatale. The knight came immediately under her spell, perhaps hypnotized by her powerful eyes, losing awareness of all but her. Although he could not understand her strange tongue, the two communicated in other ways. Reminiscent of Christopher Marlowe's passionate shepherd, he made her a garland of flowers, a bracelet, and a belt and set her on his warhorse. She in turn found strange foods for him—sweet roots, wild honey, "manna dew"—and cast a spell upon him which he mistook for words of love: "sure in language strange she said—/I love thee true." She took him to her underground grotto, where, weeping and sighing, she allowed him to comfort her even as she lulled him to sleep.

Once asleep, the knight was shaken by terrible dreams of kings, princes, and warriors all as deathly pale as himself. In vain they were warning him that he was "in thrall" or enslaved by the beautiful lady without pity. Awakening from the nightmare, the knight found himself on the cold hillside alone, the dream figures having vanished. Summer had given way to late autumn, and the beautiful lady had disappeared. The poem ends with the knight's desperate effort to explain to the questioner why he is "Alone and palely loitering." While the final stanza is pregnant with suggestion, it explains nothing. The knight's entire experience is encapsulated in the pronoun "this" (line 45), which has no grammatical antecedent. The initial speaker remains silent, perhaps shocked and befuddled by the knight's account of his experience.

Forms and Devices

This poem draws on a long tradition for much of its power and many of its effects. Ballads are divided into two categories: folk/popular and literary. Folk ballads appear early in a country's literature. They are anonymous and originate as songs. Literary ballads, on the other hand, come only after a literary tradition has been well established, and although they are modeled on a primitive poetic form, they are usually sophisticated compositions in their use of rhetorical devices to create subtle effects. Both categories of ballad share certain characteristics, many of which are evident in Keats's poem. As short narratives rarely exceeding a hundred lines, ballads relate a single event with no background or explanation. The language is simple to the point of starkness, and there is much use of dialogue, refrains, and repetition. Violent and supernatural occurrences are commonplace, and moral commentary is noticeably absent.

Although this poem was only a single evening's work (April 21, 1819), its stanzas, as Walter Jackson Bate has written in *John Keats* (1963), "have haunted readers and poets for a century and a half." Keats had become accustomed to writing iambic pentameter, so the meter here was an experiment. Much of the haunting effect that lingers in the mind long after the poem has been read comes from the stanza form of three four-stressed lines followed by a line of two stresses. The attenuated finality strikes a mournful chord. The effect is clearly seen in the first stanza: "And no birds sing."

Equally important in contributing to the tone is the heavy preponderance of dark vowels in the stressed words of generally a single syllable. Of the 289 words of the poem, all but forty are monosyllabic, and most of these contain long vowels, as in "four," "rose," "cold," "pale," and "wild." The simplicity of the language is as striking an innovation for Keats as is his departure from the comfortable iambic pentameter line. Keats's language is characteristically Spenserian in its rich density of imagery. In the early *Endymion* (1818), the richness tended to excess, blurring the outlines of description. Here, however, the balladlike starkness sets in clearly defined relief the horrid emptiness of the landscape. "The sedge has wither'd from the lake," "the harvest's done," and "cold hill's side" leave indelible marks on the memory. The effect is similar to Thomas Hardy's "Neutral Tones" (1898). The understated matter-of-factness of the narration (there is only a single exclamation) also contributes to the atmosphere of desolation.

Themes and Meanings

"La Belle Dame sans Merci" has been the subject of considerable critical attention. Bate remarks on the wide range of sources that contributed to the poem, to which may be added the strange folk ballad "Thomas Rhymer." The beautiful lady is obviously a femme fatale, an archetypal figure originating in early myth and continuing to the present in the popular image of the vamp. Bate believes the central influence to be Edmund Spenser's Duessa, who in *The Faerie Queene* (1590, 1596) seduces the Red Cross Knight. Other models readily available to Keats of warriors brought low by the wiles of beautiful women are Samson and Antony.

The identification of a specific femme fatale appears less important, however, than relating the knight's experience to the long tradition of a mortal entrammeled by a beautiful female who may possess supernatural powers. The reader is reminded of the plight of Odysseus's mariners who are bewitched by Circe in Homer's *Odyssey* (c. 800 B.C.E.). They temporarily lose their human appearance. Keats's knight fares much worse. He may be drained of his blood—he is "death-pale," as are the kings, princes, and warriors of his dream—in which case he would be the zombie victim of a vampire. He is definitely drained of his will. The irony of a knight at arms being reduced to a slave is strong indeed. His "sojourn," or rule, extends merely to the circumscribed area of desolation where "no birds sing," and his activity is reduced from roaming the countryside seeking wrongs to redress to loitering aimlessly about the lake. He is as enervated and purposeless as Alfred, Lord Tennyson's lotus eaters, as out of touch with the world of human concerns as that poet's Mariana. The knight has been victimized through no fault of his own and has suffered the irredeemable loss of his humanness. The pity is that he acquiesces to his fate; he has given up.

To be sure, all critics do not share this view that the lady is a dangerous menace. Bate, for example, sees the poem as premised on the "ultimate impossibility of contact between the human and this elusive, only half-human figure," but he has doubts that the lady is sinister, since the knight "does not actually witness the 'horrid warning' of starvation that this attempted union may bring"; he encounters it only in his dream, which may reflect his own uneasiness. Similarly, Earl R. Wasserman in *The Finer Tone* (1953) exculpates the lady from any evil intent; "she is the ideal whom the lover must pursue but whom he can never possess." The knight "is doomed to suffer her 'unkindness,' which is her nature although not her fault."

This diversity of critical opinion is testimony that the simple language of Keats's poem masks a substantial complexity of meaning. It is highly unlikely that there will ever be a critical consensus as to precisely what the poem "means." There is consensus, however, that "La Belle Dame sans Merci" is a great and unforgettable poem.

Robert G. Blake

LABYSHEEDY (THE SILKEN BED)

Author: Nuala Ní Dhomhnaill (1952-   )
Type of poem: Pastoral lyric
First published: 1988, as "Leaba Shíoda," in *Selected Poems*; English translation collected in the same volume

The Poem

"Labysheedy (The Silken Bed)" is a translation by Nuala Ní Dhomhnaill from her own Irish-language poem "Leaba Shíoda." The title refers to a small town (also identified by the spelling Labasheeda) in County Clare on the north bank of the river Shannon. The poem uses the features of the landscape as a living entity in an address to a lover, creating a mood of deep feeling and pulsing sensuality that is striking in its openness and moving in its tenderness.

The first stanza begins as a declaration of devotion, the poet speaking directly from a core of passion, describing a place of intimacy:

> I'd make a bed for you
> in Labysheedy
> in the tall grass
> under the wrestling trees
> where your skin
> would be silk upon silk
> in the darkness
> when the moths are coming down.

The physical presence of the person to whom the poem is addressed is emphasized by the focus on the body in the second stanza, which continues the tactile image of skin (metaphorically presented initially as silk), here compared to "milk being poured" so that its liquid qualities complement the sensuous textures of fine cloth. Then, in the latter part of the second stanza and the first half of the third, other attributes (hair, lips) are depicted with luscious, extravagant comparisons to the natural surroundings. In the third stanza, without pausing, the descriptive passage shifts with no change in tone to a flowing narrative of a couple walking on the banks of the river Shannon, "with honeyed breezes blowing."

The poet's adoration is exemplified in the latter part of the third stanza and the start of the fourth by a worshipful image of "fuchsias bowing down to you/ one by one" in a display of singular devotion. Then the poet returns to a direct, first-person perspective, continuing the traditional catalog of tasks that the lover would perform for the beloved:

> I would pick a pair of flowers
> as pendant earrings
> to adorn you
> like a bride in shining clothes.

The speaker then reaffirms the sentiment of the first line by repeating it with the evocative exclamation "O" preceding and the variant "in the twilight hour/ with evening falling slow" closing a quatrain with the first tight rhyme of the poem. The last stanza, another quatrain which extends and then concludes the thought of the poem's close, summarizes the spirit of the lyric; the poet anticipates the pleasure of entwined limbs wrestling "while the moths are coming down." The body consciousness of the last lines joins the couple to the physical presence of what has been described as a supportive natural setting, linking the desire of the pair to the forces that seem to govern the flow of growth and change in the world around them.

Forms and Devices

Emphasizing the importance of the Irish landscape in her work, Ní Dhomhnaill has recounted a family visit to the eastern end of the Dingle peninsula in Kerry, where her brother said "he had something special to show us." The highlight of this "special" place was a *bile*, "a sacred tree, dear to the Celts. A fairy tree. A magic tree." Ní Dhomhnaill celebrated the occasion in a poem that concludes with the query: "What will we do now without wood/ Now that the woods are laid low?"

Her personal response has been to place the features of a sacred landscape in many poems, and in "Labysheedy" the place where two lovers meet at twilight is both a figure for and a reflection of their emotions. The parenthetical title "The Silken Bed," which she added to the place name when translating the Irish into English, sets the pattern for the extended metaphor comparing feeling and geographical feature that controls the imagery in the poem. Although it is not apparent in the English version, the Irish title "Leaba Shíoda" is both a place name and a description, since the word "shíoda" means "silk." This additional meaning conveys the poet's wish to see and shape the setting so that it becomes an expression of her desires, both an inviting physical prospect and an affirmation of her admiration for the person she addresses.

The descriptive imagery that brings the place of "the silken bed" into vivid life continually connects human elements to the terrain. Skin is like silk; skin glistens like milk "poured from jugs"; the trees wrestle like human lovers; hair is likened to a "herd of goats/ moving over rolling hills" (the hills resembling the curves of the human body); lips are like "honeyed breezes." In addition, the natural world is like a chorus resonating with rhythms that parallel the emotions of the couple. The moths at darkness suggest the creatures that produce silk, and their descent echoes the lovers settling into the silken bed.

The flowers that seem to be bowing in respect to human beauty become the adornments of a bridal decoration. The gradual arrival of darkness, "the twilight hour/ with evening falling slow," suggests the building intensity of passion, and the riverside location aligns the couple with the procession of the Shannon, a traditional device to situate a human pair in concert within a poetic or symbolic life flow. The entire image pattern is augmented by the form of address, since the poet is speaking directly to the person for whom the silk bed is being prepared. The use of "I," "you," "your," then "we," and eventually "our" implies a recurring intimacy, while the attitude of reverence for the person, the place, and ultimately their joining gives the poem its mood of celebration.

Themes and Meanings

In an essay "Why I Choose to Write in Irish, the Corpse that Sits up and Talks Back," Ní Dhomhnaill mentions that "the attitude to the body enshrined in Irish remains extremely open and uncoy." It is accepted as an *nádúir*, or "in nature," and "becomes a source of repartee and laughter, rather then anything to be ashamed of." To illustrate this approach and to carry the ancient Irish tradition of regular speech as akin to song—a continuing heritage of a culture that has always admired verbal virtuosity—into the present, Ní Dhomhnaill in "Labysheedy" uses a motif common to classic folk ballads from the British Isles. To prove the truth of one's love, a person must carry out a particular series of tasks, and in "Labysheedy" these tasks are described as a means of making the body comfortable in a natural setting. The thematic thrust of the poem as the tasks are described is toward a recognition of affinities between human and natural phenomena.

The poem's other essential theme, the idea of a cultural community persisting through centuries of pressure to conform to distant (in this case, English) national standards and styles of literary expression, emerges through the depiction of the psychological mood of the poet. Against the quasi-gentile conception of proper diction for describing (or submerging) erotic impulses, the "open and uncoy" tenor of the poet's speech is offered as an appealing alternative. The calm confidence of the syntax, as the poet shifts from resolution ("I'd make") and prophecy ("your skin/ would be") to a narration in an ongoing present ("your hair is"; "we walking/ by the riverside"), then back to a projection into the future ("I would pick"), and finally to bold conjecture ("and what a pleasure it would be") is indicative of the will and volition underlying the poetic invitation.

The absence of fear, the avoidance of qualification or caution, suggests not only the self-confidence of the poet but also, by implication, a shared assumption that this type of discourse is familiar and welcome. The theme of the natural world as the true home for humanity—an understandable position in a country as beautiful as Ireland—is supported and complemented by the theme of an unfettered expression of emotion in vivid language as its most natural form of communication.

Leon Lewis

LACE

Author: Eavan Boland (1944-   )
Type of poem: Lyric
First published: 1985; collected in *The Journey and Other Poems,* 1987

The Poem

A compact lyric in free verse, "Lace" consists of thirty-five lines irregularly divided into eight sections or verse paragraphs. The title evokes a strong visual image, the significance of which becomes clear only as the poem progresses; the tatted filaments of a piece of lace represent, for Eavan Boland, the interlacings of language, sound, and sense as she labors in her notebook to compose an ideal poem. "Lace," then, is a specialized kind of lyric, because it presents the reader with a version of the writer's poetics; it is a poem about how, in Boland's view, poems can be written.

The poem begins with a sentence fragment: "Bent over/ the open notebook—." Boland's first statement, lacking both a definite subject and verb, is elliptical and oblique. She tells the reader neither who is speaking nor whom the poem is describing, information that conventionally one might expect at the beginning of a piece of writing. Readers may feel dislocated by this immediate lack of grammatical sense and empathize with the poet's apparently halting efforts to express herself in words. Readers may also find themselves implicated in that same creative process; readers too, after all, are bent over the pages of an open book, like Boland's missing subject, trying to decipher her poem. The lack of a definite "I" or "she" permits poet and reader to be drawn more closely, though tenuously, together.

The second section of the poem offers a setting, both time and place. At dusk, light is fading and clear vision becomes more difficult. The poem is located, Boland says, "in my room" at the back of the house. She places herself in relative obscurity, in a dim corner, and introduces the lyric first person—at once the poet and the dramatized speaker of the poem—not as a confident "I," but obliquely, in a possessive pronoun.

In the third section, she connects the dusk around her to the lack of poetic insight she seems to be experiencing. Asserting herself at last as a subject—"I"—she continues to doubt her talents, claiming to be looking for a language with which to express herself. She is "still" in two senses of the word, both persistently striving onward and, paradoxically, unable to make herself go on.

The fourth section consists of a single word, bringing us at last to the poem's title: "lace." Boland finds the proper word or image to express her sense of what a poem is, but for her readers, that sense is far from crystal clear. She presents the reader with a conceit, a complicated metaphorical equation—in this case of lace and poetic language—that she must explain in the body of the poem.

The fifth and sixth sections provide that explanation. Boland invokes the figure of a baroque courtier for whom poetry resembles lace: an elaborate, elegant, and finely crafted play of words tossed off with *sprezzatura* (an appearance of ease) and savoir faire to impress his peers or lovers. Such courtiers, even if they were merely princes "in a petty court," possessed a seemingly natural talent for poetic form, a talent for which Boland herself longs.

The seventh section, however, returns to the initial setting, in the dark corner of a room, and Boland reminds herself that even the apparent ease of these courtiers involves the same secluded labor over a notebook that she has undertaken. Poetry, she realizes, has never come easily to anyone, nor are its complex interlacings of sound and sense simply a matter of careless grace.

The last section of the poem, again a single line, turns on a paradox. In attempting to gain insight into "the language that is// lace," Boland discovers what the poets who seemed to achieve that light, glittering language "lost their sight for." Her own well-wrought conceit emerges not from clarity of vision but from the relative obscurity of writing a poem. Poetry, she tells us, as it strives toward vision, puts forward an elaborate form of blindness.

Forms and Devices

Boland employs two types of language in "Lace." The poem begins and ends with a barren, simple form of speech. There are no elaborate metaphors here; the descriptions are direct and unadorned, and the vocabulary is limited and unpretentious, consisting mostly of blunt monosyllables.

This type of language stands in sharp contrast to the poetically complex, elaborate diction at the poem's center, in the fifth and sixth sections that follow the introduction of the image of lace. Boland here employs abstract polysyllables such as "baroque obligation" and poeticizes her vocabulary with highly charged metaphors, as in "the crystal rhetoric/ of bobbined knots/ and bosses." In this part of the poem, she twists words together like a complicated pattern of old-style lace. Her readers can hear in the poem's diction the difference between her presently uninspired state and the baroque cleverness for which she longs.

Boland employs a clipped line of no more than eight syllables, and includes only a few words per verse. The breaks between successive lines are not necessarily determined by grammar, punctuation, or meter, or even by the poet's sense of breath. Instead, the poetry seems broken, chopped, halting, as the poet feels her way precariously into words, pausing irregularly to search for a needed expression or image. The reader follows Boland's mind in motion as she scrutinizes her own creative processes and takes notes on the apparent breakdown of smooth, effortless form—what she calls "a vagrant drift of emphasis"—and the loss of poetic self-confidence.

In contrast to her fragmented lines, however, Boland exploits interlaced patterns of sound that draw the poem together, giving the reader a sense of wholeness. While there is no formal end rhyme in the poem, many words echo one another, giving the poem musical coherence. Series of words, such as "book . . . back . . . dark . . . dusk . . . look . . . shakes" or "wrist . . . thriftless . . . crystal . . . drift . . . kisses," contain assonances, alliterations, and half-rhymes—repetitions of vowel sounds, consonants, and whole syllables—which create threads of euphony that weave through the poem.

Boland presents her readers with two sides of the creative process. On the one hand, traditional forms seem to collapse and prove insufficient; the poet expresses frustration and anxiety about her inability to create. On the other hand, she succeeds in rebuilding the "interlaced" language she wants, by means of patterns of poetic music.

Themes and Meanings

Eavan Boland typically confronts in her poems the themes of hearth and history, her sense of herself as a woman in relation to home and family, and her sense of nationality and of the Irish tradition that lies behind much of her work. In "Lace," however, neither of these issues is engaged directly. The poem is set in "the house," but that setting is never made problematic and becomes, by the end of the poem, rather a comfort, a curiously vital link with lost baroque creativity. The courtier whom Boland admires is male, his sex necessitated by the patriarchal nature of the poetic tradition from which, at the poem's outset, Boland feels ostracized. Issues of gender are not at the core of the poem's concern, however, and the courtier's maleness is not called into question as it would have been in an earlier Boland volume such as *In Her Own Image* (1980) or *Night Feed* (1982).

Instead, "Lace" sets down a basis for creativity and poetic work that is, for Boland, independent of sex, nation, or historical period. The lyric deals with the struggle to see, to attain vision, and to liberate oneself, through poetry, from the confines of everyday life, which runs its course, metaphorically speaking, in dimness and perpetual dusk. Boland wants to make a poem something light, effortless, and beautiful, but wanting is not achieving, and she discovers that, despite appearances, poetry is made not from the seemingly crystalline, other-worldly language of bygone Renaissance men, but from the very dimness and blindness that characterize her life and that certainly characterized theirs. Poetry is not an escape into light and "thriftless phrases," but a means of confronting that blindness and coming to terms with one's own apparent inability to make something clever and perfect out of the world. Boland sees value in writing poetry not because it holds any visionary keys to understanding but because of the process of confrontation and self-scrutiny that it embodies.

Basic to Boland's poetry, even before she engages the problems of nationality and sexual identity, is this principle of self-scrutiny. The poetics that "Lace" offers present an alternative to the deceptive ease of the traditional lyric, as Boland builds a viable poetic music from her apparently blocked creativity and touches, with a very critical self-consciousness, the language that is lace.

Kevin McNeilly

THE LACE

Author: Rainer Maria Rilke (1875-1926)
Type of poem: Lyric
First published: 1907, as "Die Spitze I-II," in *Neue Gedichte*; English translation collected in *New Poems*, 1964

The Poem

Rainer Maria Rilke wrote part 1 of "The Lace" in Paris, France, in the early summer of 1906, and part 2 in Capri, Italy, in February of 1907. In addition to varying in time and place of origin, the two parts also differ in form. Part 1 has three stanzas of five, four, and four lines, and alternating rhyme. Part 2, with its octave (in the original German) and sestet, is an Italian sonnet. The meter throughout is iambic pentameter, varied by Rilke's strongly rhythmic language. Both parts begin with abstract musings about the nature of human existence. Both parts end with a smile.

Contrary to what one might expect from the title, there is little description of the lace itself. In part 1, readers learn only that it is a small, densely woven piece; in part 2, that it is a flowery border. Not that Rilke's knowledge of lace was limited—a passage in his novel *Die Aufzeichnungen des Malte Laurids Brigge* (1910; *The Notebooks of Malte Laurids Brigge*, 1930, 1958) displays his familiarity with various kinds of lace: Italian work, Venetian needlepoint, point d'Alençon, Valenciennes, Binche, and pillow-laces. It is the existence of the lace, though, that is central to the poem.

In *New Poems*, Rilke was placing newfound emphasis on objects, sometimes describing them in detail, other times, as in "The Lace," seeking to extract their meaning from them. German has a word for such a poem—a "Dinggedicht," or a poem about a thing. The lace is referred to as "this thing" in both parts of the poem.

Rilke's interest in objects was strengthened by his close association with contemporary artists. From 1900 to 1902, he lived in an artists' colony in Worpswede, a village north of Bremen, Germany. Among his friends were Heinrich Vogeler, who illustrated many of Rilke's first editions; Paula Modersohn-Becker, whose early death is mourned in Rilke's "Requiem"; and the sculptor Clara Westhoff, who became Rilke's wife and introduced him to the French sculptor Auguste Rodin. Not only did Rilke admire their works, he also understood their creative personalities. It is, therefore, not surprising that, in both parts of "The Lace," his focus shifts from the lace to the lace-maker, from the artwork to the artist.

The only personal glimpse Rilke provides about the lace-maker is that she eventually went blind. His first impression is that her eyes were, perhaps, too high a price to pay for a piece of lace. Then, with astonishing directness, he apostrophizes the lady: "Do you want them back?" From this changed perspective, he understands that the lace was made with joy and still contains a trace of that joy. In fact, the very soul of the lace-maker seems present in the lace, kept alive in it long after her body has perished. The poet, with new insight, smiles at its usefulness.

In part 2, Rilke derives a lesson from the lace. It is a source of inspiration, an example of the perfect artistry to which humanity aspires. Well worth the effort, the finished product makes the artist smile.

Forms and Devices

According to the Germanist Käte Hamburger, Rilke's basic literary maneuver is the comparison, such as a simile or a metaphor. There is one of each in part 1 of "The Lace." The simile is in the second stanza: "is all your human joy here inside this thing/ where your huge feelings went, as between/ stem and bark, miniaturized?" There is a detailed analysis of this simile in Wolfgang Müller's study, *Rainer Maria Rilkes "Neue Gedichte"* (1971). Müller finds the comparison fitting in three ways: First, it stresses how small the lace is that has nevertheless taken on such significance—thin enough to fit between the stem and bark of a tree; second, it likens the process of lace-making to organic growth, since a tree adds new rings between the stem and the bark; third, when the bark is peeled off, a lacelike pattern is left on its dried inner side.

The metaphor is in the third stanza: "Through a tear in fate, a tiny interstice,/ you absented your soul from its own time." The verb in the original German is *entzogst*. The root of it, *ziehen*, means "to draw or pull," and the prefix *ent* means "away." Drawing something through a hole is fundamental to the art of lace-making. Rilke retains the basic gesture, but, instead of having the lace-maker absent herself from everyday activities by drawing threads through parts of her pattern, he has her transcend her own time by drawing her soul through a hole in fate. The commonplace is transformed. The image of lace-making conveys the idea of spiritual permanence.

Rilke's writing is persuasive without being polemical. His skillful use of questions in "The Lace" gently deemphasizes a pragmatic viewpoint without denying its validity. The sober fact of the matter is that the lace-maker went blind. While being human is fraught with changing fortunes, her fate seems particularly unkind. Rilke anticipates such a comment and avoids having to refute it by phrasing it as a question. He then effectively precludes debate by suddenly asking the lace-maker herself, by accessing the only truly knowledgeable source.

The second stanza, with its striking simile, is also phrased as a question. While stated more positively, it leaves room for doubt, as if the poet is not quite sure what the lace-maker is telling him. Not until the third stanza does her soul seem so present in the lace that he is able to employ the indicative and explain how it got there.

Proceeding from the knowledge gained in part 1, part 2 opens confidently with a lengthy rhetorical question. The poet is now sure of the deeper meaning of the lace, but, by appearing to ask, he continues to engage the reader. In a subtle series of questions, he has shifted attention from the lace-maker's ailment to her ecstasy.

Themes and Meanings

In the section of *The Notebooks of Malte Laurids Brigge* that deals with lace, looking at the family lace is something the young Malte and his mother like to do. They carefully unwind the familiar specimens from a spindle and behold their patterns with awe and wonderment yet again. By writing a second part to "The Lace" months after completing the first, Rilke is doing the same thing, taking another look at the lace, seeing something else in it, describing it in a different form.

Like any good work of art, the lace rewards repeated visits. Aesthetically pleasing, it remains the same in a changing world. It is interesting that Rilke, in part 2 of the poem, presents this permanence and perfection as particularly pleasing to adults, which has to do with his perception of the adult world as not necessarily an improvement over the world of a child, as hardly worth the effort of outgrowing "our first pair of/ shoes." Above all, adulthood seems to the poet a time of uncontrollably changing fortunes, as if one hardly gets settled when something else happens to cause a disruption.

As evidenced by the different locales in which Rilke wrote the two parts of the poem, he had no permanent home in his adult life. Rilke lived the life of a benign vagabond, traveled extensively to satisfy his curiosity about other cultures, and was a migrant guest of various admirers of his work. That was his chosen lifestyle. Multilingual, he felt at home in most of Europe and Russia. He also improved steadily as a writer, enjoying considerable success in his own time. Today, he is considered the most significant and influential German lyric poet of the first half of the twentieth century.

In "The Lace," the poet *par excellence* disregards his own accomplishments and is drawn instead to the product of what seems to have been an enviably settled lifestyle. The lace-maker's art was the fruit of years working with intricate patterns, striving for perfection. Lace-making is too complicated to be a casual pursuit, so it was usually done by intelligent ladies of the nobility whose secure lifestyles left them the time to embark on long-term projects.

Rilke admires, in the octet, the fact that the lace, the complex product of an intelligent, artistic adult mind, got made. In the sestet, he admires the perfection of the completed product. Art, unlike life, can, in gifted hands, conform strictly to a grand design and, when finished, can reflect the artist's vision, untainted by extraneous or random forces.

That argument, though, applies not only to works of fabric art. It applies equally well to musical compositions, dance choreography, visual arts, and literature. Rilke responds as one artist to another, as someone who understands the trials and rewards of the creative process, and who knows that each work, in its own way, contains some of the artist's soul.

Jean M. Snook

THE LADY IN KICKING HORSE RESERVOIR

Author: Richard Hugo (Richard Hogan, 1923-1982)
Type of poem: Lyric
First published: 1973, in *The Lady in Kicking Horse Reservoir*

The Poem

"The Lady in Kicking Horse Reservoir" refers to an actual site about thirty-five miles north of Missoula, where Richard Hugo taught at the University of Montana for the last eighteen years of his life. The poem, however, is not based on an actual drowning.

The fifty-six lines of the poem are divided into seven eight-line stanzas. The first-person speaker begins with a startlingly blunt line, mostly in monosyllables, in which he asserts that his hands, which once moved across the woman's body as the hands of a lover, have been replaced by the green algae and grasses of the lake. Instead of his ten fingers toying with her hair, ten bass "tease" it, as if they were macabre hair stylists. The poem is not a lament for his lost love, for the speaker says that he hopes to find her in the spring still tangled in the lily pads, stars reflected from her teeth.

In the second stanza, the speaker gloats in observing that while most lakes are dim a few feet down, this one is dark from the mountain range around it. He associates the woman's death with the songs of dying Indians, and he suggests that when her hands wave in the wind, they wave to the ocean, which he associates with their lost romance. In the following stanza he expands on the seashore, where they made love and where whales "fall in love with gulls." The "Dolly skeletons" of line 18 refer to Dolly Varden trout, whose watery death parallels the imagined death of the "lady" in the title. The music of the dying Indians now fades away as the "lover" bloats.

The fourth stanza begins with the terse understatement "All girls should be nicer." Instead of "windy gems," the "Indian rain" falls like arrows, and the speaker is haunted by dreams of regret and defeat; the arrows of rain sing, telling him there is no way to bring her back. In the next stanza, the speaker is reminded of a boyhood experience in which one boy was slapped and humiliated by another. The speaker in this nightmare episode recalls having tried to rescue him from the company pond. (In an interview, Hugo identified himself with both the slapped boy and the would-be rescuer who awakens to the "cold music" of failure and regret.)

In the fifth stanza, the speaker reflects on other failures: the factory that closed because "No one liked our product," the bison that multiply so fast they must be thinned out. The "hope" that he expressed so explicitly and grimly in the first stanza is now "vague," and he goes so far as to speculate that the woman's bones may be "nourished by the snow."

As the reservoir fills up with the spring run-off, the speaker imagines the woman spilling out "into weather," and he salutes her now as a "lover," not with the sarcasm of the third stanza, but in a literal sense. She has become a part of the lamented past. She is also a "mother," but in a perverse way: She will join in the irrigation of crops that "dead Indians forgot to plant." In releasing her and simultaneously associating her with unplanted crops and "dead Indians" (as opposed to the "dying Indians" of the second stanza), the speaker removes the "lady" from his obsessive anger.

The end of the poem finds the speaker "sailing west" with the arrows of rain, which now dissolve in the ocean, the site of their past romance. The "Dollys," which he envisioned in the third stanza as skeletons, are now seen as erotically "teasing oil from whales" with their tongues.

Forms and Devices

Although the free-verse line that Hugo employs in this poem varies from seven to twelve syllables, thirty-four of the fifty-six lines are within the range of blank verse (unrhymed iambic pentameter, the staple of William Shakespeare and John Milton), and it might be said that Hugo flirts with that form throughout. The first line, for example, is almost "pure" iambic pentameter, as are the last two lines of the third stanza and five lines of the sixth. Allowing for substitute and inverted feet, iambic pentameter lines occur frequently in the poem. In addition to the musical effects of this recurring but unpredictable metric regularity, Hugo often uses such sound devices as the assonantal (vowel) cluster in line 9, "lilly," "still," and "spillway," and the long *i* sounds of lines 3 and 4, "slime," "pile," and "ice." As is usually the case, such sound play creates music and adds emphasis to the statement.

What is most striking, however, is the image and metaphoric structure of the poem. A number of images and metaphors from the first three stanzas reappear, often with altered meaning or impact, in the last stanza. The recurrence involves the interplay between the landlocked reservoir and the ocean; the arrows of rain, which are connected with the defeated and dying Indians; and fish (bass, Dolly Varden, and whales—their actual status as mammals notwithstanding).

Certain key words also recur throughout the poem, and they are of special interest when they reappear near the conclusion: for example, "hope," "spillway," "lover," "foam," and "teasing." The "thundering foam" of the third stanza becomes the "dissolving foam" at the end of the poem. The ten bass that teased the woman's hair in the first stanza are transformed into the powerfully erotic metaphor of "naked Dollys" that tease oil from whales (perhaps one thinks of sperm whales here) with their tongues.

Themes and Meanings

Richard Hugo is often labeled a "regional poet," and there are strong regional elements in "The Lady in Kicking Horse Reservoir." The poem is specifically located in the Mission Range of the Rocky Mountains, and readers outside the Pacific Northwest might have difficulty with such references as those to the Dolly Varden trout, a predatory species known in the West as a bull trout. Donna Gerstenberger, in *Richard Hugo* (1983), observes that the Indians in Hugo's poems become "symbols for the dispossessed and the despairing." Hugo identifies himself with such symbols throughout his poems.

Hugo has described "The Lady in Kicking Horse Reservoir" as a "revenge poem," written from his pain and anger over a woman who jilted him and married another man. In the course of the poem, however, he exorcises the demon that has possessed him and filled him with self-destructive feelings of guilt and failure. Accordingly, the poem may be said to begin in psychological illness and end in a direction tending toward health. The dominant images of death yield to an almost comical metaphor of renewed sexual vigor.

Hugo spells out the autobiographical context of this poem in an essay from *The Triggering Town* (1979) entitled "In Defense of Creative Writing Classes." Yet it is more than a confessional cleansing ritual. Its richness has to do with the varied images and metaphors and with what might be called mythic and archetypal motifs of renewal and the return of fertility after the sterile death of winter. The ritualized symbolic death of the "lady" is similar in nature to that of the Fisher King encountered in T. S. Eliot's *The Waste Land* (1922). In that poem, Eliot draws on the ancient sacrifice of the Fisher King to assure the restoration of the land. Eliot closes his poem with apocalyptic references to a culture that disintegrates as the Fisher King, an "arid plain" at his back, shores up "fragments" against his "ruins." In the conclusion to this poem, however, Hugo associates himself with the forces of revival and renewal.

Ron McFarland

LADY LAZARUS

Author: Sylvia Plath (1932-1963)
Type of poem: Lyric
First published: 1965, in *Ariel*

The Poem

"Lady Lazarus" is an extraordinarily bitter dramatic monologue in twenty-eight tercets. The title ironically identifies a sort of human oxymoron, a female Lazarus— not the biblical male. Moreover, she does not conform to society's traditional idea of ladylike behavior: She is angry, and she wants revenge. She is egocentric, using "I" twenty-two times, "my" nine. Her resurrection is owing only to herself. This is someone much different from the grateful man of John 11:2 who owes his life to Jesus.

Given Sylvia Plath's suicide, one might equate this Lazarus with Plath. Self-destruction pervades the poem as it did her life, but she has inventively appropriated Lazarus in constructing a mythical female counterpart who is not simply equatable with herself. This common tactic of distancing autobiography tempers one's proclivity to see the poem as confessional. As confession mutates to myth, subjectivity inclines to generalized feeling.

Lady Lazarus resurrects herself habitually. Like the cat, she allows herself nine lives, including equally their creation and cancellation. The first line may stress her power over her fate, but "manage" (line 3) suggests an uneasy control. It also connotes managerial enterprise, an implication clarified when the speaker's language takes on the flavor of the carnival.

The first eight stanzas largely vivify this ugly but compelling experience. The reader sees the worm-eaten epidermis and inhales the sour breath. More cadaver than person, Lady Lazarus intends terror, however problematic her bravado. Nevertheless, she will soon smile, when time restores flesh eaten by the grave. (The smile will not prove attractive.) For the moment, however, she is only a "walking miracle" of defective parts: a shell of glowing skin, a face blank as linen, a paralyzed foot. Almost spectral, she remains finely, grotesquely palpable.

Stanzas 9 to 19 present Lady Lazarus as sideshow freak, stripper, and barker. Her emergence from the winding-sheet (perhaps a straitjacket) is a "striptease." The "peanut-crunching crowd" thrills, pruriently. She alters the introductory "Ladies and gentlemen," but her phrasing retains the master of ceremonies' idiom. Reference to her "theatrical/ comeback in broad day" plays poetically with the jargon of show business and magic.

In presenting the history of her efforts to die, Lady Lazarus assures the reader of her honor. This integrity gives continuity, making her the same woman at thirty that she was at ten. It is nothing against her that her first attempt at annihilation was accidental; it was premonitory. Eventually, intention ruled—both descent and resurrection. In the eighteenth stanza, she says that each "comeback" is, however, to the "same place" and the "same brute/ Amused shout." The prosody allows "brute" to be a noun (hence, person) in the line, an adjective in the sentence. As it is the "same brute" each time, beginning with her tenth year, and as she finally intends the destruction of "men," this brute is always the father or his replica. This explains why Plath renders the customary "Ladies and Gentlemen" as "Gentleman, ladies."

Stanzas 19 through 26 clarify Lady Lazarus's victimization at the hands of "Herr Enemy" and "Herr Doktor," who are one and the same and merely the latest incarnation of the "brute" father. The German spelling of doctor and the choice of *Herr* create the stereotype of Germanic male authority. Lady Lazarus is this creature's "baby," more particularly his "opus." Thus, this menacing figure reminiscent of Josef Mengele, of the Nazi concentration camp at Auschwitz, fathers her "art" of dying. She sarcastically repudiates his inauthentic "concern" for her but allows him his role in her fiery death and resurrection. Because she was "pure gold," he expected profit from her. He pokes among her ashes for valuable residue, but she has reduced herself to "nothing" but a "shriek." Spiritually, however, she is a virtual reliquary, which turns the tables; "Herr Enemy" will pay, and dearly, for her victimized body and consciousness. There will be a "very large charge" for "eyeing [her] scars," for discovering that her heart "really goes," even for a "bit of blood" or a "word."

Having taken up the battle with the enemy on his terms, she concludes by warning the male deity and demon that when she rises from the ashes, she consumes men as fire does oxygen.

Forms and Devices

"Lady Lazarus" plays distinctively on the ear. It blends staccato, irregular versification with a dense mixture of highly patterned sounds. End and internal rhymes, both exact and slant, are rapidly mixed and steadily joined to consonance, assonance, alliteration, and sheer repetition. At the outset, Plath makes end rhymes of "again," "ten," "skin," "fine," "linen," and "napkin" before the eleventh line. She dares, in one line, "grave cave ate" and, in another, "million filaments." The "brute" that ends line 53 is followed at once by the only slightly dissimilar "amused." Plath's prosody ingeniously restrains the metronome while rendering sound almost childlike.

The nazification of the speaker's antagonist is a perhaps hyperbolic but crucial feature of the poem. Plath once said to George Macbeth, "I see you have a concentration camp in your mind too." For Lady Lazarus, the model of her victimization is the modern slaughter of the Jews. The "Nazi lampshade" refers to the commandant's practice at Buchenwald of flaying inmates and stretching the skin, often tattooed, over a lampshade frame. The most notorious of the Nazi gas chambers and crematories were housed at Auschwitz, where blankets were made of human hair and soap from human fat. Those who emptied the ovens poked in the ashes for hidden gold wedding bands and for gold fillings missed by camp "dentists." It was at Auschwitz that the infamous and sadistically curious Doktor Mengele listened to the camp symphony, oversaw experiments on humans, and quizzically dropped in at the ovens. Hence the primal "brute" becomes "Herr Doktor" and "Herr Enemy." "Herr

God" and "Herr Lucifer," two sides of the same coin, are but extensions of the Nazi male stereotype.

To this frame of reference, Plath adds an amusing filmic touch, after the fashion of the "vampire" and the "villagers" in her poem "Daddy." "So, so, Herr Doktor./ So, Herr Enemy" parodies the stereotypical speech of Nazi officers interrogating prisoners in American war films of the 1940's. That the words are Lady Lazarus's indicates that she is exorcising the victim within her and preparing to adopt her enemy's tactics against him. She had told her nemesis to "Peel off the napkin" of her "featureless face," the manifestation of her passivity, represented as a "Jew linen."

Themes and Meanings

People who return from the edge of death often speak of it as rebirth. "Lady Lazarus" effectively conveys that feeling. It is principally, however, about the aspiration to revenge that is felt by the female victim of male domination, conceived as ubiquitous. The revenge would be against all men, though the many are rendered as singular in the poem. The text forces the reader to take the father as prototype, which drives one to read it in terms of the Electra complex. Why, one asks, is the speaker malevolent toward the father rather than amorously yearning? What has he done to inspire the hatred which has displaced love?

The poem is mythic. It leaves the father's, the male's, basic offense at the general level of brutal domination. One might rest there, taking control and exploitation as the male's by nature, practiced universally and with special vigor toward spouses and daughters. The idea will come short of universal acceptance, but the text does not disallow it.

If one looks at the "Enemy" as modeled on Plath's own father, one finds something else, though certainly no Fascist. Otto Plath's blameless offense was his death in Sylvia's childhood, which seems to have left her feeling both guiltily responsible and angry, a common reaction. One normally expects the adult child to overcome this confusion by reasonably understanding it. This poem is not about that experience; it is about the wish, however futile, to turn the tables on the father and his kind. Its dramatic overstatement of male evil may be, for one reader, an offense against fairness. For another, it may not even pertain to that problem, but only represent the extremity of long-borne suffering.

Whether the poem depicts the onset of successful revenge is problematic. Lady Lazarus has surely arrived at the point of reversing roles with her antagonist. She understands and intends to exploit his means of violent mastery, and at the last, the prefatory myth of the halting Lazarus is altered to the myth of the ascendant phoenix, the bird which immolates itself every five hundred years but rises whole and rejuvenated from its ashes. Lady Lazarus's "red hair" suggests fire, which lives (easily) off oxygen. "I eat men like air," therefore, seems the foreshadowing of victory, in the restoration of the true self and the annihilation of its detractor(s).

For a person, however, the "eating" of air is not nourishing; also, Lady Lazarus confronts men in every quarter of the universe, and her battle plan is of their design.

She is even nominally male herself. Whether the phoenix is male or female is even uncertain, though Plath preferred to think it female. Perhaps the poem ultimately envisions the tension created in the victim by the wish for revenge and the fear of its frustration.

David M. Heaton

THE LADY OF SHALOTT

Author: Alfred, Lord Tennyson (1809-1892)
Type of poem: Lyric
First published: 1832, in *Poems*; revised and collected in *Poems*, 1842

The Poem

"The Lady of Shalott," in both its original form of 1832 and in the revision of 1842, is divided into four separate narrative sections, each containing from four to six stanzas of nine lines each. The meter is predominately iambic tetrameter with an insistent and unusual rhyme structure involving double couplets and a triplet in each refrain. Alfred, Lord Tennyson took the poem's title and a few of its incidents from an anonymous medieval Italian novella variously identified as *Donna di Scalotta* or *Novella LXXXI* in the *Cento Novelle Antiche* (c. 1321). As is usual with Tennyson, this source is so altered in his retelling as to be largely unimportant for interpretation. What Tennyson retains from his source is simply a story of a lady's desperate love for the greatest of Arthurian knights, Lancelot, a love which ends in the lady's death.

The poem opens with a description of a riparian landscape: a river flowing between fields of grain down to Camelot and the sea; within this river, an island; within this island, a castle; and within the castle, the Lady of Shalott. There are enclosures within enclosures. About the island, ships sail and barges drift, but the Lady of Shalott remains unseen within the walls. Only her voice is sometimes heard by reapers at dawn; listening to her strange song, they refer to the mysterious lady as a "fairy."

This lady, the reader learns, weaves a tapestry of all the sights of the outside world that are reflected before her in a mirror hanging upon her wall. She will not look out at the world itself, only at its "shadows," for she has received a mysterious warning that if she looks to the city of Camelot, she will fall victim to a curse. The curse comes. Great Lancelot eventually rides by the window, and his splendid image in her mirror tempts the lady to look upon the man himself. As she does so, the tapestry rends, and the mirror shatters. Despairingly, in the midst of a blowing storm, the lady boards a small boat and drifts toward Camelot and death singing a final dirge. When the boat comes to Camelot bearing her silent corpse, all but Lancelot are terrified at this strange apparition. Lancelot, for whom she died loving, simply observes (almost flatly observes), "She has a lovely face/ God in his mercy lend her grace."

The narrative has the simplicity of a fairy tale, and, as in a fairy tale, causes and motivations are mysterious and obscure. The origin of the curse is never explained, and the lady has learned of it only by a strangely disembodied "whisper." Again, as in fairy tales, the transparency of the narrative surface hints at greater depths. The lady confesses after seeing a pair of lovers reflected in her mirror that she is "half sick of shadows," but her vision of the lovers is preceded by a vision of a funeral—significantly, for one later recognizes that her sickness among shadows ends finally with her death among realities. "The Lady of Shalott" remains one of Tennyson's most evocative and disturbing poems.

Forms and Devices

The most striking formal aspect of this poem is its remarkably vivid images. "The Lady of Shalott" was a favorite with Victorian painters and illustrators, who understandably delighted in picturing the crisis of the curse with its sprung tapestry and cracking mirror. Those images, and that of the lady's funeral barge at the poem's close, have been admired by many modern critics as early examples of poetic symbolism. While the magic mirror and tapestry belong to the machinery of legend and fairy tale, they seem more than props in Tennyson's hands. The lady's mirror, for example, reflects not only the outside world but also the condition of the lady herself as an outsider. Both the lady and the mirror capture images within frames, the mirror in its glass, the lady in her tapestry. This identification is pushed even further at the poem's close when the lady is described as having a "glassy countenance" as she gazes toward Camelot. Having preferred realities to shadows, having rejected the mirror's vision for her own, she becomes a mirror herself; her countenance now mirrors her coming death.

Tennyson's careful insistence on referring to the tapestry as a "web" suggests the idea of entanglement that is certainly part of the lady's condition. The insect connotations of "web" are also admissible, for this web is very much made from the lady's own substance: When it is disturbed, she dies. The careful texturing of these images reinforces, deepens, and extends their more conventional associations. The island's isolation and the temporal significance of the river current also gain by their participation in a symbolic pattern of such complexity. It is the combination of suggestive images with a relatively discontinuous, seemingly naïve narrative that lends this poem its disquieting power. The poem anticipates the modern understanding of dreams as symbol systems suspended in masking narratives. As in dreams, the narrative line is deceptively simple; the deeper significance is encoded in symbol. Since the poem is essentially about the power of dream and symbol, of image over life, its symbolic images embody the poem's theme rather than express it, which is very nearly the essence of modern poetic symbolism.

The collective effect of the symbol system in "The Lady of Shalott" is a powerful sense of narcissistic introversion. The Lady's attempt to break out of her insularity fails because she is incapable of escaping her enslavement to images. The image of Lancelot himself had been cast into her mirror from the river surface and is nothing more than another representation of the reality she cannot reach. Trapped in the immobility of her island world of images, cut off from the world of transition and change—of life, love, and death—the lady rebels against her condition by casting herself adrift into the temporal tyranny of the river current. It pulls her into the world of living men and women, but she dies in transit, singing her own death song in a funeral barge emblazoned with her own name; her isolation is never broken.

The rhyme scheme of the poem is also a means for reinforcing the sense of inescapable isolation, for it is one of the most repetitive and insistent rhyme schemes to be found in serious English poetry. The sequence *aaaabcccb* is repeated throughout the poem, and all but one stanza end with the lady's name as the final rhyme. The obsessive repetition of the name drives home her own repetitive obsessions. Images and metrical organization work together to create claustrophobia, a terrified sense of compulsive ritual that is wearying and inescapable.

Themes and Meanings

"The Lady of Shalott" has most often been read as an allegory of the artist's condition in a society indifferent or even hostile to art. The Victorian age was not, by and large, especially sympathetic to art and artists. Many Victorians believed that poetry had had its day and could offer little of use in an age of serious scientific, industrial, and social effort. Put plainly, many Victorians believed that poetry "did" nothing, that it was merely idleness and frippery. Others, perhaps no more sympathetic to the real requirements of the artist, suggested that poetry could justify itself if it celebrated the serious social achievements of the modern age—if, in other words, it put itself to work providing moral edification for the reading masses. Certainly, many of Tennyson's contemporaries took him to task for writing poems remote in their imaginative wonders from the mundane struggles and triumphs of the passing hour. Tennyson had a strong tendency to idealize the isolated, self-absorbed artist rapt in his visions of unearthly beauty, and this "art for art's sake" doctrine came in for strong criticism from well-meaning Victorian critics. "The Lady of Shalott" is, in one dimension, Tennyson's allegorical rejoinder to those utilitarian critics.

In the allegorical scheme, Camelot represents the world of commerce, politics, social responsibility, and daily life. Lancelot himself represents the temptations of worldly fame and power to which the artistic temperament succumbs at its peril. The mirror and the web represent the arts, and the lady the artist. This schematizing is reductive but not inaccurate, for the poem is at some level almost certainly a dramatization of the artist's desperate condition in a world of commercial energies, democratic sentiment, and mass standardization. The artist, like the lady, is strong only in a world of images, and the price of this strength is isolation. Like the lady, the artist's connection to the busy world of real life can only be tangential; his or her songs are at most overheard in the bustle of politics and business. In an age making insistent demands on the strenuous efforts of individuals in cooperation with social ventures, the artist may inevitably feel misgivings about his self-absorption and isolation, but the artistic temperament also knows that no reconciliation with such a world is possible except at the cost of artistic integrity. Lancelot is desired at the cost of imaginative power.

If this is Tennyson's allegorical view of the artist's position, it is a view far removed from the strong poetic faith of his Romantic predecessors such as Percy Bysshe Shelley and William Wordsworth. The great Romantic poets had believed in the transforming power of poetry. They believed that it was strong enough to act upon the real world and that the poet was a person of might—not so Tennyson, at least not in "The Lady of Shalott." If the lady is Tennyson's allegorized poet, then his poet is hiding out and is imperiled in a world of intractable fact. The lady is no match for the commercial power of Camelot; by comparison, her mirror is fragile and her web tenuous, and she turns from them only to be destroyed.

Whitney Hoth

LAGUNA BLUES

Author: Charles Wright (1935-   )
Type of poem: Lyric
First published: 1981, in *The Southern Cross*

The Poem

Charles Wright's "Laguna Blues" contains three stanzas, each with five lines, which attempt to identify the vague reasons for the poet's general malaise. Even though the poet never discovers what causes his unease in the course of this poem, he is left with a description of the California landscape around him and the quality of that uneasiness.

Although details in the poem place the setting in the coastal town of Laguna Beach, California, where Wright was living at the time he wrote it, the poem is meant to reveal more insight into the poet's emotional state than to describe the setting. The point of view wavers back and forth between actual objects within the landscape and vague references to the poet's emotional state. On a Saturday afternoon, white sheets of paper containing the poet's words lift and fall in the breeze; similarly, "Dust threads, cut loose from the heart," rise in the air and fall. The emotionally weighted objects call attention to an unsettled quality of the poet, as he proclaims, "Something's off-key in my mind." The final line of the stanza, which becomes a repeated refrain throughout the poem, emphasizes this vague distress: "Whatever it is, it bothers me all the time." The uncertainty of this uneasiness itself seems to be distressing.

Starting in the second stanza, the poet's focus gradually shifts from himself and his work before him to the things around him. He comments on the weather ("It's hot"), and he looks to a group of crows riding the ocean breezes. He mentions that he's "dancing a little dance" and "singing a little song," but because these descriptions are not accompanied by any other action, it seems clear that he means for these to be taken figuratively.

In the final stanza, the poet compares the crows to black pages that rise and fall like the white pages of paper before him. Likewise, he looks to two garden plants—castor beans and peppers—that seem to sleep in the afternoon heat. He stresses his subtle angst by repeating the refrain that "something's off-key" and that the ambiguous feeling that bothers him still bothers him "all the time."

Forms and Devices

In an interview in 1983, Wright claimed that he wrote "Laguna Blues" as one of a series of twenty poems with specific technical instructions to himself. For instance, one poem in this series was to contain no verbs in it. Another was to be written in only one sitting. "Laguna Blues," the second of this group, was an attempt to write a blues poem. (In this same interview, Wright jokingly admits that writing the blues is something "which I am incapable of doing, actually.") Therefore, some basic characteristics of the blues can be seen in the poet's techniques.

The primary form used in blues lyrics is repetition. A single phrase or line is stated, and then it is repeated, sometimes with slight variation. The third and final phrase resolves or answers the first idea with an end rhyme. The folk quality of the form allows for very loose adherence to the metrical phrasing of the music. Because of the brevity of the form, blues songs often contain gaps that are filled in through suggestion and implication, and sometimes blues singers develop narratives over the course of several short verses, expecting the listener to interpret the stories' innuendoes.

Wright takes this given form and transforms it into free-verse poetry that vaguely resembles the blues. He uses repetition in several places. For instance, the initial line of the first stanza ("It's Saturday afternoon at the edge of the world") is repeated in the same place in the last stanza, with slight variation ("It's Saturday afternoon and the crows glide down"). The penultimate line of the first stanza ("Something's off-key in my mind") is also repeated in the same place in the final stanza, with slight variation ("Something's off-key and unkind"). The final line of each stanza is the same ("Whatever it is, it bothers me all the time"). A line about dancing and singing a little dance or song is also varied within the second stanza.

Wright said that he was trying to write a blues poem, and the repetition that Wright uses—echoing lines in the first and last stanza rather than the first and second lines— merely suggests a blues form, not strictly imitating it. While this transformation gives the poem more of a literary quality than a simple set of lyrics, the song retains a subtle musical quality. Most notably, nearly every line is a sentence; this aspect creates an imagistic and disjointed narrative characteristic of the blues, rather than one that would be developed coherently, as in a more conventional literary work. The corresponding meter of each line is roughly repeated in subsequent stanzas; this metrical adherence strengthens until not only is the meter in the final lines repeated but also the exact words. The implication is that the poem could be sung in the nearly free verse folk tradition of the blues.

Themes and Meanings

Just as the form of "Laguna Blues" is derived from an imitation of the blues, discussion of its subject matter should begin there as well. Blues traditionally are songs of heartache and sorrow, often providing a catharsis for both singer and listener. Likewise, this poem seems to describe the poet's angst. Something is bothering the poet, but the source of this angst is never clearly stated. In fact, the more of the poem that is revealed, the more vague the poet becomes about whatever it is that bothers him all the time.

With so little direct clarification, that angst seems partly derived from the poem's setting. In the town of Laguna Beach, the poet is at the edge of the country, in a place of relative warmth, where crows can glide on ocean breezes. Yet "the edge of the world" also suggests a point from which he can go no farther. The poet's effort has reached a limit, and anything beyond this point must be guessed at or left unknown.

Because the poet is writing on a Saturday afternoon, he is also at the end, or "edge," of the week and may symbolically have reached the end of his ability to work. The pages ruffled in the breeze are white and perhaps contain little writing. Therefore, the scene he is describing may be an attempt and ultimate inability to capture whatever is "off-key in my mind." Even if he has been able to capture this feeling on the pages that blow "on what I have had to say," the poet's voice feels more comfortable describing his creative activity in both dance and song.

Similarly, his gaze gradually turns away from the pages he is writing on toward the flora and fauna around him. The crows and the breeze are the only things moving, as a stupor has fallen over the castor beans and pepper plants. Even as the poet looks else-where for answers, there is little that surrenders any meaning: The crows, austere scavengers, resemble "black pages that lift and fall," symbolizing any attempt to read or understand them. The plants sleep in the midday heat, suggesting that the poet too is ready to sleep the afternoon away, having accomplished little.

The single line that may give insight into the source of the poet's angst comes early in the poem: "Dust threads, cut loose from the heart, float up and fall." The poem may indeed be describing a heart that has been broken, and the poet finds opportunity in those items around him—such as the motes drifting in the sunlight—to describe what-ever is causing him pain. However, with no specific mention of a lover, the reader can-not be sure that the poem is about specific heartache, as many blues songs are. What remains is the general angst that blues inspire, as they are songs born of an oppressed race. The fragmented heart threads "float up and fall."

The poet's expectations at the beginning of the afternoon began with hope, but as the poem continues, he meets with frustration in the ability to say "whatever it is" that bothers him. All other objects in the poem also run the same path, as they rise and fall: The pages are lifted by the wind, only to fall back to the desk. The crows are borne in the air and later "glide down." The garden's plants, which likely stood tall in the morn-ing's coolness, droop in the sun. As he sits at "the edge of the world" and the end of the week, the poet has met the typical human frustration of high ideals ultimately unful-filled.

All is not lost, however. The purpose of blues is to sing, even if that singing only celebrates the singer's pain. The poet mentions that he is indeed "singing a little song" and "dancing a little dance"; therefore, if he has not achieved the goal of discovery that he intended to reach, he still has his small work of art.

Additionally, as this poem expresses the uncertainty that the poet finds himself in, he has effectively shown that something is still "off-key and unkind." The intangible and unknowable thing that bothers him "all the time" still bothers him, and the poem successfully expresses that uncertainty. Thus, as with real singers of the blues, the poet has found that some sort of heartache may still be there, but he has a song, and in communicating that sorrow to another, he has made something of beauty and truth.

Brian C. Ferguson-Avery

THE LAKE ISLE OF INNISFREE

Author: William Butler Yeats (1865-1939)
Type of poem: Lyric
First published: 1890; collected in *The Countess Kathleen and Various Legends and Lyrics*, 1892

The Poem
"The Lake Isle of Innisfree," a twelve-line poem divided into three quatrains, is a study in contrasts. The most obvious contrast is between two places: one rural (identified in the title and described throughout much of the poem), the other (alluded to only in the second-to-last line)—by implication—urban.

Innisfree is a small island at the eastern end of Lough Gill in County Sligo, Ireland. William Butler Yeats spent part of nearly every year in Sligo while growing up; he often walked out from Sligo town to Lough Gill. His father having read to him from Henry David Thoreau's *Walden* (1854), he daydreamed (as he says in *The Trembling of the Veil*, 1922, incorporated into his *Autobiography*, 1965) of living "a life of lonely austerity . . . in imitation of Thoreau on Innisfree." In 1890, while living in London, he was "walking through Fleet Street very homesick [when] I heard a little tinkle of water and saw a fountain in a shop-window . . . and began to remember lake water. From the sudden remembrance came my poem *Innisfree.*"

Yeats imagines escaping from the city to the solitude and peace of a pastoral retreat, there to live a simple life, close to nature. The first stanza states his intention and provides a prospectus for the home he will make for himself, specifying the rustic construction for his cabin and exactly how many rows of beans he will plant. The second stanza, more fancifully imagining what living there will be like, pauses over images that he associates with four different times of day: morning, midnight, noon, and evening. The third stanza reiterates his intention and for the first time suggests what motivates it: the (implied) urban setting and Yeats's nostalgia for Sligo.

The contrast between the matter-of-fact first and last stanzas and the fanciful middle stanza reinforces the contrast between the quotidian city, with its "grey" pavements, and the idealized country. The opening stanza employs no figurative language; the only figurative language in the closing stanza is the sound of waves "lapping" in "the deep heart's core." Otherwise, the language in these stanzas is straightforward and literal, emotionally neutral.

The second stanza, on the other hand, is brimming with metaphors and other figures: "peace comes dropping slow," as if it were dew; the morning wears "veils"; the cricket "sings"; the "evening [is] full of the linnet's wings." Language, imagination, and emotion all rise to a rapturous brief climax in this middle stanza before subsiding. The opening words of stanza 3, echoing the opening words of the poem, cue a return to the everyday world.

Forms and Devices

The poem's rhyme scheme is regular; all of its rhymes are exact. In each stanza, the first three lines are in hexameter, the last line in tetrameter. In these respects, the poem is perfectly regular. Its meter is iambic, though only the last line of the poem precisely conforms to the iambic pattern. In each of the other eleven lines, Yeats introduces an extra unstressed syllable just after the midpoint, and the extra syllable is in each case a one-syllable word: "now" in line 1; "there" in lines 2, 3, and 5; and so forth. Virtually all of these words could be deleted without altering the meaning of the poem. Their purpose, clearly, is to contribute not to the poem's meaning but to its sound and its tempo.

Yeats called "The Lake Isle of Innisfree" "my first lyric with anything in its rhythm of my own music. I had begun to loosen rhythm as an escape from rhetoric." The added syllables in lines 1 through 11 contribute to this loosening of rhythm (line 3 adds still another syllable; line 6 adds two more syllables); so, too, does Yeats's occasional relaxation of and variation from the basic iambic pattern. The loosening of rhythm prevented the poem's meter from being too mechanical. Absolutely regular cadence produces a monotonous, singsong effect (an aspect of what Yeats called "rhetoric"); and Yeats's "own music" was not timed by a metronome.

If "The Lake Isle of Innisfree" has something of Yeats's "own music" in it, it is not—he later realized—fully in his own voice. When he wrote the poem, he was young, and, as he recalled, "I only understood vaguely and occasionally that I must for my special purpose use nothing but the common syntax. A couple of years later I would not have written that first line with its conventional archaism—'Arise and go'—nor the inversion of the last stanza."

"Arise and go" (in line 9 as well as line 1) echoes the parable of the homesick Prodigal Son: "I will arise and go to my father" (Luke 15:18). Alexander Norman Jeffares points out that line 9 also echoes Mark 5:5: "And always, night and day, he was in the mountains" (*A Commentary on the Collected Poems of W. B. Yeats*, 1968). Such scriptural sonorities, added to the Thoreauvian quality of the first stanza's humble images and the self-consciously "poetic" diction of the second stanza ("the veils of the morning" for fog and dew; "all a glimmer"), render the poem more literary, more "conventional" than a more mature Yeats would prefer.

Themes and Meanings

"The Lake Isle of Innisfree" expresses a set of desires familiar in the modern world: to escape, to achieve peace and solitude, to be at one with nature. Yeats says almost nothing in the poem about what he would like to escape from, but his reader can easily imagine the stressful conditions of modern, especially urban, life. Such desires have been common themes in Romantic literature since the beginning of the nineteenth century, and "Innisfree" is a good example of late nineteenth century Romanticism.

Many of Yeats's early (pre-1900) poems express the feeling that, in William Wordsworth's phrase, "the world is too much with us." Poem after early poem articulates a longing for peace, for escape. The refrain in "The Stolen Child" (1886) is a seductive call to "Come away" from the world (seen as "full of weeping") "To the waters and the wild." "To an Isle in the Water" (1889) differs from "Innisfree" by expressing a wish to go away not alone but accompanied by the "Shy one of my heart." Otherwise, the poem seems to be a study, a preliminary sketch for "The Lake Isle of Innisfree."

While "The Lake Isle of Innisfree" is an early poem, it is in some respects transitional, pointing toward Yeats's mature work. As its loosened rhythms contain something of his "own music," so its images and vocabulary reveal something of his own emerging language. Again, a contrast may be drawn between the middle stanza and those that enclose it.

The middle stanza is vague, not fully in focus. What, after all, do "midnight's all a glimmer" or "noon a purple glow" mean, exactly? One might guess that the glimmering is moonlight reflected on the lake, but it would be only a guess; and who can even hazard a guess about what glows purple at noontime? One cannot be sure whether "evening full of the linnet's wings" is meant to appeal to the mind's eye or ear. Yeats would eschew such imprecise images in his mature poetry. Similarly, "glimmer" is representative of Yeats's late Victorian diction, rife with such murmurous words which, after the turn of the century, all but disappeared from his working vocabulary.

Yeats never went to Innisfree, built a cabin, or laid out bean-rows. Instead of finding a refuge on an uninhabited island, he helped found and manage the Irish National Theatre; became the central, essential figure in the Irish Literary Revival; became a prolific playwright; became, indeed, a very "public man," an Irish senator and Nobel laureate. Although "The Lake Isle of Innisfree," with its escapist wish, offers no hint of these future developments, in form and technique it contains the seeds of his future poetry. He was to transform himself from a late Victorian dreamy Romantic into the dominant poet of the twentieth century, and the transitional "Innisfree" offers a preview of that transformation.

Richard Bizot

L' ALLEGRO

Author: John Milton (1608-1674)
Type of poem: Pastoral
First published: 1645, in *Poems of Mr. John Milton*

The Poem

This 152-line poem is non-stanzaic and is written in tetrameter couplets except for the first ten lines, which are alternating trimeters and pentameters. It is a companion piece to the slightly longer "Il Penseroso," with which a detailed comparison must necessarily be made.

"L'Allegro" means "the cheerful man," and the poem describes, in pastoral terms and in his own voice, the idyllic day of such a man in the countryside. It begins with the sun rising and takes the man through the pleasures of the day until the countryfolk's bedtime. After that, the man goes to the city and enjoys his evening in more sophisticated literary company.

The poem actually begins, however, with an invocation against "loathed Melancholy," personified as a horrific creature and seen as a state bordering on madness. In place of this monster, the cheerful poet welcomes Euphrosyne, or Mirth, who, mythologically, was the daughter of Venus and Bacchus, or perhaps of Zephyrus (the west wind) and Aurora (the dawn). As neither loving nor drinking figures significantly in the poem, it must be inferred that John Milton prefers the latter, less well-known genealogy. He invites Mirth, together with "the Mountain Nymph, sweet Liberty," to take him as one of her followers, to live "in unreproved pleasures free."

The remainder of the poem is more a pastoral fantasy of what such a day spent in Mirth's company would be like than an actual description of a particular day, as one might expect to find in a Romantic pastoral such as John Keats's *Sleep and Poetry* (1817) or *I Stood Tiptoe* (1817). As in classical pastoral, the countryside is idealized, and any unpleasantness, such as bad weather or painful labor, is removed. In fact, the poet becomes a spectator rather than a participant (such as a shepherd) in the pastoral activity. He imagines the lark rising at dawn, the hunt, and the cock crowing. As the sun rises, he observes typical country work, people, and animals, especially (as befits a pastoral) sheep and shepherds.

The landscape is an impossible one, in that meadows, castles, mountains, wide rivers, and woods all jostle one another for place. Similarly, the day dissolves from a working day to a rustic holiday, focusing on the merrymaking at suppertime. The folk tell one another legends and country tales as the ale circulates. With sunset, they go to bed.

Not so the cheerful man, who imagines himself now in "towred Cities" of a distinctly medieval flavor, with "throngs of Knights and Barons bold." A tournament is being held, then a wedding feast. Then the man goes to the theater to see the comedies of Ben Jonson or the young William Shakespeare. Finally, in his bliss, the poet calls for soft music and poetry that would rouse even the god Orpheus. If Mirth can give him all this, the poet vows to live always with her.

Forms and Devices

The verse form of "L'Allegro" is delightfully lyrical. The rhythm is light and joyful, and it is the single most important factor in creating the idyllic tone of the poem. Although the meter is tetrameter, the length of line is frequently seven syllables rather than eight. Regularly placed stressed syllables dominate; in the shortened lines, along with the rhyming effect of the couplet, they provide a strong musical beat. The stressed syllables have relatively few of the longer, "dark" vowel sounds. Consonants are also soft, as in "Lap me in soft Lydian Aires/ Married to immortal verse." The *l*, *m*, and *s* sounds echo exactly the sense. The sound and the rhythm are mellifluous and flow easily in long, relaxed sentences that have none of the grammatical complexity of John Milton's later style. The vocabulary, too, is simple, avoiding pedantic or latinate words.

The only verse that suggests any harshness is the opening section. This section also demonstrates that the poet is a man of learning; even if he does not care to show it in his diction, it shows in his easy use of classical myth. The verse form here is somewhat irregular. It alternates between trimeter and pentameter, with a complicated rhyming scheme (*abbacddeec*); it is basically iambic but is sometimes broken up, as in "And the night-Raven sings." This contrast, rhythmic as well as tonal, with the rest of the poem is striking and provides a dramatic opening.

Milton's use of mythological names is accomplished, and it goes well beyond the usual pastoral naming of shepherds with Latin or Greek names. Euphrosyne's genealogies are given, and clearly Milton understands the meaning of the Greek as "she who rejoices the heart." The most significant classical allusion, though, is to Orpheus, since this forms an extended concluding image and is picked up in "Il Penseroso." In "L'Allegro," the tragedy of the myth is played down, and the beauty and enchantment of music are stressed. Orpheus lies "on a bed/ Of heapt Elysian flowers" and, with such music as the poet delights in, would have "quite set free/ His half regain'd Eurydice." The Orphic myth can still contain celebration. The poet's delight in literature also suggests his learning, and the heady mixture of pastoral and literature suggests the work of Keats a century and a half later.

The landscape descriptions, diction, and images need to be read in contrast with "Il Penseroso." Here in "L'Allegro," the diction conveys light and radiance. The lark is mentioned, rather than the nightingale of the other poem. Although both birds are symbolic of the poetic imagination, one is a bird of day, the other a bird of night. In "L'Allegro," fields fill the landscape (rather than woods); there are people instead of solitude, so the poet walks "not unseen." (In "Il Penseroso," he says, "I walk unseen.") The literature mentioned in the poems also contrasts; here, there is comedy and medieval romance, whereas there one finds epic and tragedy. The music in "L'Allegro" is country songs; in "Il Penseroso," solemn organ tones.

Themes and Meanings

A number of interpretations have been suggested for the poem—or rather, for the pair of poems. One suggestion is that the young Milton, possibly still at the University of Cambridge, or possibly recently having been graduated, was using the form of a typical student dialectic exercise to conduct an argument, such as deciding "whether day or night is the more excellent" or comparing the merits of learning and ignorance. It could also be seen as marking the poet's return from Cambridge to his father's retirement home in the Buckinghamshire countryside, expressing both his joy at country life (together with its accessibility to London) and his thoughts on his still undecided future. The poem's pastoral landscape is rustic and English; it cannot be taken for a classical setting. If Milton's thoughts, as is most likely, were turning toward the vocation of literature, then the pastoral form would be the most appropriate genre for him to begin exploring, as the pastoral was seen classically as the one for "apprentice" poets. Certainly, Milton persisted in and mastered the genre in his youth.

The poems may also be seen, as could Keats's *Sleep and Poetry*, as the youthful explorations of the aspiring poet, encapsulating the intellectual excitement in imaginative fantasies and daydreams. If this is taken as the basis for an interpretation, it is possible to go further and see the two poems as Milton's setting out a poetic program for himself. The poem becomes, thus, not so much about day and night, comedy and tragedy, as about the inspiration to be found by the young poet in idyllic nature, and the pastoral imagination founded on this and on Romance literature—inspiration that needs feeding. This is one possibility for him as a youthful, idealistic poet. The other possibility is explored in "Il Penseroso," which is perhaps the one he ultimately seems to prefer. Certainly, "L'Allegro" lacks the impressive coda to be found at the end of "Il Penseroso." The closure of the former is light-hearted, almost whimsical, and hypothetical.

Another possibility is to read the pair of poems as explorations of possible lifestyles. The life-style of "L'Allegro" puts away melancholy as a disease, an infection to be avoided at all costs. Joy is to be found in a simple and active life, close to beauty and the rhythms of everyday life, yet keeping in touch with literature and the arts. Many a young graduate must have experienced the appeal of such a life. By contrast, "Il Penseroso" embraces studiousness and "high seriousness." Milton's life followed the latter path, but it can never be known whether he made that choice at the time he was writing these poems. The poems' thematic structures are open enough to allow various interpretations, and that openness is a part of their continued attraction.

David Barratt

THE LAMENT BY THE RIVER

Author: Du Fu (712-770)
Type of poem: Ballad
First published: Written in 757; published as "Aijiang-tou," in *Jiu-jia ji-zhu Du shi,*
1181; English translation collected in *The Little Primer of Tu Fu,* 1967

The Poem

"Lament by the River" is one of the most well-known poems by Du Fu (Tu Fu). The title suggests a tragic sense aroused by scenes along the river; its function is to establish the setting and mood of the poem. The word "lament" leads naturally to the "stifled sobs" in the beginning line. The poem is written in the first person. Although "I" is never mentioned and the first person speaks through the persona of "an old rustic from Shaoling," no distinction lies between the poet and the speaker of the poem. Like most Chinese classical poets, Du Fu attempts to capture the intense feelings of his personal experience.

The poem was written in the spring of 757, after the imperial court was usurped by the rebel An Lushan. Many loyalists believed that the fall of the emperor was caused by his concubine Yang Guifei and her relatives, who gained power and wealth through nepotism. When Emperor Xuanzong escaped from the capital he was forced to have Yang Guifei put to death because of the impending mutiny of his troops. By January, 757, An Lushan had been killed in a palace coup in Loyang and his son had become the rebel emperor. Du Fu was absent from Chang'an at the time of its fall. He was probably taken by the rebels as a porter to the capital. It is possible that, while escaping from Chang'an, he paid his last tribute to the Serpentine River and was agonized by its plight.

The poem can be divided into four stanzas. The first stanza, with four lines, serves as the introduction. It portrays how on a spring day Du Fu, an old country person from Shaoling, southeast of Chang'an, walks stealthily along the Serpentine River—the river is actually a constructed waterway in the main park of Chang'an. He cannot help sobbing at the sight of the abandoned palaces along the waterside. Since the palaces are deserted, "For whom are the slim willows and new rushes green?" the poet questions rhetorically. The liveliness of nature plunges the poet into his reveries of the jostling scenes that could often be seen before the emperor was banished from the capital. The second stanza, lines 5-12, vividly captures how, at that time, the park was brightened by the royal gaiety. The maids of honor, armed with bows and arrows, lead the way for the carriage of the emperor and Yang Guifei sitting side by side. Their white horses are champing at the gold bridles. Leaning back, face skyward, one maid shoots into the clouds; two birds fall to the ground transfixed by one arrow. The third stanza, lines 12-16, shifts back to the poet's sorrowful feelings with the question, "Bright eyes and white teeth, where are they now?" Du Fu visualizes Yang Guifei's wandering soul, tainted with blood, unable to make her way back. What grieves the poet even more is the realization that there will be no way for Xuanzong, who remains alive, to communicate with his beloved Guifei, who has gone like the east-flowing water of River Wei.

It is typical of Du Fu to return to the present world in the final stanza. Lines 17-20 observe that any human with feelings, like himself, will shed tears over the tragic fate of Xuanzong and Yang Guifei, but the flowing waters and the blooming flowers along the bank remain unmoved. The last two lines correspond to the first two lines of the ballad: At dusk, the Tartar cavalry fills the city with dust. As the poet starts to move toward the south, he gazes longingly to the north. There are various interpretations regarding the "south" and "north" of this final verse. The poet is possibly heading toward Fengxiang, where the traveling court of the new emperor Suzong, son of Xuanzong, was located. His gaze to the north conveys a loyalist's mixed feelings of nostalgia and expectancy. He longs for the emperor to return to the capital.

Forms and Devices

The form of the poem falls into the category "Xinyuefu" (new court songs) in classical Chinese poetry. It resembles the style of the Western ballad, such as Samuel Taylor Coleridge's *Rime of the Ancient Mariner*; Arthur Cooper has observed similarities between these two works' poetic imagery. The poem, with twenty seven-syllabic lines, has a clear rhyme scheme in the original Chinese: Lines 1-4 rhyme with the sound *u*, while lines 5-20 maintain a basic rhyme pattern. A change of rhyme sets off the first four lines as an introduction. Iterations such as "qu . . . qu" (line 2), "jiang . . . jiang" (line 18), and "cheng . . . cheng" (line 20) add to the musical quality of the poem in Chinese.

Du Fu employs two major poetic devices: contrast and indirectness. The poem is replete with binary images. The lush green of willows and rushes is in sharp contrast with the gloom of the locked palaces. Nature's constant revival in a sense ridicules the ghost of Yang Guifei, who can never return. Thus the lover who is gone can no longer communicate with the lover who remains. Their distance is like the Wei River, which carried away Yang Guifei's body, flowing eastward, while the Sword Pass, where Xuanzong remains, stands remote to the west. The final contrast between sentimental humans and indifferent nature brings the ballad to a denouement, deepening the helplessness of human sorrows.

Poetry can be quite effective in revealing truth indirectly, and Chinese poets especially cherish indirectness in poetic expression. Although Du Fu laments the death of Yang Guifei, no explicit references to her can be found in the poem. Instead, Du Fu writes about "the first lady of the Chaoyang Palace." This lady is historically known as Zhao Feiyan, the consort of Emperor Chengdi, who reigned from 32 to 5 B.C.E.; Chaoyang was the name of the imperial palace during Zhou times. Although Zhao was slim and light like a flying swallow, while Yang was quite plump, their feminine charms for the ruler of the country were the same.

Du Fu's deliberate transplantation of the first lady of the Zhou Dynasty into the capital of the Tang Dynasty adds to the reader's poetic pleasure. Similarly, "rainbow banners" allude to Yang Guifei's extravagant sisters, who display their power and richness by riding horses with gold bridles. "River Wei" refers to Yang Guifei because her body was carried away by its waters, while the Sword Pass refers to Xuanzong because he traveled there after Yang's death. The line "the blood-soiled, wandering ghost cannot return" presents an interpretive enigma, as Yang Guifei was strangled to death on the Buddhist oratory in the Mawei Post Station, about thirty-eight miles west of the capital. Such indirectness may sorely challenge today's readers' historical knowledge. However, one may discard all allusions to history and enjoy the musical sound and beautiful imagery of the poem itself.

Themes and Meanings

Like any sophisticated poem, Du Fu's ballad allows for multiple interpretations. In spite of its autobiographical nature, it transcends personal experience and historical specifics. The universal theme of the vicissitude of human life and dynasties is enriched by Du Fu's lamentation for Yang Guifei's tragic death and the pitiful fall of Chang'an. Du Fu was the first in Chinese literature to address the theme of the love of Yang Guifei and Xuanzong, which continues to attract poets, storytellers, and dramatists today. The poet begins with sobbing for the fallen capital but ends with "weeping upon his breast" for the lover who remains as well as the lover who is gone. Death can carry away the body and even soul but cannot kill love. The pain from love is infinite.

Du Fu believed in the political function of poetry. Most of his poems contain subtle criticism of social problems. This poem shows that Du Fu sympathized with the loyalists. He attributed the fall of Chang'an to the corruption of Yang Guifei's sisters and brothers. Their abuse of power and squandering of wealth are indicated by the "rainbow banners" following the emperor and the "gold bridles" for their horses. Their reckless gaiety foreshadows the death of Yang Guifei and the emperor: Two birds drop downward at their laughter. Du Fu seems to regard Yang Guifei as innocent, like the "clear water" of the River Wei. However, because it was through Guifei's tie with the emperor that her relatives gained and abused power, her soul is soiled symbolically by the blood of victims.

Du Fu was influenced by the Taoist concept of nature; he perceived nature as indifferent and merciless. Yet humans pale by comparison with nature's powerful, reviving force and permanent beauty because their glories are transitory and they give in to emotions too easily.

Qingyun Wu

LAMENT FOR IGNACIO SÁNCHEZ MEJÍAS

Author: Federico García Lorca (1898-1936)
Type of poem: Elegy
First published: 1935, as *Llanto por Ignacio Sánchez Mejías*; English translation collected in *Lament for the Death of a Bullfighter*, 1937

The Poem

 Lament for Ignacio Sánchez Mejías is a long elegy divided into four parts corresponding to four dramatic movements. It was written to commemorate and celebrate the death of a man who many considered the bravest and most gallant matador of Spain. Ignacio Sánchez Mejías was also Federico García Lorca's great friend. In this poem, there is complete identification between poet and speaker.

 The first part of the poem, "The Goring and the Death," starts at the very hour of the tragedy—"at five in the afternoon"—and proceeds to dwell on all the horrific details of the bull ring. A child brings a white sheet; lime is spread to soak up the blood; we can see and smell the chemicals of death, the chloride and the iodine. Surprisingly, what is missing is the fallen hero himself. It is as if the speaker cannot bring himself to look at his friend, lying bleeding in the sand, and instead must concentrate on what surrounds his body. The cadence is like that of a muted, tolling bell as after every stark image, the litany-like response "at five in the afternoon" is repeated.

 The scene then shifts to Ignacio's deathbed, where the killer bull, "El Granadino," has become a bellowing nightmare that roars in triumph in the bullfighter's ears in his delirium. The clinical facts of a terrible death by gangrene poisoning are expressed poetically, but the agony cannot be hidden by beautiful words. Sensing that, again, after every image, the speaker drums into the listener the hour of the incident, until, finally, the poetic voice rises in protest at the significance of these "terrible fives."

 The same fever pitch continues into the second section, "The Spilt Blood." The speaker shouts that he does not want to see Ignacio's blood in the sand and that no one can force him to gaze on it. (In this context, it is interesting to note that García Lorca did not witness the accident and later could not bring himself to visit his dying friend, even though their mutual acquaintances pleaded with him to go.) In the poem, the speaker wants night to come and, with it, the whiteness of the moon to hide the evidence of the truth from him. He tries to calm himself by invoking images of the living bullfighter who had always "walked with death on his shoulders," and he lauds his friend's courage, grace, wit, and intelligence.

 Nevertheless, that is still not the real Ignacio, the man of flesh and blood who dies. The speaker is still trying to mask reality. In a further distancing technique—a further separation from the real, raw tragedy—Ignacio is now made the subject of medieval balladry. This entire section is written in the traditional Spanish ballad line, the romance. In addition, in another medieval echo, the poet imitates the famous cadences of another great Spanish elegy, Jorge Manrique's *Coplas por la muerte de su padre*

(1492, Verses on the Death of his Father). García Lorca, however, does not have the philosophical or religious consolation of the medieval poet. Therefore, in the concluding lines of this section, the intensity of voice rises again as the speaker insists that nothing, no symbol or image, "nor song nor flood of white lilies," can contain or justify that spilled blood.

In the third section, "The Body is Present," the verse line is lengthened as the speaker meditates on the finality and mystery of death. The stone on which the bullfighter lies is the symbol of the implacable laws of the universe, immutable for all living things: "Stone is a shoulder to carry time, with trees of tears and ribbons and planets." There is no life nor movement here, only the silence of this stone. The speaker, in protest, asks the strongest, those "men of hard voice," to stand in front of this stone, in front of this corpse and help him to discover another life for his friend and, by extension, for all humankind, but there is no hope. He then asks them to teach him a funereal song that may express adequately this horrible truth. Contrasted with the resignation of the final lines of this section, however, there still remains the lingering defiance of a friend who does not want Ignacio to accustom himself "to the death that he carries."

In the last section, "The Soul is Absent," the speaker talks quietly to the dead man. The "you" of his address is juxtaposed to the final "I" of the closing verses as the speaker insists that he is the only one who can, or wants to, remember the bullfighter. All other things and people of this world must forget, but the memory of Ignacio lives on because this poet can sing of his life and death.

Forms and Devices

The poetry of García Lorca is difficult to translate because of the complex associations of his verses, which are an amalgam of surrealistic images, personal trademark symbols, and traditional Spanish poetic and thematic echoes. His genius lies in the ability to fuse these disparate elements into one fluid, musical whole. *Lament for Ignacio Sánchez Mejías* is a master example of this poetical transmutation.

García Lorca was also a great playwright, and this poem can be described as a verse drama in four acts. Images and allusions are utilized as props or metaphoric icons which link the action and lead the listener/spectator to the artistic denouement. Two of these devices are color and the recurring image of the animal protagonist of the *corrida*, the bull.

Lament for Ignacio Sánchez Mejías starts *in medias res*. The reader is not actually present at the fatal goring; only its consequences are seen as if in a blurred black-and-white film. All color is stripped away as, one by one, dreamlike white objects appear and then fade away into others. The white of a sheet covering the body dissolves into that of lime, cotton wool becomes "arsenic bells," and the "sweat of snow," white eggs. These surrealistic images contrast sharply with the jarring simplicity of the refrain, just as white objects stand in contrast to the steady flowing of the red blood which the speaker cannot yet look upon or even bear to mention. Yet both he and the listener/spectator know it is there. In this first section, the animal that physically causes Ignacio's death announces the coming of this death. Agent becomes symbol.

In the second section, so resonant with traditional Spanish echoes, the roaring bull becomes plural and is transformed into the ancient stone bulls of Guisando, archetypal symbols of Spanish endurance and pride, and mute evidence of man's impermanence on earth. These figures, "almost death and almost stone," in their turn are metamorphosed into "the bulls of heaven." Celestial forces, they represent the fatality which seemed to surround Sánchez Mejías; they are the "black bulls of sorrow."

This black overcomes the white images of consolation which try to palliate the reality of death, but "no white frost of the light," that is, reason, can hide the blood which now "comes singing," forcing itself into the poet's sight. The speaker had asked the moon to hide with its white light the blood of his friend. The moon, as a symbol of death, is one of the definitive images of García Lorca's poetry. Here, its coldness cannot quench the fever of memory.

The dominant color of the third section is gray; the reds and whites mist away into "pale sulfurs" and "rain showers." Even noise and movement seem to harden into the cold gray stone on which Ignacio lies and which gives "no sound, nor crystal, nor fire." The speaker hopes without hope that his friend's spirit can break free of the physical death which fetters him. The bulls become part of the earthly impedimenta which weigh down on him, preventing his escape. (The living Sánchez Mejías could not resist this siren song; he had to return to the ring one more time.) "The Soul is Absent" has no colors, no bulls, no stone, nor indeed anything for Ignacio. These symbols are only for the living.

Themes and Meanings

The physical setting of *Lament for Ignacio Sánchez Mejías* is quintessentially Spanish: An Andalusian bullfighter, singled out by fate, dies defiantly in the ring. Its philosophical setting is a meditation on life and death. Two men, in the poem, must face this ordeal. Ignacio dies, but it is his friend who must deal with the implications of this tragedy. This personal poem symbolizes the universal dilemma of all human existence, what Miguel de Unamuno y Jugo called "the tragic sense of life." Human beings desire the eternal but are confronted with the seeming finality of death, which must come at a specific time and place. This sense of an implacable fatality is overwhelming in the first part as the reader is continuously reminded that Ignacio's death struggle must begin at a specific, inevitable moment (García Lorca was convinced that Sánchez Mejías had to die: "Ignacio . . . did everything he could to escape from his death, but everything he did only helped to tighten the strings of the net").

Much has been made of the ancient Spanish "culture of death," the idealization of those who deliberately place themselves in the greatest danger; much has been made also of García Lorca's identification with, and admiration of, this concept, in which (paradoxically) the continual defiance of death can be seen as an affirmation of life. It is appropriate to remember that García Lorca, criticizing those who wanted to abolish bullfighting, said: "I think it is the most cultured festival that exists anywhere in the world. It is the only place where one can go in safety to contemplate Death surrounded by the most dazzling beauty."

Sánchez Mejías, against the advice of all his friends, had come out of retirement because he missed the danger and excitement and was killed while performing a foolhardy maneuver in the ring. In the poem, García Lorca eulogizes Ignacio's "appetite for death and the taste of its mouth" and recalls the "sadness that was in your valiant gaiety." This sadness reflects the belief that man's existence is terminal; therefore, Ignacio's courage is all the more to be praised.

In *Coplas por la muerte de su padre*, Jorge Manrique compares the lives of men to rivers that flow into the sea, but this sea is not eternal oblivion. It signifies the passage from mortality to eternity. Fortified by his fate, Manrique's father accepts death with a Christian resignation. In García Lorca's poem, however, the poet keeps repeating, "Now it is all over," and in a direct rejection of the optimistic message of the earlier work, he cries out, "Go, Ignacio . . . Sleep, fly away, rest. Even the sea dies."

Nevertheless, in one important sentiment, the final message of both poems, so far apart in time and philosophy, seems to coincide. Manrique, although he stresses that all mortal things are transitory and worthless, still clings to the hope that his father will be remembered; valiant deeds and a good life can endure, and his son's elegy will reinforce that memory. García Lorca, too, sings so that his brave friend will live on in his words, but there is one significant difference: García Lorca believed that poets were mediums, bridges between different worlds; consequently, only through a poet could the dead make themselves known authentically to the living. Together, poet and friend can overcome the oblivion of death.

This interlocking of destinies has provided a poignant, historical background to the reading and interpretation of this poem. García Lorca identified strongly with the death of his friend; "Ignacio's death is like mine, the trial run for me," he stated. It frightened him that the animal that killed the bullfighter was called "El Granadino" (the one from Granada), an epithet that was applied to García Lorca himself. *Lament for Ignacio Sánchez Mejías* has been interpreted as a premonition of its author's own death; García Lorca was murdered in 1936 by Nationalists in the Spanish Civil War. García Lorca's life and death have been inextricably woven into the metaphoric richness of this work.

Charlene E. Suscavage

LAMENT FOR THE MAKARIS

Author: William Dunbar (c. 1460-c.1525)
Type of poem: Ballad
First published: 1508, as "I that in heill wes and gladnes," in *The Chepman and Myllar Prints*; collected in *The Poems of William Dunbar,* 1932

The Poem

"Lament for the Makaris" is a poem in twenty-five stanzas, each of four lines with a rhyme scheme of *aabb* and a recurring refrain. Although written in a ballad form, William Dunbar's poem is actually a meditation on serious moral and religious issues, including what for his time would have been the most important of all, the afterlife. The poem is about mutability and transition, including the transition from life to death, and what the human response to those changes should be. Death is a central concern because, as Dunbar notes in his repeated refrain, *"Timor mortis conturbat me"*: "The fear of death confounds me."

In order to emphasize the shifting, uncertain nature of the world, Dunbar points out that the powerful and educated are subject to death. Neither position, wealth, nor learning will protect a person from the inevitable end. Dunbar then narrows his focus from the broader society to a very specialized group with whom he was familiar, the "makaris" (poets of Scotland and England) who have died. There is a further twist, for the poem's subtitle is "Quhen He Wes Sek" (when he was sick), and it has been speculated that Dunbar may have himself been very ill at the time the poem was composed. At such a time, meditation on life and, especially, death would be expected. This would be particularly true for Dunbar, who was a priest, most likely in the Franciscan order.

"Lament for the Makaris" is written in the dialect known as "Middle Scots," which was the traditional literary language of Scotland during the period from the latter half of the fifteenth century through the early part of the seventeenth century. Middle Scots and English derived from essentially the same sources; their syntactic patterns are almost identical. The major differences are in vocabulary, pronunciation, and spelling, and these differences are clearly evident in "Lament for the Makaris."

Dunbar has been regarded by many scholars and critics as the finest lyric poet in the British Isles in the period between Geoffrey Chaucer and Sir Thomas Wyatt, and this work clearly displays his ability to produce a consistent, powerful, and moving poem that combines genuine sensitivity and insight with a high level of poetic technique and skill. The individual lines are relatively short, each having four main stresses, but Dunbar avoids the sense of choppiness or abruptness that readers sometimes find in a similar, nearly contemporary poet, the Englishman John Skelton.

As Dunbar constructs his poem, the central theme of mutability and death is introduced; then the topic is further considered by a roll call of famous Scots and English writers who have died; finally, Dunbar closes the poem by acknowledging that he, too, will die and noting that such is the common fate of all human beings. For that reason, he concludes, people must do their best to live proper lives.

Forms and Devices

Dunbar is an extremely skilled and competent poet, and "Lament for the Makaris" is a carefully constructed work. There are twenty-five stanzas, each of four lines of rhyming couplets with a running refrain, "*Timor mortis conturbat me.*" This pattern, which developed in earlier French court poetry and was transported to England and Scotland, is known technically as "kyrielle" verse.

The refrain is from the religious ceremony known as the Offices for the Dead, and its repetition at the end of each stanza drives home one of the poem's central points: In the midst of life one is surrounded by death and should live accordingly. For a moralizing, religious poet such as Dunbar, this point entailed opposing a *carpe diem* (seize the day) philosophy; instead of living for the moment, people should constantly and consistently behave well in order to deserve a life after death.

By using this running refrain and by restricting his verses to quatrains, Dunbar has imposed a limit on himself: He has, essentially, only three relatively short lines (four strong beats per line is his pattern) in which to present his meaning in each stanza. Further, since each stanza ends with the refrain, his rhyme scheme is limited, since line 3 must always match the "*conturbat me*" of the final line. The overall impact of the repetition and inevitable rhymes is to emphasize the repetitive and inevitable natures of change and death themselves, which constantly recur in human life.

Dunbar's syntax is simple and direct. He uses a number of parallel constructions, especially in the earlier, establishing portion of the poem. Stanza 8, for example, compares the "campion in the stour," the "capitane closit in the tour," and the "lady in bour." These three people are similar in having privileged positions in late medieval society; they are also all similar in being subject to inevitable death.

This parallelism is found elsewhere in the poem, again emphasizing the transitory nature of existence. Human beings, Dunbar notes in stanza 3, are "Now sound, now seik, now blith, now sary [sorry]/ Now dansand mery, now like to dee [die]." The language of the poem suggests that these changes occur with such speed that they may in fact seem simultaneous states: A person is happy and alive one moment, sick or even dead the next.

The metrical pattern of the poem reinforces this sense of inevitable change. Like the syntax, it is simple, even basic. The essential, almost unvarying, rhythmic pattern gives four strong stresses to each line—one of the oldest and most consistent metrical forms in English and Scots literature. Its presence here serves a dual purpose: to underscore the sense of inevitability and to link this specific poem with other verse from the past. This latter point becomes important during the long central section of the poem, in which Dunbar commemorates and laments the other "makaris" or poets who have died.

The rhyme pattern also helps give the poem a sense of inevitable pattern. The regularity of the *aabb* scheme encourages the reader to expect the same message to be repeated from stanza to stanza, and the recurring refrain further emphasizes this sense of continuity and human mortality.

Themes and Meanings

The themes of "Lament for the Makaris" may be found in the very pattern of the poem itself. Dunbar constructed his poem in order to examine, in logical progression, the various forms of mutability in this temporal existence, especially as they affect his fellow poets.

Stanzas 1 through 12 are concerned with mutability in general. In particular, stanzas 1 through 4 function as a sort of introduction, first telling readers that the poet, once healthy and happy, is "trublit now with gret seiknes." This leads him to consider in stanza 5 how changeable the human condition is, especially in its final change, from life to death: "On to the ded gois all Estatis."

In stanzas 6 through 11 Dunbar works out in some detail how all stations and conditions of human life are subject to this iron law. The poem specifically details how knights, clerks (that is, scholars), physicians, noble women, magicians, astrologers, rhetoricians, logicians, and even theologians are not spared from death. No matter how great their position or extensive their knowledge, they all must share the common human fate.

So must poets, as Dunbar acknowledges in stanza 12: "I se that makaris," he admits, are among those who "gois to graif." For the remainder of the poem, except for a concluding stanza, he focuses on a list of twenty-four Scots and English poets who have died. He begins with three of the most prominent, whose work had an influence on his own poetry: Geoffrey Chaucer, John Lydgate, and John Gower. Although their verse is immortal, they have been devoured by death.

So have others, and the poem catalogs them, a list of the more notable "makaris" of the British Isles of the period. Although the emphasis is on Scots writers, Dunbar's cosmopolitan outlook is shown by the inclusion of a number of English writers as well. Finally, Dunbar concludes the list by bringing it up to his own time, noting that his contemporary poet, Walter Kennedy "In poynt of dede lyis veraly."

With this, the poem uses its final two stanzas to bring the work back to its underlying theme: that the transition from life to death is not to be escaped by any human being, including William Dunbar: "Sen he hes all my brether tane,/ He will nocht lat me lif alane" (Since he has all my brethren taken,/ He will not let me live alone). The only recourse is to prepare for death—to deserve salvation in the next world, since there is no permanence in this one.

Michael Witkoski

LAMENTATIONS

Author: Louise Glück (1943-   )
Type of poem: Poetic sequence
First published: 1980, in *Descending Figure*

The Poem

"Lamentations" consists of four brief lyric poem sequences in free verse. Each sequence has its own title: "The Logos," "Nocturne," "The Covenant," and "The Clearing." Individual sequences contain from three to four stanzas each. These vary from two to seven lines in length, and the lines themselves mimic the stanzas through the economy of words used.

The title of this poem, "Lamentations," suggests mourning for something irrevocably lost. It especially recalls the Old Testament's Hebrew prophets lamenting the folly of the Children of Israel and their resultant separation from Jehovah. There are also correspondences between Louise Glück's sequence titles and the New Testament gospel of Saint John. For example, the title of the first sequence, "The Logos," recalls John's story of Jesus Christ, as the gospel of John opens with the phrase, "In the beginning was the Word." One definition of "word" in this context is the Greek word *logos*. "The Logos" can be described as cosmic reason or, according to ancient Greek philosophy, as the source of world order and intelligibility. The title of "The Logos" therefore suggests a story of cosmic origins and mythical figures that echoes both Greek and Christian mythology. Indeed, the poem's first stanza describes archetypal figures of a woman—described as "mournful"—and a man. These figures in turn recall the Genesis story of the Garden of Eden and the origins of humankind. The figures are not alone, according to the poem: "god was watching."

The second sequence, "Nocturne," indicates, if not a literal setting, a mood of dusk, with a landscape bathed in twilight that projects feelings of both human warmth and "panic." Here the reader begins to feel a division between the figures from the preceding sequence: There are three distinct entities, "the man, the woman, and the woman's body." The unity of "The Logos" sequence, in which there is woman with man "branching into her body," is gone. With night comes separation and fear.

The result of this fear is an attempt to procure security in the third sequence, "The Covenant": "Out of fear, they built a dwelling place." However, this attempt at unity is thwarted by the "child [who] grew between them." The division of "man" and "woman" as well as the realization of a child's dependence upon them force the figures from the first sequence to realize that they are now "mother and father." They are responsible, and like the god who watched them in "The Logos," they watch the developing "small discarded body" of their creation.

The final sequence, "The Clearing," speaks further of the separation and alienation begun in "Nocturne." Even the familiar becomes strange: "Nothing was as before," and language, the source of communication, is compared with wounds that show distinctly on the "white flesh" of humans. God, now spelled with a capital *G*, leaves the children of his creation and ascends into heaven. This final separation between the creator, God, and his children is not openly lamented; instead it is quietly described from the viewpoint of God, who, the narrator muses, must have been awestruck by the beauty of Earth when seen for that first time "from the air." There is a sense in this closing stanza of both despair at the separation of God from his Creation and wonder at the beauty of that Creation.

Forms and Devices

"Lamentations" abounds with rich mythic imagery that serves as the poem's touchstone. The four sequences recall the days of Creation that began with the word, or *logos*, and ended with night. "The Covenant" echoes the Genesis Creation story, in which God makes a covenant between himself and "the man" and "the woman." At the conclusion of six days of Creation, God rests from his work and calls it "good." "Lamentations" ends with a corresponding note with the lines, "How beautiful it must have been,/ the earth, that first time" as God saw it when He "leapt into heaven."

"Lamentations" sets archetypal figures against a backdrop of nature. The man, woman, and child are seen within a world of stripped-down imagery. Readers see the primitive beginnings of humankind, set within a natural world of flowers, beasts, day, night, and they are made aware of the minimal human needs of shelter, warmth, security, and food. The simple, direct imagery of "Nocturne" illustrates the tone of the poem with images of a "forest," "hills," "dusk," "reeds," and "leaves." Beasts, "wolves," and "the man, the woman" populated this environment. "Nocturne" concludes with a line reminding one of the moon glancing off night trees with a "moan of silver." Such mythic images are explicit metaphors for fundamental human impulses and emotions.

Glück's sparse language mirrors her use of mythic imagery. Her style in this poem is characteristically pared, chopped, and brief. Calvin Bedient, in an essay in *Parnassus* (Summer, 1981), compares her style to Ezra Pound's Imagist poetry, full of "hard light, clear edges." In an essay published in the *American Poetry Review* (September/ October, 1993), Glück wrote: "I am attracted to the ellipsis, to the unsaid, to suggestion, to eloquent, deliberate silence . . . they haunt because they are not whole; though wholeness is implied." Her style is exhibited in the tightly compressed sequences, stanzas, lines, and words of "Lamentations." Each of its sequences has no more than four stanzas, and no line has more than nine words. The lines themselves are also clipped, with no more than three or four stresses. Lines from the second stanza of "The Logos" illustrate these tendencies: "But god was watching,/ They felt his gold eye/ projecting flowers on the landscape."

Despite the poem's brevity, the poetic sequence suggests the entire cycle of creation, and elemental human emotions of "panic," hunger, and isolation. These themes are explored in a simple language that leaves much to the reader's imagination. Everything is reduced to a minimum, as if the poet—like the god in "The Logos"—"want[s] to be understood" but cannot adequately explain.

Themes and Meanings

The title of "Lamentations" encapsulates a central concern that is developed throughout the poem. The instant of creation in the poem occurs at the beginning, the genesis, of separation and loss. "Birth, not death, is the hard loss," Glück wrote in "Cottonmouth Country" from her first book, *Firstborn* (1969). Helen Vendler writes in *Part of Nature, Part of Us: Modern American Poets* (1980) that Glück's "parable" passes from creation "through splitting and panic to birth and authority . . . [to] language and estrangement." The lament is a moan of mourning, "a slow moan," for a time when man, woman, and child were not dissolved into distinct, separate beings whose only source of communication hinges on "words," the language which the poem compares to "wounds" on "white flesh."

The woman faces a double alienation: She is divided from the man, and the angels see that the division also includes "the woman, and the woman's body." It is from this "woman's body" that "a child grew between" her and the man. There is isolation from the nuclear family, but also from her own flesh. The child's beseeching as it "reached its hands" toward the man and woman makes them realize that they must take responsibility for their creation, as they are now the highest authority. All is built upon this premise. From the realization of authority, humanity is fully realized, and the figures try to understand and imagine the god who created them.

The attempt to conceive God's view of the earth shines a ray of hope into the landscape of the poem. It portrays the capacities of humankind's imagination and leaves a sense of wonder, "How beautiful," in the last stanza. A flicker of faith is expressed throughout the poem that the power of creative imagination can heal the wound of the alienated self and bring it into contact with the external world and other human beings. The poem projects an intense need to create meaningful language, to make the world familiar as a respite against the isolation so keenly described. Language, while being depicted as the final example of human estrangement, has the potential to redeem the divided relationships within the poem. Language attempts to express the wild beauty of human imagination so that there is, along with lamentation, elation. The poem tries, through the use of archetypal imagery, to bring the reader to a greater understanding of the world through Glück's vision, communicated by the shared medium of language.

Tiffany Werth

LAMIA

Author: John Keats (1795-1821)
Type of poem: Narrative
First published: 1820, in *Lamia, Isabella, The Eve of St. Agnes, and Other Poems*

The Poem

Lamia is a narrative of 708 lines of rhymed couplets, divided into two parts of approximately equal length. The major source is a brief passage in Robert Burton's *The Anatomy of Melancholy* (1621) describing the marriage of Menippus Lycius, a twenty-five-year-old "philosopher" of "staid and discreet" decorum, to "a phantasm in the habit of a fair gentlewoman." She is exposed at her wedding by Apollonius as "a serpent, a lamia," upon which she, her house, and all who were in it instantaneously disappear. John Keats embellishes Burton's bare narration with the story of Hermes' love for a mysterious forest maiden, irresolvable thematic complexities, and passages of ornate description.

Lamia opens with words that echo the "Once upon a time" of the fairy tale, an appropriate beginning for a narrative that features nymphs, satyrs, and gods and has as its central figure a lamia, a supernatural creature represented as a serpent with the head and breasts of a woman and reputed to feast on the blood of children. Keats transformed this traditional demoniac figure into a character of considerable sympathy. Equally original is his depiction of the traditional classical woodland deities being driven away by King Oberon and his fairy throng at some indefinite time after the action of this poem takes place.

The narrative begins with the ardent Hermes surreptitiously leaving his throne on Mount Olympus to find in the forest of Crete the beautiful nymph by whom he has been smitten. Even after a thorough search, he fails to find her, because a lamia has made her invisible to shield her from the lustful satyrs. Instead, he encounters "a palpitating snake . . . of dazzling hue." The snake (the lamia) agrees to reveal the maiden's presence if Hermes will restore her to her previous woman's form. Oaths are made. At once Hermes sees the "nymph near-smiling on the green." The beautiful creature begins to fade but is restored by Hermes, and the two fly into the green woods, never to grow "pale as mortal lovers do."

The lamia undergoes a violent metamorphosis into Lamia, a virgin of supernal beauty in love with young Lycius, a student in Corinth whom she has seen on one of the many psychic trips she made "when in the serpent prison-house." As quick as thought, she is in Corinth and meets Lycius, who is musing in "the calm twilight of Platonic shades." He falls in love with her at first sight and swoons "pale with pain" when she tells him that "finer spirits cannot breathe below/ In human climes, and live," ironically presaging her own demise and stating one of the poem's possible themes. Relenting, she "threw the goddess off, and won his heart/ More pleasantly by playing woman's part." On the way to her mysterious palace, unknown to any but "a few Persian mutes," they encounter the aged Apollonius, the sage teacher and "trusty guide" of Lycius. Lamia instinctively trembles, and Lycius for the first time in his life looks upon his "good instructor" as the "ghost of folly haunting [his] sweet dreams."

After living for an indefinite period of time shut off from the world with Lamia in her "purple-lined palace of sweet sin," Lycius is moved by pride to show her to his friends. Rejecting her pleas to continue as they are, he invites many guests to their marriage feast. Apollonius appears, uninvited, and with good intentions of saving his pupil from becoming a "serpent's prey," exposes Lamia. She turns deathly pale and vanishes. Lycius in turn dies, and the poem concludes as the guests wind "the heavy body" in "its marriage robe."

Forms and Devices

Lamia was written in 1819, Keats's wondrous year that began with "The Eve of St. Agnes" and concluded with *The Fall of Hyperion* (1856). In this period of creativity unparalleled in English poetry, Keats, ever the experimenter, mastered many literary forms and effects. In *Lamia* he returned to the pentameter couplet, which he had used two years earlier for the lengthy *Endymion* (1818). In the interim, he had studied John Dryden's couplets. Dryden's influence is seen in the heightened control of language over thought that is displayed in *Lamia*. Here there is little of that impression one has when reading *Endymion* that the progression of thought is often determined by the need for a rhyme, although Keats occasionally sacrifices English word order for the expedience of a rhyme, as in "Fast by the springs where she to bathe was wont" or "Soft went the music the soft air along." In this poem Keats minimizes the monotony of the couplet form by enjambment, internal stops, and frequent Alexandrines. The poem concludes with a triplet, which gives a strong sense of finality.

Lamia is rich in rhetorical devices: alliteration ("purple-lined palace of sweet sin"), allusion ("she lifted her Circean head"), metaphor ("a moment's thought is passion's passing bell"), simile ("His mind wrapp'd like his mantle"); personification ("Love, jealous grown of so complete a pair/ Hover'd and buzz'd his wings"), and periphrasis ("star of Lethe" for Hermes, "a bright Phoebean dart" for sun ray). The most important device is imagery. As in "To Autumn," Keats appeals to every sense (including a sense of motion) to involve the reader in the experience of the poem. Especially vivid are the descriptions of Hermes in quest of the nymph, the "gordian shape of dazzling hue," and Lamia's pleasure palace. These descriptions are as colorful and rich in detail as those of "The Eve of St. Agnes." "Green" and "pale" are motifs signifying vitality and death. In the last fifty lines, auditory images become particularly important as the sounds of pleasure in Lamia's palace are replaced by a "deadly silence" that is pierced by the shrieks of Apollonius.

Themes and Meanings

The possible meanings of *Lamia* have elicited extensive critical commentary. While it is evident that Keats did not envisage the character of Lamia as the demoniac creature of tradition, it is far from clear whether she is a femme fatale or the fragile victim of Apollonius's rationality. The character of Apollonius is equally ambiguous: Is he the cold-hearted destroyer of beauty and joy or the good teacher of high ideals? Even Lycius is problematic. To what extent is the tragic ending attributable to his desire to provoke the envy of others? Further, does he hubristically reject human limitations to aspire to that pure pleasure known only by the immortals? These questions defy definitive answers.

The central conflict in *Lamia* may be taken to be either between responsibility and wanton hedonism on the one hand or between ethereal beauty and murderous rationality on the other. The problem is that, in either case, the text can support both views. Lamia's benevolence is illustrated by her protection of the beautiful nymph from the lustful creatures of the forest—but why was she imprisoned in a serpent's body in the first place? Apollonius's positive character is established by his desire to save Lycius from wasteful self indulgence—but why does he laugh maliciously when he discovers Lamia's identity?

It is probable that Keats himself was of a divided mind regarding his characters and their actions. Recurrent themes in his poetry are the power of art to capture the essence of human passions permanently, the power of the gods to enjoy for eternity the highest of human joys that last for but a moment on this earth, and the danger to humans of mingling with the gods. These themes are especially prominent in the poems of 1819, written only two years before his death.

The most problematic passage in *Lamia* is the one in part 2 that begins, "What wreath for Lamia? What for Lycius?" Keats appears to enter into the poem in a personal way, coming down on the side of Lamia against Apollonius, asking, "Do not all charms fly/ At the mere touch of cold philosophy" and asserting that "Philosophy will clip an angel's wings." These sentiments embody the anti-intellectual bias of Romanticism, a bias seen earlier in William Wordsworth's lines "Our meddling intellect/ Misshapes the beauteous forms of things:—/ We murder to dissect." Keats's denunciation of rational inquiry, which he sees as destroying the mystery of beauty, is a personal intrusion upon a narrative which to that point had been as objectively delivered as one could reasonably expect. The passage does not answer the many questions which the poem raises, but it does suggest that Keats in his heart sided with Lamia.

Robert G. Blake

THE LANDSCAPE NEAR AN AERODROME

Author: Stephen Spender (1909-1995)
Type of poem: Meditation
First published: 1933, in *Poems*

The Poem

Stephen Spender's "The Landscape near an Aerodrome" is a poem of thirty lines arranged into six stanzas of five lines each. The poem is a description of the flight of an airplane and its landing at an urban airport. Such a flight would still have been a somewhat unusual event in the 1930's, and the speaker meditates upon the meaning and significance of the airplane, the landscape over which it flies, and the airport ("aerodrome" means airfield or airport) at which it arrives. The title suggests that the focus of the poem is the landscape, but in the first stanza the speaker describes the airplane. It is "More beautiful and soft than any moth/ With burring furred antennae feeling its huge/ path/ Through dusk." In the first line, therefore, Spender announces his perspective: Modern machinery surpasses the traditional beauty of nature. However, nature is not completely lacking in the description of this machine: It has "furred antennae" like the moth to guide it through the air, but it is directed toward its destination by human design rather than by instinct. Significantly, it is gliding with "shut-off engines," so there is no discordant sound of mechanical engines. Its descent is gentle, and it does not disturb the "charted currents of air."

The second stanza shifts from an appreciative description of the airplane to the perspective of its passengers, who are "lulled" by its gentle descent. The landscape over which they travel is given human attributes: It is described as "feminine" and "indulging its easy limbs/ In miles of softness." This is a landscape both natural and suburban, and its softness is attributable to the broad patterns of farms and meadows unbroken by the hard, masculine buildings and monuments of the city. As stanza 2 continues, the passengers' eyes "penetrate" the beginnings of a town where "industry shows a fraying edge." The attitude toward the industrial landscape is neutral: "Here they may see what is being done."

In the next stanza, the passengers look past the "masthead light" of the landing ground and "observe the outposts/ Of work." The chimneys are "lank black fingers" that appear "frightening and mad." These negative images are quite different from the descriptions of the airplane and the farmlands. The urban landscape is broken and mournful: The "squat buildings" look "like women's faces/ Shattered by grief," and the surrounding houses moan. The airplane then flies over a field where boys are playing. In contrast to the first stanza, Spender now sees positive value in things that are linked to nature: The shouts of joy that accompany the boys' active play are like the cries of "wild birds." However, those cries "soon are hid under the loud city." The urban world is a nightmare of sound and broken visual images, in direct contrast with the airplane that can fly high above it.

In the last stanza, the airplane finally lands. Its passengers are met by a "tolling bell/ Reaching across the landscape of hysteria." The landscape is one of madness, intensifying the nightmarish images of the previous descriptions of the city. Industry and the military are dwarfed by the mad bells of religion, "the church blocking the sun." The freedom of the airplane in the sky is now destroyed by the institutions of industry and religion.

Forms and Devices

The meter of "The Landscape near an Aerodrome" is primarily iambic with some trochaic substitutions, and the line length is hexameter with a few pentameter variations. For example, the first line is iambic pentameter, but the second shifts to iambic hexameter. The poetic purpose of these lines of uneven length is unclear, however, and seems more arbitrary or accidental than designed.

The major poetic device used to describe the airplane and the rural landscape over which it flies is personification. The farmland, for example, is described as a "feminine" landscape with "easy limbs." Metaphor and simile become the dominant figures of speech in the poem as it develops from the early contrasts between the natural and the mechanical. The airplane is metaphorically seen as a moth with fur and antennae, although it is more beautiful. Similes tend to appear later: The urban houses "remark the unhomely sense of complaint, like a dog/ Shut out and shivering at the foreign moon," and the chimneys are "like long black fingers/ Or figures, frightening and mad." The change from the playful "winking" world of the airplane to the grimy city is dramatic. In a more positive simile, the boys at play are described as being "like wild birds." Their cries, however, are "hid under the loud city." The sound images are the crucial poetic device that Spender uses to establish the contrast between the natural and the urban landscapes. The gliding airplane makes no noise, but the city is loud. The tolling bell of the oppressive church is even louder, and it is inescapable. This onerous institution is also "blocking the sun" and bringing darkness upon the land, blotting out the promise of new technology and the freedom to pass effortlessly over the seas.

Themes and Meanings

The positive treatment of a mechanical subject in the first part of the poem is typical of the poets of the 1930's (particularly those in the W. H. Auden, Stephen Spender, and Louis MacNeice group) as well as the earlier Futurists. In poems such as "The Funeral" and "The Express," Spender celebrates the machine and those who work with it. To these poets, the airplane is poetically more significant and beautiful than the objects of nature that for centuries were considered the proper subject of poetry. In contrast with such old themes, the airplane is a sign of progress, flying over the sea and carrying the passengers gracefully to their destinations. It suggests the birth of a new era that requires poets to follow advances in technology and science.

An important change in the poet's perspective occurs in the second part of the poem. The images describing factories are negative, and the children's play is drowned out by the city's noise. The machines of the city are noisy in contrast with the silent and gliding airplane. The reason for this change is at least partly related to the portrayal of the dominant church that blocks the sun and has a tolling bell louder than industry or the batteries of the military. The progress signified by the machine has been undone by the presence of a church that demands allegiance to its history and myths. The landscape that began free as the wind and "feminine" is now dominated by negative images, such as shivering dogs, mad "figures," and women's grieving or hysterical faces—the "landscape of hysteria."

The condemnation of the church and other traditional institutions that are deemed responsible for the oppression of the masses is an important part of Marxist ideology and was a staple of the work of many poets of the 1930's. They believed that it was necessary to destroy such ideologically powerful institutions in order to bring into being a new world in which there would be economic freedom for ordinary people. Auden made it clear that he believed changes in technology would lead to changes in people when he said, "New styles of architecture, a change of heart."

James Sullivan

LANDSCAPE WITH TRACTOR

Author: Henry Taylor (1942-   )
Type of poem: Lyric
First published: 1983; collected in *The Flying Change*, 1985

The Poem

Henry Taylor's "Landscape with Tractor" is a mid-length poem in free verse, written in twelve four-line stanzas. Although mildly evoking the pacing and feel of blank verse, the poem employs no formal metrical device. In terms of its carefully plotted visual arrangement and disciplined emphasis on rhythm, however, "Landscape with Tractor" establishes and maintains a sense of order and control that reinforces its principal thematic concerns.

The poem is written in the first person, with the speaker relating an apparently hypothetical event in the form of long rhetorical questions. The most unusual aspect is the fact that the speaker continually addresses his reader or listener as "you"; because the person being addressed is also the person performing the apparently hypothetical actions of the poem, the actions are also performed by "you" ("you're mowing," "you keep going," and so on). This device suggests a deliberate attempt on the part of the speaker to distance himself from the action of the poem. It also lends this startling poem its unique character, reinforcing its playful equivocation and offhanded ambiguity.

The poem begins with a rhetorical question that serves as both the formal and thematic locus of the poem. Asking the reader "How would it be if you . . . ," the speaker plunges into a surrealistic narrative reminiscent of the fictive musings of Magical Realists such as Jorge Luis Borges or Franz Kafka. The poem proposes a situation in which a man—perhaps the narrator, perhaps not—perfunctorily mows his three-acre lawn with a "bushhog" (a small tractor or mowing machine), sinking further into the numbing mundaneness of the task as the narrative progresses. Just when he seems to have completely lost himself in his work, a bizarre and unforeseen tableau presents itself in his otherwise pastoral landscape.

A dead body is lying in a yet unmowed patch of grass "maybe three swaths" from where the man is cutting. At first he offers himself some more rational, palatable explanation of this grotesque, unsettling image. "It's a clothing-store dummy, for God's sake," he consoles himself. A seeming realist, doubting to the last moment the possibility of an encounter with something so patently bizarre as a corpse, the speaker candidly dismisses the scene, musing ironically that "People/ will toss all kinds of crap from their cars." In a few more moments, however, he realizes the truth of the situation. An anonymous car "from the city" has apparently discarded a body "like a bag of beer cans." The mower's inherent connection with the obligations of the human condition—as well as his practical urge to get things done—lead him to alert the authorities; two country doctors dutifully arrive and "use pitchforks/ to turn the body, some four days dead, and ripening." The cause of death is immediately apparent; the person has been shot.

According to the narrator, weeks pass and no one "comes forward to identify the body." He repeats the question "how would it be?" only now in a redefined context. Initially the speaker regards the idea of encountering a dead body as an abstract concept to be debated. Now it becomes a reality, lending new urgency to the problem: Just how *would* it be? In the closing stanzas the speaker directly addresses a "you" that is clearly meant to be anyone claiming to be a part of humanity. You clearly wish to "go on with your life"—putting gas in the tractor, for example—but cannot easily dismiss the glimpse into mortality revealed in the vision of the "thing not quite like a face/ whose gaze blasted past you at nothing" as the decomposing corpse was gathered and taken away.

Forms and Devices

Taylor is best characterized as a narrative poet. His work is rich with the flavor of a storytelling tradition inherited from his Quaker roots. Thus many Taylor poems, "Landscape with Tractor" being no exception, are replete with the techniques and trappings of a good story—setting, character, conflict, and resolution (or at least a yearning for resolution). Taylor's meticulous attention to visual arrangement and structure reinforce a central theme of the work, the role of the artificer in the execution of his art. "Landscape with Tractor" concerns the storyteller as much as it does the story, and its appearance on the page shows the reader just how much presentation can impact interpretation. The tight, regularly arranged stanzaic pattern suggests at every moment, in an otherwise stylistically unobtrusive poem, the omnipresent hand of the artisan. Likewise, the call-and-response pattern suggested by the poem's rhetorical questions reminds the reader that poetry may be as much about the nature and practice of questioning itself as it is about providing "answers" to life's most stirring questions.

The dead body and the bushhog-steering man mowing stand out as the two images in "Landscape with Tractor" that convey the most resonance. Each suggests a wealth of interpretive possibilities, some of which have already been alluded to. For example, the corpse, as well as the man's enigmatic attraction toward it, may represent the human psyche's fascination with its own mysterious destiny. Further, the body might be said to represent the enigma of death itself. A somewhat genteel, contemporary incarnation of Everyman, the mowing man is the thoughtful but slightly jaded persona through whom the problem of this poem is viewed.

The style of Taylor's language should also be noted. A poem quite accomplished in its mastery of idiom, "Landscape with Tractor" provides in its speaker an absorbing version of the rural "gentleman farmer," although with a unique postmodern spin. This late-twentieth century man of the country is clearly exiled from "the city" by choice, not by birthright. His general attitude is revealed by the playful and slightly irreverent use of phrases such as "for God's sake" and "Christ!" At points Taylor instills a wry flippancy into his persona, a figure self-admittedly "with half [his] mind on something [he'd] rather be doing." By the final lines of the poem, however, his genial manner regarding what he has witnessed has dissolved into a disturbing sobriety brought on by the realization that the dead woman's image will remain with him, will "stay/ in that field" that houses his memory and conscience until he himself dies.

Themes and Meanings

The three primary thematic concerns of "Landscape with Tractor" are the nature of unexpected change, the contemplation of mortality, and the inexplicable connection between human beings. In his review of Taylor's *The Flying Change* for *The New York Review of Books* (May, 1986), Peter Stitt views the first of these themes, the consequences of change and mutability, as the thematic core of the book. Stitt observes that Taylor seeks to portray the "unsettling change," the "rent in the veil of ordinary life." Clearly "Landscape with Tractor" explores this idea extensively; the speaker's unexpected encounter with a dead body awakens in him the realization that change, even extreme change, lurks clandestinely around every bend in the human journey.

Perhaps the most disquieting kind of change looming on the human landscape is one's own inevitable death. The speaker's moment of facing his own mortality, depicted in his uneasy confrontation with the "ripening" corpse, reflects Taylor's second preoccupation. Death, especially as the result of sudden and unexplained violence, is a theme that dominates much of Taylor's work, especially in memorable poems such as "Barbed Wire," from *The Flying Change*, and "A Voltage Spike," from Taylor's 1996 collection *Understanding Fiction*. In these poems violent, sudden, and seemingly meaningless deaths force both the poet and the speaker to recognize the tenuous nature of life and to examine the consequences that stem from this realization. A final thematic concern, and one that perhaps distinguishes "Landscape with Tractor" from other Taylor poems, is its concern with the inexplicable but strongly felt bond between human beings. For Taylor, an elusive but undeniable bond links all of humanity, a bond that is unquestionable but very difficult to articulate.

Gregory D. Horn

LANDSCAPE WITH TWO GRAVES
AND AN ASSYRIAN DOG

Author: Federico García Lorca (1898-1936)
Type of poem: Lyric
First published: 1940, as "Paisaje con dos tumbas y un perro asirio," in *Poeta en Nueva York*; English translation collected in *Poet in New York*, 1955

The Poem

As one might imagine from the title, "Landscape with Two Graves and an Assyrian Dog" is an unusual poem. The title suggests a painting of some sort—not an ordinary one, but a Surrealist painting such as Federico García Lorca's fellow Spaniard Salvador Dalí might create. Such a painting almost always attempts to capture, on canvas, the illogical and imagistic nature of dreams.

García Lorca attempts something similar in his poem. The poem is relatively short, consisting of three stanzas easily contained on one page. It is written in free verse with lines of varying length. García Lorca also uses jagged, discordant language, which, when combined with the form and length of the poem, serves to mirror the ephemeral and illogical nature of a dream.

One thinks of dreams as making an appeal to the subconscious to discover or work out something. García Lorca makes the same appeal in his poem. The poem begins: "Friend/ get up and listen/ to the Assyrian dog howl." Each of the three stanzas begins the same way, by urging a friend to arise and listen. The poem is written in the first person, as are most of García Lorca's poems, and the speaker is most likely García Lorca himself. It is possible that García Lorca is trying to rouse a friend, but because of the commands, the reader feels that García Lorca is speaking directly to him or her, thus reaffirming this sense of urgency.

The poem shifts from this type of command to the poet's description of his surrealistic vision, about which he is warning the reader. In this vision, there are, among other things, "cancer's three nymphs," "mountains of red sealing wax," and a horse with "an eye in its neck." All of these images help build suspense and create an overwhelming feeling of terror.

García Lorca uses this technique effectively in stanza 2: "Wake up. Be still. Listen. Sit up in your bed." The poet does not plead or cajole; rather, he commands, as if he and the reader are in danger. And indeed, this seems to be the case because the howling of the dog is suddenly transformed into a "purple tongue" that disperses "terrifying ants and the liquor of irises." These images appear to represent two disparate elements—the frightening, swarming, regimented material world and the soft, pure, natural world. By transforming internal concerns into external symbols, García Lorca blurs the boundaries between the real and the symbolic.

This blurring of boundaries, the horrific images, and the fact that García Lorca urges his friend to arise, all suggest that the poem is a nightmare from which García

Lorca is attempting to awaken his friend or the reader. The final stanza, however, is simply the first three lines of the poem repeated. The sleeper never awakens. Readers are left with the realization that the poem is not a nightmare, but the singing of the nightmarish quality of the real world, from which they will never "awaken."

Forms and Devices

The most striking aspect of "Landscape with Two Graves and an Assyrian Dog" is the imagery. The images García Lorca uses are not the picturelike images one finds in the poetry of William Carlos Williams (which one can literally picture, such as "a red wheel/ barrow/ glazed with rain/ water"), but images one can picture both consciously and subconsciously. García Lorca's images are images formed in the psyche. For example, when he says, "The grass of my heart is somewhere else," he is speaking of the vital, natural, basic elements that are dear to him but are now lost.

García Lorca does not use these images to describe something, but to convey a mood or to express emotion. In this poem, García Lorca is profoundly stirred, excited, and his mind is racing, making wild associations at the speed of light. The images are so strong that the poem revolves around them. The odd juxtaposition of the images, one of his most startling techniques, creates an odd poetic tension that infuses each line with power.

One's reaction to this poem is not intellectual, but emotional. Unlike many modern American poets, García Lorca does not attempt to encapsulate an idea in his poems, but instead attempts to translate the sensory nature of things into language. In "Landscape with Two Graves and an Assyrian Dog," this is especially evident, because we see García Lorca express the mysteries of being human through subconscious intuitions. He does this with force and passion; the poem builds up so much momentum that it seems it could explode at any moment.

The result of García Lorca's insight is that he creates a new understanding, one more real than reality. The images do not make "logical connections"; instead, they cross boundaries and connect elements of the subconscious that appear frighteningly vivid and stark. For example, the first stanza closes: "And the moon was in a sky so cold/ that she had to tear open her mound of Venus/ and drown the ancient graveyards in blood and ashes." Because of the odd juxtaposition of the already odd images, it is difficult to explain what this passage "means," but one can discuss the mood it conveys.

The aura surrounding this passage is one of death, which coincides with the title of the chapter in which this poem appears in *Poet in New York*, "Introduction to Death." In the poem, the moon mutilates herself, which in turn "drowns" (smothers) the graveyard in blood and ashes. This act of violence covers the dead (the graveyard) in traditional symbols of death (blood and ashes), as if to suggest that the dead are now more profoundly dead. This passage is a classic example of what García Lorca calls *duende*—which is the sense of the presence of death. He believes that for a poem to be truly powerful and magical, it must possess *duende*, which this poem does.

Themes and Meanings

Just as it is difficult to explain what a García Lorca image means, it is almost as difficult to attempt to offer the meaning of a García Lorca poem. "Landscape with Two Graves and an Assyrian Dog" is certainly no exception, but the tone of the language and the images suggest that the poet is concerned with the recognition of horror and that this poem is a confession of that recognition.

García Lorca wrote this poem when he was staying on a farm in the Catskill Mountains in upstate New York. The owner of the farm, who was visibly suffering from cancer, owned a huge, half-blind dog that slept right outside García Lorca's room. The terror that these elements elicited in the poet became the genesis for the poem.

Though he has been labeled a Surrealist, in poems such as this one, García Lorca transcends Surrealism. The French Surrealist poets would remain in the dreamlike world mentioned earlier, but García Lorca breaks out of the nightmare to take the world head-on, shocking as it may be. What is horrific about the poem is not that it is the transcription of a nightmare, but that it is ultimately about reality. The horrors of deformity and of people suffering—the horrors of everyday life—are far more terrifying than the horrors of the imagination.

Reality frightens him so deeply because one can never escape it. One can wake up from a dream or simply stop imagining, but one cannot elude the suffering one must experience as a human being. This theme of unavoidable grief is reaffirmed in the second stanza of the poem. García Lorca warns his friend, and the reader: "Here it comes toward the rock. Don't spread out your roots!/ It approaches. Moans. Friend, don't sob in your dreams." Clearly something inescapable and terrible is coming and is bringing sadness with it.

García Lorca does not want the reader to remain sleeping, though; he urges him or her to wake up and listen to the dog howl: One cannot ignore the horrors of the world by living in a dream world or by covering one's eyes or ears. One must wake up and listen; one must embrace what one fears. For García Lorca, facing up to what he fears is his only method of conquering it, and it acts as his muse to create art. He writes with his eyes, his ears, his teeth, his hair, his heart, and his blood. Because his entire being is assaulted, his entire being composes poetry.

As stated earlier, this is a poem of confession. García Lorca confesses that to him the sky and the earth engender death, that he has lost something vital to his existence, that he loves, and that he is afraid. He confesses that he and a child he loves "lived inside a knife for a hundred years," suggesting that even his innocence has been ravaged. Essentially, the poet confesses to being human, and he accepts the tribulations of this responsibility through the force of his poetry which, to use his own words, even now remains "a conscious rocket of dark light, let off among the dull and torpid."

Dean Rader

LAPIS LAZULI

Author: William Butler Yeats (1865-1939)
Type of poem: Meditation
First published: 1938, in *New Poems*

The Poem

This fifty-six-line poem is dedicated to Harry Clifton, who gave to William Butler Yeats on his seventieth birthday an eighteenth century Chinese carving in lapis lazuli, an azure-blue semiprecious stone. It was a traditional scene representing a mountain with temple, trees, paths, and tiny human beings about to climb the mountain. Yeats uses the carving to meditate on the role of art in an essentially tragic world.

The poem begins by acknowledging certain complaints from "hysterical women" who say that they "are sick of the palette and fiddle-bow,/ Of poets that are always gay." The implication is that artists are frivolous and irresponsible, playing around in the face of imminent disaster instead of doing something to save the world. Unless something "drastic" is done, the hysterical voices go on,

> Aeroplane and Zeppelin will come out,
> Pitch like King Billy bomb-balls in
> Until the town lie beaten flat.

The second stanza does not deny the probability of violence, but it deplores the hysterical wailing and defends art as a way of coping with tragedy. Yeats uses the Shakespearean analogy that all the world is a stage and further states that the play enacted there is always tragedy. "There struts Hamlet, there is Lear,/ That's Ophelia, that Cordelia." All these Shakespearean characters die. Yet, when the curtain is about to fall, they do not "break up their lines to weep." They transcend their fate, for "They know that Hamlet and Lear are gay;/ Gaiety transfiguring all that dread." They are an expression of everyone's fate, for everyone dies.

The triumph of the tragic hero is to play that role with dignity and grace, finding beauty and inspiration in the performance. Even though the curtain drops on a "hundred thousand stages," tragedy "cannot grow by an inch or an ounce."

The third stanza presents a sweeping look at the course of history, with its endless succession of civilizations. The poet imagines them as a great caravan, coming on foot, by ship, on camels, horses, and mules. "Old civilisations put to the sword./ Then they and their wisdom went to rack." Moreover, their great art died as well. He gives one example: the superlative achievements of Callimachus, an ancient Greek sculptor, "Who handled marble as if it were bronze." Only a scrap of his art remains. "All things fall and are built again,/ And those that build them again are gay." In other words, the joy of life is in the process of creating; it exists in the journey itself, not in some goal or object at the end of the trail which is going to live forever.

The fourth stanza, shorter than the others, introduces the carving in lapis lazuli.

Three Chinese men, one apparently a serving man carrying a musical instrument, are climbing toward a "little half-way house." Above them flies a long-legged bird, a crane, conventional Chinese symbol of longevity. The last stanza elaborates how the carving brings delight to the beholder. It evokes an imaginative journey that goes beyond the scene frozen in stone. The poet participates mentally in the climb and imagines the two old men sitting under flowering trees at the half-way house, listening to mournful music. They stare out on "all the tragic scene" below: "Their eyes mid many wrinkles, their eyes,/ Their ancient, glittering eyes, are gay."

Forms and Devices

The poet makes sensitive use of sound devices and connotations, the first stanza combining colloquial phrases ("sick of," "beaten flat") with explosive words and repeated consonants ("drastic . . . done," "King Billy bomb-balls") to suggest the hysterical, bombastic tone of the women. "King Billy" may have associations with English-Irish conflicts but also brings to mind "Kaiser Bill," a popular term for Kaiser Wilhelm II, German emperor during World War I. Although zeppelins, rigid-framed airships, were obsolete as war machines in 1936, when Yeats wrote this poem, he remembered the zeppelin bombing raids on London during World War I. In 1936, the Germans reoccupied the Rhineland; other events in Europe were leading up to World War II. The threat of war was real enough, therefore, but the tone of the first stanza suggests that a melodramatic, frenzied reaction to that threat is not helpful.

The poet ironically points to dramatic art as offering a better model for learning to bear human tragedy than public screaming and moaning or the condemnation of artists. He maintains the note of violence, however, by equating the real tragedy of modern war with the descending final curtain of the play. "Black out; Heaven blazing into the head:/ Tragedy wrought to its uttermost." The term "Black out" carries multiple, contradictory connotations. The final curtain blacks out the play, as a falling bomb blacks out human life. "Heaven blazing into the head," however, suggests enlightenment or transfiguration from that fatal blow that ends the play or the individual life. Thus, that which seems most terrible may be that which reveals heaven. The vision of heaven is itself an artifice, and it must be kept alive, often in defiance of the "real" world of political action and armed conflict.

The rest of the poem retreats into a calmer, more contemplative tone, assuming the viewpoint of eternity. The attention shifts from the everlasting recurrence of violence and death to the equally everlasting reality of life and creativity. Everything is in process. Even static arts celebrate and suggest motion: Callimachus "Made draperies that seemed to rise/ When sea-wind swept the corner." The poet's appreciation of the lapis lazuli carving does not rest in the reality of the stone itself but in the imaginative recreation of a living scene it inspires. This is the magic of art—it leads the beholder beyond itself to partake again of the joy of creativity. The poet has not only defended art and artists but also demonstrated art in action.

Themes and Meanings

When Yeats uses the term "gay" in describing the old men's "glittering eyes," he is obviously not using the word in exactly the sense that the women do who speak of "poets that are always gay." The women intend some conventional meaning such as indulgence in wine, women, and song in utter disregard of the serious business of life. Yeats's meaning is closer to an intense consciousness, actually heightened by an understanding of the seriousness, indeed the tragic nature of life.

At about the same time that Yeats received the gift of the lapis lazuli carving, he wrote in a letter, "To me the supreme aim is an act of faith and reason to make one rejoice in the midst of tragedy." Moreover, in his rather esoteric prose work, *A Vision* (1925, revised 1937), in which he discussed his private psychological and historical mythology, he asserted, "We begin to live when we conceive of life as tragedy."

According to Yeats, each psyche is suspended mentally and emotionally between contraries, sometimes referring to some subjective inner validity, sometimes focused on some objective empirical evidence. Indeed, one cannot develop or expand consciousness except in a struggle to unify one's own contradictory interpretations of existence. Yeats says that "only the greatest obstacle that can be contemplated without despair, rouses the will to full intensity."

Obviously, the greatest obstacle one can imagine is death itself. The hysterical women are assuming that the threat of death is peculiarly significant in their particular, objective moment of history; therefore, one should suspend all other activities in the present emergency. Yeats is pointing out that the threat of death is the constant human condition, neither more nor less tragic than it ever was. What is needed is courage and a way to contemplate disaster with some measure of equanimity. Art, which may indeed seem to pull one into a different reality, may help one to "transfigure all that dread."

Another Yeats poem of this period, "Sailing to Byzantium," deals again with old men, but as more appropriately withdrawn into a subjective vision of reality:

> An aged man is but a paltry thing,
> A tattered coat upon a stick, unless
> Soul clap its hands and sing, and louder sing
> For every tatter in its mortal dress.

In warfare, persons of all ages become, like old men, more aware of the imminence of death. For them, here is an even greater urgency to transcend fate and to teach the soul to "clap its hands and sing."

The singer speaks for life, not death. In "A General Introduction for My Work," Yeats wrote, "The heroes of Shakespeare convey to us through their looks, or through the metaphorical patterns of their speech, the sudden enlargement of their vision, their ecstasy at the approach of death." While social crisis should bring forth an active response to empirical danger, it should not silence the singers. Human beings must live in two worlds: the material, objective world where all men die, and the mental, imaginative world where the soul abides and joy is possible.

Katherine Snipes

LAST NIGHT WITH RAFAELLA

Author: David St. John (1949-   )
Type of poem: Lyric
First published: 1990; collected in *Terraces of Rain: An Italian Sketchbook*, 1991

The Poem

David St. John's "Last Night with Rafaella" consists of twenty-six "stanzas" varying in length from a single line to nine lines, a classic free-verse or open-form poem. As is typical with this form of poem, there is no fixed or predominant meter, rather a sweeping musical cadence that is the hallmark of a long, open lyric.

In 1984, St. John received the Prix de Rome Fellowship in literature, awarded by the American Academy and Institute of Arts and Letters, and spent a year in Rome, where he began work on "Last Night with Rafaella." The poem is a recollection of an evening the speaker in the poem spent in long conversation with Rafaella, a makeup artist in the world of high fashion. Rafaella is "a sophisticated,/ Well-traveled woman, so impossible/ To shock," while the speaker wants to talk about "changing [his] life," "The spiritual life," and his own "Long disenchantment with the ordinary world."

Roughly, the first half of the poem takes place in one of the "outside tables" of the café "Rosati" in the "Piazza del Popolo." Here the speaker muses about "Doing something meaningful—perhaps/ Exploring a continent or discovering a vaccine," while Rafaella strokes the back of his wrist. The other "meaningful" activities the speaker considers are "Falling in love or over the white falls/ Of a dramatic South American river!—"

The spectrum of meaningful activities purposefully ranges from the prototypical greatness achieved by an explorer or scientist to the ordinary drama of falling in love, or the extraordinary drama of falling over a waterfall, to let the reader know the speaker does not take his musing completely seriously. Rather, the poem—and the poet—seem pointedly self-aware. The reader cannot help but infer a kind of self-sardonic, American-poet-in-Europe-on-a-fellowship tone in this early section of the poem. The fact that the speaker feels "comfortable there" in the piazza with Rafaella and trusts her advice, "a woman who, with the ball of her exquisite thumb,/ Carefully flared rouge along the white cheekbones/ Of the most beautiful women in the world," casts Rafaella in both a dominant and frivolous role.

In an interview, St. John talked about Rafaella as a strong woman, an "activating character," and the speaker in the poem as passive. The speaker in this poem is tentative and lacks the presence of Rafaella, who travels in circles of "famous, even notorious" designers, and who bring "tears to the eyes/ Of contessas, movie stars, and diplomats' wives." Fashion that brings tears to the eyes is either unutterably beautiful, or St. John is not so subtly mocking the whole industry of which Rafaella is a part.

The second half of the poem fully explores the sensuality that is introduced with lines about Rafaella: "A friend who'd/ Often rub the opal on her finger so slowly// It made your mouth water." The speaker in the poem is tantalized by Rafaella telling him "what it would be like/ To feel her tongue addressing [his] ear." The scene then shifts from the café to Rafaella's bedroom, where the speaker views a small tattoo just above her hip bone, by moonlight. He then runs his finger along her collarbone, circles the tattoo—the "shy angel"—while the stars shift "in their rack of black complexities above." The poem ends with an image of Rafaella's hair falling on the speaker's shoulder "To some whole other level of the breath." This sonorous but ambiguous phrase suggests Rafaella is indeed powerful, at least as powerful as life-giving breath; yet breath is fleeting and must be repeated.

Forms and Devices

The speaker in "Last Night with Rafaella" is charmed by her; he rhapsodizes about her sensual gestures (slowly rubbing an opal on her finger until she makes his "mouth water"). As the two lie in bed together, St. John includes a rather obvious sexual image— "wind knocking at those stiff/ Umbrella pines along her garden's edge." Most of his references to Rafaella are beautiful, subtle, and lyrical, however. He describes the ball of her thumb as "exquisite," the small tattoo "just above her hip bone" as a "dove in flight or an angel with its/ Head tucked beneath its wing."

When Rafaella speaks in the poem, she makes a strikingly beautiful, deceptively simple observation:

> *Do you know how to tell a model?*
> *In fashion, they wear tattoos like singular beads*
> *Along their hips,*
> > *but artists' models*
> *Wear them like badges against the daily nakedness,*

She goes on to give the example of Celestine, who "has above one nipple that/ Minute yellow bee and above/ The other an elaborate, cupped poppy." The two similes Rafaella utters, tattoos like "singular beads" or "badges," serve to distinguish the two types of models—and perhaps the two types of women—who wear their tattoos or clothing as ornament or a kind of armor against nakedness.

The speaker thinks about Rafaella's observation as he listens to "the owls marking the distances" as they hunt in the night sky. This image, coupled as it is with "geometries/ Of the dark," is a striking one. This marking or measuring imagery continues as the speaker traces the "delicate winged ridge of her/ Collarbone, running the harp length of [her] ribs." It should come as no surprise that Rafaella's tattoo is on her hip, ornamental rather than protective, a dove or an angel, and that her ribs form a harp. Here St. John offers the possibility that Rafaella is a transcendent, spiritual being, or that she offers the speaker a vehicle for the transcendence he seeks.

The final lines of the poem complete the vision of her lyrical beauty and power as her hair falls "in coils,// Like the frayed silk of some ancient tapestry,/ Like the spun cocoons of the Orient—/ Like a fragile ladder." These rich, luxurious images also hold a suggestion of ancient wisdom and of the means, albeit a fragile means, of reaching "a whole other level of the breath," of consciousness. These images, occurring as they do at the poem's end, leave the reader a final perception of Rafaella as both a strong and ethereal beauty, capable of assisting the speaker in reaching the meaningful life he says he seeks in the opening lines.

Themes and Meanings

"Last Night with Rafaella" is one of what is considered St. John's "Pasolini sequence," or poems written about his year in Rome. The speaker in the poem may be seen as the passive, languorous poet, who drinks, sits, and converses with Rafaella, seeking an end to his disenchantment with "the ordinary world," to his ennui, and to his romantic longing. In this view of the speaker's position in the poem, Rafaella is the stronger, more centered, more knowing figure. Yet, as already acknowledged, the speaker also casts Rafaella in a more frivolous role, a makeup artist for fashion models, sophisticated in only the most superficial sense of the word. St. John may be subtly humorous here, even ironic about his life as a poet, seeking meaning perhaps too passively at the hands of fashion models.

However, this view is belied by the lush, richly sensual, even mystical images surrounding Rafaella, particularly in the second half of the poem. It is hard to ignore that the stars shift "in their rack of black complexities above," as Rafaella's hair falls on the speaker's shoulder, and that that very hair is likened to a ladder that leads to "some whole other level of breath." It may be the natural movement of the constellations across the waning night sky, but it seems more likely that Rafaella is the bearer of some cosmic significance, some transcendent power, and that sexual communion with her has the ability to dissolve spiritual as well as physical boundaries.

It may be more than mere coincidence that Rafaella is the feminine form of Raphael, who stands as one of the most evolved painters of the High Renaissance, whose approach to art meant that a painting was no longer the mere portrayal of an event, but a translation and interpretation of its subject matter through its composition. Everything in a Raphael painting is aimed at harmonious balance, wherein the movement of the body becomes understood as an analogy for the animation of the spirit, and each individual figure becomes an inseparable part of the whole. Rafaella may be Raphael's true namesake, weaving the mystery of the sacred into what St. John has called the "slow dance of men and women."

Linda Bannister

LAST POEM

Author: Ted Berrigan (1934-1983)
Type of poem: Lyric
First published: 1988, in *A Certain Slant of Sunlight*

The Poem

In the work of Ted Berrigan, the mode of modernism sometimes called kitsch or camp, in which everything becomes jokey, a parody of serious intentions, received a new lease on life. In reading his work, one must keep in mind that the sentiment it contains is probably being mocked rather than uttered naïvely. Yet ultimately the sentiments are very likely being uttered with a degree of naïve genuineness that is protected by a campy tone; the poet can then deny having meant them too seriously. For all of his sophistication—Berrigan lived in Manhattan throughout his poetic career— he cultivated his naïveté and was able, behind his affectation of simplemindedness, to stay simple to the end.

"Last Poem" is at once more and less than its title may suggest. The title is dramatic. Does the poem represent a deathbed dictation? Was it discovered in Berrigan's will? Is it a farewell to the pursuit of poetry? At the same time, it is flat in tone, uninspired, the merest chronological notation. From its position in *A Certain Slant of Sunlight* (1988)—about halfway through the book—one deduces that it is in no absolute sense a last poem, but rather the most recent poem Berrigan had written at that time. The title becomes another joke, an undercutting of readerly expectations and of the grand poetic tone of yesteryear that Berrigan so often targeted.

From one point of view, however, the title can gain more than these meanings. The poem concerns a strike and violent strikebreaking event in a working-class English community. It is dedicated to Tom Pickard, a poet from Northeast England, and by its vocabulary ("When you were just a wee insolent tyke") and other clues ("Management set upon us/ Jarrow boys"), one finds that "Last Poem" is a sort of dramatic monologue, with Berrigan speaking as if he were Pickard or one of Pickard's mates or forebears. (Jarrow is a shipbuilding center in Tyneside, near Pickard's home; there was a landmark strike and strikebreaking there.) The poem ends, "They/ outnumbered us 5 to 1; & each had club/ knife or gun. Kill them, kill them, my/ sons. Kill their sons."

Acted upon, this poem would become literally the last poem for those killed. On the other hand, one can see in a feud that spans generations the futility of all attempts at finality; every attempt to strike the final blow leads only to further acts of revenge. If read in this light, the poem becomes ironic in that its title is undercut by the events, or at least by the would-be events, referred to at its end. The poem then becomes a sympathetic yet ironically distanced act of comradeship, the American Berrigan understanding the social situation of his friend yet not wanting to allow him to continue in his attitude without trying subtly to show him something important that Berrigan has discerned about that attitude. Perhaps, however, Berrigan is simply saying that a time comes when poetry can do no more and the time for killing begins.

Forms and Devices

This eleven-line free-verse poem employs the dialect of Northeast England—Tyneside—on occasion to imply, rather than perform, a dramatic monologue. Although the subject, a strikebreaking, is serious, the tone is comic. "I am the man yr father & Mum was," it begins, making a man out of Mum. This confusion of genders yields to a confusion of dialect tones, for "wee insolent tyke" and other working-class terms are laid next to expressions such as "days of infamy" and "ensuing brouhaha," taken from journalistic diction. The "Kill them, kill them, my/ sons. Kill their sons" at the close has the violence of farce, not of tragedy, largely because of the lack of preparation for it. The farce shows the tragic aspect in another light—sublime vengeance becomes ridiculous mechanical reactiveness.

Berrigan's refusal to enter with formal seriousness any of the issues his poems raise operates as a critique of the conventions of serious poetry. By an ironic twist, this refusal itself becomes, therefore, a serious formal gesture. His homespun, slap-dash ways implicitly ask why others persist in climbing on a rhetorical high horse before addressing reality so earnestly, since reality happens anyway, like it or not. All the poems in *A Certain Slant of Sunlight*, in common with Berrigan's production overall, exude this casual, down-home air of spontaneity, and when one learns something of how they were written, this does not seem surprising.

Alice Notley, the poet's widow, in her introduction to this posthumous book, reveals that it was initially written on postcards, the postcards having been supplied by Ken and Ann Mikolowski of the Alternative Press. Berrigan's method of composition on these cards—of which five hundred were sent to him, each measuring $4\frac{1}{2}$ by 7 inches—is also discussed by Notley, who says that her husband would give a handful of the cards to someone and ask that person to write a few words on them. Among those who collaborated in this way with Berrigan were Allen Ginsberg, Steve Carey, Greg Masters, Joanne Kyger, Steve Levine, Tom Pickard, Jeff Wright, Eileen Myles, Anne Waldman, and herself. It seems likely, therefore, that the poem dedicated to Pickard was also a collaboration with him.

Themes and Meanings

Berrigan collaborated with many poets in his lifetime, and a certain carelessness about ownership—of both words and possessions—was a part of the challenge that these poets raised to bourgeois society. Berrigan's poetry flourished in the 1960's and early 1970's, in the years when the counterculture had such momentum, and revolutionary possibilities were—to an extent—realizable. Such techniques of collaboration as the "exquisite corpse" method (each person writes a line, folds the paper over, and passes it to his neighbor) began with the Surrealists but were revived by Berrigan and his peers in the interests of encouraging community. A sort of utopianism, a kind of anarchy, and surely the old wish to shock the bourgeoisie were at once context and theme for Berrigan and his collaborators. These poets often composed while stoned on marijuana or hallucinogenic drugs; alcohol and amphetamines were also popular. To their detractors, this was mere self-indulgence, producing work of little consequence that would soon fade from attention. An illuminating hierarchy of precedence can be discovered for such a procedure, however, including Arthur Rimbaud's advice to poets to derange and disturb their senses, the better to see through society's false orders.

These writers, among whom Berrigan was prominent, might not have believed in possessiveness, but this did not mean that the material was a matter of indifference to them. Alice Notley remarks that postcards hold appeal as materials for poetry, being readily graspable, compact, and manageable. Indeed, the tendency of ownership to interfere with one's fascination with a given material, be it a landscape ("Get off my property!") or another person ("That woman is my wife, you cad!"), should be obvious enough to all, and one need seek no further for a connection between these two terms of an only apparent contradiction.

As for the way in which these themes connect with "Last Poem," the reader need only consider that what is being reported in the poem concerns a union, a brotherhood of shared concern, being beaten up and killed by thugs representing property owners. From this act of repression and murder flows endless harm, the poem reveals, corrupting even those who, as victims of violence, should best understand why violence ought not to be used.

David Bromige

LAST THINGS

Author: William Meredith (1919-   )
Type of poem: Meditation
First published: 1970, in *Earth Walk: New and Selected Poems*

The Poem

"Last Things" is a forty-seven-line meditation that is divided into four stanzas. Included in William Meredith's 1970 collection, *Earth Walk: New and Selected Poems*, "Last Things" is one of the thirteen new poems that make up the opening section of the collection; it is the last poem—the impact poem—of the opening section.

In the eleven-line first stanza, the poet observes a porcupine crossing a road. The porcupine's movements are described as reminding him of other "relics": "Possum, armadillo, horseshoe crab." They seem "arthritic with time." The porcupine and the other creatures are neither cute nor graceful, and "In all their slowness we see no dignity." The porcupine is "oblivious," though, to its standing on the evolutionary chart, and at the end of the stanza "he falls off/ Deliberately and without grace into the ferns." Meredith moves to a completely new location in the thirteen-line second stanza. He describes the situation of a different type of relic, old cars in a junkyard. The contents and arrangement of the junkyard are detailed. The "old cars" have been "kept for the parts"; there are "Fenders and chassis and the engine blocks." The rows in the junkyard conjure up the image of "an old orchard" that follows "the contours of the hill." The cars and their various parts are on display for the purpose of being picked clean to satisfy the needs of still-functioning cars. The last line of the stanza makes it clear what role the functioning cars play: "Cars the same age are parked on the road like cannibals."

In the fifteen-line third stanza, the poet transports the reader to Africa and focuses on "Statues of soldiers and governors and their queen" that were once erected by the Englishmen who had come to that continent. The statues now lie ignored in a field "where the Africans put them." Meredith speaks rather generously of the soldiers and governors, who "did their best" and who for the most part were not "plunderers." Nevertheless, those people and the statues of them that were left behind have been forgotten. The statues have "chipped extremities," rest "in a chipped regalia," and "lie at angles of unaccustomed ease." Only the African lichen confers any "grandeur" on the statues; lichen is a crustlike plant, consisting of fungus and green algae, that grows on rocks. The natural world may have given the statues a certain grandeur, but "men have withheld it."

The closing eight-line stanza introduces the ancient Greek world and the legend of Prometheus. The poet speaks of "fallen gods" that were chained to a cliff. This allusion refers to Prometheus, who, in Greek mythology, had committed a crime against the gods and therefore was chained to a mountain where a vulture would eat his liver by day; it was restored by night so that the process was never-ending.

Using the mythical story as the foundation of the last stanza, Meredith speaks of "Time" being "without forgiveness." "Time" also "intermittently" "sends the old, sentimental, hungry/ Vulture compassion to gnaw on the stone/ Vitals of each of us." No one is exempt from this process. Both old and young must be prepared "for the unthinkable/ Event he foresees for each of us—a reckoning, our own." The seemingly random subject matter of the previous stanzas is tied together by the reckoning foreseen for all things.

Forms and Devices

William Meredith began his poetic career by writing academic verse. Over the years, he slowly shifted toward a more open poetry that tends to be straightforward and personal. Like several of the other new poems of *Earth Walk*, "Last Things" flows with conversational ease. Meredith does not completely abandon formal constraints, though; he still capitalizes the first letter of each line, for example, but the line and stanza lengths vary. The balance of "Last Things" stems from the maturity of a poet who has learned to create poignant verse without always relying on formal poetic forms. Each stanza stands on its own as a description of a creature or object that, for whatever reason, has become a relic. In the first stanza it is the porcupine, in the second it is old cars, in the third it is statues, and in the last it becomes personal—it is "each of us." The cumulative effect creates a powerful conclusion. The title "Last Things" immediately introduces the reader to the idea of end results, and Meredith uses concrete images to build a moral case for his point of view.

In "Last Things," Meredith employs both metaphor and simile. "Tunnel of woods" and "freckled light," in the first stanza, enhance the description of the locale. When the creatures of the stanza become "like burnt-out galaxies," Meredith has chosen an appropriate simile to clarify the position these creatures have in the evolutionary scheme of things. In the second stanza, hills are described as being "as choppy as lake water," and rows of junkyard cars "are irregular only as an old orchard is." In the last line of the stanza, cars "are parked on the road like cannibals." The third stanza can be fully understood only with the reader having some knowledge of the English colonization of Africa. Meredith does not make vague references that would be understood only if footnotes were used—it is not his purpose to seem scholarly at the expense of the reader—but he does expect his reader to be schooled in the Western tradition. This becomes even more evident in the last stanza, where the mythological references enhance the personal perspective that concludes "Last Things."

Sound also adds to the power of "Last Things." Alliteration is used subtly; Meredith is never heavy-handed or showy. "Light," "Larger," and "life" are sprinkled throughout the first lines of the opening stanza. In each of the stanzas, sound casts its spell on the reader; well-chosen words make the conversational tone seem effortless. "Last Things" succeeds because of its seamless combination of all these techniques.

Themes and Meanings

"Last Things" is a poem of inevitability. Time seems always to control the race, but, as Meredith presents the story, there will be a "reckoning" in which "compassion" can be an ingredient in the final judgment. In each of the stanzas, the poet sees a relic and observes how it exists in the contemporary world. The porcupine of the first stanza seems ludicrous to the casual observer. "He moves with the difficulty of relics." The porcupine is "oblivious" to how it is observed. Meredith makes the point that how a creature is viewed by humans does not necessarily stand as the indicator of the true value of that creature. This only becomes clear, however, after one reads the entire poem. The porcupine moves at its own pace and answers to time accordingly. The junkyard of cars of the second stanza will be picked clean, so as to equip other cars that still ride the open road. The "old cars" are man-made relics, and they have become a feast for "cars parked on the road like cannibals." There is even an element of dark humor in the image of cars ready to strike "like cannibals." Yet Meredith has a larger—and more eternal—theme in mind, and the final two stanzas complete the moral picture.

The English soldiers and governors of the third stanza had struggled to make the best of things on the African continent. Meredith notes that the majority of them were "men of honor" and that the natural environment has conferred "an antique grandeur" on the statues left behind. Their own country forgot about them, and, ironically, "more dreadful shapes of the ego" can be found "In the parks and squares of England."

In the final stanza, there is the image of the mythological "fallen gods" being "chained, immortal" to a cliff. The story of Prometheus is a gruesome one. He had taught people about fire and in doing so had angered the Greek gods. The gods therefore chained him to a mountain where a vulture would gnaw at his liver. In "Last Things," Meredith uses the mythological foundation to speak about time and how it shows no "forgiveness." Yet the vulture of "Last Things" is "compassion," and it will "gnaw on the stone/ Vitals of each of us." In a discomforting way, Meredith is presenting a comforting thought. There may be "an unthinkable/ Event," but it does not need to be feared by those who were neglected during their lifetime. The relics of "Last Things" all deserve better, and, as the poet presents it, all creatures and things will be judged by time. More "compassion" should be exercised by everything on Earth. Meredith is thoughtful without being ponderous, and in "Last Things" he has an effective moral voice without resorting to strident preaching.

Michael Jeffrys

THE LAST TRAIN TO MALAKHOVKA

Author: Andrei Voznesensky (1933-   )
Type of poem: Lyric
First published: 1960, as "Poslyednyaya Zlyektrichka"; English translation collected in *Antiworlds, and the Fifth Ace,* 1967

The Poem

Written in the late 1950's, Andrei Voznesensky's "The Last Train to Malakhovka" illustrates the poet's concern for the fate of his fellow human beings in an increasingly alienating and depersonalized world and reflects his belief in the revitalizing power of poetry. Like much of Voznesensky's early work, "The Last Train to Malakhovka" is intended to be read aloud. The translation by poet Jean Garrigue preserves many of the aural qualities of the original Russian, although Garrigue's interpretation does not rhyme, using blank verse instead. The poem is divided into ten four-line stanzas; lines vary from four to eleven syllables.

The opening stanzas present the passengers on the late train to Malakhovka, a rundown suburb of Moscow known for its prostitutes and its criminal element. The poem's first line introduces switchblade-carrying toughs, and the next depicts a rough group of girls whose gold-capped teeth mark them as members of an underclass, possibly gypsies. The stanza closes with a glimpse of the conductors napping. The second stanza reveals a division among the passengers. Tired workers sleep in the front of the coach; the rougher, rowdier group is at the rear. This is where the poet, introduced in the third stanza, chooses to ride, among the "Thieves and guitars." The back of the train, noisy and littered with trash, is likened to a gypsy camp. In the midst of the din, the poet begins to recite "First Frost," a comparatively uncomplicated verse also written by Voznesensky in 1959.

This poem describes a young woman talking in a telephone booth on a cold night; the "first frost" of the title refers both to the weather and to the pain of the conversation the young woman is having with a lover who is leaving her. "First Frost" fails to capture the attention of the young men on the train because, as stanzas 6 and 7 indicate, they are too callous and self-absorbed to care either about the girl in the poem or about her flesh-and-blood double sitting nearby. This young woman is described in the eighth stanza as someone who has been sexually used and discarded by a number of men like the ones currently ignoring her. The accuracy of the poet's perception is demonstrated in the penultimate stanza as the young woman indicates that she has listened carefully and taken the poet's words to heart. In the final stanza, she detrains with a graceful and surprising leap that causes the other passengers to view her as remarkable: "Astounding everyone/ You leap to the platform—/ Purer than Beatrice." The closing vision, which alludes to the figure of Beatrice in Dante's *La divina commedia* (c. 1320; *The Divine Comedy,* 1802), inspires Voznesensky's poet to compose "The Last Train to Malakhovka," thus giving the work a circular structure.

Forms and Devices

Voznesensky is noted for his virtuosity, and in "The Last Train to Malakhovka" he takes full advantage of the flexibility that the Russian language affords, a flexibility not available in English. As a result, translation cannot reproduce some of the formal features of the original, yet Jean Garrigue's version remains faithful to the spirit of the Russian. Garrigue's translation re-creates a sense of a train moving over uneven patches of track and preserves the rich aural qualities through ornamental alliteration and assonance. For example, in the opening line, initial sounds in stressed syllables are repeated in the phrase "fancy flick knives," and the terminal assonance of "knives" and "smiles" in lines 1 and 2 suggests the rhyme pattern of the original Russian.

The repetition of sounds also softens the tone of the early verses, working against the dinginess and potential danger of the scene. Wordplay and punning inject a playfulness that corresponds to the possibility of excitement and liveliness described in the latter portion of the second stanza and indicate that the poet feels at ease with his traveling companions. When he begins to recite "First Frost," the rear of the train is noisy, "where jigs/ A hubbub of drunken strings." The inattentiveness of the young men in his audience is explained as resulting from "rackets of their own," alluding both to the noise they are making and to their own, most likely shady, interests.

These playful qualities, combined with some commonplace description, such as "Cigarette butts, a litter of/ Spat-out sunflower seeds," disguise the sophistication of the structure. The poem's syntax underscores the relationships among the passengers, who fall into two distinct groups but share a common destination. The unsavory-looking riders are introduced in fragmented phrases, while the hardworking, law-abiding people appear in completed clauses; however, a vague pronoun reference and inverted construction in the opening line of the second stanza connect them: "They're all nodding, our workaday citizens." The antecedent of "They" first appears to include the rough gang from the first verse, which is composed entirely of phrases and ends in an ellipsis; however, it is "our workaday citizens" who are nodding—the ruffians are wide awake. The initial ambiguity connects, if only for a brief time, the separate groups, and hints at thematic significance.

Syntax in the seventh stanza is revealing as well. The young woman who will emerge as a major figure by the poem's end is introduced almost incidentally: "this one here/ All bangs, plastered with powder." The indefinite pronoun "one" and the subordinate construction in which she is described illustrate her insignificance. The terminal stop at the end of the line cuts off further description—unlike lines ending in ellipses, which suggest unfinished thought—so that the woman is left faceless; the words "plastered with powder" have nothing to describe but the indefinite pronoun "one" from the previous line.

The most dramatic structural device in "The Last Train to Malakhovka"is the description of Voznesensky's "First Frost," which, significantly, is never quoted exactly. In the latter work "A girl is freezing in a telephone booth," "Glass beads in her ears," and winter can be seen "glittering on her cheek"; in "The Last Train to Malakhovka" the poet recites a piece "About a girl who's crying/ In the glassy night of a telephone booth," while the girl who is listening to him is "shining with tears" in the overheated coach. Because the imagery is similar but not identical, the two poems maintain a distinct identity, although the meaning of each is changed by the existence of the other.

Themes and Meanings

As Voznesensky skillfully demonstrates with "The Last Train to Malakhovka," the meaning of his work reaches outside of the boundary of a single poem. His individual poems function as discrete units, but they are interconnected, and meaning expands from specific to general. Not surprisingly then, the poet's particular concern with the sexual objectification of women, reflected in his sympathetic treatment of the young girl in "The Last Train to Malakhovka," is but one manifestation of what he views as a general depersonalization afflicting all who live in technologically advanced societies. In this poem, as in much of his other work, trains represent the ill effects of mechanization, speeding in a single, predetermined direction, physically separating humans from the natural world and from one another, and finally threatening individual identity. Images of separation and fragmentation abound: the segregation of passengers, the failure of the poet to gain the attention of the young men, the namelessness and facelessness of the young woman. It is this fragmentation, however, not human nature itself, that accounts for the asocial behavior of the young men on the train, their potential for violence, and their disregard for others.

In spite of the sordid world and sorry beings he depicts in poems such as "The Last Train to Malakhovka," Voznesensky seems to believe that humans are essentially good and that poetry can reveal that goodness. Poetry can work against depersonalization and fragmentation by reasserting the individualized voice. However, to speak authentically, the poet must continually seek new forms of expression, lest the uniqueness of his voice be stifled by lack of variation. By maintaining his individuality in this way, the poet can identify safely with others without loss of self. At this point, he or she can communicate effectively. Even a simple verse such as "First Frost" can succeed because the poet's sentiment is genuine. Although the young thugs in the train cannot appreciate his sincerity, the young woman who does is transformed, and her transformation causes a reaction from the others.

The optimism of the poem's closing is qualified, however, by the circularity of the structure and by the fleetingness of the image. Poetry may cleanse and revitalize, but the effects are immediate and temporary. The poet's work is ongoing, and in this respect he is much like the "workaday citizens" on the train. Neither heroic figure nor tortured soul, Voznesensky's poet retains his ordinariness and, with it, the connection to his fellow travelers essential to the success of his mission.

K Edgington

LATIN NIGHT AT THE PAWNSHOP

Author: Martín Espada (1957-   )
Type of poem: Lyric
First published: 1990, in *Rebellion Is the Circle of a Lover's Hands*

The Poem

Martín Espada's "Latin Night at the Pawnshop" is a short lyric poem of nine lines divided into two stanzas. The first stanza consists of merely three lines, while the second stanza consists of six. Under the title, Espada indicates that the poem is of a particular time and place by stating "Chelsea, Massachusetts/ Christmas, 1987." The poem was inspired by a specific event, a specific vision. Espada happened to be passing the "Liberty Loan/ pawnshop" in Chelsea, Massachusetts, on the Thursday before Christmas, and a flood of images rushed into his consciousness. It was his usual routine to walk from his law office to the district court in Chelsea. Thursdays at the district court are considered "eviction day." On this particular day, Espada took the time to look in the pawnshop window and noticed the musical instruments inside. It would take months, however, before Espada was able to turn this mere glance into a moving poem.

The opening stanza introduces "The apparition of a salsa band." This salsa band is "gleaming in the Liberty Loan/ pawnshop window." Born to Puerto Rican immigrants himself, the poet is struck by the instruments that are in the window. There is a "Golden trumpet," a "silver trombone," "congas," "maracas," and a "tambourine." These instruments made vibrant music in the past, but they are now relegated to a pawnshop in Massachusetts with "price tags dangling." For the poet, the price tags conjure up the frightful and sad image of a "city morgue ticket/ on a dead man's toe." The poem ends with this image. The instruments have had the life taken out of them. A whole culture has been discarded and shown little or no respect.

"Latin Night at the Pawnshop" is only one of the gripping poems that Espada included in his collection *Rebellion Is the Circle of a Lover's Hands*. Espada and Camilo Pérez-Bustillo also translated the poems of the collection into Spanish in order to make *Rebellion Is the Circle of a Lover's Hands* a bilingual collection. In the author's note, Espada expresses his hope that by translating the poems into Spanish he could "communicate with the peoples of Latin America" and also "bridge the gap between those Latinos . . . who speak English . . . and those . . . who speak predominantly Spanish."

Recognized as one of the leading activist poets in the United States, Espada speaks forcefully through his poems concerning the inherent value of all Hispanic cultures and their rich histories. In "Latin Night at the Pawnshop," he has taken the chance occasion of passing by a pawnshop during the Christmas season and universalized the all-too-painful fate of much of Latino expression in the vast Anglo world of North America.

Forms and Devices

Throughout *Rebellion Is the Circle of a Lover's Hands*, Espada writes powerfully about how hardworking Latinos have toiled without much recognition for their efforts. He also writes movingly and boldly about how discrimination has forced millions of Latinos to live in poverty and to not fully realize their potentials. The opening image of a salsa band as an "apparition" gives "Latin Night at the Pawnshop" a dreamlike introduction. Knowing that the poem takes place during the Christmas season only adds to its mystical nature. While the traditional images of Christmas usually include carolers or Santa Claus spreading good cheer, Espada is struck by a salsa band having been relegated to a pawnshop.

To the poet, this band is "gleaming" in the window. For one reason or another, these beautiful instruments have been discarded. Someone may have been in desperate need of ready cash and, therefore, had to part with one or more of these precious musical instruments. The trumpet may be "Golden" and the trombone may be "silver," but it is of no matter at this point in time, at this particular Christmas season. There is no telling how long the instruments have had to languish in the pawnshop, but they were perhaps pawned so that a Latino family could have a holiday meal, pay the rent, or bail a loved one out of jail. While these speculations may seem wild or off-base to the reader, these are the typical issues that Espada raises in his poems, deals with as a lawyer, and struggles with as a Latino activist in contemporary North America.

In the first stanza of "Latin Night at the Pawnshop" the poet tells the reader what he thinks he sees in the "Liberty Loan" pawnshop. The stanza ends with a colon, and the second stanza presents the list of instruments included in this salsa band. The reader can imagine how loud they would be if given half a chance. In their present situation though, the instruments all have "price tags dangling" from them. It is a tragedy that these instruments must remain stuck inside a pawnshop. By introducing the simile of the price tags hanging "like the city morgue ticket/ on a dead man's toe," Espada makes this tragedy all the more gripping. This is an extremely jarring image: The instruments, the music, and the past are all dead. The instruments once were part of a vibrant salsa band that brought joy to those who played and heard them, but they are now no more than an apparition or ghost of that former band. Like so many body parts that once made up a living person, the trumpet, the trombone, and the other instruments are now merely dead reminders of what they once were.

Themes and Meanings

Espada is a poet, a lawyer, and a teacher. No matter what professional hat Espada has worn, he always has strived to fight for social justice. His first book of poetry, *The Immigrant Iceboy's Bolero*, was published in 1982. With each critically acclaimed collection of poems that followed, Espada continues to give voice to the oppressed Latinos who have struggled to carve out a life for themselves and their families. *Rebellion Is the Circle of a Lover's Hands* won both the 1990 PEN/Revson Award and the Paterson Poetry Prize. "Latin Night at the Pawnshop" is only one of the poignant free verse poems that fill the collection. Never shrill or pedantic, the poet paints vivid portraits of Latinos who have been wronged in one way or another. While political poetry can tend to put readers on edge, Espada's success as a poet stems from his ability to tell the human story behind any tragedy. He stated that he does not wish for anger to "overwhelm a poem or group of poems." While intensity of feeling is one of Espada's strengths as a poet, he never goes about hammering a reader over the head with a strident diatribe that would only do a disservice to the subject matter.

Rebellion Is the Circle of a Lover's Hands is divided into two sections: "If Only History Were Like Your Hands" and "To Skin the Hands of God." "Latin Night at the Pawnshop" is one of the twenty-two poems that can be found in the first section. As with other poems of this section, including "Revolutionary Spanish Lesson," "The New Bathroom Policy at English High School," and "Shaking Hands with Mongo," Espada details a personal history, a personal story to which any attentive reader can relate. The political poet must walk a fine line in order not to lose the very readers he wishes to inform and educate.

The title "Latin Night at the Pawnshop" introduces a humorous tone to the poem. It may be a dark humor that takes a morbid turn by the end of the poem, but the impact is enhanced by this tone. The seemingly insignificant fate of various musical instruments has been expanded to speak for an entire culture driven to death by either intent or neglect. The Christmas message of goodwill toward all seemingly has fallen on deaf ears. In "Latin Night at the Pawnshop," Espada convincingly conveys to the reader through clear direct language that one should pay respect to all cultural expressions no matter how foreign or removed they are from one's own.

Jeffry Jensen

LE MONOCLE DE MON ONCLE

Author: Wallace Stevens (1879-1955)
Type of poem: Meditation
First published: 1918; collected in *Harmonium*, 1923

The Poem

"Le Monocle de Mon Oncle" is one of the longer poems in Wallace Stevens's first collection, *Harmonium*. It consists of twelve eleven-line stanzas of flexible blank verse. Its title has multiple reverberations, as its sound play and its French title distance the poem from the author. Readers are asked to accept that they are looking through the uncle's monocle and not the poet's own eyes. The title turns the poem into a kind of dramatic monologue, except that the poem's emphasis is not on characterizing the speaker, as is generally the case in a true dramatic monologue, but on posing and answering, or attempting to answer, philosophical questions. It presents a persona who is aging, disappointed in love, and skeptical about religion. This world-weary speaker explores the nature of desire and inquires how desire translates into art.

Beginning with a mocking speech, perhaps part of a quarrel, the narrator examines his relationship with a woman, presumably his wife. He proceeds to examine the nature of the man-woman situation in general. His tone is of fatigue, disappointment, and withdrawal. He describes an apparent rejection and compares the present with the past: "The radiant bubble that she was." He is aware of how old he has become and of how he is edging toward death: "I am a man of fortune greeting heirs;/ For it has come that thus I greet the spring." The poem develops a meditation on sex and death as the speaker muses on his worn-out love, the aging of the body, and sexual confusion, and wonders how these things relate to the creation of art. Sexual "verve" is a source of poetry, but what if that fails? What is left for the artist or poet to draw on?

The speaker concludes that the waxing and waning of sexuality is not all there is. He claims, "There is a substance in us that prevails," but this "basic slate" remains undefined and not entirely satisfactory. It is true that there is another wellspring for art besides sexual longing that is longer lasting: metaphysical desire. This longing too is unsatisfiable, and the speaker discusses the lack of credibility in traditional religion and compares the two kinds of desire: "The honey of heaven may or may not come,/ But that of earth both comes and goes at once." Picturing himself and his love as "two golden gourds" overripe and ready to rot on the vine, he considers the irony of the human situation: Signs of earth's fruitfulness are in evidence, but this kind of fulfillment is not for the aging; on the other hand, metaphysical fulfillment remains beyond his grasp. He retreats into resignation, pondering what growing old has taught him and how different his perspective is now from what it was when he was young.

It is significant that this tired philosopher appears in Stevens's first collection, accompanied by Crispin of "The Comedian as the Letter C," who is also a played-out questioner but one who has been fully satisfied in sex and love—to the extent that these elements of his life took the place of art. It would seem that neither indulgence nor denial was fully effective in producing artistic creativity.

Forms and Devices

Blank verse is a suitable form for this philosophical poem; its division into twelve eleven-lines stanzas provides a sense of order and completion. The rhythm is flexible rather than metronome-like. The casual, conversational rhythm helps to develop the character of the speaker as well as to present the issues. Figurative language abounds. In fact, the poem is a series of metaphors presented and then explained self-consciously by the narrator. Since this is a poem of meditation by an invented character, the metaphors show the speaker's rather precise, pedantic way of looking at the world. They are often parables to explain the positions explored in the poem. The speaker describes angels riding mules down from the heavens, while "centurions guffaw and beat/ Their shrilling tankards on the table-boards." He then explicates: "This parable, in sense, amounts to this," the explication being the passage quoted above about the "honey of heaven" as contrasted with "that of earth." The motifs in the poem underscore its theme of mortality: fruit, ripe and rotting; a frog, suggesting the human grotesque; and a mystical tree, which, in its self-replenishment, may suggest the inexhaustibility of nature.

The images of nature suggest the limits of the individual life in contrast with the life force. Images of fluttering birds appear in the last section, and these movements may suggest the helplessness and fragility of the individual. The birds also suggest a contrast between the perceptions of youth and age:

> A blue pigeon it is, that circles the blue sky,
> On sidelong wing, around and round and round.
> A white pigeon it is, that flutters to the ground,
> Grown tired of flight . . .

The blue pigeon may suggest participation, what Stevens calls in another title "The Pleasure of Merely Circulating." The white pigeon is aware of being "tired," and circling has changed to a downward fluttering. Both the images explained by the speaker and those left for the reader to unravel express the speaker's sense of exclusion and his need to find another source of self-definition besides sexual love. The speaker is self-mocking but nevertheless serious about his predicament.

Themes and Meanings

"Le Monocle de Mon Oncle" is a poem about art, as are, on one level, all of Stevens's poems. This poem explores the relationship of sexuality to art. The poem's argument is relatively direct, and meanings are not hidden in symbols or allusions. Some critics hold that Stevens's disappointment in marriage resulted in this poem. Stevens's engagement was protracted because he wanted to be in a position to support his beautiful fiancé Elsie Moll before marrying her. During his long engagement, he wrote her voluminous letters that showed her role as his muse; after the marriage, it is clear from the letters that passion cooled fast. Stevens apparently needed to admire his muse from afar. To have her fail as a source of poetry may have made him raise the issue of the role of sexual love in the creative drive and may have made him look for a substitute—not only for her but also for the whole male-female procreative-creative impulse. The speaker asks: What source can bring forth art, if not that one? How can older poets write at all, if they are not impelled by the same energy that brings them to their lovers' arms? Although Stevens may have separated himself from his speaker with a French title, these are his questions too. What about metaphysical desire as the replacement for physical desire? Although metaphysical longing is powerful, it is uncertain of fulfillment. The "honey of heaven" is too vague and unreliable. Nevertheless, it is desire, whatever the object, that brings poetry into being. Unfulfilled desire is the underground stream that also feeds this poem.

Whether or not Stevens's own relationship is the basis of the poem, it examines this issue persistently and obsessively. Like so many of his other works it is elegiac in tone, perhaps regretting a remembered or imagined period of full participation in love and in life. The reward of aging—wisdom—is not sufficient to replace youthful drive, although wisdom itself contributes to art. The poetry of age has wisdom, while the poetry of youth has verve; it seems impossible to have both. This problem is one cause for the speaker's ironic resignation.

"Le Monocle de Mon Oncle" is one of several poems in which Stevens creates older, somewhat pedantic speakers to reflect on art and its relationship to life. The tone of self-mockery may seem to undercut the conclusions reached by the narrators, but even this affected self-awareness may be considered a part of the artist's perspective, especially in Stevens's early poems. The speaker of "Le Monocle de Mon Oncle" may be seen as a counterpart to T. S. Eliot's ineffective suitor in "The Love Song of J. Alfred Prufrock," except that "Mon Oncle" has the wisdom to look beyond his own insecurities in an attempt to make sense of his situation and find a valid source for his art.

Janet McCann

LEARNING A DEAD LANGUAGE

Author: W. S. Merwin (1927-   )
Type of poem: Lyric
First published: 1956, in *Green with Beasts*

The Poem

W. S. Merwin's "Learning a Dead Language" begins with a stark and disconcerting statement that takes the breath from one's lungs: "There is nothing for you to say." The poem ends with the same statement. In between, the reader is told how to learn a dead language. One must listen and listen again, and remember even when what one remembers doesn't make sense. A language can only make sense, the poem implies, all at once. Imagine staring at Egyptian hieroglyphs before the Rosetta Stone was found, staring and staring again, memorizing the physical forms of the hieroglyphs but having no idea what they might mean. Then one clue makes sense of it all.

In second person throughout, "Learning a Dead Language" almost reads like instructions for a Buddhist spiritual exercise: "you must/ learn first to listen . . . you must therefore/ learn to be still when it is imparted,/ and, though you may not yet understand, to remember." In this discipline, one is told to practice one of the most strenuous forms of self-denial, that of silence, total and long, perhaps the lifetime of silence practiced by mystics both Eastern and Western. It is within the sound chamber of such a silence that one learns to listen. The poem suggests that what one hears when one listens is the dark, inarticulate presence of this dead language. This language constitutes a total order, a sense of self and world, that is unattainable until one learns the art of hearing a language that does not speak.

This will not be easy. The poem says that one must understand the whole language before one can understand any of its parts. Unfortunately, though, one "can learn only a part at a time," and to understand the least part, one has to "perceive/ the whole grammar in all its accidence/ and all its system."

It appears that learning this dead language might, then, be impossible, and it is characteristic of Merwin's poetry that it asks the reader to abide within such paradoxes. In this, he is a mystic poet, evoking the dark that is light, the silence that speaks, the knowing that is unknowing, the enterprise that goes nowhere. The poem promises, only faintly, that silence and long listening may finally result in comprehension. At most, one might hope to hear the passion that once made the dead language live and thus bring oneself into partial accord with a form of wisdom that is inconceivable within the languages that now circulate the globe.

Forms and Devices

The most notable stylistic feature of Merwin's "Learning a Dead Language" is its remarkable flatness of tone, its lack of passion. The poem develops as a set of direct, cool, almost leaden statements. The deadness of tone seems deliberate, adopted to support one of the poem's chief thematic concerns, which is that the grammatical death of a language is also the demise of its formative, life-giving passion. The language of the poem tries—by means of its lack of tone and its lack of color, image, sensuous detail of any sort—to suggest the absence of this vitalizing passion.

Stylistically, the mode of direct statement is very different from Merwin's later distinctive style, which is oblique rather than direct, evocative rather than assertive, associative rather than sequential, and syntactically malleable rather than firm. Every aspect of style in "Learning a Dead Language" serves to make the language of the poem rigid, hieratic, and devitalized, almost as if "it," this language of the poem, *were* the dead language, awaiting the rebirth of one more passionate and more whole. The poem is, if anything, forbidding, like a closed iron door, challenging the reader not to enter.

Similarly, the structure of the poem is stolid and regular, unlike the "open forms" of Merwin's later work. Merwin, in fact, was one of those who tried to revive and reformulate what modernist poets called "free verse." For many contemporary poets, Merwin's was the most significant voice in defining the idea and practice of "open form" verse—poetry that was built upon temporal air rather than ideas of symmetry, regularity, measure, permanence, poetry that was composed of breath, emptiness, inconclusion. In distinguishing itself from modernist practice, which cultivated and parodied "cultural voice," Merwin's poetry sought an impossible voice, the voice prior to and uninformed by culture, the voice of pained and basic being in the world. This, primarily, is why he is often called a primitivist poet.

"Learning a Dead Language" is, unlike Merwin's signature work, filled with symmetry and regularity. The stanzas are all sestets, six lines long; the line lengths are regular and keep very close to iambic pentameter. Each stanza, after the first, begins with a clause that involves remembrance, usually its salvific and formative functions, so that there is a kind of refrain or chant in the poem of "remember, remember, remember." Finally, the ending of the poem returns to the beginning: "There is nothing for you to say." This circular structure tends to close the poem. Such strong closure is very unlike Merwin's later work, which usually ends on a halftone, a faint or indeterminate utterance or image.

It may, however, be possible to read the ending of the poem more openly: If one has listened and learned, one is full and has no need to speak. The repetition may, then, be repetition with a difference.

Themes and Meanings

Though stylistically, "Learning a Dead Language" is a work in the formal style of Merwin's long and accomplished apprenticeship (in his first four books, he masters and exhausts formal style), it very much prefigures his major thematic concerns—his preoccupation with silence, with the inefficacies and failure of language and his desire to find a purer, more poetic, less implicated and virulent language than those that now flow from human tongues.

When Merwin evokes language in his later poems, it is often the "language" of silence rather than that of words. "What is the silence?" he asks in "Some Last Questions," and the answer is, "As though it had a right to more." In "The Cold Before the Moonrise" (another poem from *The Lice*, 1967), he says he would like to speak the language "Of frost stirring among its/ Stars like an animal asleep," a "language" that is wordless, to be sure, and almost inaudible.

Although "Learning a Dead Language" can be described quite literally as a poem about reviving a language that is no longer current, it can also be understood as a poem about discovering or rediscovering Edenic or Utopian language. Many of the poems in Merwin's later work are poems about finding or recovering a language that, so to speak, "really works." This language would be one that seems really to name the passions and the things of this world, and holds them without harm. It would be a language that is, in a way, disempowered, incapable of abusing the world and its creatures, and perhaps even dysfunctional, incapable of being reduced to communication or information, incapable of being commercialized and consumed.

There is in Merwin's work, both early and late, a deep reluctance to speak. Speech is so often to the side of what one might say; speech is so often banal, ugly, manipulative, and, in poetry, exquisite but impoverished.

In "Learning a Dead Language" and in all of his poems that ruminate on language or the silence that language violates, W. S. Merwin is very much a voice of the twentieth century. While many contemporary voices speak of the joyous delights of language and how one might play with it, Merwin speaks of the grief that accompanies it.

Anne Shifrer

LEARNING EXPERIENCE

Author: Marge Piercy (1936-   )
Type of poem: Narrative
First published: 1969, in *Hard Loving*

The Poem

"Learning Experience" focuses on a boy who is about to take an examination to determine whether he will be subject to being drafted into the United States Army. The twenty-two-line poem is written in free verse that conforms to no predetermined rules and follows no particular meter. It is one long, unified stanza. The title of the poem is ironic. The boy, who is sitting in a classroom in Gary, Indiana, is supposed to be "learning" how "to think a little on demand," but he is bored, and the teacher's lessons on "dangling participles" are not going to teach him much about life. In the world outside he will undergo a learning experience, certainly, but one that has little to do with "French irregular verbs" and "Jacksonian democracy," with the material listed on an English or history syllabus. The speaker of the poem is a teacher who has come "out on the train from Chicago" to Gary to teach English grammar.

History forms a backdrop to Marge Piercy's poem and to the plight of the boy in the Gary classroom. In 1965 President Lyndon Johnson authorized General William Westmoreland, commander of U.S. troops in Vietnam, to commit soldiers to the battlefield. Therefore, at the time of this poem, American soldiers are fighting in Vietnam, and more young men are being drafted into the Army every day. The second crucial historical aspect is that in March, 1951, President Harry Truman had issued an executive order deferring the draft for college students of adequate scholastic standing. There would be no second chance for those who failed the college aptitude test that would permit a student deferment.

In line 11, halfway through the poem, it is revealed that "The time of tomorrow's draft exam is written on the board." This fact points to, and explains, the final line of the poem, which says that tomorrow the boy "will try and fail his license to live." Because the boy has been too bored to learn enough in school, he will fail the exam and ultimately will be drafted into "Today's Action Army," qualifying for an education in "death that hurts."

Forms and Devices

One of Piercy's primary interests in delineating history is to make the lessons of the past part of a learning experience that prevents the repetition of past horrors. History can be a kind of moral instruction. The significance of place—where the boy is, physically, socially, and politically—is crucial to the poem. A series of nine prepositional phrases using the word "in" points to where he is: "in the classroom/ in Gary, in the United States, in NATO, in SEATO/ in the thing-gorged belly of the sociobeast,/ in fluorescent light in slowly moving time/ in [thick] boredom."

In the poem's twenty-two lines, twenty-two prepositional phrases attest the weight of the preposition "in" in the poem. To be "in" something is to be contained, and perhaps, as here, trapped. He is trapped by the situation of his life, which has left him few options. Were the war not raging, he might go to work in the steel mills that "consumed his father." As it is, if he had been more interested or studied harder in school, he might be able to attend college and avoid the draft; he will not have this chance. Yet academic pursuits are shown as unappealing as well; a simile describes classroom boredom as "thick and greasy as vegetable shortening."

Marge Piercy refers to Gary, Indiana, in her first novel, *Going Down Fast* (1969). Here, early in her career, she taught English composition and questioned the merit of a learning experience such as that experienced by the boy. Piercy notes that Gary, named for a judge who acquired a reputation for hangings, was a steel-mill town "you never forget you came from" (*Going Down Fast*).

NATO and SEATO are both treaty alliances to which the United States belonged (the North Atlantic Treaty Organization and Southeast Asia Treaty Organization, respectively). Both were established largely to stop the international spread of communism. Being "in" these organizations widens the trap containing the boy far beyond Gary and even the United States. Moreover, the boy is "in the thing-gorged belly of the sociobeast"—the sociobeast emblematic of a capitalist, consumer-oriented society that has turned into a monster and begun consuming its own material and members. It may remind one of the "military-industrial complex," a term often used in the 1960's to refer to the complicity between industry and the "war machine" dedicated to fighting the Vietnam War.

Would it be better, the poem asks, to be alive in a world of scholastic obfuscation or to be drafted into the Army and sent to Vietnam, the Dominican Republic, or Guatemala? The juxtaposition of an education represented by a curriculum of lifeless facts with that of the instruction provided by the Army defines the complexity of the "learning experience" portrayed in the poem.

Themes and Meanings

The central issue in the poem is what constitutes a worthwhile education or "learning experience." The poem examines the teaching role of history, but Piercy also raises a number of points regarding education. Classroom learning often seems to have little relevance to the world outside or to what a young adult will need to know to thrive in that world. Classroom education often seems to consist of exercises such as mastering the conjugation of French irregular verbs before students have yet experienced life, but it is also an attempt to get them to "think a little on demand."

The boy in the poem, and thousands of others like him in the late 1960's, because of their lack of interest in the classroom, were literally "bored to death." Perhaps the education system, stuffing him with "lectures on small groups" in classrooms with "green boards and ivory blinds," has failed them. Piercy's interest in history and in the process of education led her to depict a learning experience in which established systems fail to preserve what Americans value in life. It could be argued that young people, like the boy in Gary, are America's finest resource and that they are of more value than steel.

What the boy is learning in the classroom has ill-prepared him for the experience of living his life. The classroom—and the Army, for that matter—may elicit learning experiences of a type, but those experiences cannot truly be equated with education. The series of prepositional phrases allied in the poem point to dead-end places: the classroom, the city of Gary, the United States of America, NATO, SEATO. All are leading the boy to "Today's Action Army." On the other hand, academic success would offer the boy a draft deferment but would give him in return a life of deathlike boredom.

Sue B. Walker

LEDA AND THE SWAN

Author: William Butler Yeats (1865-1939)
Type of poem: Sonnet
First published: 1924, in *The Cat and the Moon and Certain Poems*

The Poem

"Leda and the Swan" is a sonnet that, like the Italian or Petrarchan sonnet, divides into an octave that presents a narrative and a sestet that comments on the narrative. Although the rhyme scheme of the first eight lines follows the typical Shakespearean form (*abab, cdcd*), the next six lines follow the expected Petrarchan (*efg, efg*) rhyme scheme.

The octave essentially describes the god Zeus's forced and unannounced impregnation of Leda and her ineffectual human efforts at resisting this sudden implosion in her "loosening thighs." The sestet's first sentence has been called William Butler Yeats's most brilliant sentence and even the capstone of his magnificent *The Tower* (1928). This line reveals the consequent engendering of the Greek Age of Homer (but Aeschylus, Euripides, and even Vergil also profit), because springing from this union of the king of the gods and the mortal woman were both Helen of Troy, who caused the Trojan War, and Clytemnestra, who slew the returning, conquering Agamemnon at the war's end—primary themes of the Greek Age. The second sentence of the sestet poses a question not so relevant to the Greeks, who, thinking often of women as booty, rather accepted the inexorable, blind run of fate and the inevitability of tragic human destiny. The poem's final question, however, is highly relevant to Yeats's ultimate meaning:

> Being so caught up,
> So mastered by the brute blood of the air,
> Did she put on his knowledge with his power
> Before the indifferent beak could let her drop?

The fated and tragic character of the Greek mentality, in which superhuman deities (often all too human in their emotional rages of jealousy, anger, vengeance, and lust) would sport with nearly helpless human creatures, is immediately clear and powerfully felt at the opening of the poem: "A sudden blow." Zeus never courted Leda, never announced his coming (as, say, God told Mary through His archangel Gabriel), and never spoke a word throughout. The enormous tension is heightened by the seeming casualness of the nearly regular iambic pentameter of the first line. "Great wings" creates a midline spondee (a double-accented foot), in order to stress Zeus's overwhelming power. Leda, as a mere mortal (and a woman), has no active role in this drama: She suffers the divine play of human destiny to be acted out through the medium of her frail body. Like the Genesis story in which the woman causes the fall from grace, this is a male-dominated myth. Yeats, with his leading rhetorical questions, however, can at the same time retain the inextricable bond between mortal beauty and its tragic passing even while he transcends the contexts of both the Greek and the Judeo-Christian myths.

Forms and Devices

The sonnet's extreme precision allows much to be said and implied, and Yeats further compacts this poem's terseness by using synecdoche: Only the "wings," "webs," and "bill" are attacking; only Leda's "fingers," "nape," and "thighs" are resisting. Only a "wall," "roof," and "tower" represent the Greek siege of Troy, though it was a war waged for ten years to recover Helen. The richness of the symbols, especially as they function organically within Yeats's overall poetic context, is astounding.

References to Helen of Troy, in particular, and to many enduring myths of the Greek, Celtic, Christian, Buddhist, or Byzantine eras abound in Yeats's poems. Because the central dedication of all Yeats's work as a poet-seer (the true bard of human culture) was always to the mystical, he was drawn constantly to the deep, still waters of humankind's most profound illuminations, which he tirelessly labored all his life to mold into a unity of vision. The framework upon which he would weave this unified tapestry of mythology was provided by *A Vision* (1925, 1937); however, the mystical "voices" who communicated the ideas of *A Vision* (through the medium of his wife Georgie's automatic writing) guided him carefully so that he would not take the finger (of the system) for the moon (of the mythological poetry): "We have come," they insisted, "to give you metaphors for poetry."

Yeats's *A Vision* is an elaborate system of the cycles of human ages, with archetypal as well as individual incarnations within the various gyres—both Helen, sprung from Leda, and Yeats's own beloved Maud Gonne, for example, appear in phase fourteen of the "Phases of the Moon." Yet grasping all the terrifying, vague features of Yeats's system may not be as important in this case as simply catching the large clues Yeats offers at the start of the final book of *A Vision*. There he explains that the present time, 1925, is nearing the peak of one "Historical Cone" of the gyre (the spiraling wheel of time that waxed from the year zero to the year 1050 and wanes to its nadir in the twentieth century). The text of this fifth book of *A Vision* starts off with the next critical clue, "One must bear in mind that the Christian Era, like the two thousand years, let us say, that went before it, is an entire wheel." As if to be certain that the complex gyres, wheels, phases, and cones of his visionary symbology do not intrude upon the poetry, Yeats calls the final book of *A Vision* "Dove or Swan" and reprints there, as a kind of epigraph to the final chapter, the entire text of "Leda and the Swan."

Yeats means for one to see "Leda and the Swan" in the broad context of *A Vision* if one is to understand its meaning: As the Swan-God's impregnation of Leda initiated the Greek age, so did the Dove-God's impregnation of Mary initiate the Christian age. Since mythic ages last about two thousand years, this age must be on the cusp of a new revelation—an idea Yeats explores in "The Second Coming."

Themes and Meanings

In Yeats's mythological poetry, the Christian revelation is not the only divinely inspired one; it is not unique. It does, however, share an honored place in concert with the world's other great religious myths—though its truth is not everlasting. Things thought to be true for too long (for Yeats, that time is about two thousand years) eventually can no longer be believed: Myth is symbols in motion, for Yeats as for William Blake, and the symbols must always be renewed. After their validity is exhausted, myths undergo change, flux, and rebirth. Indeed, the very heart of the prevailing myth contains the seeds of its own destruction. That is one reason why "Leda and the Swan," depicting the very inauguration of the predestined Greek era, concludes with the one question whose real answer is beyond the pale of the Greek imagination: Could Leda fathom Zeus's knowledge before being dropped? Perhaps more to the point, can the poem's reader comprehend the heart mysteries here? The real answer is beyond the merely logical categories of yes and no, since the real poem transcends the categories of the myths it utilizes to lead the reader to an inward vision. One might assume that no Greek would imagine Leda, being but a vessel for that august era, could "put on his knowledge with his power." The question simply would not pertain.

In sharp contrast to Leda, the Virgin Mary must have understood much, since she was given a choice: the Christian Annunciation is like a proposal, and Mary had free will in accepting the role of being the mother of God because Christianity cherishes informed free will as the Greeks cherished fated human destiny. Unlike the "brute blood of the air," the Dove of the Christian age is holy, aphysical, and otherworldly. To even think of the Virgin's "loosening thighs" would be sacrilegious, and any question of her sexual arousal would simply not pertain. There are built-in parameters, limitations, and presuppositions in every mythology, yet therein lies the nemesis of the Christian dispensation: Under Plato's influence, the body (the "mere flesh") for the Christian myth is all but irrelevant. In the end, the reign of the Dove, like the reign of the Swan, must pass away—for no myth can embody all truth, and certainly not for all time. If Leda, as mortal life, as vehicle for beauty that is inherently tragic, and as aesthetic affirmation, is momentarily thought of as the poet, the artificer of eternity, the bard of wisdom, then the implosion of the divine into the human can be understood in a yet more profound manner: as Annunciation not divorced from Epiphany.

Yeats intends ultimately to share with his reader the visionary truth of this conjunction of the divine and the human: It is not merely a symbol of what has already happened historically at Bethlehem or beneath some Olympian cloud, for both Dove and Swan pass away. The fortunate reader of Yeats, however, if not prejudiced against the brute flesh or biased in favor of the fleshless spirit, can, by meditating upon these symbols that pass away, attain the visionary moment of knowledge and power, the timeless now where (as Yeats described it in "Among School Children") the dancer need not be distinguished from the dance.

Paul R. La Chance

LEGAL FICTION

Author: William Empson (1906-1984)
Type of poem: Meditation
First published: 1928; collected in *Poems*, 1935

The Poem
   "Legal Fiction" is a closely argued sixteen-line poem of four quatrains. A legal fiction is any point in law which is deemed to be true even though in reality it either is a nonsensical point or has no existence. The legal fiction involved here is one of property ownership. The poem explains that in buying any piece of land, the space below and above it are included in the sale, being deemed to be part of the property. That is to say, property has a three-dimensional existence rather than a two-dimensional one.
   William Empson links this fiction to a cosmic and mythic view of space: the space below extends logically to the center of the earth, where every radius ("long spikes") must necessarily meet. "Your rights reach down where all owners meet." Mythically, this is where hell has been placed, at least in the traditional "three-decker" universe. Similarly, the space above extends logically *ad infinitum.* Mythically again, this is where heaven is situated. From a mythical viewpoint, then, the legal fiction of property ownership states that "you own land in Heaven and Hell."
   Empson then extends this fictional concept of property ownership in two ways. First, he defines the geometrical shape of this legal configuration as a cone or "growing sector," with its point at the earth's center and the top "growing" as space extends outward (or upward). Second, he considers the earth's rotation about its axis: "your spun farm's root still on that axis dwells," where "still" could mean ambiguously "continuously" or "without movement," the central point of a turning sphere being deemed not to rotate. The fact, however, is that "Earth's axis varies"; there is no still center after all, so that the whole cone is not fixed, but "wavers . . . at the end."
   In this tightly argued meditation, the conclusion is built around three contradictions or paradoxes arising from this fiction. First, in putting "short stakes" around their property, owners are actually buying up rights to boundless volume: They are getting much more than they bargained for. Second, far from buying something fixed, in which to settle down, a property owner is "a nomad yet," because the bought space is continuously moving. Finally, in buying something material, owners are actually buying into the mythical.
   The image that Empson leaves in conclusion is that of a lighthouse whose beams penetrate the darkness of space. They form a cone, just like the shape of the property. The beam flashes "like Lucifer, through the firmament." The figure of Lucifer, traditionally a name for Satan or the devil, thus forces the theological dimension of heaven and hell into the reader's consciousness. Life is less certain, less solid, than humans suppose. They are inevitably involved with questions of ultimacy, of final judgment,

and, however uncertainly and tentatively, they must acknowledge the depths and heights of which human life consists.

Forms and Devices

Although he wrote during a period of modernist and experimental verse, Empson's poems remain traditional in stanza form and rhyme scheme. Here the quatrain form is used, each stanza being clearly completed by a period. The alternating rhymes are marked as clearly. The lines have a basic iambic pentameter, but the demands of Empson's density of expression typically push extra spondees into the line. Thus there is no easy rhythmical reading of the verse: It has to be read in controlled speech rhythms that move toward prose, and one must follow the punctuation carefully to retain the sense of the argument.

Both diction and imagery are interesting in the poem. The diction at first appears to be solidly legal: "law," "real estate," "flat" (apartment), "citizen," "owners," and especially "your rights." The use of "you" is typical of Empson; it challenges the reader much more directly than "we" or "they," and with "you" he is forcing the readers' rights on them. However, the materiality of this diction is constantly challenged—for example, by the oxymoron "the nomad citizen." (One may wonder how a nomad can own a "high flat," let alone overlook a piece of real estate.)

Although the "rights" mentioned here are apparently property rights rather than human rights, the two concepts merge "at earth's centre," where the separateness and exclusiveness of property rights are countered by the communality of human rights "down where all owners meet." In the end, too, "nomad" merges with the owner, since the space owned is so vast and is not actually fixed, but shifting. The stability that owning land brings is a delusion: People are still as much moving, restlessly even, whether they own property or not.

One strand of the imagery, as stated earlier, involves the traditional view of hell, earth, and heaven as three layers of existence. However, the cone image is more reminiscent of Dante's Inferno, where hell is depicted as a series of narrowing circles running from the surface of the earth down into its center. For Dante, only the worst villains are located at the lowest points, whereas Empson keeps the traditional image of the whole of hell being down there. The combination of the two schemes would seem impossible, but Empson's geometrical logic keeps the conceit powerfully alive.

The other strand of imagery transforms the cone into a beam of light, first from a lighthouse, finally reduced to a candle. A certain ambivalence lies in this light image, since the lighthouse flashes are compared to Lucifer, who, while originally an angel of light (literally the name means "light-bearer"), has become prince of darkness. In the same way, one's "central cone" is dark; one sees not the candle wavering but its shadow. What emerges from the poem is a sense of the darkness of space as well as the darkness of the earth's center: Human life only flashes or gleams intermittently in this darkness.

Themes and Meanings

Although he was still an undergraduate at Cambridge University when he wrote this poem, Empson's poetic formulation and style were already remarkably well developed. The dense intellectualism of its style and its avoidance of direct emotional expression could easily render the poem an exercise in that mental puzzlement often devoted to crosswords. However, the sheer philosophic power behind it gives it movement and coherence. In fact, "Legal Fiction" is one of the easier poems to decipher in Empson's first volume of poetry. In reading other poems in the volume, certain themes, motifs, and images emerge to help in the elucidation of any one poem.

For example, the excitement of space travel and the new theories of cosmology then current is evident, as in the poems "Camping Out" or "Dissatisfaction with Metaphysics," in which Empson writes: "New safe straight lines are finite though unbounded." As did the Metaphysical poets of the early seventeenth century, whom he much admired, he seeks to unify cosmological and other scientific discovery with metaphysics and theology through the medium of poetry. The poet thus becomes the polymath. Good examples of such poems are "This Last Pain," in which heaven and hell are featured frequently, and "The World's End," in which notions of the world's circularity are viewed cosmologically and eschatologically—no end comes to mean no purpose; everyone has to define their own.

Empson's theological interest is not that he has a religious faith—far from it—but that within literature, theology has been given mythical forms that people still need to explore mentally. As he stated in his study *The Structure of Complex Words* (1951), "myths are where incompatibles are joined." The key phrase in the poem is thus "real estate of mind." In Empson's poem "Letter 1," the cosmos becomes the typical image for inner space or being. The fear expressed in that poem is that both inner and outer space will merely be a void. In "Arachne" he writes similarly of "his gleaming bubble between void and void." In "Legal Fiction," that fear does not seem so urgent, and an allusion to a Jungian notion of a feared "shadow" self is not developed.

Throughout his life Empson conducted an argument with another intellectual poet whose imagination was cosmic, seventeenth century poet John Milton. Empson could quote Milton's epic *Paradise Lost* by heart. In his scholarly work *Milton's God* (1961), he takes issue with Milton's adherence to the traditional Christian view of heaven and hell and of God as the just, perfect Creator. For Empson they are still needed, in revised forms, as literary fictions to help people come to terms with an otherwise amoral, purposeless, though magnificent cosmos. Lucifer becomes the central ambiguous figure, as he was for William Blake and other Romantic poets.

"Legal Fiction," then, is part of Empson's attempt to remap the cosmos now that God is not there. The "contradiction and conflict" that Christopher Ricks saw as "the foundation of his poems" here is that of the human condition, in touch with and capable of acting in dimensions of good and evil, yet uncertain how to find a true and fixed place in which to own such possibilities.

David Barratt

LEGEND

Author: Hart Crane (1899-1932)
Type of poem: Lyric
First published: 1926, in *White Buildings*

The Poem

"Legend" is a short poem of five stanzas of varying length. It is written in free verse and has elegiac qualities evidenced in the seriousness of the emotional statement being made about its topic: Hart Crane's lament for a homosexual experience or (more likely) relationship recalled from his youth. His lost love has now become "legend" to him, and the poet ponders the meanings of this passing.

Although the poem is written in the first person, the poet refers explicitly to himself one time only; he creates an aura of subtlety about his work by couching most of the important statements in passive voice. Crane does not much address or even seem aware of the reader; it is as though he were whispering a secret to himself.

The first stanza is the shortest one, containing only two lines. Crane positions himself in front of a "silent" mirror where, it "is believed," that "Realities plunge in silence by . . ." The redundancy of having a "silent" mirror in which reality plunges in "silence" is effective. His topic, in both its sexual and emotional nature, requires an absence of noise not only to preclude discovery but also to provoke an intensity in thought. Crane does not say who does the "believing," but the believer is identified in the next stanza, where he is revealed to be the poet himself.

The reader does not yet know that the implicit "now" of the second stanza refers to the poet in the "noon," or middle age, of his life. He asserts that he is not "ready for repentance." He is not sorry, by any means, for the experience which will be labeled "legend" in the last line of the poem. Nor is he ready "to match regrets"—a statement which may indicate that his lover had regretted the relationship, though not repented it. "Kisses" remain the most operant part of reality, the "only worth all granting."

The third stanza begins with another operative passive, "It is to be learned." The poet then defines the "It" as "This cleaving and this burning"; that is, he describes the intertwined sexual and emotional makeup of the love. "Cleaving" suggests an attempt on the part of the poet to hold on to his personal legend; just as readily, "burning" indicates the intensity of this relationship both in terms of its culmination in the past and unquenchable desire for its return in the present. The "one who/ Spends out himself again" is another indirect reference to the poet himself and a reference to masturbation.

The next stanza is the most enigmatic in the poem. The "Twice and twice" is explainable, however, in terms of the reference to the "unwhispering . . . mirror" at the end of the stanza. The poet counts himself as one and his reflection in the mirror of his soul as two; his love is compounded because the identity of his legend-lover is also embodied in his own, so there are two such reflections; that is, they are "Twice and twice."

The important part of the last stanza is the concluding two lines, in which the poet explains the title of the poem by mentioning the "legend"—the personal love kept alive and made greater in love, emotion, and accomplishment in time. Crane attempts to expand the meaning of his expression by moving from the personal to the plural. He writes "for all those," and the personal legend of the title becomes, collectively, "their" legend.

Forms and Devices

The most important poetic devices in "Legend" are imagery and metaphor; each stanza contains elements that help the poet express the condition of his soul. The most important image is that of the mirror. Crane sees himself in the mirror, literally, but he also sees the reflection of his homosexual lover. Both are silent, and both are to be believed because the mirror does, in fact, reflect reality. The mirror is silent, "un-whispering," but it works to make "Realities" evident.

In the second stanza, the rather commonplace metaphor of the moth and the flame appears. A moth is attracted to the beauty of the flame which destroys it; such is the case of the poet and his legendary lover. The reflection in the mirror is both of himself and of his lover, but at least one of these will destroy the other. Later, in the fourth stanza, a "smoking souvenir" is mentioned, a reference to the burned remnants of the relationship. It is the result of the "burning" mentioned in the middle stanza.

Explicit and implicit sexual images abound in the poem. The mirror is indicative of masturbation and narcissism as well as homosexuality. The "cleaving and burning" of the third stanza literally and emotionally indicate the sex act, on one hand, and an intense longing for a departed lover on the other. The "Spends out himself again" is another reference to masturbation. The "smoking souvenir" of the fourth stanza at once refers to the burning moth of the second and to an expended phallus. The "Bleeding eidolon," or phantom, may be similarly explicated; it indicates a spent penis as well as the memory of his lost lover. Even so, the most explicit reference to the sex act occurs in the final stanza, where the poet records a "constant harmony" that has been achieved "drop by caustic drop." The reference is both to masturbation and to the following announcement of the "legend"-lover, the homosexual relationship of his youth. "Drop by caustic drop" can be explained as a reference to orgasm; the "constant harmony" means that the significance of such a relationship has never wavered or faltered. Finally, it is called a "Relentless caper," which ironically shows that it is not a caperish prank at all.

Themes and Meanings

The primary matter of "Legend" is the exposition of a mature man looking back to make a statement about a relationship of his youth in order to determine the lasting if not lingering effects. The poet expresses an intense desire for his return to this past relationship. At the same time, he explores its impact as a defining characteristic of his present identity.

The mature poet writing of a relationship from his youth knows that the way the relationship seemed then was not what he now considers it to be. Hence, there is the title and the use of the word "legend" in the last line of the poem. The love from his youth has, to a certain, insurmountable extent, made his love life, if not the essence of his being, what it is at the time the poem is being written—that is, in the "noon" of the poet's life. The relationship has left the poet fixed forever as one who can explain himself and the meaning of his existence only in terms of what had happened in his youth. He had not merely permitted but actually willed that this love would become a lover for all seasons and years and lives, one whose memory now could provide an unquenchable "constant harmony" not evident during the actual relationship of his youth.

As indicated in the fourth stanza, to believe in a mirror is to believe in oneself and the reality of oneself. The lover as object has become the lover as subject; one who is different, at least in memory, has become one who is the same. The result is a concord not only for the individual but also for "all those who step/ The legend of their youth into noon." The meaning of the poem is not universal, but it does have an audience and application far beyond that of the poet himself.

Finally, it must be maintained that the poem is not strictly about a homosexual relationship from the poet's youth, even though this factor gives clear sustenance to the poem's existence. The poem pertains to all individuals in the "noon" of their lives who would fondly look back at relationships from their youths in order to give them significance which they probably neither had nor deserved. Had they truly been what the poet romantically imagines them to be, then they would not be history. They can rightly be described as "Bleeding eidolons." They remove the life-blood from one's present, denying temporal happiness.

Carl Singleton

A LEMON

Author: Pablo Neruda (Neftalí Ricardo Reyes Basoalto, 1904-1973)
Type of poem: Ode
First published: 1957, as "Oda al limon," in *Tercer libro de odas*; English translation
collected in *Selected Poems of Pablo Neruda,* 1961

The Poem

"A Lemon" is an ode (an ode was originally a vehicle of praise, either civic or lyrical in nature, intended to be sung in public) written in highly flexible free verse and composed of four stanzas. Pablo Neruda wrote three volumes of what he called "odas elementales" ("elementary odes"), which were translated together into English as *The Elementary Odes of Pablo Neruda* in 1961. As in all those poems, the subject matter is a seemingly "unpoetic," simple, ordinary object.

The poem opens with a wild and sensuous image of "lemon flowers/ loosed/ on the moonlight." In the next several lines, the sense of smell dominates; the lemon blossoms become "love's/ lashed and insatiable/ essences,/ sodden with fragrance." As the poem moves from the sense of smell to sight, the blooming flowers are suddenly transformed into yellow lemons. Continuing the stanza's vertical movement (from moonlight to the tree to the earth), the lemons fall from their branches—which are likened to a planetarium—to the earth below.

Once the lemons drop to the earth, they are no longer described in romantic terms but rather in practical terms; they become the "Delicate merchandise!" referred to in the opening line of stanza 2. Thus the images of moonlight, love, and lemon blossoms alluded to in the previous stanza are superseded by images of bustling harbors and bazaars where lemon becomes "barbarous gold," a commodity to be bought and sold. The pace of the poem quickens.

Next the poet focuses his attention upon the individual buyer of the lemon. This person cuts the fruit and opens it, finding "the halves/ of a miracle" within. The simple fruit becomes elevated to the level of the extraordinary. Comparing the fluid that emerges from the cut lemon to blood flowing from a cut vein, the poet describes the fluid as "a clotting of acids." Alluding to the first stanza, in which the lemons are fixed like stars in the firmament, the second stanza describes how the juice of the lemon "brims/ into the starry/ divisions"—that is, the symmetrical divisions of the pulp of the cut lemon. Next the poet conjures up images of the creation of the world and the garden of Eden, referring to lemon juice as one of the essences of life, one of "creation's/ original juices." In the final lines of the stanza, the lemon's rind is compared to a house, the proportions of which are both "arcane and acerb," secret and bitter.

In the third stanza, the lemon is further endowed with a sense of reverence. The movement of the opening line continues the action of cutting the lemon, portrayed in stanza 2. Here the visual image is of another house, a "cathedral" that remains when the knife slices into the lemon's core. At this point in the poem, cutting the lemon becomes a religious experience. The sliced lemon contains "alcoves," "acidulous glass," and topaz-colored drops; these drops are described as "altars,/ aromatic facades."

The final stanza of the poem unites the religious and metaphysical imagery of the previous stanzas. For the first time in the poem, the poet addresses the reader directly, using the pronoun "you." The act of holding a cut lemon is likened to holding "half a world," "the gold of the universe." The lemon half returns its holder to the elemental forces of nature, to Mother Earth, with "a breast and nipple/ perfuming the earth." In the last two lines of the poem, there is a play on words that changes the biblical phrase "and the Word was made flesh" to "a flashing made fruitage."

Forms and Devices

Unlike the poems in Neruda's *Residencia en la tierra* cycle (1933-1947)—in which readers are always somewhat outside the system because of the complex language and content, mere spectators whose function is to admire the poet and his extraordinary experiences with the ordinary matter of, for example, wood, wine, and celery—the poems in the Elementary Odes series reverse the situation. These poems, including "A Lemon," are designed to draw the reader directly into the process of wonder and discovery.

The poem is designed as a didactic construct, helping the reader to see and to speculate on the extraordinary significance of the world in which he or she lives. For this reason, the poem (as is the case with most of the Elementary Odes) ends with a kind of philosophical maxim summarizing the lesson in order to help the reader comprehend the poem's practical import.

In "A Lemon," as in most of the poems in *The Elementary Odes of Pablo Neruda*, the basic formal pattern is as follows: The elemental subject is introduced, transformed, and then summarized at the end. At the outset of the poem, the subject announced by the title is metaphorized promptly so as to bestow it with a certain level of poetic dignity. It is introduced indirectly (with the hint of lemon-blossom fragrance), then directly in the object of the lemon itself. The subject is more completely transformed later in the poem; the juice of the ripe yellow lemon cut in half is associated with religious imagery and precious gemstones, elegant and noble points of comparison for a simple lemon. Instead of simply dropping to the ground when ripe, the lemon is depicted as traveling from the heavens (the planetarium) above to the earth below.

Finally, in the poem's conclusion, the religious/philosophical dimension predominates as the speaker philosophizes on the significance of the elemental. The speaker of the poem, addressing the partaker of the lemon directly, reminds him or her that partaking of the fruit connects that individual with the miracle of the universe and its creation in the garden of Eden. This individual is partaking of no simple, ordinary fruit but becomes part of the "diminutive fire of a planet."

Themes and Meanings

The major theme of Neruda's "A Lemon" is the unsuspecting and hidden poetry of ordinary objects surrounding humankind. Neruda saw in his new poetics (that is, the poetics following the *Residencia en la tierra* cycle) an aesthetic that resisted an excess of sophistication; its object was to draw the poet toward rather than away from everyday reality. This embracing of reality was a welcome return to the sources, to what was simply human: his family, his native village, the modest lives of his childhood friends.

In the poem "A Lemon," Neruda renders the elemental object of the lemon purely and directly. By gaining insight into the grandeur of the lowly and the sublimity of the trivial, the ode attempts to open the world to imaginative re-creation.

Although "A Lemon" is not an overtly political poem, as are the poems of the *Residencia* series, by his choice of subject matter Neruda's poem conveys an ideological meaning. The return to, and exaltation of, nature in the poem is a political act, in that in praising what is positive and essential there is a silent accusation against whoever would abuse and exploit the resources of the Americas. More important, in choosing the simple language and style for the Elementary Odes, Neruda was clearly motivated by a deeply held political belief: A leftist poet must reject "elitist" styles; he must write simply and clearly for the people. To Neruda, the poet should not be isolated in his or her ivory tower away from the human community but should be part of that community.

The new aesthetics exemplified in "A Lemon" aimed at strengthening the ties between the poet and the people. The elevation of common objects constituted a leveling of poetic subject and the breaking down of class distinctions, as if reducing all things to the same standard by investing the lowliest with a humble dignity of their own.

Genevieve Slomski

THE LEMON TREES

Author: Eugenio Montale (1896-1981)
Type of poem: Lyric
First published: 1925, as "I limoni," in *Ossi di seppia*; English translation collected in *Selected Poems*, 1965

The Poem

"The Lemon Trees" is the second poem in Eugenio Montale's collection *Ossi di seppia* (*Bones of the Cuttlefish*, 1984) and the first poem of the series entitled "Movimenti" ("Movements"). It consists of forty-nine lines in free verse, divided into four stanzas of various lengths. In addition to introducing an important image in the poem—the lemon trees themselves—the title suggests a connection with the first composition of the book. First, it recalls the orchard mentioned in the opening poem and suggests to the reader that images of nature will continue to figure as prominently in the following compositions as they did in the first ("wave of life," "garden," "beating of wings," "solitary strip of land"). Furthermore, the Italian "I limoni" echoes the title of the first poem, "In limine" ("On the Threshold"), hinting that both poems together serve an introductory function in the collection.

As in "On the Threshold," the poet begins by addressing the reader with an imperative: "Listen." He thus impresses on the reader the urgency of his message and invites him to consider carefully not only what he has to say but also the way he says it, that is, the language of the poem. In the opening lines, he tells the reader that he will break with the laureate poets of the past and select for his poems objects, places, and language from his personal experience, rather than those dictated by tradition. He declares his individuality in the line "I, for my part, prefer." In the Italian, this declaration is strengthened by the use of the first-person singular pronoun in addition to the verb form. The poet then proceeds to take the reader down a path to "grassy ditches" where children hunt for eels and through cane fields to a lemon orchard. In the second stanza, he explains how "the war of the diverted passions" of his soul is miraculously calmed by the breeze in the "friendly boughs" and by the smell of the earth and the lemon trees. The orchard offers a haven to the poet and a point of contact with the elements of nature.

The poet begins the third stanza with another imperative, this time telling the reader to "see." He reveals at this time his desire to discover in the orchard the "ultimate secret,/ . . . the thread to disentangle which might set us at last/ in the midst of a truth," which will offer hope to him and other "dislodged Divinit[ies]." In the fourth stanza, however, his reverie is broken, and time brings him back to the present moment, in which his soul has grown bitter in the depressing winter darkness of the city. This spell is nevertheless broken one day when he chances to see, growing amid the ruin of the city, a lemon tree, whose golden fruit fills his heart with the song of sunlight.

Forms and Devices

Montale's strength as a poet lies in his ability to present the essence of an object or scene by paring it down to the core of its reality using a precise and exacting selection of diction, syntax, and composition. The objects in Montale's work are generally things common to most readers, but in the poems they take on a very personal meaning for the poet. Sometimes, the image or action of a poem can be traced to a specific event in Montale's life. Nevertheless, an understanding and appreciation of his poetry does not demand a thorough knowledge of his biography. Furthermore, Montale draws his images in such stark, graphic detail that he distances himself from the composition, allowing the individual reader to find his or her own meaning in the suggestiveness of the poem's symbols.

Several images appear frequently in Montale's poetry. For the most part, he takes his scenes from nature, in particular from the country and coast of Liguria, where he spent his youth. Montale often portrays nature as a harsh and brutal force, at times hostile, at times merely indifferent to humankind. In "The Lemon Trees," however, nature is a refuge for the poet from the harshness of modern society; it is a *locus amoenus* or a paradisiacal garden in which he hopes to find peace. Indeed, he describes the trees as "friendly boughs," and it is in the orchard that his impoverished soul finds its "share of riches/ and it is the scent of the lemon-trees." The city, instead, represents the barren, hostile world, which swallows up the individual and chokes off his life.

The lemon trees themselves play an important role in the poem. The poet knows the orchard well, and just as the scent of the fruit is "inseparable from earth," so are the memories, feelings, and thoughts associated with the lemons inseparable from his soul. When he sees the lemon tree in the courtyard at the end of the poem, he is able to transcend the decadent world in which he lives to find beauty and truth. In addition, Montale refers at the beginning of the poem to the classical poets' laurel, which to him represents a tradition void of life and without a voice for modern society. He breaks with tradition and chooses as his symbol the more common, more modest lemon tree, which for him is real, alive, immediate, and significant.

Another important image in "The Lemon Trees" is the boy (or boys, as in the Italian) mentioned in the first stanza. As in other of Montale's poems ("Dance of the Children" and "The End of Childhood," for example), the child symbolizes youthful vigor and curiosity, the simplicity of a past world unfettered by the concerns of modern society, and the power of the human spirit to survive. In "The Lemon Trees," the poet recalls his own childhood and finds in that memory the inspiration to continue down familiar paths to the orchard, where he hopes to find a way to rejuvenate his weary, adult soul.

Montale also uses the various elements of language to suggest the meaning of the poem. For example, because all the verbs in "The Lemon Trees" are in the present tense, the poem takes on a sense of immediacy. The poet's memories of hunting for eels, of going down into the orchard, and of seeing the lemon tree in the courtyard become present experiences through the act of poeticizing. The use of the present tense thus serves to erase the boundaries between past, present, and even future, much as the sight of the lemons in the courtyard lifts the poet out of the tedious world to which time has returned him into the timelessness of revelation.

Themes and Meanings

At the outset of his study *Eugenio Montale's Poetry: A Dream in Reason's Presence* (1982), Glauco Cambon says that *Ossi di seppia* " . . . is first and foremost a rhapsody of the four elements, Nature's essentiality confronted by a tried consciousness that keeps wavering between utter disenchantment and glimpsed ecstasy in the reiterated endeavor to regain contact with the lost bliss of childhood." Placed at the beginning of the collection, "The Lemon Trees" introduces the poet's search for something that makes sense of and brings meaning to his experience in the natural world and disperses the uncertainty in his soul. The narrator descends into the stillness of the orchard in hopes of finding there, by some miracle, an answer. He finds only "an unquiet sweetness," helpful but far from satisfying. It is only later, when the poet finds himself in the middle of the "clamorous cities," that he experiences the miracle of the lemon trees. Through a mistake of nature—a fruitful lemon tree growing in the middle of the wintery city—his soul is nourished and "the war of the diverted passions" is momentarily suspended. The answer is not complete, and one senses that the narrator will soon find himself again firmly planted in the world, but this burst of light and understanding, which has come only after a long period of darkness, enraptures his soul and encourages him to continue his search with hope. He cherishes the miracle all the more because of its unexpected arrival.

This poem is also the first step, the first movement, in the search for life to which the reader is invited in "On the Threshold." Like "Nature," as described in the third stanza of "The Lemon Trees," poetry often seems on the verge of giving up its secret, of revealing a thread whereby it can be understood, but in the end the reader is left somewhat disillusioned by the lack of a clear answer. Only in another time and place when one least expects it does a flash evoke the memory of the "song" and reveal its significance. In reference to the persona in Montale's poem "Arsenio," Ghan Shyam Singh, in *Eugenio Montale* (1973), notes that "Everything he sees around him—familiar sights and sounds as well as natural phenomena—becomes a means of self-discovery for him and represents a milestone in the exploration of reality. . . . In such a mood of metaphysical contemplation, he finds the distinction between the real and the illusory, the near and the far, the personal and the impersonal, momentarily annulled. . . . [His] profound and perspicuous awareness of himself as well as of the world outside him brings him in touch with the embryonic forces of life." In "The Lemon Trees," the lemons serve as a mediator between the poet's past and present, and his seeing them inspires him with understanding of his present life in terms of the past. Poetry is similarly the mediator between the poet and the reader, and it serves to unite them over the distance of time and space.

Cameron K. Deaver

LENINGRAD (1941-1943)

Author: Edward Hirsch (1950-   )
Type of poem: Elegy
First published: 1984; collected in *Wild Gratitude*, 1986

The Poem

Edward Hirsch's "Leningrad (1941-1943)" describes in vivid and sometimes hallucinatory images the horror of the German blockade of that city during World War II. The blockade lasted 526 days, but the actual assault on the city continued much longer. Hirsch tells his story in seven sections of six three-line stanzas each, unrhymed, with almost no caesuras or end-stopped lines. Sharon Olds's poem "Leningrad Cemetery, Winter 1941" is a moving companion piece, though much shorter, on the same subject.

The poem opens with a cacophony of animal sounds in section 1, as of zoo creatures gone mad from bombardment, such a nightmare that "we knew it had begun in earnest." The chaos of animal terror—of "wild dogs/ Howling like dirges," "three mad sables roving through the streets," and "polar bears wailing"—climaxes in a chilling stanza that describes "the sky speaking/ German," "the night wearing a steel helmet,/ And the moon slowly turning into a swastika." These menacing images establish the historical reality and foreshadow the unspeakable events immediately following.

Harrison Salisbury's *The 900 Days: The Siege of Leningrad* (1969) tells the whole story in almost unbearable detail, devoting one chapter, "The Blood-Red Clouds," to the destruction of the Badayev food warehouses, and although Hirsch does not name them it is obvious that his section 2 dramatizes the Badayev event as he speaks of the "crumbling wooden depots of food/ Climbing in swollen clouds into the sky." Sections 3 and 4 mourn the human misery of nights in cold rooms during the 1941-1942 winter of record-setting low temperatures and of "days when dying will seem as/ Easy as sitting down in a warm, comfortable/ Overstuffed chair and going back to sleep." The sick endure in hospitals with no heat or light, and "The bodies keep piling up in the corridor."

Salisbury tells of an admiral who gave his leather briefcase to a starving woman, who returned several days later with a dish of meat jelly made from the briefcase. In Hirsch's section 5, this becomes "A thin jelly made of leather straps." Hirsch's references to eating dogs and cats "without disgust" are corroborated by Salisbury, who adds that after the siege kittens brought high prices in the convalescing city, eager for the recovery of warm, human values. The final triplet of section 5 alludes to the cannibalism that Salisbury describes in the degraded Haymarket section of the city: "But I won't gouge at another human body;/ I won't eat the sweet breasts of a murdered/ Woman, or the hacked thighs of a dying man."

In Salisbury's account, a stock of cottonseed cake meant to be burned in ships' furnaces was heated to high temperatures to neutralize its poisons and all four thousand tons of it added to the bread rations. Hirsch speaks in section 6 of "Cellulose and cottonseed cakes and dry meal dust" as standard fare. One of Salisbury's photos depicts a woman pulling a sheet-wrapped corpse on a child's sled, a common occurrence commemorated in Hirsch's lines "And then one day the bodies started to appear/ Piled on the bright sleds of little children . . . ." Hirsch's "scent of turpentine hanging in the frosty air" is explained by Salisbury's note that the cemetery-bound trucks loaded with corpses were all drenched with turpentine. Hirsch ends his elegy for the Leningrad victims with the only words available to the survivors: "Somehow we lived."

Forms and Devices

Hirsch's seven sections are generally discrete in their subjects but cohere in a unity of impression, and the enjambed triplets carry a smooth flow of imagery and rhythm. The seven sections roughly follow the course of the ordeal, with the destruction of the food warehouses, the ensuing hunger and cold, the increasing desperation marked by the burning of books and furniture and the eating of human flesh, through to the final image of the scraping away of the "dead flesh" of their death-in-life experience. The only narrator identified is the "we" that speaks for the survivors in honor of their dead.

No one metrical foot prevails, but anapests carry much of the pulse of sound, as in "Howling like dirges," "screeching like children," "Careening around," and "smashing their cages"—all from section 1. Moreover, although feminine endings are not as dominant in succeeding stanzas, of the eighteen lines in section 1, thirteen end with unstressed syllables, nicely complementary to the many anapests scattered throughout the lines. The poem's fourth line—"It began with the shrieking of peacocks"— illustrates the deft use of both the anapest and the feminine ending, and perhaps the best summary of Hirsch's metrics is that he has a superb ear for rhythm and phonetics. Stanzas picked at random always yield alliteration and assonance. Section 2, stanza 4, describes the burning of the food storehouses:

> It was like seeing hundreds of waves of
> Blood rolling over the city at dusk and then
> Hanging in heavy layers under the stars.

Assonance is heavy in "hundreds," "Blood," "dusk," and "under," while "hundreds," "Hanging," and "heavy" alliterate. As a final example, the first triplet of section 4 reveals strong sibilance in "So," "must," "survive," "must," "sick," "civilians," "shiver," and "stretchers."

The imagery of the panicked animals in section 1 suggests a mad, surrealistic scene entirely appropriate to the brutal vignettes from Hieronymous Bosch that follow. The "stomach of the city," with its "charred/ Sugar and fresh meats," catches in brilliant ambiguity the starvation facing the populace, and the "old man who saw his own small intestine/ Drifting like a balloon over his wife's head" suffers a vision straight from Salvador Dalí.

Some of the images are emotionally exhausting. In section 4,

> A red soldier tears his mouth from a bandage
> And announces to a young nurse, 'Darling,
> . . . .
> Tanks are what we need now, beautiful tanks,
> Beloved tanks rolling over the barren fields
> And playing their music in the pink sky.'

Section 7 mourns the "soldier cradling a kneecap in his palms" and the "children watching the soft red fluids/ Of their intestines flowing through their fingers."

Themes and Meanings

The magnitude of Hirsch's theme emerges in the numbers. Salisbury gives for Hiroshima a death count of 78,150, with 13,983 missing and 37,426 wounded. Although all figures have to be estimates, Salisbury says that in the blockade of Leningrad more than ten times as many died than at Hiroshima. Excepting the millions who died in the Holocaust, no larger group has ever been elegized.

Images of human misery dominate Hirsch's narrative, relieved only by reminders of the people's courage. The conflagration at the Badeyev food warehouses was a catastrophe, as all realized at the time, yet only a few hungry children "cried out or screamed in pain." In Peter the Great's "white showcase," the sufferers dream at night of "the sweetness of surrender," yearning for the days of "women with bright parasols/ Strolling down the wide Parisian boulevards." Memories of "men cruising in black limousines" ward off the words "typhoid" and "cholera" and dampen the sirens' "wailing" throughout nights of uneasy sleep. During these hard days when resignation and death beckon seductively, rest is forbidden, for "you must spend your life digging/ Out trenches with a shovel, staying awake."

Everyone's endurance is challenged by the need to work to eat and fight to survive, even as the corpses accumulate in the hospital corridors. A "dazed girl" embodies the spirit of the survivors as she keeps shouting, "'But I *can*/ Fight the Nazis!'" Honor still prevails among those who try to "relinquish judgment" of those whose desperation drives them to measures that would ordinarily shame them. Even the severest hardships can be borne with patience, for "we got used to icicles in our chests" and to "the fires falling from the sky/ At dusk." Worst of all, with "the staircases jammed with corpses" and the turpentine smell everywhere, "We got used to leaving our dead unburied." Yet iron will triumphed over "empty stomachs" and "ankles in chains," even over "a heavy iron collar wrapped tightly/ Around our necks." Hirsch's poem is a saga of courage under duress.

Such powerful human sympathy is not unique in Hirsch's work. His "Three Journeys" testifies eloquently to the goodness of the poor and humble as he observes a bag lady on a "terrible journey" past the overflowing supermarket and the record store. She reminds Hirsch of the destitute Romantic poet John Clare, walking eighty miles over bad roads, "hungry, shy of strangers." The bag lady "sprawled out on a steaming vent" brings to mind Clare "lying down in an open dike bottom." Hirsch's moving declaration of love for the mad Clare is perhaps a fitting memorial for the starving millions in Leningrad, those who survived on grass, bark, and jelly made from meat straps:

> Tonight when I lie down in the dark
> in my own bed, I want to remember
> that John Clare was so desperately hungry
> after three days and nights without food
> that he finally knelt down, as if in prayer,
> and ate the soft grass of the earth,
> and thought it tasted like fresh bread,
> and judged no one, not even himself,
> and slept peacefully again, like a child.

Frank Day

LENORE

Author: Edgar Allan Poe (1809-1849)
Type of poem: Elegy
First published: 1831, as "A Paean"; collected in *The Raven and Other Poems*, 1845

The Poem

"Lenore" is a poem of twenty-six lines in four stanzas, reflecting on the death at a young age of the fair Lenore. Most likely, the Lenore remembered in this poem is the same "rare and radiant maiden whom the angels name Lenore" who is mourned in another of Edgar Allan Poe's poems, "The Raven."

"Lenore" is a poem with at least two different speakers. The second and fourth stanzas are enclosed in quotation marks; the first and third, while not marked, are clearly spoken by a character or characters, not by an omniscient narrator. Beyond the quotation marks and a noticeable shift in tone and attitude, there is no indication who is speaking anywhere in the poem. Most critics have assumed that the poem presents a dialogue between Guy De Vere, Lenore's grieving lover, and the family or priest of the dead woman.

The first stanza is addressed to Guy De Vere. In formal and very poetic language, the stanza announces the death of Lenore. She is described as a "saintly soul" and "the queenliest dead that ever died so young," and yet there is no real mourning in this stanza. The stanza comments on the general sadness of a young woman dying, but there is no specific regret that Lenore herself has died. The tone is solemn and reverent but not truly sorrowful. The speakers ask De Vere why he has not cried.

The second stanza is spoken by De Vere. The tone here is much less restrained. The speaker rages against the speakers of the first stanza, calling them "wretches" and blaming them for their "evil eye" and their "slanderous tongue." They never loved Lenore, he tells them, but loved only her wealth. It would be shameful hypocrisy for them to read the burial rite or sing the funeral song. She died to escape from their unkindness.

The original speakers reply to De Vere's accusations in the third stanza. Again, there is little emotion in the speech. More platitudes about death and heaven are uttered, and De Vere is urged to calm himself. He is now only angry because Lenore has died, "Leaving thee wild for the dear child that should have been thy bride."

The fourth and final stanza is spoken by De Vere. He notes that Lenore's soul has risen to heaven from its turmoil on earth, and begs the others to leave off their rituals of mourning so that Lenore will not hear them. As for himself, he concludes, he is glad for Lenore that she is finally away from the "fiends" who tormented her in life. He will not mourn her at all but "waft the angel on her flight with a Paean of old days."

Forms and Devices

In revising "Lenore" for the final time in 1845, Poe made changes to emphasize differences in tone between the speakers of the poem. Death is a subject requiring great solemnity, but Poe worked within that framework to create drama as well.

Even the way the lines of the poem appear on the page contributes to the solemnity of tone. In an earlier version of "Lenore," each of the subsequent version's long lines was divided into two or three shorter lines. For example, the first stanza contained the lines "See, on yon drear/ And rigid bier,/ Low lies thy love Lenore!" The effect of these short lines is to lighten the tone. The "drear/bier" rhyme is emphasized because of the pauses that naturally occur at line breaks, and the iambic meter is heightened for the same reason. The resulting rhythm gallops—it is difficult to make the lines sound mournful. When Poe combined short lines into lines of iambic heptameter, he made them look and sound more dignified. The long lines and short stanzas look to the eye more weighty than do short irregular lines with complicated patterns of indentation.

More important, the revisions changed the sound of the lines, making them more suitable for exploring death and grief. Compare the three lines quoted above with their revision: "See, on yon drear and rigid bier low lies thy love Lenore!" The new line drops the internal punctuation and capitalization; the internal rhyme thus becomes less obtrusive—although it remains to add melody and beauty to the line. Read aloud or silently, the long line "sounds" more hushed, reverential.

Poe was a master at choosing words whose vowels and consonants would echo the feeling he was trying to convey. Consider the repetition of the *l* at the end of the same line: "low lies thy love, Lenore." The sound is quiet and formal as the empty rituals for Lenore are mouthed. The first stanza is full of these repeated consonants: "flown forever," "saintly soul," "dirge for her the doubly dead in that she died so young." The beauty of these words and sounds is undeniable—even though it is revealed in stanza 2 that the beautiful words are empty and false.

The second stanza, in which the grieving Guy De Vere rails against Lenore's hypocritical family, is harsher in sound as well as in meaning. Every line in stanza 1 is end-stopped, contributing to the regular, formal rhythm and tone. The reader encounters frequent strong punctuation (primarily dashes) within the lines, and two of the five lines are enjambed. The stanza's third line, for example ("By you—by yours, the evil eye,—by yours, the slanderous tongue"), is punctuated five times internally and not at all at the end. The result is a much less regular rhythm. The sound is more like that of a man enraged, with abrupt stops and irregular phrasing.

Poe uses these devices throughout the poem to establish contrasts between the false formality of the dead woman's family and the sincere emotionality of Guy De Vere.

Themes and Meanings

Critics have been baffled by "Lenore" for more than one hundred years. There is no consensus as to what the poem is about, or who the speakers are, or even how many speakers there are. Most of the clues to the poem's meaning actually lie outside the poem, in Poe's other writings.

In "The Philosophy of Composition," Poe claimed that the most poetical topic was the death of a young woman. Further, he wrote, the best speaker to utter the mournful lines was the grieving lover. Poe went back to this idea again and again, creating poems such as "Ulalume," "The Raven," and "Annabel Lee."

The woman Lenore is typical of the dead women mourned in Poe's poetry. Her youth is emphasized; the phrase "died so young" occurs three times in the first two stanzas. Both the grieving lover and the other speaker refer to her innocence and her place in heaven. She is radiantly beautiful, in death as in life. Even the woman's name is identifiable as a Poe creation. Lenore takes her place with Annabel Lee, Ulalume, Ligeia, Morella, Eleonora, Helen, and others—the letter *l* seemed to Poe somehow fitting for the name of a dead, loved woman.

The identity of the lover as Guy De Vere seems clear enough from the first stanza of the poem. Since he is addressed directly in stanza 1, it seems only logical that it is he who speaks the next stanza and the fourth stanza, which are framed in quotation marks. De Vere might be expected to wish for the return of his love, but this mournful lover does not. Rather, he is glad that she has finally escaped the suffering inflicted upon her by false friends and family.

In fact, the "wretches" are never identified in the version of the poem Poe finally left. Yet two earlier versions of the poem provide clues to their identities. The earlier versions clearly blame "friends" and "false friends" for Lenore's suffering, and the 1843 version identifies Lenore as "yon heir," suggesting that family members are among the mourners.

The dramatic purpose of the poem, then, is to establish a contrast between the sincere feelings of Guy De Vere, Lenore's intended, and the false sentiments of her friends and family. The formal, ritualistic lines in stanzas 1 and 3 may be spoken by the group of mourners or perhaps, as has been suggested, by the officiating priest.

While critics have disagreed about its precise meaning, all agree that this poem—like many of Poe's poetical works—is more significant for its sound than for its thematic significance.

Cynthia A. Bily

THE LESSON

Author: Charles Simic (1938-   )
Type of poem: Narrative
First published: 1977, in *Charon's Cosmology*

The Poem

"The Lesson" is a short narrative poem in free verse, its seventy lines divided into six stanzas of varying lengths. The title suggests that the poem will focus upon an event or series of events from which the poet gained new knowledge. Such events are often characterized by irony, as they tend to overturn one's comfortable assumptions about the nature of things—sometimes violently, sometimes comically, sometimes, as in "The Lesson," both.

The poem is written in the first person, which gives the events that it describes the authority of actual experience and the poignance of personal recollection. One is encouraged to assume that the lesson mentioned in the poem's title was learned by the poet himself. He speaks directly to the reader in a tone both retrospective and confessional. As one reads, one believes that one is being taken into the poet's confidence and invited to share the knowledge he has gained.

The poem opens with a sudden, ironic revelation as the poet realizes that he has in some way been deluded his entire life, has been "the idiot pupil/ of a practical joker." The words that the poet chooses to describe his revelation foreshadow the complexity of the narrative he is about to unfold, as they accuse both his own foolishness and the cruelty of his experience for the ignorance which the poem will explain and dispel. Having realized himself to be the victim of a malicious joke, the poet intends to be a victim no longer.

In the next stanza, the poet recounts the foolishly passive ways in which he accepted as true and wise all that he was earlier taught. He revered his teachers unreflectingly. He repeated his lessons "like a parrot"—that is to say, with accuracy but without understanding. In happy ignorance, he accepted the proposition that his lot in life was constantly improving. The third stanza continues and brings to a climax the delusion which the poet mistook for education, detailing his conviction that life had some hugely felicitous "pattern" and purpose, that history itself was headed, as the "intricate plot/ of a picaresque novel" is headed, toward some inevitable happy ending.

Beginning with the word "unfortunately," stanza 4 signals the unraveling of the poet's delusion. As the evidence of his personal memory accumulated, it began to overshadow the memory of things learned merely by rote. The poet came to see, in all the details of life, ambiguous, troubling "beginnings" rather than happy endings. Ominous images, such as that of the urinating soldier and the "shadows of trees on the ceiling" were preludes to even more ominous situations, such as starvation. In stanza 5, the happy delusion is entirely replaced by the waking nightmare of the "prison train." Reality was no longer on the gladsome, ever-ascending path of a picaresque novel but rather on the iron tracks of a railway headed toward a frightening, unknown confinement.

The closing stanza defines this nightmarish awakening as the undeluded poet's new classroom. The practical joke is ended, and it is the poet who laughs. His situation is as terrifying and ambiguous as his laughter at "the memory of [his] uncle/ charging a barricade," but his situation is at last real, at last entirely his own.

Forms and Devices

As with all of Charles Simic's best poems, "The Lesson" expertly demonstrates what may be called the art of artlessness. Vivid but spare, direct but unrhetorical, the poem communicates its profoundly dramatic theme with seemingly little need for the traditional devices of poetry. "The Lesson" resonates with the qualities of actual, unrehearsed speech, and those qualities create an immediate trust on the part of the reader for what the poet recounts.

Yet there is an art to what "The Lesson" achieves, and this consists of a number of devices employed in their purest forms. Chief among these is the irony already discovered in the poem's title. From thence onward through every stanza, ironic reversals provide the literal energy for Simic's meaning. What was taken for knowledge turns out to be ignorance. What was revered as wisdom turns out to be folly. The implacable reality of human progress turns out to be a vain dream, as nightmare images (starkly recalled from Simic's own memories of his childhood in Nazi-occupied Yugoslavia) come to represent the sole and unprogressive reality of "The Lesson."

The poem concludes upon the richest and most disturbing of its ironies: The poet's own laughter at his "long and terrifying" delusion. In a situation where one might more reasonably expect to witness gestures of outrage or tears of shame, the reader is surprised by laughter, an irony which allows Simic to make the depth of his revelation as astonishing to the reader as it evidently was to him.

All the rest of the poem's devices function under the aegis of this irony. There are rich puns. The "pupil" in line 4 represents the poet not only as a student but also as an eye which takes in all that it sees without the judgment vital to real vision. The "plot" in line twenty-five suggests a conspiracy as well as the story-line of a novel. Such puns enable Simic's irony to function at the very basic level of language itself. Crucial metaphors—the teacher as "practical joker," the teacher's lesson plan as an entertaining but finally unrealistic "picaresque novel," and the poet's new, undeceived reality as a "classroom/ austerely furnished/ by my insomnia"—signal the various stages of the poet's awakening.

It is the imagery of "The Lesson," however, that embodies Simic's irony most effectively. These images, which the poem dismissively introduces as "trivial detail," turn out to be anything but trivial, as it is the "haircut of a soldier," "the shadows of trees," the "prison train," and the final image of the poet's uncle "charging a barricade/ with a homemade bomb" which accumulate in the poet's mind and there overwhelm the imageless, stale, and facile generalizations of his so-called education. The images are his real teachers, and as such they constitute the reality of "The Lesson."

Themes and Meanings

In keeping with the artful artlessness of "The Lesson," the themes of the poem are virtually identical with its techniques and the narrative it tells. What happens in the poem—the ironic transpositions of ignorance and knowledge—is the poem's meaning. "The Lesson" participates in the traditional expression of Western culture's most fundamental theme: the journey from innocence to experience.

The greater part of this theme hinges upon the identity of the "practical joker" of stanza 1. He can be God, history, society, or any source of ideology and idealism that sets itself apart from and above the stubbornly ambiguous realities of any life as it is lived in real time. However one pictures him, this practical joker is the source of the "wise pronouncements" and disembodied generalizations, the myths of progress and predetermined fate that the poet ingenuously parrots in stanzas 2 and 3. Like the tenets of Europe's Utopian Socialists and of America's doctrine of Manifest Destiny, these illusory precepts are as insidious as they are charming because they always subordinate historical means to supra-historical ends. They devalue reality in order to inflate the value of the dreams in which they so stridently and, in the case of the poet's teachers, so convincingly believe.

By countering such abstractions with the vital, animate images of the poem's latter half, Simic establishes the dignity of objects and of persons, no matter how unlovely, no matter how frightening, in a world which more often than not tends to degrade them in the name of supposedly higher purposes. Accordingly, "The Lesson" recounts a brief history that, in the context of the poet's life, details the excesses of history's idealism and the cruel practical joke which that idealism plays on people and things. It is the finally positive theme of this poem that asserts the victory of reality over idealism through the process of the poet's awakening. As he begins to linger "more and more/ over the beginnings" (represented by the poem's crucial images) and less and less over the ends preached to him in the classroom, the poet begins to understand the irreducible uniqueness of everything that exists. Every life is its own school, and its lessons cannot truthfully be translated into generalizations. That is why the poet exclaims, "Forgive me, all of you!" near the poem's end, for he had come dangerously close to imposing the tyranny of an ideal pattern upon the stubbornly independent objects in his life. "The Lesson" is a poem about the ways in which origins refuse to become ends, in which the infinite originals in any one life refuse to become stereotypes. Heard in this context, the poem's final laughter is indeed a laughter of joy, of liberation.

Donald Revell

LETTER FROM A DISTANT LAND

Author: Philip Booth (1925-   )
Type of poem: Epistle/letter in verse
First published: 1955; collected in *Letter from a Distant Land*, 1957

The Poem

"Letter from a Distant Land" is an epistolary poem of 163 lines in three stanzas. The title is derived from a quotation (which Philip Booth borrows as an epigraph) from Henry David Thoreau's *Walden* (1854). In this classic of American literature, Thoreau describes his adventure of living at Walden Pond, near Concord, Massachusetts, between 1845 and 1847.

In a brief passage, Thoreau, speaking to other writers, declares that part of a writer's work should be a simple account of his or her life, "some such as he would send to his kindred from a distant land." Booth makes images of Walden and nature central to his poem, and "Letter from a Distant Land" is Booth's response to Thoreau's challenge. Booth measures who and where he is in relation to who and what he aspires to be; Thoreau and *Walden* are his yardsticks.

To understand Booth's effort, it is necessary to know that in *Walden* Thoreau sought to discover the nature of true being, the essence of life. By withdrawing from society and living as a recluse, Thoreau lived in harmony with nature. As a result, he came to understand new spiritual truths; he discovered the oneness of creation and its manifold beauty. His message in *Walden* is that humanity needs to rediscover that core of value and meaning.

The first stanza of "Letter from a Distant Land" is dominated by the image of nature, the pleasant world in which the poet lives and in which he nurtures his spiritual strength. Booth quickly sounds his theme of "living halfway" in this world where it is difficult to feel comfortable and completely at home. At his back is the airfield with its gleaming jets that are a constant reminder of the world on the brink of war. Seeing them and hearing them mitigate his sense of being fully part of nature, where the woods are his "chapel" and where he half confesses and finds "absolution in the wind."

In the second stanza, the dominant image is of the jet planes that quickly metamorphose into "great sharks with silver fins that foul the ocean air" and prey on man. The jets represent the great destructive power of the modern state. As Booth meditates on them, he remembers his own participation in the "last war" (World War II) as a pilot and concludes that he "owes several debts" in relation to that participation. The remainder of the stanza deals with his efforts to live on and in harmony with the land, to protect nature, and to live by his own hard labor.

The long final stanza of eighty-four lines moves toward a resolution of the conflict facing the poet. The stanza opens with an image of radar and enemies, which the poet contrasts with the imagery of a walk through the woods, "half-way towards dawn."

The lake is still "half Thoreau's," although the area has been made into a tourist attraction. The poet meditates on the transformation of Thoreau's world and ends the poem with an affirmation of hope despite these changes. He declares his love for the land, though he still feels like a stranger in it.

Forms and Devices

The form in which Booth expresses these ideas is the epistolary form of poetry, the letter, specifically a letter to a spiritual "kinsman." Booth adopts iambic pentameter as his primary meter and employs a complex pattern of off-rhyme in tercets (terza rima), rhyming *aba, bcb, cdc, ded* throughout the poem. This strict pattern accomplishes several objectives. The iambic pattern is that of speech and thus helps establish the sense that the poet is engaging in direct speech. The intricate pattern of rhyme provides for a tight structure of thought and image, but one that is disguised by the use of off-rhyme. The result is a carefully crafted poem, one suitable for delivery to a spiritual master.

Another formal device is the contrast of two sets of images: the mechanical and the natural, the jet planes and the birds and trees. These images are part of the structure of the poem's three long stanzas, yet they are subsumed under the more pervasive image of "halfway." Throughout the poem, this reference to halfway takes on new and richer meaning.

The entire poem is based on a sense of a half-realized life, a half-realized sense of purpose. This sense of half-realization is attributable in part to the allusion to *Walden*. Thoreau's vision of the complete life is very strict and demanding, and though Booth is attempting to live it, he falls short in his own estimation. *Walden* or no *Walden*, however, Booth sees himself at a halfway point with his life.

Where he is is not only a place, it is also a state of mind. Thus, when he describes the place he lives as "halfway between the airfield and your pond," he not only describes the physical location but also reveals the fact that he has been able to free himself only in part from the concerns of the world, its history, its conflicts, and its stresses. That world is symbolized by the airfield and its jets that play so great a part in the development of the poem.

Themes and Meanings

The theme of the poem is the need of the poet to connect himself with a previous, perhaps more innocent time and to establish a sense of himself in the present. Although he is ostensibly writing a letter to Thoreau, he is also using the poem as a vehicle to declare his own sense of connectedness and purpose, the "strange love in a distant land" with which the poem ends.

Part of the problem of identity for Booth is his perception of the encroachment of the machine that threatens the land, the chain saws that "rape a virgin stand to stumps" and that have "more power than has ever been seen before." They desecrate the natural landscape: "an orange oil tank flaws the spring; girders bloom with concrete blocks." In addition to the incursion of the machine, time has wrought additional havoc: wars, inflation, tourists, pollution. "Tight-paired jets" write "cryptic warnings on the thin blue air." The jets symbolize not only the present but also a future dominated by machines and by violence.

Booth's view of the mechanization of modern life is a step beyond that of Thoreau, who in *Walden* found a place for the railroad as symbol of the new age of the machine. Like Walt Whitman in *Democratic Vistas* (1871), Thoreau saw the machine as part and parcel of his transcendental vision. It was all part of the transformation of the world, a new vehicle for humanity to reach a state of higher development. Apparently neither Thoreau nor Whitman foresaw that modern science and technology would lead to the destruction of the environment. For Philip Booth, that destruction made great inroads on the quality of life and on the state of nature.

Booth takes this whole situation one step further: For him, the world is on the verge of war. This poem was written in the early years of the Cold War, in which the United States and the Soviet Union maintained hostile relations with each other and believed each nation sought the destruction of the other. The image of the jet overhead and the carcass of a "traffic-flat" skunk suggest a vulnerable world subject to imminent and total destruction. Booth recognizes, though, that war and death are not some new part of American life. He points out that Thoreau wrote *Walden* during a period of great violence and war. This was also the time when the issue of slavery was tearing the country apart.

Booth sees himself, a century after Thoreau, crossing "the middle-ground/ toward hope." Despite the fact that America has changed dramatically and that new and more potent dangers have emerged, Booth declares that he must make do with what he has and ask only that nature provide him with a home and the wisdom that was granted to Thoreau. Like Thoreau before him, he believes his salvation will come from hope and love derived from reverence for and appreciation of nature.

Richard Damashek

LETTER OF TESTIMONY

Author: Octavio Paz (1914-1998)
Type of poem: Lyric/Meditation
First published: 1987, as "Carta de creencia: Cantata," in *Árbol adentro*; English translation collected in *The Collected Poems of Octavio Paz: 1957-1987*, 1987

The Poem

"Letter of Testimony" is a long meditative poem in free verse. Divided into three parts, it is subtitled "Cantata" and concludes with a nine-line coda.

The poem begins at dusk, that uncertain moment between light and dark that can stand perfectly as a symbol for the flow of time. As day darkens, so does the page on which the poet is writing. Once again the reader is in touch with one of Octavio Paz's favorite scenarios for his long meditative poems: the writer writing at night.

Writing supposes a curious kind of conversation that is almost three-way: The poet talks to himself and to the woman he loves (in this case Paz's wife, the subject of most of his late poems). Writing, or the conversation that it stands for, should be natural, the way a tree talks to the air, or the way water flows or fire sparks. As always, however, Paz realizes only too well the multifarious nature of words. If words are bridges between objects in the world and human consciousness, they are also "traps, jails, wells." Nevertheless, as they define and describe, they do create meaning and character: "that word is you." Words are bridges to the past (as in the poem "San Ildefonso Nocturne"), and here they lead to a memory evoked by the author of his wife as a child, sleeping at the age of nine among the mimosa, near the city of Meknes in Morocco.

Part 2 reiterates the slippery nature of words but emphasizes that they speak to humans, reveal what they think and are. Love, a universal and particular theme for Paz, also requires a word that, like all others, is equivocal. Paz recalls, in poetic and sometimes unclear allusion, famous statements about love in Western literature and philosophy, some of which have their basis in the works of Plato and Dante and in Neoplatonism. In this tradition, love has been spiritualized, driven to ascend a ladder of perfection. Others, however, less fanciful, think of love as a fever, a kind of sickness. Paz insists on combining the physical with the spiritual, refusing to give precedence to either body or soul. He rejects the "Platonic One," the term for complete union, in favor of the notion that love is always a matter of two people, always searching, never quite finished.

Part 3 returns to specifics, the afternoon once more, the poet writing. The conversation (writing) is renewed; lovers are evoked in the figures of Miranda and Ferdinand from William Shakespeare's *The Tempest* (1611). In the coda, Paz says that although human beings have been condemned to abandon the Garden of Eden, perhaps a form of love is to learn how to walk through the world, to stand natural like a tree, and to continue talking (writing poetry).

Forms and Devices

Paz is at pains to underline what he conceives to be the musical structure of his poem. "Cantata" refers to a musical composition that can comprise a chorus, solos, and recitatives. It is music for voices and, in this case, for the conversation and meditation on the meaning of love and the fact that the spoken word is one of the ways that love defines itself. A "coda" is a passage that brings a composition to a close, and in this poem it contains Paz's statement that to learn to love is to learn to live in harmony with nature.

In terms of the contents, Paz also follows a musical pattern. He is fond of introducing a theme, developing it in the form of variations, and, at the conclusion of the poem, returning to the main theme. In "Letter of Testimony," the theme of time appears, followed by the writing of poetry, which cues a discussion of the slippery nature of words; love is introduced and confronted with time. Finally, the poem returns to the scene with which it began, now altered by the passage of time.

Paz's talent for metaphor is, as always, evident. One can see in the early lines a favorite device wherein he allows one metaphor to develop into another. The "page" on which he writes encourages the notion of a "leaf" and this, in turn, leads into the idea of a tree dropping its leaves. "Letter of Testimony" is part of a volume of poems called *Árbol adentro (1976-1987)* (1987; *A Tree Within*, 1988). The tree appears in the coda, and thus one can see that symbols and metaphors are stated, developed, and returned to, following the paradigm of a musical composition.

The afternoon itself at the opening of the poem stands for time, and the "dark river" that files away at the edge of things is Paz's expression of one of humankind's oldest symbols for the movement of time and life: the river.

In the midst of his flow of lyrical meditation, Paz is given to catching the reader's attention with a particularly striking metaphor. Above the nine-year-old girl sleeping in the arms of mimosa, a hawk circles. Paz notes the compulsiveness of this action by a wonderful line: "In love with geometry/ a hawk draws a circle." In part 3, the poet accents the importance of touch to lovers with the image: "To love is to have eyes in one's fingertips." In part 1, Paz indulges in an extended use of similes: "like running water . . ./ like a still puddle . . ./ like fire." The similes also function as anaphora, that is, the repetition of words at the beginning of a line.

Paz's love of pairing opposites, a characteristic feature of much of his poetry, appears also in this poem. To underscore the paradox of love, he gives it a series of contraries. Life is both a gift and a penalty, a rage and a holiness, a wound out of which blooms the rose of resurrection.

Themes and Meanings

"Letter of Testimony," as the title implies, confirms several of Paz's enduring themes: time, language, and love. Time hovers over nearly everything that he has written, an ever-present witness to human mortality. (It is interesting to note that Paz speaks very little about death, but much about time, the existence of which leads to the demise of individuals.) Time presides over "Letter of Testimony" in the first stanza.

Throughout this poem, as in his other writings, Paz eschews the creation of moments outside time and even refuses the refuge offered to artists, that of claiming the immortality of art. Love (and art) can create a sense of timelessness, but the ultimate boundary is still time: "Love, timeless island,/ island surrounded by time." Love itself in its surges imitates living and dying.

The ability to use language is one of the defining characteristics of a human being and therefore makes humans dependent on what language can and cannot do. Philosophers and writers have made this one of the common themes of the twentieth century, and Paz in his essays and poetry has constantly discussed what it means to use words. Words are symbols, labels, but not the things themselves; nevertheless, they are all that human beings have, and they give to things a kind of reality. This is particularly true when it comes to distinguishing an individual: "That word is you,/ that word/ carries you from yourself to yourself." Language expresses us.

Writing poetry is one of the most special ways imaginable of employing language, and viewed in this light, it is easy to understand why Paz makes so much out of the writing of poetry in his work. Poetry thrives on the paradoxical reality of words.

In later life, along with the theme of language, love occupies a preferential place in the poet's themes. Paz's achievement as a poet has been to glorify love as an imperious life force without yielding to the temptation to romanticize it or indeed to overidealize it. Love is part of history; like every other human activity it is time bound. One must distinguish it from lust. Desire (lust) is pointless (a mask of death) unless it permutes into love, which is barely an instant in biological history, but enough for invention (or transfiguration) to occur: "the girl turns into a fountain,/ her hair becomes a constellation."

One form of deifying love goes back to Plato and his enormous influence in Western civilization. It was to split the body from the soul and assign to the latter the highest stage of love. Paz recognizes that the corporal senses bring about love, and that the fusion of two bodies does not lead into the disappearance of both in the "Platonic One." Rather, "to love is two,/ always two," longing perhaps to be one but never complete.

The calm statement in the coda caps an impressive career: Love is perhaps a way of learning to see and to live in the world and to be in relationship with the world as are the elements of nature.

Howard Young

LETTER TO LORD BYRON

Author: W. H. Auden (1907-1973)
Type of poem: Epistle/letter in verse
First published: 1937, in *Letters from Iceland*

The Poem

"Letter to Lord Byron" was written during and after a trip to Iceland. W. H. Auden and fellow poet Louis MacNeice had approached Faber, the British publishing firm, and proposed a travel book. Faber accepted and gave the poets the money to finance the trip. Auden, not being a travel writer, had no real idea what to write on for the book, but he had brought a copy of Lord Byron's *Don Juan* (1819-1824) along to read. He decided to write a verse letter to Byron, informing the poet, who died in 1824, what was happening in the Europe of the 1930's. As such, "Letter to Lord Byron" has more digressions than it does Byron; indeed, one might claim that the poem is almost solely composed of digressions.

The poem comprises five unequal parts, all written in rime royal, all discursive and conversational in tone. The actual trip to Iceland that served as the occasion for the poem is mentioned, but in passing and at irregular intervals. References to the journey serve merely as a frame for what Auden really wants to say.

Part 1 begins with a direct address to Byron, apologizing for disturbing him. Auden—there is no point in insisting on a persona here, since the poet makes no pretense of developing any voice other than his own—mentions that he is in Iceland awaiting the arrival of the rest of his fellow travelers, and he discusses why he chose to address the letter to Byron. Auden had brought Byron's *Don Juan* and a novel by Jane Austen with him, but he finds both what he has to say and his medium for saying it more attuned to Byron. He talks about his choice of a form and then begins to give a defense of light verse, a form not highly prized in the literature of the twentieth century.

Part 2 initially describes a little of Auden's immediate reaction to Iceland, but soon he begins to talk of recent developments in Europe. He acquaints Byron with the changes of taste in England, the confusion of the class system because of industry— "We've grown, you see, a lot more democratic,/ And Fortune's ladder is for all to climb"—and then imagines how modern publicity would make a celebrity of Don Juan. After a quick glance at the art scene, Auden begins discussing "the spirit of the people," finding a conscious rejection of heroism for economic comfort: "'I may not be courageous, but I save.'" This spirit is inimical to that of Byron, so Auden next imagines Byron returned to modern realities, but this is not a heroic age: "In modern warfare, though it's just as gory,/ There isn't any individual glory."

Auden begins part 3 just before setting off for an excursion into the countryside of Iceland. Auden once again affirms his liking for light verse and announces that he shares Byron's belief that William Wordsworth is "a most bleak old bore." This observation leads naturally enough into a discussion of landscape, then proceeds to a lengthy consideration of the estrangement of the artist from society—an estrangement that Auden traces to the nineteenth century.

Part 4 begins on ship heading back to England. Auden quickly summarizes what he gained from the trip, his main accomplishment being learning to ride a pony. Then, triggered by his returning home, he begins to tell his own biography. Starting with a glance at his passport and his own Icelandic ancestry, Auden takes a general, and generally light-hearted, look at his own character, eventually pronouncing, "'Your fate will be to linger on outcast/ A selfish pink old Liberal to the last.'" Then he begins to recount his upbringing, his early interest in machinery, school days during World War I, his adventures with headmasters (which allows him an attack on "Normality" and a defense of eccentric teachers), the incident that led him first to write poetry, his days at the University of Oxford, then his time spent in Berlin on family money, his return to England, and his teaching at a boarding school. He finally gets to his work in documentary filmmaking as the boat reaches the dock.

Part 5 is by far the briefest of the sections; Auden does, however, manage to touch on the coming war, labor difficulties, his essential Englishness, and the proper place to send his "Letter to Lord Byron." He finally pictures Byron lounging with other poets in heaven ("Are Poets saved? Well, let's suppose they are") and apologizes for the length of the "letter that's already far too long,/ Just like the Prelude or the Great North Road"; he then justifies the poem's size when he closes: "As to its length, I tell myself you'll need it,/ You've all eternity in which to read it."

Forms and Devices

"Letter to Lord Byron" is an obvious response to *Don Juan*, which Auden was reading at the time. Exactly why Auden chose a different form for "Letter to Lord Byron" is unclear. *Don Juan* is written in ottava rima, which consists of stanzas of eight lines of iambic pentameter with the first, third, and fifth lines rhyming with one another, as do the second, fourth, and sixth. The verse form is completed with lines 7 and 8 forming a rhyming couplet.

Auden claims, "I want a form that's large enough to swim in,/ And talk on any subject that I choose." Certainly, Byron found ottava rima appropriate for expansive, digressive verse. Auden acknowledges this: "Ottava Rima would, I know be proper,/ The proper instrument on which to pay/ My compliments." He states that if he did use it, however, he would "come up a cropper." Certainly such a claim should be taken with more than the proverbial grain of salt. First of all, rime royal, which Auden chose, is as difficult a form as ottava rima; second, even though at the time he was a poet still in his twenties, Auden had already shown himself to be a master of form. Clearly his claim of deficient skills should not be considered seriously.

Perhaps Auden believed that Byron had already done as much as one can with ottava rima in the comic mode. In choosing rime royal, Auden selected an expansive form that had not been utilized with any great success at length since Geoffrey Chaucer's *Troilus and Criseyde* (1382), which was not a humorous poem. Rime royal consists of seven-line stanzas of iambic pentameter, with the first and third lines rhyming and the second, fourth, and fifth lines rhyming. The verse then closes with a rhyming couplet composed of the sixth and seventh lines. In effect, the form is identical to ottava rima with the fifth line omitted. What this omission does is make the verse end with two pairs of rhyming couplets.

Regardless of the reason for his choice, rime royal left Auden with the repetition of rhyme and the drawing together of the closing couplet so helpful to humorous verse. Like Byron, Auden makes extensive use of feminine, or multisyllabic, rhyme, the bounce of which tends to have a comic effect: "At least my modern pieces shall be cheery/ Like English bishops on the Quantum Theory." He also echoes Byron in calling conscious attention to his supposed deficiencies in poetry: "Et cetera, et cetera. O curse,/ That is the flattest line in English verse."

Themes and Meanings

It would be impossible in this brief space to discuss adequately all the themes of "Letter to Lord Byron." The poem by design is without design; themes are introduced, dropped, and picked up again, sometimes merely touched on, at other times discussed in detail, and always with a lightness of tone. Topics include the psychology of twentieth century man and the isolation of the artist from society.

Auden tells Lord Byron that people have the "same shape and appearance" and "haven't changed the way that kissing's done" but that modern man is "another man in many ways." He says that the contemporary man is best portrayed by cartoonists such as Walt Disney. This man "kicks the tyrant only in his dreams,/ Trading on pathos, dreading all extremes;/ The little Mickey with the hidden grudge."

This is economic man, bred "on Hire-Purchase by Insurance," fearing admonishment by "tax collector and a waterboard." He makes no pretense to the heroic, as "'Heroes are sent by ogres to the grave./ I may not be courageous, but I save.'" He dares to "give his ogreship the raspberry/ Only when his gigantic back is turned." He is caught in his fears, but he fears even more to escape into uncertainties, so his oppressor knows that his comfort makes him a slave: "The ogre need but shout 'Security,'/ To make this man, so lovable, so mild,/ As madly cruel as a frightened child." This is not a time for the disinterested hero, for those who risk their lives for the cause of others as Byron did for Greek independence.

Auden begins his consideration of the artist and society with the Augustan age. He speaks of two arts; one was dependent on "his lordship's patronage" and was more of an aristocratic pursuit. This form of "high" art Auden personifies in Alexander Pope. The other form of art was "pious, sober, moving slowly,/ Appealing mainly to the poor and lowly" and is personified in Isaac Watts. These arts were very different, but Auden is unusually emphatic as to the central point: "The important point to notice, though, is this:/ Each poet knew for whom he had to write." He makes the assertion that art must be attendant—that is, must serve a particular class with whom the artist shares similar concerns. What art must not be is independent.

Yet this is just what has happened. Auden writes that each man naturally wants his independence, but for the artist, such independence is disastrous. Until the Industrial

Revolution, the artist had to depend on the patron and please the taste of the patron or the class: "He had to keep his technique to himself/ Or find no joint upon his larder shelf."

When the artist was able to declare his independence, however, he "sang and painted and drew dividends,/ But lost responsibilities and friends." At first there was great experimentation and euphoria; Auden writes of his imagined Poet's Party: "Brilliant the speeches improvised, the dances,/ And brilliant too the technical advances." Soon, however, the artist is ignored by the public that he scoffs at rather than serves and is left alone with only his technique. At the Poet's Party, some "have passed out entirely in the rears;/ Some have been sick in corners; the sobering few/ Are trying to think hard of something new." Technique is now everything; the audience is gone, and art becomes solipsistic.

Auden does mention that this applies more to the visual arts; even at "the Poet's Party," the majority "of the guests were painters." The case applies in a lesser way to literature, though the onus of meaning generally attached to words does make most writing more accessible than the other arts.

This is but one of many themes running through "Letter to Lord Byron," but it is particularly noteworthy in being one of the first instances where Auden is consciously rejecting the opaque style that brought him fame in his twenties and is attempting to reach out with plainer speech to a wider audience, in effect beginning to distrust the vatic nature of his early verse.

Robert Darling

LETTERS TO A PSYCHIATRIST

Author: May Sarton (1912-1995)
Type of poem: Poetic sequence
First published: 1972, in *A Durable Fire: New Poems*

The Poem

As the title suggests, "Letters to a Psychiatrist" is a series of letters in verse. They are six in number, written to Marynia F. Farnham, the author and psychiatrist to whom *A Durable Fire: New Poems*, the collection in which these poems first appeared, is dedicated. As a sequence of poems, these six letters in verse, though varied in length and form, move from Christmas, 1970, the time of the first poem, through Easter, 1971, the time of the fifth poem. The movement of the sequence is at once linear and circular. The first-person narrator, a patient of Marynia the psychiatrist, is modeled on May Sarton herself, a poet/artist who, while singing songs of praise to Marynia, moves from a state of suicidal depression to a state that is more whole, conscious, and integrated by the poem's end, an action of change made possible by the vehicle of the accepting and skilled therapist.

The eulogy to Marynia begins with "Christmas Letter, 1970." Consisting of five numbered parts, the numbers provide slight shifts to the ongoing, interior lyrical narrative, an internal dialogue from the "I" of the poem to Marynia, sometimes referred to as "she," sometimes addressed directly by name, and sometimes addressed as "you." In this first poem, Sarton establishes Marynia metaphorically as an "angel" of wisdom, someone so gifted in her profession that she allows those wounded ones, like the narrator herself, to go deeply into themselves to begin the process of healing. The second poem in the sequence, a sixteen-line poem with four stanza breaks entitled "The Fear of Angels," continues the eulogy to the psychiatrist. The poet expands the angel metaphor: The psychiatrist is described as one whose brightness and almost-divine presence allows the patient to drop her defenses in order to go deeper into herself.

"The Action of Therapy," the third poem, is similar to the first poem in structure, a long poem in verse divided, in this case, into six parts. Sarton begins this poem with a whirlwind, a dangerous time when "The psyche nearly cracked/ Under the blast," a metaphor linking the chaos of nature to the turmoil of the individual psyche. Darkness and storm, earthquake and whirlwind evoke a destructive passion that has blasted the narrator to the core. Yet the poem centers on the healer, the psychiatrist Marynia who, as the "psychic surgeon," has the angelic power to accept, give, heal, and bless. Without judgment, with "Simple acceptance/ Of things as they are," Marynia allows the patient to dig into her past, allows the patient to love her in a structured but nonthreatening and nonjudgmental atmosphere, and thereby allows the patient to break the spell her own mother had over her. To give and to receive love, to be receptive and teachable, are some of the actions of therapy. The psychiatrist is once again eulogized in glowing terms of light, transformation, and transparency—the soul's realm.

The fourth poem, entitled "I Speak of Change," is the pivotal poem in the sequence. An eighteen-line poem with no stanza or numbered breaks, it is more formally structured than those that have preceded it. Indeed, the tight structure serves to mirror the poem's content: the lesson of passion contained (a recurring theme in Sarton's poetry). The poet begins with the couplet, "Tumult as deep and formal as in dance/ Seizes me now for every scheduled hour." The tension between chaos and order, passion and detachment is resolved by merging these two seemingly opposite impulses. Here the psychiatrist and poet meet, representing, on a figurative level, the reconciliation of elements in the poet's own psyche. Indeed, reconciled opposites inform the poem: words and silence, light and darkness, distance and closeness. The narrator indicates the relationship has served growth and change and has allowed the narrator/ patient/poet to become more fully and authentically herself.

The fifth poem, entitled "Easter 1971," is a celebration of the riches that have come from the patient-therapist relationship; it is also a celebration of the poet's aloneness. The narrator knows that an epiphany is near, and she celebrates the antiphonies of opposite forces, named in the poem as "fervor and detachment," two qualities that Sarton herself believes to be necessary for the poet/artist. In the last line of this poem, the narrator calls the psychiatrist-patient relationship "a structured, impersonal, and holy dance."

In "The Contemplation of Wisdom," the last poem in the sequence, the narrator speaks of the inevitable severing of the relationship with the psychiatrist and contemplates the wisdom she has gained. The narrator accepts more fully the life of one who has to live on the edge, the artist's life, and shows acceptance of her darkness and loss. Once again the narrator eulogizes the psychiatrist: "I summon up fresh courage from your courage." She ends with the acceptance of the psychiatrist's love as the key that will help her with her solitary poet/artist's life.

Forms and Devices

These poems abound with references to the natural world of plants and animals; light and dark; seasons, earth, water, and sky; and earthquakes, storms, and fire. Used as both metaphors and images that inform the poetic landscape, these references make it clear that human beings, with their capacity for suffering and joy, also belong to this natural kingdom. The personal psyche can be blasted just as a tree struck by lightning can be blasted or the earth, rent by an earthquake, can be blasted. Juxtaposed with these natural images are images of transcendence, an arena of experience belonging to both God and humans.

Sarton begins "Christmas Letter, 1970" with "These bulbs forgotten in a cellar,/ Pushing up through the dark their wan white shoots,/ Trying to live—." Used metaphorically as a part of the narrator/poet that is lost in unconsciousness, the bulbs, a symbol of potential beauty and transformation (the flower), serve as that potential for growth that is acknowledged yet "forgotten," that part of the narrator's own psyche that wants realization. Sarton, who speaks lovingly in her journals of gardening, writes, in her *Journal of a Solitude* (1973), a non-fiction journal she was writing even as she composed the poems for *A Durable Fire*, "For a long time, for years, I have carried in my mind the excruciating image of plants, bulbs, in a cellar, trying to grow without light, putting out *white* shoots that will inevitably wither. It is time I examined this image."

Juxtaposed with the natural world in these poems is the more transcendent world of angels and God, a nonetheless human world that incorporates mystery, wisdom, and rebirth as well as the great "Unknown." The movement toward reconciliation of these seemingly opposite forces contributes to the tension of this sequence. The human rises to the divine in the person of Marynia, described again and again as "an angel," one who has "superior powers." Marynia is also emblematic of a surrogate mother figure, the divine Mother, the Eternal Feminine. The divine also descends to the human in the figure of Christ, a symbol of transcendence and rebirth but also of suffering (his earthly life leading up to the Crucifixion). In the fifth part of the third poem, "The Action of Therapy," Sarton writes, "In middle age we starve/ For ascension," clearly indicating that in maturity the interior psychological drive is for transcendence, which means, for Sarton, a drive for love and connection, for earthly communion and wisdom. "The cruel ascension/ Toward loss" described in part 3 of "The Action of Therapy" epitomizes the narrator's struggle to transcend humankind's animal nature by merging into it and accepting loss and change.

The Christian holidays of Christmas and Easter are integral to the sequence and parallel the narrator's struggle. Christmas, symbolic of Christ's birth, is, in the Christian tradition, a time of joy and hope for the world. It is also, for many, a time of loneliness and depression. In part 2 of "Christmas Letter, 1970," the reader hears Marynia's voice through the interior dialogue of the narrator/patient: "'Yes,' you say, 'of course at Christmas/ Half the world is suicidal.'" Sarton also draws the parallel between vulnerable infant love, which the Christ child also represents, and the vulnerable love of the patient for the psychiatrist, a love that, in parts of the sequence, appears naïve in its ubiquitous adoration, a naïveté that is clearly a part of the process of therapy. The patient, like the vulnerable infant and the "homeless cat" mentioned in part 1 of this same poem, is "hungry" and "starving." This animal need for food, symbolic of the narrator/patient's need for love and acceptance, will be satisfied by a meeting of the divine presence, symbolized in the literal as well as figurative Marynia, one who is associated with both the human and divine mother. Words such as "food," "nourish," "restore," "save," "shelter," "provide," and "mother" surround Marynia throughout these poems as do words such as "angel," "goddess," "power," "light," "mysteries," and "blessed." The narrator/patient/poet must, like the Christ child, integrate the human and divine into herself. She does this through the meeting with the literal and figurative Marynia, who, as a psychiatrist with "superior powers," represents for the patient mother love, divine love, and transcendent love.

As Christmas connotes both joy and suffering, Easter connotes both as well. In the Christian tradition, Easter represents Christ's death and suffering as epitomized in the crucifixion; Easter also represents Christ's rebirth and resurrection. In "Easter 1971," the narrator has been, through "the action of therapy," figuratively resurrected. She writes, "I come to this Easter newly rich and free/ In all my gifts." Celebrating both the richness of her own gifts as a poet and her "winter poverty," the aloneness and detachment required for a writer, the narrator has come to a fuller acceptance of her self. Though the poet feels reborn through "the action of therapy," she nevertheless must struggle, as all humans do, with loneliness, suffering, and loss. Wisdom, the topic of the last poem, is, Sarton implies, the true meeting place that is both God-like and human, the reconciliation of the human and divine soul.

Themes and Meanings

"Letters to a Psychiatrist" is a poem about the interior journey, a theme that has occupied Sarton in her novels, fiction, and poetry. While "Letters to a Psychiatrist" explores the unique relationship between psychiatrist and patient, it also explores the human journey of suffering, pain, depression, and loss as well as the human journey of growth, love, and transcendence. Although the patient/narrator is modeled on Sarton herself, it is most important to realize that any poem, if it works at all, should not require an exhaustive search into the poet's own life and psyche to be understood, for good poetry speaks of the largesse of the human experience, however idiosyncratic the subject or even the poet may seem. However, because Sarton's life and art are so closely related, her themes can be better understood by looking at a few of her own words.

In *Journal of a Solitude*, Sarton writes, "Here in Nelson [New Hampshire] I have been close to suicide more than once, and more than once have been close to a mystical experience of unity with the universe." This preoccupation with both the realm of suffering and the realm of transcendence, the mystical realm, is what, most of all, informs these poems. Though Marynia F. Farnham was Sarton's real therapist, readers will realize, if they look at the poems themselves rather than Sarton's life, that Marynia must also be seen as a facet of Sarton herself and, by implication, as a facet of the feminine, if not the divine feminine, in every person.

Though the decision to exclude talk about the relationship between Farnham and Sarton in *Journal of a Solitude* was left to critic and editor Carolyn Heilbrun, Sarton herself argued, "There are still many people who believe that going to a psychiatrist is an admission of failure or an act of cowardice . . . I am a fruitful person with a viable life and I believe it would be helpful for people to know that I have had help and did not fear to ask for it." This quote is important because Sarton's personal life and her art are almost inseparable; yet, paradoxically, because she is an artist, her art is at once larger than her personal life.

Once again, though Marynia was a real, living person, this woman, through the action of the poems themselves, becomes much larger than a simple woman or a psychiatrist in the same way the narrator of these poems becomes much larger than Sarton the writer and poet. While the meanings and themes of this poetic sequence are based on what happened in Sarton's real life, they are also much more than what happened;

they are about emotional involvement and emotional detachment (stereotypically and traditionally represented in Western culture as the feminine/masculine) as well as the human/divine nature in each person that aspires to self-knowledge, understanding, love, and wisdom. As far as the patient/narrator/poet is concerned, Sarton asks, in *Recovering: A Journal* (1980), "Is there anyone, I sometimes wonder, who is not wounded and in the process of healing?" thereby aligning each reader with her narrator.

Though some of Sarton's critics have criticized the poems in *A Durable Fire* for not confronting "the emotional issues she writes about with candor, openness, or a sufficient sense of honesty," the strength of the poems in "Letters to a Psychiatrist" is that they transcend that which is purely personal. Human beings all suffer from lack of growth and unconsciousness, like those bulbs "forgotten" in a dark cellar that begin the sequence. While on one hand "Letters to a Psychiatrist" is a eulogy to Marynia, this poetic sequence also concerns, at its core, the struggle toward integration of all the disparate parts that make people human, the struggle to integrate the feminine within themselves, the struggle to integrate the open and vulnerable child with the mature, suffering, and more cynical adult, and the struggle of the poet to integrate the passionate and emotional lover with the more rational detached artist, "those antiphonies/ Where the soul of a poet feeds and rests." Finally, this poem is about the journey of the psyche and the self toward what Sarton calls "Total awareness," toward "a new landscape" where "souls, released at last,/ Dance together/ On the simple grass."

Candace E. Andrews

LEVIATHAN

Author: W. S. Merwin (1927-   )
Type of poem: Narrative
First published: 1956, in *Green with Beasts*

The Poem

   W. S. Merwin's "Leviathan" is written as "imitation" poetry. The poem replicates old english poetry in both thematics and poetic technique. Merwin, following in the footsteps of Ezra Pound, has seen fit to describe the human condition in the twentieth century by using vehicles of poetry established during the Anglo-Saxon period some twelve to fifteen hundred years earlier. In particular, the lonesome, brooding qualities of figures in earlier English poetry are revisited as modern alienation, despair, and isolation. In the manner of Anglo-Saxon poetry, the poem is entirely in the third person, which permits the poet to comment about human nature while appropriately remaining detached himself. The title word "leviathan" means any large sea animal. It was originally applied to various animals such as crocodiles or sea turtles, but today it commonly signifies the whale, the meaning Merwin has in mind.

   The first dozen lines or so of the poem provide a description of the leviathan, here seen initially as the "black sea-brute bulling through wave-wrack." The whale is then shown in action moving through the waves, creating vast havoc, and in his environment, where he "overmasters" the sea-marches to find "home and harvest."

   The whale's size and actions make him "frightening to foolhardiest/ mariners." He plows through the ocean waves so as to create terror in the hearts of those who view him. All of nature receives the impact of his presence. When the whale is last seen, he is diving into the "cold deep . . . drowning."

   The speaker of the poem then places the leviathan in the context of human history and identifies his association with humankind by listing a series of biblical references. Specifically, the reader is reminded that the whale was the first creature made by God and that Jonah was held by the whale for three days and nights. After describing him as the "curling serpent" of the ocean (yet another biblical reference, this time to the Garden of Eden), Merwin compares him to Satan himself in the phrase "lost angel." Finally, the main point of the poem is made: It is humanity that is the new leviathan; that is, humankind has now come to occupy the same position in the cosmos that was once held by the great whale. It is the human race that has come "to herit earth's emptiness."

   In the concluding sentences of the poem, Merwin returns to the whale in action. The leviathan, now identified as both whale and humanity, is left in an isolated state, "cumbered with itself." The Creator, perhaps, has made no advancement in moving from whales to humans; both existences are isolated, functional, and mechanical. Both creatures dominate their environments, but neither experiences any peace or fulfillment.

Forms and Devices

"Leviathan" makes expert use of the themes and techniques of Old English poetry. Merwin exactingly captures the mood and atmosphere of the Anglo-Saxon mind-set in so far as brooding, isolation, and immobility (or at least pointless mobility) are concerned. The poem is an extended metaphor in which the life of man is compared, never contrasted, with the life of the whale. Humanity, too, is alone in a universe in which the environment is hostile yet sufficiently controlled; other creatures experience fear and dread in the presence of whales or humans; and there is an understood fear and dread of contact within the species.

As is the case with Old English poetry, the verse is highly alliterative; in this poem, in fact, every line contains alliteration, a feat not always accomplished by the ancients themselves. Every line has a marked caesura, a formal break, often rendered by punctuation, in the middle of the line. There is no end rhyming of the lines, and there is no fixed number of syllables. "Lines" are composed of four feet; four heavily stressed words or syllables are paired with unstressed ones. In addition, as is the case in Old English poetry, the language is forceful and direct, and kennings are used. In many Old English poems, Christian scribes later added Christian elements in an attempt to depaganize the themes of the poems. Merwin, too, has incorporated such elements into his work here. In every way, the poet has written a twentieth century poem by prescriptively following the requirements of form and theme used by the earliest English poets.

Themes and Meanings

The most important theme of "Leviathan" can be readily derived from the overall metaphor of the poem: Humanity has both replaced and displaced whales as the dominant being on earth, and its own existence is entirely similar to that of the original dominating animals. Both entities are large, pervasive, and given too much to thought; both are "hulks" in their own environments; both are frightening to other creatures, here called "mariners"; and, finally, both are trapped in the "dark of night," trying hopelessly to escape but unable to do so because the darkness is pervasive.

Humanity, then, is likened unto that which is leviathan. Like the whales, humanity lives trapped in the "emptiness" of life. Individuals wait in the stillness, trying to focus with one eye, unable to see because there is nothing to see. Existence is a struggle not so much for survival against nature, but for survival against the nothingness of life.

Merwin has taken the commonplace expressions about life voiced by the earliest English poets and has realized connections, associations, and direct applications between then and now. Alienation is the force against which all struggle and never win; the best to be hoped for is a benign acceptance of the emptiness that can only control and rule until the end of one's life. The poet does not provide a voice in the wilderness so much as a voice in the depths of the ocean of despair. Life has no meaning, purpose, or direction; each individual trapped in his own isolation and immobility, here represented only by the voice of the poet, lives like a "lost angel/ On the waste's unease."

Like the ancient poets, Merwin introduces Christian elements into this background with puzzling results that seem forced. The poet legitimizes the biblical creation, the story of Jonah and the whale, and Satan seen as lost angel. The end of the poem definitely recognizes the presence of a "Creator," although the reference is hard to understand. Traditional Christian belief would hold that humankind is the ultimate creation of God, his perfection and self-definition made in His own image. For Merwin, this is not so; the "sea curling . . . is the hand not yet content/ Of the Creator." Humanity, then, is not the final product of God's efforts, and humankind is far more akin to the beasts, represented by the whales, than to the Creator Himself. Appropriately, then, humankind "waits for the world to begin" because there is no evident or operant direction and plan to the present world, or to the present existence of human beings.

Essentially, the poem is "existential" in outlook, perspective, and meaning, although it is unique in poetry because of the poet's successful juxtaposition of an earlier form with contemporaneous thought and belief. Merwin's poem effectively serves to remind the reader that the recognition of an absence of meaning in life, as well as the understanding that each isolated individual must somehow discover and define life and its meaning for himself, did not start with nineteenth century pronouncements that God is dead. Such thinking has always been apparent in poetry written in English. All great thinkers and sensitive people have been aware that humanity can be rightfully compared with "that curling serpent that in the ocean is," knowing full well the earth is an empty place that must be filled with individual efforts made in isolation. Such was the life of leviathan when it dominated the planet, and such is the existence of each person.

Carl Singleton

THE LIAR'S PSALM: REPENTANCE

Author: Andrew Hudgins (1951-   )
Type of poem: Meditation
First published: 1984; collected in *The Never-Ending*, 1991

The Poem

"Repentance" is one of four poems which together constitute a longer work entitled "The Liar's Psalm." The epigraph that precedes "The Liar's Psalm" states the subject and sets the tone for the entire work. It is a quotation from the beast-fable, "Reynard the Fox," one of the many medieval versions of the adventures of an immoral predator who manages through cunning to avoid the punishment he deserves. The epigraph begins by pointing out that, while it takes neither "art nor cunning" to tell the truth, a skillful liar "may do wonders." Motivated by the "hope of gain only," he can rise high in the secular world or in the Church. Almost as an afterthought, the speaker adds that, though lying is indeed an "art," it inevitably ends in "misery and affliction."

With its emphasis on Reynard's accomplishments rather than his downfall, this epigraph establishes the ambivalent tone that is evident throughout "The Liar's Psalm." Andrew Hudgins, the poet, cannot but admire a creature with the artistic talent of the fox; on the other hand, Andrew Hudgins, the moralist, knows that though truth may seem dull, lies are the devil's instrument.

"Repentance" is the second segment in "The Liar's Psalm." It is preceded by "Homage to the Fox," in which the fox's gifts are praised and his worldly success emphasized, while the truth is characterized as both cowardly and unimaginative. The section that follows "Repentance" is called "Judas, Flowering." In it, the speaker says that his hero and presumably his model is Christ's betrayer, Judas. Again, the deceiver is shown as being a fascinating character, unlike pedestrian truth. In the last section of "The Liar's Psalm," "treachery" is again honored; it is far more valuable, the speaker says, than "love" and "hope." There is, however, a puzzling comment in the final lines of the poem. The speaker admits that on occasion he does believe that the moon (light, good, and truth) might eliminate the darkness of the night sky, or evil, but he hastens to add that such a notion is merely proof that he can deceive even himself.

Like the other segments of "The Liar's Psalm," "Repentance" exalts fiction above fact, lies above truth. What the speaker repents is his own failure to lie. He sees truth as powerless; not only can it not keep the persona's father from dying, but it also keeps the son miserable, anticipating grief. The speaker rejects logic, the supposed servant of truth, for in actuality it has "no god": it can be used to prove anything.

Having rejected both reality and logic, the speaker now vows never again to "insult" those he cares about "with the actual." He recalls and regrets the times he told the truth and hurt those he loved—his mother, his wife, a friend, his brother. From now on, he resolves, he will lie to others and believe the lies they tell him. At the end of the poem, the speaker asks forgiveness for his past skepticism, for behaving like Thomas the Apostle, who would not believe that Christ had indeed risen from the dead until Thomas had placed his hand in Jesus's wounded side.

Forms and Devices

Though Hudgins often utilizes blank verse for his poetry, "Repentance" is written in a mixture of forms. Some of the lines are conventional blank verse—for instance, "and I repent logic, which has no god: it will do." Other lines are either shorter or longer but still regular and iambic: "So I have made this vow" and "of apple pie, a black chrysanthemum, a job—I could go on." Sometimes anapests dominate, as in "It is nothing against principalities, against powers." Occasionally the meter becomes so uncertain as the line progresses that Hudgins seems to have forgotten metrics altogether, but when that happens, he soon returns to a regular pattern, if not necessarily to iambic pentameter. For example, after "or with their densities. They are not worth their flawed kingdoms," is followed by a line which begins with three iambic feet, "And neither do I love" before veering away from regularity. However, Hudgins is a careful craftsman, and there is method in what might seem to be metrical madness. To emphasize a point, for example, he uses simple words and a simple, regular pattern, as in the first four words of the poem and in the later "So I have made this vow."

Hudgins's imagery is as varied as his metrics. Some of it is grand and abstract, such as the Miltonic "principalities" and "powers" and the references to "gods" and "kingdoms." On the other hand, much of it is taken from the everyday world. Reality, like manual labor, will "blister" his hands and "make them raw." Logic is compared to a "taxi," lies to self-indulgences like "a piece/ of apple pie," and when in the past the speaker "attacked/ with actuality," he used the "blade" of a knife.

There are often surprising juxtapositions of images in "Repentance." For example, the list of minor "gifts" to oneself (clothing, pie, a flower) ends with a matter of major significance in life, "a job." Similarly, when the speaker lists the truths that he regrets telling, he moves back and forth between moral flaws and matters of taste or appearance. Thus he appears to give the same importance to adultery and theft as to making an unfortunate choice in clothing or simply being too fat.

Often Hudgins is classified with Carson McCullers and Flannery O'Connor as a southern gothic writer. In this poem the final image is more graphic than the biblical original, for here the speaker has his finger not on, but "knuckle deep" in the wound. The earlier reference to human flesh, "sliced from my thighs," is also grotesque. In both cases, however, and throughout the poem, Hudgins places his dramatic, concrete imagery at the service of profound philosophical concepts.

Themes and Meanings

In "Homage to the Fox" and "Judas, Flowering," the speaker glorified evildoers because, as the epigraph points out, they are both interesting and successful. However, the epigraph ends by noting that evil results in "misery and affliction." Certainly it did for Judas, who committed suicide and presumably is spending eternity in Hell. It is obvious, then, that though Hudgins's persona may be deceived, the poet is not. Instead, he is using his speaker to demonstrate how human beings are seduced by evil and specifically by lies and lying.

"Repentance" differs from the segments before and after it in that, here, lying is not shown as a way to worldly power but as a positive good. For example, people would be happier, the speaker argues, if they could not anticipate the deaths of those they love. The knowledge God gave humankind, then, is a burden, not a blessing. The persona then insists that it is lies, not facts, that make a person happy. For one thing, reality is limited, while the human imagination can invent possibilities "six times a second." Even if these dreams do not come true, anticipation alone can bring one great delight.

It is difficult to refute this argument, especially when one broadens it to include in the category of "lies" all the works of the imagination. If one were to divide the world on that basis, as a writer Hudgins must be on the side of lies, and so would everyone be who has chosen to read this poem. Hudgins now proceeds to another argument in favor of lies: that they are kinder than the truth. As has been noted, his examples of cruelty vary from the trivial, such as a comment about an unbecoming dress, to scathing attacks on character traits, such as "stinginess." In a peculiar reversal of Christian doctrine, then, one hopes to be "blessed" with lies, rather than being damned by telling the hurtful truth.

Having pointed out the value of lying to oneself and to others, the persona carries his argument one step further, insisting that one should also believe all the lies one is told. Since he then alludes to Thomas's encounter with the risen Christ, one might read the final lines as a suggestion that faith is a matter of believing in untruths. However, the allusion itself contradicts that implication, for Thomas felt real flesh. His doubts, therefore, were beside the point, for he did not create or imagine Christ. "The Liar's Psalm," then, is not an argument for evil, but an examination of humanity's susceptibility to it. Thus the speaker in the final section of the poem foolishly rethinks his brief moment of faith, while in "Repentance" the liar somehow manages to miss the important truth: that when he decides to "repent the actual," he is rejecting the God who does not lie.

Rosemary M. Canfield Reisman

LIBERTY AND PEACE

Author: Phillis Wheatley (1753?-1784)
Type of poem: Meditation
First published: 1784; collected in *The Poems of Phyllis Wheatley*, 1966

The Poem

"Liberty and Peace," by Phillis Wheatley, is a sixty-six-line meditation celebrating the genesis of the United States of America as a country separate from Great Britain: "Lo! Freedom comes." Written after the successful end of the Revolutionary War as a companion piece to her tribute to George Washington, "To His Excellency General Washington," Wheatley describes in "Liberty and Peace" the figure of "Peace," a woman "divinely fair,/ Olive and Laurel bind[ing] her golden Hair," descending from heaven to grace the new country, called "Columbia," with her presence after the long years of turmoil: "So Freedom comes array'd with Charms divine." "Peace," a messenger from heaven, comes to earth to force the tyrannical "Britannia" to "submit to Heaven's decree" and allow America to detach itself from its colonial forebears.

Wheatley's poem recounts the numerous years of repression that America had suffered from its colonial master, Great Britain, primarily due to the superiority of her natural gifts: "Each Art and Science now with rising Charms/ Th' expanding Heart with Emulation warms." As a "Realm of Freedom," America's impending rivalry with Britain caused great jealousy: "E'en great Britannia sees with dread Surprize,/ And from dazzl'ing Splendor turns her Eyes!" Consequently, Wheatley says, Britain began a series of controlling measures upon America to keep it from becoming a power in its own right: "Britain, whose Navies swept the Atlantic o'er,/ And Thunder sent to every distant Shore."

America's rebellion, meant to finally shake off Britain's restrictive policies regarding American trade—its "Manners cruel" and "Thirst of boundless Power"—is supported by France ("For Galia's Power espous'd Columbia's cause"). King Louis XVI, remarks Wheatley, "Sees the fierce Wrong, and to the rescue flies," since Britain's "Tyrants" are abhorrent to the observing eyes of other countries. The Revolutionary War was not, however, without its costs, as Wheatley so carefully demonstrates. The "fraternal Arms" of Britain and America battled, killing many people and destroying much property. Wheatley reports that the earth itself complained at being soaked with "kindred Gore," and that Britain's soldiers "plunder'd" America's "Treasures" and burned Charlestown: "In one sad hour the savage troops despoil." Only France, "fair Hibernia," Wheatley says, was moved enough to enter the fray and assist the new country in it struggle for freedom.

However, these losses were mitigated by peace's return at the end of war: "And in her Train Commerce and Plenty shine," as America begins open trade with other countries: "Hibernia, Scotia, and the Realms of Spain:/ And great Germania's ample coast." The war being over and peace between nations restored, Wheatley saw a grand future rising for the new country and celebrated both the richness of America's natural resources and the strength of its determined citizenry. With the return of peace after the cessation of the "Din of War," even Britain could return to a peaceful reconciliation with the new country: "Now sheathe the Sword that bade the Brave attone/ With guiltless Blood for Madness not their own."

Forms and Devices

Like all but five of Phillis Wheatley's surviving poems, "Liberty and Peace" is a poem that relies primarily on the English neoclassical devices of the heroic couplet: end rhyme, iambic pentameter, and the caesura. Wheatley's imitation of Alexander Pope apparently led her to attempt to duplicate, more or less successfully, the form of his rhyming couplets, along with all the problems inherent in the use of such forms. The irregular spelling and punctuation of eighteenth century English made Wheatley dependent on the frequent use of elision and odd pronunciation of certain words to maintain the required iambic pentameter: "Britain, whose Navies swept th' Atlantic o'er."

Further, she sometimes duplicated the worst faults of the neoclassical tradition in the use of clichés, stale syntax, and overapplication of personification. "Liberty and Peace," in particular, is a good example of this neoclassical fault because of Wheatley's depiction of not only the inanimate qualities of "Liberty" and "Peace" but also the warring countries of the Revolutionary War as personages: "Columbia," "Britannia," and "Hibernia"—a veritable surfeit of personification.

Like Wheatley's elegies, "Liberty and Peace" also tends to be somewhat impersonal and artificial in sentiment; despite its morbid content, the line "And mutual Deaths, all dealt with mutual Rage" lacks any real suggestion of sympathy and horror at the real bloodshed taking place literally around the young poetess. Again, however, like the faults of language seen in "Liberty and Peace," Wheatley's lack of sentiment tends to be the fault of her reliance on the English neoclassical tradition in verse rather than any lack of poetic ability.

Wheatley's imitation of Pope was not always a bad thing, however, as numerous critics have noted. Quite a number of Wheatley's most elegant and fluid lines bear the marks of Pope's fluency of thought and sublime expression: "She, the bright Progeny of Heaven, descends/ And every Grace her sovereign Step attends." That she could connect such inspired imagery to events happening in her life, albeit events of such dramatic importance as the Revolutionary War, demonstrates her ability to give an elevated, historical perspective to day-to-day colonial life.

The companion poem to "Liberty and Peace," "To His Excellency General Washington," received such high favor that its subject, George Washington, personally invited Wheatley to visit Cambridge for the purpose of meeting the then general in 1776. When the young poetess died in 1784, her death was noted in *The Boston Magazine* and *The Independent Chronicle* as a loss not just to the African American community of the day but also to the reading public as a whole. "Liberty and Peace" helped establish Wheatley as an American poet of note, a title still with her.

Themes and Meanings

Any analysis of any work written by Wheatley would be incomplete without a basic understanding of the unusual life circumstances of the author. Unlike most of her poetic contemporaries, whose lives were graced by wealth and privilege, Wheatley stood out during her era as being one of a very few published black authors and probably the only published black female author. In contrast with such writers as Thomas Godfrey and Anne Bradstreet, Wheatley was not a native of her homeland but was brought to America during her early childhood and raised as a slave, albeit a privileged one, in the house of John Wheatley, a fairly well-to-do tailor in Boston.

Further, at the time that her earliest poems were written, Wheatley had been speaking and writing English for only ten years and suffered constantly from ill health. Certainly good fortune played a large part in establishing Wheatley's poetic fame, but it should also be noted that only a very facile mind could have absorbed such as mass of cultural information as Wheatley did during her youth. Wheatley's training consisted of astronomy, some ancient and modern geography, considerable Bible knowledge, grammar and rhetoric, and classic literature—training that resulted in the poetess's considerable fluency in Greek and Latin, her favorite work being Pope's translation of Greek poet Homer. For any young woman, let alone a household slave, such training was the mark of accomplishment and great natural ability.

Given her status, then, such works as "Liberty and Peace" stand out as being marks of not a good, but rather an exceptional, intellect for a very young woman—merely thirty-one at the time of her death—of African descent living as a slave. Her first poem, "An Elegiac Poem on the Death of George Whitefield," written in 1770, was the work of a seventeen-year-old servant girl. Nevertheless, the poem attracted the attention of many of the best and brightest in the Boston literary community. *The London Magazine: Or, Gentleman's Monthly Intelligencer* quickly reviewed the 1773 edition of Wheatley's works and found it to be vigorous and admirable.

Such late works as "Liberty and Peace," dealing as it does with the society-shaking events of the Revolutionary War, attracted a great deal of admirable press—not least those of George Washington and the governor of Massachusetts. The primary themes, those of loyalty to one's country and God, further inspired admiration among Wheatley's readers. Wheatley's poetic references to the Muses and other mythological figures placed her in the same literary camp as her inspiration, Alexander Pope, which, given his popularity at the time of Wheatley's writing, did not hurt in establishing a consistent audience for Wheatley's creative talents. Again and again, critics of Wheatley's poems have emphasized that she should have a lasting place in history, if not for exceptional poetic ability then definitely for the perseverance of her literary spirit and her patriotic tributes to her adopted country.

Julia M. Meyers

THE LIBRARY

Author: Timothy Steele (1948-   )
Type of poem: Lyric
First published: 1993; collected in *The Color Wheel*, 1994

The Poem

Timothy Steele's lyric poem "The Library" is written in eight stanzas of nine lines each employing an *ababccdbd* rhyme scheme. The poem describes a person coming out of a university library in Southern California at the end of the day, who is struck by a series of increasingly significant contrasts. While walking out of an air-conditioned library, the speaker is blasted by the hot, dry Santa Ana winds in the heat of the day. He seeks refuge on a bench in the sculpture garden where he begins to compare his world with ancient worlds of Greece and Rome. He thinks how times have changed from handwritten to printed books, now as often on microfilms and disks as on paper. That the wealth of ancient literature was largely lost is a point of regret for the speaker: "Thoughts of the art and science thus destroyed/ Leave me a little empty and unnerved." Though the poem is about loss, it is not a lament.

Pursuing the personal connection he feels to art and literature, the speaker trusts that "Technology now limits what is lost," and, he reasons, literature exists best in the minds of living people. He thinks of "The Library as Mind," an interesting organic concept, but abruptly shifts his attention to the more manageable details of ordinary life.

With careful attention, the sixth and seventh stanzas of the poem move through the tasks associated with closing the library for the night. The speaker pauses to think about the last checkouts from the circulation desk, the turning off of the lights on each of the aisles, and the librarians and staffers, whose days are insulated from their outside cares.

How the present is preserved for the future emerges as another theme of the poem through the last few stanzas as the speaker's attention is attracted to a squirrel looking for a nut to bury. In the little animal's "nosing round, compelled to hoard/ By instinct, habit, and necessity," the speaker sees his instincts, as well as those of the librarians, as keepers of culture to save and protect books and other such artifacts out of habit and the sense that it must be done. Presumably, after putting the pieces together, the speaker goes home.

Forms and Devices

The nine-line rhymed stanzas follow a nearly perfect pattern, with the exception of stanza 6. In stanza 6, the three *b*-line rhymes—"truer," "viewer," and "through a"—require the reader to slide "through" them as one word so as not to disturb the *ababccdbd* scheme. The lines are largely end-stopped. The first and second, and seventh and eighth lines of each stanza use enjambment, the technique of continuing an idea over two lines without pausing. The poem follows an accentual syllabic meter that creates an even flow and rhythm.

Steele mixes images of nature with those from history and culture. He also infuses the poem's latter half with detailed descriptions of the closing of the library. Stanza 1 sets the natural scenes as the speaker leaves the library at closing time. Because of the Santa Ana winds, the "grainy sunlight pours/ Through eucalypti whose peeled bark strips beat/ The trunks to which they cling like feeble sleeves." The simile here is clear and precise: The bark strips look like sleeves of an old shirt or jacket flapping frailly in the wind. Throughout the poem attention is paid to the sounds of the natural world as well as to its appearance, giving the poem additional texture and fullness.

The shelter the sculpture garden's bench offers from the winds gives the speaker time to wonder if the library of today might still be called a "cultural oasis." While it houses books, the speaker says he feels as if he is "playing Faustian video games" when using the computer to track books. At the end of the second stanza, the speaker thinks of how Plato, the Greek philosopher, spoke against the power of literature to subvert people's reason and make them want more than they could achieve. There is a connection between scientist-magician Johann Faust, who sold his soul so he could live forever, and Plato, as technology has a way of making people think that whatever is saved on the computer will be safe forever.

In stanza 3, the speaker ponders how the ancient philosophers and scholars would react to the idea of a database. They would be amazed at "words and software joined and sync-ed." The innovations of the technological library strike the speaker as similar to what likely happened when an unnamed early scholar decided that poems should look different from prose "And first gave lyric measures lineation." He is not opposed to changes in the library; he simply wonders what their long-term effectiveness will mean to reading and to preserving written materials.

The flapping of a banner on the nearby art gallery and the fight of two birds over an edible carob pod do not break the speaker's concentration, as he gets deeper into the idea of the contrasts between ancient and modern cultures. Thinking of Rome, Alexandria, and Pergamum, three ancient centers of learning, the speaker seeks to establish the importance of the library in both his life and in the society at large. The success of the allusion that ends stanza 4 depends on the recognition of three commonalities: During the Hellenistic period, poets enjoyed great freedom of expression and were supported in their writing by the royal courts, especially in Alexandria, where the Ptolemic kings were great book collectors; the ancient world's writing gave rise to what today is thought of as literature, with the contents of the libraries being treated as war prizes by conquering armies; and the early librarians were scholars and poets who composed handbooks, glossaries, and anthologies of quotations to promote literature. These ancient libraries were eventually destroyed, and Steele, though he leaves the reader some sense of the significance of the names of the three cities, presumes the reader will be able to make the full connection between the allusions and the poem at hand.

It is also worthwhile to know that Pergamum was famous for its bronze statues celebrating the victories of Kings Attalus and Eumenes, which feature both the conquerers and their victims in dramatic poses capturing the ferocity of battle and the courage of the combatants. This image links the end of stanza 4 to the earlier reference within it to Auguste Rodin's sculpture *Walking Man*, which the speaker can see from the bench. *Walking Man* is one of Rodin's characteristic pieces, which like *The Man with the Broken Nose* reflects his notion that unfinishedness is an artistic aesthetic of its own. Such pieces have a quiet forcefulness about them, which causes the viewer to shift expectations from figural realism to the fragment of the person Rodin made his subject. As Steele moves into the fifth stanza, the issue becomes whether new technology will save learning "from any partial holocaust."

The turning point in "The Library" comes when the speaker changes from the line of thought of "The Library as Mind" to consider how "the details of closing time" are more important. The last line of stanza 7 enjambs into the first of stanza 8 as the speaker is returned to the present moment by the squirrel and the wind blowing some leaves around. The squirrel traces his path down the sycamore tree "as though along a corkscrew's thread," lending a feeling of unity in natural elements. The implied comparison of the squirrel's impulse to preserve itself and the speaker's to preserve his love of learning despite the physical changes in the library, though not quite a metaphysical conceit, suggests humans and animals are among "the frail" who must preserve themselves against larger forces which, like the seasons, might overwhelm the unprepared.

Through carefully chosen evocative language, literary and historical allusions, and a simply understood narrative line, Steele offers a full picture of the physical landscape that constitutes the external setting of the poem and the mental landscape the first-person speaker inhabits. The attention to detail at all levels gives the poem a suitably large scope and makes the speaker a more fully drawn character within the poem. First-person address invites the reader to share the moments the poem describes.

Themes and Meanings

The speaker's love of learning and of the library is evident throughout the poem. He is curious about the ways libraries have served and continue to serve as culture. In the poem's seventy-two lines, Steele is able to address the past, present, and future of not just the library but also intellectual life as a whole. Underlying the history of the library in the ancient world is the theme of resilience. Although countless irreplaceable literary treasures have been lost, more books have taken their places. Naturally, the speaker is worried not only about the fate of the books but also about what role the physical library will have in a virtual world.

As a poet and literary scholar, Steele is drawn to the subject of his poem as part of his own life (his wife is a librarian as well). That he is interested in the question of the library as cultural oasis raises the questions of what culture is and what people must do to preserve it. Though not personified, the library is in fact a living record of literary expression, alive with the signs of past, present, and future human creativity and intellect. Seated between nature and culture, the speaker of "The Library" ultimately asserts his faith in the enduring order of things in the world.

Beverly Schneller

LIBRETTO FOR THE REPUBLIC OF LIBERIA

Author: Melvin B. Tolson (1898-1966)
Type of poem: Epic
First published: 1953

The Poem

Melvin B. Tolson, a professor of English at Wiley College in Marshall, Texas, and author of a collection of poems entitled *Rendezvous with America* (1944), was appointed poet laureate of Liberia by that African nation's president, William V. S. Tubman, in 1947. Tolson was commissioned to compose a poem to celebrate Liberia's centennial. He spent six years at the task, and the book-length *Libretto for the Republic of Liberia* was eventually published in 1953. While he might have fulfilled this commission with a flattering poem, Tolson had a much more ambitious idea. He told an interviewer in 1965, "I, as a black poet, have absorbed the Great Ideas of the Great White World, and interpreted them in the melting-pot idiom of my people. My roots are in Africa, Europe, and America." This self-image as an intellectual synthesizer of world culture informs his poem.

Tolson produced an epic poem in the tradition of Vergil's *Aeneid* (c. 29-19 B.C.E.), presenting Liberia's history in terms of a grand mythology, recounting significant events, and attaching symbolic resonance to the deeds of great leaders. The poem is divided into eight sections—each given the title of one of the notes in the *do-re-mi* musical scale—which Tolson thought of as the rungs on a ladder. Each section brings the reader (and the poet) closer to attaining an overview of history. Because *Libretto for the Republic of Liberia* is intended to be an epic poem, this view of history—like Dante's in *The Divine Comedy* (c. 1320) or John Milton's in *Paradise Lost* (1667) and *Paradise Regained* (1671)—includes past, present, and future.

Section 1, *"Do,"* opens with a series of questions about the Eurocentric view of Africa as a mysterious continent, the very shape of which suggests "a question mark." The meaning of the independent black nation of Liberia is the question that Tolson must answer. He contends that Liberia's unique history makes it "A moment in the conscience of mankind." *"Re,"* the next section, presents the history of Africa before the slave trade began, citing the Songhai Empire, the great city of Timbuktu, and other precolonial centers documented in works by J. A. Rogers and in W. E. B. Du Bois's *The World and Africa* (1947). In section 3, Tolson describes the establishment of Liberia as a haven for freed slaves from the United States sponsored by the American Colonization Society. He describes these settlers as "Black Pilgrim Fathers" because their return to Africa in 1820 reverses the direction of the voyage of the Mayflower exactly two hundred years earlier. The section ends with a leap forward in time to 1942, when airfields in Liberia were a staging area for Allied bombers in World War II.

Section 4 presents images of predatory nature juxtaposed with the refrain "in the interlude of peace," symbolizing Liberia's struggle to remain independent while European nations partitioned the rest of the continent into colonial possessions. Section 5, *"Sol,"* emphasizes that the Liberian settlers must survive perilous conditions, but in addition they are charged with the task of refuting Europe's racist judgment of African inferiority. Tolson counters such views with a series of African proverbs, beginning: "Africa is a rubber ball;/ the harder you dash it to the ground,/ the higher it will rise." The next section, *"La,"* recounts the heroic efforts of Jehudi Ashmun, the white American missionary who devoted his life to help establish the Liberian settlement.

Section 7, *"Ti,"* is a 232-line tour de force of literary allusions and intricate rhyme schemes that attacks European imperialism and the Eurocentric misreading of history that supported the exploitation of other continents. The final *"Do"* section—which rivals *"Ti"* for inventive density—is a vision of a glorious African future that will herald a new era of genuine peace and international cooperation. In this coming age, after centuries of turmoil, Tolson predicts that it will become possible for human beings to balance "the scales of Head and Heart."

Forms and Devices

In form, *Libretto for the Republic of Liberia* may be considered an irregular ode, but its eight-hundred-line length and historical subject matter also qualify it as a modernist epic comparable with Hart Crane's *The Bridge* (1930) or Ezra Pound's much longer *Cantos* (1925-1968). Tolson's poem also has some stylistic similarities to these works. However, as the title suggests, he intended *Libretto for the Republic of Liberia* to be a grand song joined by many voices.

Tolson's dividing of the poem into sections titled with notes from the musical scale indicates that each section has its own distinct tonality, allowing the poet to use a number of different poetic forms. Since a libretto is ordinarily understood to be the words for an opera, this arrangement suggests that Tolson intends the reader to understand that his words form the "meaning" of each musical note. Music is ordinarily thought of as an abstract or nonreferential art form, but there are African traditions suggesting that specific notes or musical tones have specific meanings. Indeed, the tones produced by the West African *dundun* (or "talking drum") can simulate words in a tonal language such as Yoruba. Tolson studied African proverbs extensively, and his use of them in the poem indicates his concern that *Libretto for the Republic of Liberia* would embody traditional African artistic elements.

The poetic techniques that Tolson most often employs in this poem are metaphors and highly concentrated allusions (references to other literary works). As in his earlier long poem "Rendezvous with America," he also devises different rhyme patterns for each section of the work.

Tolson's complex structure of literary allusions and historical references is similar to the juxtapositions found in Pound's *Cantos*, and he directs the reader to his sources with footnotes in the manner of T. S. Eliot's *The Waste Land* (1922). The range of references documents Tolson's own scope of knowledge and suggests a curriculum for the reader's further education. The scope of these references supports Tolson's belief that culture and knowledge are not limited by racial, geographical, or political boundaries; he cautions the reader not to ignore "the dusky peers of Roman, Greek, and Jew" in attempting to assess the progress of human civilization, to which all of the world's cultures have contributed. The dedicated reader of *Libretto for the Republic of Liberia* can seek out the specific references behind the poem's allusions and, by so doing, gain a deeper understanding of Tolson's argument and his unique mental associations. To use a musical analogy, exploring this level of the poem is like focusing on the bass line of a familiar song; suddenly one becomes aware of a delightful new set of designs and parallel inventions. When Tolson alludes to a line from Rudyard Kipling's 1897 poem "Recessional," for example, he is leading the reader to the idea that the advent of an independent, peaceful future for African nations must necessarily also involve the recessional or retreat of the exploitative European colonialism that Kipling's poem celebrated.

Section 5 demonstrates that, while he was an avid student of European literature, Tolson's approach to writing this epic poem includes the traditions of the West African *griots*, the oral historians and bards described in Tolson's footnote as "living encyclopedias." Just as those poets were responsible for memorizing the genealogies of the families in their region, Tolson's poem contains the stories of the Reverend Jehudi Ashmun, the Reverend Robert Finley of the American Colonization Society, and Liberia's first president, Joseph Jenkins Roberts. Although he employs the elevated language suitable to an epic poem, Tolson does not provide a straightforward narrative structure. The reader who consults encyclopedia entries on Liberia and the American Colonization Society can learn many of the historical details needed to follow Tolson's references.

Themes and Meanings

In vivid contrast to the beginning of *Libretto for the Republic of Liberia*, in which the shape of the African continent suggests to Tolson a question mark or a skull, the poem's concluding section presents a series of glowingly positive images. The poem's final prophetic section, the musical scale's resolving "*Do*," is written in verse paragraphs reminiscent of the Bible or Walt Whitman's *Leaves of Grass* (1855). Here Tolson depicts the continent via the metaphor of the Futurafrique—imagined as a fast train, supersonic airplane, or ocean liner. This promise of a glorious modernistic future is followed by Tolson's vision of a Parliament of African Peoples.

Earlier in the poem, Tolson quotes (in French) the nineteenth century rationalization for slavery and the colonization of Africa based on the argument that "alone of all the continents, Africa has no history" or civilization. It is against this claim that he offers his vision of the continent's future. Rather than devoting the poem to a list of great African leaders or a chronicle of memorable precolonial achievements, Tolson refutes the myth of African inferiority with a catalog of African proverbs that testify to the wisdom and experience of the continent's peoples. Finally, Tolson presents Liberia not only as a nineteenth century refuge for American slaves but also (as a result of its heroic survival) as a beacon of global promise, the coming fulfillment of humankind's best possibilities as reflected in the nation's motto, "The Love of Liberty Brought Us Here."

Lorenzo Thomas

THE LIE

Author: Sir Walter Ralegh (c. 1552-1618)
Type of poem: Satire
First published: 1608, in *A Poetical Rapsody*; collected in *The Poems of Sir Walter Ralegh*, 1929

The Poem

Given that "The Lie" is now Sir Walter Ralegh's best-known poem, it would be ironic if the French critic Pierre Lefranc were correct in his assertion, in *Sir Walter Ralegh, Ecrivain, L'oeuvre et les idées* (1968), that it was not written by Ralegh. The earliest known manuscripts, which date from approximately 1595, are unsigned, as is the first printed version in Francis Davison's *A Poetical Rapsody* (1608). Lefranc argues that the poem is obviously the work of a Puritan, which Ralegh emphatically was not. Lefranc further argues that the poem is too clumsy and tedious to be Ralegh's. The vast majority of English critics, however, agree that the attribution is correct, claiming that the impression of Puritan sentiment is derived from a too-literal reading of a satire and observing that the poem's rhythm, based on iambic trimeters with five initial trochaic feet, closely resembles poems that are unmistakably Ralegh's. The English critics also disagree with the contention that the poem is clumsy or tedious, although its tempo is certainly furious enough to give it a reckless quality, and it hammers home its point with a rain of blows whose quantity is suggestive of overkill.

The thirteen stanzas of "The Lie" comprise a series of instructions addressed to the soul, famously characterized as "the body's guest," demanding that it strip away the poses and pretenses with which social life is armored. Each six-line stanza concludes with an injunction that any reply should be stoutly met: The last line of each stanza (except the thirteenth) is a variant of the phrase "and give the world the lie." Following the introductory stanza, the main series moves through three phases. In the first phase (a single stanza) the soul is commanded to tell the court that "it glowes,/ and shines like rotten wood" and the Church that "it showes/ whats good, and doth no good."

In the second phase, which comprises three stanzas, the soul is instructed to address itself more generally to potentates, "men of high condition," and "them that brave it most." The potentates are gently reminded that they are "not loved unless they give"; the men of high condition are attacked far more vituperatively because "their purpose is ambition/ their practise onely hate"; the third group, by contrast, is let off more lightly than the addressees of any other stanza, it merely being said that "they beg for more by spending,/ Who in their greatest cost/ like nothing but commending." In the third and longest phase (seven stanzas), the soul is commanded to penetrate the illusion, each in its turn, of zeal, love, time, and flesh; age, honor, beauty, and favor; wit and wisdom; "Phisicke" (medicine), skill, charity, and law; fortune, nature, friendship, and justice; arts and "schooles" (philosophy); and faith, manhood, and virtue. The last stanza gives the screw of cynicism one last turn in conceding that "to give the lie,/ deserves no lesse then stabbing" but notes triumphantly that "no stab thy soule can kill."

Forms and Devices

"The Lie" is a poem about disillusionment, and its method is admirably suited to its subject, for disillusionment is a process that proceeds by inexorable degrees, stripping one layer of falsity after another until the last is gone. Ralegh employs the repetitive rhythm of the poem to build up a relentless surge that cannot be interrupted until it has taken its corrosive task to its logical end point. The suggestion of overkill that seems tedious to Lefranc is, in fact, entirely appropriate to the project.

Disillusionment is the principal stock-in-trade of satire, which was newly fashionable as a device when "The Lie" was written. The satirical method is one of contemptuous exaggeration that magnifies faults so aggressively that no half measures are tolerated. "The Lie" accepts this extremism wholeheartedly, accelerating as it moves through its phases of generality to the point at which each of the soul's addressees is condemned by a single, dismissive adjective: "Tell fortune of her blindnesse,/ tell nature of decay,/ Tell friendship of unkindnesse,/ tell justice of delay." The poet is not stating that all these things are worthless but that they are flawed. The essence of the poem's argument is that nothing is perfect—except for the soul itself, the measure of all these things that "no stab . . . can kill."

Because the form and devices of the poem are determined by its subject matter, which reflects and embodies the process and progress of disillusionment, care must be taken in evaluating the implications of its argument. In spite of its relentlessly downbeat thrust, the poem is not as nihilistic as it might appear at first glance, nor is it atheistic or puritanical as its early detractors suggested. "The Lie" is not atheistic because all its charges are directed against earthly institutions and human endeavors. It is not puritanical because it makes no distinctions and offers no policies. It is, in fact, entirely concerned with admitting and accepting the truth and not at all concerned with organizing behavior. It advises the inner being to be perceptive and suspicious of all imposture, but it advises no more than that. It is an angry poem, but its wrath is wry rather than righteous, directed inward rather than outward; although the soul is directed to do a great deal of "telling," the entities that are to be told are ideas rather than actual individuals. The soul that the author is admonishing is his own and so are the ideas; the only person who is under attack is the poet himself.

When the soul is told to "Tell Potentates they live,/ acting by others action," Ralegh undoubtedly has his former patron Queen Elizabeth in mind, just as he has the earl of Essex, the rival who replaced Ralegh as Queen Elizabeth's favorite, in mind when he refers to "men of high condition," but what he is doing is instructing himself to recognize and understand their agendas. The next stanza, addressed to "them that brave it most" (who else but Ralegh?), asks that he should also recognize and understand his own agenda and its built-in flaws. The whole composition is a matter of the poet standing aside from himself and looking back with a coldly clinical and uncompromising eye. Such an imaginative sidestep is not unprecedented, but the measure of

"The Lie" as a literary work is the authority, economy, and forcefulness of the manner in which that self-analytical act is accomplished.

Themes and Meanings

No one knows exactly when "The Lie" was composed, but it surely does not belong to the 1580's when Ralegh's career was in the ascendant. When he was knighted in 1584, he was given a monopoly in the highly profitable wine trade and authorized to conquer and colonize distant lands in the queen's name; for some years thereafter, he was on top of the world, and he spent forty thousand pounds of England's taxes on exercises of bravado for which tobacco and the potato must have seemed precious little recompense. No man in that position would have written "The Lie," although the stanza that exhorts the soul to "Tell them that brave it most,/ they beg for more by spending" might well refer back to such golden days.

There is a strong temptation to assign "The Lie" to the year 1592, when Ralegh, who had been displaced from the queen's affections by Essex, was nevertheless sent to the Tower of London for making love to one of her maids of honor (Bess Throckmorton, his future wife). It is easy enough to imagine Ralegh whiling away the time of his not entirely just incarceration with exactly such reflections on folly and excess. If Ralegh did write "The Lie" during his first spell in the Tower, its lack of nihilistic implication is clearly demonstrated in his subsequent career. By 1595, he was out adventuring again, this time financed from his own coffers.

If Ralegh did spend his first incarceration in "giving the lie" to all the delusions to which he had formerly fallen prey, perhaps it is both entirely natural and beautifully ironic that he spent so much time thereafter manufacturing illusions to sell to others. The Scottish philosopher David Hume described Ralegh's *The Discoverie of the Large, Rich, and Bewtiful Empyre of Guiana* (1596) as "full of the greatest and most palpable lies that were ever attempted to be imposed on the credulity of mankind." After being imprisoned by King James I on suspicion of treason, he talked his way out again—though not for thirteen years—with tasty rumors of El Dorado, the fabled city of gold that he set out in search of in 1616. James eventually had him beheaded in 1618 for piracy against the Spanish (whose Princess Infanta was about to marry Prince Charles), but such was the sympathy of the people that no other victim of the royal axe is credited with quite so many stirring last words, including "What matter how the head lie, so the heart be right?" For all its froth and fury, the heart of "The Lie" is right.

Brian Stableford

LIFE IN AN ASHTRAY

Author: John Meade Haines (1924-   )
Type of poem: Lyric
First published: 1993, in *The Owl in the Mask of the Dreamer: Collected Poems*

The Poem

"Life in an Ashtray" is a free-verse poem of twenty-three lines divided into nine stanzas of no more than three lines each. The poem personifies cigarettes and follows them through their brief "lives." Written in 1970, it might be seen as an allegorical commentary on American existence at that time. The poem's tone, at first glance, seems bleak and fatalistic and probably reflects John Haines's attempt to capture the emotional aura of the country in the late 1960's and early 1970's. Known as a nature writer, Haines nevertheless found himself affected by the political and social unrest of this era. He writes, "For a time in the late 1960's I was preoccupied with events in the outside world—politics, social conflict, all that absorbed so many of us at the time . . . but on the whole I was too far from the events themselves for them to dominate my poems as convincingly as the wilderness world had up until that time."

This tight, elegant metaphor belies that statement. The poem opens with cigarettes speaking in the first-person plural. In the initial stanza, the poetic creatures describe themselves: "our thin white paper skins," "freckled collars," and "little brown shreds for bones." The second verse introduces action and the first hint of futility: "we begin with our feet in ashes,/ shaking our shoes/ in a crazy, crippling dance." The third stanza is the only one that includes a direct reference to the ashtray in the title. These lines define the ashtray as the characters' entire "world" with the cigarettes skating on its "metal rim."

The initial three stanzas of three lines each are followed by two of two lines, a move that builds urgency into the poem. It echoes the hapless burning of cigarettes toward their inevitable end with an abrupt reference to "the only people born tall,/ who shrink as they grow." Haines then returns to three verses of three lines each. In these, he elaborates on the different aspects of a cigarette's life. When the cigarette tries to speak, it produces only smoke and coughing. As it ages, the "yellow glare" of its eyes turn red, and its feet stomp to "put out the fire." The poem ends with a three-line stanza followed by one line set alone: "And always the old ones crumpling,/ crushed from above/ by enormous hands,/ the young ones beginning to burn." Poetry should speak to everyone in the same way a piece of artwork does. It can cut through barriers of culture and race and nullify questions of science, which really are only comments on the world outside the human heart. The successful poem takes a familiar subject and employs it simply, almost deceptively, to reach something deep inside its reader, something responding out of recognition in a truly visceral way. Although "Life in an Ashtray" works on many different levels, the final line evokes such a gut response. It seems to blend all of the various images into a single archetype, that of an endless cycle that concludes only to immediately repeat itself.

Forms and Devices

"Life in an Ashtray" is an extended metaphor (or even conceit) using personification and imagery. In *The Wilderness of Vision: On the Poetry of John Haines* (1996), William Studebaker explores mysticism in Haines's work. His essay asserts that Haines takes metaphor beyond its accepted definition of implied comparison into the realm of allegory and parable: "His poems are passageways, intersecting symbols, allegories to extra-ordinary consciousness as it grows and fills every silence. . . . Through metaphoric logic, he joins the preternatural and the temporal, announcing a fresh perception of reality." It is far easier in the health-conscious days that have followed the writing of this poem to link mysticism with nature (as seen in the bulk of this poet's work) than it is to discern any kind of equation between mysticism and cigarettes. However, such was not always the case. In her books, Ayn Rand likens the tiny glow of the cigarette to the campfire around which aboriginal man gathered for comfort, company, and myth-making. When Haines wrote this poem in 1970, smoking was a pervasive, acceptable part of American life. He chose to use the cigarette in this sense, then, as a common denominator for the struggle of being human. Perhaps it is only the passage of time that makes the idea of utilizing cigarettes and an ashtray as a trope for life in modern American society seem unusually fanciful and places this particular metaphoric poem in the conceit category.

The use of the first person in "Life in an Ashtray" gives the poem its sense of immediacy. How different it would read if it began "In *their* thin white paper skins." Haines chose to include the reader, thus making the fate of the poetic characters more personal and inescapable. The fact that it is a plural use of the first person widens the scope to all of society in a fatalistic, lemmings-to-destruction way. The careful reader will also notice that Haines selects verbs to reinforce the powerlessness he wishes to portray in this metaphor. The action words "shake," "skate," "shrink," "prod," "dissolve," "stomp," "crumple," and "crush" all underscore the feeling of a society caught up in something that cannot be stopped by individuals. Alliteration is applied sparingly in "Life in an Ashtray." The few examples—"shaking our shoes/ in a crazy, crippling dance"—subtly assist the narrative flow.

Themes and Meanings

Haines maintains that writing, for him, is "a necessary undertaking, a means by which I place myself in the world." Although he feels his political poetry was not as convincing as his wilderness work, "Life in an Ashtray" is strong enough to discount that belief. It is a sharp, witty, and incisive look at America in the days of flower children, protests, and the Vietnam War. Written in 1970, this poem is found under "Interim: Uncollected Poems from the 1970's" in his collection *The Owl in the Mask of the Dreamer.* Originally a homesteader in Alaska, Haines left his solitary life in 1969 and returned to live in society. In addition, he both divorced and remarried in 1970. It is a dangerous game to try looking into the mind of the poet to deduce his thoughts based on the outward appearance of his life. However, it would probably be safe to say that Haines was experiencing some major life changes at the time he wrote this poem.

He also turned forty-seven in 1970. Many people have their first encounter with a slowing body during their forties, which often brings on thoughts of mortality.

Allegorical poems such as this typically display interpretations on several levels. "Life in an Ashtray" portrays, first, the excellent physical description of what happens as a cigarette burns and the careful personification of how the cigarette views life. Then the larger societal connotation emerges. Finally, the personal meaning appears, or rather two personal meanings appear: one for the poet and one for the reader. The fifth and sixth stanzas illustrate this nicely:

> Prodded by hired matches,
> we'd like to complain,
>
> but all our efforts to speak
> dissolve in smoke
> and gales of coughing.

These words create an almost literal picture of a Vietnam War-era demonstration. Uniformed personnel ("hired matches") confront marchers and reward their attempts to be heard with tear gas. More personally, the reader identifies with the poet's effort to chronicle those moments in life when thoughts and ideas go unrecognized, becoming as useless and ephemeral as smoke.

"Life in an Ashtray" again meshes three different meanings at the end. The reader easily sees the motions of a chain-smoker who grinds out a finished cigarette and lights another. Also clearly recognizable are both the worn-out oldster whose weight of years has crushed the need to fight and the fiery young protester who believes fiercely in cherished ideals. On a personal note, the meaning deepens to reflect the feelings of one approaching later years who looks back on vigorous youth with a sense of loss. Readers see a consistent return to various themes throughout Haines's career, and chief among these is his use of cycles. In this poem, the perpetual rhythm of the cigarette smoked to its end only to be replaced by another echoes the wheel of life and death, thus revealing a universal pattern. "Life in an Ashtray" chooses to leave the reader on the upbeat of that cycle rather than its necessary conclusion. Such a sense of the absolute vitality of life remains a familiar theme in Haines's work.

Sue Storm

LIKE WALKING TO THE DRUG STORE, WHEN I GET OUT

Author: Joyce Carol Oates (1938-   )
Type of poem: Epistle/letter in verse
First published: 1994; collected in *Tenderness*, 1996

The Poem

"Like Walking to the Drug Store, When I Get Out" is a letter in free verse with eight stanzas and a short, cryptic "PS." The title of the poem is also the final line in stanza 6 and is a statement of the utter nonchalance with which the writer of the "letter" regards his impulse to violence, even murder. Although initially a confusing phrase, the title becomes a nugget of clarity when it appears within the poem. The speaker is a prison inmate, a convicted child molester, who writes a letter to the "famous" author Joyce Carol Oates, threatening her (indeed all unimprisoned, free persons) with vicious murder: "I'd just grab a baseball bat and I'd beat you/ till your brains leaked out." The chilling aspect of the inmate's harangue is his insistence that he "wouldn't feel a thing." It would be "just like walking to the drug store."

The poem is written in the first person in the voice of an obviously male sociopath. Clearly obsessed, deeply paranoid, and intensely bitter, the prisoner has time on his hands and vitriol in his pen. He has written to Oates five times previously, and, although he promises this letter is the last, it is quickly clear to the reader that he is an obsessed fan. He has seen Oates's picture in the paper in Iowa City, the location of a federal penitentiary where the reader may assume the letter writer has been imprisoned for the last "6½ years." It is intriguing that, in fact, Oates the poet writes this letter/poem to herself, to Oates the famous fiction writer, in the persona of an inmate, in the ungrammatical language that an ill-educated criminal might actually use.

The letter writer of the poem is vengeful as well, despising those who have "done everything [they] want/ to [him]" and promising repayment for the insults and confinement he has suffered. He states that he has no remorse, that he feels no guilt or shame. In stanza 6, he wonders if he should not have committed mass murder—"four or five hundred people"—to make his mark on society. The reader is led to wonder if this is anguished exaggeration or monomaniacal raving. At the poem's close, the inmate insists he is not a child molester and spits out a wild accusation, calling everyone on the outside "capitalist swine" who are molesting their "own sons & daughters" with the express permission of the Constitution! The reader cannot be sure which of the freedoms guaranteed by the Constitution the prisoner is railing against, but it is clear that freedom and recognition are what he desperately wants.

The last stanza zeroes in on Oates again. The prisoner repeats that he is not a child molester, bluntly claiming that he likes grown women but that Oates is "too old" for him. The final threat is chilling indeed: "Believe me if I started murdering people/ there'd be none of you left." The reader is left feeling no doubt that the writer of the letter would make good on this promise.

The poem ends with a cryptic "PS" that is almost an epithet: "The U.S. started World War II." Clearly, the inmate's anger goes well beyond Oates: The entire United States government (and the American people) are to blame for World War II and, more important, for his imprisonment, his tragic life, his crimes. The "you" that the prisoner addresses in the poem is Joyce Carol Oates, but it is also all other people who have shunned or ignored him. Oates so skillfully constructs this persona that readers leave the poem feeling that the prisoner holds them personally responsible for his fate.

Forms and Devices

It is ironic that a poem such as "Like Walking to the Drug Store, When I Get Out" appears in a collection of poems Oates titles *Tenderness*. The poem is the antithesis of tenderness: It sits on the edge of violence for eight stanzas, each line a taut threat spit out between the clenched teeth of the angry prisoner who writes the letter. The poem begins with the salutation of a traditional letter, "Dear Joyce Carol." The writer assumes familiarity in using Oates's first names but, interestingly, does not sign his own name at the end of the letter. The reader must conclude that something prevents his signature, perhaps latent fear or embarrassment, or that perhaps the poet omits it intentionally. It could be anyone. Through this omission, Oates may be indicating that all people experience extreme states of mind; taking responsibility for them is terribly difficult. The prisoner's bravado is not strong enough to allow him to reveal his identity. He is, like many of Oates's characters, trapped by his circumstances.

He is, quite literally, in prison, but he is also imprisoned by his unfulfilled need. The lines of the poem vibrate with his frustration that his story will not be told, that he will not "make his mark." His primary regret is not his crimes but that his crimes have not made him famous. The matter-of-fact diction, profanity, spelling errors, and awkward constructions contribute to the realism of the poem. The hyperbolic political accusations punctuate the text of the poem and contribute to the reader's impression that these are the ravings of a madman. The run-on, breathless structure of the lines ("In my whole life I burglarized a 7-11, some nickels & dimes/ & busted open a stamp machine/ & some cars & cashed a couple checks") conveys a desperate self-righteousness. The voice in the poem is unmistakable. The diction and syntax are chillingly realistic. There is nothing quite so frightening as a threatening letter, particularly when the author is a violent criminal, a convicted child molester, and an aspiring murderer. The absence of formal poetic devices such as metaphor, the loosely narrative structure, and the conversational (and occasionally profane) tone of the poem contribute to its realism. After reading the poem, one feels almost as if Oates has simply recopied an actual letter she received from a deranged fan.

Themes and Meanings

"Like Walking to the Drug Store, When I Get Out" is much more than a threatening letter. It is an embodiment, in the person of Oates's own psychotic "pen-pal," of the rage and hostility society's outcasts feel. One cannot be sure whether or not the prisoner writing the letter in the poem is a real-life or a fictional person, but Oates, like most celebrities, has been threatened several times by persons who might be considered mentally disturbed and dangerous. In a *Writers at Work* interview (1981), she recalls a time when she was not allowed to teach a large lecture class at the University of Windsor because, during the previous night, one of her students had received a phone call from an angry, distraught man who announced he intended to kill Oates. The poem is about the irrational anger the prisoner feels toward Oates and others, but it is also about the palpable terror he is able to inspire in the reader.

The reader feels victimized just as Oates must have in the above threatening situation. The end result of the poem is to make the reader feel hunted and powerless. When one is the object of a fantasy or an imagined slight or wrongdoing and the fantasy is uncontrollable (by the imaginer *or* the victim), it is truly terrifying. Oates is often asked why her writing is so violent, a question she considers insulting and sexist, as though a woman cannot explore dark, intense, violent themes successfully. Oates is particularly effective at creating the violent, vengeful, obsessive persona in "Like Walking to the Drug Store, When I Get Out." It is, perhaps, a fulfillment of traditional gender roles that the victim in the poem is female (Oates herself) and the victimizer is masculine (the prisoner). Regardless of their sex, readers are likely to be unsettled by this poem. There is an undercurrent of madness in the persona of the letter writer: He is self-absorbed, self-righteous, and self-deluding. Furthermore, his final threat is directed at the reader as well as Oates. The "you" in the poem is truly the "you" reading the poem: "Believe me, if I started murdering people/ there'd be none of you left." All of these combine to make him terrifying and terrifyingly real.

Linda Bannister

LILACS

Author: Amy Lowell (1874-1925)
Type of poem: Lyric
First published: 1925, in *What's O'Clock*

The Poem

"Lilacs" is a poem of 109 lines of free verse separated into four stanzas. The first and third stanzas are of unequal length; the first is a long stanza of fifty-two lines, and the third has twenty-seven lines. The second and fourth stanzas are fifteen lines each. Another asymmetry in the poem is that stanzas 1, 2, and 4 begin with the same five brief lines: "Lilacs,/ False blue,/ White,/ Purple,/ Colour of lilac." By contrast, the association of lilacs with New England that is mentioned briefly in stanza 1 is developed in the opening lines of stanza 3: "Maine knows you,/ Has for years and years;/ New Hampshire knows you,/ And Massachusetts/ and Vermont."

Also interesting is the change in perspective as the poem progresses. In the first three stanzas Amy Lowell speaks to the lilacs directly, addressing them as "you." In the first stanza, she mentions the timelessness of the lilacs and lingers on their details: their heart-shaped leaves and the crooks of their branches. From precise physical detail the poem moves to the acts of lilacs, and it becomes apparent that they are more than mere flowering shrubs. She describes the effect they have on preachers, schoolboys, housewives, and clerks, typical New England figures. Wherever the lilacs occur they have a beneficial effect, as when they call to the clerks and cause them to write poetry.

Lowell refers to the Persian origin of lilacs in the second stanza, comparing their exotic beginning with the domestic attitude the shrub has adopted in New England: "A curiously clear-cut, candid flower,/ Standing beside clean doorways,/ Friendly to a house-cat and a pair of spectacles." Lowell is still speaking directly to the lilacs, but the sensibility of the speaker is clear. She has a sharp eye and a profound attachment to nature, and she is deeply grounded in the New England of the poem. Although "I" is not used yet, it is reasonable to assume that the speaker is the poet herself rather than an assumed persona.

In the third stanza, Lowell connects the lilacs to specific New England places, such as Cape Cod and Maine. She also specifies, and repeats, the time of year, May, when the lilacs are most profuse and associates the flowers with a luminous series of spring nature images. Lowell finally reveals herself fully in the fourth stanza, where "I" appears for the first time. She claims both lilac and New England as her own in a metaphor in which she becomes both the flower and the place. The poem builds to a powerful, almost triumphant ending as she "sings" the lilacs as her own.

Forms and Devices

"Lilacs" uses many of the techniques of the Imagists, a group of poets bound by similar ideas who were active roughly between 1905 and 1917. The group was first led, and perhaps defined, by poet and critic Ezra Pound with the help of another American poet, Hilda Doolittle (H. D.). Lowell became identified with the group in 1913 and displaced Pound as leader in 1915. She organized the group to carry out a publicity campaign to free poetry from the "tyranny" of rhyme, regular meter, and other traditional devices. Under Lowell's leadership the annual anthology, *Some Imagist Poets*, was published for three years and contained statements of Imagist theory. The Imagists believed in short poems structured around a single image or metaphor, clarity and concreteness of detail, economy of language, and an avoidance of abstract meaning or "message." Imagist poems generally were concerned with presenting an object or scene for the direct understanding of the reader.

The patterns of stanza openings and length first establish expectations in the readers' minds and then cause a small shock of surprise when the patterns are broken. This asymmetry affects both the eye and the ear and is characteristic of free verse, which was widely used by the Imagists.

The poem is structured around the lilacs of the title, the central image. An image refers to sensual impressions that the poem reproduces in the mind of the reader. Lowell carefully establishes the visual image of the lilacs by listing their colors and their shapes, "great puffs," at the beginning of three stanzas. She mentions the fragrance of the flowers in the first stanza and, since odors are difficult to describe, brings it to life by describing the effect the fragrance has, primarily on New England clerks in customhouses. The lilacs are personified—they acquire human characteristics. They are as active as the people: They tap the window, run beside the schoolboy, and persuade the housewife that her husband is pure gold.

Repetition is an important device in the poem. The five identical, very short lines that open stanzas 1, 2, and 4 acquire an incantatory quality, as if the colors of the lilacs have some magical power. The repetition also keeps the image fresh in readers' minds as the poem explores other aspects of the shrub in addition to its appearance. "New England," first introduced in the seventh line of the poem, is repeated several times, each time becoming more specific until it culminates in the final metaphor.

Not only are images repeated, but sentence structure tends to fall into patterns as well. In the first stanza, Lowell establishes a pattern of subject/verb when she addresses the lilacs: "You are . . ./ You were . . ." and repeats the pattern eight times. In the third stanza Lowell expands the meaning of lilacs in a series of metaphors, one of which plays on the figure used in stanza 1 that describes lilac leaves as "heart-shaped." Here she speaks of "the leaf-shapes of our hearts," an implied metaphor that connects the human and botanical world in a concise phrase. Everywhere, Lowell exhibits an economy of language. Seven lines in sequence begin with "May is . . . " and pile up images in a series of tight metaphors.

The climax of a poem occurs when a series of sentences that repeat words from previous sentences build to a high point of force or excitement. This high point occurs in the fourth stanza, when the two major images that are repeated many times in the poem are fused with the speaker when she reveals herself overtly for the first time. Lowell switches to the first person, a tradition in lyric poetry. The effect is dramatic;

the poem suddenly changes from an ode to lilacs to a powerful personal statement. Stanza 4 effectively unites all the imagery in one extended metaphor. Lowell identifies herself as the lilac with roots and leaves, and then with New England. In the lyrical line "Lilac in me because I am New England," she uses synecdoche, a type of metaphor in which a small part stands for the whole.

Themes and Meanings

Lowell was descended from a distinguished colonial family that included James Russell Lowell, the nineteenth century poet and Harvard professor; her brother, Abbott Lawrence Lowell, president of Harvard University; and later the Pulitzer Prize-winning poet Robert Lowell. Amy Lowell also won the Pulitzer Prize in 1926, posthumously, for her book *What's O'Clock*. Her impassioned identification with New England is an affirmation of her life and heritage; it is difficult to separate the Lowells from the history of Massachusetts.

Although Lowell's work has been criticized for dealing too exclusively with vivid images and neglecting emotional values, when "Lilacs" is judged by the Imagist ideals that shaped it, the poem is successful. The poem is composed primarily of concrete nouns that describe the appearance of the lilacs in exquisite detail, from their individual flowers to the way they appear in the New England landscape. The concern with appearance, color, and light in the poem illustrates Imagist ideas and has led some critics to associate the movement with Impressionism, the art movement.

Perhaps the most overt expression of Imagist ideas is the absence of a deeper meaning to "Lilacs" than what is stated. There is no "message" or hidden meaning. The poem is a clear statement of what lilacs mean to the poet; she identifies lilacs with the New England of her ancestors and, finally, with herself. Significantly, the poem achieves interest not because of its meaning, which is relatively simple, but because of Lowell's technique, which communicates the meaning in a vivid and unique way.

Sheila Golburgh Johnson

LINES COMPOSED A FEW MILES ABOVE TINTERN ABBEY

Author: William Wordsworth (1770-1850)
Type of poem: Lyric
First published: 1798, in *Lyrical Ballads*

The Poem

This 160-line poem is autobiographical, written in the first person and in the poet's own persona. The poem is subtitled "On Revisiting the Banks of the Wye During a Tour." It is set at Tintern, a ruined abbey next to the River Wye in the West of England.

The poet opens with the observation that five years have passed since he was last there. He continues with a description of the peaceful landscape. Line 23 marks a transition in time and place. He recalls that in moments of weariness in noisy towns, the memory of this landscape has calmed and restored him in body and mind. These pleasant feelings promote kind and loving actions in life. They also bring with them a more sublime gift: transcendental experiences, beyond the everyday state of consciousness, which William Wordsworth was to refer to in his later poem *The Prelude* (1850) as "spots of time."

The poet describes such an experience as a serene and blessed mood capable of lightening life's burdens. The awareness leads into a state of such deep rest that the breath and heartbeat are suspended, though the mind is wide awake—"we become a living soul." In this joyful and harmonious state, the poet says, sense perception is directed inward. There are no objects of perception for the eye to see. Instead, the perception is opened to the inner spiritual life that informs creation.

At line 66, the poet shifts his attention to comparing his passionate, unthinking, animal-like enjoyment of the landscape five years ago with his more philosophical response now—underscored by "the still, sad music of humanity." Now, he is also aware of a spiritual presence imbuing nature's many forms and the mind of man, impelling both the perceiving consciousness and the objects of perception. This awareness inspires his mature love for nature, which fosters and nourishes his finest thoughts and feelings.

The final section of the poem centers on the poet's sister Dorothy, who accompanies him. In her "wild eyes," he recaptures the passion of his youth. He says a prayer for Dorothy, confident that Nature never betrayed the "heart that loved her." Nature's sublimating effect on the mind is proof against evil, unkindness, and world-weariness, and preserves one's faith that the world is full of blessings.

A prayer for Dorothy's old age begins at line 135. The poet asks that her mind might be a dwelling-place for beautiful forms and sounds, just as in the past he has been restored and uplifted by memories of this landscape. If her life should then be tainted with fear or pain, then the memory of his prayer will bring healing thoughts. If they are separated by then, she will not forget that they stood together on the banks of the Wye. Nor will she forget that on his second visit, this place was dearer to him, both because it had grown in significance in his mind and because Dorothy was with him.

Forms and Devices

The imagery of the poem in many cases brings out contrasts between opposites. For example, the "blessed mood" (line 38) is introduced, then defined in terms of its opposite value: In the lines that follow, the key words are "burthen," "mystery," "heavy," "weary weight," and "unintelligible." Then, in line 42, the burden built up over three lines is suddenly lifted in the resolution "Is lightened." The line rests in a momentary pause in which all tension is released.

The poet goes on to build an experience of an opposite kind—an account of the transcendental experience that nullifies the burden. The opposites within this description take the reader into the realms of the paradoxes of spiritual experience: The expected motion of the blood and breath is set against their state of suspension; the deep rest of the body is set against the alertness of the spirit. Also noteworthy is the "presence" (line 95) that "disturbs" him with "joy"—an apparent contradiction that makes intuitive sense.

A similar process of juxtaposition of opposite values is at work in the poet's tribute to nature. In rhetorical style and over several lines, the poet builds a sense of the power of nature to fortify the human spirit, in such words as "joy to joy," "inform," "impress," "quietness and beauty," and "feed with lofty thoughts." Then, in symmetrical structure, the negative influences are detailed. Evocative use of alliteration is made in "the sneers of selfish men," and "greetings" set against "no kindness" is a telling paradox. Yet the passage does not rest on the negative side: The reader is moved along to the resolution (lines 133-135), a moving affirmation of life's joys and fullness.

The poem is in the blank verse form of iambic pentameter, with five feet per line, each foot consisting of a weak and a strong stress. Though this metrical form closely approximates natural spoken English, it is capable of evoking immense grandeur, as one sees in the passage describing the "presence" of nature (lines 94-103). The music of this passage can be fully appreciated only when it is read aloud. The rhetorical device of repeating the introductory phrase "and the . . ." creates an ecstatic effect of an accumulation of blessings. The spondees (two consecutive strong stresses) combined with long vowel sounds add particular emphasis to certain images: The first two syllables of "round ocean," and "blue sky" are examples. The imagery also adds to the sense of the "presence" pervading nature as a vital being: A "dwelling" normally refers to something belonging to a person; the air is "living"; the spirit "rolls through all things."

Themes and Meanings

The central theme of the poem is typically Wordsworthian: the interactive relationship between the perceiving awareness, "the mind of man," and nature. In the poet's view, perception is as much active and creative as passive and receptive. Reality depends upon the quality of the onlooker's perception, and this changes with time. The poet's youthful perception of the area around Tintern Abbey was different from that of his mature view. Five years later, his mature perceptions are less passionate and more thoughtful. He no longer sees nature as divorced from the human condition (lines 91-94).

He has developed the ability to see a level of reality beyond sensory impressions—the spirit underlying the myriad forms of nature, which animates and unites perceiver and objects of perception. For example, the description of the Tintern landscape (lines 4-23) is noteworthy for the blurring of distinctions between objects: the orchards that melt into the woods, the farms green to the door, the smoke among the trees—all bespeak a synthesizing, unifying perception.

Central to Wordsworth's vision are "spots of time" (*The Prelude*)—profound spiritual experiences that he describes as having a renovating, uplifting, and nourishing virtue. In "Lines Composed a Few Miles Above Tintern Abbey," worldly cares are twice referred to in terms of heaviness or burdens (lines 39-40, 55). Set against them is the ability of the "serene and blessed mood" to lighten their weight (line 42). More important, these experiences culture joy and harmony in the poet's awareness, allowing him to "see into the life of things." This theme is expanded in the extraordinary vision of the one spirit pervading nature and human consciousness in lines 94-103. The poet's moments of communion with nature endure, independent of inhospitable surroundings. Amid the noise of towns and cities, his spirit would turn to this landscape for regeneration—emphasizing the power of the human spirit to create its own reality.

Yet a tension runs through the poem that pulls against this affirmative theme. In Dorothy's "wild eyes," he recaptures his youthful passion, but one senses an underlying yearning for "what [the poet] was once"—and is no longer. Similarly, he prays that her memories will render her mind "a mansion for all lovely forms" in her later years, but he is preoccupied with the pain and grief she may suffer. He anticipates separation from her and his consequent inability to "catch from [her] wild eyes these gleams of past existence." Such thoughts reveal a deep anxiety about the passing of time and the decline and loss it may bring.

Many readers identify a lack of conviction behind Wordsworth's protest (lines 86-89) that he does not mourn the passing of the "dizzy raptures" of his youth and note a wistfulness in his references to that time being past (lines 84-86). In his assertion that maturity brings "Abundant recompence," he seems to be trying to convince himself that the gain is worth the loss. In this respect, this poem invites comparison with "Ode: Intimations of Immortality" (published in 1807). The "Ode" was inspired by Wordsworth's "sense of the indomitableness of the spirit within me" (annotation by Wordsworth, compiled in 1843 by Isabella Fenwick) yet at the same time is an elegy to the "visionary gleam" of his youthful perception of nature.

Claire Robinson

LINES FOR THE PRINCE OF VENOSA

Author: Lars Gustafsson (1936-   )
Type of poem: Narrative
First published: 1972, as "Rader för Hertigen av Venosa," in *Varma rum och kalla*;
   English translation collected in *The Stillness of the World Before Bach*, 1988

The Poem

Lars Gustafsson's "Lines for the Prince of Venosa," as translated by Yvonne L. Sandstroem, is a narrative poem of approximately 875 words. The poem is written in free verse with irregular line and stanza lengths. Although the predominant configuration is two-line stanzas with occasional one-line stanzas for emphasis, the five parenthetical stanzas are more irregular, varying from one to eight lines. The unpredictable line and stanza patterns reinforce the free-flowing nature of the narrative in which the speaker describes an aimless journey through time and space. Although the poem begins in November, 1971, in Sweden, it quickly moves to an encounter with nineteenth century composers Anton Bruckner and Gustav Mahler in Egypt's Sinai desert. During the course of his travels, the speaker meets, in person and in daydream, a number of well-known historical figures, but he never encounters the poem's title character, Prince Venosa.

The narrator of "Lines for the Prince of Venosa" is clearly intended to be the poet himself. This point is made clear when the speaker, a writer, complains about a newspaper review that reads: "Gustafsson, above all, is unnecessarily *learned*." This offhand comment about Gustafsson's writing reinforces the whimsical tone of the entire narrative. The poem begins by dismissing "Robinson," apparently Daniel Defoe's Robinson Crusoe, because "he was nothing but a character in an adventure story." Next, the narrator finds himself in Gothenburg (Göteborg in Swedish), the second-largest city in Sweden, talking with people who do not "understand" him. Then he travels to the university town of Lund, where a supposedly learned professor prophesies a series of events that actually occurred years before.

Next is a trip to the Sinai with Mahler and Bruckner, who are pictured as wearing "soulful little eyeglass frames." The two composers accompany the speaker on a tour of the monastery of Saint Catherine, reputed to be the oldest inhabited Christian monastery, in Egypt's Sinai desert. The tour prompts a bizarre discussion on the distinction between the way that ordinary people are buried and the way that bishops are buried in Saint Catherine's monastery. While commoners' bones are sorted by body parts, bishops are buried with their bones intact. Bruckner theorizes that on Judgment Day the bishops must "*pull themselves together*," and Mahler agrees that they must "*get on their legs* quickly to take command."

With no clear transition, the narrator finds himself back in Sweden riding a train to Karlstad for a literary reading where he is to share the lectern with two writers of primitive verse: an old Lapp woman and a football player. During the train ride, the speaker fantasizes a meeting between Jack Kerouac, American hero of the Beat generation, and "a little psychiatrist in gold-frame glasses," apparently Sigmund Freud, who died in 1939. The narrator pictures Kerouac getting the best of Freud in their discussion concerning the differences between the definitions of neuroses and inhibitions by Kerouac's suggestion that they drop their trousers on the count of three.

During the uncomfortable literary reading, the narrator fantasizes that he spots in the audience Maria d'Avalos, the beautiful wife of the Prince of Venosa. When he meets her again at the bar of a local hotel, the speaker is so struck with Donna Maria's beauty that he blurts out a question about the young woman's husband. He remembers too late that the sixteenth century composer had ordered his wife and her lover murdered. However, Donna Maria's graceful, noncommittal reply about her husband's beautiful music shakes the narrator out of his reverie and sends him back to snowy Sweden where his dog happily welcomes him home.

Forms and Devices

In "Lines for the Prince of Venosa," Gustafsson uses two techniques that are typical of American poet T. S. Eliot. The first is the deliberate omission of transitions, a technique that forces the reader to actively participate in the poem in order to arrive at some kind of understanding. For example, Gustafsson's poem begins with a reference to a Romantic nineteenth century novel set on a tropical island and immediately shifts to late twentieth century Sweden. Gustafsson expects the reader to supply the transition.

A second Eliot-like device is the use of multiple allusions that only a widely educated reader would recognize. Even the narrator-poet jokes that reviewers complain that Gustafsson's erudition seems "unnecessary." Although place names such as "Gothenburg," "Lund," and "Värmland" would be familiar to Gustafsson's Swedish readers, other references are more obscure. While the three composers, Venosa, Mahler, and Bruckner, may also be known to the reading public, they are hardly as well known as Johann Sebastian Bach or Wolfgang Amadeus Mozart. Also, "Robinson" is mentioned with the expectation that the reader will fill in "Crusoe," and one wonders whether a Swedish audience would understand the jokes about "wholesales Whitman" and Kerouac's first-class Atlantic passage.

A third technique, one that is a distinct departure from Eliot's style, is the humor laced throughout the poem. The picture of the supposedly erudite Professor Ehrenswärd "sucking a milk carton/ as if it were a mother's nipple" while he poetically describes farmers as "proletarians of the plow" is perfectly delicious due to the juxtaposition of the professor's puerile actions and his alliterative word choices. References to "Mahler and Bruckner" as both a "congenial firm" and a logical name for a delicatessen serve as perfect counterpoints to both composers' ponderous music. In addition, the imagined argument between the freewheeling Kerouac and the stuffy Freud ends with Kerouac's scatological test of inhibitions.

Themes and Meanings

In spite of the lighthearted tone, "Lines for the Prince of Venosa" is a serious poem about what it means to be an artist. The three themes that the poem considers are the artist's need for fame and for affirmation of his or her work, the artist's needs as a human being, and the artist's search for truth. The most immediate concern is the need for affirmation of one's work. Most of the artists that Gustafsson mentions had difficulty finding popular acceptance. For example, Mahler's reputation was hampered by his unpopularity as an exacting conductor and by the fact that he was a Jew. Even though Bruckner had written three masses that were performed in Linz, Austria, he was treated in Vienna like a rustic outsider. Walt Whitman's poetry, with its disjoined lines, likewise languished in obscurity. Of himself, Gustafsson says that people in Gothenburg do not understand him "(as usual)" and that the press considers him too "*learned*." However, the narrator's own appreciation of Mahler and Bruckner is qualified by the description of their symphonies as being interminably slow and ponderous in order "to convince us that death isn't so bad after all." Whitman's disconnected rhyming catalogs are juxtaposed with the piles of disjointed body parts found in Saint Catherine's monastery. Finally, Defoe's widely read novel is dismissed because it is only "an adventure story/ that everyone's read before."

The second theme, the artist's needs as a human being, is tied to the meaning of home. For Prince Venosa, home became a place of shame rather than a place of rest and comfort. Even the Renaissance composer, who was noted for his devotional masses, did not possess faith strong enough to forgive his wife for her infidelities. In contrast, the narrator is happy to settle for a wifeless homecoming with only a bouncy dog to greet his arrival. Concerning the meaning of home, the narrator comments that one will always "find a way home," but he warns that it will not be the same safe haven that was left behind.

The most important theme is the artist's search for truth, a concept that the poet uses interchangeably with the concept of beauty. The following lines occur three times in the poem: "Yes/ beauty is the only thing that lasts." The first comment ends the pontifical professor's lecture, and the third is part of Donna Maria's cocktail chatter about her husband's music. In spite of the comical contexts, the reveries that follow these lines indicate the serious purposes of the poem. The first reverie begins with a comparison of beauty to stones, both of which are not only long lasting but are also "pure and simple." Then, both the first and second reverie continue the comparison by commenting on what is inside the stone. The narrator says that certain types of quartz trap water that is "older than all the seas in our world." Furthermore, this water, never having been exposed to light, is both clean and pure. The darkness inside the stone stands in sharp contrast with the blinding but often sterile light in the mountains of the Sinai and other sterile areas of the earth. Gustafsson suggests, then, that truth is ancient, pure, and encased in darkness or in misunderstanding. Therefore, it is the task of often-misunderstood artists to release the truth, but the price that artists pay for their efforts may be high indeed.

Sandra Hanby Harris

LISTEN!

Author: Vladimir V. Mayakovsky (1893-1930)
Type of poem: Lyric
First published: 1914, as "Slushaite!"; collected in *Polnoe sobranie sochinenii*, 1955; English translation collected in *Mayakovsky: A Poet in the Revolution*, 1973

The Poem

"Listen!" is one of several short lyric poems of existential questioning by Vladimir Mayakovsky that appeared in the first issue of *Pervyi zhurnal russkikh futuristov* (*First Journal of the Russian Futurists*) in 1914. The poem combines youthful angst about the writer's insignificance in the vast universe with a self-assured mastery of his idiom and technique. In the preceding year, Mayakovsky had published his first lyric collection and had produced and starred in an autobiographical play in verse, *Vladimir Mayakovsky*. In "Listen!" Mayakovsky entertains the possibility, somewhat perversely for a Futurist who rejected all of humankind's past beliefs, that there is a God, arguing, from the ancient position, that God must have set the stars in the sky.

Mayakovsky makes an appeal to pure intuition for proof of the existence of God: He begins three lines of his thirty-line poem with "You know" (*ved'* in Russian), a nervous, rhetorical colloquialism sometimes left untranslated and sometimes translated as "surely?" The appeal to intuition is continued in five more lines, all beginning with "That means," another nervous colloquialism that urges causality, connection, or equivalence. Thus:

> You know—if they light up the stars—
> That means—somebody needs them?
> It means—someone wants them to be there?
> It means—someone calls that spit pearls?

The irreverent and colloquial language characteristic of Mayakovsky is softened here by an almost childlike tone in his choice of words. Pure, direct rhetoric and almost conventional imagery are used to express his thoughts. The poem is particularly poignant in the context of his other works, which make clear that his childhood had ended early, even before his six months of imprisonment and solitary confinement as a sixteen-year-old Bolshevik schoolboy. The naïve tone is suitable to his final rhetorical question of whether the stars are lit up to ensure that every single evening, above the roofs of humankind, at least one star will always shine.

While the poem is sometimes ambiguous about whether the "somebody" who needs the stars is God or humankind, the central section makes clear that humans need both the stars and the God who gives them those stars. The unnamed "somebody," an uncharacteristically humble figure who replaces Mayakovsky's habitual "I," begs for stars as a pledge of good faith. "Somebody" kisses God's hand but does not ask for the father figure's love directly: The gift of stars is enough. The stars alone will rid him of fear and make him feel "all right."

In the poem that followed "Listen!" entitled "And Yet," a more mature, worldly tone reasserts itself. The anonymous "somebody" is replaced by Mayakovsky in the first person, who speaks defiantly of prostitutes who worship him. The poet predicts that God will read Mayakovsky's books and weep and will then rush about the heavens showing them to his acquaintances. "And Yet" was followed by "Petersburg Again." In this third poem of ontological questioning, the universe has become menacing, a "cannibalistic" fog blocks out the stars, and God is an absurd, distant, and rejected figure who looks down from the sky with irrelevant dignity "like Leo Tolstoy." In its structure, however, "Listen!" is by far the most innovative of the three poems.

Forms and Devices

"Listen!" is a short but complex work. Its level of technical control makes the categorization of free verse almost irrelevant, although the poem does not follow traditional rules of versification. It is divided into three parts: the introduction, the body, and the conclusion. The first and last parts mirror each other like the *aba* form of a classical sonata movement. The rhythmic structure consists of a mixture of feet and lines of varying lengths. Feet of three syllables tend to predominate, with the key word "Listen" being a dactyl in the original. However, Mayakovsky builds up tension with feet of four, then five, then six syllables, always with a stress on the final beat. He then delivers punchlines of a single word for further contrast. Trochees are also used to provide a cross-rhythm to the polysyllabic feet, as if working against them. While not perfectly regular, a structure clearly emerges from the alternation of lines of increasing length and lines of a single word.

The one-word lines acquire a lyrical, expressive prominence: "Listen," "Sobs," "Begs," "Swears," and "Yes." Each of the exceedingly long lines gives prominence to its final word, which contains the long-awaited stress. Mayakovsky is able to create a rhyme scheme that utilizes much longer jumps from rhyme to rhyme than are found in traditional poetry. His rhymes are not perfect but tend toward assonance. The word "star" (*zvezdá*) rhymes boldly with "yes" (*da*) and again with itself across cosmic gaps in space. In his advice to aspiring proletarian poets in *Kak delat' stikhi?* (1926; *How Are Verses Made?*, 1970), Mayakovsky observed: "Without rhyme (understanding the word in a wide sense) poetry falls to pieces."

Parallel constructions are underlined by the very structure of Russian and have long been prominent in Russian style. They have a strong role to play in Mayakovsky's work. With parallels at both the beginnings and the ends of lines, and with the end of the poem reflecting its beginning, this poem could scarcely be more highly structured despite its use of free verse. On the finer scale of sound, Mayakovsky's use of alliteration provides the final organizing factor. In the Russian, the sound "z" shines forth, beginning with "star" itself and echoing in the repeated words "light up" and "that means." Other alliterations deliberately restrict the poem's palette of sound, focusing meaning with impassioned intensity.

Themes and Meanings

While his formal education was interrupted early, Mayakovsky read widely and eclectically. He was aware of the far-flung origins and echoes of the themes of stars, God, and the cosmos, from the Bible to the nineteenth century Russian classics. In Russian literature, "Listen!" most nearly echoes the lyric poetry of Mikhail Lermontov, a tragic rebel who despised "the establishment," who was very partial to polysyllabic rhythms, and who was profoundly affected by the stars shining over the Caucasus, the region of Biblical grandeur and solemnity that was Mayakovsky's birthplace. Lermontov's works are filled with angels, demons, stars, clouds, and cosmic space, all conversing with one another. His cosmic imagery, inspiring a series of works by the painter Mikhail Vrubel, was very much in vogue in the years preceding the Russian Revolution of 1917. Mayakovsky had studied art while Lermontov, the self-taught amateur, could sketch. In a final, unfortunate parallel, Mayakovsky and Lermontov both wrote about the impulse to self-destruction.

Mayakovsky's persona of the street urchin, usually expressed as an impudent orphan cynical beyond his years, is tempered in "Listen!" by an unexpectedly childlike, naïvely questioning, and vulnerable voice. The child is on familiar terms with the father-God whom he importunes with his huge request for stars; the child rushes to him, trusting and hopeful, so as not to be "late" (as if to dinner) and kisses his "veiny" hand (an obligatory gesture of child to parent in prerevolutionary Russia). The possibility of a cosmic parent is left open in this poem, and all mockery is hushed. It may represent a turning point in Mayakovsky's relationship to God that hangs between the trust of a self-effacing child (a nameless "somebody" who finds comfort in faith) and the disillusionment of the youth who mocks the face of God to the skies, who wishes to set his own name everywhere and yet who proclaims that this very self-assertion, which in effect replaces the need for God, is a "tragedy."

The stars of the cosmos continued to be a key image for Mayakovsky throughout his life. The long poem *Oblako v shtanakh* (1915; *The Cloud In Trousers*, 1960) ends with the beautiful metaphor, "The universe is asleep/ its huge ear,/ star-infested,/ rests on a paw." His last lyric poem, "Past One O'Clock," from which he quoted in his suicide note, ends with the immortal lines: "Night has laid a heavy tax of stars upon the sky./ In hours like these you get up and you speak/ To the ages, to history, and to the universe."

D. Gosselin Nakeeb

THE LISTENERS

Author: Walter de la Mare (1873-1956)
Type of poem: Lyric
First published: 1912, in *The Listeners and Other Poems*

The Poem

"The Listeners" is a single-stanza poem of thirty-six lines, rhyming *abcb*. The title suggests the focus of the poem: It is not on the poem's human traveler, but on the phantom listeners who await him. The poem is written in the third person, to allow the reader to observe, objectively, the traveler first and then the listeners, and to remain behind with the listeners when the traveler hastily departs at the poem's close.

The poem begins *in medias res*, with the traveler knocking on a moonlit door in an unknown place. It is this sense of the unknown, with all its ambiguities, that controls the tone and mood of the poem. The place in the forest where the traveler finds himself is deserted and overgrown with brambles; the sense of isolation and strangeness causes the lonely human visitor first to knock on the door of the turreted house, then to smite it, and finally to smite it even louder, as his cries receive no response.

One soon discovers, however, that it is only he who is perplexed and lonely in this nighttime scene; nature ignores the phantoms, as is seen by his horse contentedly champing the grasses and by the bird in the house's turret being disturbed, not by anything eerie or frightening in the natural scene, but by his voice and loud knocking. The scene reinforces one of Walter de la Mare's common themes: Human beings are estranged from both the natural and the social worlds, and are puzzled and even frightened by the unfathomable mystery at the heart of life.

This sense of mystery is deepened by the power of hints and suggestions—in Wallace Stevens's terms, of innuendos and inflections. Why is the traveler here? Evidently to keep some promise, perhaps to those who are no longer alive, since he is "the one man left awake" (line 32). Something, though, has caused him to come to this lonely and isolated place in the middle of the night and compelled him to cry out repeatedly to a deserted house, without entering to see for himself who or what might be there.

De la Mare builds on the paradoxes and ironies inherent in the situation, opposing the "lonely" traveler to the "lone" house, and his standing "still" because he is perplexed and wondering to the "phantom listeners" who are "still" in the sense of being quiet (and perhaps dead). Yet even while the traveler feels in his heart their strangeness and stillness, his horse continues to crop the "dark turf," naturally oblivious to these human fears.

The poem ends with a shift in focus from the lonely traveler to the silent listeners; while he rushes to flee the scene, they remain behind in the returning silence. De la Mare's effort to coalesce verbal sounds and verbal symbols is nowhere more evident than in this poem, and especially in the soft sibilance of the *s* sounds in the final lines.

Though the traveler has departed, readers are left wondering what has happened to those to whom he has made a promise as well as what this promise might be.

Forms and Devices

De la Mare uses several poetic strategies to make "The Listeners" effective. His language, for example, is quite simple and ordinary, an apt contrast to the strange and eerie quality of the setting. None of his words causes a reader to search out their meanings in a dictionary; it is as if he wants to convince readers that the world he is portraying is the actual world in which they live. With the exception, perhaps, of the turret on the house, none of the concrete details is exotic or arcane. The strangeness, in other words, is in the atmosphere created by the mind of the traveler, not in ordinary reality.

The repetition of words is also effective: knocking, still and stillness, and listening are prominent. There is a general absence of metaphor and simile as well; it is the language of the setting itself, dark, empty, still, listening, which creates a mood of sadness, loneliness, and emptiness.

It is perhaps the rhythm, however, which is the most striking stylistic component: de la Mare uses a basically anapestic rhythm (two unstressed syllables followed by a stressed syllable), more commonly used in rollicking ballads or sea chanteys, to communicate a sense of urgency and anxiety in the situation. Indeed, for many readers, it is difficult to be left behind in the forest at the poem's end. When the traveler leaves, one wishes to leave with him, rather than to stay behind with the phantom listeners.

Themes and Meanings

"The Listeners" is a poem about an unsuccessful quest for clarity and meaning in an inscrutable universe. Like Herman Melville and Stephen Crane, Walter de la Mare sees humans caught in a web of circumstance that drastically limits their personal freedom and prevents them from making full connections with either nature or other people. Yet, paradoxically, it is this yearning for a harmony and wholeness in the natural and social worlds which is always just out of reach that convinces people that personal integrity and fidelity to commitments, responsibilities, and attachments is what makes them most human, and what keeps them from the dark terrors of a universe which, while not openly hostile or malevolent, still ignores the human presence.

One question which occurs to many readers is why the poem is entitled "The Listeners" and not "The Traveler," since the initial focus is on the human traveler who comes to this distant and lonely scene. Although the focus is at first centered on "the one man left awake" or alive (line 32) who speaks with a "voice from the world of men" (line 16), that focus shifts in an important way to the "host of phantom listeners" (line 13) that dwell in this strange house. These listeners not only listen but also stand "thronging" (line 17) the dark stair that goes down to an empty hall, yet they answer his cries only with their "stillness" (line 22). Are they the ghosts of those persons the traveler is hoping to meet, and guardians of this lost house, those to whom the traveler made some promise that was so binding that he is coming to this forsaken spot in the middle of the night to keep his word? The reader cannot tell; de la Mare does not want readers to be sure, though they can perhaps guess. The poet wants readers to be left behind in this strange and eerie place, after the traveler has gone—left behind, alone, with the listeners.

The focus of the poem is much more on tone and mood than it is on theme. Like the traveler, readers experience the loneliness, bewilderment, and anxiety that is part of living in a world which they do not—and cannot—fully comprehend. In "The Listeners," Walter de la Mare has made excellent use of what Ernest Hemingway called "the fifth dimension" in literature: He has deliberately omitted details in the material, especially details which would explain the context of the situation. He does this not to confuse readers, but to cause them to wonder, and to engage with him in the mutual enterprise of seeking to comprehend at least partially what is finally incomprehensible: their nature as individual persons, their relations with one another, and their place in the physical world in which they live.

Clark Mayo